COMPUTERS AND INFORMATION PROCESSING

Concepts and Applications ○ **with BASIC**
Fourth Edition

Steven L. Mandell
Bowling Green State University

West Publishing Company
Saint Paul ○ New York ○ Los Angeles ○ San Francisco

COPY EDITOR: Sheryl Rose
ILLUSTRATIONS: Rolin Graphics
COMPOSITION: Parkwood Composition Service

A study guide has been developed to assist you in mastering concepts presented in this text. The study guide reinforces concepts by presenting them in condensed, concise form. Additional illustrations and examples are also included. The study guide is available from your local bookstore under the title, *Study Guide to Accompany Computers and Information Processing: Concepts and Applications Fourth Edition*, prepared by Steven L. Mandell.

Photo Credits appear following index

COPYRIGHT © 1979   By WEST PUBLISHING COMPANY
COPYRIGHT © 1982   By WEST PUBLISHING COMPANY
COPYRIGHT © 1985   By WEST PUBLISHING COMPANY
COPYRIGHT © 1987   By WEST PUBLISHING COMPANY
                    50 West Kellogg Boulevard
                    P.O. Box 64526
                    St. Paul, MN 55164-1003

Printed in the United States of America

95 94 93 92 91 90 89 88   8 7 6 5 4 3 2

Library of Congress Cataloging-in-Publication Data

Mandell, Steven L.
  Computers and information processing.

  Rev. ed. of: Computers and data processing.
3rd ed. © 1985.
  Includes index.
  1. Electronic data processing.   2. Electronic
digital computers.   3. BASIC (Computer program
language) I. Mandell, Steven L.   Computers and
data processing.   II. Title.
QA76.M27472 1987b   004   86-29012
ISBN 0-314-32151-9

CONTENTS

INTRODUCTION TO INFORMATION SYSTEMS   55

HARDWARE 75

MICROCOMPUTERS 179

8

TELECOMMUNICATIONS AND DISTRIBUTED COMPUTING 215

SYSTEM SOFTWARE   245

SOFTWARE DEVELOPMENT   269

● CONTENTS

MANAGEMENT INFORMATION SYSTEMS AND DECISION SUPPORT SYSTEMS   395

COMPUTERS IN OUR LIVES: TODAY AND TOMORROW 469

APPLICATION SOFTWARE SUPPLEMENT   527

BASIC SUPPLEMENT   B-1

PREFACE

The revision work associated with the fourth edition of this text has been even more productive and enjoyable than the efforts involved with the three earlier editions. Feedback from instructors using the text has been an excellent source of ideas for making improvements. When it comes to improving content, nothing can replace the actual classroom testing of material. While prior editions of this text have been highly successful, a great deal of care went into updating and refining the latest edition. The final result is a fourth edition textbook vastly improved in structure and substance.

It is appropriate at this point to thank the following people who reviewed the book and provided invaluable comments based on their experience using the third edition of *Computers and Data Processing*.

David Anderson
Cuyahoga Community College, Ohio

Dennis Boyer
Mt. San Jacinto College, California

John DaPonte
Southern Connecticut State University

Arvind D. Doegirikar
The College of St. Rose, New York

Jim Gross
University of Wisconsin Center

Harvey Hershey
Wayne County Community College, Michigan

Joan Krone
Ohio State University

Richard J. McCowan
State University of New York at Buffalo

Gregory L. Smith
Colorado State University

Paul Will
State University of New York at Oswego

Brother Bernard Zalewski
University of Dayton, Ohio

● New Features

Readers familiar with the third edition of the text will notice several changes incorporated in the fourth edition:

● Title change from *Computers and Data Processing* to *Computers and Information Processing* reflects the change in the way the processing of data is viewed in business
● New articles and highlights
● New and updated corporate applications
● Redesigned Concept Summaries with clearer and more concise reviews of key topics
● New chapter on information processing
● Increased coverage on the computer industry and professional associations
● New chapter on application software for mainframes
● Rewritten chapter on microcomputers
● Rewritten chapter on programming with emphasis on top-down design
● Rewritten BASIC supplement with emphasis on structured programming
● New application software for microcomputers supplement covering word processing, data managers, electronic spreadsheets, and integrated software
● New software Users Guides provide maximum hands-on flexibility
● New appendix covering commercial networks
● Increased coverage on the impact of computers on our society

The most inspiring lectures on computers that I have had the good fortune to attend were presented by Rear Admiral Grace Hopper (Ret.), a leader in the development of early computers. In analyzing her material, which always seemed so interesting, it became apparent to me that no new concept was permitted to remain abstract. Rather, actual examples were described, encouraging the listener to visualize their applications. Following Admiral Hopper's example, each chapter in this book is followed by an application that shows how a corporation implements the concepts presented.

Several other important features are included within each chapter. The introductory section serves a dual purpose: as a transition between chapters and as a preview of material. An article with high interest appeal draws the student into the chapter. Highlights containing interesting computer applications or controversial topics are interspersed throughout the chapter to maintain reader interest. Concept summaries permit the student to review quickly the important key topics covered in the chapter. Chapter summary points and review questions are also provided. A comprehensive glossary and index are placed at the end of the text.

Throughout the development of this book the emphasis has been on orienting material to students. All incorporated approaches are designed to assist students in the learning process. Important concepts are never avoided regardless of their complexity. Many books on information processing emphasize one of two aspects of the subject—either informational relationships or computer capabilities. This book attempts to balance and blend both subjects.

In order to provide for a variety of teaching situations, there are two versions of this text available; first, a version with a complete, expanded BASIC Supplement, and second, a language-free version.

● Supplementary Educational Materials

The study guide for this text includes numerous materials for student reinforcement. The instructor material is designed to reduce administrative efforts. Transparency masters are provided to adopters of the text as well as color slides (with a written script) of a tour of a modern computer facility. For qualified adopters there is also available a set of full color transparencies. WESTEST II and Micro Test II, computerized testing services with over one thousand questions, are available from West Publishing Company.

Available to qualified adopters of this version of the text is the greatly improved West Educational Software Series version 2.5. Included in the series are WestWord, a word processor; WestCalc, an electronic spreadsheet; WestGraph, a graphics package; and WestData, a data manager. The 2.5 version of the software, available for a number of microcomputers, has been extensively redesigned so that it is more like commercial software both in appearance and capability.

For those courses which emphasize a hands-on application software component, four new Software User's Guides will be available. These workbooks offer maximum flexibility because the instructor has the choice of using popular commercial software, which may or may not be installed in the college or university, or using the greatly improved West 2.5 software. The Guides also complement the text's new microcomputer applications supplement.

The four versions are:

● Software User's Guide: West 2.5 Version-IBM + MS DOS (for the IBM and MS DOS computers)
● Software User's Guide: Professional Software Version-IBM (for use with already-purchased Lotus 1-2-3, dBase III, WordStar and WordPerfect commercial packages)
● Software User's Guide: EducateAbility Version
● Software User's Guide: West 2.5 Version-Apple (for Apple II-family computers)

West 2.5 (IBM and Apple) and EducateAbility software accompany their respective workbooks, whereas commercial software for the Professional Version (Lotus 1-2-3, dBase III, WordStar and WordPerfect) must be provided by users.

These guides, which introduce students to word processing, spreadsheets, database management, and graphics software, can greatly enhance the classroom learning experience. Each software Guide comes with a data disk for completing exercises in the text and an easy-to-run WestSoft 1.0 simulated applications disk.

Other West software available to accompany the text includes West Tutor and WestSoft. WestTutor is a BASIC tutorial developed from the BASIC Supplement of the text. The diskette is designed to complement the BASIC material as a computer-assisted instructional device. The tutorial also includes an on-demand dictionary of terms from the BASIC Supplement. WestSoft consists of a series of simulations demonstrating home banking, a personality profile test, a ticket office manager, an information service, and a dental office manager. Students can learn to use the basic functions of these computer applications following step-by-step instructions at the bottom of each screen. All the West software is designed to be used in conjunction with both Chapter 8, Microcomputers, and the Application Software Supplement.

● Acknowledgments

I wish also to express my thanks to the people who reviewed the chapters and supplement new to the fourth edition of this book. Their thoughtful comments and suggestions were instrumental to the successful completion of *Computers and Information Processing*.

Jim Gross
University of Wisconsin Center

Harvey Hershey
Wayne County Community College, Michigan

Joan Krone
Ohio State University

Richard J. McCowan
State University of New York at Buffalo

Paul Will
State University of New York at Oswego

Brother Bernard Zalewski
University of Dayton, Ohio

Many individuals and companies have been involved in the development of the material for this book. The corporations whose applications appear in this book have provided invaluable assistance. Many professionals provided the assistance required for completion of a text of this magnitude: Norma Morris and Michelle Westlund on manuscript development; Melissa Landon on photos; Sarah Basinger, Sue Baumann, Laura Bores Stump, and Susan Moran on chapter development; Irene Bulas on the BASIC Supplement; Meredith Flynn on the Application Software Supplement; Lynnette Radigan, Monica Bulas, and Sara Fetterman on instructor material; Ken Wise on student material; Shannan Benschoter, Linda Cupp, Kathleen Shields, and Christine Custer on manuscript preparation; and Robert Slocum and Rochella Thorpe on the index.

The design of the book is a tribute to the many talents of William Stryker. One final acknowledgment goes to my publisher and valued friend, Clyde Perlee, Jr., for his encouragement and ideas.

Steven L. Mandell

1 INTRODUCTION TO INFORMATION PROCESSING

1

○ ARTICLE
The Future's Arrived

Robert Gray
Contributor

When my father was about 9 years old, his father took him on a long trip from their farm in Pennsylvania to Kill Devil Hill, a place on a cold, windy beach in North Carolina. A small crowd of people there had come to watch a couple of backyard tinkerers try out their newfangled contraption. People were skeptical, but many, including my grandfather, wanted to believe. When he read that Orville and Wilbur Wright had mounted an engine on their machine and were going to try it out before Christmas, he decided to see it for himself. So he packed up his little boy and made the trip out to the isolated Atlantic beach.

My father used to tell me about that historic December day in 1903. He and my grandfather had ventured down on the train and hitched a ride from the station in a buggy with some other people. They didn't arrive in time to see several flights attempted earlier that day, but according to one of the men in the crowd, "Those fools are going to keep on flying that thing until they break it or kill themselves."

It was cold that day, and a steady wind was blowing in off the ocean. Dad was at the bottom of the hill, about 300 feet from where the brothers were readying their machine. Finally, the shout came down the hill, "Everybody move back. It's going to go!"

Dad watched intently as the noisy engine was fired up, and the strange-looking machine began moving downhill. Suddenly, about halfway down, it jumped into the air! The craft bobbled up and down a couple of times before it smoothed out, and it was 30 or 40 feet up when it passed my father and grandfather. It made a slow turn to the right as it followed the beach to the south. When the craft landed, about a minute later, it was more than 800 feet

away, and the crowd started running to the landing site. My grandfather just stood there for a minute. "Son," he exclaimed, "you just saw the future!"

We all experience, at one time or another, something so startling that we realize that the world has changed somehow and the future has arrived. Sometimes, the change infiltrates our culture so gradually that we don't realize until later just what happened. For instance, in my life, television became an everyday artifact while I was in the Air Force. When I joined, in 1953, nobody I knew had a set. When I got out in 1957, everybody had one. It was a drastic change in our lifestyle, but it snuck up on me.

I remember Sputnik, and Echo, and Friendship 7; each time I thought, "Here comes the future again." But I wasn't really an eyewitness to these events. They didn't touch me personally the way the Wright Flyer touched my father and grandfather. Then, a few months ago, I had a firsthand, personal encounter with the future. I was awakened by a spaceship! So were a lot people along the coast of Southern California. What we heard was the sonic boom as the Space Shuttle came in across the shoreline. My first thought was, "It's like something out of a Ray Bradbury story. A spaceship woke me up!"

Then I realized this was not my first personal encounter with the future. A couple of years ago I bought my first computer, and my life has been different ever since. My own computer. A couple of years ago, I would have called that science fiction. Now, I almost take it for granted.

When you think about it, you realize that the advent of the affordable personal computer is a more fundamental and far-reaching change in our world

than the space shuttle is. Millions of personal computers have been sold already, and the number is growing by leaps and bounds. In a couple of years, they'll be as common as the telephone. Each computer changes the world for its owner.

A few years ago, Alvin Toffler wrote a book called *Future Shock*, in which he said that changes are happening too rapidly for most people to assimilate. This failure to adjust causes shock, and a refusal to acknowledge that we have to change, too. People suffering from "future shock" live in yesterday, and resist the new technology. If you're reading this, you're probably interested in computers already, and that's a good sign that you're adapting nicely to the future. Don't ever decide that "This is it," and lock up your mind. There's always tomorrow, and there's a lot more future coming.

● **In the last decade, computers have helped to create the information society that we live in, and already we are taking them for granted, much as we do our television sets. What does the future hold? Artificial intelligence? Computers made of living material? You can be sure that whatever it is, it will change the way we live.**

● Introduction

A July 19, 1976, *U.S. News and World Report* article on the computer revolution began, "The changes the computer has made already in American life are insignificant compared with the startling advances predicted for the coming decade." At the time, small banks argued that automated teller machines gave an unfair advantage to the larger institutions that could afford the equipment, and shoppers protested the use of scanners and the Universal Product Code in grocery stores. People could no longer count on sending checks to creditors without sufficient funds to cover them with the idea that they could make a deposit before the checks would clear. And the microcomputer was the "new kid on the block," provided you had the energy to build one from a kit. People had an inkling that computers were changing their lives.

A decade later, the *U.S. News* statement is still true. We will experience even greater changes in the next decade as new technology permits more startling uses for computers. This chapter examines some current uses for computers, the basic terminology of computers, and the classifications of computers we might find in almost any kind of business.

● Computers Today

Yesterday's **computers** were tools for scientists, mathematicians, and engineers. When computers became commercially available, only the largest businesses acquired them, often just for the prestige of owning one. Today, there are many types and applications of computers. **Hardware,** the tangible parts of a computer, ranges from equipment that fills a large room to computers that fit on a lap. **Software** provides instructions to the computer for doing anything from pointing out a good spot to drill for oil to playing realistic games about making and losing money.

There's no doubt that computers are a part of life. In a single day, you come into contact with computers more often than you would think:

● Your morning newspaper was written, edited, and typeset on computers.
● Your late-model car contains a computer chip that governs the fuel mixture and controls emissions from the car's exhaust.
● Your pharmacist consults a data base and warns you that your new medication will not be as effective if taken with milk.
● At the grocery store, the clerk slides your groceries over a counter-mounted scanner that reads coded data about each item into a computer.
● At home, you slip a potato into the microwave oven. Once you punch in the length of time and degree of heat, a computer takes over and controls the baking process.
● The televised evening newscast receives information from an elaborate computer-controlled communications network.
● You can get cash at the bank even though it is closed because you will use the automatic teller machine.
● The "Miami Vice" theme song and many other themes and commercial jingles consist of music that was created using a computer.

These are just a few of the computer applications you might experience in a day. Businesses, governments, research laboratories, and many other organizations deal with so much information every day that it would be almost impossible to proceed without computers.

COMPUTERS IN BUSINESS

Hardly a day goes by when we do not make a computer-controlled business transaction. Each time we visit the bank, use a credit card, pay a bill, or buy groceries, a computer lurks behind the scene, recording each transaction. Computers can process data in a fraction of the time it would take to perform the same jobs manually, reducing paperwork and costs.

Until recently, computer capabilities were limited primarily to large businesses and corporations due to the expenses associated with purchasing a computer system. As the cost of computer hardware decreased, more small businesses were able to use computers. Many computer **programs** for small computers are now available for handling typical business activities, and almost any entrepreneur can purchase the hardware and software needed for a complete accounting system.

Computers in business provide many services. Airlines, travel agencies, and hotels use extensive networks of computer equipment for scheduling reservations. Branches of a business can be connected by communication lines across the country. Businesses use computers for performing clerical duties, preparing documents, sending messages, and sharing data. Since computers work very fast, handle large amounts of data, and provide results exactly when needed, they seem almost indispensable in banking, manufacturing, management, and office functions.

Banking

A bank processes huge amounts of paper and figures daily. Checks, loan records, deposits, savings clubs, and investment plans must be processed. The balances of all accounts must be kept up to date. Funds and data must be exchanged among banks. Banks across the country use computers to facilitate these activities. Banks also use computers for the clerical and communications procedures found in most businesses.

Many banks now offer automated services, such as direct deposit of checks into customers' accounts by their employers and automatic payment of bills. No cash or checks actually change hands. Customers can also request that a regular amount be transferred from checking accounts to savings accounts. Most banks also offer twenty-four-hour banking services in which a computer-controlled machine, the automatic teller machine, permits customers to do their banking day or night (see Figure 1–1).

Manufacturing

Computers have done much to increase productivity in industry. Manufacturing involves designing and building products. It takes extensive

planning and scheduling to accomplish this. Computers can help manufacturers handle the routine scheduling of inventory, machinery, and labor.

Engineers use computers in drawing plans for products, machines for building those products, and machines for building the machines that make the products. During the manufacturing process, computers are used in controlling the operation of machinery (see Figure 1–2). Computers are also helpful in testing prototypes of products. Among the products we use every day that may have been designed by computer are car seats, lenses in sunglasses, sport shoes, and other sports equipment.

Management

The essence of any business is communication, and computers are becoming an essential part of business management by facilitating communication. Preparing documents and analyzing financial data are two of the applications most frequently used by managers to save time and make tasks easier. At the headquarters of Mobil Oil, Norman James, manager of analysts and controls, uses an IBM PC to complete annual budget reports. Using the PC, James is able to complete a report in ten days that once took four to six weeks to complete.

Because computers make it so easy to generate and **retrieve** information, many managers find they suffer from information overload. It is well known in business circles that 80 percent of management decisions are based on 20 percent of the data, but that 20 percent must be the right data. In some cases, graphically represented data helps focus the important data. Comparisons, relationships, trends, and other essential points can be spotted more easily using graphics such as bar graphs, pie charts, and line graphs (see Figure 1–3).

Office Automation

If we believe the advertisements on television and in business magazines, the office as we now know it is doomed. Gone will be the typewriters, the bulky desks, the cumbersome filing cabinets, the impromptu "conferences" at the water fountain, and the endless rows of clerks and secretaries. Recent developments in communications, information storage and retrieval, and software have changed the office environment. Organizations are realizing that computer technology is efficient, cost effective, and necessary in handling the exploding amounts of data. The increasing amount of reporting required by federal government agencies particularly lends itself to computer technology in the office.

● **FIGURE 1–3**
Bar Graph
This bar graph was created using graphics software.

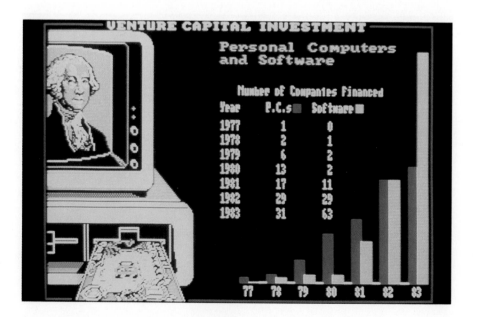

● COMPUTERS AND INFORMATION PROCESSING

Almost every office function—typing, filing, and communications—can be automated. The term applied to the integration of computer and communication technology with traditional office procedures is **office automation.** Among the specific applications in office automation are word processing, information retrieval, electronic mail, teleconferencing, and telecommuting (see Chapter 16). The most widely adopted application is **word processing.** At least 75 percent of U.S. companies use some form of word processing. Word processing aids in preparing text and bypasses the shortcomings of traditional writing and typing.

COMPUTERS IN OTHER AREAS

No area of enterprise seems without computers nowadays. Scientists build computer models of airplane crashes in order to determine the "crash behavior" of airplanes, which in turn helps aircraft designers plan safer seats, windows, and fabrics to decrease fire hazards during a crash. Ecologists use computers in monitoring environmental problems like acid rain and suggesting solutions. Engineers use computers to design replacements for damaged bones. Educators use computers in the classroom to perform chemistry experiments that might otherwise be dangerous. There seems to be no limit to computer applications.

The federal government is the largest user of computers in the United States. This fact is not surprising when one considers the many government agencies that collect, process, and store information about the population. Typical examples are taking the U.S. census every ten years, processing the millions of income tax returns received each year, maintaining the large data bases in the Library of Congress and Federal Bureau of Investigation, and managing the welfare and social security systems (see Figure 1-4).

● **FIGURE 1-4**
FBI Data Base
FBI computer operators are preparing some of the many magnetic tapes for storage in the bureau's huge tape library.

● Enhancing Human Performance

Some of us who use computers find that they almost become extensions of ourselves—our minds and our bodies. Perhaps the seeds were sown in the days of video games when we reacted quickly to information on the screen by manipulating a joystick or trackball. Now we discover that computers provide immediate feedback to the data we enter, and we can improve our performance in work, education, and sports.

Portable computers have made it possible to record and analyze data in almost any work environment. Rapid feedback from data entered at the work site helps managers solve problems quickly.

Sports doctors and biomechanical engineers are using computers to study movement of athletes and test strength and endurance.

Students from various engineering disciplines learn to use the PS 300 family of computer graphics systems at the Center for Computer Assisted Engineering at Colorado State University. Students working in the computer graphics lab are solving complex design and engineering problems using today's most advanced hardware and software.

A flight simulator "flies" through a visual scene created from actual photographs by LTV Aerospace & Defense Co. The simulator's visual environment can use photos taken from satellites and high-altitude aircraft. The photos are updated 30 times per second.

Computers are used in the areas of science and medicine for routine clerical functions. More importantly, in just seconds they can make calculations and test designs that human beings could not complete unaided in months. Data analyzed by computers may be collected by satellites for military intelligence and environmental planning, by seismographs for earthquake prediction, by CAT scans for medical diagnosis, and by sensors for determination of toxicity levels. For example, a crisis such as the life-endangering gas leak at the Union Carbide plant in Bhopal, India, might have been prevented with computerized warning systems.

Educators are becoming more involved in computer use, too. A frequently asked question in the past ten years has been, "Will the computer replace the teacher?" The answer, of course, is "no" but computers can help teachers and students with their work. Computers become private tutors for students who need extra help or additional challenges. Computers are used in helping students learn programming languages such as Pascal or BASIC. Videodisks combined with computers offer a learning aid that, unlike books, includes motion and sound. Using videodisk lessons, students can see reproductions of the early colonists preparing for the Revolutionary War or the Wright brothers trying out their first airplane. They can interact with lessons about current events and watch news footage from old newscasts.

Computer use does not end at school or at work. Increasingly, American families are buying computers for use at home. At first, they may play games, but later they realize the tremendous potential of home computers in gathering information. Using the telephone lines and specially equipped computers, people can call a commercial data base such as CompuServe for information about the stock market, current events, historical background, or sports (see Figure 1–5). Word processing, filing, and financial planning are popular home uses, too.

We have seen how computers can be powerful tools in both large-scale applications and everyday functions of our lives. By knowing how computers work, what they can do, and what their problems and benefits are, we can use computers to their best advantage.

● Overview of Information Processing

The terms **data processing** and **information processing** are often used interchangeably by many people. The difference in meaning between the terms is subtle, and in the context of this book, a distinction must be made. Data processing refers to the steps involved in collecting, manipulating, and distributing data to achieve certain goals. Using computers for data processing is called **electronic data processing (EDP).** The term *data processing* has historically been used to mean EDP.

The objective of all data processing, whether manual or electronic, is the conversion of data into information that can be used in making decisions. The term *information processing*, then, is used when referring to all the steps involved in converting data to information, including the use of processed information for decision making.

What is the difference between data and information? **Data** refers to raw facts collected from various sources, but not organized or defined

● **FIGURE 1–5**
Computers at Home
This computer is being used for controlling the home environment, including heating, lighting, and security.

in a meaningful way. Data cannot be used to make meaningful decisions. For example, a bank manager may have very little use for a daily list of the amounts of all checks and deposit slips from the branch offices. But once data is organized, it can provide useful information—perhaps in the form of a summary report giving the dollar value and total number of deposits and withdrawals at each branch. **Information** is processed data that increases understanding and helps people make intelligent decisions (see Figure 1–6). To be useful, information must be accurate, timely, complete, concise, and relevant. It must be delivered to the right person at the right time in the right place. If information fails to meet these requirements, it fails to meet the needs of those who must use it and is of little value.

DATA ORGANIZATION

For effective processing, data should be organized in an integrated way so that the anticipated need of users for information can be met. Therefore, data items are placed in groups from the smallest unit, the bit, to the largest unit, the data base. Each category is described below.

1. Bit. Data is represented by on and off states of the computer's electronic circuitry (see the section on Analog and Digital Computers below). The symbols that represent on and off are the binary digits 0 and 1. Each 0 or 1 is called a **bit,** short for **bi**nary dig**it.** The bit is the smallest unit of data a computer can handle.

2. Character. There are obviously more letters and numbers than two but the computer only recognizes the two. Therefore, combinations of 0s and 1s are used to represent **characters**—letters, digits, and special symbols such as %, #, or $. In the employee name E. J. Barnes, the characters are the two periods, the two spaces, and the letters E, J, B, a, r, n, e, and s.

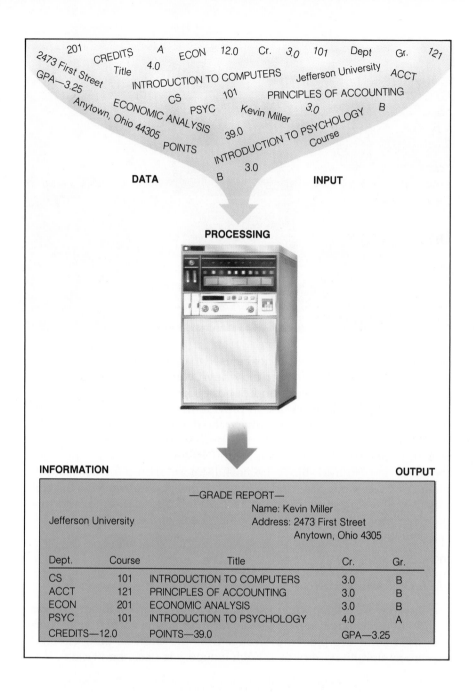

3. Field. A business firm maintains specific data about its employees, such as home address, social security number, hourly wage, withholding tax, gross income, and so on. Each of these categories is called a **field.** A field is a collection of related characters that conveys a unit of information.

4. Record. A collection of fields that relate to a single unit is a **record.** An inventory record might consist of fields for item number, item name, description, price, supplier, quantity on hand, and location.

5. File. A grouping of related records is a **file.** All the client records for a construction firm would constitute the firm's client file.

6. Data base. Today's sophisticated software provides a method of structuring data called a **data base** that satisfies a wide variety of information needs and multiple functions. All of a company's employee files, inventory files, client files, and much more would constitute a data base.

This book uses the terms *bit, character, field, record, file,* and *data base* as described (see Figure 1–7). The following sections discuss data processing relevant to computers and introduces the requirements, the steps involved, and the advantage of computers in data processing.

THE DATA FLOW

In deriving information from data, the data is manipulated, or processed. All processing follows the same basic flow: input, processing, and output. Each step is described in detail below.

Input

Input is the process of capturing data and putting it in a form that the computer can "understand." Input includes both the data that is to be manipulated and the software.

Data can be input into a computer by typing on a keyboard, using a scanning device such as the wands found in a department store or the counter-mounted scanners found in grocery stores, speaking into a microphone connected to the computer, or running a magnetic tape or disk. Such devices are described in greater detail in Chapters 4 and 5.

Input involves three steps:

● Collecting the raw data and assembling it at one location.
● Verifying, or checking, the accuracy and completeness of data, including both the facts and the programs. This step is very important since most computer errors are due to human error.
● Coding the data into a machine-readable form for processing.

● **FIGURE 1–7**
Organization of a Data Base

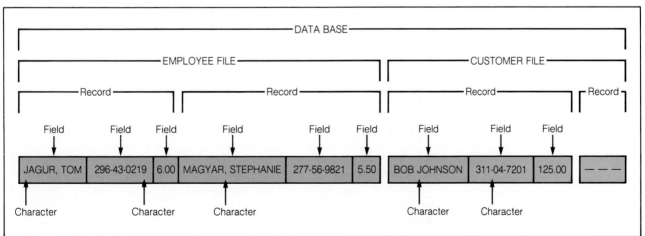

Processing

Once the data has been input, it is processed. **Processing** occurs in the part of the computer called the **central processing unit (CPU),** examined in Chapter 4. The CPU includes the circuitry needed for performing arithmetic and logical operations and **primary memory.** Primary memory is the internal storage that holds programs and data used in immediate processing.

Once an instruction or data is stored at a particular location in primary memory, it stays there until new data or instructions are written over the old material. The same data can be **accessed** repeatedly during processing, or the same instructions can be used repeatedly to process many different pieces of data.

Processing entails several types of manipulations (see Figure 1–8):

● Classifying, or categorizing, the data according to certain characteristics so that it is meaningful to the user. For example, sales data could be grouped according to salesperson, product type, or customer.
● Sorting, or arranging, the data alphabetically or numerically. An employee file may be sorted by social security number or by last name.
● Calculating, or figuring, the data arithmetically or logically. Examples include computation of students' grade-point averages, customers' bank balances, and employees' paychecks.
● Summarizing data, or reducing it to concise, usable forms. All grades for all students in all classes can be summarized by grade point averages, naming those students who earn a place on the dean's list. Sales figures can be summarized by salesperson in order to provide a list of those salespersons who received orders greater than that month's goal.
● Storing, or retaining, data on storage media such as magnetic disks, tapes, or microfilm for later retrieval and processing.

Output

After data has been processed according to some or all of the steps above, information can be distributed to the users. There are two types of **output:** soft copy and hard copy. **Soft copy** is information that is seen on a televisionlike screen or monitor attached to most computers. It is temporary; as soon as the monitor is turned off or new information is required, the old information vanishes. **Hard copy** is output printed in a tangible form such as paper or microfilm. It can be read without using the computer and can be conveniently carried around, written on, or passed to other readers. Hardware that produces hard copy includes printers, discussed in Chapter 5.

Three steps are necessary in the output phase of data flow:

● Retrieving, or pulling, data from storage for use by the decision maker.
● Converting, or translating, data into a form that humans can understand and use (words or pictures displayed on a computer screen or printed on paper).
● Communicating, or providing information to the proper users at the proper time and place in an intelligible form.

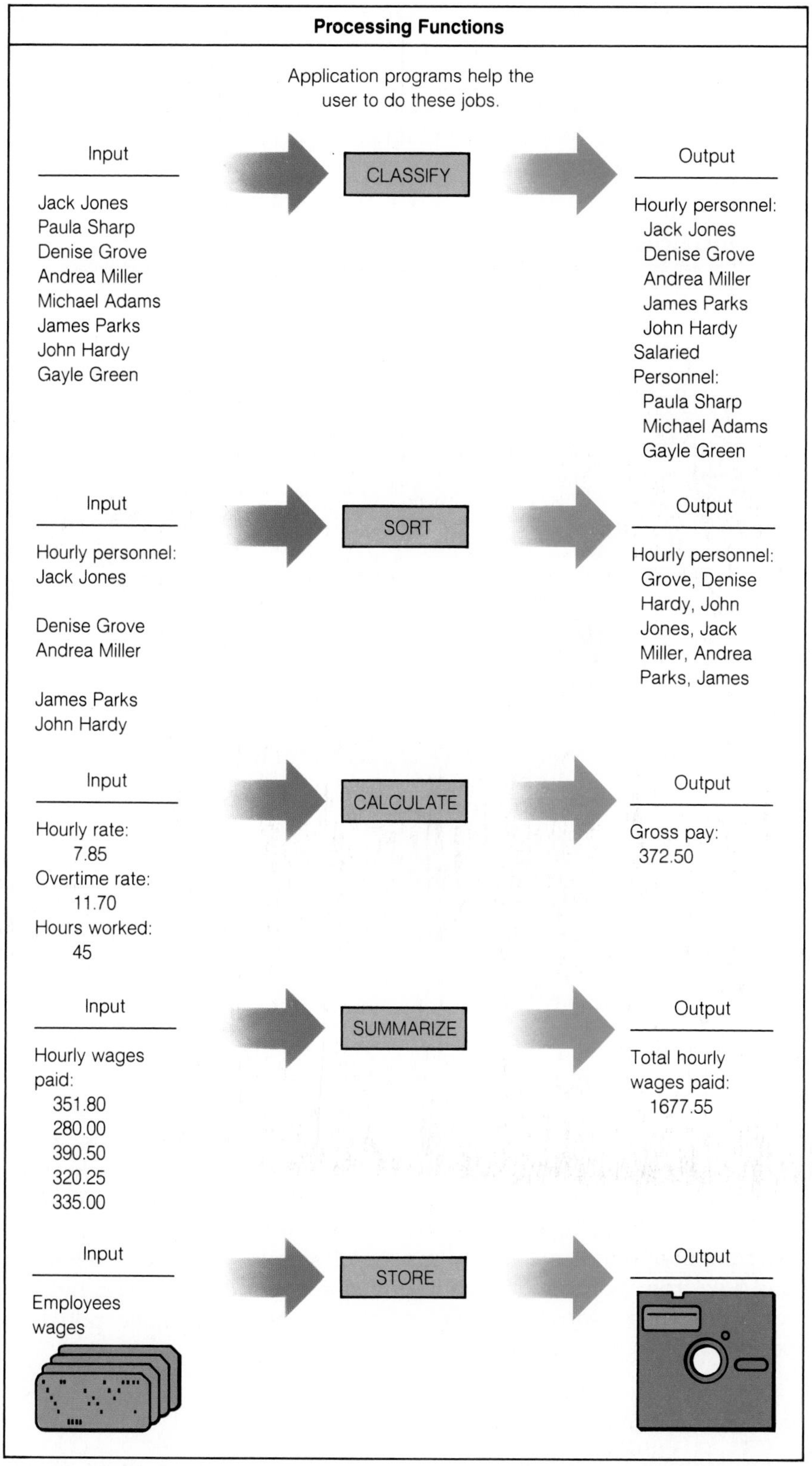

Processing Functions

Application programs help the user to do these jobs.

Input

Jack Jones
Paula Sharp
Denise Grove
Andrea Miller
Michael Adams
James Parks
John Hardy
Gayle Green

CLASSIFY

Output

Hourly personnel:
Jack Jones
Denise Grove
Andrea Miller
James Parks
John Hardy
Salaried
Personnel:
Paula Sharp
Michael Adams
Gayle Green

Input

Hourly personnel:
Jack Jones

Denise Grove
Andrea Miller

James Parks
John Hardy

SORT

Output

Hourly personnel:
Grove, Denise
Hardy, John
Jones, Jack
Miller, Andrea
Parks, James

Input

Hourly rate:
7.85
Overtime rate:
11.70
Hours worked:
45

CALCULATE

Output

Gross pay:
372.50

Input

Hourly wages
paid:
351.80
280.00
390.50
320.25
335.00

SUMMARIZE

Output

Total hourly
wages paid:
1677.55

Input

Employees
wages

STORE

Output

● **FIGURE 1–8**
Processing Functions

Information processing is monitored or evaluated in a step called **feedback.** Over time, the information provided through this processing may lose its effectiveness. Feedback is the process of evaluating the output and making adjustments to the input or the processing steps to ensure that the processing results in good information.

Overview of Information Processing

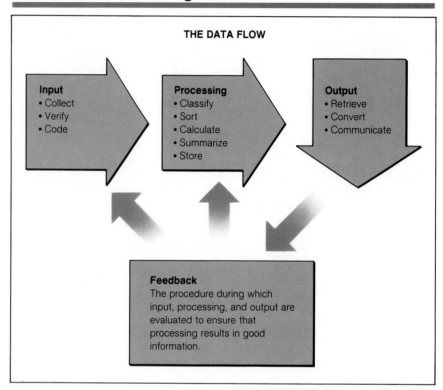

THE DATA FLOW

Input
- Collect
- Verify
- Code

Processing
- Classify
- Sort
- Calculate
- Summarize
- Store

Output
- Retrieve
- Convert
- Communicate

Feedback
The procedure during which input, processing, and output are evaluated to ensure that processing results in good information.

OPERATION OF COMPUTERS

Many people envision an electronic marvel with mystical powers when they hear the word computer. A computer, however, performs only those tasks that a person has directed. It has no intelligence of its own and must rely on human intelligence and instructions for performing any task.

A computer handles data by means of simple yes/no operations. It pulls data from storage, acts on it, and stores it again, directed by programs that determine the yes/no, on/off, or conducting/nonconducting operations of its circuits.

Analog and Digital Computers

When we refer to computers in this book, we are talking about digital computers. There are also analog computers. **Analog computers** measure changes in continuous physical or electrical states, such as pressure, temperature, voltage, length, volume, or shaft rotations. A gasoline pump uses an analog device that measures the quantity of gasoline pumped to the nearest tenth of a gallon and the price of that gasoline to the nearest penny. Another analog device is a speedometer. Here, driveshaft rotations are measured and converted to a pointer that indicates the speed of the car.

On the other hand, **digital computers** count. In a digital computer, data is represented by discrete "on" and "off" (conducting/nonconducting or yes/no) states of the computer's electronic circuitry. Numbers, letters, and symbols are represented by a code based on the binary number system, a number system consisting of two digits, 1 and 0. This number system is well suited to represent the on/off states of electric current. The digital computer must convert all data to binary form.

Results from digital computers are more accurate than results from analog devices. It is not uncommon for a car's speedometer to be off by one or two miles per hour. Some digital computers, however, can provide results accurate to hundreds or even thousands of decimal places. These precise computers are used in scientific applications. For business applications, results accurate to only a few decimal places are sufficient. Computer manufacturers design digital computers with varied capabilities that meet the varied needs of the users of these machines. The computers discussed in this book are digital computers.

The Computer Advantage

Within the limitations of its circuits, a computer can perform three basic functions:

1. Arithmetic operations (addition, subtraction, multiplication, division).
2. Logical comparisons of relationships among values (greater than, less than, equal to).
3. Storage and retrieval operations.

If the three functions named above are all a computer can do, then why use a computer? People use a computer because it is a very fast machine, its circuits are reliable, and it can be used to store vast amounts of data.

SPEED. Two physical factors control the speed of a computer: the switching speed of its electronic components (switching the state from on to off, or switching the direction the current travels, for example) and the distances that electric currents must travel within the circuits. By packing circuits closer together and increasing the switching speed, engineers have been able to increase vastly the speed of the computer. Other factors that affect computer speeds are the language used in writing programs, the amount of data a computer can handle at one time, and the amount of data and instructions readily available in the computer's primary memory.

Modern computers can perform millions of calculations in one second. Their speed is fast reaching the physical limitation of the speed of light, 186,000 miles per second. Generally, computer speed describes the time

A Tale of Two Bugs

The story of the first computer bug has become a legend. In the summer of 1945, something went wrong with the Mark II, a large electromechanical machine used by the Department of Defense. Though the machine was not working properly, the operating personnel could find no obvious problems. A continued search revealed a large moth beaten to death by one of the electromechanical relays. The moth was pulled out with tweezers and taped to a log book (now exhibited in the Naval Museum at the Naval Surface Weapons Center, Dahlgren, Virginia). "From then on," said Rear Admiral Grace Hopper, one of the people working with the machine, "when the officer came in to ask if we were accomplishing anything, we told him we were 'debugging' the computer." So the phrases "bugs in the program" and "debugging the program" became popular in describing programming errors.

Few people realize, however, that the use of the word *bug* to mean an error is at least a hundred years old. Thomas Alva Edison introduced the word in a letter to Theodore Puskas, Edison's representative in France, on November 13, 1878. He wrote:

I have the right principle and am on the right track, but time, hard work, and some good luck are necessary too. It has been just so in all of my inventions. The first step is an intuition, and comes with a burst, then difficulties arise—this thing gives out and then that—"bugs"—as such little faults and difficulties are called—show themselves and months of intense watching, study and labor are requisite before commercial success—or failure—is certainly reached.

So now you have it—A Tale of Two Bugs.

required to perform one operation and is measured in terms of nanoseconds and other small units (see Figure 1–9). In the past, the time required for performing one addition ranged from 4 microseconds to 200 nanoseconds. In the future, it may be 200 to 1,000 times faster.

ACCURACY. The accuracy of a computer applies to the inherent reliability of its electronic components. The same type of current passed through the same circuits yields the same results each time. We take advantage of this aspect of circuitry every time we switch on an electric device. When we turn on a light switch, we expect the light to go on, not the radio or a fan. The computer is reliable for the same reason: Its circuitry is reliable. A computer can run for hours, days, and weeks at a time, giving accurate results of millions of activities. Of course, if the data or programs submitted to the computer are faulty, the computer will not produce correct results. The output will be useless and meaningless, illustrating the human error involved. This is called garbage in—garbage out (GIGO) and is fundamental in understanding computer "mistakes."

STORAGE. Besides being very fast and reliable, computers can store large amounts of data. Some data is held in primary memory for use during immediate operations. The amount of data held in primary memory varies among computers. Some small computers hold as few as 16,000 characters, and large computers can hold billions of characters. Data can also be recorded on magnetic disks or tapes (see Figure 1–10); this **secondary storage** makes a computer's "memory" almost limitless. Secondary storage holds data that is not immediately needed by the computer.

Similarly, vast quantities of data stored in paper files would become extremely bulky and require substantial storage space. Further, the job of manually extracting data from such files would become increasingly tedious and time consuming as the size of the files increased. Data can be stored electronically in considerably less space and retrieved in a fraction of the time needed by manual methods.

The ability of the computer to store, retrieve, and process data, all without human intervention, separates it from a simple calculator and gives it its power and appeal to humans. So while humans can perform the same functions as the computer, the difference is that the computer can reliably execute millions of instructions in a second and store the results in an almost unlimited memory.

● **FIGURE 1–9**
Divisions of a Second

UNIT	SYMBOL	FRACTIONS OF A SECOND
Millisecond	ms	one-thousandth (1/1,000)
Microsecond	μs	one-millionth (1/1,000,000)
Nanosecond	ns	one-billionth (1/1,000,000,000)
Picosecond	ps	one-trillionth (1/1,000,000,000,000)

Computer Functions

- The computer performs three functions: arithmetic operations, comparison operations, and storage and retrieval operations.

- A computer's appeal is based on its speed, accuracy, and memory.

- A computer's internal memory is called **primary storage,** and media used to hold data outside the computer constitute **secondary storage.** Secondary storage makes the computer's memory almost limitless.

● Computer Classifications

Computers are categorized by size, capability, price range, and speed of operation. It is becoming increasingly difficult to distinguish among the different classifications of computers, however, because smaller computers have increasingly larger primary memories and are able to handle an increasing number of **peripheral devices** such as printers and secondary storage devices. The four major categories of computer systems are supercomputers, mainframes, minicomputers, and microcomputers.

SUPERCOMPUTERS

Supercomputers are the largest, fastest, most expensive computers made (see Figure 1–11). They process data at speeds exceeding 400,000,000 to 600,000,000 operations per second. The computers act so fast that their chips must be surrounded by a liquid coolant to prevent melting.

Research in supercomputer development has become a heated race between the United States and Japan. Whoever develops and commercializes technology improving supercomputers will have the competitive

● **FIGURE 1–10**
Tape Storage
This woman adjusts a tape drive for running one of many magnetic tapes her company uses for storing data.

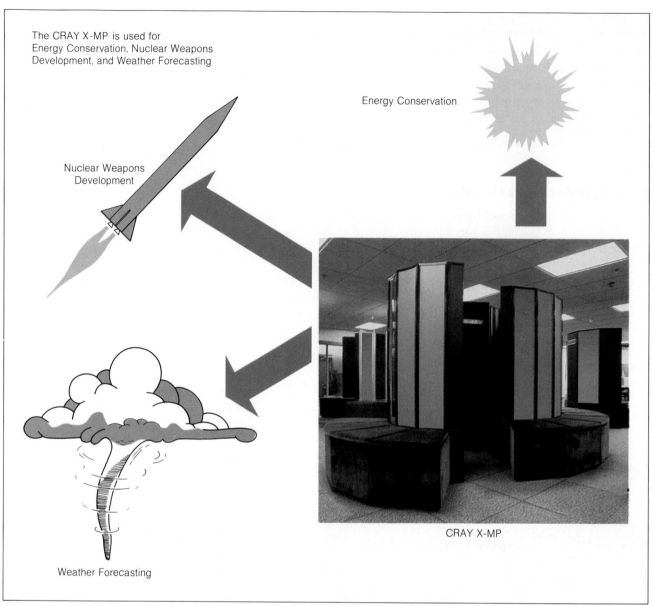

The CRAY X-MP is used for Energy Conservation, Nuclear Weapons Development, and Weather Forecasting

Energy Conservation

Nuclear Weapons Development

Weather Forecasting

CRAY X-MP

● **FIGURE 1–11**
The Cray X-MP Supercomputer System

edge in all computer-related industries, an important consideration for both economics and national defense. Companies developing supercomputers include Cray Research, Fujitsu, and ETA Systems, Inc.

Only a few supercomputers are produced each year because the manufacturing cost is high and the market is limited. Each supermachine costs several million dollars to develop and install. In addition, software development for supercomputers is much more complex and expensive because the design of the machines is so much different from the design of less powerful computers. To justify costs this high, an organization must be very large and must need to process millions of instructions very quickly or maintain large data bases.

Demand for supercomputers is increasing, however. In 1980, there were only 21 supercomputers in the world. Today, 142 supercomputers are busy crunching numbers, and the appetite for them seems insatiable. Even universities are beginning to install supercomputers for their extensive research projects.

Supercomputers are used for figuring lengthy and complex calculations. Scientists use them in weather forecasting, oil exploration, energy conservation, seismology, nuclear reactor safety analysis, and cryptography. In addition, supercomputers are used for simulations in nuclear energy research and stress tests in automotive and aircraft design.

MAINFRAMES

During the 1960s, the term *mainframe* was synonymous with CPU. Today the word refers simply to a category of computers between the minicomputer and the supercomputer.

Mainframes operate at very high speeds and support main input and output devices that also operate at very high speeds. They can be subdivided into small, medium, and large systems. Most mainframes are manufactured as "families" of computers. A family consists of several mainframe models varying in size and power. An organization can purchase or lease a small system and, if processing needs expand, upgrade to a medium or large system. Purchase prices may range from $200,000 to several million dollars for a large mainframe with peripherals. Mainframes are used chiefly by large businesses, hospitals, universities, and banks with large data processing needs (see Figure 1–12).

A mainframe creates a fair amount of heat, requiring cooling systems. It cannot be plugged into a standard electrical outlet, therefore it needs special electrical wiring. It may rest on a special platform so that its wires and cables can be housed beneath it. Because a mainframe operates

● **FIGURE 1–12**
IBM System/370/155 Mainframe

day and night and provides access to a large amount of data, access to it must be controlled for security reasons. These factors add to its cost.

Because of their sophistication and size, mainframe computers are sold or leased with a great deal of support from the vendor. The vendor may invest considerable time and money in helping a customer select and install a mainframe. Once the system is installed, the vendor spends additional effort training the customer's employees from top executives to clerical workers to use the system, servicing and repairing the mainframe, and solving questions and problems that arise periodically. Major mainframe manufacturers are IBM, Burroughs, Honeywell, NCR, and Sperry.

MINICOMPUTERS

Minicomputers were developed in the 1960s for doing specialized tasks. They were smaller, less powerful, and less expensive than the larger computers available at that time. As they became increasingly sophisticated, their capabilities, memory size, and overall performance have overlapped those of mainframes. The more powerful minicomputers are called *superminis*.

Minicomputers are easier to install and operate than mainframe computers. They take up less floor space than mainframes; they may fit on a desk, or they may be as large as a file cabinet (see Figure 1–13). They require few special environmental conditions. Minicomputers can be plugged into standard electrical outlets and often do not require facilities such as air conditioning and special platforms. Prices for minicomputers

● **FIGURE 1–13**
Minicomputer System with Peripherals

● COMPUTERS AND INFORMATION PROCESSING

range from a few thousand dollars to two or three hundred thousand dollars.

Minicomputers are used for multiuser applications, numerical control of machine tools, industrial automation, and word processing. They are also used in conjunction with communication facilities for sharing data and peripherals or serving a geographically dispersed organization. They can use **packaged software,** that is, standardized, commercial software developed for solving general problems such as preparing a general ledger or payroll.

A minicomputer system can easily be enlarged to meet the needs of a growing organization since it can be implemented in a modular fashion. For example, a hospital may install one minicomputer in its outpatient department for record keeping and another in the pharmacy or laboratory. As additional minicomputers are installed, they can be connected to existing ones to share common data.

In the late 1970s and early 1980s, the minicomputer industry grew at a rate of 35 to 40 percent annually. Today, the market for minicomputers is weakening. The increased capabilities and improved software of microcomputers has led to the increased use of microcomputers in traditional minicomputer markets. Many companies now link microcomputers with mainframes or existing minicomputers to hold down equipment investment costs and still meet processing needs. This practice, however, creates new security problems for many corporations.

Manufacturers of minicomputers include Digital Equipment Corporation (DEC), Hewlett-Packard, Data General, Honeywell, General Automation, Burroughs, Texas Instruments, Wang Laboratories, Prime Computer Inc., and IBM. Minicomputers are available from the vendors.

MICROCOMPUTERS

Once technology had advanced to the point where many circuits could be etched onto a single silicon chip, the **microprocessor** was developed. A microprocessor is a chip that contains the portions of the CPU that control the computer and perform arithmetic and logic operations. It may contain some primary storage also. The microprocessor became the foundation for the **microcomputer,** also called the personal computer.

Microcomputers are the most popular type of computer today. They may fit on a desktop or in a briefcase (see Figure 1–14). Some microcomputers designed for home use cost as little as $100, and some microcomputers for professional use may cost as much as $10,000. Most microcomputers are single-user systems.

The prefix *micro* applies more to size and cost than to capability, because current microcomputers are very powerful for their size. Microcomputers cannot perform as many complex functions as today's large computers and have much smaller primary memories; however, technology continues to give them more speed and memory at decreasing costs. One important aspect of microcomputer design involves the development of user-friendly hardware and software; that is, equipment that is easy to use and easy to learn to use. The concern for user friendliness has overflowed into the development of other computers, too.

Microcomputers are available in computer stores, office supply stores,

● **FIGURE 1–14**
Apple IIc
This couple uses their Apple IIc for
many home applications.

and department stores. In some cases, they are sold much as an appliance like a television or videocassette recorder. Software for microcomputers is often packaged, but many users like the challenge of developing their own and many businesses need custom-developed software. Chapter 8 provides a detailed discussion of microcomputers.

CONCEPT
SUMMARY 1–3

Factors to Consider in Buying a Computer System

	SUPER-COMPUTER	MAINFRAME	MINI-COMPUTER	MICRO-COMPUTER
Cost	Several million dollars	$200,000 to several million dollars	A few thousand to two or three hundred thousand dollars	$100 to $10,000
Other facts	Largest, fastest computer. Good for complex, lengthy calculations. Hard to justify costs. Software development complex.	Additional costs: platforms, security, wiring, air conditioning. Vendor support. Easily upgraded to next size in family.	Fits in small space. Uses standard electrical outlets. Often needs no air conditioning. Expandable in modular fashion. Micros rapidly approaching minicomputer capabilities.	Can fit on desk or lap. Many applications. Can be linked to mainframes or minicomputers. Newer computers and software are user-friendly.

● Summary Points

● Computers are powerful tools in many areas such as business, manufacturing, banking, government, education, and personal use. Most of today's transactions and procedures involve computer equipment, office automation, and data bases.

● Electronic data processing, often called simply data processing, involves the use of computers in collecting, manipulating, and distributing data to achieve goals. The terms *hardware* and *software* describe the physical components of a computer and instructions or programs used in electronic data processing.

● Data refers to unorganized, raw facts, and information is data that has been organized and processed so that it can be used in making intelligent decisions.

● For effective data processing, data is organized in meaningful units. The units, from smallest to largest, are bit, character, field, record, file, and data base.

● Converting data into information follows this pattern: input, processing, output.

● Input involves collecting, verifying, and coding the data.

● Processing involves classifying, sorting, calculating, summarizing, and storing data.

● Information retrieved and converted so that it can be communicated to the user in an intelligible form is output.

● Analog computers measure the change in continuous physical or electric states, and digital computers count data in the form of yes/no, on/off, conducting/nonconducting states of electronic circuitry. The digital computer must convert all data to binary form, a form based on the binary number system of two digits, 0 and 1.

● The computer performs three functions: arithmetic operations, logic comparisons, and storage and retrieval operations.

● A computer's appeal is based on its speed, accuracy, and memory.

● A computer's internal memory is called primary storage. Media used to hold data outside the computer constitute secondary storage. Secondary storage makes the computer's memory almost limitless.

● Computers are categorized by size, capability, price range, and speed of operation. The four classifications are supercomputer, mainframe, minicomputer, and microcomputer.

● Advances in technology have blurred the distinctions between the classifications of computers, so that some minicomputers have capabilities as great as mainframes and some microcomputers have capabilities as great as minicomputers.

● Many companies are linking microcomputers to existing systems to increase capabilities yet hold down costs.

● Review Questions

1. In your job or school today, name some ways that computers affect you. Relate these ways to applications discussed in the first section of this chapter.

2. Distinguish between data and information in the context of data processing. Give some examples.

3. Define data processing. Why is it often referred to as EDP?

4. Describe the relationship that exists among data within a data base, mentioning the bit, character, field, record, file, and data base.

5. Using data that a store might collect when you purchase groceries, describe the five types of manipulations that may occur in the processing stage of the data flow.

6. Name the three basic functions that a computer can perform.

7. Although computer processing is essentially error free, mistakes can and do occur. What is meant by the phrase "garbage in—garbage out"? Name two procedures mentioned in the discussion of the data flow that could prevent GIGO.

8. Describe two types of storage involved in data processing. Why is the computer's "memory" almost limitless?

9. For what purposes might you use a supercomputer? Have you heard of any uses other than the ones mentioned in the text? What are they?

10. What market trends are currently causing the downturn in sales of mainframes and minicomputers?

COMPANY HISTORY

The largest newspaper in the country with a circulation of more than two million, *The Wall Street Journal,* began more than a hundred years ago as a two-page publication known as the *Customers' Afternoon Letter.* The *Letter* was the brainchild of Charles H. Dow and Edward D. Jones, two financial news reporters who worked for a New York news agency. The two men formed Dow Jones & Company and were soon joined in their publishing efforts by Charles M. Bergstresser.

The *Letter,* which was delivered to subscribers in the Wall Street area, appeared each afternoon and summarized the financial bulletins that were issued during the day. Charles Dow added a daily feature called the Dow Jones Average, a stock price index based on a formula he devised. The publication prospered and, soon after Clarence W. Barron joined the staff, the *Letter* became a full-fledged newspaper called *The Wall Street Journal.* The first issue of *The Wall Street Journal* was printed on July 8, 1889, cost two cents, and was four pages long. Although the *Journal's* stories emphasized business and finance, general news stories appeared in the first issue and continue to this day.

The *Journal's* reputation and circulation grew. Clarence Barron bought a controlling interest in the company following the death of Charles Dow in 1902. Barron increased circulation, expanded news coverage, and introduced modern printing equipment during the years in which he controlled the paper. A Pacific Coast edition of the *Journal* was first published eight days before the stock market crash of 1929.

With the collapse of the stock market, the *Journal* fell upon hard times. Circulation dropped as the financial community struggled to survive. Help came from Barney Kilgore, who was named managing editor in 1941. The changes in the paper that Kilgore implemented exist today. He insisted the paper acquire a broader

scope, including all aspects of business, economics, and consumer affairs. Kilgore also made the Pacific Coast edition of the paper a duplicate of the Eastern edition.

Serving the readers promptly was another of Kilgore's goals. This goal provided the impetus for a Southwest edition of the *Journal* in 1948 complete with a printing plant in Dallas. Although three editions of the paper ensured that readers all over the country would have access to up-to-the minute news, the diverse locations created technical problems of a new magnitude. How could the same newspaper with the same staff of writers and editors be published in different locations around the country? The answer involved the use of a new technology. Once stories were typed, they were coded on perforated tape and passed through a reader that converted the stories into electrical pulses. The pulses were sent via telephone lines to linecasters and then were automatically set into type.

Continued circulation growth and expansion in news coverage brought the *Journal* worldwide fame. A number of the paper's writers received the Pulitzer Prize. Old printing plants were replaced, and early in the sixties, a breakthrough came on the production front. Microwave transmissions were used to send full-page images from one plant to another. By the mid-seventies, all *Journal* printing plants were using a sophisticated internal communications system. A central computer directed typesetting in multiple printing plants.

COMPUTER USAGE TODAY

Today, computers play an essential role in getting news stories into print. A complicated electronic network transports stories from the point of origin to the homes and offices of subscribers. Personal computers and computer consoles are used with word-processing software to write and edit stories. Once a story has been written and edited, it is transmitted by facsimile from New York to Chicopee, Massachusetts. There it is entered into a computer system that electronically transmits the story to another computer at the research facilities in South Brunswick, New Jersey. From South Brunswick, the story is sent by telephone lines to computer-controlled, high-speed photocomposition typesetters located in production plants across the country. Typeset stories are output on strips of paper that are then laid out and pasted onto pages. At this point, the pages may undergo one

APPLICATION

of two routes. They may be photographed, with printing plates made from the film and the plates set onto high-speed presses. Or they may be made into paper proofs, which in turn are scanned by a laser beam and transmitted via satellite to other printing plants. Computer-controlled printing systems can print fifteen copies per second. Once printed, the papers are automatically labeled with a computer-produced label, bundled, and loaded on trucks that carry the papers to distribution points.

Computers are used in a number of other ways at *The Wall Street Journal*. Financial systems are run on IBM mainframes using MVS/XA and VM operating systems. A computerized advertising system provides page makeup information and produces invoices. Circulation services are kept current on a Sperry computer that contains a master file of all subscribers. Each printing plant is sent a list of subscribers daily.

When Charles Dow and Edward Jones began their two-page *Afternoon Letter* in a tiny basement office, they could hardly have imagined the magnitude to which their news organization would grow.

DISCUSSION POINTS

1. Describe how computers are directly involved in bringing stories to print.
2. Other than bringing stories to print, how are computers used at *The Wall Street Journal*?

2 THE EVOLUTION OF COMPUTERS

A Birthday Party for ENIAC

Philip Elmer-DeWitt
TIME

A few weeks after Kay McNulty graduated from Philadelphia's Chestnut Hill College in 1942 with a degree in mathematics, she got a job at the Army's Ballistic Research Laboratory as a human "computer," calculating artillery trajectories. For three years she did the kind of mind-numbing mathematical drudgery—punching numbers into a mechanical calculator and copying down the results—that in those days was measured in "girl hours." Then she was invited by the University of Pennsylvania's Moore School of Electrical Engineering to help J. Presper Eckert and John Mauchly put the finishing touches on a new kind of computing device called ENIAC (for Electronic Numerical Integrator and Computer). That machine and its descendants were destined not only to make her old job obsolete but to change the world profoundly.

One day last week McNulty (now the widowed Mrs. John Mauchly), Eckert and 500 computer enthusiasts gathered at a "black-tie optional and hackerwear essential" party at Boston's Computer Museum to celebrate the 40th anniversary of the dedication of the first all-electronic digital computer. On that day in 1946, ENIAC in 20 seconds performed a mathematical calculation that would otherwise have required 40 girl hours to complete.

By every measure, ENIAC was an imposing machine. It weighed 30 tons and occupied a space as large as a boxcar. Its 40 modular memory and processing units, each housed in a 9-ft. high black metal cabinet and bristling with dials, wires and indicator lights, filed a room the size of a small gymnasium. Its 18,000 vacuum tubes radiated so much heat that industrial cooling fans were needed to keep its circuitry from melting down.

ENIAC was the technological wonder of its day. Programming the machine could take as long as two days as "coders" armed with detailed instructions fanned out among the panels, setting dials and plugging in patch cords in an arrangement that resembled an old-fashioned telephone switchboard. Data were fed into ENIAC in the form of IBM punch cards; a million cards were required for the monster's first assignment, a top-secret numerical simulation for the still untested hydrogen bomb. Every time a tube burned out, which happened twice a day at the start, a technician had to rummage among the tangle of wires to locate and replace the dead component. To prevent rodents from nibbling at ENIAC and destroying vital parts, Eckert recalled at the anniversary party, the scientists captured some mice, starved them for several days and then fed them bits of the insulating materials used in the machine. Any pieces the mice seemed to favor were removed from ENIAC and replaced with less tasty parts.

Anticipating the gung-ho spirit of their spiritual successors in Silicon Valley, the ENIAC team members worked with demonic intensity. "Eckert was completely devoted to the machine," recalls John Grist Brainerd, the project director. "He would work on it day and night, and worry, worry." Two cots were installed on the ground floor of the Moore School so that the exhausted computer scientists could rest near their cherished machine. "When it finally turned on, everyone was elated," recalls Kay Mauchly. "It seemed like every day was a happy day."

Those happy days soon came to an end. A month after the ENIAC's public unveiling, Eckert and Mauchly re-signed rather than turn their patent rights over to the university. Five years later they developed the first commercial computer, UNIVAC 1, but business reversals forced them to sell their fledgling computer company to Remington Rand. The final insult came in 1973. Seeking to invalidate Mauchly and Eckert's patent for "the" electronic computer, Honeywell convinced a federal judge that Mauchly had based his ideas for ENIAC on the work of a computer pioneer named John Atanasoff. The patent was dismissed, and Mauchly and Eckert lost legal claim to one of the great inventions of the 20th century.

ENIAC was decommissioned in 1955, having churned out military and scientific calculations for nearly a decade. Today its cabinet-size modules are scattered among several museums and institutions. Four remain at the Moore School, gathering dust and cobwebs in a foyer off the old building's main hallway. Nearby, someone has hung a contemporary computer chip and a sign that says it all: "In less than 40 years, advances in microelectronics technology have enabled the digital computer with performance far superior to the ENIAC to be placed on a one-quarter-inch piece of silicon."

● **Technological advancements come when the technology of the past is mixed with the innovation of the present. Researchers today can see in their projects the same potential to revolutionize information processing that Eckert and Mauchly saw in ENIAC.**

2

● Introduction

Although the computer is a relatively recent innovation, its development rests on centuries of research, thought, and discovery. Advances in information-processing technology are responses to the growing need to find better, faster, cheaper, and more reliable methods of handling data. The search for better ways to store and process data is not recent. Data-processing equipment has gone through generations of change and improvement. An understanding of the evolution of data processing is especially helpful in understanding the capabilities and limitations of modern computers.

This chapter presents a discussion of significant people and events that led to the development of the modern computer. Each of the four computer generations is described. An overview of the computer industry including both the hardware and software industries is presented. The chapter concludes with brief descriptions of several professional associations.

● The Technology Race

True electronic computers entered the technological revolution only about forty-five years ago. They can be traced through a long line of calculating and recording methods that began with tying knots in pieces of rope to keep track of livestock and carving marks on clay or stone tablets to record transactions.

Later, the abacus, a device made of beads strung on wires, was used for adding and subtracting (see Figure 2–1). The **abacus,** along with hand calculations, was adequate for computation until the early 1600s when John Napier designed a portable multiplication tool called **Napier's Bones,** or Napier's Rods. The user slid the ivory rods up and down against each other, matching the numbers printed on the rods to figure multi-

● **FIGURE 2–1**
The Abacus
The abacus is still used by some Chinese as the primary calculating device. It is also a popular desk accessory and educational toy.

plication and division problems. Napier's idea led to the invention of the slide rule in the mid-1600s.

These tools were anything but automatic. As business became more complicated and tax systems expanded, people needed faster, more accurate aids for computation and record-keeping. The idea for the first mechanical calculating machine grew out of the many tedious hours a father and his son spent preparing tax reports. Once this machine was introduced, the way opened for more complex machines as inventors built upon each succeeding development. The race for automation was on.

EARLY DEVELOPMENTS

In the mid-1600s, Blaise Pascal, a mathematician and philosopher, and his father, a tax official, were compiling tax reports for the French government in Paris. As they agonized over the columns of figures, Pascal decided to build a machine that would do the job much faster and more accurately. His machine, the **Pascaline,** could add and subtract (see Figure 2–2). Much as an odometer keeps track of a car's mileage, the Pascaline functioned by a series of eight rotating gears. But a market for the Pascaline never grew. Clerks and accountants would not use it. They were afraid it might replace them at their jobs and thought it could be rigged, like a scale or a roulette wheel.

About fifty years later in 1694, the German mathematician Gottfried Wilhelm von Leibniz designed the **Stepped Reckoner** that could add, subtract, multiply, divide, and figure square roots. Although the machine did not become widely used, almost every mechanical calculator built during the next 150 years was based on it.

● **FIGURE 2–2**
Blaise Pascal and the Pascaline
The Pascaline worked very well for addition, but subtraction was performed by a roundabout adding method.

The first signs of automation benefited France's weaving industry when Joseph-Marie Jacquard built a loom controlled by punched cards. Heavy paper cards linked in a series passed over a set of rods on the loom. The pattern of holes in the cards determined which rods were engaged, thereby adjusting the color and pattern of the product (see Figure 2–3). Prior to Jacquard's invention, a loom operator adjusted the loom settings by hand before each glide of the shuttle, a tedious and time-consuming job.

Jacquard's loom emphasized three concepts important in computer theory. One was that information could be coded on **punched cards.** A second was that cards could be linked in a series of instructions—essentially a program—allowing a machine to do its work without human intervention. A third concept was that such programs could automate jobs.

The first person to use these concepts in a computing machine was Charles Babbage, a professor at Cambridge University in England. As a mathematician, Babbage needed an accurate method for computing and printing tables of the properties of numbers (squares, square roots, logarithms, and so on). A model of his first machine worked well, but the technology of the day was too primitive for manufacturing parts precise enough to build a full-sized version (see Figure 2–4).

Later, Babbage envisioned a new machine, the **analytical engine,** for performing any calculation according to instructions coded on cards. The idea for this steam-powered machine was amazingly similar to the design of computers. It had four parts: a "mill" for calculating, a "store" for holding instructions and intermediate and final results, an "operator" or system for carrying out instructions, and a device for "reading" and "writing" data on punched cards. Although Babbage died before he could construct the machine, his son built a model that worked from Babbage's notes and drawings. Because of the ideas he introduced, Babbage is known as the father of computers.

● **FIGURE 2–3**
The Jacquard Loom
Although other weavers had already designed looms that used punched cards, Jacquard refined the idea and he receives credit for the invention.

● **FIGURE 2–4**
Charles Babbage and the Difference Engine
Even very slight flaws in the brass and pewter rods and gears designed for a larger version of the difference engine threw the machine out of whack and invalidated results.

Punched cards played an important role in the next advance toward automatic machines. Dr. Herman Hollerith, a statistician, was commissioned by the U.S. Census Bureau to develop a faster method of tabulating census data. His machine read and compiled data from punched cards. These cards were the forerunners of today's standard computer card. Thanks to Hollerith's invention, the time needed to process the census data was reduced from seven and a half years in 1880 to two and a half years in 1890, despite an increase of thirteen million people in the intervening ten years (see Figure 2–5).

Encouraged by his success, Hollerith formed the Tabulating Machine Company in 1896 to supply equipment to census takers in western Europe and Canada. In 1911, Hollerith sold his company, which later combined with twelve others as the Computing-Tabulating-Recording Company (CTR).

In 1924, Thomas J. Watson, Sr. became president of CTR and changed the name to International Business Machines Corporation (IBM). The IBM machines made extensive use of punched cards. After Congress set up the social security system in 1935, Watson won for IBM the contract to provide machines needed for this massive accounting and payment distribution system. The U.S. Census Bureau also bought IBM equipment.

During the late 1920s and early 1930s, **accounting machines** evolved that could perform many record-keeping and accounting functions. Although they handled the U.S. business data-processing load well into the 1950s, they did little more than manipulate vast quantities of punched cards. These machines were limited in speed, size, and versatility.

The first real advance toward modern computing came in 1944 when Howard Aiken's team at Harvard University designed a machine called the **Mark I.** This machine, the first automatic calculator, consisted of seventy-eight accounting machines controlled by punched paper tapes.

● **FIGURE 2–5**
Herman Hollerith and the Tabulating Machine
Hollerith's code fit the grid of twelve rows and eighty columns on his cards. Once data was punched onto the cards, a tabulator read the cards as they passed over tiny brushes. Each time a brush found a hole, it completed an electrical circuit and caused special counting dials to increment the data. The cards were then sorted into 24 compartments by the sorting component of the machine.

The U.S. Navy used the Mark I for designing weapons and calculating trajectories until the end of World War II.

Regardless of its role in computer history, the Mark I was outdated before it was finished. Only two years after work on it was begun, John Mauchly and J. Presper Eckert, Jr. introduced the first electronic computer for large-scale, general use at the University of Pennsylvania Moore School of Engineering. This machine was called the **ENIAC,** short for **Electronic Numerical Integrator and Calculator** (see Figure 2–6). It represented the shift from mechanical/electromechanical devices that used wheels, gears, and relays for computing to devices that depended upon electronic parts such as vacuum tubes and circuitry for operations.

The ENIAC was a huge machine; its 18,000 vacuum tubes took up a space eight feet high and eighty feet long. It weighed thirty tons and gobbled 174,000 watts of power. It could multiply two ten-digit numbers in three-thousandths of a second, compared with the three seconds required by the Mark I. At the time, the ENIAC seemed so fast that scientists predicted that seven computers like it could handle all the calculations the world would ever need.

The ENIAC had one major problem. Operating instructions had to be fed into it manually by setting switches and connecting wires on control panels called plugboards. This was a tedious, time-consuming, and error-prone task. In the mid-1940s, the mathematician John von Neumann proposed a way to overcome this difficulty. The solution involved the **stored-program concept,** the idea of storing both instructions and data in the computer's primary memory. Although Eckert and Mauchly actually conceived of the stored-program concept long before von Neumann, they had not outlined a plan for its use.

Von Neumann's principles spurred the development of the first stored-program computer in the United States, the **EDVAC (Electronic Discrete Variable Automatic Computer).** The EDVAC's stored instructions de-

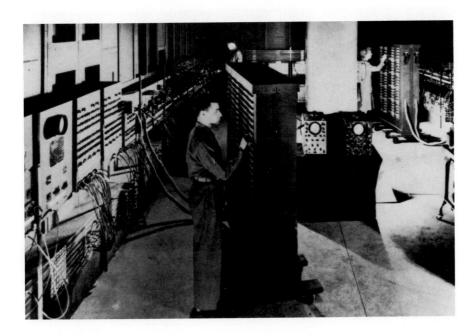

● **FIGURE 2–6**
The ENIAC
The ENIAC's first job was calculating the feasibility of a proposed design for the hydrogen bomb. The computer was also used for studying weather and cosmic rays.

creased the number of manual operations needed in computer processing. This development marked the beginning of the modern computer era and the information society. Subsequent refinements of the computer concept have focused on speed, size, and cost (see Figure 2–7).

FIRST GENERATION: 1951–1958

Improvements in computer capabilities are grouped in generations based upon the electronic technology available at the time. The first generation of computers—based upon the designs of the ENIAC and EDVAC—began with the sale of the first commercial electronic computer. This machine, called the **UNIVAC I,** was developed by Mauchly and Eckert, who had approached Remington Rand for financing (see Figure 2–8). Remington Rand (today Sperry Corporation) bought Mauchly and Eckert's company and propelled itself into the computer age with a product that was years ahead of the machines produced by competitors. In 1951, the first UNIVAC I replaced IBM equipment at the U.S. Census Bureau. Another UNIVAC was installed at General Electric's Appliance Park in Louisville, Kentucky. For the first time, business firms saw the possibilities of computer data processing.

The UNIVAC I and other **first-generation computers** were huge, costly to buy, expensive to power, and often unreliable. They were slow compared to today's computers, and their internal storage capacity was limited. They depended upon the first-generation technology of vacuum tubes for internal operations. The masses of **vacuum tubes** took up a lot of space and generated considerable heat, requiring an air-conditioned environment. Vacuum tubes could switch on and off thousands of times per second, but one tube would fail about every fifteen minutes. Too much time was wasted hunting for the burned-out tubes (see Figure 2–9).

● **FIGURE 2–7**
John von Neumann and the EDVAC
As it turned out, two groups of people were working simultaneously on a stored-program computer. Scientists at Cambridge University in England were building the EDSAC (Electronic Delay Storage Automatic Computer). The EDSAC received the title of first stored-program computer, although it was completed only a few months before the EDVAC.

● **COMPUTERS AND INFORMATION PROCESSING**

● **FIGURE 2–8**
The UNIVAC I
The most popular business uses for the UNIVACs were payroll and billing.

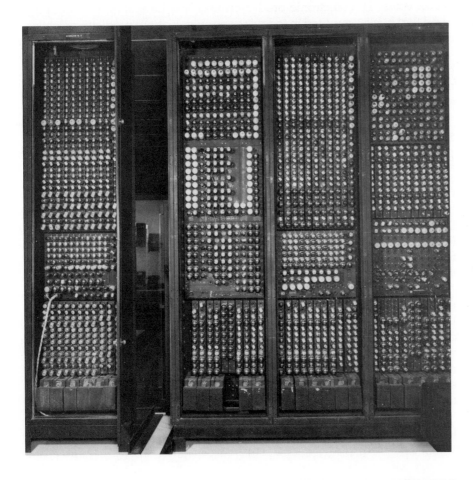

● **FIGURE 2–9**
Racks of Vacuum Tubes
Vacuum tubes were used in the architecture of first-generation computers.

Augusta Ada Byron, Countess of Lovelace

While Charles Babbage was struggling through the development of his difference engine in the mid-1800s, he was not alone. Working by his side was Augusta Ada Byron, daughter of the poet Lord Byron and later Countess of Lovelace. Lady Lovelace was considered a mathematical genius and her work with Babbage has earned her the title of the first programmer.

Lady Lovelace began working with Babbage in 1842 after translating from French to English a paper about his difference engine. Her interest heightened as she worked on the project, and the following year, when she was twenty-eight years old, Lady Lovelace added some of her own ideas to Babbage's. The paper, as it turned out, tripled in length because of her additions.

One of Lady Lovelace's ideas that earned her the title of first programmer was what we now refer to as the concept of a *loop*. She had observed that it was often necessary to repeat the same sequence of instructions to perform a single calculation. She discovered that by using a single set of cards and a conditional jump instruction, the calculation could be performed with a fraction of the effort.

Lady Lovelace continued to work with Babbage until her tragic death from cancer at the age of thirty-six. Babbage was once again left alone to continue with his labor. Neither Lady Lovelace nor Babbage lived to see the fruits of their efforts. In honor of her work, a high-level programming language (used chiefly by the U.S. government) was named Ada.

Punched cards were used to enter data into the machines. Internal storage consisted of **magnetic drums,** cylinders coated with magnetizable material. A drum rotated at high speeds while a device poised just above it either to write on the drum by magnetizing small spots or to read from it by detecting spots already magnetized. Then the results of processing were punched on blank cards.

Early first-generation computers were given instructions coded in **machine language.** Preparing the program or instructions was extremely tedious and errors were common. In order to overcome this difficulty, **symbolic languages** were developed. Symbolic languages use mnemonic symbols to represent instructions. For example, ADD would stand for addition. These symbols were easier for people to use than the strings of 0s and 1s of binary code, but the computer had to translate each symbol into machine language. A special set of language-translator programs was developed for this job. Rear Admiral Grace Murray Hopper of the U.S. Navy worked with a team that developed the first of these programs.

In the early 1950s, the public was not yet aware of the amazing computing machines. This changed with the 1952 presidential election. After analyzing only 5 percent of the tallied vote, a UNIVAC I computer predicted that Dwight David Eisenhower would defeat Adlai E. Stevenson. CBS doubted the accuracy of the prediction and did not release the information to the public until the election results were confirmed by actual votes. The electronic prediction became the first in a burgeoning trend that has culminated in today's controversy about predicting election results from East Coast tallies before polls are closed on the West Coast.

Business acceptance of computers grew quickly. In 1953, Remington Rand and IBM led the infant industry, having placed a grand total of nine installations. By the late 1950s, IBM alone had leased one thousand of its first-generation computers.

SECOND GENERATION: 1959–1964

Four hardware advances led to the **second-generation computers** of the early 1960s: the transistor, magnetic core storage, magnetic tapes, and magnetic disks. **Transistors** replaced the vacuum tubes of first-generation machines. A transistor is a small component made of solid material that acts like a vacuum tube in controlling the flow of electric current (see Figure 2–10). Using transistors in computers resulted in smaller, faster, and more reliable machines that used less electricity and generated much less heat than the first-generation computers.

Just as transistors replaced vacuum tubes as primary electronic components, **magnetic cores** replaced magnetic drums as internal storage units. Magnetic cores consisted of tiny rings of magnetic material strung on fine wires. Each magnetic core was placed at the intersection of a vertical and a horizontal wire. To turn on a core, half the electricity needed was run through each wire. Thus, only at the intersection of specific wires would a core become charged. In this way, groups of cores stored instructions and data (see Figure 2–11).

The development of magnetic cores resulted from the U.S. Navy's need for a more advanced, reliable high-speed flight trainer. Known as Whirlwind I, the navy project was one of the most innovative and influential projects in the history of the computer. Because of the high speed with which instructions and data could be located and retrieved using magnetic cores (a few millionths of a second), the Whirlwind allowed the real-time processing necessary in flight simulation. (Real time describes the ability of the computer to provide output fast enough to control the outcome of an activity.) The development led to other real-time functions such as air traffic control, factory management, and battle simulations.

This new type of internal storage was supplemented by external storage on magnetic tapes and disks. During World War II, the Germans used huge, heavy steel tapes for sound recording. Plastic magnetic tapes eventually replaced the metal tapes, and later were tried for recording computer output. Output was recorded as magnetized spots on the tape's surface. Another by-product of sound recording, the platter, led to the introduction of the magnetic disk. Much as a record is "accessed" on a jukebox, magnetic disks allowed direct access to data, contributing to the development of real-time activities such as making airline reservations. Both disks and tapes greatly increased the speed of processing and storage capacities, and replaced punched cards for storage.

During this period, more sophisticated, English-like computer languages such as COBOL and FORTRAN were commonly used (see Figure 2–12).

● **FIGURE 2–10**
Transistors
Transistors were mounted close together and connected with tiny, flat wires on small cards called circuit boards.

● **FIGURE 2–11**
A Frame of Magnetic Cores
An assembled core unit looked much like a window screen.

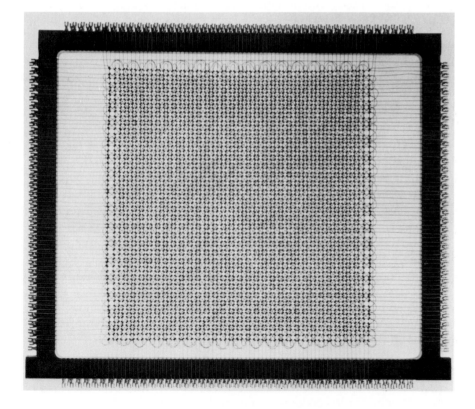

THIRD GENERATION: 1965–1970

At the same time that transistors were replacing vacuum tubes, Jack S. Kilby of Texas Instruments and Robert Noyce at Fairchild Semiconductor were separately developing the **integrated circuit (IC).** Using their own methods, they discovered that the components of electronic circuits could be placed together—or integrated—onto small chips. Soon a single silicon chip less than one-eighth inch square could hold sixty-four complete circuits. This seems crude to us since today's chips may contain as many as five hundred thousand transistors.

The chips marked the beginning of **third-generation computers,** computers that used less power, cost less, and were smaller and much more reliable than previous machines. Although computers became smaller, their internal memories increased due to the placement of memory on chips (see Figure 2–13).

A major third-generation innovation resulted when IBM realized that its company was turning out too many incompatible products. The company responded to the problem by designing the System/360 computers, which offered both scientific and business applications and introduced the family concept of computers. The first series consisted of six computers designed to run the same programs and use the same input, output, and storage equipment. Each computer offered a different memory capacity. For the first time, a company could buy a computer and feel that its investment in programs and peripheral equipment would not be wasted when the time came to move to a machine with a larger memory. Other manufacturers followed IBM's lead, and before long, more than 25,000 similar computer systems were installed in the United States.

Other developments in this period included minicomputers. Although these machines had many of the same capabilities as large computers, they were much smaller, had less storage space, and cost less. Use of remote terminals also became common. Remote terminals are computer

A DEC Third-Generation Minicomputer
The development of minicomputers allowed many small businesses to acquire computer power since the costs were much less than the costs of mainframes.

terminals located some distance away from a main computer and linked to it through cables such as telephone lines.

The software industry also began to emerge in the 1960s. Programs to perform payroll, billings, and other business tasks became available at fairly low costs. Yet software was rarely free of "bugs," or errors. The computer industry experienced growing pains as the software industry lagged behind advances in hardware technology. The rapid advancements in hardware meant that old programs had to be rewritten to suit the circuitry of the new machines, and programmers skilled enough to do this were scarce. Software problems led to a glut of computer-error horror stories: a $200,000 water bill or $80,000 worth of duplicate welfare checks.

FOURTH GENERATION: 1971–Today

Although the dividing lines between the first three generations of computers are clearly marked by major technological advances, historians are not so clear about when the fourth generation began. They do agree that in **fourth-generation computers** the use of magnetic cores had been discontinued, replaced by memory on silicon chips.

Engineers continued to cram more circuits onto a single chip. The technique by which this was accomplished was called **large-scale integration (LSI),** which characterized fourth-generation computers. LSI put thousands of electronic components on a single silicon chip for faster processing (the shorter the route electricity has to travel, the sooner it gets there). At this time, the functions that could be performed on a chip were permanently fixed during the production process.

This Is a Personal Computer?

Back in 1966 you could own a "personal computer" . . . if you had room to house a used vacuum tube monster, and if you could afford to buy a used transistor computer at $4,750 or $5,000—in 1966 dollars. The alternative was to build your own.

To build a computer required the skills of a true Renaissance person. You had to know a lot about electronics, back-plane wiring, metal working, plastics, and scrounging! With luck, you could acquire some old equipment. Sometimes magnetic drum memories were available, but they had to be salvaged from equipment that had been sledgehammered before being discarded. Used teletype machines became input/output devices. It was a frustrating, time-consuming "hobby."

Then the first home-built computer kit, the Mark 8, came out in 1974. The Mark 8 was built completely from scratch; there was no power supply, no screen, no keyboard, no case, no software. Very few were built. In 1975 the MITS Altair 8800 was introduced. If you ordered one, you got a blue board with an 8080 microprocessor chip; 256 bytes of random-access memory (RAM); no read-only memory (ROM); no interfaces to the outside world; no software; but lots of diagrams, assembly instructions, and solder. Once the computer was built, you used a teletype machine to enter programs. You wrote your own software; there was no word processing program, checkbook balancer, or data filer. The whole business bore little resemblance to personal computing as we know it today!

Ted Hoff, an engineer at Intel Corporation, introduced an idea that resulted in a single, programmable unit, the **microprocessor** or "computer on a chip." He packed the arithmetic and logic circuitry needed for computations onto one microprocessor chip that could be made to act like any kind of calculator or computer desired. Other functions, such as input, output, and memory, were placed on separate chips. The development of the microprocessor led to a boom in computer manufacturing that gave computing power to homes and schools in the form of microcomputers.

As microcomputers became more popular, many companies began producing software that could be run on the smaller machines. Most early programs were games. Later, instructional programs began to appear. One important software development was the first electronic spreadsheet for microcomputers, VisiCalc, introduced in 1979. VisiCalc vastly increased the possibilities for using microcomputers in the business world. Today, a wide variety of software exists for microcomputer applications in business, school, and personal use.

Currently, **very-large-scale integration (VLSI)** is replacing large-scale integration. In VLSI, thousands of electronic components can be placed on a single silicon chip. This further miniaturization of integrated circuits offers even greater improvements in price, performance, and size of computers (see Figure 2–14). A microprocessor based on VLSI is more powerful than a roomful of 1950s computer circuitry.

Trends in miniaturization led, ironically, to the development of the largest and most powerful of computers, the supercomputers. By reducing the size of circuitry and changing the design of the chips, companies that manufacture supercomputers were able to create computers powerful enough with memories large enough for computing the complex calculations required in aircraft design, weather forecasting, nuclear research, and energy conservation (see Figure 2–15). In fact, the main processing unit of some supercomputers is so densely packed with miniaturized electronic components that, like the early mainframe computers, it needs to be cooled and is submerged in a special liquid coolant bath that disperses the tremendous heat generated during processing.

Scientists today are working on experimental chips that can perform more than a million calculations in a single second and electronic devices so small that 30,000,000 would fit on a single one-quarter-inch-square chip. Some computer experts say that trends in chip design, supercomputers, and computer languages that resemble human speech suggest a fifth generation of computer development. And some believe that tiny computer circuits can be grown from the proteins and enzymes of living material such as *E. coli* bacteria. With the breakneck pace of computer development in the past forty-five years, nothing seems surprising now.

● The Computer Industry

Because computers have become powerful machines that have played a significant role in our country's growth and economic development in the last thirty years, the phrase *the computer industry* could include a variety of topics. In this section we will examine briefly the hardware and software industries and vendor maintenance and support.

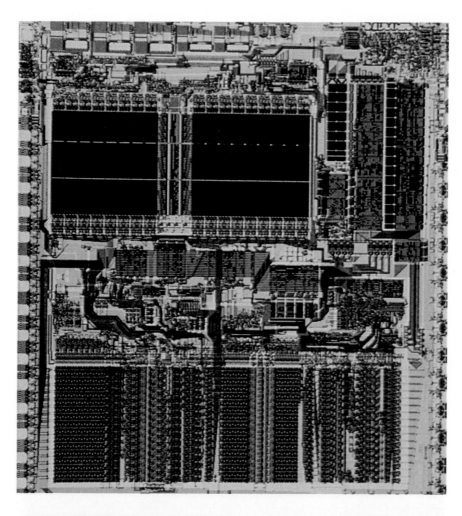

● **FIGURE 2–14**
A Motorola MC 68000 16-Bit Microprocessor
This microprocessor was designed on the principles of very-large-scale integration.

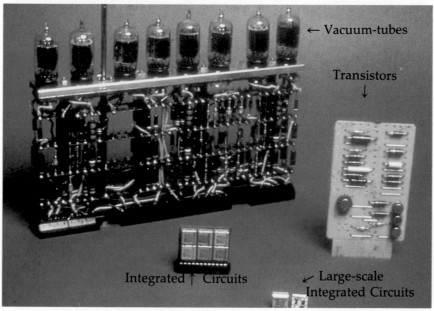

← Vacuum-tubes

Transistors
↓

Integrated ↑ Circuits

↙ Large-scale
Integrated Circuits

● **FIGURE 2–15**
First-, Second-, and Third-Generation Components
Vacuum tubes gave way to transistors and transistors gave way to chips in the effort to reduce the size of computer components.

The Technology Race: Generations of Computer Development

PERIOD	CHARACTERISTICS
First Generation 1951–1958	Vacuum tubes for internal operations. Magnetic drums for internal storage. Limited internal storage. Heat and maintenance problems. Punched cards for input and output. Slow input, processing, and output. Low-level symbolic languages for programming.
Second Generation 1959–1964	Transistors for internal operations. Magnetic cores for internal storage. Increased internal storage capacity. Magnetic tapes and disks for external storage. Reductions in size and heat generation. Increase in processing speed and reliability. Increased use of high-level languages.
Third Generation 1965–1970	Integrated circuits on silicon chips for internal operations. Increased internal storage capacity. Compatible systems. Introduction of minicomputers. Emergence of software industry. Reduction in size and cost. Increase in speed and reliability. Operating systems on external storage media.
Fourth Generation 1971–Today	Large-scale integration for internal operations. Development of the microprocessor. Introduction of microcomputers and supercomputers. Greater versatility in software. Introduction of very-large-scale integration. Increase in speed, power, and storage capacity.

THE HARDWARE INDUSTRY

The hardware industry encompasses manufacturers of computer equipment, including makers of different sizes of computer systems (microcomputers, minicomputers, mainframes, and supercomputers) and makers of peripheral devices such as monitors, disk drives, communications equipment, and printers.

There are many hardware manufacturers in existence today, but the number of manufacturers of large computer systems is fairly limited, primarily due to the huge capital investment required to produce large systems. The leading manufacturer of large computer systems is IBM.

Burroughs, NCR, Sperry-Univac, Control Data, and Honeywell are all major competitors in the large-system market (see Figure 2–16). Some of these companies, such as IBM and Honeywell, also compete in the production of minicomputer systems against Digital Equipment Corporation, Hewlett-Packard, Data General, and Wang Laboratories, among others. In the last few years some Japanese companies have begun to manufacture large computers, creating more competition in the international market. The leading Japanese manufacturers are Toshiba, Fujitsu, and Hitachi.

There are far fewer supercomputers built than any other type of computer. Cray Research and Control Data are the leading manufacturers of these powerful systems. For information on manufacturers of microcomputers see Chapter 8.

Large computer vendors do more than sell their systems. A computer is useless to an organization that lacks the knowledge needed to operate it. Most vendors provide support services along with the initial purchase. These services normally include education and training for all levels of users from top executives to data-entry personnel. Training can involve classes and seminars or self-study in which users pace their own learning while studying manuals and practicing hands-on exercises. Other services such as maintenance and repair may be included in the purchase or lease price of a computer system. Recent technological advances have contributed to an average yearly decline of 15 to 20 percent in hardware costs. In contrast, service costs have increased significantly each year, making good vendor support after the initial purchase even more important to users.

Since a large percentage of the money spent on hardware goes toward the purchase of peripherals such as printers, monitors, and disk drives, many of the major companies mentioned earlier also produce peripheral equipment to support their computers. For example IBM and Hewlett-

● **FIGURE 2–16**
IBM 4341 Mainframe

Packard manufacture printers, monitors, and disk drives (see Figure 2–17). Leading exclusive manufacturers of peripherals include NEC (monitors), Epson (printers), and Kodak (disk drives).

Because of rapidly changing technology in the computer industry, many new product announcements are made over the course of a year. New technology leads to new companies. Often, new companies will introduce a product that incorporates the latest technology, creating a highly successful business year. One successful year may be followed by a lean year when a competitor introduces an even more sophisticated product a short time later. Many times in the past, situations such as this have led to the failure of peripheral companies, so the market is in a constant state of flux.

THE SOFTWARE INDUSTRY

Early computer systems came complete with software that was specially designed to operate on a specific system. Most of the software consisted of **operating systems** and **utility programs** designed by the manufacturer. Users were responsible for designing programs to meet their own specific needs, and companies hired programming staffs to write the programs in-house. Companies found this practice very expensive and looked for other ways to solve their programming needs. During this period, a court decision (1969) forced IBM, the industry leader, to "unbundle" its software or offer hardware and software for sale separately. This action, more than any other, led to the development of independent software companies and the emergence of a new industry.

Early software companies often consisted of one person working at home and developing a clever idea. Today there are thousands of software companies in existence, creating programs capable of running on all sizes and brands of computers. Many companies specialize in producing a particular type of program to satisfy a particular industry or need, while other companies create "generic" software for a variety of applications. A few software companies work under contract, custom-designing programs to meet the needs of specific customers. Some hardware companies still offer their own company-designed software to hardware buyers. Of all the options presently available to users, off-the-shelf software is generally the most cost-effective because programming is labor-intensive and requires a high degree of skill.

● Professional Associations

As computers have taken a more important role in all phases of our lives, the number of people choosing careers in computer-related fields has increased. Societies have been formed that increase communication among professional people in computer fields. The purposes of these societies vary, but most attempt to share current knowledge through the publication of professional journals and encourage the ongoing professional education of members.

AFIPS

The American Federation of Information Processing Societies (AFIPS), organized in 1961, is a national federation of professional societies established to represent member societies on an international basis and to advance and disseminate knowledge of these societies. There are two categories of AFIPS participation: (1) member societies that have a principal interest in computers and information processing and (2) affiliated societies that, although not primarily concerned with computers and information processing, have a major interest in this area. Some of the prominent constituent societies of AFIPS are the Association for Computing Machinery (ACM), the Data Processing Management Association (DPMA), the Institute of Electrical and Electronic Engineers (IEEE), and the American Society for Information Science (ASIS). Affiliated societies of AFIPS include the American Institute of Certified Public Accountants (AICPA) and the American Statistical Association (ASA).

ACM

The Association for Computing Machinery (ACM) is the largest scientific, educational, and technical society of the computing community. Founded in 1947, this association is dedicated to the development of information processing as a discipline and to the responsible use of computers in increasingly complex and diverse applications. The objectives of the association are:

● To advance the science and art of information processing, including the study, design, development, construction, and application of modern machinery, computing techniques, and programming software.
● To promote the free exchange of ideas in the field of information processing in a professional manner, among both specialists and the public.
● To develop and maintain the integrity and competence of individuals engaged in the field of information processing.

The ACM has established special interest groups (known as SIGs) to address the wide range of interests in the computing field. For example, SIGSMALL was established for ACM members interested in small computers; SIGPLAN, for those interested in programming languages; and SIGCSE, for those interested in computer science education.

DPMA

Founded in Chicago as the National Machine Accountants Association, the Data Processing Management Association (DPMA) was chartered in December 1951. At that time the first electronic computer had yet to come into commercial use. The name "machine accountants" was chosen to identify persons associated with the operation and supervision of punched-card equipment. The society took its present name in 1962.

DPMA is one of the largest worldwide organizations serving the information-processing and management communities. It comprises all levels of management personnel. Through its educational and publishing

● HIGHLIGHT

The Hackers

If you believe the media, you believe that hackers are nasty little boys who hunch over their microcomputers and modems and break into the world's securest computer systems. Unfortunately, many hackers have wreaked havoc in computer systems. By the time he was sixteen, one famous hacker had "crashed" a DEC TOPS-10 operating system, and later a CDC Cybernet system—supposedly crash-proof—through computers at the University of Washington.

But many hackers are persistent and hard-working. They stand by their own code of ethics: Never say, "You can't do that!" Although some hackers have frequently violated the formal rules of computer use, others have created word processing programs, spreadsheets, graphics programs, video games, and personal computers.

In November 1984, 150 of the best computer hackers gathered at an abandoned army base in Marin County, near San Francisco. The group included Lee Felsenstein, the organizer of the Home Brew Computer Club; Andy Hertzfeld, who wrote the Macintosh ROM for Apple; Doug Carlston, the president of Broderbund Software; Steven Levy, who wrote *Hackers: Heroes of the Computer Revolution*; Charles Moore, who invented the computer language FORTH; Steven Wozniak, who developed the Apple I and Apple II computers; and many others.

The group of famous hackers argued about whether all software should be free, about whether microcomputers or mainframes were best, and about whether hacking had received a bad name from the media. They also decided that it was important to keep in touch. After all, you never know when one hacker might be able to help another!

activities, DPMA seeks to encourage high standards in the field of data processing and to promote a professional attitude among its members.

One of DPMA's specific purposes is to promote and develop educational and scientific inquiry in the field of data processing and data-processing management. It sponsors college student organizations interested in data processing and encourages members to serve as counselors for the Boy Scout computer merit badge. The organization also presents the "Computer Sciences Man of the Year" award for outstanding contributions to the profession.

ASM

The Association for Systems Management (ASM), founded in 1947, is headquartered in Cleveland, Ohio. The ASM is an international organization engaged in keeping its members abreast of the rapid growth and change occurring in the field of systems management and information processing. It provides for the professional growth and development of its members and of the systems profession through:

- Extended programs in local and regional areas in the fields of education and research.
- Annual conferences and committee functions in research, education, and public relations.
- Promotion of high standards of work performance by members of the ASM and members of the systems profession.
- Publication of the *Journal of Systems Management*, technical reports, and other works on subjects of current interest to systems practitioners.

The ASM has five technical departments: data communications, data processing, management information systems, organization planning, and written communications. An ASM member can belong to one or more of these departments.

ICCP

The Institute for Certification of Computer Professionals (ICCP) is a non-profit organization established in 1973 for the purpose of testing and certifying the knowledge and skills of computing personnel. A primary objective of the ICCP is to pool the resources of constituent societies so that the full attention of the information-processing industry can be focused on the vital tasks of development and recognition of qualified personnel.

The establishment of the ICCP was an outgrowth of studies made by committees of the DPMA and the ACM, which developed the concept of a "computer foundation" to foster testing and certification programs of the DPMA, including the certificate in data processing (CDP) examination, which DPMA had begun in 1962. All candidates for the CDP examination must have at least five years of work experience in a computer-based information system environment. The examination consists of five sections: data-processing equipment, computer programming and software, principles of management, quantitative methods, and system analysis and design. Any qualified person may take the examination; he or she must successfully complete all five sections to receive the certificate. Another certification, the certificate in computer programming (CCP), recognizes experience and professional competence at the senior programmer level. Candidates for this certification must also pass a basic five-part examination.

The ICCP is involved in improving existing programs and establishing new examinations for various specialties. A framework for a broad spectrum of tests and the relationship of these tests to job functions and curricula is under development.

SIM

The Society for Management Information Systems (SIM) was founded in 1968 to serve persons concerned with all aspects of management information systems in the electronic data-processing industry, including business system designers, managers, and educators. The organizational aims include providing an exchange or marketplace for technical information about management information systems and enhancing communications between MIS directors and executives responsible for the management of the business enterprises. SIM also offers educational and research programs, sponsors competitions, bestows awards, and maintains placement programs.

Professional Associations

ASSOCIATION	PURPOSE
AFIPS	To represent member societies on an international basis and to advance and disseminate knowledge of the member societies
ACM	To develop information processing as a discipline and promote responsible use of computers in diverse applications
DPMA	To encourage high standards in the field of data processing and to promote a professional attitude among members
ASM	To keep members abreast of rapid change and growth in the field of systems management and information processing
ICCP	To test and certify knowledge and skills of computing personnel
SIM	To provide an exchange or marketplace for technical information about MIS and to enhance communication between MIS directors and executives

● Summary Points

● Humans have been searching for ways to calculate answers to problems and keep track of the results for thousands of years. Early attempts to succeed at this goal include the abacus, Napier's Bones, Pascal's and von Leibniz's machines, and Jacquard's punched cards.

● Charles Babbage, the father of computers, designed the analytical engine, a machine that was similar in design to a computer, but it was doomed to failure because it was too advanced to be produced by the technology of its time.

● Punched cards played an important role in the advance toward automatic machines when Dr. Herman Hollerith designed a tabulating machine that could read census data from the 1890 census punched onto cards.

● Hollerith's tabulating machine became the basis for a company that Thomas Watson joined. Today that company is known as IBM. During the 1920s accounting machines evolved that could perform many record-keeping and accounting functions.

● Howard H. Aiken invented the first large-scale electromechanical automatic calculator, the Mark I. The first general-purpose electronic digital computer, ENIAC, was built by John W. Mauchly and J. Presper Eckert. It was huge and required tremendous amounts of electricity, but it was much faster than the Mark I.

● To solve the problem of manually feeding operating instructions into ENIAC and setting switches, John von Neumann proposed the idea of storing both instructions and data in the computer's primary memory. This is the stored-program concept. The first computer of this type in the United States was called EDVAC.

● First-generation computers relied on vacuum tubes for power and used magnetic drums for storage. Instructions were coded in machine language until symbolic languages (mnemonic symbols representing instructions) were invented.

● Second-generation computers were characterized by magnetic core memory and transistors for power. Internal storage was supplemented by external storage on magnetic tapes and disks. More sophisticated, English-like languages such as COBOL were commonly used.

● The integrated circuit developed by Jack S. Kilby of Texas Instruments and Robert Noyce at Fairchild Semiconductor led to the third computer generation. These machines were even smaller, faster, and more powerful than computers in earlier generations. They were also less costly, more reliable, and used less electricity.

● A major three-generation innovation resulted when IBM developed the System/360 computers, the first series designed to run the same programs and use the same input, output, and storage equipment. Other developments in this period included minicomputers and the emergence of the software industry.

● Fourth-generation computers rely on large-scale integration and very-large-scale integration to cram more circuits onto a chip. Ted Hoff, an engineer at Intel Corporation, introduced the microprocessor, or "computer on a chip."

● Trends in miniaturization led to the development of the largest and most powerful of computers, the supercomputers. These machines perform complex calculations required in aircraft design, weather forecasting, nuclear weapons research, and energy conservation.

● Scientists today are working on experimental chips that can perform calculations faster than ever before. With all the technological developments taking place today, some scientists feel we are on the threshold of a fifth computer generation.

● The hardware industry encompasses manufacturers of computer equipment, including makers of different sizes of computer systems (microcomputers, minicomputers, mainframes, and supercomputers) and makers of peripheral devices such as monitors, disk drives, communications equipment, and printers.

● The leading manufacturer of large computer systems is IBM, with Burroughs, NCR, Sperry-Univac, Control Data, and Honeywell all active competitors in the large-system market. The leading Japanese manufacturers of large systems are Toshiba, Fujitsu, and Hitachi.

● Large computer vendors may offer support services to users. While hardware costs are declining, costs associated with training, maintenance, and repair are increasing, making good vendor support an important consideration for potential buyers.

● A large percentage of the money spent on hardware goes toward the purchase of peripherals such as printers, monitors, and disk drives. Rapidly changing technology leads to the rise and fall of many makers of peripheral equipment.

● Early computer systems came complete with software that was specially designed to operate on a specific system. A court decision in 1969 forced IBM, the industry leader, to "unbundle" its software or offer hardware and software for sale separately. This action, more than any other, led to the development of independent software companies.

● Today software companies offer users many options to meet their computing needs, from custom-designed programs to off-the-shelf software. Off-the-shelf software is generally the most cost-effective way of meeting needs because programming is labor-intensive and requires a high degree of skill.

● As more and more people have chosen careers in computer-related fields, societies have been formed that increase communication among professionals. The purposes of these societies vary, but most attempt to share current knowledge through the publication of professional journals and encourage the ongoing professional education of members. Some of these societies are AFIPS, ACM, DPMA, ASM, ICCP, and SIM.

● Review Questions

1. What contributions did Pascal and von Leibniz make to the development of computers?

2. In what ways did the development of a loom by Jacquard affect the development of computing devices?

3. How was Babbage's analytical engine similar in design to modern computers?

4. What was the first automatic calculator? What machine made the Mark I become outdated even before it was finished? How did this machine differ from the Mark I and other earlier computing devices?

5. Explain the stored-program concept.

6. What were some of the drawbacks of first-generation computers?

7. What replaced vacuum tubes and magnetic drums in second-generation computers? What advances were noteworthy in storage?

8. What significance did the IBM System/360 computers have in the third computer generation?

9. How did large-scale integration lead to the miniaturization of fourth-generation computers?

10. Explain how a court decision that forced IBM to unbundle its software led to the growth of the software industry.

National Semiconductor

National
Semiconductor
Corporation

COMPANY HISTORY

As transistors replaced vacuum tubes in second-generation computers, the demand for this special circuitry grew. National Semiconductor Corporation was founded in 1959 in Danbury, Connecticut, to help meet the growing demand for the new technology. Despite this demand, the business of manufacturing transistors was filled with problems, which National Semiconductor worked hard to overcome. In 1964, Peter Sprague secured a major interest in the struggling company, and in 1966, he acquired Molectro, a small integrated circuit company based in Santa Clara, California. When Charles Sporck was named president and chief executive officer of National a year later, company headquarters were moved from Danbury to Santa Clara, an area known today as "Silicon Valley."

Today, Silicon Valley is known throughout the world as the center of new computer technology, and National is known as a leader in the high-tech industry. The company has evolved from a small transistor manufacturer into one of the foremost developers of advanced semiconductor and system products. National manufactures more than 5,000 types of integrated circuits and has introduced more than 150 new products.

Although the company now manufactures a wide variety of products, in 1959 National began modestly with just three product lines. Transistors, the first of many National product lines, are still produced in large numbers at the Danbury, Connecticut, plant. Linear integrated circuits (ICs), a second product line, are used in computers, communications equipment, instrumentation, stereos, radios, TVs, and other consumer products. Today, National boasts the world's broadest linear line. The third of the three product lines combines transistors or ICs and other components in the same package, called a hybrid. Today, National is the world's largest standard hybrid manufacturer.

By the middle of the third computer generation in 1968, sales increases and newer technology prompted National to add two more product lines. Logic devices,

which are used to perform mathematical and logical operations in computers, became a standard product. Also added to the product line were MOS memory integrated circuits. The tiny, high-density ICs were put to use in computers and instrumentation systems.

As the product lines expanded and National's reputation for manufacturing quality products grew, sales increased. The demand for National products spread throughout the world. National was faced with the challenge of meeting product demands overseas without production facilities in foreign countries. To meet worldwide demands and ensure effective participation in European and Far Eastern markets, in 1969 the company expanded its manufacturing operations to Hong Kong, Singapore, Germany, and Scotland.

The year 1971 brought an industry slowdown, but National continued its pattern of growth and expansion. Microprocessors were added to the product line in 1972 to meet the needs created by fourth-generation computers. The production of memory systems was the company's first step beyond the manufacture of components and into entire systems. Datachecker, a National supermarket point-of-sale system, led the industry in rate of new installations. More new products helped the company survive during the 1975 downturn, which many feel was the worst the industry ever faced. While other companies suffered, sales at National increased by 10 percent.

NATIONAL TODAY

The company continued expanding its product line by developing the world's first "talking" cash register and medium- and large-scale general-purpose computers. In fact, National installed more of these computers worldwide than any other IBM compatible mainframe supplier. Investments in research and development continue to reflect National's commitment to the development of new products and process technologies.

National may now be on the verge of a new era in integrated circuit development. The Semiconductor Division is producing a gate array product line. Gate arrays make it possible for customers to create their own proprietary products from a standard set of logic gates. National has introduced three processors that compete with IBM's 4341 systems. The company has also diversified and added more point-of-sale systems to meet the needs of all retail market segments.

Today, National is a world leader in the world's highest technology industry. National employs more than 32,000 people in twenty-nine countries and has annual sales approaching $2 billion. Integrated circuits, of which the company manufactures more than 5,000 types, account for approximately 60 percent of sales. National's other business segment, digital systems, includes IBM-compatible mainframes and peripherals, point-of sale systems for the retail industry, and microcomputer products.

DISCUSSION POINTS

1. What are the first three products that National manufactured?

2. How did National counter the industry slowdown in 1971 and continue the company's pattern of growth and expansion?

3 INTRODUCTION TO INFORMATION SYSTEMS

Surveying The Data Diddlers

Philip Elmer-DeWitt
TIME

A brokerage-firm margin clerk sitting at a keyboard in Denver changes a few letters on a computer screen and magically transforms 1,700 shares of Loren Industries stock worth $1.50 each into the same number of Long Island Lighting shares selling for more than ten times that price. A keyboard operator processing orders at an Oakland department store changes some delivery addresses and diverts several thousand dollars' worth of store goods into the hands of accomplices. A ticket clerk at the Arizona Veterans' Memorial Coliseum issues full-price basketball tickets, sells them and then, tapping out codes on her computer keyboard, records the transactions as half-price sales.

These are among the cases brought to light in a new study released last week by the National Center for Computer Crime Data, a Los Angeles research firm. The results of the survey, the first comprehensive study of people who have been prosecuted under computer-crime laws, suggest that although teenagers like the members of Milwaukee's widely heralded "414" gang are a real annoyance, the most serious losses are caused by electronic miscreants who are a good deal older and not half so clever. "Generally, these are unsophisticated crimes," says the center's director, Jay Bloom-Becker. "The myth that computer crime is this romantic activity done by geniuses and involving millions of dollars is just that—a myth."

One of the more surprising results of the survey is how few cases it turned up. Canvassing 130 prosecutors' offices in 38 states, BloomBecker was able to uncover only 75 computer crimes. This suggests either that the problem is grossly exaggerated or that victims are not reporting incidents that, if publicized, might expose the vulnerability of their computer systems. Moreover, many of the so-called computer criminals, like the Oakland subway riders accused of using folded $5 bills to coax free Bay Area Rapid Transit tickets from computerized coupon dispensers, had only the most rudimentary knowledge of the machines they manipulated.

Most misdeeds boiled down to what Donn Parker, a computer-crime watcher at SRI International, calls "data diddling"—entering false numbers at a keyboard. To pay for his wife's drug purchases, for example, a programmer at a savings and loan company in Los Angeles transferred $5,000 into his personal account and tried to cover up the switch with phony debit and credit transactions. The error was picked up in a routine bank audit. Among the 15 programmers and ten students nabbed, the offenses committed most often were thefts of software and telecommunications services. The rest of the crimes were scattered among a rogues' gallery of electronic lowlife that included seven bank tellers, five unskilled laborers, two computer-company executives, a TV reporter and a former Los Angeles County deputy sheriff.

A case gleaned from the prosecutors' files involved one of their own. Last August, Jefferson County (Colo.) District Attorney Nolan Brown was convicted of computer crime, forgery and abuse of public records in a ticket-fixing case. Hoping to reduce his automobile-insurance rates, Brown had asked a motor vehicle bureau employee to delete a pair of speeding tickets from the department's computer system. He was sentenced to five days in jail, fined $2,000, placed on four years' probation and ordered to perform 200 hours of community service. He also resigned. Thus Brown lost a $73,000-a-year job to save some $400 worth of insurance premiums, a clear signal that, at least for him, computer crime does not pay.

● **At the same time that the information society is changing the kinds of work people do, it is also changing the kinds of crimes they commit. Since the evidence is often only electrical current that lasts for a few microseconds, detection of these crimes is not keeping pace.**

● Introduction

Historically, the United States became a world power as an industrial society. The birth of our country and the industrial revolution both occurred during the late eighteenth century. A wealth of natural resources and innovative ideas from people who worked hard to make their ideas succeed made the United States a dominant economic and political force. As an industrial society, most of our workers were employed in jobs related to manufacturing. The agricultural and service industries also employed large numbers of workers.

This chapter discusses how technology developed to meet information needs as the United States evolved from an industrial to an information society. The chapter includes discussions on the value and qualities of information. The term *system*, so frequently associated with computers, is defined, and the relationships among systems, subsystems, and information systems are explored. The chapter also examines the ways businesses use information systems.

● The Information Society

The United States has evolved from an industrial society to an information society. As the need for information developed, Herman Hollerith's tabulating machine was one of the first attempts to streamline the collection and dissemination of information. Little did Hollerith realize that his machine would lead to the birth of another revolution—the information revolution.

Increasingly, during the first half of the 1900s, technology focused on developing machines, such as accounting machines, that would help meet growing information requirements. By 1950, the year that marks the beginning of the first computer generation, information needs had grown so rapidly that workers employed in information-related jobs outnumbered workers in the industrial sector. Predictions for the future suggest that the total number of information workers will soon surpass the total combined number of workers in industry, agriculture, and service.

Information is increasing at an astounding rate. Of the total amount of information known today, 75 percent became available in the last twenty years. To keep track of this information each year, workers in the United States alone process 35 billion sheets of paper! But not all the information is useful. Systems to process this information are in great demand. In the following section, we discuss the qualities that make information meaningful.

THE QUALITIES OF INFORMATION

How can we determine if the information received from an information system is appropriate for decision making? For example, suppose a sales report is based on data that are entered in a computer carelessly. If errors occur at the time of data entry, then information in the sales report will be inaccurate. The computer jargon used to describe this situation is **"GIGO,"** or **"garbage in-garbage out."**

To determine if information is meaningful and appropriate for decision making, managers must ask themselves if information is timely, relevant, accurate, verifiable, and complete. If the answers to these questions are positive, then the information is appropriate for decision making.

The timeliness of information is important because information frequently loses its value as it ages. Different management levels need varied types of information. At the lowest level, decisions focus primarily on the routine, operational aspects of a business, so information must be current. For example, a warehouse manager needs up-to-the-minute reports on inventory levels to fill orders promptly. A report generated last year would be useless in determining inventory levels for the current week. At higher management levels, long-range planning may require information that spans a longer period of time. A future sales campaign may be based on sales figures that span a five-year period and reveal past sales trends.

Even the most timely information is irrelevant if it does not contribute to making decisions more easily or more successfully. Extraneous information can complicate decision making. A company comptroller needs the financial records of each department in the company to perform an audit, but the plant maintenance schedule for the past year would be irrelevant to the comptroller.

Decision making also requires accurate (error-free) information. The degree of accuracy acceptable to most decision makers depends on the circumstances. When decisions must be made quickly, there are trade-offs between speed and accuracy. Information produced quickly may not be error free. If the gauges in a chemical plant indicate that a toxic leak is about to occur, it may be advisable to institute emergency measures first and check the accuracy of the gauges later. When more time can be spent gathering data, however, greater effort should be made to ensure that the resulting information is accurate.

Accurate information is verifiable. In other words, it can be confirmed. Verification can be accomplished in different ways. One approach compares the new information with other information that is accurate. Another approach rekeys the raw data and compares the processed information with the original. A third approach traces the information back to its original source. This method is called an **audit trail.** An audit trail describes the path that leads to the data on which information is based. A decision maker evaluates the audit trail description to verify the accuracy of information. Any well-designed information system should include a plan for an audit trail. Information that cannot be verified cannot be depended on for decision making.

Before making decisions, managers must determine if the information is complete or if more is needed. Timely, accurate, relevant, and verifiable information may be meaningless if it is not complete. Circumstances influence this decision because in some situations, incomplete information may not hamper decision making, whereas in others it could lead to disastrous consequences. For example, a fire department will respond to a report of a fire in a chemical plant immediately. Once on the scene, however, fire fighters need more information to fight the fire effectively. The chemicals inside the building affect decisions about techniques used to combat the blaze.

Qualities of Information

QUALITY	EXPLANATION
Timely	Information frequently loses value as it ages. Different management levels have different information needs.
Accurate	Information should be without errors. The degree of accuracy depends on different circumstances.
Verifiable	The accuracy of information can be confirmed by comparing, rekeying, or performing an audit trail.
Relevant	Information should contribute to making decisions more easily or more successfully. Extraneous information can complicate decision making.
Complete	Information may be meaningless if it is not complete. Circumstances help determine if more information is needed.

● Systems

A **system** is a group of related elements that work together toward a common goal. A system is made up of input, processes, and output. **Input** enters the system from the surrounding environment and is transformed by some **process** into output. Information can flow within the system or between the system and its larger environment. Most **output** leaves the system and flows into the external environment. Some may remain in the internal environment.

A system requires **feedback,** which can come from either internal or external sources. Feedback keeps the system functioning smoothly. In system theory, a system's primary goal is survival. Feedback helps the system survive by pinpointing the system's strengths and weaknesses (Figure 3–1).

A newspaper is an example of a system with input, processes, output, and feedback. Input consists of the news items that are collected by reporters. The writing, editing, typesetting, and printing of the stories is the process that turns the news items into output (the printer paper). Feedback to this system may come from internal or external sources. The opinions of the publisher are a source of internal feedback. Letters to the editor from readers and changes in subscriptions are sources of external feedback.

Many systems are subsystems of larger systems. A newspaper is a subsystem of the media industry. The media industry is a subsystem of the national economy, and the national economy is a subsystem of the world economy. In a business, payroll, accounts receivable, and accounts payable can all be subsystems of the accounting system.

A SYSTEM'S INTERACTION WITH OTHER SYSTEMS

Each system can be viewed in terms of inputs, processes, outputs, and feedback mechanisms, but the boundaries between systems are not al-

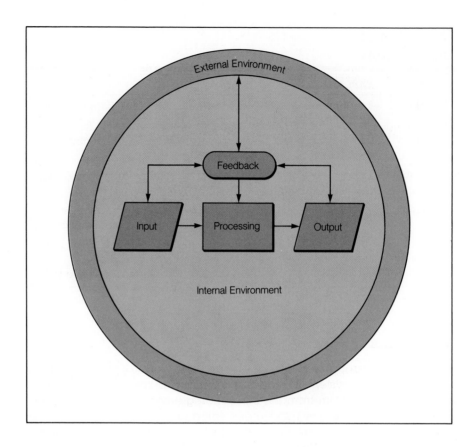

ways easy to define. Neither are the elements of a system that might stand alone as systems in themselves. The determination of boundaries and elements depends on the level or scope at which one views the system. In medicine, for instance, a general practitioner views the human body as the system, whereas an ophthalmologist views just the eye as the system.

The fact that one system may be a subsystem of another, larger system is an important concept in system theory. It implies the existence of interaction among systems. All these concepts can be applied to an information system.

THE ORGANIZATION AS A SYSTEM

The concepts of system theory can also be applied to organizations. These have groups of related elements (departments and employees) working together toward common goals (survival, growth, or profit). Figure 3–2 shows a state university as a subsystem of a larger system, the community. The university uses inputs from the surrounding environment and transforms them into useful outputs.

As shown in Figure 3–2, the university is affected by external factors beyond its control. The economy; federal, state, and local legislation; and competition from other universities are examples of external factors. Internal factors affecting the university include the quality of its faculty

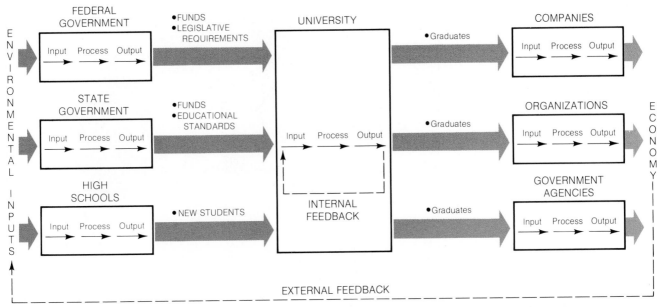

● **FIGURE 3–2**
The University as an Interacting System

and students, relationships among administrators, departmental relations, and internal communication channels. An analysis of its information needs must consider both internal and external factors.

Each department in the university is a subsystem within the university. The goal of each department is to educate students according to predetermined standards. But each department must interact with other departments. The history department must obtain enrollment and eligibility information from the registrar. The registration department must find out from the bursar's office which students have not paid their tuition.

External information, such as the number of high school graduates, SAT scores, and new tax laws affecting education, comes from state agencies among others. Information about present and future economic conditions that will affect university enrollments is supplied by external sources such as federal agencies. Some of the many interactions are shown in Figure 3–3.

● Components of an Information System

Information is data that have been processed and made useful for decision making. Decision makers use information to increase knowledge and reduce uncertainty. Organizations cannot function without information. An information system, therefore, is designed to transform data into information and make it available to decision makers in a timely fashion. There are many components of an information system. These are simply the parts that can be identified in the system. The components of an information system—hardware, software, data, and people—are discussed in the following sections.

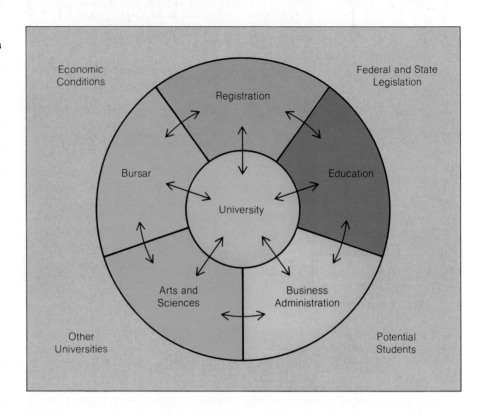

HARDWARE AS PART OF AN INFORMATION SYSTEM

In a computer-based information system, hardware consists of equipment, or the parts of the computer that can be seen. Several kinds of hardware may be part of an information system. Since hardware is discussed in more detail in Chapters 4–6, this section is limited to a brief explanation of how hardware fits into an information system.

Input Equipment

Input equipment is used to place data in the computer. Many kinds of equipment are used for this function (Figure 3–4). Several factors affect the type of equipment chosen for inputting data. These include cost considerations, size limitations, speed requirements, and ease of use.

Processing Equipment

Processing equipment includes the parts of a computer-based information system that perform operations on data placed in the computer. Processing occurs inside the computer's CPU and cannot be seen.

Output Equipment

Output equipment transfers processed data or information from one location to another. It moves information or data processed in the CPU either to another location for storage or to a display device such as a screen to be seen by a user.

Storage Devices

Storage devices are the remaining category of equipment. Once processed, data and information are often stored. Storage media such as tapes, tape drives, and disks perform this function. Tapes and disks hold data that may be used again for processing. They also hold information that has already been processed. Storage devices are an important part of an information system because they allow the input-processing-output cycle to be repeated with minimal effort.

SOFTWARE AS PART OF AN INFORMATION SYSTEM

Without specific instructions provided by software, a computer-based information system would not function. Software programs are specific

● **FIGURE 3-4**
Input Equipment

sequences of instructions needed to run computers. Programs may be either general-purpose **system programs** that run the computer itself or **application programs** that are designed to solve a particular user need. Both types of programs are described in detail in later chapters.

Because it supplies all types of operating instructions to the computer, software plays a significant role in the inputting, processing, and outputting phases of computers. Software may even give procedural instructions to people operating the computer.

DATA AS PART OF AN INFORMATION SYSTEM

Before they can flow through an information system, data must be collected and changed into a form on which the computer can operate. Although collection methods vary widely, the most common data input method is using a keyboard to "type" the data. Data can also be input directly from sources by scanning devices. Remember that data refers to raw facts collected from various sources, but not organized or defined in a meaningful way. Information is processed data that helps people make intelligent decisions. Processing data through an information system involves the manipulation of data by the CPU. As noted earlier, processed data are either organized and output to a device such as a CRT or printer, or they are placed in storage for future use.

PEOPLE AS PART OF AN INFORMATION SYSTEM

People are an essential part of an information system. They bring the parts together and coordinate all activities within the system (Figure 3–5). One of the many ways to categorize the people in an information system is by the roles they perform: designers, operators, users, and clients. The first three groups, designers, operators, and users, must receive special training to make the system operate smoothly.

● **FIGURE 3–5**
People are an important component of an information system.

● COMPUTERS AND INFORMATION PROCESSING

People who design information systems may help clients determine the needs that the system will fulfill. The designers also select the hardware to meet those needs and develop the instructions (software) that will control the hardware.

Operators actually run the computer equipment. They make sure the computer is turned on and running properly. They also check and enter data. Operators frequently serve as the liaison between people functioning in other jobs. They may even be responsible for making minor equipment repairs.

Users interact directly with the information system. They provide input or use the output in their jobs. Often they are clerks or data-entry personnel. Clients, on the other hand, may not interact directly with the system, although they do benefit from it in other ways. A customer purchasing a product through a computer-based information system benefits when the product is received even though the customer does not have direct use of the computer.

For example, many mail-order catalog businesses operate computerized information systems from which their customers benefit. Lands' End, a Wisconsin-based, mail-order business, sends monthly catalogs to its customers. To place an order, a customer fills out an order form (including information such as catalog number, quantity, price, color, and size) and sends the form to Wisconsin. A data-entry clerk receives the order form and enters the appropriate order information into the computer system. The order information is transmitted to a terminal in a warehouse where shipping clerks select the requested items from the stock and send the items to the customer. The customer, who receives the correct item, indirectly benefits from the system.

Components of an Information System

HARDWARE	SOFTWARE	DATA	PEOPLE
Input hardware	System programs	Input	Designers
Output hardware	Application programs	Process	Operators
Processing hardware		Output	Users
Storage devices		Store	Clients

● The Value of Information

The number of businesses and organizations with computer-based information systems is growing. Companies find that combining hardware, software, data, and people to create information systems is so successful that the term **synergism** is frequently used to describe the relationship. Synergistic relationships are those in which the combined efforts of all the parts are greater than the sum of the efforts of each part operating independently.

Many corporations still do not take advantage of all the possibilities available to them through their computer systems. Others, realizing the potential, are beginning to reorganize, using their information system as the foundation. As a result, they are discovering opportunities that were not feasible before.

American Airlines, for example, used technology to create a "sideline" that blossomed into an entirely new business. When American was forced to stop listing its own schedules first on Sabre, the computerized reservation system it developed for travel agents, it simply began charging the agencies a fee to use the system if they did not make their bookings on American. Sabre alone was expected to make its parent company $170 million in revenues last year.

It wasn't until the early 1980s that information became a strategic marketing tool. The development of personal computers meant that executives no longer had to rely on overworked data-processing departments to access corporate information, because it was right at their fingertips. They did not have to understand the technological aspects of the information system to use it. But having access to information is not enough. To get the edge in the technology race today, managers must use it creatively. It is an ongoing battle, and a business in the lead today may be caught napping by another, more innovative business tomorrow.

Science has many synergistic relationships. In chemistry, an area in which synergism abounds, tensile strength is one example. Chrome-nickel steel has a tensile strength of approximately 350,000 pounds per square inch. That figure exceeds, by 100,000 pounds per square inch, the sum of the tensile strengths of each of several elements that, when combined, form chrome-nickel steel. In other words, the whole is greater than the sum of the parts.

A political campaign is another area in which we can observe synergistic relationships. Suppose a politician must decide the most effective way to use personal appearances, television ads, and direct-mail flyers in a campaign. The candidate knows that when used one at a time, a direct-mail flyer will generate 5,000 votes, personal appearances will generate 7,000 votes, and television ads will generate 10,000 votes. If each tactic is used in three separate months, the politician can depend on receiving 22,000 votes. However, voter surveys show that if all three tactics are used the month before an election, the combined effect will generate 30,000 votes. With this information, a knowledgeable politician might choose to operate a campaign that uses all three tactics the month before the election.

Regardless of the situation—political campaign or information system—combining resources for maximum effectiveness demonstrates good management practice. A person working alone to input data in an information system is slow and prone to making errors. A computer can input data faster and more accurately than the human, but the computer can only input data that are in computer-readable form. Human and computer working together can input huge amounts of data with a high degree of accuracy.

After the input phase, data can be processed and turned into useful information. The question that businesses face is, since a computer-based information system is a major expense, what value does that processed information have to the organization?

Decisions are made with the hope that they will produce the best outcome either by maximizing or minimizing a result. A major consideration in determining the value of information is whether it reduces the uncertainty that surrounds the outcome of a decision. A decision is generally chosen from among a number of options, or choices, each with a different degree of uncertainty. The degree to which information reduces uncertainty determines its value to the organization or firm.

Businesses quantify the value of information by determining the cost of obtaining the information and comparing that with the cost of making a decision without the information. If the cost of obtaining information exceeds the negative consequences of making a decision without the information, then the information loses its value to the firm.

● How Businesses Use Information Systems

Businesses use computer-based information systems in a variety of ways. There are probably as many uses of information systems as there are activities to be performed. When computers were first introduced to businesses, the machines were used to solve specific processing problems.

● **COMPUTERS AND INFORMATION PROCESSING**

Little emphasis was placed on centralized planning or on using computers in the most effective way to benefit the entire organization. The primary applications for computers were clerical and record-keeping tasks. Today, computer use has expanded and developed into information systems that include all types of applications from record keeping to operational functions to strategic planning. In the following sections, we examine how computer-based information systems are used for some of these.

ACCOUNTING/PAYROLL

Payroll, a record-keeping function, is a frequently used application of an information system in the accounting departments of most businesses (Figure 3–6). Chapter 2 noted that accounting machines were one of the first forms of automated machines. Accountants continued the tradition by being one of the first professions to use electronic computers. Since one purpose of accounting is to maintain and represent financial data accurately, the speed, accuracy, and memory advantages offered by computers make them ideal for accounting applications.

A payroll system designed to compute wages for hourly employees has many informational requirements. A typical payroll system computes taxes and appropriate deductions for each employee. Vacation time and sick leave must be reflected in paychecks. Checks and W-2 forms must be printed. A payroll system must also accommodate changes in employee information, such as address or number of deductions. Although these information requirements are complex, most systems break the requirements into phases and fulfill the requirements without error.

SALES/ORDER PROCESSING

In the area of sales, order processing is a frequent application of an information system. Order processing must provide for a fast and ac-

● **FIGURE 3–6**
Payroll systems are widely used forms of information systems.

○ HIGHLIGHT

Rebirth of a Company

Once an industry nearly buried in paperwork, the wholesale drug-distributing industry now benefits from information systems. Since the 1970s, smaller companies have been forced out of the industry by technology. They either would not or could not invest in computerized systems. The remaining companies now compete to see who can profit the most from technology.

McKesson Corp., today's leading drug distributor, nearly sold out in the early 1970s. Instead, it invested nearly $125 million into modernization. Handwritten and phoned-in orders were eliminated by giving customers hand-held electronic devices that both compiled the order list and placed the order. Computers were used to reorganize warehouses. Orders were filled in days, rather than weeks. McKesson then developed Economost, a service that provides customers with marketing reports about their products.

Today, nearly all wholesalers offer similar services, including supplying pharmacists with in-house computers that transmit orders and keep important data on customers. McKesson even processes insurance forms in bulk for their customers. By providing such services, wholesalers can often "lock-in" their customers. According to the National Wholesale Druggists' Association, 65 percent of all pharmaceutical products are now distributed by wholesalers, compared with 45 percent in 1970. But competition is fierce, and drug distributors continually use their information systems to keep ahead of the game.

curate movement of customer orders. A computerized inventory system is often used in conjunction with order processing. By combining the two in the same information system, orders can be filled more quickly, accurately, and efficiently.

Most businesses have customers who place orders in person, by phone, or by mailed requests. Items are also returned for credit. An information system must be designed to handle all these situations.

An inventory control system can help process orders. Inventory control systems facilitate sales by preventing delays in filling orders that are caused by running out of stock. For example, a computerized inventory system may indicate reorder points when inventory levels are low. Inventory control systems also help keep costs down by making sure that warehouses do not become overstocked with items that tie up operating capital.

MANUFACTURING/MATERIALS REQUIREMENT PLANNING (MRP)

Manufacturers transform raw materials into finished products. Although this sounds simple, the process involves many complex activities. Products must be designed and engineered, raw materials must be purchased, components must be assembled, and facilities and equipment must be scheduled. **Materials requirement planning (MRP)** assists in the planning, purchasing, and control of raw materials used in the manufacture of goods (Figure 3–7).

A well-designed MRP system has many interacting subsystems. Inventory control regulates the quantity of raw materials available. The scheduling of facilities helps eliminate wasted machine time and sched-

● **FIGURE 3–7**
MRP is being used increasingly by manufacturers.

uling conflicts. Engineering systems assist in designing and testing new products. Sophisticated engineering systems speed up the design process and hold down cost by eliminating the need for building and testing prototypes (Figure 3–8).

HUMAN RESOURCES MANAGEMENT/PERSONNEL

Human resources management departments are involved in many functional areas of businesses. Services such as relocation, benefits, training and development, policies and procedures, and personnel/record keeping may all fall under the human resources department.

Personnel/record keeping is a functional area ideally suited to computerization because the volume of processed information is large and records must be updated frequently. Most organizations keep employee records in a centralized data base to which additions, deletions, and other changes are made. Each record may include information such as the employee's name, address, phone number, social security number, date of hiring, job assignment, salary, and performance ratings. Human resource management emphasizes planning and control. By computerizing the personnel/record-keeping functions, organizations can reach this goal.

● Summary Points

● The United States has gradually evolved from an industrial society to an information society. Since 1950, workers employed in information-related jobs have outnumbered workers employed in the industrial sector.

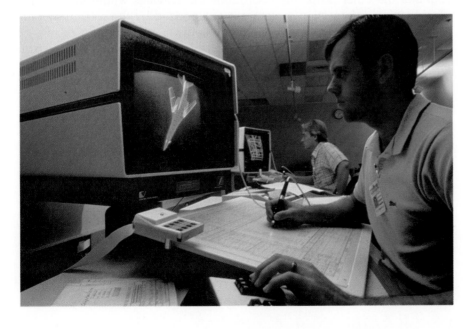

● **FIGURE 3–8**
Using computers to assist in product design and engineering can speed up the design process and reduce manufacturing costs.

- As information needs increase, information systems are in great demand for processing information and presenting it in meaningful ways to decision makers.
- To be meaningful and appropriate for decision making, information must be timely, relevant, accurate, verifiable, and complete. Information that meets these criteria is suitable for decision making.
- A system is a group of related elements that work together toward a common goal. A system includes inputs, processes, outputs, and feedback. Many systems are subsystems of larger systems.
- The boundaries between systems are seldom easy to define. Neither are the elements of a system that might stand alone as systems in themselves. The determination of boundaries and elements depends on the level or scope at which we view the system.
- The concepts of system theory can be applied to an organization. It has a group of related elements (departments and employees) working together toward a common goal (survival, growth, or profit).
- The four main components of an information system include hardware, software, data, and people. These components are the parts that can be identified in the system.
- Hardware consists of equipment, or the parts of the computer that can be seen. An information system has several kinds of hardware. Input equipment is used to place data in the computer. Processing equipment performs operations on data placed in the computer. Output equipment transfers data or information from one location to another. Storage devices hold data that may be used again for processing. They also hold information that has already been processed.
- Software consists of the specific sequences of instructions required to run computers. Software programs are either general-purpose system programs or specific application programs.
- Once collected, data can be input, processed, output, or stored.
- People are a necessary part of an information system, for they bring together the other parts and coordinate all activities within the system. People in an information system are categorized by the roles they perform: designers, operators, users, and clients.
- Synergistic relationships are those in which the combined efforts of all the parts are greater than the sum of each part operating independently.
- One consideration in determining the value of information is whether it reduces the uncertainty that surrounds the outcome of a decision. The degree to which information reduces uncertainty determines its value to the organization or firm.
- Businesses quantify the value of information by determining the cost of obtaining the information and then comparing that with the cost of making a decision without the information.
- Businesses use computer-based information systems in different ways to meet the needs of management, employees, and customers. Payroll, order processing, materials requirement planning (MRP), and human resources management are types of information systems commonly used in businesses.

● Review Questions

1. Using a historical perspective, explain why information-related jobs outnumber other kinds.

2. How can managers determine if information is meaningful and appropriate for decision making?

3. What do the information traits of accuracy and verifiability mean?

4. What is the purpose of feedback? Give an example of how feedback works.

5. Think of an example of a system. Describe its inputs, processes, and outputs. Using this system, describe a larger system of which it is a part.

6. Without software, a computer-based information system would not function. What function do system programs and application programs play in an information system?

7. Explain how synergism affects the performance of an information system. Describe a synergistic effect not explained in the chapter.

8. How can a business manager determine the value of information to the firm?

9. Explain how businesses quantify the value of information. At what point does information begin to lose its value to a firm?

10. What is materials requirement planning?

PRUPAC

COMPANY HISTORY

Prudential Property and Casualty Insurance Company (PRUPAC) is a wholly owned subsidiary of the Prudential Insurance Company of America, the largest life insurance company in the United States. The company markets four types of insurance—private passenger auto, homeowners, personal catastrophe liability, and dwelling fire insurance—through Prudential agents. A relatively young organization, PRUPAC was created in 1971, after studies indicated an interest on the part of the public in dealing with one agent for all their personal insurance needs: life, health, auto, and homeowner. At the same time, Prudential recognized a need to keep its agents competitive with those of several large property and casualty insurers (who had begun marketing life and health insurance through subsidiary companies) by adding auto and homeowners insurance to their portfolios.

PRUPAC began its operations in June 1971, in a one-room office in Chicago, with 18 employees. By the end of that year, it had 112 employees and insured 14,200 cars and homes in Illinois alone. Within five years, the company had expanded countrywide, insuring nearly 1.5 million risks; its staff numbered more than 3,000. Today, with the same size staff, PRUPAC insures about two million cars and homes, making it one of the fifteen largest personal-line property and casualty insurers in the country.

GENERAL COMPUTER USE

Such rapid expansion would not have been possible without computers. Prudential bought its original computers in the early 1950s, when the first commercially available vacuum tube models appeared. As the computer evolved during the following decade, so did Prudential's applications. By the time PRUPAC was founded in 1971, it could build on the software and

hardware expertise of its parent company and start its corporate life as a fully computerized operation. Unlike many of its competitors, PRUPAC never had to undergo the expense, both in time and personnel dislocation, of converting a massive, manual record-keeping system to a computerized information system. This heavy reliance on computers right from the start enabled the company to handle more business with fewer people in less time, making explosive growth financially and operationally feasible.

The basic product sold by insurance companies is an intangible: the promise to pay should a loss occur. The concrete embodiment of that promise is the insurance contract and all the records and paperwork that go with it. Computerized information systems have made it possible to handle the millions of transactions involved both efficiently and economically.

Besides the computer systems that handle the records dealing with policyholders, their bills, and their claims, other systems help manage the finances of the company. These are the common general ledger, accounts payable, accounts receivable, tax, and payroll systems used by most companies, although they are specifically tailored for PRUPAC's needs.

Although the basic product of insurance is simple—a promise to pay for a loss—the trick is in knowing how much to charge so that all losses can be paid off and the company can make a profit without charging rates so high that customers go elsewhere. This is the realm of the actuaries, trained specialists in the mathematical discipline of probability theory. In addition to past experience with losses, the kinds of people who have had losses, and the circumstances under which those losses occurred, actuaries must take into consideration economic projections regarding inflation, return on investment, and so forth. Capturing and analyzing this mass of statistical data would be an awesome task without computer assistance. The computer has enabled insurance companies to analyze and adjust their rates on a more timely basis than previously possible.

All of these systems are part of the information system that helps senior management understand what is happening with the company's business and financial picture before a crisis occurs. These include systems for projecting and planning for the future, analyzing current results against set objectives, and facilitating corrective action.

TELECOMMUNICATIONS AND MICROCOMPUTERS

Although PRUPAC was born a child of the computer age, since its founding in 1971 there have been two major technological advances, telecommunications and microcomputers, that have affected both the company's organization and its people. The growth of telecommunications and on-line storage capacity has changed the structure of the organization and the way it operates. Telecommunications and on-line storage allow access to millions of records in a central location from anywhere in the company. Once accessed, the records can be updated quickly. The advent of the microcomputer, on the other hand, brought the power of the computer out of the data-processing center and placed it in the hands of the layperson.

Perhaps the most outstanding example of microcomputer use at PRUPAC is at the point of sale. Rating insurance policies is a complex process. For example, variables in quoting an auto insurance premium in most states include, but are not limited to, the age, sex, and marital status of the driver, the kind of car, how far the car is driven each year, what use is made of the car, where the car is garaged, whether the driver has any points or convictions for motor vehicle violations, which of a dozen or more possible coverages the driver wants and in what amounts, and so forth. Add to these factors the number and ages of the drivers and the number of cars owned, and the calculations in figuring a rate are formidable.

To facilitate the rate process, PRUPAC furnished agents with a loose-leaf binder containing numerous rate tables, rating rules, and worksheets to guide the agent through the necessary calculations. Even with this aid, though, calculating rates often took fifteen or more minutes during which prospective clients waited and fidgeted. Recalculating the premium with different coverages or different amounts to try to tailor a package to meet the client's needs meant going through the whole process again.

Portable Sharp 1500A computers came to the rescue of beleaguered agents. These machines can fit easily into a briefcase or jacket pocket, yet they provide more than 22K of storage. To use the small computers, agents key in a policy and the client's answers to a series of questions. Most of the answers can be entered in the computer with a single keystroke (Y for "Yes"; N for "No"). When all necessary data have been input, the computer calculates all the rates and displays a final figure. The entire process, including keying in data, takes no more than five minutes. When rates change, the portable machines are reprogrammed in agency offices via modems and telephone lines.

At PRUPAC, computers, from large information systems to tiny portables, play an important role in the day-to-day operations of the company.

DISCUSSION POINTS

1. Explain how starting corporate life as a fully computerized operation helped PRUPAC gain an edge over the competition?

2. Discuss the benefits that hand-held computers have created in PRUPAC, its agents, and its customers.

4 HARDWARE

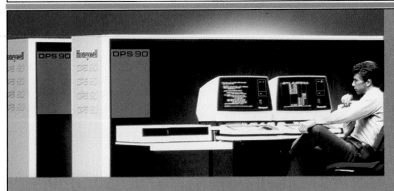

○ ARTICLE

A Maker of Chips That Won't Forget

John Paul Newport Jr.

Fortune

Now would not seem the time to launch a semiconductor company. Industry overcapacity and sluggish computer sales are battering earnings for most major players. Undaunted, Dallas Semiconductor, a year-old private company headed by industry veterans Charles "Vin" Prothro, shipped its first products in November and aspires to grow from $3.5 million in sales this year to $26 million in 1986 and $100 million by 1988.

The company is placing its bets on a basketful of intriguing technologies and a devout determination to avoid selling commodity chips that are all too vulnerable to attack from low-cost Oriental producers. Says Michael Bolan, director of marketing, "The semiconductor industry long ago learned to make the same products cheaply. Our goal is to make unique products cheaply."

Dallas Semiconductor's first products exploit an innovation pioneered by United Technologies' Mostek subsidiary—former stomping ground of Prothro and Bolan, two other Dallas Semiconductor co-founders, and a dozen of its engineers. The idea is to mate lithium batteries—the buttonlike cells found in some wristwatches—and a type of memory chip known as CMOS, for complementary metal oxide semiconductor. Because CMOS chips require extremely small doses of energy, high-quality lithium batteries can keep them energized for ten years or longer—kicking in whenever the electric current that normally powers them kicks out. This is significant because most memory chips that can be added to or erased at will forget everything when power is cut. For many applications that's okay; memory can be preserved on floppy disks or other devices. But having crash-proof memory is crucial on, say, vital medical equipment and mundane products like cash registers that need to keep running totals of the day's take.

Chips to protect software, which Dallas Semiconductor will introduce in July, may be the product to put the technology over the top. For about $5 each, the company will sell a blank "key"—an integrated circuit and lithium battery in a plastic case about the size of a postage stamp—to software vendors who will program it with fiendish codes of their own devising. A matching code will be embedded in the software packages sold with the key. Only when the user inserts the key into a socket connected to his computer's innards—a device costing about $10—will the program work. Software publishers are clamoring for theft-stopping solutions. The big question is whether software houses will be gutsy enough to force buyers to install the socket—a job a layman can handle but might rather avoid.

This summer Dallas Semiconductor also plans to start operating a laser capable of etching semiconductor chips with super precision, which it will use to customize chips even in the final stages of production. Next year it will put to work a powerful machine for implanting patterns of ions deep inside silicon structures. Both pieces of equipment will put the company on the cutting edge of the technology for adapting chips to a customer's specifications on short notice. "All the major developments in this industry have been decided by the marketplace, not by planning," says marketing man Bolan. "Our cardinal promise is not to fall in love with any one product."

● **Nonvolatile microchips and security devices for commercial software are two hardware advances allowing a new company to grow in an otherwise stagnant market. This market state, as much as anything else, is helping to push the technology forward.**

● Introduction

A general understanding of electronic data processing is possible without undertaking a detailed study of computer technology, just as a general understanding of how a car operates is possible without undertaking a detailed study of the internal combustion engine. However, with cars as well as computers, a general understanding of the machines' capabilities and limitations may be useful.

This chapter focuses on the parts of a computer system. The central processing unit, or CPU, and its key components are identified and their functions explained. The chapter also examines various forms of primary storage and briefly discusses read-only memory (ROM) and programmable read-only memory (PROM). Data representation in relation to computer processing is discussed. Binary, octal, and hexadecimal number systems are covered along with computer codes. The chapter concludes with a brief discussion of code checking.

● Central Processing Unit

The **central processing unit (CPU)** is the heart of the computer system. It is composed of three parts that function together as a unit. These parts are the control unit, the arithmetic/logic unit, and primary storage. Each part of the CPU performs its own unique functions (see Figure 4–1).

While the CPU incorporates all three components, the control unit and the arithmetic/logic unit are often referred to collectively as the **processor.** A processor may incorporate one or more circuit elements, or "chips." In a large computer, the processor may be built on several circuit boards in boxlike structures or frames, hence the term *mainframe.* Processors in microcomputers have been shrunk in size to fit onto a single plug-in chip and are referred to as microprocessors.

When data and programs enter the CPU, they are held in primary storage. Generally the primary storage that holds the data and programs is a form of semiconductor memory called **random-access memory (RAM).** RAM is the working area of the computer. Since RAM is volatile, or nonpermanent, data or programs will be erased when the electric power to the computer is turned off or disrupted in any other way. When any changes or results are to be saved, they must be saved on an external form of storage, for example, on disks or magnetic tapes.

To begin work, data and programs to be manipulated are written into RAM. What happens to the contents of RAM depends on the processor. The processor, as stated earlier, consists of two processing units: the control unit and the arithmetic/logic unit. The **control unit** maintains order and controls activity in the CPU. It does not process or store data; it directs the sequence of operations. The control unit interprets the instructions of a program in storage and produces signals that "command" circuits to execute the instructions. Other functions of the control unit include communicating with an input device in order to begin the transfer of instructions and data into storage and, similarly, communicating with an output device to initiate the transfer of results from storage.

The manipulation of the data occurs in the **arithmetic/logic unit (ALU)** of the CPU. The ALU performs arithmetic computations and logical op-

● **FIGURE 4–1**
Computer System Components

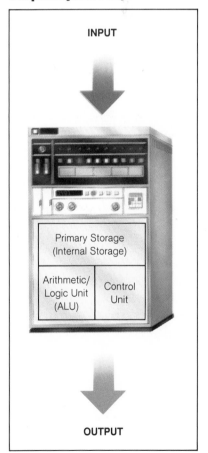

INPUT

Primary Storage
(Internal Storage)

Arithmetic/
Logic Unit
(ALU)

Control
Unit

OUTPUT

erations. Arithmetic computations include addition, subtraction, multiplication, and division. Logical comparisons include six combinations of equality: equal to, not equal to, greater than, less than, equal to or greater than, and equal to or less than. Since the bulk of internal processing involves calculations or comparisons, computer capabilities often depend upon the design and capabilities of the ALU.

Primary storage (also known as **primary memory, internal storage/ memory,** or **main storage/memory**) holds instructions, data, and intermediate and final results of processing. At the start of processing, data is transferred from some form of input media by an input device to primary storage, where it is stored until needed for processing. Data being processed and intermediate results of ALU calculations are also stored here. After all computations and manipulations are completed, the final results remain in memory until the control unit causes them to be transferred to an output device. See Concept Summary 4–1 for a review of the central processing unit.

CONCEPT SUMMARY 4–1

Components of the Central Processing Unit

COMPONENT	FUNCTION
Control Unit	Maintains order Controls CPU activity Directs sequence of operations
Arithmetic/Logic Unit (ALU)	Manipulates data Performs arithmetic computations Performs logical operations
Primary Storage	Holds instructions, data and intermediate and final results of processing

● Instructions

A computer functions by processing a series of instructions. Each computer instruction has two basic parts: the operation code and the operand. The **operation code (op code)** indicates to the control unit what function is to be performed (such as ADD, MOVE, DATA, or COMPARE). The **operand** indicates the primary storage location of the data on which to operate. (Op codes and operands will be discussed in more detail in Chapter 12.)

The computer performs instructions sequentially, in the order they are given, unless instructed to do otherwise. This **next-sequential-instruction** feature requires that instructions be placed in consecutive locations in memory. Otherwise, the computer would be unable to differentiate between instructions and data. Since input must be brought into the computer for processing, a separate area must be designated for the input. The output generated by processing also requires an area isolated from the instructions (see Figure 4–2).

Input to a computer can take many forms. In one form, data and instructions can be entered in the computer from magnetic tape by pressing keys on a terminal keyboard. Another method relies on data that is stored on magnetic disks. No matter what method is used to enter data in a computer, once the process begins, the control unit directs the input device to transfer instructions and data to primary storage. Then the control unit takes one instruction from storage, examines it, and sends electronic signals to the ALU and storage, which causes the instruction to be carried out. The signals sent to storage may tell it to transfer data to the ALU, where it is mathematically manipulated. The result may then be transferred back to storage.

After an instruction has been executed, the control unit takes the next instruction from the primary storage unit. Data may be transferred from storage to the ALU and back several times before all instructions are executed. When all manipulations are complete, the control unit directs the storage unit to transfer the processed data (information) to the output device.

The most widely used output devices are printers, which provide results on paper; visual-display units, which project results on televisionlike screens; and tape and disk drives, which produce machine-readable magnetic information. (These devices will be discussed in Chapters 5 and 6.)

If more than one input record is to be processed, the steps that have been described will be repeated for each record. These steps can be summarized as shown in Figure 4–3. Notice that, like humans, computers can only execute one instruction at a time. The power of computers comes from the fact that they can work at incredibly high speeds.

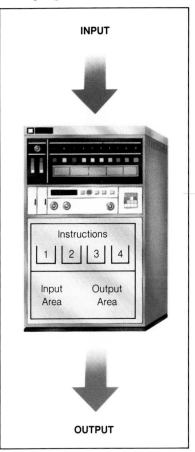

Stored-Program Concept

In Chapter 1 a program was defined as a series of instructions that direct the computer to perform a given task. In early computers, instructions had to be either wired on control panels and plugged into the computer at the beginning of a job or read into the computer from punched cards in distinct steps as the job progressed. This approach slowed down processing because the computer had to wait for instructions by a human operator. To speed up processing, the memory of the computer was used to store the instructions as well as the data. This development, the **stored-program concept,** was significant; since instructions were stored in computer memory in electronic form, no human intervention was required during processing. The computer could proceed at its own speed— close to the speed of light!

Modern computers can store programs. Once instructions required for an application have been determined, they are placed into computer memory so the appropriate operations will be performed. The storage unit operates much as a tape recorder. Once instructions are stored, they remain in storage until new ones are stored over them. Therefore, it is possible to execute the same instructions over and over again until the instructions are changed. Executing the same instructions over and over is known as reading. Storing new instructions is called writing. This characteristic, therefore, is known as **nondestructive read/destructive write.** Each series of instructions placed into memory is called a **stored program,** and the person who writes these instructions is called a **programmer.**

● **FIGURE 4–3**
CPU Operations

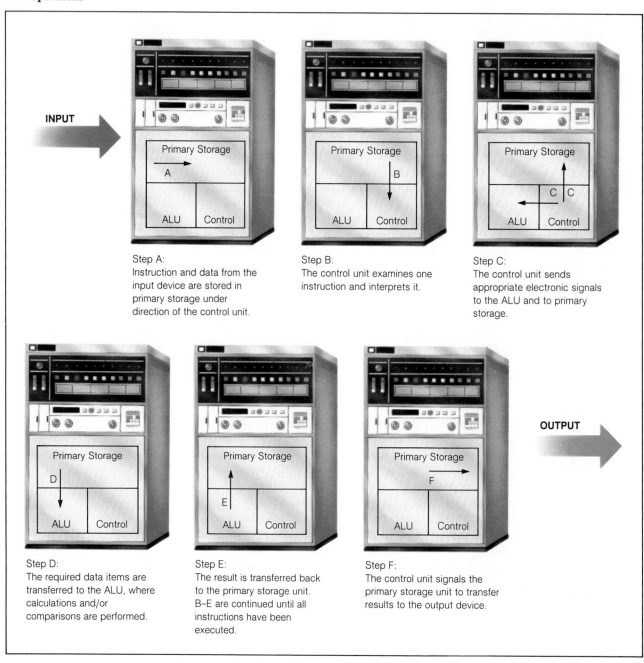

INPUT

Step A:
Instruction and data from the input device are stored in primary storage under direction of the control unit.

Step B:
The control unit examines one instruction and interprets it.

Step C:
The control unit sends appropriate electronic signals to the ALU and to primary storage.

Step D:
The required data items are transferred to the ALU, where calculations and/or comparisons are performed.

Step E:
The result is transferred back to the primary storage unit. B–E are continued until all instructions have been executed.

Step F:
The control unit signals the primary storage unit to transfer results to the output device.

OUTPUT

● Storage

STORAGE LOCATION AND ADDRESSES

In order to direct processing operations, the control unit of the CPU must be able to locate each instruction and data item in storage. Therefore, each location in storage is assigned an **address.** One way to understand this concept is to picture computer storage as a large collection of mailboxes. Each mailbox is a specific location with its own number or address (see Figure 4–4). Each can hold one item of information. Since each location in storage has a unique address, items can be located by use of stored-program instructions that give their addresses. Sometimes data at some locations must be changed, added, or deleted during execution of the program. A **variable,** or symbolic name for the kind of data to be changed, represents a location to the programmer who writes the instructions.

To understand variables, consider this example. Suppose the computer is directed to subtract TAX from GROSS PAY to determine an employee's salary. Suppose further that TAX is stored at location 104 and has a value of 55.60 and that GROSS PAY is stored at location 111 and has a value of 263.00. To determine an employee's salary, the programmer instructs the computer to subtract TAX from GROSS PAY. The computer interprets this to mean that it should subtract the contents of location 104 from the contents of location 111.

Programmers must keep track of what is stored at each location, and variables help in this task. It is easier for the programmer to use names such as TAX and GROSS PAY and let the computer translate them into addresses assigned to storage locations. The term *variable* means that while the variable name (the storage address) does not change, data stored at the location may. The values of TAX and GROSS PAY are likely to change with each employee. The addresses of TAX and GROSS PAY will not.

● **FIGURE 4–4**
**Each Mailbox Represents a Storage
Location with a Unique Address**

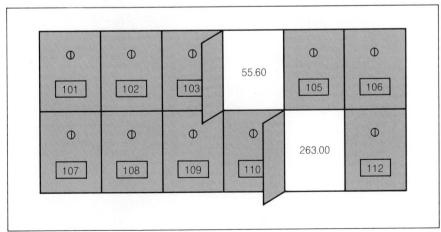

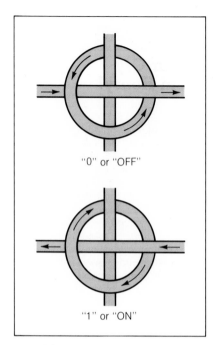

● **FIGURE 4–5**
Magnetizing a Core

● **FIGURE 4–6**
This memory chip can hold as much data as thousands of cores.

PRIMARY STORAGE

Primary storage is all storage considered part of the CPU. It may, in some cases, be supplemented by **secondary storage** (also called **auxiliary,** or **external storage),** which is separate from the CPU. Information is transferred between primary and secondary storage through electrical lines. The most common secondary storage media are magnetic tapes and magnetic disks. Secondary storage media are discussed more fully in Chapter 6.

First-, second-, and third-generation computers contained primary storage units composed of magnetic cores. Each core could store one **bit** (short for *binary digit*). When electricity flowed through the wires making up the cores, a magnetic field was created. The direction of the magnetic field determined which binary state a core represented. A magnetic field in one direction indicated an "on" (1) condition; a magnetic field in the other direction indicated an "off" (0) condition (see Figure 4–5).

Technological developments have led to the use of semiconductors in primary storage units. **Semiconductor memory** is composed of circuitry on **silicon chips.** Each chip, only slightly bigger than one core, can hold as much data as thousands of cores and operate at significantly faster speeds. Storage for most computers in use today consists mostly of semiconductors (see Figure 4–6).

Semiconductors are designed to store data in locations called **bit cells,** which are capable of being either "on" or "off." An "on" state is represented by a 1, an "off" state by a 0. The bit cells are arranged in matrices of eight rows by eight columns. Unlike core memory, semiconductor memory does not store data magnetically. With semiconductor memory, electrical current is sent along the wires leading to the bit cells. At the points where the electrically charged wires intersect, the bit cells are in "on" states. The remaining cells are in "off" states (see Figure 4–7).

There are many different kinds of semiconductor memory, but most

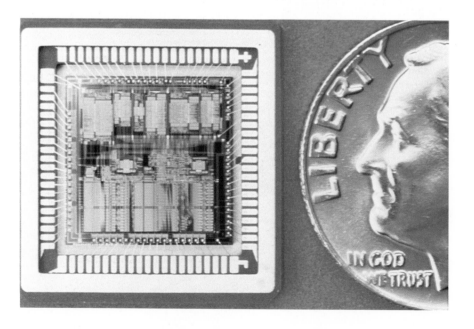

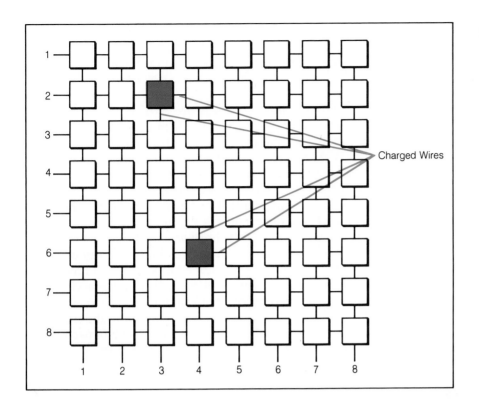

require a constant power source. Since they rely on currents to represent data, all stored data are lost if the power source fails and no emergency (backup) system exists. Core memory retains its contents even if the power source fails because it relies on magnetic charges rather than on currents. Despite this disadvantage of semiconductor memory, its speed makes it a more popular form of memory than core.

A form of memory called **bubble memory** has been introduced as a replacement medium for both primary and secondary storage. This memory consists of magnetized spots, or **magnetic domains,** resting on a thin film of semiconductor material. The magnetic domains (called bubbles) have a polarity opposite that of the semiconductor material on which they rest. Data are stored by shifting positions of the bubbles on the surface of the material (see Figure 4-8). When data are read, the presence of a bubble indicates a 0 bit. Bubbles are similar to magnetic cores in that they retain their magnetism indefinitely. They are much smaller than magnetic cores and store more data in a smaller area. A bubble memory module only slightly larger than a quarter can store 20,000 characters of data. While some manufacturers are using bubble memory in computers, high cost and production problems have led to the limited use of bubble memory.

READ-ONLY MEMORY (ROM)

Computers are capable of performing complex functions such as taking square roots and evaluating exponents. Such functions can be built into

● **FIGURE 4-8**
Bubble Memory

the hardware or software of a computer system. This provides the advantages of speed and reliability, since the operations are part of the actual computer circuitry. Building functions into software allows more flexibility, but carrying out functions built into software is slower and more prone to error.

When functions are built into the hardware of a computer, they are placed in **read-only memory (ROM).** Read-only memory instructions are **hard-wired** and cannot be changed or deleted by other stored-program instructions. Since ROM is permanent, it cannot be occupied by common stored-program instructions or data and can only be changed by altering the physical construction of the circuits. Sometimes ROM chips are called *firmware.* Building instructions into ROM makes the distinction between hardware and software less clear cut (see Figure 4–9).

Microprograms are a direct result of hard wiring. Microprograms are sequences of instructions built into read-only memory to carry out functions (such as calculating square roots) that otherwise would have to be directed by stored-program instructions at a much slower speed. Microprograms are usually supplied by computer manufacturers and cannot be altered by users. However, microprogramming allows the basic operations of the computer to be tailored to meet the needs of users. If all instructions that a computer can execute are located in ROM, a complete

● **FIGURE 4–9**
ROM Chip

new set of instructions can be obtained by changing the ROM. When selecting a computer, users can get the standard features of the machine plus their choice of the optional features available through microprogramming.

Read-only memory is different from nondestructive read. With nondestructive read, items stored in memory can be read repeatedly without loss of information. New items can then be stored over old ones if the stored program instructs the computer to do so. Read-only memory, on the other hand, is hard-wired into the computer and can only be changed by rewiring.

A version of ROM that can be programmed by the end user is **programmable read-only memory (PROM).** PROM can be programmed by the manufacturer, or it can be shipped "blank" to the end user for programming. Once programmed, its contents are unalterable. With PROM the end user has the advantages of ROM along with the flexibility to meet unique needs. A problem with it, though, is that mistakes programmed into the unit cannot be corrected. To overcome this drawback, **erasable programmable read-only memory (EPROM)** has been developed (see Figure 4–10). EPROM can be erased but only when it is submitted to a special process, such as being bathed in ultraviolet light. Concept Summary 4–2 presents a review of RAM and ROM.

REGISTERS

Registers facilitate the execution of instructions by acting as temporary holding areas for instructions and data. They are located in the CPU but are not considered part of primary storage. Registers can receive information, hold it, and transfer it very quickly as directed by the control unit of the CPU.

A register functions much as a standard pocket calculator does. The

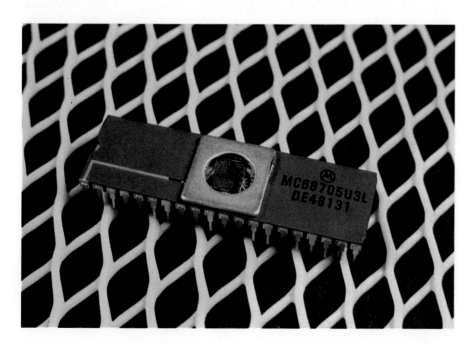

● **FIGURE 4–10**
EPROM Chip

RAM and ROM

RAM	ROM
Stands for random-access memory	Stands for read-only memory
Form of primary storage for holding temporary data and instructions	Form of primary storage for holding permanent data and instructions
Volatile: Programs and data are erased when the power is disrupted	Permanent: Programs and data remain intact even when power is off
	Other forms of ROM: PROM—Programmable ROM EPROM—Erasable PROM

person using the calculator acts as the control unit by transferring numbers from a sheet of paper to the calculator. This paper is analogous to the primary storage unit of the CPU. When the calculation is complete, the calculator displays the result. The person (control unit) then transfers the result displayed on the calculator (register) back to the sheet of paper (primary storage). This process is very similar to the way most modern computers work. Intermediate calculations are performed in registers, and the final results are transferred back to primary storage.

CACHE MEMORY

Cache memory, also called a high-speed buffer, is a portion of primary storage used to speed the processing operations of the computer. Cache memory serves as a working buffer or temporary area to store both instructions and data that must be accessed, often by the program being executed. By storing the data in a temporary area of primary storage, the need to continually access secondary storage for the data or instructions is eliminated. Although more expensive than primary storage, cache memory increases processing speeds, which sometimes warrants its use.

● Data Representation

Humans communicate information by using symbols that have specific meanings. Symbols such as letters or numbers are combined in meaningful ways to represent information. For example, the twenty-six letters of the English alphabet can be combined to form words, sentences, paragraphs, and so on. By combining the individual words in various ways, we construct various messages. This enables us to communicate with one another.

The human mind is much more complex than the computer. A computer is only a machine; it is not capable of understanding the inherent meanings of symbols used by humans to communicate. To use a computer, therefore, humans must convert their symbols to a form the computer is capable of "understanding." This is accomplished through binary representation and the "on" and "off" states discussed earlier.

BINARY REPRESENTATION

Data is represented in the computer by the electrical state of the machine's circuitry: magnetic states for core storage, current for semiconductor storage, and the position of magnetic bubbles for bubble memory. In all cases, only two states are possible, "on" and "off." This two-state system is known as a **binary system,** and its use to represent data is known as **binary representation.**

The **binary (base 2) number system** operates in a manner similar to the way the familiar **decimal number system** works. For example, the decimal number 4,672 can be analyzed as follows:

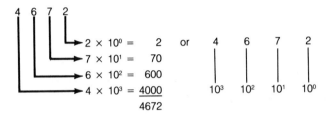

Each position represents a specific power of 10. The progression of powers is from right to left; that is, digits further to the left in a decimal number represent larger powers of 10 than digits to the right of them (see Figure 4–11).

The same principle holds for binary representation. The difference is that in binary representation each position in the number represents a power of 2 (see Figure 4–12). For example, consider the decimal number 14. In binary, the value equivalent to 14 is written as follows:

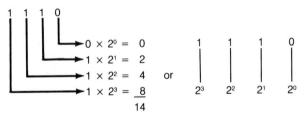

● **FIGURE 4–11**
Decimal Place Value

10^5	10^4	10^3	10^2	10^1	10^0
100,000	10,000	1,000	100	10	1

● **FIGURE 4–12**
Binary Place Value

2^6	2^5	2^4	2^3	2^2	2^1	2^0
64	32	16	8	4	2	1

● HIGHLIGHT

Static Can Zap a Microprocessor!

When you were little, you probably scuffled along the carpet to build up static electricity and then "zapped" somebody. The snap that was felt and heard—to the chagrin of its receiver—is called electrostatic discharge (ESD). Ten steps on a nylon rug can build up 10,000 to 20,000 volts of static electricity in your body.

While humans may not feel a low-voltage ESD, a microprocessor surely can! A glip, gremlin, or glitch in computer operations can be caused by a discharge of only 2,000 volts of static electricity. During winter months, when indoor temperature is high and humidity low, a stroll across an office carpet can generate up to 30,000 volts of static electricity—enough to do permanent damage to a computer or software.

Static can be transferred to the system either by contact charging (for example, a person touching the key on a computer terminal), or by induction charging (electric fields radiating from such items as clothing or polyethylene bags). A shirt sleeve, for example, can generate enough static electricity to destroy most PROM (programmable read-only memory) chips. Other sources of static electricity include waxed, painted, or varnished surfaces; vinyl flooring; synthetic garments; styrofoam; electrostatic copiers, spray cleaner; and plastic-covered chairs and desks.

When completing a computer system plan, a company should include the cost of antistatic floor mats, antistatic agents in spray bottles or towelettes; and ionizers, devices that neutralize charged electrons. Protecting a system this way is much cheaper than repairing blown microcircuits or recovering lost data.

As a further example, the value represented by the decimal number 300 is represented in binary form below:

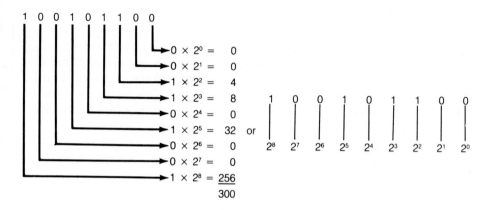

As indicated by the examples above, the binary number system uses 1s and 0s in various combinations to represent various values. Recall that each digit position in a binary number is called a bit. A 1 in a bit position indicates the presence of a specific power of 2; a 0 indicates the absence of a specific power. As in the decimal number system, the progression of powers is from right to left.

OCTAL NUMBER SYSTEM

Although all digital computers must store data as 0s and 1s, the sizes of the storage locations vary. Storage locations within primary memory are referred to as **words,** and one word is equal to one "mailbox" (see discussion on storage locations and addresses in this chapter). Word sizes are measured in bits and are typically 8, 16, 24, 32, 48, and 64 bits in length.

The **octal (base 8) number system,** which uses digits 0 to 7, can be employed as a shorthand method of representing the data contained within one word, or addressable memory location. In the case of 24- and 48-bit word size computers, the octal number system provides a shorthand method of representing what is contained in memory. This is true because three binary digits, or bits, can be represented by one octal digit and both 24 and 48 are divisible by three.

As noted above, three binary digits can be represented by one octal digit. This is done by considering the first three binary place values from right to left that sum to seven, the highest single digit value in the octal number system.

```
1  1  1
│  │  │
│  │  └─→ 1 × 2⁰ = 1
│  └──→ 1 × 2¹ = 2
└───→ 1 × 2² = 4
                  ─
                  7
```

If we wanted to represent a binary value that was contained in a 24-bit word as an octal value, it could be converted as follows:

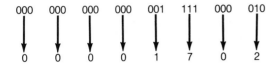

The octal value can be converted to its decimal equivalent. The octal number 1,702 is equivalent to the decimal number 962. Consider the conversion below, keeping in mind that each digit of the octal number represents a power of 8.

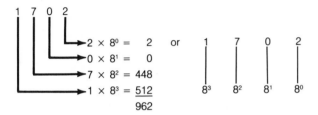

For another example, the value represented by the decimal number 10,000 is displayed in octal form below:

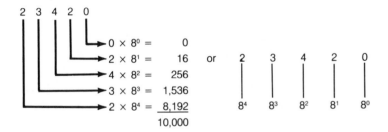

HEXADECIMAL NUMBER SYSTEM

When a program fails to execute correctly, it is sometimes necessary to examine the contents of certain memory locations to discover what is wrong. This can be done by obtaining a printout, or **dump,** of the contents of the memory locations (see Figure 4–13). If everything were printed in binary representation, the programmer would see page after page of 1s and 0s. Error detection would be difficult.

To alleviate this problem, the contents of storage locations in computers can be represented by the **hexadecimal (base 16) number system.** In the hexadecimal number system, sixteen symbols are used to represent the digits 0 through 15 (see Figure 4–14). Note that the letters A through F designate the numbers 10 through 15. The fact that each position in a hexadecimal number represents a power of 16 allows for easy conversion from binary to hexadecimal, since 16 is equal to 2^4. A single hexadecimal digit can be used to represent four binary digits.

```
9000D203  9000C11E  41330004  4650C05A
0010E020  C1220064  E020C186  006407FE
40F0F740  40F0F840  4040F540  40F2F340
40404040  40404040  40F2F340  40F2F340
40F4F640  40F2F540  40F1F240  40F2F440
4040F640  40F6F640  40F8F540  40404040
40F0F840  40F2F540  40F3F140  4040F540
F2F5F640  F7F8F940  F1F2F540  F6F2F440
00000005  00000005  00000006  00000007
0000000F  00000010  00000015  00000017
00000018  00000018  00000019  00000019
00000035  00000035  00000037  00000038
00000055  00000055  00000060  0000007D
0000022B  0000022B  0000022B  0000022B
0000022B  00000315  F0E3C8C5  40E4D5E2
E2D6D9E3  C5C440C1  D9D9C1E8  F1F5F5F5
F5F5F5F5  F5F5F5F5  F5F5F5F5  F5F5F5F5
F5F5F5F5  F5F5F5F5  F5F5F5F5  F5F5F5F5
```

As noted above, four binary digits can be represented by one hexadecimal digit. This is done by considering the first four binary place values (from right to left) that sum to 15, the highest single digit value in the hexadecimal number system.

$$
\begin{array}{r}
1 \times 2^0 = 1 \\
1 \times 2^1 = 2 \\
1 \times 2^2 = 4 \\
1 \times 2^3 = \underline{8} \\
15
\end{array}
$$

● FIGURE 4–14
Binary, Hexadecimal, and Decimal
Equivalent Values

BINARY SYSTEM (PLACE VALUES)				HEXADECIMAL EQUIVALENT	DECIMAL EQUIVALENT
8	4	2	1		
0	0	0	0	0	0
0	0	0	1	1	1
0	0	1	0	2	2
0	0	1	1	3	3
0	1	0	0	4	4
0	1	0	1	5	5
0	1	1	0	6	6
0	1	1	1	7	7
1	0	0	0	8	8
1	0	0	1	9	9
1	0	1	0	A	10
1	0	1	1	B	11
1	1	0	0	C	12
1	1	0	1	D	13
1	1	1	0	E	14
1	1	1	1	F	15

A binary value contained in a 32-bit word as a hexadecimal value could be converted as follows:

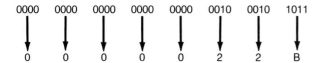

The hexadecimal value can be converted to its decimal equivalent. Keep in mind that each digit of the hexadecimal number represents a power of 16.

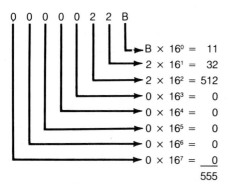

$$B \times 16^0 = 11$$
$$2 \times 16^1 = 32$$
$$2 \times 16^2 = 512$$
$$0 \times 16^3 = 0$$
$$0 \times 16^4 = 0$$
$$0 \times 16^5 = 0$$
$$0 \times 16^6 = 0$$
$$0 \times 16^7 = 0$$
$$555$$

COMPUTER CODES

Many computers use coding schemes other than simple binary notation to represent numbers. One of the most basic coding schemes is called **four-bit binary coded decimal (BCD).** Rather than represent a decimal number as a string of 0s and 1s (which gets increasingly complicated for large numbers), BCD represents each decimal digit in a number by using four bits. For instance, the decimal number 23 is represented by two groups of four bits, one group for the "2," the other for the "3." Representations of the number 23 in four-bit BCD and in binary are compared below:

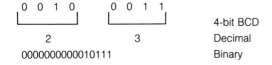

0 0 1 0	0 0 1 1	4-bit BCD
2	3	Decimal
0000000000010111		Binary

The representation of a three-digit decimal number in four-bit BCD consists of three sets of four bits, or twelve binary digits. For example, the decimal number 637 is coded as follows:

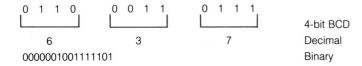

0 1 1 0	0 0 1 1	0 1 1 1	4-bit BCD
6	3	7	Decimal
0000001001111101			Binary

Use of four-bit BCD saves space when large decimal numbers must be represented. Furthermore, it is easier to convert a four-bit BCD to its decimal equivalent than to convert a binary representation to decimal.

The four-bit code allows sixteen (2^4) possible unique bit combinations. We have already seen that ten of them are used to represent the decimal digits 0 through 9. Since that leaves only six remaining combinations, this code in practice is used only to represent numbers.

To represent letters and special characters as well as numbers, more than four bit positions are needed. Another coding scheme, called **six-bit BCD,** allows for sixty-four (2^6) unique bit combinations. Thus, six-bit BCD can be used to represent the decimal digits 0 through 9, the letters A through Z, and twenty-eight characters, such as the period and the comma.

The four rightmost bit positions in six-bit BCD are called **numeric bits.** The two leftmost bit positions are called **zone bits** (see Figure 4–15). The zone bits are used in various combinations with the numeric bits to represent numbers, letters, and special characters.

Another approach to data representation is an eight-bit code known as **Extended Binary Coded Decimal Interchange Code (EBCDIC).** An eight-bit code allows 256 (2^8) possible bit combinations. Whereas six-bit BCD can be used to represent only uppercase letters, eight-bit EBCDIC can be used to represent uppercase and lowercase letters and additional special characters, such as the cent sign and the quotation mark. The EBCDIC bit combinations for uppercase letters and numbers are given in Figure 4–16.

In EBCDIC, the four leftmost bit positions are zone bits, and the four rightmost bit positions are numeric bits. As with six-bit BCD, the zone bits are used in various combinations with the numeric bits to represent numbers, letters, and special characters.

The **American Standard Code for Information Interchange (ASCII)** is a seven-bit code developed cooperatively by several computer manufacturers who wanted to develop a standard code for all computers. Because certain machines are designed to accept eight-bit rather than seven-bit code patterns, an eight-bit version of ASCII called **ASCII-8** was created. ASCII-8 and EBCDIC are similar, the key difference between them being in the bit patterns used to represent certain characters.

Bits, as described, are very small units of data; it is often useful to combine them into larger units. A fixed number of adjacent bits operated on as a unit is called a **byte.** Usually, one alphabetic character or two numeric characters are represented in one byte. Since eight bits are sufficient to represent any character, eight-bit groupings are the basic units of memory. In computers that accept eight-bit characters, then, a byte is a group of eight adjacent bits. When large amounts of storage

● **FIGURE 4–15**
Bit Position in 6-Bit BCD Representation

ZONE BITS		NUMERIC BITS			
B	A	8	4	2	1

● **COMPUTERS AND INFORMATION PROCESSING**

○ HIGHLIGHT

Easy-to-Do Conversion

It's easy to convert whole decimal numbers to binary numbers, or to numbers in any other base, for that matter. Simply get out your handy-dandy pocket calculator and push the buttons for conversions!

Seriously, there is an easier way than the subtraction method. It's the division multiplication method. All you do is divide the number by the value of the base until nothing is left to divide. The remainders of each division, written in each place starting with the ones place, form the new equivalent number. Here's how it works in base 2:

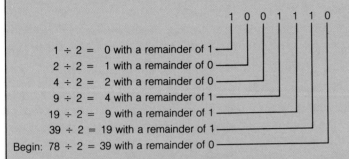

```
                    1   0   0   1   1   1   0

      1 ÷ 2 =   0 with a remainder of 1
      2 ÷ 2 =   1 with a remainder of 0
      4 ÷ 2 =   2 with a remainder of 0
      9 ÷ 2 =   4 with a remainder of 1
     19 ÷ 2 =   9 with a remainder of 1
     39 ÷ 2 =  19 with a remainder of 1
Begin: 78 ÷ 2 = 39 with a remainder of 0
```

Now convert the decimal number 325 to a base 2 number. Did you get 101000101? Very good! So try something more difficult: Change 325 to a base 8 number. Was your answer 505? Good! That means 5 in the 64s place, 0 in the 8s place, and 5 in the 1s place. Try some more problems you make up. Check them with your calculator!

Character	EBCDIC Bit Configuration	Character	EBCDIC Bit Configuration
A	1100 0001	S	1110 0010
B	1100 0010	T	1110 0011
C	1100 0011	U	1110 0100
D	1100 0100	V	1110 0101
E	1100 0101	W	1110 0110
F	1100 0110	X	1110 0111
G	1100 0111	Y	1110 1000
H	1100 1000	Z	1110 1001
I	1100 1001	0	1111 0000
J	1101 0001	1	1111 0001
K	1101 0010	2	1111 0010
L	1101 0011	3	1111 0011
M	1101 0100	4	1111 0100
N	1101 0101	5	1111 0101
O	1101 0110	6	1111 0110
P	1101 0111	7	1111 0111
Q	1101 1000	8	1111 1000
R	1101 1001	9	1111 1001

● **FIGURE 4-16**
EBCDIC Representation: 0–9, A–Z

are described, the symbol **K** (for kilobyte) is often used. Generally, one K equals 1,024 (2^{10}) units. Thus, a computer that has a 256K bytes of storage can store 256 × 1,024, or 262,144, characters.

CODE CHECKING

Computers do not always function perfectly; errors can and do occur. For example, a bit may be lost while data is being transferred from the ALU to the primary storage unit or over telephone lines from one location to another. This loss can be caused by varied factors such as dust, moisture, magnetic fields, or equipment failure. Thus, it is necessary to have a method to detect when an error has occurred and to isolate the location of the error.

Most computers accomplish this by having an additional bit, called a **parity bit,** or **check bit,** at each storage location. Computers that use parity bits are specifically designed always to have either an even or an odd number of 1 (or "on") bits in each storage location. If an odd number of 1 bits is used to represent each character, the characters are said to be written in **odd parity.** If an even number of 1 bits is used to represent each character, the characters are written in **even parity.** Internal circuitry in the computer constantly monitors its operation by checking to ensure that the required number of bits is present in each location.

For example, if the six-bit BCD code is used, a seventh bit is added as a check bit (see Figure 4–17). Suppose the number 6 is to be represented in six-bit BCD using odd parity (see Figure 4–18). In this case, the check bit must be set to 1, or "on," to make the number of 1 bits odd. If a parity error is detected, the system may retry the read or write operation occurring when the error was detected. If retries are unsuccessful, the system informs the computer operator that an error has occurred.

Notice that the checking circuitry of the computer can only detect the miscoding of characters. It cannot detect the use of incorrect data. In the previous example, for instance, the computer circuitry could determine whether a bit had been dropped, making the representation of the number 6 invalid. However, if the number 5 had been mistakenly entered into the computer instead of 6 (for example, because of incorrect keying of a card), no error would be detected.

● **FIGURE 4–17**
Bit Positions of 6-Bit BCD with Check Bit

CHECK BIT	ZONE BITS		NUMERIC BITS			
C	B	A	8	4	2	1

● **FIGURE 4–18**
Detection of Error with Parity Check (Odd Parity)

	C	B	A	8	4	2	1
Valid — →	1	0	0	0	1	1	0
Invalid— ←	1	0	0	0	0	1	0

● **COMPUTERS AND INFORMATION PROCESSING**

● Summary Points

● The central processing unit, the heart of the computer, is composed of three parts: the control unit, the arithmetic/logic unit (ALU), and primary storage. The control unit maintains order and controls what is happening in the CPU; the ALU performs arithmetic and logical operations; and the primary storage unit holds all data and instructions necessary for processing.

● Instructions are placed in consecutive locations in memory so that they can be accessed consecutively. This is called the next-sequential-instruction feature.

● The stored-program concept involves storing both data and instructions in the computer's memory, eliminating the need for human intervention during processing.

● The nondestructive read/destructive write characteristic of memory allows a program to be re-executed, since the program remains intact in memory until another is stored over it. The computer executes instructions sequentially (as accessed in consecutive location in memory) unless instructed to do otherwise.

● Each location in storage has a unique address, which allows stored-program instructions and data items to be located by the control unit of the CPU as it directs processing operations. Variables (names for storage addresses) are often used by programmers to facilitate data location.

● One method of storing data in primary storage uses electrical currents to set magnetic cores to "on" and "off" states. Another form of storage is semiconductor memory, which uses circuitry on silicon chips. Semiconductor units are smaller and faster than cores, but they usually demand a constant power source. Bubble memory consists of magnetized spots that rest on a thin film of semiconductor material. These bubbles retain their magnetism indefinitely and have the ability to store much more data in a smaller space than core memory.

● Read-only memory (ROM), part of the hardware of a computer, stores items in a form that can be deleted or changed only by rewiring. Microprograms are sequences of instructions built into read-only memory to carry out functions that otherwise would be directed by stored-program instructions at a much slower speed.

● Programmable read-only memory (PROM) can be programmed either by the manufacturer or by users to meet unique needs. Thus, it provides greater flexibility and versatility than ROM.

● Registers are devices that facilitate the execution of instructions. They act as temporary holding areas and are capable of receiving information, holding it, and transferring it very quickly as directed by the control unit of the CPU.

● Cache memory is a portion of primary storage designed to speed the CPU's processing of instructions or data.

● Data representation in the computer is based on a two-state, or binary, system. A 1 in a given position indicates the presence of a power of 2; a 0 indicates its absence. The four-bit binary coded decimal (BCD) system uses groups of four binary digits to represent the decimal digits 0 through 9.

- The six-bit BCD system allows for sixty-four unique bit combinations; alphabetic, numeric, and twenty-eight special characters can be represented. Both EBCDIC and ASCII-8 are eight-bit coding systems and are capable of representing up to 256 different characters.
- Octal (base 8) and hexadecimal (base 16) notation can be used to represent binary data in a more concise form. For this reason, the contents of computer memory are sometimes viewed or printed in one of these notations. Programmers use these number systems to help in locating errors.
- Parity bits, or check bits, are additional bits in a coding scheme used to detect errors in the transmission of data. They can only detect the miscoding of characters and cannot detect the use of incorrect data.

● Review Questions

1. Name the three major components of the central processing unit (CPU) and discuss the function of each.

2. What is the difference between the operation code and the operand?

3. What is meant by the next-sequential-instruction feature?

4. How does the nondestructive read/destructive write feature of a computer work?

5. What technological developments have occurred in primary storage media and what impact have these developments had on modern computers?

6. How does the concept of read-only memory relate to microprogramming?

7. Why are computer codes necessary? What advantages does EBCDIC offer over six-bit BCD?

8. Why are concepts of the binary number system important to an understanding of digital computers?

9. What relationship do the first four binary place values (from right to left) have with the hexadecimal number system?

10. What is the purpose of code checking? By using a parity bit, or check bit, can incorrect data be detected?

11. Convert the following binary value to an octal value. Then convert the octal value to a decimal value.

101100101

IBM

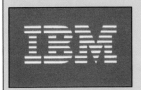

GENERAL CORPORATE INFORMATION

In the 1880s, Herman Hollerith developed a mechanical method of processing census data for the United States Bureau of Census. His method included two devices: one that coded population data as punched holes in cards and another that sensed the data. The success of his method led Hollerith to form his own company in 1896 to manufacture and sell these devices. In 1911, the company became part of the Computing-Tabulating-Recording (CTR) Company, which manufactured commercial scales and tabulating and time-recording equipment. In 1924, CTR became the International Business Machines (IBM) Corporation.

Today, IBM is a leader of the worldwide data-processing community and is the leading vendor of mainframe computers. IBM's Entry Systems Division is the second largest producer of small computers. IBM's products include data-processing machines and systems, information processors, electric typewriters, copiers, dictation equipment, educational and testing materials, and related supplies and services. Most products can be either leased or purchased through IBM's worldwide marketing organizations.

IBM'S FAMILY SERIES

IBM's major business is information handling. IBM computers range from small, powerful minicomputers to ultra-high-performance computers for high-speed, large-scale scientific and commercial applications. The wide range of computer applications in scientific, industrial, and commercial areas today requires machines of different sizes and capabilities. For example, a computer used to forecast the weather has capabilities different from those of a computer used mainly for payroll processing. Consequently, computers with similar characteristics are usually grouped together into a family, series, or system. The family members differ from each

other in range of available memory, number of input-output channels, execution speed, and types of devices with which interface can be established.

For example, IBM's Series/1 is a family of low-cost, versatile, small computers. These computers are modular—that is, the user can acquire as much or as little processing power as needed. The Series/1 includes two processor versions. One, the 4952 processor, is available in three models. All offer 32K to 128K bytes of primary storage. Data can be transferred through input-output channels at a rate of 832,000 bytes per second, and the processor has a cycle time of 2,100 nanoseconds. The 4952 Model C processor offers the same functional capabilities and contains an integrated diskette drive.

IBM also offers software to accompany the Series/1. Like the hardware, it is modular. The Series/1 was designed to facilitate extensive communication networks. Several processors and terminals may be tied together and share the same data. The Series/1 can also be used as a "front-end processor," or a link between a variety of peripherals and a central, or host, computer. The modular design and great flexibility of the Series/1 give users of all types and sizes a number of data-processing alternatives. Areas of application for the Series/1 include distributed processing (where there is a need for data entry, remote job entry, and inquiries to files); commercial applications (such as billing, inventory control, and sales analysis); sensor-based applications (materials and component testing, machine and process control, and shop floor control); and graphics.

In comparison, IBM's System/370 is a family of general-purpose large computers readily adaptable to many applications. The System/370 models' main storage capacities vary from 65,536 bytes to 8,388,608 bytes. Model 168, designed for large-scale, high-speed scientific and commercial applications, has the largest main storage capacity. Its scientific applications range from nuclear physics and theoretical astronomy to weather forecasting. The Model 168 can be used commercially as the control center of complex airline reservation systems, coast-to-coast time-sharing networks, and process control systems. The power and speed of these advanced systems are primarily the result of improved circuit technology. The machine cycle time of the System 370 devices is as fast as 80 nanoseconds, eight times faster than that of the Series/1 computers.

One of IBM's more recent advances is the System/38 family, a general-purpose data-processing system that supports both interactive and batch applications. Since the System/38 is designed as a growth system for some of IBM's previous computers, conversion techniques have been developed to allow the user to convert to the new System/38 with as little reconstruction as possible.

The unique aspect of the System/38 is its use of a high-level "architecture" that involves a new use of hardware technology. The actual hardware is separated from the instruction set by two layers of microprogramming. Storage capacities range from 524,288 bytes to 2,097,152 bytes of primary storage. The System/38 is capable of translating secondary storage addresses to main storage addresses.

The System/38 is composed of a processing unit, main storage, disk storage, console display, diskette drive, and optional I/O and communications facilities. One of the optional I/O devices is the IBM 5250 Information Display System, which consists of several models of display stations and printers.

Finally, the IBM 5520 Administrative System is an office system that integrates shared logic and resource characteristics. It is compatible with System/370 communications and data bases. It features text processing and document distribution. Through the text-processing functions, users can create, revise, share, print, and store documents. The file-processing function can merge fields from one or two files with text to create reports or repetitive letters. Arithmetic expressions, if/else logic, record update, and multiple stored procedures provide a data-processing-like function for administrative users. The document distribution feature has the capability to forward documents to other offices in the same building or across the country. There are four models, which differ in processing power and the amount of fixed and auxiliary storage they support.

Table 4–1 summarizes the major IBM series and their various models. As data-processing requirements have expanded, hardware capabilities such as those provided by IBM have been developed to give the necessary support.

DISCUSSION POINTS

1. What characteristics do computers within a family have in common?

2. How do computers within a family series differ from each other?

● Table 4–1
Major IBM Computers

SERIES	MODELS	DATE INTRODUCED	COMMENTS
700	701	1953	Vacuum tubes
			Magnetic core
	702		
	704		
	705		
Type 650		1954	Magnetic-drum machine
1400	1401	1960	
	1410		Oriented to business
7000	7070	1960	Transistors, business-oriented
	7074		Scientific-oriented
1620		1960	Scientific-oriented, decimal minicomputer
1130		1962	Integrated circuits, small, special-purpose
1800		1963	Integrated circuits, small, special-purpose
360	20	1965	
	25		Systems
	30		designed for
	40		
	44		
	50		all purposes- business
	65		and scientific
	67		
	75		
	85		
	90		
	91		
System/7		1970	Replacement for 1800
System/3		1969	Midismall computer
370	115	1973	
	125		IBM's most popular system- extends capabilities of System/360
	135		
	138		
	145		

SERIES	MODELS	DATE INTRODUCED	COMMENTS
	148		
	158		
	168		
	3031	1977	IBM's most powerful processors
	3032		
	3033	1980	
System/32	3081	1975	Small system for business
System/34		1977	Small system for business
Series/1		1976	Versatile small computer for experienced users
system/38		1973	Powerful, general purpose supporting extensive data bases
5100		1975	Portable computer
5110		1978	Small business computer
5120		1980	Small business system
5520		1979	Administrative office system
Datamaster		1981	Small system with data, word processing
Personal Computer		1981	Microcomputer for home and office
	AT	1984	Increased speed and memory
	XT		
Series/3090	200	1985	Powerful business system
	400		
PS/2	30	1987	XT Compatible small system for business
	50		
	60		
	80		

5 INPUT AND OUTPUT

○ ARTICLE
Biometrics Has a Touch for Spotting Phonies

Eleanor Johnson Tracy
Fortune

While poets have long extolled the uniqueness of each individual, biometrics technology is making a business out of it. Biometrics is the science of taking a biological characteristic, such as a fingerprint, and quantifying it. Devices that can do this are being installed at military bases and other places that now employ guards to screen admissions. Eventually, biometrics may be economical enough to use in verifying the identity of bank customers.

The virtues of biometrics are clear. I.D. cards and credit cards can be filched or forged, and identification numbers can be forgotten by their owners or found out by strangers. But nobody can palm off his fingerprints as someone else's.

Biometrics is still an infant industry, with scarcely $5 million in factory sales last year. But Joseph P. Freeman, whose market research firm in Newtown, Connecticut, tracks the security business, projects sales of about $100 million a year by 1990. Freeman believes biometric devices will make their first big inroads by replacing guards who check photo badges in high-security areas.

Fingermatrix of White Plains, New York, is shipping a product that will guard access to a U.S. naval intelligence command post in Norfolk, Virginia. Bolstered by this invention, the stock of Fingermatrix, which sold at $4.75 a share a year ago, recently traded at $7.25. Yet the nine-year-old company has yet to make a dime: it lost $4 million on sales of $110,000 in fiscal 1984.

The device, which scans fingerprints, is user-friendly. A person puts his finger, any finger, in a slot on a scanning machine (see picture). Within five seconds a microprocessor translates the print into digital code—256 bytes per finger—and matches it against codes stored in the computer's memory.

Other ways of fingering the good guys come from two California companies, Stellar Systems of San Jose and Identix Inc. of Palo Alto. A subsidiary of Wackenhut, which sells guard services and security systems, Stellar markets a product that recognizes a person's hand when it is placed on a scanning device. The University of Georgia is using Stellar machines to identify students eligible to eat in its cafeteria. Indentix, founded in 1982, raised $2.25 million to develop a fingerprint device. Early this year the FBI bought a system to control access to, of all places, an area where fingerprints are processed.

Another biometrics technique relies on scanning blood vessels in the retina. A device that uses this method is produced by Eyedentify Inc., based in Beaverton, Oregon. The product is a machine fitted with what looks like a pair of binoculars. A person simply looks into the eyepieces and presses a button. Identification is quicker than you can say Sherlock Holmes.

Fingermatrix hopes to cash in on the potentially huge market in electronic banking. Banks are promoting debit cards, which holders can use to get cash at automated teller machines or to debit their bank accounts when they buy merchandise. Consumers might feel more secure if strangers couldn't steal their cards and siphon money from their accounts. Biometrics could eliminate the cards, though consumers would have to supply an I.D. number to permit the computer to make swift matchups without searching its entire memory.

At $7,000 to $10,800 each, the various biometric devices are cheaper than guards but are too costly to install at every automated teller machine or cash register. Fingermatrix thinks that if its machine were mass-produced, the price would drop from $10,000 to perhaps $3,500 and eventually go lower. It would need to. Some bankers say $2,000 is the most they would pay; others say $500 would be tops.

● **Who gets to input and output data has become a major issue in the information society. The Fingermatrix machine could easily provide a means of controlling access to database data.**

◯ Introduction

A computer system is much more than a central processing unit with different kinds of storage. Auxiliary devices enter data into and receive output from the CPU. Data input and information output are important activities in any computer-based system because they are the communication links between people and the machine. If these interfaces are weak, the overall performance of the computer system suffers. This chapter describes the primary media used for computer input: punched cards, magnetic tape, and magnetic disks. The growing field of source-data automation is also examined. A discussion of printers, the basic medium for computer output, concludes the chapter.

◯ Data Input

PUNCHED CARDS

Punched cards were used in data processing long before the digital computer was developed. Punched cards were used with early digital computers as a means of entering data. Although they are not as widely used today as they once were, punched cards occasionally still serve as a means of entering data into computers. They are also often found as user-oriented documents, such as time cards, invoices, checks, and turnaround documents. A turnaround document is often used for utility bills. Typically, a turnaround document consists of two parts, with a perforation in the middle. One part of the document is the customer's record of the bill, and the other part contains information about the customer's account. After the customer receives the bill, the card is torn apart on the perforation. The customer keeps the designated portion and returns the other portion to the utility company along with a payment.

Whatever the use, the standard punched card has eighty vertical columns and twelve horizontal rows (see Figure 5–1). It is called an **eighty-column punched card,** or a **Hollerith card,** after its developer Herman Hollerith. Each column can contain a single letter, number, or special character. Data is recorded as holes punched in a particular column to represent a given character. The pattern of holes used to represent characters is known as the **Hollerith code.**

The eighty-column punched card is divided horizontally into three sections. The lower ten rows are **digit rows,** which can represent any digit from 0 through 9. The upper three rows are called **zone rows.** The very top of the card is called the *print zone.* It displays the actual character punched into a card column in a form easily read by humans.

Data is generally grouped together and punched in specific columns on punched cards. Recall from Chapter 1 that a group of related characters treated as a single unit of information is called a field. On punched cards, a field is composed of a group of consecutive columns (see Figure 5–2). When one punched card contains all the necessary data about a transaction, it is called a **unit record,** a complete record. Figure 5–2 also illustrates a unit record—a card containing all data pertaining to the sale of a particular item.

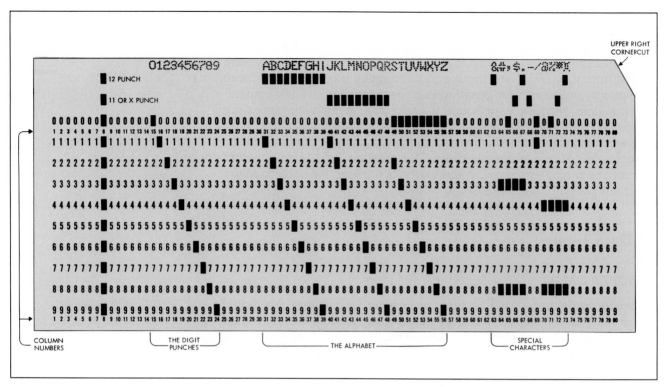

- **FIGURE 5–1**
**Eighty-Column Punched Card and
Hollerith Code**

Eighty-column punched cards do present some disadvantages as a means of recording data. When records require more than eighty columns, two or more cards must be used. This hinders processing since punched-card machines are designed to operate on only one card at a time. Also, when less than an entire card is needed for a record, the remaining space is left unused and wasted. Still another disadvantage of punched cards is the possibility of mutilation during handling. Mutilation hinders the processing of punched cards.

Data is most commonly recorded on punched cards using a **keypunch** (see Figure 5–3). An operator reads a source document and transcribes the data from the document onto cards by pressing keys on a keyboard that is similar to a typewriter. The machine automatically feeds, positions, and stacks the cards, allowing the operator to concentrate on the keying operation.

Even though several steps in the keypunch process are automated, keypunching is still the slowest and most costly operation in any computer system. One person is needed to operate each machine, and much time is spent keying and checking data. For these reasons, data entry by keypunching is not used on many computer systems today.

KEY-TO-MAGNETIC MEDIA

Punched card systems require much mechanized movement and have many limitations. **Key-to-tape** and **key-to-disk** machines were developed to help solve the limitations of punched card systems. With key-to-tape

Field

PUNCH CT D	ORDER NO.	ORDER DATE			SALESPERSON NO.	CUSTOMER NO.	STATE	CITY	QUANTITY	ITEM DESCRIPTION	ITEM NO.	UNIT PRICE	UNIT COST	SALES AMOUNT	COST AMOUNT	GROSS PROFIT	PUNCH RT CTR
		MO	DAY	YR													

Record

and key-to-disk machines, data is entered in much the same fashion as with the card punch, but the data items are stored as magnetized spots on the surface of a tape or disk. The data can be stored indefinitely because the spots retain their magnetism until they are replaced with new data. The ability to reuse tapes and disks overcomes a major disadvantage of punched cards, which cannot be reused. Tapes and disks can also store much more data in a smaller space. For example, between 1,600 and 6,250 characters are commonly stored on one inch of magnetic tape. Data stored on tape or disk can be read into the CPU hundreds of times faster than data stored on cards. Thus, use of magnetic tape or disk significantly increases the efficiency of data-processing operations.

There are two types of key-to-tape configurations available to users, and with both types data are recorded on magnetic tape in reels, cartridges, or cassettes. The first type, a **stand-alone key-to-tape device,** is a self-contained unit that takes the place of a keypunch device. An operator keys the data onto magnetic tapes, cartridges, or cassettes which are then collected from all the stand-alone devices. Next, data from the various media is combined onto a single magnetic tape which is used for computer processing. The second type of key-to-tape configuration, a clustered key-to-tape device, uses several keyboards linked to one or two magnetic-tape units, which accept data from the operators and combine it as keying takes place. This configuration eliminates the extra step needed for the stand-alone devices. **Clustered key-to-tape devices** tend to be less expensive than stand-alone devices because the hardware for recording data onto the tape is centralized. Clustered devices are used in applications where large quantities of similar data are keyed. One advantage of both configurations is that data on the tape can be checked for accuracy and corrected prior to being forwarded to the computer for processing.

A typical key-to-disk configuration consists of several keying devices connected to a minicomputer (see Figure 5–4). Data is keyed onto magnetic disks. Before that, however, the data is usually stored and checked for accuracy by the minicomputer using stored-program instructions. If an error is detected, the system interrupts the operator and waits until a correction has been entered.

An increasingly popular data-entry system is the key-to-diskette system. A **flexible** (or **floppy**) **diskette** is used instead of the conventional (hard) disk. The data is entered on a keyboard, displayed on a screen for error detection, and recorded on diskette. A key-to-diskette system can operate as a stand-alone device or in a cluster configuration. Data recorded on the diskettes is collected and pooled onto a magnetic tape for computer processing.

The key-to-magnetic media offer several advantages over traditional punched-card input:

- Magnetic tapes, disks, and diskettes are reusable.
- Errors can be corrected by backspacing and rekeying correct data over the incorrect data.
- The devices work electronically rather than mechanically and are much quieter.
- Operators transcribe data faster.
- Record lengths are not limited to eighty characters; however, most key-to-magnetic media systems can accommodate data in an eighty-column format, allowing use of old programs written to accept punched-card records.
- Storage on tape, disk, or diskette is much more compact, which reduces handling and saves storage space.

Perhaps the biggest disadvantage to key-to-magnetic systems is that they cost more than punched card systems. Generally, magnetic systems are cost-effective where large amounts of data are prepared for processing on medium-sized or large computers.

SOURCE-DATA AUTOMATION

Data entry has traditionally been the weakest link in the chain of data-processing operations. Although data can be processed electronically at extremely high speeds, significantly more time is required to prepare and enter it into the computer system.

Consider a computer system that uses punched cards for data input. The data is first written on some type of coding form or source document. Then they are keypunched onto cards by an operator. Next, the data may be verified by duplication of the entire keypunching operation. Incorrect cards must be keypunched and verified a second time. After all data has been recorded correctly on cards, operations such as sorting and merging may be required before the cards can be read into the computer. Generally, card files are copied onto magnetic tape for later input to the computer, because magnetic-tape files can be read into the computer much faster than card files. Figure 5–5 diagrams this process.

● **FIGURE 5–4**
Key-to-disk configurations are often connected to minicomputers such as this one.

● COMPUTERS AND INFORMATION PROCESSING

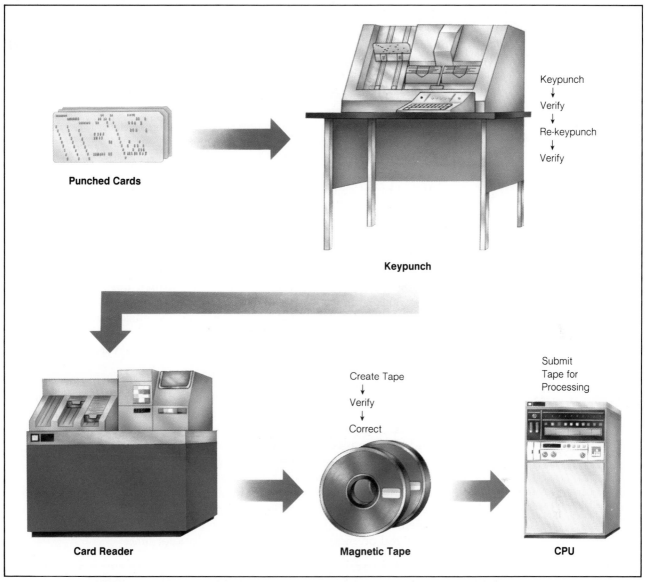

Keypunch
↓
Verify
↓
Re-keypunch
↓
Verify

Punched Cards

Keypunch

Create Tape
↓
Verify
↓
Correct

Submit
Tape for
Processing

Card Reader

Magnetic Tape

CPU

● **FIGURE 5–5**
Traditional Keypunch Data Entry Process

This method of entering data into the computer is time-consuming and expensive. Some organizations have turned to the key-to-magnetic media systems to simplify keypunching operations. Another approach to data collection and preparation which is gaining in popularity is called **source-data automation.** This process collects data about an event, in computer-readable form, when and where the event takes place. By eliminating the intermediate steps used in preparing card input, source-data automation improves the speed, accuracy, and efficiency of data-processing operations.

Source-data automation is implemented by several methods. Each requires special machines for reading data and converting it into machine language. The most common approaches to source-data automation are discussed in the following paragraphs.

Magnetic-ink was introduced in the late 1950s to speed check processing in the banking industry. Because magnetic-ink characters can be read by both humans and machines, no special data conversion step is needed. Magnetic-ink characters are formed with magnetized particles of iron oxide. Each character is composed of certain sections of a seventy-section matrix (see Figure 5–6). The characters can be read and interpreted by a **magnetic-ink character reader.** This process is called **magnetic-ink character recognition (MICR).**

With MICR each character area is examined to determine the shape of the character represented. The presence of a magnetic field in a section of the area represents a 1 bit; the absence of a magnetic field represents a 0 bit. Each magnetic-ink character is composed of a unique combination of 0 bits and 1 bits. When all sections in a character area are combined and translated into binary notation in this manner, the character represented can be determined. MICR devices automatically check each character read to ensure accuracy.

Processing bank checks is a major application of magnetic-ink character recognition. The magnetic-ink characters are printed along the bottom of the check (see Figure 5–7). The **transit field** is preprinted on the check. It includes the bank number, which is an aid in routing the check through the Federal Reserve System. The customer's account number appears in an **"on-us" field.** A clerk manually inserts the amount of the check in the **amount field** after the check has been used and received at a bank.

All magnetic-ink characters on checks are formed with the standard fourteen-character set shown in Figure 5–8. Other character sets may be used in other applications. As the checks are fed into the MICR device, it reads them and sorts them by bank number at a Federal Reserve Bank and by account number at the issuing bank. In this manner, checks are routed back to each issuing bank and then back to its customers. A MICR device can read and sort hundreds of checks per minute.

In another form of source-data automation, optical recognition devices read marks or symbols coded on paper documents and convert them into electrical pulses. The pulses can then be transmitted directly to the CPU or stored on magnetic tape for input at a later time.

● **FIGURE 5–6**
Matrix Patterns for Magnetic-Ink Characters

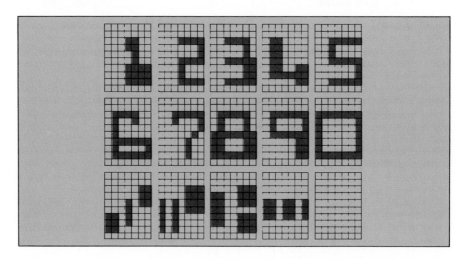

● **COMPUTERS AND INFORMATION PROCESSING**

FIGURE 5–7
Magnetic-Ink Character Recognition

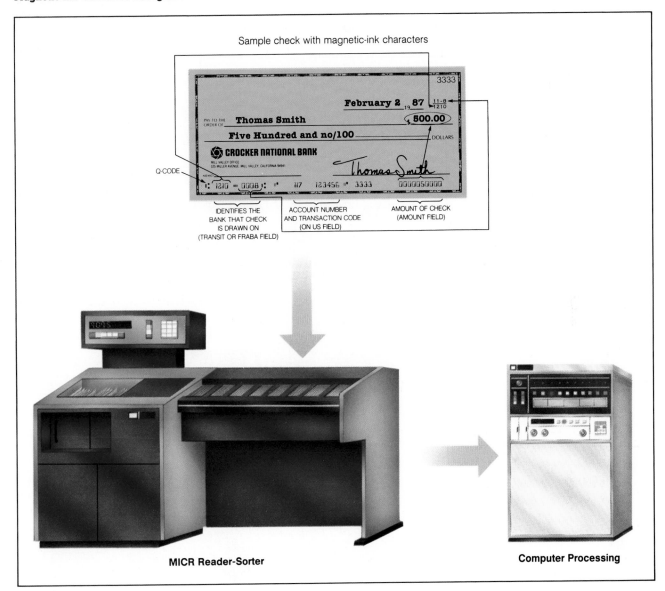

Sample check with magnetic-ink characters

3333

February 2 19 87   11–8
                    1210

PAY TO THE
ORDER OF   **Thomas Smith**   **500.00**

Five Hundred and no/100   DOLLARS

CROCKER NATIONAL BANK

MILL VALLEY OFFICE
125 MILLER AVENUE, MILL VALLEY, CALIFORNIA 94941

Q-CODE

MEMO

1210   0008   117   123456   3333   0000050000

IDENTIFIES THE
BANK THAT CHECK
IS DRAWN ON
(TRANSIT OR FRABA FIELD)

ACCOUNT NUMBER
AND TRANSACTION CODE
(ON US FIELD)

AMOUNT OF CHECK
(AMOUNT FIELD)

MICR Reader-Sorter

Computer Processing

FIGURE 5–8
Magnetic-Ink Character Set

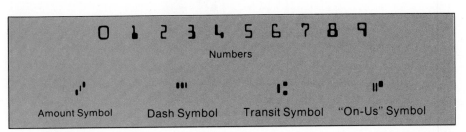

0 1 2 3 4 5 6 7 8 9

Numbers

Amount Symbol   Dash Symbol   Transit Symbol   "On-Us" Symbol

The simplest approach to optical recognition is known as **optical-mark recognition (OMR),** or **mark-sensing.** This approach is often used for machine scoring of multiple-choice examinations (see Figure 5–9). A heavy lead pencil is used to mark the location of each desired answer. The

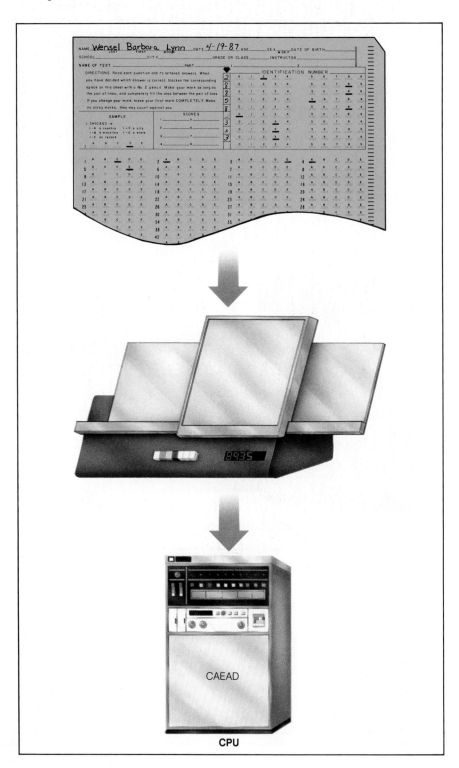

● COMPUTERS AND INFORMATION PROCESSING

marks on an OCR document are sensed by an **optical-mark page reader** as the document passes under a light source. The presence of marks in specific locations is indicated by light reflected at those locations. As the document is read, the optical-mark data is automatically translated into machine language. When the optical-mark page reader is directly connected to the computer, thousands of forms of the same type can be read and processed in an hour.

Optical-mark recognition is also used in order writing, inventory control, surveys and questionnaires, and payroll applications. Since optical-mark data is initially recorded by people, forms that are easy for them to understand and complete must be devised. Instructions, with examples, are generally provided to aid those who must use the forms. Good design helps prevent errors and lessens the amount of time required to complete forms.

Another type of optical reader, the **bar-code reader,** can read special line, or bar, codes. Bar codes are patterns of optical marks that represent information about the object on which the code appears. Some bar codes in use today are shown in Figure 5–10. They are suitable for many applications, including **point-of-sale (POS) systems,** credit card verification, and freight identification to facilitate warehouse operations.

● **FIGURE 5–10**
Bar Codes

Data is represented in a bar code by the widths of the bars and the distances between them. Probably the most familiar bar code is the **Universal Product Code (UPC)** found on most grocery items. This code consists of pairs of vertical bars, which identify both the manufacturer and the item, but not the item's price. The code for each product is a unique combination of these vertical bars. The UPC symbol is read by a hand-held **wand reader** (see Figure 5–11) or by a fixed scanner linked to a cash register-like device (see Figure 5–12). The computer system identifies the product, its brand name, and other pertinent information and uses this data to find the item's price. It then prints out both name and price. The computer keeps track of each item sold and thus helps the store manager to maintain current inventory status.

Optical-character readers can read special types of characters known as **optical characters.** Some **optical-character recognition (OCR)** devices can read characters of several type fonts, including both uppercase and lowercase letters. The most common font used in OCR is shown in Figure 5–13.

A major difference between optical-character recognition and optical-mark recognition is that optical-character data is represented by the shapes of characters rather than by the positions of marks. However, both OCR and OMR devices rely on reflected light to translate written data into machine-readable form.

Acceptable OCR input can be produced by computer printers, adding machines, cash registers, accounting machines, and typewriters. Data can be fed into the reader via a **continuous form** such as a cash register tape or on **cut forms** such as phone or utility bills. When individual cut forms are used, the reader can usually sort the forms as well.

The most advanced optical-character readers can read handwritten characters. However, handwritten characters must be neat and clear; otherwise, they may not be read correctly. Because handwriting varies

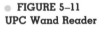
● **FIGURE 5–11**
UPC Wand Reader

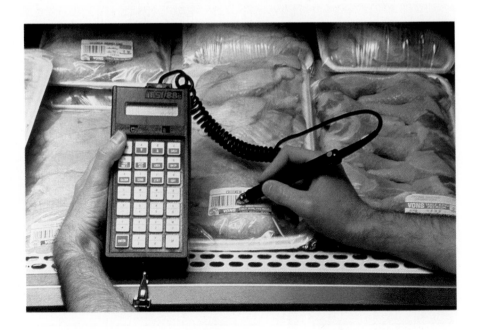

● **COMPUTERS AND INFORMATION PROCESSING**

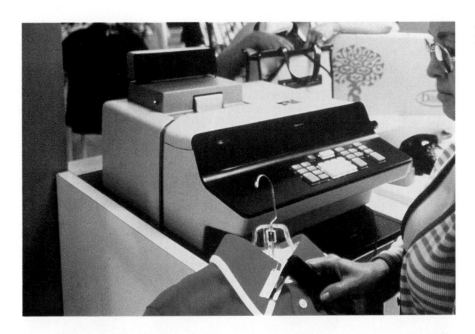

widely from individual to individual this system is not foolproof. Devices that must read handwriting are often very slow. Any characters that cannot be interpreted are rejected by the optical-character readers.

Machine-produced optical-character recognition has been used in credit card billing, utility billing, and inventory-control applications. Hand-written optical-character recognition has been used widely in mail sorting. The reliability of optical-character recognition systems is generally very good.

Remote terminals collect data at its source and transmit the data to a central computer for processing. Generally, data are transmitted over telecommunication equipment. The many types of remote terminals available can increase the versatility and expand the applications of the computer.

Remote terminals that perform the functions of a cash register and also capture sales data are referred to as **point-of-sale (POS) terminals.** Such terminals have a keyboard for data entry, a panel to display the price, a cash drawer, and a printer that provides a cash receipt. A POS terminal typical of those found in many supermarkets is pictured in Figure 5–14.

● **FIGURE 5–13**
OCR Characters

```
A B C D E F G H I J K L M N
O P Q R S T U V W X Y Z , ▪
$ / ✱ - 1 2 3 4 5 6 7 8 9 0
```

What do blue jeans and computers have in common? A lot, if the jeans are made by Levi Strauss & Co. and the computer by Light Signatures, Inc. Light Signatures has been working with Levi Strauss to protect the jeans manufacturer from counterfeiters. That's right, counterfeiters! Not the money kind, but the jeans kind.

Makers of counterfeit jeans manufacture a product that closely resembles the Levi line. To add authenticity to the fake pants, a counterfeit label is stitched on the rear of the jeans.

Light Signatures uses a high-intensity light beam to spot fakes. Each label on a genuine pair of Levi's jeans has a unique fiber composition. When a high-intensity light beam is focused on a label, the unique fiber pattern appears like a shadow. The fiber pattern is focused on a solid-state sensor in a hand-held computer with light-sensitive elements. The computer analyzes the fiber pattern and compares it to a numeric code, also on the label. If the two match, the jeans are authentic. Levi Strauss is so pleased with the success of the Light Signature system that they have expanded its use to other product lines.

The next time you pull on a pair of Levi's jeans, check out that label. It could be hiding some top-secret information!

● FIGURE 5–14
Point-of Sale Terminal with Fixed Scanner

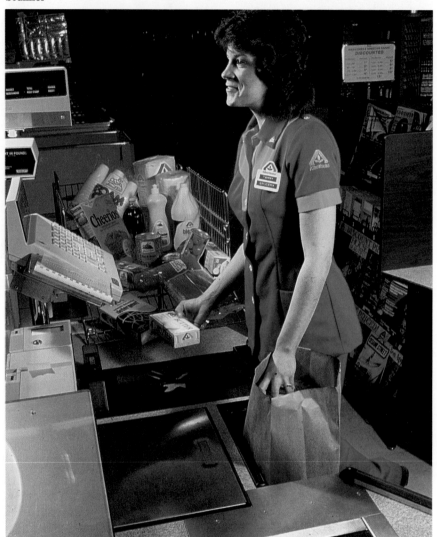

Some POS terminals have wand readers that can read either the Universal Product Code (UPC) or the OCR characters stamped on or attached to an item. The sale is registered automatically as the checkout person passes the wand reader over the code; there is no need to enter the price via a keyboard, unless the wand malfunctions. Thus, POS terminals enable sales data to be collected at its source. If the terminals are directly connected to a large central computer, useful inventory and sales information can be provided almost instantaneously to the retailer.

Touch-tone devices are remote terminals used together with ordinary telephone lines to transfer data from remote locations to a central computer. The data is entered via a special keyboard on the terminal. Generally, slight modifications must have been made to the telephone connection to allow data to be transferred over the line (see Figure 5–15).

There are several types of touch-tone devices. One reads a magnetic strip on the back of plastic cards and is often used to verify credit card transactions. Another stores large amounts of data on a magnetic belt similar to a magnetic tape before transmitting it. This type of terminal is best suited for large-volume processing. Concept Summary 5–1 reviews the various types of data input.

Types of Data Input

CONCEPT
SUMMARY 5–1

TYPE OF INPUT	METHOD OF IMPLEMENTATION
Punched Card	Keypunch
Key to Magnetic Media	Key-to-Tape System Key-to-Disk System Key-to-Diskette System
Source-Data Automation	Magnetic-Ink Character Recognition (MICR) Optical-Mark Recognition (OMR) Bar-Code Reader Optical-Character Recognition (OCR)

Enhancing Creativity and Entertainment

Computers have redefined the limits of art and music. They have made possible the creation of images and sounds once found only in dreams. Professional artists and entertainers use minicomputer and mainframe equipment to create animation and surrealistic scenes and to superimpose human actors upon computer-generated backgrounds. However, advances in microcomputer technology and software provide increased computer power to any of us who want to explore our ideas.

The various elements of this image, called "Road to Point Reyes," were designed separately and then combined with the help of special compositing software.

Courtesy of Lucasfilm, Ltd.

COMPUTERS AND INFORMATION PROCESSING

This image was created using Lumena® software by Time Arts, Inc. It combines video digitizing, hand drawing, image manipulation, enhanced resolution, and color mapping effects.

WorldKey Information Service hostess Carmen Pena uses the touch-sensitive screen to transmit a picture, over a two-way video connection, to a guest at a remote terminal location in Epcot Center.

San Francisco's public TV station, KQED, employs a multi-user CompuPro system to supply 25 kinds of information on more than 4000 TV programs and then formats it into schedules, logs, newspaper listings, publicity releases and more.

⦿ Information Output

PRINTERS

Computer **printers** serve a basic function: printing processed data in a form humans can read. This permanent, readable copy of computer output is often referred to as **hard copy.** To produce hard copy, the printer first receives electronic signals from the central processing unit. In an **impact printer,** these signals activate print elements, which are pressed against paper. **Nonimpact printers,** a newer development, use heat, laser technology, or photographic techniques to print output.

Impact Printers

Impact printers come in a variety of shapes and sizes. Some print one character at a time, while others print one line at a time. Printer-keyboards, dot- or wire-matrix printers, and daisy-wheel printers are the three principal character-at-a-time devices.

The **printer-keyboard** is similar to an office typewriter (see Figure 5–16). All instructions, including spacing, carriage returns, and printing of characters, are sent from the CPU to the printer. The keyboard allows an operator to communicate with the system; for example, to enter data or instructions. Printer-keyboards produce output at a relatively slow rate.

Dot-matrix (also called **wire-matrix**) **printers** are based on a design principle similar to that of a football or basketball scoreboard. The matrix is a rectangle composed of pins, usually seven pins high and five pins wide. Certain combinations of pins are activated to represent characters. For example, the letter A and the number 3 are formed by a combination of pins being pressed against paper (see Figure 5–17). The dot combi-

● FIGURE 5–16
Printer Keyboard

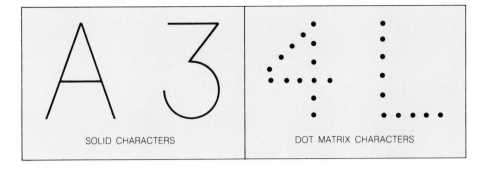

SOLID CHARACTERS   DOT MATRIX CHARACTERS

nations used to represent various numbers, letters, and special characters are shown in Figure 5–18. Letter- or typewriter-quality characters produced by dot-matrix printers contain more dots placed closer together. Dot-matrix printers can typically print up to fifteen characters per second or 900 characters per minute.

Daisy-wheel printers use a daisy wheel, which is a flat disk with petal-like projections (see Figure 5–19). Daisy wheels come in several type fonts that can be interchanged quickly to suit application needs. The daisy-wheel printer offers high-quality type and is often used in word-processing systems to give output a typewriter-quality appearance. Daisy-wheel printers can produce up to 3,000 characters per minute.

Types of line-at-a-time printers include print-wheel, chain, and drum printers. A **print-wheel printer** typically contains 120 print wheels, one for each of 120 print positions on a line (see Figure 5–20). Each print wheel contains forty-eight alphabetic, numeric, and special characters. Each print wheel rotates until the desired characters move into the corresponding print position on the current print line. When all wheels are in their correct positions, a hammer drives the paper against the wheels and an entire line of output is printed. Print-wheel printers can produce about 150 lines per minute, which makes them comparatively slow.

● **FIGURE 5–19**
Daisy Print Wheel

● **FIGURE 5–18**
Dot-Matrix Character Set

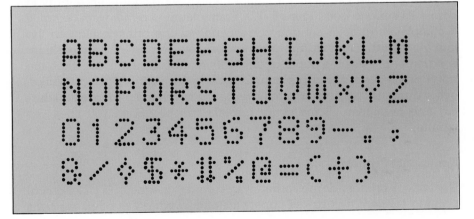

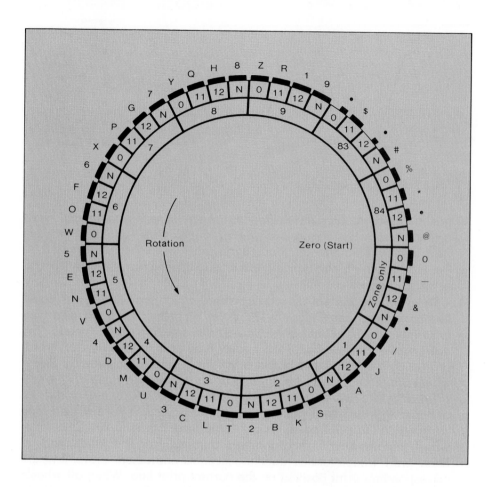

A **chain printer** has a character set assembled in a chain that revolves horizontally past all print positions (see Figure 5–21). There is one print hammer for each column on the paper. Characters are printed when hammers press the paper against an inked ribbon, which in turn presses against appropriate characters on the print chain. The fonts can be changed easily on chain printers, allowing a variety of fonts, such as italic or boldface, to be used. Some chain printers can produce up to 2,000 lines per minute.

A **drum printer** uses a metal cylinder with rows of characters engraved across its surface (see Figure 5–22). Each column on the drum contains a complete character set and corresponds to one print position on the line. As the drum rotates, all characters are rotated past the print position. A hammer presses the paper against the ink ribbon and drum when the appropriate character is in place. One line is printed for each revolution of the drum, since all characters eventually reach the print position during one revolution. Some drum printers can produce 2,000 lines per minute.

Nonimpact Printers

Nonimpact printers do not print characters by means of a mechanical printing element that strikes paper. Instead, a variety of other methods

● **COMPUTERS AND INFORMATION PROCESSING**

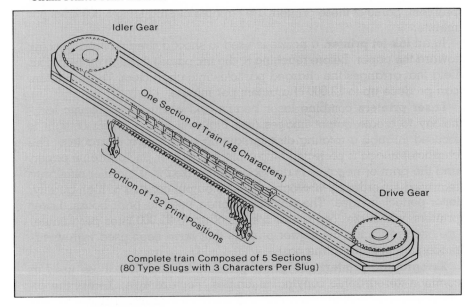

Computers and Sports

are used. Electrostatic, electrothermal, ink-jet, laser, and xerographic printers will be discussed here.

An **electrostatic printer** forms an image of a character on special paper using a dot matrix of charged wires or pins. The paper is moved through a solution containing ink particles that have a charge opposite that of the pattern. The ink particles adhere to each charged pattern of the paper, forming a visible image of each character.

Electrothermal printers generate characters by using heat and heat-sensitive paper. Rods are heated in a matrix. As the ends of the selected rods touch the heat-sensitive paper, an image is created.

● FIGURE 5–22
Print Drum

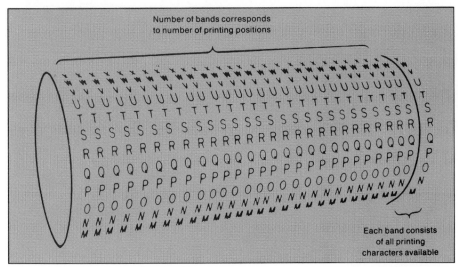

Both electrothermal and electrostatic printers are relatively quiet in operation. They are often used in applications where noise may be a problem. Some of these printers are capable of producing 5,000 lines per minute.

In an **ink-jet printer,** a nozzle is used to shoot a stream of charged ink toward the paper. Before reaching it, the ink passes through an electrical field that arranges the charged particles into characters. These printers can produce up to 12,000 characters per minute.

Laser printers combine laser beams and electrophotographic technology to create output images (see Figure 5–23). A beam of light is focused through a rotating disk containing a full font of characters. The character image is projected onto a piece of film or photographic paper, and the print or negative is developed and fixed in a manner similar to that used for ordinary photographs. The output consists of high-quality, letter-perfect images. The process is often used to print books. Laser printers, which can operate at speeds of up to 21,000 lines per minute, are often replacing the slower printers that have been used with word-processing systems in the past.

Xerographic printers use printing methods much like those used in common xerographic copying machines. For example, Xerox, the pioneer of this type of printing, has one model that prints on single 8½-by-

● **FIGURE 5–23**
Laser Printer

● **COMPUTERS AND INFORMATION PROCESSING**

11-inch sheets of plain paper rather than on the continuous-form paper normally used. Xerographic printers operate at speeds of up to 4,000 lines per minute.

Since nonimpact printers involve less physical movement than impact printers, they are generally much faster. They offer a wider choice of type faces and better speed-to-price ratios than impact printers, and their technology implies a higher degree of reliability because they use fewer movable parts in printing. The disadvantages of nonimpact printers include the special paper requirements and/or poor type-image quality of some printers and the inability of the printers to make carbon copies. However, nonimpact printers can produce several copies of a page in less time than it takes an impact printer to produce one page with several carbon copies.

New printing systems now on the market combine many features of the printing process into one machine. For example, collating, routing, hole punching, blanking out of proprietary information, and perforating may be performed. Some printers produce both text and form designs on plain paper, reducing or eliminating the need for preprinted forms. For a summary of the types and speeds of impact and nonimpact printers, see Concept Summary 5–2.

VISUAL DISPLAY TERMINALS

Visual display terminals are output devices that display data on cathode-ray tubes (CRTs) similar to television screens (see Figure 5–24). A typical screen can hold twenty-four lines, each containing eighty characters. These terminals supply what is known as **soft copy** output. This means that the screen image is not a permanent record of what is shown. CRTs are well suited for applications involving inquiry and response, where no permanent (printed) records are required, and can be used

Impact and Nonimpact Printers

CONCEPT SUMMARY 5–2

IMPACT PRINTERS	SPEED
Printer-Keyboard	Very slow
Dot Matrix	Up to 900 characters per minute
Daisy Wheel	Up to 3,000 characters per minute
Chain Printer	Up to 2,000 lines per minute
Drum Printer	Up to 2,000 lines per minute
NONIMPACT PRINTERS	**SPEED**
Electrostatic	Up to 5,000 lines per minute
Electrothermal	Up to 5,000 lines per minute
Laser	Up to 21,000 lines per minute
Xerographic	Up to 4,000 lines per minute
Ink-jet	Up to 12,000 characters per minute

for capturing data to be transmitted to the screen for verification as it is keyed.

Visual display terminals have some advantages over printers. First, they can display output much faster than printers—some CRT terminals can display up to 10,000 characters in a second. Also, they are much quieter in operation than impact printers. It is usually possible to connect a printer or a copier to a CRT terminal, making it possible to obtain hard-copy output of the screen contents.

Another type of CRT, known as a **graphic display device,** is used to display drawings as well as characters on a screen. Graphic display devices are generally used to show graphs and charts, but they can also display complex curves and shapes. Graphic display devices are being used in highly technical fields such as the aerospace industry to aid in the deign of new wing structures. They are also being used heavily in computer-assisted design/computer-assisted manufacturing (CAD/CAM) areas where objects can be designed and tested and the manufacturing process specified on the computer system in an interactive fashion.

◯ Summary Points

● Data is recorded on punched cards by means of a card punch/key-punch machine. Data is typed from source documents by an operator. Options like automatic skipping and duplicating are available on most keypunches.

● The unit record concept implies that all necessary data pertaining to a transaction is contained on one punched card.

● The major disadvantages of punched cards are length limitations, possible mutilation during handling, and slow processing speed. Also, large card files take up space and increase handling costs.

Key-to-magnetic media are increasingly used because they overcome the disadvantages of punched cards. Tapes, disks, and diskettes allow easy correction of errors, are reusable, can store more data in less space than cards, and can transfer data much faster than cards.

Source-data automation refers to collection of data at the point where a transaction occurs. Common approaches to source-data automation employ optical-recognition devices and other types of remote terminals.

Magnetic-ink characters can be read by humans and also by machines, since they are magnetically inscribed. Magnetic-ink character recognition (MICR) devices can convert the magnetic characters into machine code for computer processing. MICR devices are used extensively by the banking industry for processing checks.

Optical-mark recognition devices can sense marks made with a heavy lead pencil and convert them into machine code. Other optical-character recognition devices are capable of reading bar codes, documents printed in various type fonts, and even handwritten characters. The main advantage of optical-character recognition is that it eliminates the intermediate process of transcribing data from source documents to an input medium.

Remote terminals can collect data at its source and transmit it over communication lines for processing by a central computer. Each device satisfies distinct needs for input and output. Which device is most appropriate for a certain application depends on the particular input/output requirements.

Printers provide output in a permanent (hard copy) form, which people can read. Impact printers can be classified as either character-at-a-time (such as printer-keyboards, dot-matrix printers, and daisy-wheel printers) or line-at-a-time (such as print-wheel printers, drum printers, and chain printers).

Nonimpact printers use more recent technological developments such as photographic, thermal, or laser techniques to print output. They are faster than impact printers, offer a wider choice of type faces, better speed-to-price ratios, and are very reliable.

Visual display terminals display data on cathode-ray tubes (CRTs). Typically a CRT screen can hold twenty-four lines each containing eighty columns of soft copy output. A graphic display device can display drawings as well as characters.

○ Review Questions

1. What is a field? List three fields that illustrate a record pertaining to the sale of a particular item.

2. Without considering any one particular input medium, does an input record have to be limited to eighty characters or less? Explain your answer.

3. Explain what is meant by a unit record.

4. What are some of the advantages and disadvantages of key-to magnetic media?

5. Explain source-data automation.

6. Discuss three types of optical-recognition devices. Indentify applications in which each type can be used.

7. What is the Universal Product Code (UPC)?

8. Discuss the two major divisions of types of printers. Which type uses the newest technology.

9. Distinguish between character-at-time and line-at-time printers, giving examples of each.

10. Describe what is meant by a point-of-sale (POS) system. Which retailers might be using POS systems?

11. What is the difference between soft copy output and hard copy output?

Wendy's International Inc.

COMPANY HISTORY

Wendy's International Inc., the fourth largest restaurant chain in the world, began with the dream of R. David Thomas, Wendy's founder and senior chairman. That dream became a reality in Columbus, Ohio, in 1969 when Thomas named his first restaurant after his daughter Melinda Lou, nicknamed "Wendy" by her brother and sisters.

Today, Wendy's has nearly 3,500 restaurants in all fifty states and eighteen countries overseas. Systemwide sales have grown from less than $300,000 in 1970 to nearly $2.7 billion in 1985. Wendy's was the first chain to exceed $1 billion in sales in its first ten years and reached the one-thousandth and two-thousandth restaurant opening marks faster than any competitor.

More than two million customers are served each day in Wendy's Old Fashioned Hamburgers restaurants. These customers rank Wendy's as the number one hamburger chain in the country, as evidenced by the company's top ranking in the prestigious "Tastes of America Survey" conducted by *Restaurants and Institutions* magazine.

To operate an organization as large and as successful as Wendy's requires extensive use of computers. About ten years ago, computer technology was introduced to automate the accounting and financial functions. As these applications proved successful, Wendy's invested more money in equipment to computerize other areas of operation.

Between 1977 and 1979, Wendy's developed and implemented data processing through a local service bureau computing facility (CompuServ). By 1979, the company created an information systems organization to transfer and develop basic applications for in-house processing. Payroll, general ledgers, accounts payable, and sales audit systems were developed on a central-

ized basis. Inputs for these systems were manually derived from field locations and processed at headquarters. Pertinent reports for field management and site locations were mailed through a courier service organization. These procedures were workable until Wendy's business grew and the number of stores and locations also grew at a significant rate.

Computer-based technologies were needed at the store level to accommodate the growth in (1) the number of product offerings, (2) the number of different types of raw materials, (3) the management control functions needed to adequately run a larger sales-based store, and (4) the amount of information needed to manage the business competitively. The years 1982–1985 brought significant investments in minicomputers at the area locations.

CURRENT COMPUTER USE

Currently, Wendy's network consists of 1,200 stores with POS systems (IBM 3683-84), 25 area locations with minicomputers (Series/1), and a Corporate Data Center with IBM/3081K and IBM 3033 computers. Approximately 300 personal computers are in use with field locations using 150 of these. Applications for PCs include word processing, electronic mail, data-base access, spreadsheet analysis, crew scheduling, product analysis, sales projections, and so on. The network is a means of obtaining data/information through daily polling of the stores. This creates a data base for (1) daily sales, (2) product mix reporting, (3) audit applications, (4) financial accounting, and (5) price elasticity analysis and other marketing applications.

Wendy's use of point-of-sale (POS) systems is extensive. The 1,200 stores equipped with POS systems use the systems predominantly for cash register operations and management control. Specific applications include customer receipts, cash control, inventory control, labor scheduling, sales analysis, slogans on receipts, and point-of-purchase displays. Application software for the POS systems is developed internally by programmers using assembler language. Changes in the software (such as price changes or on-site messages) are downloaded from headquarters. A Field Operations Support Center is maintained twenty-four hours a day seven days a week to support problem resolution at the store level. When operation reports are requested by man-

agement in corporate headquarters, Series/1 minicomputers located at area offices poll the POS systems located in retail outlets and collect the data required for the reports. Machines at corporate headquarters in turn poll area offices and gather the data collected by the minicomputers. On occasion, the process is reversed when reports such as financial statements and marketing reports are sent back to remote locations from corporate headquarters.

Each area office at Wendy's is equipped with an IBM PC/XT and peripherals. The major uses of these machines are for restaurant operation systems and electronic mail. The restaurant operation systems are used to project certain operating requirements, such as raw products and personnel, on a weekly basis.

The trend in the restaurant industry is to have a communication network within the corporation that can serve the stores, field locations, and corporate offices with a data/information flow that is fast and cost efficient. At Wendy's, computers are helping make fast and efficient operations a reality.

DISCUSSION POINTS

1. How are personal computers used at Wendy's?
2. Describe how point-of-sale systems are used to prepare operation reports for management at Wendy's.

6 STORAGE DEVICES

Memory Takes a Quantum Leap

Kelly Costigan Science Digest

In recent years, significant achievements have been made in producing smaller, more powerful personal computers. Now the computer world is poised for another revolution—this one in the enhancement of computer memory capability. The breakthrough?

Optical disks are finally making their debut for use with large computers. The technology behind this new storage device is already known to consumers who have bought compact 4.75-inch audiodisks or laser videodisks. But with its application to larger 12-inch disks, the impact—in terms of greater office efficiency and instant access to information—is expected to be enormous. And when smaller disks designed for personal computers come out at the end of this year, the revolution will be in full swing.

Most magnetic disk drives used today are capable of storing kilobytes or megabytes (thousands or millions of bytes) of data. But the new optical memories can store gigabytes—billions of bytes. On just one side of the larger disks now being manufactured, it is possible to store 100 times more data than can be stored on the highest capacity magnetic disk and 2,500 times more than on the lowest.

Until now, optical technology has been used on prerecorded compact disks: like a phonograph record, the disks cannot be altered by the user. Several companies, however, have developed a similar laser-based technology that allows you to record—but only once.

Workhog

For data-processing firms, libraries and government agencies, the capacity to log in hundreds of thousands of documents and records represents a tremendous opportunity. It frees them from reliance on warehouses full of magnetic tapes and less durable and more cumbersome microfiche and microfilm.

"This product is meant for people who are fed up with having to store reams of information on tape," says John Messerschmitt, vice-president of the North American Philips Corporation. "It's great if you have a tremendous need for information."

The optical disk now manufactured for large computers by Alcatel Thomson offers a storage capacity equivalent to 10 hard magnetic disks or 20 magnetic tapes. Thomson's Gigadisc 1001, which includes a 12-inch disk and drive, can store two gigabytes. It sells for about twice as much as a magnetic disk drive.

Another optical disk that recently entered the market is being manufactured by Optical Storage International (OSI). Equipped with the same storage capacity as Thomson's, it will cost $7,000. This disk can transfer data from its memory to the computer at a rate of 300,000 characters per second—considerably slower than the 3 million delivered by the most high-powered magnetic disk drive. But OSI, like other optical-disk manufacturers, expects to improve that rate soon.

Today almost all computers rely on magnetic tape or disks for data storage. The foundation of this technology lies in charged magnetic particles. These iron oxide crystals are "read," and each charge is interpreted as a zero or one—the digital signal that, when combined with others, signal that, when combined with others, indicates a letter or character.

Optical disks outperform magnetic devices because the amount of space required to store equivalent amounts of information is physically smaller.

Reading with a Laser

Like a record, a laser disk contains information along thousands of circular tracks. In one technique, the digital signal stems from a laser beam reflecting off tiny bubbles or flat spots and registering, respectively, a one or a zero. Since these bubbles are smaller than the magnetic crystals, more of them can fit on a disk.

To record data, laser light is aimed at the disk's recording layer, made of metals such as gold-platinum alloy. The laser's heat causes a micron-size bubble to rise. To retrieve the data, the laser—at a lower power—scans the tracks.

For now, industry observers maintain that optical disks will augment, but not replace, the magnetic memories in the commercial and industrial sectors because they can't be erased and reused. But once erasable optical storage is developed, along with smaller, 5.25-inch disks for microcomputers, the picture could change dramatically. Both of these objectives are being pursued by several companies. This year OSI expects to start mass-producing optical disk drives to sell for under $1,000 for a wide range of personal computers. The drives can store a quarter of a billion bytes per side. Manufacturers are working to reduce this price further, to be more competitive with floppy disk drives, now about $4,000.

In the meantime, optical technology is having a decisive impact elsewhere. The Drexler Technology Corporation, which already offers a small disk for memory storage, has gone a step further. It is producing a wallet-size card for $1.50 that can store the equivalent of an 800-page novel. The Drexon Laser Card can be slipped into a home computer that has an optical photodetector.

Reprinted with permission from *Science Digest*.

● **A trademark of the computer revolution has been miniaturization, first as a result of the transistor, which was followed by the integrated circuit and the microprocessor. Now the effects of miniaturization are becoming evident in storage devices such as the optical disk.**

● Introduction

Organizations store large amounts of data for a variety of purposes. Many businesses commonly store data regarding their employees, customers, suppliers, inventory levels, sales figures, and expenses in addition to the specific types of data required to perform their particular business functions. Organizations that use electronic methods of processing data must store it in computer-accessible form. The arrangement of computer-based files and ultimately, the type of media used for data storage, depends on the needs and constraints of the organization. Each type of storage media has certain characteristics that must be considered.

This chapter examines the two most popular types of data storage media, magnetic tape and magnetic disk, and two of the most common types of file arrangement using these media (sequential and direct-access). Emphasis is placed on the storage media used with mainframe computer systems. Storage devices commonly used with microcomputers will be covered in more detail in Chapter 8. Considerations concerning mass storage devices and future trends in data storage are also covered.

● Classification of Storage Media

A computer system generally includes two types of storage: **primary storage** and **secondary** (or **auxiliary storage**). Primary storage, discussed in Chapter 4, is part of the CPU and is used to store instructions and data needed for processing. Semiconductor memory, the circuitry on silicon chips capable of extremely fast processing, is the most widely used form of primary storage. Bubble memory is also in limited use.

In most cases, the amount of data required by a program or set of instructions exceeds the capacity of primary storage. To compensate for limited primary storage, data can be stored on secondary storage devices. Secondary storage is not part of the CPU. The most common types of secondary storage are magnetic tapes and magnetic disks. Mass storage devices are useful in some situations. Media such as punched cards and magnetic drums can also be used but they have become outdated. Secondary storage media cost much less than primary storage. Therefore, they make the storage of large amounts of data economically feasible for most organizations.

Secondary storage media are connected to the CPU. Once data has been stored on a secondary storage device, it can be retrieved for processing as needed. However, the retrieval of items from secondary storage is significantly slower than retrieval from primary storage. After processing has been completed, the data or results can be written back onto the secondary storage media (see Figure 6–1).

● Sequential-Access Media

MAGNETIC TAPE

A **magnetic tape** is a continuous plastic strip wound onto a reel, quite simiiar to the tape used in reel-to-reel audio recorders. The magnetic tape's plastic base is treated with an iron oxide coating that can be magnetized. Typically, the tape is one-half inch in width. It is wound in lengths from 400 to 3,200 feet. Some magnetic tapes are also packaged in plastic cartridges and cassettes for use with personal computers.

Data is stored on magnetic tape by magnetizing small spots of the iron oxide coating on the tape. Although these spots can be read (detected)

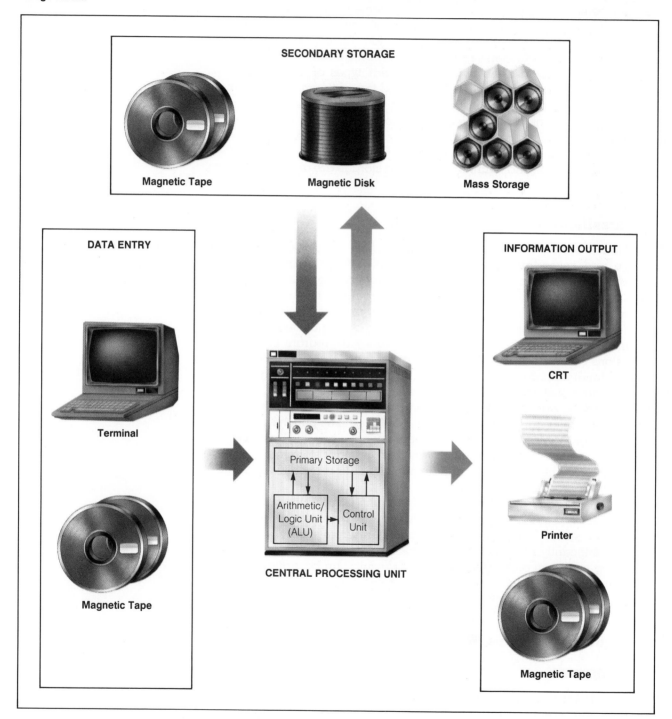

SECONDARY STORAGE

Magnetic Tape

Magnetic Disk

Mass Storage

DATA ENTRY

Terminal

Magnetic Tape

CENTRAL PROCESSING UNIT

Primary Storage

Arithmetic/ Logic Unit (ALU)

Control Unit

INFORMATION OUTPUT

CRT

Printer

Magnetic Tape

● COMPUTERS AND INFORMATION PROCESSING

by the computer, they are invisible to the human eye. Large volumes of information can be stored on a single tape; densities of 1,600 characters per inch are common, and some tapes can store up to 6,250 characters per inch. A typical tape reel 2,400 feet long can store as much data as 24,000 pages of double-spaced text and costs between $20 and $30.

The most common method of representing data on magnetic tape uses a nine-track coding scheme, although other coding schemes are also used. When the nine-track method is used, the tape is divided into nine horizontal rows called **tracks** (see Figure 6–2). Data is represented vertically in columns, one character per column. This method of coding is identical to the Extended Binary Coded Decimal Interchange Code (EBCDIC) used to represent data in primary storage. In this way, eight bits and eight of the nine tracks are used to represent each character. The ninth bit, and ninth track, functions as a parity bit.

A magnetic tape is mounted on a **tape drive** when a program needs the data it contains (see Figure 6–3). The tape drive has a **read/write head** (which is actually an electromagnet) that creates or reads the magnetized bits as the tape moves past it (see Figure 6–4). When the read/write head is reading data, it detects the magnetized spots and converts them into electrical pulses to send to the CPU. When writing data, the

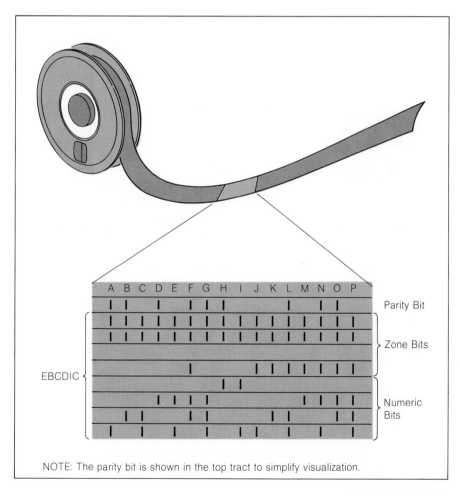

● **FIGURE 6–2**
Nine-Track Tape with Even Parity

NOTE: The parity bit is shown in the top tract to simplify visualization.

Magnetic Tape Drive

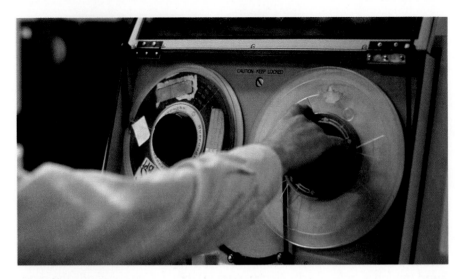

● FIGURE 6–4
Recording on Magnetic Tape

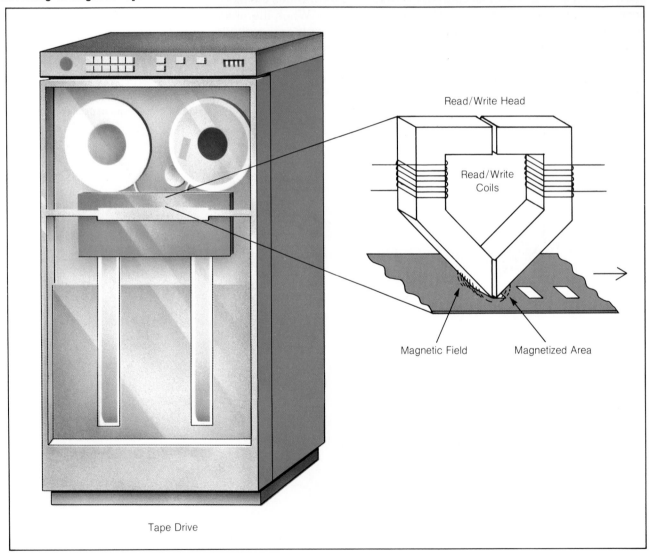

Read/Write Head

Read/Write Coils

Magnetic Field

Magnetized Area

Tape Drive

head magnetizes the appropriate spots on the tape and erases any data stored there previously.

Individual records on magnetic tape are separated by **interrecord gaps (IRGs),** as shown in Figure 6–5. These gaps do not contain data but they perform a specific function. When a tape is being read, its entire contents are rarely read all at once. Rather, it is stopped when the end of a record is reached. The tape must then be accelerated to the proper speed before the next record can be read accurately. If this were not the case, the result would be similar to what happens when a phonograph record is played at the wrong speed. The IRG gives the tape time to regain the proper speed before the next record is read. The length of the IRG depends on the speed of the tape drive. If the tape drive is very fast, longer gaps are needed. A slower tape drive will require shorter gaps.

If the records stored on a tape are very short and the IRGs are long, it would be possible for the tape to be more than 50 percent blank, causing the tape drive to stop and accelerate constantly. To avoid this situation, records may be grouped, or blocked, together. These **blocked records,** or **blocks,** are separated by **interblock gaps (IBGs)** as shown in Figure 6–6. Instead of reading a short record and stopping, then reading another short record and stopping, the read/write head reads a block of records at one time and stops, then reads another block and stops, and so forth. Using the interblock gap method of reading data has two advantages over the interrecord gap method:

1. The amount of storage available on the tape is used more efficiently.
2. The number of read/write operations required is significantly reduced, which makes the use of computer time more efficient.

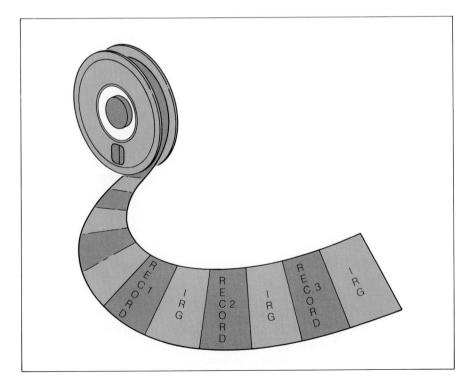

● **FIGURE 6–5**
Magnetic Tape with Interrecord Gaps

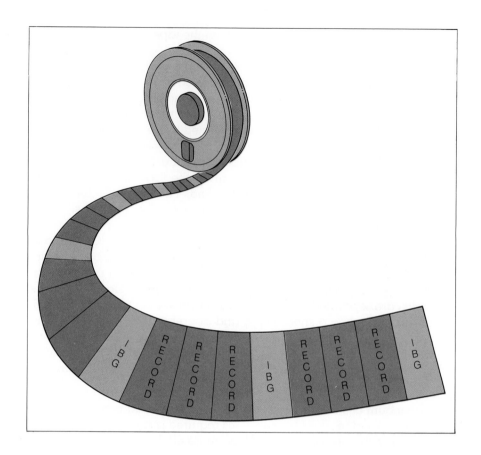

CASSETTE TAPE

Small computer systems may not need a large amount of secondary storage. For these systems, **tape cassettes** and tape cartridges have been developed. Tape cassettes look like those used in audio recording; some can even be used with a typical cassette player/recorder. The major difference between the two types of tape cassettes is the tape itself: tape cassettes used for storing data have a high-quality digital recording tape (see Figure 6–7).

The recording densities for tape cassettes range between 125 and 200 characters per inch. They are usually between 150 and 200 feet long. Tape cartridges, on the other hand, can store from 200 to 800 characters per inch and they are available in standard lengths of 300, 450, and 555 feet (see Figure 6–8).

The advantages of using magnetic tape as a means of data storage include the following:

● Data can be transferred between magnetic tape and the CPU at high speeds.
● Magnetic tape records can be any length, while punched card records are usually limited to eighty characters.
● Because of their high recording densities, magnetic tapes store a large amount of data in a small amount of space.
● Magnetic tape can be erased and used over and over again.

- Magnetic tape provides high-capacity storage and backup storage at a relatively low cost.
- Magnetic tape is perfectly suited for sequential processing. It is the most common storage medium for systems utilizing sequential processing.

Use of magnetic tape has the following disadvantages:

- Since magnetic tape is a sequential medium, the entire tape must be read from beginning to end when changes are made in the data. The

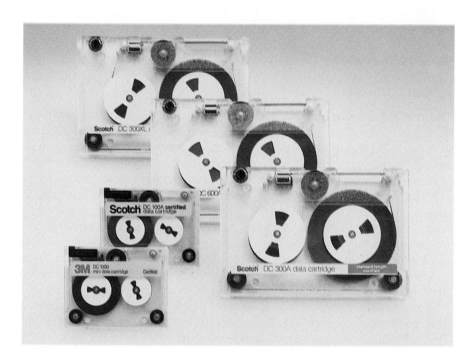

● **FIGURE 6–8**
Tape Cartridge Used for Data Storage

amount of time required to retrieve data precludes its use when instantaneous retrieval is required.

● All tape and reel containers must be properly labeled to identify the contents.

● Humans cannot read the data stored on magnetic tape. To see the data stored on tape, the contents of the tape must be printed.

● Environmental factors can distort data stored on magnetic tape. Dust, moisture, extreme heat or cold, and static electricity can alter the data.

CONCEPT SUMMARY 6-1

Characteristics of Magnetic Tape

FEATURES	ADVANTAGES	DISADVANTAGES
A continuous strip of plastic tape wound onto a reel	Transfers data between tape and the CPU rapidly	Data must be read sequentially
Tape is treated with a magnetizable iron oxide coating	Records can be any length	Tapes require proper labels for content identification
Data are represented as magnetized spots on the surface of the tape	Stores large amounts of data in a small space	Environmental factors can distort data stored on tape
Data are accessed sequentially	Erasable and reusable	Humans cannot read the data stored on tape
	Low-cost backup media	
	Well suited for sequential processing	

● Direct-Access Media

MAGNETIC DISK

The conventional **magnetic disk** is a metal platter fourteen inches in diameter, coated on both sides with a magnetizable material such as iron oxide. In many respects, a magnetic disk resembles a phonograph record. However, it does not have grooves etched onto its surface as a phonograph record has. The surface of a magnetic disk is smooth.

A magnetic disk does store and retrieve data in much the same fashion as a phonograph record is played. The disk is rotated while a read/write head is positioned above its magnetic surface. Instead of spiraling into the center of the disk as the needle does on a phonograph record, the read/write head stores and retrieves data in concentric circles. Each circle is referred to as a *track*. One track never touches another (see Figure 6–9). A typical disk has between 200 and 500 tracks per side.

In most disk storage devices, several disks are assembled to form a **disk pack** (see Figure 6–10). The disks are mounted on a central shaft. The individual disks are spaced on the shaft to allow room for a read/

Track 199

Track 000

● FIGURE 6–10
Disk Pack

write mechanism to move between them (see Figure 6–11). The disk pack in Figure 6–11 has eleven disks and provides twenty usable recording surfaces. The top and bottom surfaces are not used for storing data because they are likely to become scratched or nicked. A disk pack may contain anywhere from five to one hundred disks.

A disk pack is positioned in a disk drive when the data on the pack is to be processed. The **disk drive** rotates all disks in unison at speeds up to 3,600 revolutions per minute. In some models, the disk packs are removable; in others, the disks are permanently mounted on the disk drive. Removable disk packs allow disks to be removed when the data they contain is not needed (see Figure 6–12). Users of removable disk packs typically have many more disk packs than disk drives.

The data on a disk is read or written by the read/write heads located between the disks. Most disk units have one read/write head for each disk recording surface. All the heads are permanently connected to an

● **FIGURE 6–11**
Side View (a) and Top View (b) of a Disk Pack

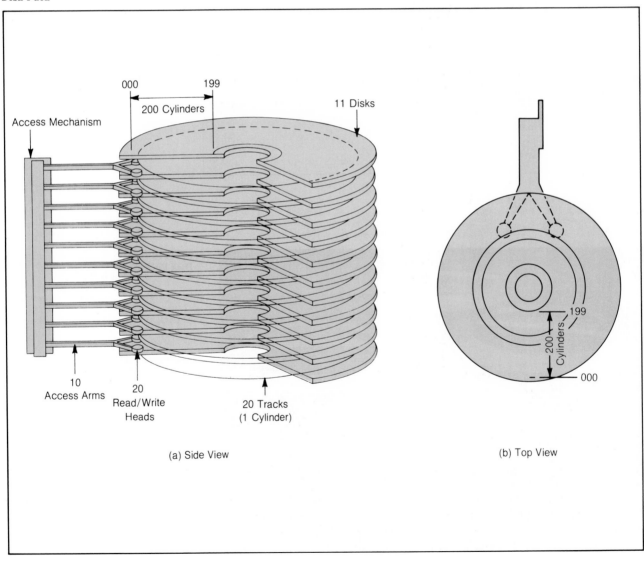

● **COMPUTERS AND INFORMATION PROCESSING**

Are you interested in finding the answer to an obscure point of ancient Hebrew law? Then travel to Bar Ilan University in Tel Aviv, Israel, and pose your question to the Responsa Project—a data base that stores the contents of 250 volumes of rabbinical statements and judgments on legal questions. That's the equivalent of 50 million words!

Responsa are questions and answers about religious issues. There are more than 3,000 volumes of responsa altogether, and eventually 500 volumes will be stored on disks. The volumes stored thus far contain information on Jewish life in Europe and North Africa. The information covers a time span from the Middle Ages to the twentieth century.

Scholars use the data base to find information about a variety of topics that affected Jewish life in earlier times. But scholars are not the only users of this unusual data base. Sociologists, historians, economists, and linguists have all made use of the Responsa Project. Information that once would have taken months of devoted research can now be located in minutes. Graduate students, quick to accept the new technology that made the project possible, are using the data base to write dissertations that otherwise would not be written.

Lawyers are among the most enthusiastic users of the data base. Until a few years ago, Israeli law was based on British common law. Currently, in the event of a conflict, Hebrew law takes precedence. Attorneys use the data base to find evidence that will support their clients' positions.

access mechanism. When reading or writing occurs, the heads are positioned over the appropriate track by the in-and-out movements of the access mechanism.

When data stored on the surface of one disk in the disk pack is required, all heads move to the corresponding tracks on the surfaces of the other disks because they are connected to the same access mechanism. Since all the read/write heads move together, they are positioned over the same tracks on all disk surfaces at the same time.

Some disk units have one read/write head for each track. The access time is much faster with this type of disk unit since the access mechanism does not move from track to track. Units such as this are rarely used because they are very expensive. The placement of data on the disk pack, therefore, can be an important factor if the amount of access time is critical. When access time is an important factor, it is best to store data that is accessed most frequently on the same or adjacent tracks of the disk surfaces. This will reduce the motion of the read/write heads and thus reduce the access time.

Each track on a disk can store the same amount of data even though the tracks get smaller toward the center of the disk. Consider a disk pack with 4,000 usable tracks (20 surfaces × 200 tracks per surface) on which 7,294 characters can be stored on each track. The disk pack could conceivably store 29,176,000 characters of data (4,000 tracks × 7,294 characters per track).

The computer locates data stored on a magnetic disk by its disk surface number, track number, and record number. These numbers make up the data's **disk address.** The disk address of a record is stored immediately before the record (see Figure 6–13). Disk records are separated by

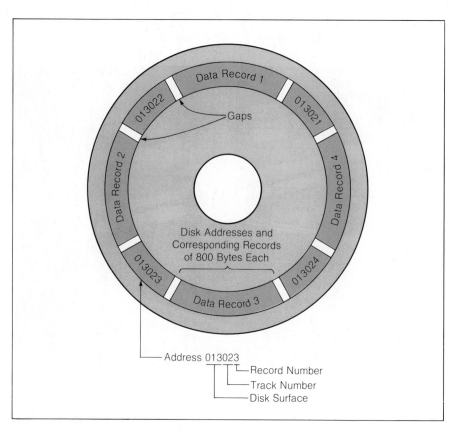

gaps similar to the interrecord gaps on magnetic tape. However, the presence of gaps in each track reduces the amount of data that can be stored on a disk. Therefore, the usable storage capacity in the disk pack described in the previous paragraph would be slightly less than the potential 29,176,000 characters.

Since disks provide direct access, they are typically used to store data that is accessed frequently. Depending on the disk drive, it is possible for up to 850,000 characters to be read per second.

FLOPPY DISK

● **FIGURE 6–14**
Floppy Disk

The **floppy disk, flexible disk,** or **diskette** was introduced in 1973 to replace punched cards as a medium for data entry, but it can also store programs and data files (see Figure 6–14). Floppy disks are made of plastic and coated with a magnetizable oxide substance. In most respects, they are miniature magnetic disks. Since the diskettes are relatively inexpensive (some sell for as low as $3), they are popular for use with microcomputer systems and point-of-sale terminals. They are reusable, easy to store, and weigh less than two ounces. Because floppy disks are removable, they provide added security for a computer system; they can be stored in a safe if necessary. Floppy disks can even be mailed.

Data are stored on a floppy disk as magnetized spots in tracks, as on conventional magnetic disks, and are addressed by track number and sector number (see Figure 6–15). The read/write head accesses the disk

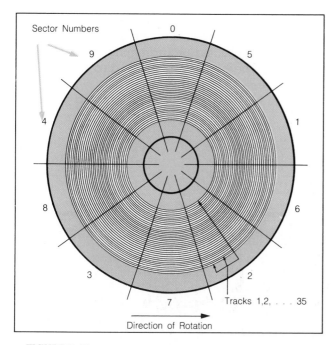

● **FIGURE 6–15**
Sectors and Tracks on a Floppy Disk

● **FIGURE 6–16**
Parts of a Floppy Disk

through the oblong or rectangular opening in the jacket, called the *read/write notch* (see Figure 6–16). It moves back and forth to read the data or write data to the disk. Unlike the one used in hard disk systems, this read/write head actually rides on the surface of the disk rather than being positioned slightly above it. The disk rotates at a speed of 360 revolutions per minute (as compared to as many as 3,600 revolutions per minute for hard disk drives).

Magnetic disks have several advantages over magnetic tapes:

● Disk files on magnetic disks can be organized sequentially and processed in the same way as magnetic tape, or they can be organized for direct-access processing.
● The fast access time offered by magnetic disk storage allows data files to be accessed or changed immediately.
● Quick response can be made to inquiries (normally, response is made in seconds).
● With the appropriate software, a single transaction can simultaneously update or change several files stored on disks.

The major disadvantages of magnetic disk storage include the following:

● Magnetic hard disks are a relatively expensive storage medium; their cost may be ten times more than magnetic tape in terms of cost per character stored. However, reductions in disk cost and the introduction of floppy disks are making these storage devices more affordable.
● When data stored on a disk is changed, the original data is erased and the new data is stored in its place. Therefore, magnetic disks provide

no backup file. Data can be lost if there are inadequate provisions for error checking and backup files.

● Disk storage requires more complicated programming to gain access to records and to update files. The hardware itself is also highly complicated; skilled technicians are needed to maintain it.

● Security may be a problem because of the ease of gaining access to data stored on disk files.

CONCEPT SUMMARY 6–2

Characteristics of Magnetic Disks

FEATURES	ADVANTAGES	DISADVANTAGES
A metal platter coated on both sides with a magnetizable material	Files can be organized for sequential or direct-access storage	More expensive than magnetic tape
Data are represented as magnetized spots on the surface of the disk	Data can be accessed immediately	Requires backup files so data is not lost when changes are made
Disks come in varying sizes	Files can be altered simultaneously	Requires complex programming to gain access to files
		Easy access to data may pose security problems

● Mass Storage

As stated earlier, accessing data and instructions from primary storage is very fast because it requires no physical movement of hardware devices. The speed of electricity is, in effect, the only limiting factor. However, the capacity of primary storage is limited and also very expensive. Disk storage is less expensive and provides direct-access capabilities, but even disk storage tends to be expensive when very large amounts of data must be stored for direct-access processing.

To meet the need for a low-cost method of storing vast amounts of data, mass storage devices have been developed. They allow rapid access to data. Large files, backup files, and infrequently used files can be placed in mass storage at a relatively low cost.

One type of mass storage uses a cartridge tape as the storage medium (see Figure 6–17). The cartridges are similar to cassette tapes and permit sequential access of data. The high-density tape used requires 90 percent less storage space than common magnetic tapes. A mass storage system such as this can hold the equivalent of up to 1,000 tape reels. Tape mounting is controlled by the system, rather than by a human operator, and tends to be much faster than the traditional operator-controlled mounting of magnetic tapes.

Mass storage is not limited to high-density magnetic tape. A mass storage system for minicomputers using small floppy disks as the storage medium has been introduced. However, unlike the cartridge system described above, most mass storage systems such as this require extensive physical movement because the needed files must first be found and then mounted (or loaded) mechanically before data can be read or written. Although direct access is possible, the retrieval time is relatively slow (although still measured in seconds) compared to systems utilizing magnetic tapes or disks.

● Trends in Data Storage

CHARGE-COUPLED DEVICES

As technology continues to advance, smaller, faster, and less-expensive storage devices will become commonplace. Advances are rapidly being made in semiconductor and laser technology. An innovation in semiconductor technology is the development of **charge-coupled devices (CCDs)** for use in data storage. CCDs are made of silicon similar to semiconductor memory. They are nearly 100 times faster than magnetic bubble memory

A New Job for an Old Disk

Are you looking for a compact way to store 100,000 typewritten pages? Then perhaps you should consider storing those pages on a compact disk.

A standard compact disk is 4.7 inches in diameter. That is enough storage space for 500 million bytes of data. By comparison, the standard single-sided, single-density floppy disk used with many microcomputers is capable of storing only 500,000 bytes. The compact disk can store 1,000 times more bytes than a floppy disk!

Information stored on a compact disk is encoded by pinpoint laser beams that burn tiny pits on the surface of the disk. Each disk can store vast amounts of information, but once the information has been stored on the disk, it cannot be changed or erased. This limits its use.

In the past, compact disks have been used mainly for reproducing high-quality music recordings, but makers of compact disks are searching for new markets for the disks. Many disk makers think that the compact devices are well suited for electronic publishing. Large data bases or many smaller data bases could be stored on one disk. Once a data base was recorded on a disk, it could be sold to users. This approach would allow users to bypass current database systems that require access through a commercial network.

In the educational market, compact disks could hold an entire curriculum for a course such as a foreign language. Another use for the disks involves software. Due to the vast storage capacity of compact disks, both a program and its documentation could fit on the same disk. When a user had a problem with a program, he or she could consult the documentation stored on the disk for help in solving the problem.

but are somewhat slower than semiconductor RAM. As in semiconductor memories, data in CCDs can be lost if a power failure occurs. CCDs are used primarily with large computer systems such as minicomputers and mainframes.

LASER TECHNOLOGY

Laser technology provides an opportunity to store mass quantities of data at greatly reduced costs. A **laser storage system** can store nearly 128 billion characters of data at about one-tenth the cost of standard magnetic media. In a laser storage system, data is recorded when a laser beam forms patterns on the surface of a polyester sheet coated with a thin layer of rhodium metal. To read data from this sheet, the laser reflects light off the surface, reconstructing the data into a digital bit stream. Data stored by laser resists alterations and any attempt to change it can easily be detected. Therefore, it provides a very secure storage system. In addition, unlike magnetic media, laser storage does not deteriorate over time and it is immune to electromagnetic radiation. Another advantage is that there is no danger of losing data as a result of power failures.

A more recent development is a laser system used as a mass storage device for minicomputers. This system uses a helium-neon laser, delivering about ten milliwatts of optical power to a disk coated with a film of a nonmetallic substance called tellurium. Data is recorded when the laser creates a hole approximately one micrometer in diameter in the film. The disk used in this system is thirty centimeters in diameter and can store ten billion bits on its 40,000 tracks. The data cannot be erased once it is written, so this system is best suited for archival storage purposes or when a large volume of permanent data must be maintained online.

Another development in laser technology is the optical, or laser, disk (see Figure 6–18). **Optical disks** are much faster than hard disks but are still fairly slow compared to semiconductor RAM. One big advantage, though, is their large capacity. A single optical disk can hold more than 600 megabytes of data. That is over 225,000 pages of manuscript or the entire contents of the *Encyclopaedia Britannica* with space left over. Bits of data are stored on an optical disk as the presence or absence of a tiny pit burned into the disk by a pinpoint laser beam. A single line one inch long contains about 5,000 pits, or bits, of data.

RAM DISKS

Accessing data on disks is relatively slow compared to the speed at which a microprocessor can manipulate data. **Random-access memory (RAM) disks** are currently the only type of storage device that can approximate the speed of a microprocessor. A new peripheral device using RAM chips is now available (see Figure 6–19). A RAM card that contains RAM chips plugs into the computer in the same slot as the disk drive card. The computer treats the RAM card just as it does a disk drive. Even though RAM disks are not separate physical disks, they function like regular diskettes. A RAM disk instructs the computer to set aside storage space in RAM to function like a disk. A typical RAM disk used with a micro-

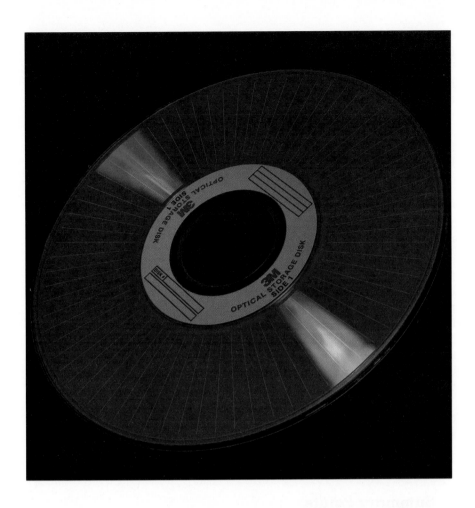

● FIGURE 6–18
Optical Disk

● FIGURE 6–19
RAM Disk Chip

Optical disks provide the highest storage density of any medium. They have been designed to serve archival functions, storing very large amounts of data to be accessed occasionally, but rarely, if ever, changed. These, for the most part, are produced for use with large computer systems. A similar technology designed for use with microcomputers involves the harnessing of compact-disk players which are a recent innovation in the audio field. The units are called CD-ROM (compact disk ready-only memory) players.

Knowledgeset Corp. is currently offering a CD-ROM with an electronic encyclopedia. Other data bases are in the works as well. The CD-ROM technology offers an efficient, inexpensive means of storage. Data bases can be kept in-house offering much quicker access than on-line data bases. Reduced on-line services costs can help frequent users pay for the units relatively quickly.

The CD-ROM player's use is pretty much limited to housing data bases right now. There is no software currently available that will work with CD-ROM, since no data can be changed on the disks. It's possible, however, that special software could be prepared to work with the disks in the future.

computer stores up to 265K of data and has a retrieval rate fifty times faster than a floppy disk.

The advantage of using RAM disks is speed. Data stored in RAM can be transferred from one part of RAM to another faster than it can be transferred from a disk to RAM. The disadvantage of RAM disks is that they require a continuous power supply. As with any internal memory, when the power supply is discontinued, data is erased from memory. However, some manufacturers provide battery backup units for use with RAM disks in case of a power failure.

JOSEPHSON JUNCTION

The **Josephson junction** is a form of primary storage named for Brian Josephson, a British Nobel Prize winner. Josephson junctions are in an early stage of development. When the technology for these devices is perfected, the speed at which primary storage operates is estimated to increase tenfold. Current semiconductor memory is slower than that proposed with Josephson junctions because of the environment in which it is housed. By surrounding the circuits in liquid helium, the Josephson junction will eliminate the resistance to the flow of electricity that exists in semiconductor memory. The use of the Josephson junction, along with other technological advances, is expected to lead to further reduction in the size of computer hardware.

Technology advances so rapidly that accurate predictions of what future storage media will be like is nearly impossible. Even though the state of the art changes from day to day, the objectives of making storage less expensive, faster, and more compact will continue to be pursued.

● Summary Points

● Secondary storage, which is not part of the CPU, can store large amounts of data and instructions at a lower cost than primary storage. The most common secondary storage media are magnetic tapes and magnetic disks.

● Access to data in secondary storage can be either sequential or direct. Magnetic tapes on reels and cassette tapes provide sequential-access storage. Hard magnetic disks and floppy disks provide direct-access storage.

● Magnetic tape consists of a plastic base coated with iron oxide. Data is stored as small magnetized areas on the surface of the tape.

● Records are separated on magnetic tape by interrecord gaps (IRGs). When the tape is stopped while reading records, these gaps allow the tape to regain the proper speed before the next record is read.

● Data is often recorded on magnetic tape in groups of records called blocks. Blocks are separated from each other by interblock gaps (IBGs). Blocking reduces overall input/output time and also makes more efficient use of available storage.

● Tape cassettes are similar to audio cassettes. They can store up to 200 characters per inch and are used when small amounts of storage are required.

- A disk pack is positioned on a disk drive, which rotates all disks in the pack in unison. Some disk packs are removable; others are permanently mounted on disk drives.
- Magnetic disks provide direct access to data. Any record can be located by referring to its address—disk surface number, track number, and record number.
- Floppy or flexible disks provide low-cost, direct-access storage. Floppy disks are easy to store and are frequently used with minicomputers and microcomputers.
- Mass storage devices are appropriate when large amounts of data must be stored at low cost. Commonly used mass storage media are cassette and cartridge tapes and floppy disks. Floppy disk mass storage devices provide direct access, but the retrieval time is much slower than with standard disk storage.
- Advances in technology continue to make storage devices faster, smaller, and less expensive. Recent innovations are charge-coupled devices, laser storage systems, RAM disks, and the Josephson junction.
- Optical disks allow faster access to data than hard disks, but they provide fairly slow data retrieval compared to RAM. The advantage of optical disks as a storage medium is their storage capacity.
- A RAM disk is an area of RAM that temporarily functions like a storage diskette.
- Josephson junction technology allows primary memory to be housed in liquid helium to eliminate the resistance to the flow of electricity in semiconductor memory.

● Review Questions

1. Distinguish between primary storage and secondary storage. Name three common secondary storage devices.
2. Which storage media provide direct access? Which provide sequential access?
3. What is the function of interrecord gaps (IRGs) in magnetic tape storage?
4. Explain the purpose of blocking records with an interblock gap (IBG).
5. What is a disk pack?
6. Name the three components of a record's disk address.
7. Discuss the advantages and disadvantages of magnetic tape storage.
8. Discuss the advantages and disadvantages of magnetic disk storage.
9. Describe two types of mass storage devices.
10. Explain how a laser storage system stores data. What is the main advantage of a laser storage system?

Eastern Airlines

EARLY DEVELOPMENTS

The second largest air passenger carrier in the free world, Eastern Airlines, began its existence as a tiny mail carrier on May 1, 1928. The company was called Pitcairn Aviation, Inc., after its founder and owner Harold F. Pitcairn. Pitcairn had already established a reputation as an aircraft manufacturer when he decided to go into the airmail business.

The first customer for the new airline was the federal government. In a contract with the government, Pitcairn agreed to haul the mail for $3 a pound. At the time, the entire Pitcairn fleet consisted of eight single-engine, open-cockpit biplanes flown by a motley collection of pilots whose flying experiences ranged from barnstorming to World War I combat. The original contract with the government specified air coverage for a route 792 miles long from New Brunswick, New Jersey, to Atlanta, Georgia. Even before the first run began, though, a second contract was signed establishing another route between Atlanta and Miami. Together, the routes formed a 1,411-mile "eastern airline."

On the first day of operation, May 1, 1928, the government gave Pitcairn's company so much mail that it was necessary to operate a double schedule. When the first two planes took off from New Brunswick, New Jersey, on May 1, word of the new air service quickly spread. Hundreds of curiosity seekers poured onto the landing fields at stops along the route to see the first air mail deliveries.

In 1929, Pitcairn sold the successful mail carrier to North American Aviation, Inc., and the name of the company was changed to Eastern Air Transport, Inc. The airline soon expanded and added passenger service six days a week. More and more routes were added for both mail and passenger service, and new "modern" planes such as the eighteen-passenger Curtiss Condor became the standard. Even with the Con-

dor, though, a trip from New York to Miami took almost fourteen hours and included ten stops along the way.

With World War I flying ace Edward Rickenbacker joining Eastern in 1935, the company survived some lean years during the Depression. "Captain Eddie" took charge of the organization and quickly turned losses into profits. In 1938, Rickenbacker and six associates bought the company for $3.5 million. Rickenbacker became president and general manager, and under his guidance Eastern thrived for the next three decades.

The 1970s found Eastern, like many other airlines, struggling to remain profitable. Help came in the form of another famous aviator—this one from the space age. Colonel Frank Borman, an astronaut of Apollo 8 fame, took over as president and chief executive officer. Borman revitalized the company through cost control measures and innovative employee motivational techniques.

The difficult years of the early seventies were followed by several profitable ones—until deregulation struck. Before airline deregulation, the Civil Aeronautics Board controlled all decisions concerning routes, fares, and virtually every other issue, large or small, for the thirty-six interstate air carriers. After deregulation, competition intensified as discount air fares became commonplace among the new entries in the air carrier field.

MODERNIZATION

To compete, Eastern continued to expand and modernize, and computers played an important role in the modernization program. In 1981, the company introduced an innovative computerized reservations and ticketing system called SYSTEMONE. It was marketed to travel agencies, government travel departments, and commercial accounts and played a key role in building passenger traffic. SYSTEMONE offers a feature called Direct Access, which was pioneered by Eastern. It provides the advantages of multiaccess to data and information stored in a computer system without the disadvantages.

A single-access system stores current data about schedules, reservation availability, and fares for only one carrier. Most prospective passengers want information about several airlines. Multiaccess systems allow access to several airlines, but each airline may have its own procedures for accessing stored information. To effectively use information stored in a multiaccess system,

the user needs to know all the formats and procedures used by all the participating airlines—a hopelessly complex task.

Eastern's Direct Access bypasses both the problem of insufficient information in a single-access system and the complexities of dealing with a multiaccess system. Direct Access offers users one set of formats and procedures for accessing up-to-date information about all the carriers that participate in the system. Airlines that participate in the Direct Access system link their computers to Eastern's computer, and their stored information is automatically reformatted when it is accessed by Eastern's computer. All reformatted information stored in the Eastern computer uses one set of inputs, procedures, and outputs. This information includes airline schedules, fare quotes and itinerary pricing, passenger names,

ticketing and itinerary invoicing, seat reservations, boarding passes, and ground transportation information. Any user participating in Direct Access can obtain up-to-date information from the system simply by knowing a single set of procedures.

SYSTEMONE and Direct Access are helping Eastern survive in what has become a difficult period for commercial air carriers.

DISCUSSION POINTS

1. Discuss how computers helped Eastern modernize ticketing and reservation operations.
2. What are the disadvantages of both single-access and multiaccess storage systems?

7 FILE ORGANIZATION AND DATA BASE DESIGN

A Tax-Return Company Wants a Bigger Gross

Eleanor Johnson Tracy
Fortune

It may come as a surprise to a lot of taxpayers that their accountants—including partners in Big Eight firms—ship tax returns off to an obscure Texas company, Computer Language Research Inc., for processing. The company's main business, Fast-Tax, chalked up $88.4 million in revenues handling tax returns last year. The key to Fast-Tax's success with its 8,000 clients lies in sophisticated software systems that can process 220 different federal personal and corporate income tax forms and 1,100 state forms. Fast-Tax plugs a customer's data into computers that review as many as 100 alternatives to find the smallest allowable tax bite.

Chairman Francis Winn, now 67, started the business in 1964 by preparing individual returns for well-heeled Texans. He soon branched out into oil and gas partnerships; a highly complex one involving 2,500 people generated a return 166,000 pages long—"enough to stretch from Dallas to Oklahoma City," boasts President Stephen Winn, 38, son of the founder. Word of that feat spread from the oil patch to Dallas offices, and soon the company was preparing returns for corporations and tax professionals as well. Two years ago the company went public, selling 2.2 million shares at $21 each. The Winn family controls some 80% of the common stock, worth about $80 million today.

Fast-Tax employs 175 programmers, and prides itself on taking on the most complicated jobs in the business. Declares Robert Wells of Peat Marwick, "Fast-Tax has always been a leader, a year or two ahead in each stage of development, from laser printing to getting involved with microcomputers." Computer Language is not counting on Fast-Tax alone for future growth, however. A simplified federal tax system could chill the two-thirds of Fast-Tax's business that now comes from processing U.S. returns. Even without tax simplification, there's little room for expansion in the tax-processing business.

So computer Language has just introduced a new system, Sprinter, which can electronically generate practically any kind of business form, from corporate tax returns to Medicare applications. Like Fast-Tax, it depends on proprietary software. The company's biggest prospects: the federal government and major insurance companies. With Sprinter, for instance, an insurer need not keep some 40,000 different forms in inventory. Instead, he calls on Sprinter to produce the forms through his computers when and where he needs them.

Stephen Winn has invested heavily in developing and testing Sprinter. As a result, earnings on last year's $98.2 million in revenues were $6.6 million, down 23% from 1983's $8.5 million on sales of $85.2 million; the company's stock has tumbled to $7 a share. But the market for paper forms is $5 billion a year, more than 20 times the size of the tax-return-processing business, and Winn is betting that Americans will keep filling out a lot more than tax returns in the years ahead.

● **The preparation and filing of corporate and complicated personal taxes, and the subsequent processing by the IRS, are tasks requiring the use of a number of large data bases. In fact, the IRS keeps one of the three biggest data bases in the United States.**

● Introduction

All organizations maintain a wide variety of files containing data about employees, customers, inventory levels, production, sales, and other information pertinent to the organization. An organization's method of processing this data is determined largely by specific job requirements. To aid in the processing of data, an organization can tailor its files to meet certain objectives. For example, files can be structured to minimize overall processing time and to increase processing efficiency.

This chapter examines three types of file arrangement, or data design: sequential, direct-access, and indexed-sequential. It describes representative applications of these methods to illustrate how they are used and discusses the characteristics of each method. The chapter also explains the concept of a data base and how it uses physical and logical data design.

● File Processing

File processing is the activity of updating permanent files to reflect the effects of changes in data. Files can be organized in several ways, with or without a computerized system. Without computers, files must be recorded on paper and updated manually. For example, consider the case of American Sporting Goods, a small supplier of sports equipment. The company carries an inventory of 110 items, supplies equipment to thirty customers and maintains a staff of twenty employees. All of American Sporting Goods' records are kept on paper and transactions are recorded manually.

Every time a customer places an order, a clerk must prepare a sales order. The customer's file is checked to obtain all necessary data about the customer, such as billing address, shipping address, and credit status. The clerk fills in the type and quantity of item ordered, and the sales order is sent to the warehouse where the inventory is stored. At the warehouse, an employee determines if the requested items are available. To do this, the employee must actually count the number of items in stock. If the items are available, they can be packaged and prepared for shipping. If the order cannot be filled, the employee must prepare a backorder. The sales order is sent on to the accounting department where the customer's bill is prepared. In the accounting department, a clerk checks the company catalog to determine the current cost of each item on the order. The total bill is calculated, including tax and shipping charges. The total amount is recorded on the customer's record, and the order is then shipped.

Even this simplified transaction includes many time-consuming activities. In addition to handling customer orders, the company must prepare monthly payrolls, purchase orders to replenish inventory supplies, sales reports, and many other types of transactions. The American Sporting Goods Company could save time and money by computerizing its activities.

Several computerized files could be designed to facilitate American Sporting Goods' operations. An employee file could be set up containing records for each employee. An employee record might contain the employee's home address, social security number, company identification number, hourly wage, withholding tax bracket, and gross income. In order for this data to be used in a variety of ways by several departments, it must be stored in a file accessible by all departments that require the data. Figure 7–1 shows a portion of an employee file and reintroduces several terms useful in a discussion of data design. Recall from Chapter 1 that a field is one data item, a record is a group of data items related to a single unit, and a file is a group of related records.

The company could also use an inventory file with one record for each item carried in inventory. Each record could contain a description of the item, its cost, the quantity in stock, and information about the manufacturer of the item. Finally, a customer file containing fields such as billing and shipping addresses, current balance due, and credit status would be useful.

Each of these files would be accessed, or read, in different ways. For example, the entire employee file would be read every time the payroll was prepared. The inventory file, however, would only need to be accessed one record at a time; that is, only one record would be read each time an order was placed for a certain item. The customer file would be accessed in two ways. When a customer placed an order, only the record containing the data about that customer would be read. The entire file

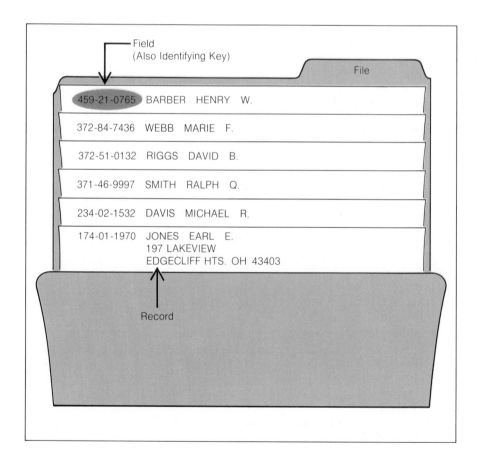

● **FIGURE 7–1**
Employee File for the American Sporting Goods Company

would be read each time the American Sporting Goods Company prepared customer bills or needed a report on overdue accounts.

Methods of File Access

An important consideration in determining the best file design for an organization is the manner in which data will be retrieved. The access method can be either batch or online, depending on how fast data must be retrieved.

BATCH FILE ACCESS

With **batch file access,** all transactions to be processed are gathered for a certain period of time and then processed all at once. The period of time for which transactions are gathered before processing may be one work shift (eight hours), one calendar day (twenty-four hours), or any other logical time period dictated by the information needs of the user.

Batch file access is most useful when current information is needed only at set times, rather than at all times. For example, student grades can be processed at the end of a term or employee payrolls at the end of a pay period.

ONLINE FILE ACCESS

Online file access provides the ability to retrieve current information at any time. Each time a transaction occurs, the affected records are updated at the same time. Online file access is often used for inventory control, airline reservations, and banking transactions.

File Designs

Different access methods require different file designs. If a data file requires batch file access, the best file design may be a **sequential file design.** If online access is needed, a **direct-access file design** or **indexed-sequential file design** must be used.

SEQUENTIAL FILE DESIGN

If a particular record must be found in a file and the number of records in the file is very small, then it may not be difficult to search the file from beginning to end to find the desired record. For files containing large numbers of records, however, this method is impractical. A special ordering technique is needed so that records can be retrieved more easily. For this reason, records may be arranged according to a **key** value. The key is one data field chosen to identify the record. Since a key is used to locate a particular record, it must be unique; that is, no two records in a file can have the same key value. In Figure 7–1, the social security number field is used as the key. Social security numbers are excellent keys for employee records because no two people in the United States have the same number. An employee record is located by searching for the appropriate value in the social security field. The key value in an inventory file could be the item number. When records are ordered according to their key values, a sequential file is formed.

Updating involves two sets of files: the **master file** and a **transaction file.** The master file is the file containing all existing records. The transaction file is the file containing the changes to be made to the master file. During the updating process a third file, the new master file, is created. The old master file is organized in sequential order according to the key field but the transaction file may be organized in any order. To speed the updating process, the transaction file should first be sorted according to the same key as the one used in the master file.

To update a file, the computer compares the key of the first master file record with the key from the first record in the transaction file. If the keys do not match, the computer writes the record to the new master file as is and reads the next record on the master file. When a match between the master and transaction records occurs, the computer updates the master record. If a transaction record has no matching master record, the computer may generate an error message.

Some transactions may add a new record, while others may delete an existing record. Since records are stored one after another on a sequential file, these types of transactions cannot be handled using the old master file alone. To allow for the insertion or deletion of records, a new master file is created whenever changes are made to the old master file. Each master record not deleted from the file must be written into a new master file, whether or not it is changed during the update. The process of creating an entirely new master file each time transactions are processed is called **sequential processing.**

With sequential processing, there is no direct way to locate the matching master record for a transaction. Each time a certain master record is to be updated, the entire master file must be read and a new master file created. Since this makes updating one record in a file very time-consuming, transactions are collected over a period of time and processed in one run (see Figure 7–2). Therefore, batch file access must be used with sequential file design.

The amount of time required to update a record with sequential processing includes the time needed to process the transaction, read and rewrite the master file until the proper record is reached, update the master record, and finish rewriting the master file. To reduce the time needed, the transactions are sorted in the same order as the master file. For security, the old master file and the transaction records are kept for a period of time; then, if the new master file is accidentally destroyed, it can be reconstructed from the old master and the transaction files. In many instances, two generations of old masters are kept, giving rise to "father" and "grandfather" backup copies.

Example of Sequential Processing

The preparation of customer bills is well suited to sequential processing. Customers' bills are usually prepared only at scheduled intervals. Standard procedures apply and large numbers of records must be processed.

Processing customer records results in the preparation of bills for customers and updates of the amounts they owe. Magnetic tape is an appropriate medium for this application because the customer records can be arranged in order by customer number and processed in sequence accordingly.

The procedure for preparing the billing statements involves the following steps:

1. The transaction records indicating which items have been shipped to customers are keypunched and verified. One card is used for each item

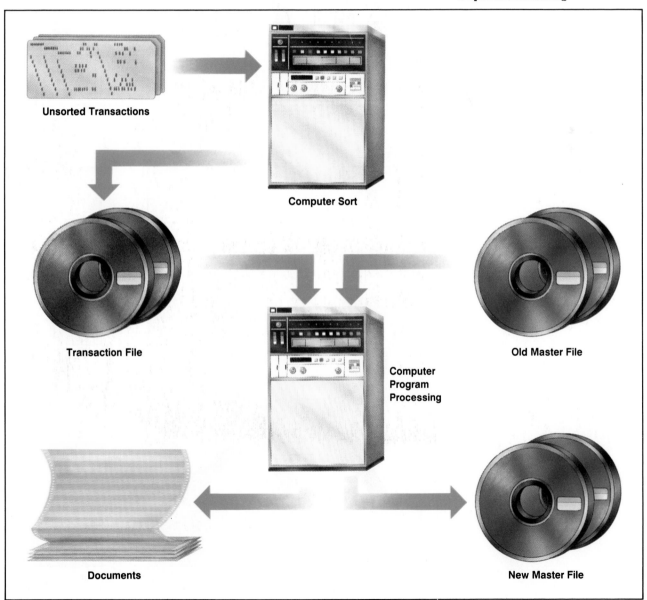

Unsorted Transactions

Computer Sort

Transaction File

Old Master File

**Computer
Program
Processing**

Documents

New Master File

shipped. The key-to-tape operation also provides a report of invalid transactions so that they can be corrected (see Figure 7–3a).

2. The transaction records are sorted according to customer number because the customer master file is arranged in order by customer number (see Figure 7–3b).

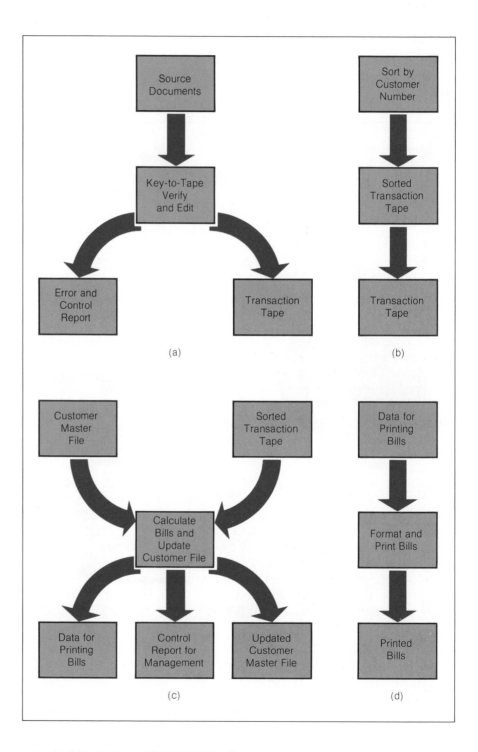

3. The sorted transactions are used to update the customer master file. The process involves reading the transaction records and master records into primary storage (there may be more than one transaction record for a master record). The master record is updated to reflect the final amount owed by the customer, and a report is usually printed for management. For example, during the billing update, the computer may print a listing of customers who have exceeded their credit limits (see Figure 7–3c).

4. The customers' bills are prepared from the data generated in Step 3 (see Figure 7–3d).

Making Inquiries to Sequential Files

How inquiries into a sequential file on magnetic tape are handled depends on the type of inquiry. Consider the following inquiries into the employee file shown in Figure 7–1.

1. List the records of employees with social security numbers 234-02-1532 and 372-84-7436.

2. List all employees from the area with zip code 43403.

The employee file is sequenced according to social security number. In the first case the file will be searched for the correct social security numbers from the beginning of the file, but only the key of each record will be checked. As soon as the required social security numbers are located and the required records listed, the search is stopped. Of course, if the numbers are in the last two records on the file, then the entire file must be searched.

For the second inquiry, the entire file will again have to be searched. In this case, the zip code field of each record must be checked to see if it matches 43403. This illustrates one problem with referring to a non-key field on sequential files. If an inquiry is based on a field other than the key, a great deal of time may be wasted in the search process. To alleviate this problem a second employee file, ordered by zip code, could be created; however, this approach requires multiple files with duplicate data.

Assessment of Sequential File Design

Sequential processing and file design are suitable for applications with high **activity** and low **volatility.** Activity refers to the proportion of records processed during an updating run. Volatility refers to the frequency of changes to a file during a given time period. Examples of applications with high activity and low volatility (requiring large numbers of records to be updated at specific times) include payroll processing, updating the addresses of magazine subscribers, and preparing student grades.

Advantages of sequential processing and file design include the following:

- It can be cost-effective when at least half the records in a master file are updated during one processing run.
- The design of sequential files is simple.
- Magnetic tape, a low-cost medium, can be used to maximum advantage.

The disadvantages of this method of processing include the following:

- The entire master file must be processed and a new master file written even when only a few master records have to be updated.
- Transactions must be sorted in a particular sequence; this takes time and can be expensive.
- The master file is only as up-to-date as the last processing run. In many instances, using information from a master file that has not been recently updated results in the use of old, and sometimes incorrect, information.
- The sequential nature of the file organization makes it difficult to provide information for unanticipated inquiries such as the status of a particular record.

DIRECT-ACCESS FILE DESIGN

Direct-access file designs also use the key field of the records but in a different way from sequential design. The key field provides the only way of accessing data within a direct-access file design. Therefore, records are not stored in any particular order.

The data record being sought is retrieved according to its key value, so records before or after it are not read. Usually, a mathematical process called **randomizing** or **hashing** is applied to the record key, with the result of the process being the storage addresses of the record. The address is usually a number of five to seven digits that is related to the physical characteristics of the storage medium. When a file is created, this address determines where the record is written. During retrieval, the address determines where to locate the record. Another way to obtain the address of a record is to place the record keys and their corresponding addresses in a **directory** (see Figure 7–4). During processing, the computer searches the directory to locate the address of a particular record.

Direct-access file design is much more efficient than searching an entire data file for a particular record. It is useful when information must be updated and retrieved quickly and when accurate information is crucial. A common application of direct-access file organization is for airline seat reservations. Accurate information about available flights and seats must be available at all times so that flights are not overbooked.

In contrast to a batch-processing system, a direct-access system does not require transaction records to be grouped or sorted before they are processed. Data is submitted to the computer in the order it occurs, usually using an online access method. **Direct-access storage devices (DASDs),** such as magnetic-disk drive units, make this type of processing possible. A particular record on a master file can be accessed directly, using its assigned keys, and updated without all preceding records on the file being read. Only the key to the record needs to be known. Thus, up-to-the-minute reports can be provided. For example, assume Ralph Smith's address in the employee master file in Figure 7–1 had to be changed. With direct-access processing, the computer can locate the record to be updated without processing all records that precede it. Figure 7–5 shows how direct-access processing would be used in a business.

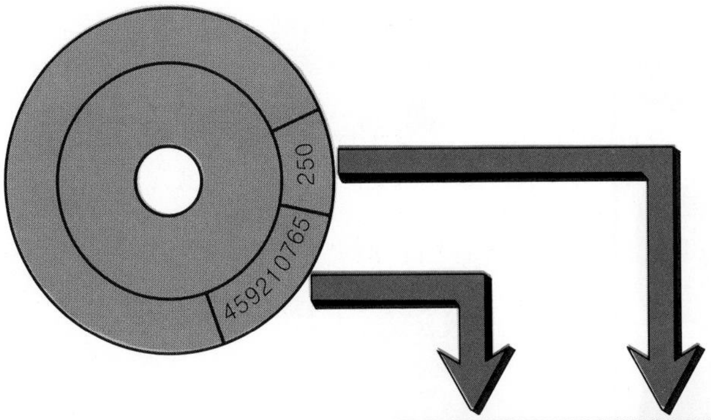

Social Security Number	Address
459210765	250
372847436	829
372510132	301
371469997	677
234021532	425
17401970	712
⋮	⋮
⋮	⋮

FIGURE 7–4
Sample Directory for Social Security Number

Making Inquiries to Direct-Access Files

To see how direct-access files handle inquiries, refer to the two inquiries discussed in connection with sequential files:

1. List the records of employees with social security numbers 234-02-1532 and 372-84-7436.
2. List all employees from the area with zip code 43403.

With regard to the first inquiry, the records of the two employees can be located directly, assuming the social security number is used as the key.

The approach used for the second inquiry will depend on the organization of the file. If the file is large and much processing is done based on a geographic breakdown of employees, a directory using zip codes and their record addresses can be created (as in Figure 7–6). However,

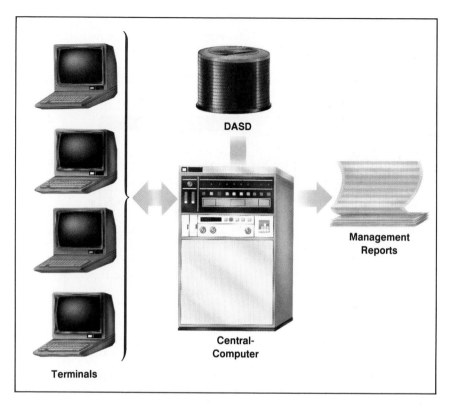

if there are not many employees and processing is seldom based on the geographic breakdown of employees, a directory to locate employee records by zip code may have little value. In this case, the situation is the same as with sequential files—the entire file must be read to obtain the desired information.

Assessment of Direct-Access File Design

Direct-access processing and file design is suitable for applications with low activity and high volatility. Examples of applications with low activity and high volatility (requiring only a few records to be updated frequently) include banking operations and hotel and airline reservation systems.

Advantages of direct-access processing and file design are the following:

● Transaction data can be used directly to update master records via online terminals without first being sorted. Transactions are processed as they occur.

● The master file is not read completely each time updating occurs; only the master records to be updated are accessed. This saves time and money.

● Gaining access to any record on a direct-access file takes only a fraction of a second.

● Direct-access files provide flexibility in handling inquiries.

● Several files can be updated at the same time by use of direct-access processing. For example, when a credit sale is made, the inventory file can be updated, the customer file can be changed to reflect the current

● **FIGURE 7–6**
Directory for Zip Codes

ZIP CODE	ADDRESS
43403	12043
43403	12140
44151	12046
44153	12143
44200	12146
44201	12045

164

accounts receivable figure, and the sales file can be updated to show which employee made the sale. Several runs would be required to accomplish all of these operations if sequential processing was used.

Disadvantages of direct-access design include the following:

● During processing, the original record is replaced by the updated record. In effect, it is destroyed. (In batch processing, a completely new master file is created, but the old master file remains intact.) Consequently, to provide backup, an organization may have to make a magnetic-tape copy of the master file weekly and also keep the current week's transactions so that master records can be reconstructed if necessary.

● Since many users may have access to records stored on direct-access devices in online systems, the chances of accidental destruction of data are greater. Special programs are required to edit input data and to perform other checks to ensure that data is not lost. Also, there exists the possibility of confidential information falling into unauthorized hands; additional security procedures are necessary to reduce this risk.

● Implementation of direct-access systems is often difficult because of their complexity and the high level of programming (software) support that such systems need.

INDEXED-SEQUENTIAL FILE DESIGN

Sequential processing is suitable for applications in which the proportion of records processed in an updating run is high. However, sequential files provide slow response times and cannot adequately handle file inquiries. On the other hand, direct-access processing is inappropriate for applications like payroll where most records are processed during a single run. When a single file must be used for both batch processing and online processing, neither direct-access nor sequential file organization is appropriate. The same customer file that is used in a weekly batch run for preparing bills by the accounting department may be used daily by order-entry personnel to record orders and check credit status. To some extent, the limitations of both types of file design can be minimized by using another approach to file organization, indexed-sequential design.

In this structure, the records are stored sequentially on a direct-access storage device according to a primary key. A **primary key** is a field that will be unique for each record on the file. In addition, secondary keys can also be established. **Secondary keys** are fields that are used to gain access to records on the file but may not be unique. For instance, if zip code is chosen as a secondary key, there may be several records with the same value. Records on an indexed-sequential file can be accessed randomly by using either the primary or one of the secondary keys, or the file can be read sequentially, in primary key-sequential order.

The method used to gain access to a record on an indexed-sequential file is a little different from the method used for a direct-access file. Every record on an indexed-sequential file may not have its own unique address. Rather, several records may be grouped together and one address given for the entire group. An index table is created for all fields that are primary or secondary keys. The index table lists the value of the key (such as social security number) and the corresponding address on the direct-access storage device at which the group containing that record can be found. A key given by the user is matched against the index table to get an approximate address for the required record. The computer then goes to that location on the direct-access storage device and checks records sequentially until the desired record is found. In the case of secondary keys, all records with that key may be retrieved.

Figure 7–7 shows the employee file from Figure 7–1 set up as an indexed-sequential file. The primary key is a social security number,

● **FIGURE 7–7**
The Physical Layout of Records on a Disk for Indexed-Sequential Design

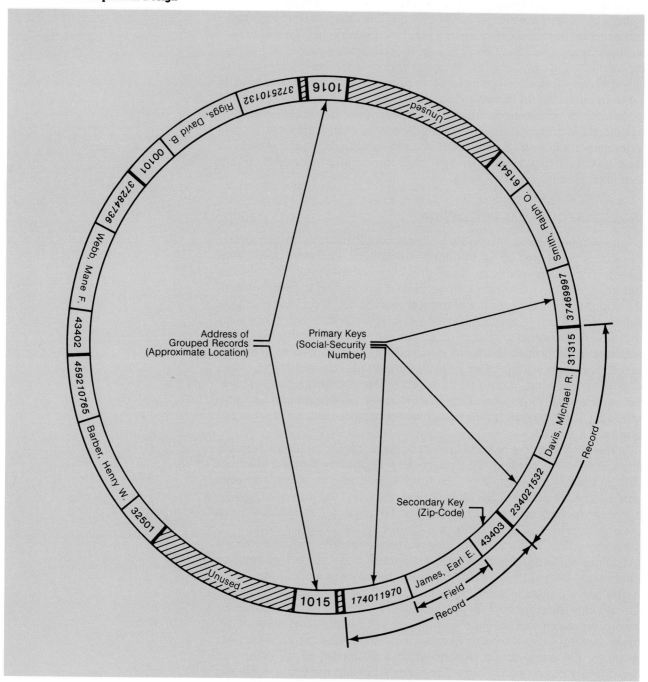

● **COMPUTERS AND INFORMATION PROCESSING**

while zip code is a secondary key. Notice how the records are in sequence according to the social security number on the file. To locate an employee with a zip code of 43403, the computer goes to the index table for zip code (see Figure 7–8). Next to the value 43403 is the address on the direct-access storage device at which the group containing that record can be found, 1015. The computer goes to that address and reads each record in the group until the one with zip code 43403 is found. In this case, it is the first record in the group.

Thus, an indexed-sequential file provides direct-access capability. Since all the records are ordered according to a primary key, it also allows efficient sequential processing.

Making Inquiries to Indexed-Sequential Files

The customer file referred to earlier in this chapter is an example of a file suitable for indexed-sequential processing. The file could be read sequentially for the billing operation. In addition, it could be accessed one record at a time for order-entry transactions. The following steps outline the procedures involved in preparing a customer order:

1. A customer sends an order to American Sporting Goods for equipment. The clerk receives the order and enters the customer number on a visual display terminal. This number acts as a key to the file.
2. The index to the customer number on the customer file is searched until it is located. The record's approximate address is used to begin the search on the disk file. Once at that location, records are searched sequentially until a match is found between the number entered and the appropriate record. Once the appropriate record is found, the information appears on the terminal's screen. The clerk verifies shipping and billing addresses.
3. The order is entered at the keyboard, and a sales order is generated by a printer connected to the system.
4. The customer's record is updated to reflect the current order.

Assessment of Indexed-Sequential File Design

Indexed-sequential files have a built-in flexibility that is not available with either sequential or direct-access designs. They work well in an environment where transactions are batch processed and inquiries require the fast response of direct-access processing.

● **FIGURE 7–8**
Index Tables of Primary and Secondary Keys

PRIMARY KEY (Social Security Number)		SECONDARY KEY (Zip Code)	
Number	Address	Number	Address
174–01–1970	1015	00101	1016
234–02–1532	1015	31315	1015
371–46–9997	1015	32501	1016
372–51–0132	1016	43402	1016
372–84–7436	1016	43403	1015
459–21–0765	1016	61541	1015

Advantages of indexed-sequential design include the following:

- Indexed-sequential files are well suited for both inquiries and large processing runs.
- Access time to specific records is apt to be faster than it would be if the file were sequentially organized.

Disadvantages of indexed-sequential design include the following:

- More direct-access storage space is required for an indexed-sequential file than for a sequential file holding the same data because of the storage space required for indexes.
- Processing time for specific record selection is longer than it would be in a direct-access system.

CONCEPT SUMMARY 7–1

Comparison of File Designs

	Sequential	Direct-Access	Indexed-Sequential
Types of Access	batch	online	batch or online
Data Organization	sequentially by key value	no particular order	sequentially and by index
Flexibility in Handling Inquiries	low	high	very high
Availability of Up-to-Date Data	no	yes	yes
Speed of Retrieval	slow	very fast	fast
Activity	high	low	high
Volatility	low	high	high
Examples	payroll processing billing operations	airline reservations banking transactions	customer ordering and billing

● Data Bases

Organizations such as hospitals, banks, retailers, and manufacturers have special information needs. Usually, data is collected and stored by many departments in these organizations. But this often results in the duplication of data. A hospital, for example, may keep files on patients treated in the emergency room. If a patient is then admitted, separate records may be compiled and kept for admissions, surgical procedures, X-rays, insurance, and billing purposes. The patient's name, address, personal physician, and medical history might be repeated in most or all of the records.

A data-base approach to file design treats all data from every department as one entity. A **data base** is a single collection of related data that can be used in many applications. This data is stored on a direct-access device, such as a disk. Data is usually stored only once in a data base, which minimizes data duplication.

In a data base, data is stored in such a way that the same data can be accessed by many users for various applications. Data elements are grouped to fit the needs of all departments in the organization rather than the needs of one particular application.

In addition to reducing the duplication of data, data bases increase efficiency. When a data element is updated, the change needs to be made only once because the data files are shared by all users. Once the update is made, current information is readily available to all departments.

The task of determining the design of data in a data base is the responsibility of the system analyst and data-base analyst. A **system analyst** is the interface between users and the system programmers. The **data-base analyst** is responsible for the analysis, design, and implementation of the data base. Together, they try to model the actual relationships that exist among data elements. The physical design of the data base is performed by the data-base administration (DBA) team. The DBA team must consider the problems of data redundancy, access time, and storage constraints in order to develop a logical design that works for the physical records and files actually stored in the data base.

The key to a successful data base is to incorporate more than one physical file into a logical file. What one user views as a logical unit of data may include data from several files. For example, if a user needs an employee's identification number, address, and salary, all that information can be obtained from two files, the personnel file and the payroll file (see Figure 7–9).

Data-base systems depend on direct-access storage devices (DASDs) to allow easy retrieval of data elements. The capabilities of DASDs are needed to handle the many logical relationships that exist among data elements. Combinations of data elements can be retrieved from a number of DASDs.

STRUCTURING DATA

Data elements in a computer file can be arranged in many ways according to how they are related to one another. These relationships, called **data structures,** represent the ways in which data elements can be joined together in logical ways. The user determines the way in which the elements are linked. The most common data structures are the simple, hierarchical, network, and relational structures. These data structures determine the possible ways in which data contained in a data base can be organized.

The Simple Structure

The **simple structure** is a sequential arrangement of data records. All records are viewed as independent entities, as illustrated in Figure 7–10. Each record in this file has five characteristic fields called **attributes**—name, title, education, department, and sex. If the records are ordered—

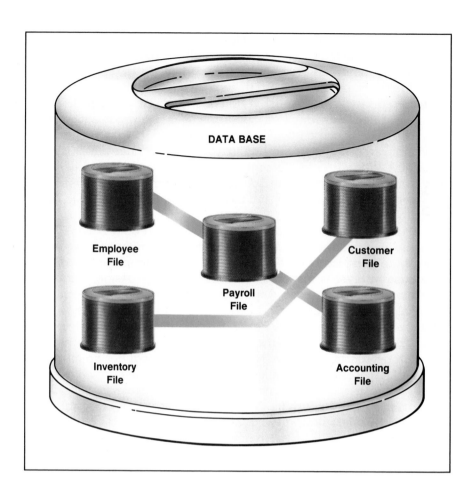

that is, arranged in a specific sequence—then the list is referred to as
a **linear structure.** Simple file structure is appropriate for generating
large reports but cumbersome for handling inquiries. To overcome this
limitation, an **inverted structure** can be used. The inverted structure
contains indexes for selected attributes in a file, similar to those used in
indexed-sequential files; the addresses of records having those attributes
are also listed so that these records can then be referenced by these
addresses. Figure 7–11 demonstrates an inverted file. Thus, the indexes

● FIGURE 7–10
File with Simple Structure

ADDRESS	NAME	TITLE	EDUCATION	DEPARTMENT	SEX
018021	Borgelt	Asst. Prof.	Ph.D.	Marketing	Male
018024	Henkes	Professor	D.Sc.	Management	Male
018046	Pickens	Instructor	M.S.	Accounting	Male
018020	Deluse	Asst. Prof.	Ph.D.	Marketing	Female
018016	Kozak	Assoc. Prof.	Ph.D.	Accounting	Male
018412	Gadus	Assoc. Prof.	Ph.D.	Accounting	Male
018318	Cross	Asst. Prof.	M.B.A.	Management	Female

NAME		TITLE		EDUCATION		DEPARTMENT		SEX	
Value	Address	Value	Address	Value	Address	Value	Address	Value	Address
Borgelt	018021	Instructor	018046	M.S.	018046	Marketing	018021	Male	018021
Henkes	018024	Asst. Prof.	018021	M.B.A.	018318		018020		018024
Pickens	018046		018020	Ph.D.	018021	Management	018024		018046
Deluse	018020		018318		018020		018318		018016
Kozak	018016	Assoc. Prof.	018016		018016	Accounting	018046		018412
Gadus	018412		018412		018412		018016	Female	018020
Cross	018318	Professor	018024	D.Sc.	018024		018412		018318

● FIGURE 7–11
File with Inverted Structure

rather than the actual files can be searched, and complex inquiries can be handled easily.

An advantage of the inverted structure is that it enables a variety of inquiries to be handled quickly and efficiently. A major disadvantage is that the attributes to be used in searches must be indexed. In some cases, the indexes for a particular file may be larger than the file itself.

The Hierarchical Structure

When a primary data element has many secondary data elements linked to it at various levels, it is called a **hierarchical** (or **tree) structure.** The primary data element is the parent element. Each parent may have many children (secondary elements) related to it, but each child may have only one parent. Figure 7–12 shows a hierarchical structure. A is the parent of B1 and B2; B1 is the parent of C1, C2, and C3; and so forth. The

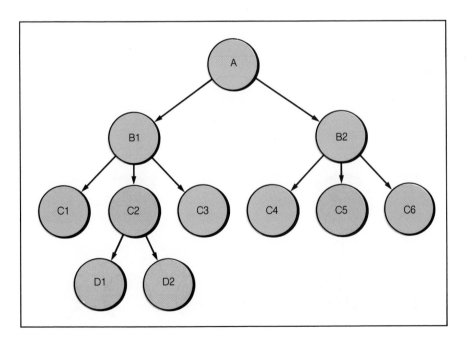

● FIGURE 7–12
Hierarchical Data Structure

organization of corporations is typically a hierarchical structure. A school system may use the hierarchical data structure for its student records. Figure 7–13 shows the relationship between data elements of a student's course schedule. A student's social security number is linked to the courses in which the student is enrolled. Each course is linked to one teacher, a meeting time, and a room number. Therefore, if the principal needs to know where a particular student is at 1:00, for example, he or she could enter the student's social security number into the computer and the student's course schedule would be displayed on the terminal screen.

A problem with hierarchical data bases is that data stored at the lower levels can only be accessed through each successive parent on the levels above. Second, relationships between the elements are created at the same time as the data base; therefore, these relationships cannot be altered at a later time.

The Network Structure

Similar to the hierarchical data structure, a **network structure** allows a parent data element to have many children, but it also allows a child to have more than one parent. With this structure, any data element can be related to any other data element. There is no longer a simple hierarchy of data elements with relationships flowing only from a high level to a lower level. Data elements at a lower level can be related to elements at a higher level although these structures are quite complex. Figure 7–14 graphically illustrates this structure.

Figure 7–15 shows the relationship between data elements of a student course file. Each course is related to a student, a teacher, a meeting time, and a room number. Courses may have two parents, a student social security number, and a teacher. With this relatively simple example, the principal could locate either a student or a teacher by entering the student's social security number or the teacher's name.

● FIGURE 7–13
Student Course Schedule Shown in a Hierarchical Data Structure

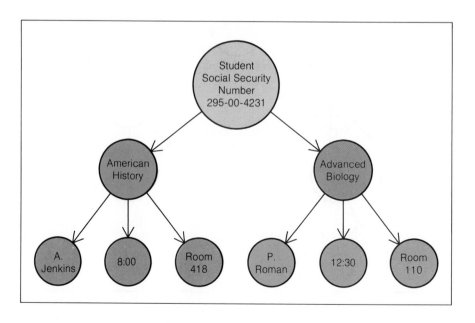

● COMPUTERS AND INFORMATION PROCESSING

The Relational Structure

The newest type of data base is the **relational structure.** Relational data bases were developed to provide a more user-friendly approach to this type of data accessing. Although relational data bases are easy for the user to access, they are the most sophisticated of the types of data bases discussed here. A relational data structure places the data elements in a table (called a relation) with columns and rows. The rows represent records, and the columns represent fields or individual data elements. With this structure, a data element can be related to other elements in the column in which it is located or to elements in the row in which it is located. With a relational data structure, the user can access either the

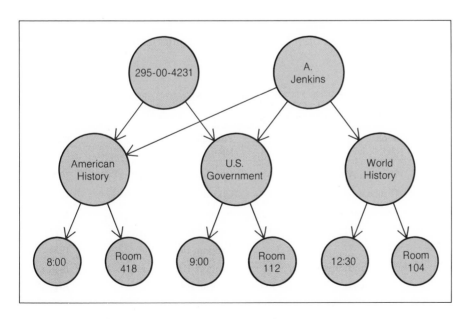

● FIGURE 7–15
Student Course Schedule Shown in a
Network Data Structure

data elements that comprise a record (one row) or the data elements contained in one field (one column). It is also possible to join two or more relations to develop a third relation or to select records within a record according to user-specified criteria.

Figure 7–16 shows a relational data structure of authors, books, publishers, and copyright dates. Each record contains one author, book publisher, and copyright date. For example, Ernest Hemingway, *The Sun Also Rises*, Charles Scribner's Sons, and 1926 make up one record. Each record has an author field (Hemingway), book field (*The Sun Also Rises*), publisher field (Charles Scribner's Sons), and copyright date field (1926).

Each data element has a unique location in the table identified by the column number and row number. The row and column numbers are called subscripts. For example, the subscript (1,5) identifies the data element James Joyce, located in column 1, row 5.

This sample data structure might be used at a bookstore. A clerk could then obtain the record with J. R. R. Tolkien data, for example, or a list of all book titles carried at the store (the data elements in one field).

DATA-BASE MANAGEMENT SYSTEMS

An organization can use a **data-base management system (DBMS)** to help set up a data base. A DBMS is a set of programs that serves as the interface between the data base and the programmer, operating system, and users. With a DBMS, the programmer does not have to pay attention to the physical nature of the file; the programmer's main concern is the specific data the program needs.

A DBMS can perform the following functions:

- Organizing the data into logical structures that model the actual relationships among the data elements.
- Storing the data required to meet the needs of multiple users.
- Providing for concurrent retrieval and updating of data.
- Arranging data to eliminate data duplication.
- Providing privacy controls to prevent unauthorized access to data.

● **FIGURE 7–16**
Relational Data Structure

		COLUMNS (FIELDS)			
		Author (1)	Book (2)	Publisher (3)	Copyright (4)
	(1)	Ernest Hemingway	The Sun Also Rises	Charles Scribner's Sons	1926
	(2)	F. Scott Fitzgerald	The Last Tycoon	Charles Scribner's Sons	1941
ROWS (RECORDS)	(3)	Richard Adams	Watership Down	Avon	1972
	(4)	J. R. R. Tolkien	The Silmarillion	George Allen 7 Unwin	1977
	(5)	James Joyce	Ulysses	Random House	1934
	(6)	William Faulkner	The Sound and the Fury	Random House	1946
	(7)	J. D. Salinger	The Catcher in the Rye	Bantam Books	1945

ASSESSMENT OF THE DATA-BASE APPROACH

Using a data base has a number of advantages:

● Data redundancy is minimized.
● Data can be stored in a manner that is useful for a wide variety of applications.
● Updating involves only one copy of the data.
● The system can handle requests that previously may have spanned several departments.

Limitations of the data-base approach include the following:

● An error in one input data record may be carried throughout the data base.
● Design and implementation of a data-base system requires highly skilled, well-trained people.
● Major attention must be given to the security of the system since all the data resources of the organization are collected in a place that is readily accessible to data-base users.
● Traditional processing jobs may run more slowly.

● Summary Points

● Batch file access methods require transactions to be gathered for processing at one time.
● Online file access methods provide the ability to retrieve data and update data at any time.
● In sequential file design, all data is stored in sequential order on a master file; it may be ordered by some key field. Transactions to be processed against the master file are stored on a transaction file. Transactions are usually collected and processed against the master in one batch. During processing, transactions are matched against the master file, and the master file is updated. Updates to the master file are made by writing a new master during processing. The entire master file must be read when sequential processing is used.
● Batch access methods are generally used with sequential file designs.
● In direct access processing, records are accessed according to their key. The computer determines the location of the record on the disk by a transformation process on the key or by using a directory. Once the physical address is known, the record can be retrieved.
● Direct-access file designs are accessed using online methods.
● Indexed-sequential processing is used when the same file may be required for sequential processing and single-record updates. A primary key is used to identify each unique record, and records are stored in sequence according to the primary key. Secondary keys are set up for those fields used to gain access to the file. The computer uses the key value to determine the approximate physical location of the record (or records), and then reads the records sequentially until the desired one is found.

- A data base is a grouping of data elements structured to fit the information needs of all departments of an organization. The data base reduces data duplication and increases efficiency and flexibility.
- Data within a data base can be structured in many ways. Four ways are the simple structure, the hierarchical structure, the network structure, and the relational structure.
- In a simple structure, records are arranged sequentially. Inverted structures are used to index files with simple structures by attributes which are characteristic fields.
- In a hierarchical structure, a given parent element may have many children but a given child can have only one parent. In network structures, on the other hand, a parent can have many children and each child can also have more than one parent.
- The newest type of data base structure, the relational structure, has data elements placed in tables called relations. The rows represent the records and the columns contain each record's fields.
- A data-base management system is a set of programs that provides (1) a method of arranging data to limit duplication; (2) the ability to make changes to the data easily; (3) the ability to handle direct inquiries.

● Review Questions

1. What are the two most common methods of accessing a data file?

2. Define the term *key*. Explain the use of a key in sequential processing.

3. How does the use of a key in direct-access processing differ from sequential processing?

4. Distinguish between a master file and a transaction file.

5. Explain the similarities between indexed-sequential processing and sequential processing.

6. Explain the similarities between direct-access processing and indexed-sequential processing.

7. How does the computer use a directory during data retrieval?

8. Explain what a data base is.

9. How can a data base be structured to respond to a variety of inquiries?

10. Name three advantages of using a data base.

11. Explain different types of data structures that are used to organize data bases.

12. How does the inverted file structure assist in the handling of inquiries?

Superx

GENERAL COMPUTER USE

The success of Superx drugstores is due largely to one philosophy: The pharmacy is the heart of the business, and concern for the health of the customers and their families lies within the professional and quality service of that pharmacy. In 1960, when the Kroger Company decided to go into the drugstore business, they began by purchasing a chain of New Jersey drugstores. From the purchase of those stores, the Superx philosophy of the drugstore management evolved.

Computers play an integral part in the operation of Superx Drugs, Inc. Their introduction into store operations in 1980 effected dramatic changes. Automating pharmacy procedures created additional time for more meaningful consultation between customers and pharmacists. Use of hand-held wand scanning devices in the product-ordering process improved clerk productivity and reduced errors. Electronic cash registers began to capture sales and gross profit information for evaluation of advertising effectiveness.

The Superx general office staff relies heavily on computers to capture, maintain, and report all information associated with daily store operations. A communications network linking all stores, offices, and data centers provides for electronic movement of data seven days a week, twenty-four hours a day. Major system applications that depend on this network include store ordering, product distribution, prescription billing, and financial reporting.

DATA RECORD STORAGE

One of the primary reasons for the success of the computerized pharmacy system is the method by which the data records are stored in the computer. Superx selected an IBM-supplied utility called IAM (Index Access Method). This utility allowed the retrieval of data records as well as the efficient management of data storage space on a disk.

The IAM method of data record storage has several requirements in defining a file structure. The first requirement is that all data records to be retained in the file must be the same length. IAM cannot accommodate variable length records in a single file. The second requirement is that all data fields in the data record must be the same length and position. This allows standardization of the data elements. A third requirement is the selection of the "key" field in the data record. The key is used to access each data record and therefore must be unique to each data record. When a specific data record is required, the key is used to locate the data record in the file.

The IAM method of storage provides a rapid retrieval of data records by storing the keys of each data record in index blocks. An index block contains a group of the keys and points to the location on the disk of each associated data record. The index blocks are stored in multiple levels depending on the size of the data file. They are linked in a series of levels until they point directly to the data records. The method of index block storage from a high level to lower levels to data records gives a cascading effect for data record lookups. This downward flow is the basis for a speedy retrieval of a requested data record.

At the heart of the computerized pharmacy system is a series of intricately related IAM files. The most important of these is the customer information file. The cus-

tomer data record contains the personal data for each person—name, address, phone number, birthdate, and so on. To furnish a unique key to each customer, the name is processed through a hashing algorithm, which generates a unique hash value. Identical names, such as John Smith, will produce identical key values. When a duplicate hash value is found, a sequence byte is incremented and a unique key is created.

The customer data record also contains a link to another important file in the pharmacy system, the prescription history file. This file contains information about each prescription filled for each customer. As a new prescription is filled or an old one is refilled, a new entry is made in the prescription history file. To allow the pharmacist to review the customer's prescription history, each prescription is linked by the order in which it was filled. Also stored in this file for each prescription is the link to the drug item file.

The drug item file contains the data records for each drug item in the pharmacy system. The data records are made up of the information about each item, such as drug name, strength, package size, DEA class, pricing breakdown, and so forth. This file is updated weekly from a corporate data base to ensure that all information is up-to-date.

The files for the computerized pharmacy system are a network of interdependent data files. Each file contains pieces of information that individually mean very little, but when used in conjunction with one another, form the basis of a successful computerized application.

DISCUSSION POINTS

1. Describe the general use of computers at Superx.
2. How is the Index Access Method used for file storage at Superx? Discuss the requirements in the definition of a file structure.

8 MICROCOMPUTERS

●ARTICLE
The Great Personal Computer Con/

Tim Hartnell
Creative Computing

It may be harsh news, but those who market potential computers have been conning us for years.

Be honest. What do you *really* do with your personal computer? I don't mean the things you tell people when they ask (so you can disguise the fact that every disk you own is filed with bootleg copies of games like *Space Cobbler* or *Smash Hell Out of the Alien*), I mean the things that you actually do.

Several times I've been interviewed regarding personal computers and inevitably (after the obligatory question "Are computer games leading us to raise a race of people who can solve problems only by blowing up their opponents?") the wise interviewer will say, "Well, I've thought about it, and there is nothing I can see that I would use a computer for at home."

And when I thought about it seriously, I realized that I didn't have much idea of what people really did with personal computers or why they bought them. I know what the marketers of personal computers *say* you can do. And this is where the con comes in.

There are two main approaches they use. The first one runs like this: "Buy a computer or your child will be hopelessly left behind at school and will be handicapped for life." I reject these claims absolutely because (a) they attempt to arouse parental guilt and feelings of inadequancy; and (b) because they are just plain lies. This direction can hardly, to my mind, be one in which the answer to "what do

you need a personal computer for?" can be found.

The second main way to sell personal computers seems to be the "use the computer as a Gee Whiz Aid around the house." Balance your checkbook on it, store recipes on it, catalog your books.

In *Time* magazine last year, the results of a survey of owners of personal computers were published. The results showed that 49% of those surveyed *claimed* they used their computers for "balancing their checkbooks." Bunkum. I suggest the people who drew up the survey questions and analyzed the results should have been a bit more critical. I bet that nearly all (if not all) of the 49% ticked the "balance my checkbook" box because they didn't want to be seen as someone who just plays games."

It seems to me that many of the reasons manufacturers give us for buying a computer are either lies or are so utterly irrelevant as to suggest that those drawing up the advertising don't have a clue as to what the products would be used for.

What do *you* use your computer for (or, if you don't have one, what do you think you would use it for?) If you are like most of my computer-owning friends you spend a lot of very satisfying time just "mucking about" with it—writing programs, typing in stuff out of books and magazines, expanding your programming knowledge, playing with commercial software.

As well, you may use it—as more and more people appear to be

doing—as a word processor for letters and reports, or for keeping control of a mailing list for your club. However, I'll bet you spend most of the time just "mucking about" with your computer.

People don't ask, when they see your car in the driveway or notice an electronic organ in your home, "What do you do with it?." You feel you are entitled to have a musical instrument to muck about on, with no intention of giving a concert at the Lincoln Center, and you can drive for pleasure without feeling you must one day be a racing driver or drive a cab around town. Why should a computer be different?

It is the quintessential toy. It is an infinite passageway that can lead you and your mind just about anywhere you choose. You do not have to use it (or feel you must defend why you are not so using it) as a poor substitute for a stack of file cards or a calculator and the back of an envelope. When Faraday was asked the use of that newfangled stuff "electricity," he turned the question back on the enquirer by saying "What's the use of a newborn baby?"

The personal computer is still a newborn baby. We are still at the horse and buggy stage of computing. At present, computers are pretty dumb and in need of constant direction.

And here's where the "telephone" and the title comes in. I believe that fairly soon (within six years) computers will be much like present day telephones.

You don't need an instruction book or a four-week course to use the telephone. You see someone do it or you have 12 seconds of instruction and you can use a phone for life.

This will happen with computers. And when it does, when you can just get one, talk to it and get it to talk back to you and do what you want it to do without hassle or misunderstanding, the personal computer will really have arrived. Once it has come to this, no one will ask "why do you need one around the house?"

Until the era of the Hartnell Telephone-Like Computer, there is just one way to answer those people who want to know what use a personal computer can possibly be. Assume a sage-like expression, raise one eyebrow like Mr. Spock about to go boldly where no man has been before, look fixedly at your enquirer, and ask softly "What is the use of a newborn baby?" That'll shut 'em up.

● **In addition to being used for game playing and check balancing, microcomputers are being used in homes by students for writing papers and by adults bringing work home from the office.**

● Introduction

Few technological changes equal the impact that microcomputers have had on our lives in so short a period of time. In just one decade, microcomputers evolved from primitive toys for hobbyists to sophisticated machines that far surpass the early mainframe computers in both speed and capabilities. The small machines have become so common that they now appear in every area of our lives, from work to play.

The proliferation of microcomputers has introduced a new set of options and vocabulary to explore. For example, a description of an Apple IIc may include the following: 128K RAM, 40/80 column display, two serial ports, a mouse/game port, one built-in disk drive, a connector for a second disk drive, and outputs for composite and RGB monitors, with an RF modulator to drive a television set. This chapter examines the terms and hardware associated with microcomputers and describes some unique aspects and ramifications of using the machines.

8

● Microcomputers: An Overview

Microcomputers, also called personal computers or home computers, are the smallest computers. They differ from minicomputers, mainframes, and supercomputers in capability, price, and size. The list of things they can do is rapidly expanding, however, and clear distinction no longer exists between their capabilities and those of the next class of computers, minicomputers. Some microcomputers, often referred to as supermicrocomputers, are so powerful that they are being used instead of minicomputers by some organizations. (These machines are discussed later in the chapter.)

Microcomputers can usually sit on a desk top (see Figure 8–1). They are less expensive than minicomputers and mainframes, due largely to their less complex and less expensive operating systems. Microcomputer prices range from about $100 to $15,000.

● **FIGURE 8–1**
Microcomputer.
Microcomputers, the least expensive
category of computers, are general-
purpose machines used in many applications in homes, schools, and offices.

The prefix *micro* should be thought of as applying more to size and
cost than to capability. Microcomputers are very powerful for their size.
Today's microcomputers exceed the power of the early room-sized mainframe computers. Although they cannot perform as many complex functions as the large computers available today, technology continues to
give them more speed and more memory at an ever-decreasing cost.

THE NEW TECHNOLOGY

The invention of the microprocessor ushered in the fourth generation of
computers in 1971. The microprocessor is a single chip containing arithmetic and logic circuitry as well as control capability for memory and
input/output access (see Figure 8–2). It controls the sequence of operations and the arithmetic and logic operations. It also controls the storage
of data, instructions, and intermediate and final results of processing,
much as the CPU of a mainframe computer does. A mainframe's CPU
contains a series of integrated circuits, however, and is much more complex than the microprocessor.

Microprocessors quickly increased in power while they decreased in
size. This combination of power and miniaturization paved the way for
microcomputers as they exist today.

The first microprocessor was not even designed for microcomputers.
Ted Hoff, an engineer at Intel, designed the first microprocessor chip for
a Japanese company that wanted an integrated, programmable circuit
chip for its line of calculators. At the time, calculators used several circuit
chips, each chip performing only one function. Hoff's chip, the Intel 4004,
could be programmed to perform numerous calculator functions.

The Intel 4004 had a very limited instruction set (the fundamental logic
and arithmetic circuitry), could not perform many functions, and could
manipulate only four bits of data at a time. By 1974, however, micropro-

cessors could manipulate eight bits of data at a time. Popular early eight-bit chips still in use today are the Zilog Z-80, Intel 8080, and Motorola 6809. These powerful eight-bit microprocessors were used in the first microcomputers, among them the MITS Altair 8800.

Ed Roberts, the founder of a company called MITS, foresaw the start of the microcomputer revolution. He developed a computer that could be built from a kit, the Altair 8800. In January 1975, his computer received cover billing in *Popular Electronics* magazine (now *Computers and Electronics*). The computer came unassembled for $397 or fully assembled for $498. It used the Intel 8080 microprocessor, had only 256 bytes of RAM, and offered no software. Yet the Altair 8800 created so much interest that MITS received more than 5,000 orders. This response indicated that the market for microcomputers was well worth pursuing. Other microcomputers in kit form followed: the Scelbi-8B, the Sphere I, the Jolt, and the Mike. Most featured from 1K to 4K of memory.

In 1976, not long after the introduction of the Altair, Stephen Wozniak, an employee of Hewlett-Packard, finished building a small, easy-to-use computer. His computer, the Apple I, used the MOS 6402 microprocessor chip, which cost $20. Steven Jobs, a friend of Wozniak's and a former Hewlett-Packard employee, persuaded Wozniak to leave Hewlett-Packard and start a business with him. The two men raised $1,300 and began building Apple computers. Their first commercial microcomputer, the Apple II, was a huge success (see Figure 8–3). Since then, Apple has produced a series of computers, including the Apple II Plus, Apple IIe, Apple IIc, the Macintosh, and the Macintosh Plus.

Both Wozniak and Jobs have left Apple and are working on new ideas in computer technology and applications. Apple's chairman is now John Sculley, whom Jobs brought in from Pepsi Cola Company in order to improve Apple's efficiency.

● FIGURE 8–3
Steven Jobs, Stephen Wozniak, and
the Apple II.

The year 1976 was a busy one in microcomputer development. Commodore Business Machines, headed by Jack Tramiel, had acquired MOS Technology, the semiconductor manufacturer that was developing the 6502 microprocessor. The chip was incorporated in the Commodore PET. Tramiel also sold the 6502 chip to Apple and Atari.

In 1977, the PET was introduced at an electronics show and received tremendous enthusiasm from those attending the show. Later, Commodore developed two popular and inexpensive computers, the VIC 20 and Commodore 64 microcomputers. Commodore's product line has expanded to include the Amiga and the Commodore 128 Personal Computer.

Today, Jack Tramiel is the chairman of the board of Atari. His philosophy—to provide more sophisticated technology for home computer users—is culminating in the introduction of the ST line of computers, the eight-bit Atari EX microcomputer, and a portable computer, the Atari XEP.

Meanwhile, the chairman of Tandy Corporation, John Roach, was busy persuading Tandy president Charles Tandy to manufacture a microcomputer and market it through Radio Shack stores. Roach's marketing sense led him to believe that the distribution potential of Radio Shack stores would help make Tandy's computer a success. He was right. Radio Shack offered the first opportunity for a consumer to walk into a retail store and purchase a low-priced personal computer. The TRS-80 Model I used the Zilog Z-80 microprocessor. The TRS-80 microcomputer Models I, II, III, and 4, the portable TRS 200, and the advanced TRS 2000 have made Radio Shack and Tandy Corporation a driving force in the microcomputer industry.

Industry giant IBM entered the microcomputer race in 1981 under the leadership of chief executive officer John Opel. The IBM Personal Computer (PC), developed under the direction of the late Philip D. Estridge, quickly became the standard in small business computers. IBM's reputation as a producer of high-quality business products quickly helped boost the sales of the PC. The IBM PC uses the Intel 8086 microprocessor, which can manipulate sixteen bits of data at a time. The success of the IBM PC prompted other microcomputer manufacturers to develop sixteen-bit computers. IBM then introduced the IBM PC jr and the more advanced IBM PC XT and IBM PC AT (see Figure 8–4).

Since 1974, more than 150 companies have introduced microcomputers. Some, such as DEC, Wang, Hewlett-Packard, and NCR, were already established manufacturers of larger computer systems. Others were new companies attempting to capture a share of the booming new industry. Not all the companies were successful. A number, among them Osborne Computer, Texas Instruments, and Timex Sinclair, were forced either to abandon their efforts or to regroup.

The shakeout of microcomputer companies is not over, and the market for microcomputers is still growing, although at a slower rate than it did in the early 1980s. Prices of microcomputers should continue to decline while more and more capabilities are added. Two factors affecting the microcomputer market are more powerful microprocessors and better manufacturing methods.

Today, sixteen-bit and thirty-two-bit microprocessors are common in microcomputers. So far, the most powerful microprocessor is the sixty-four-bit microprocessor developed by Control Data Corporation. This chip has not yet been implemented in any commercial microcomputers.

Microprocessors are being used for controlling the functions of many devices other than microcomputers. They are commonly found in microwave ovens, calculators, typewriters, sewing machines, vending machines, traffic lights, and gas pumps. Current-model cars have microprocessors that control the ignition system, the flow and mix of gasoline, and the timing of sparks.

● FIGURE 8–4
IBM PC.

Early Microcomputers and Their Microprocessors

MICRO-COMPUTER	YEAR INTRODUCED	MANUFACTURER	MICRO-PROCESSOR
Altair 8800	1974	MITS	Intel 8080
Apple II	1976	Apple Computer	MOS 6502
PET	1977	Commodore	MOS 6502
TRS-80 Model I	1977	Tandy Corporation	Zilog Z-80
IBM PC	1981	IBM	Intel 8086

THE MACHINES THEMSELVES

Most microcomputers today are desktop models (see Figure 8–5). They are small enough to place on a desk, but too large to carry around easily. A fairly versatile system includes the computer, a keyboard for input, a disk drive or two as storage devices, and a monitor and a printer for output. Other peripheral devices can be added to most systems.

Inside the computer itself is a main system board, often called the motherboard, that holds the microprocessor, other circuits, and memory chips (see Figure 8–6). The system board may contain slots for plugging in cards that expand the capabilities of the computer. For example, you can insert cards for adding memory, changing the number of characters

● **FIGURE 8–5**
Desktop computers fit on the surface of work spaces but are too large to be carried around comfortably.

per line that appear on the monitor, or using printers, modems, voice recognition units, music synthesizers, and bar code readers (see Figure 8–7). Of course, there is a limit to the number of cards that can be added at once.

"Closed systems"—which cannot be easily opened for access to the system board—have ports used for plugging in peripherals (see Figure 8–8). A port may be designed for serial communication, in which the bits are transferred one at a time much as people pass through a turnstile, or parallel communication, in which the bits are transferred eight at a time much as cars drive down an eight-lane expressway.

● FIGURE 8–7
Add-on Card.

Cables for telephone connections and printers require serial ports, but parallel ports are also used for communicating with some printers.

Although most computers are desktop models, there are three other major groups of microcomputers: portables, transportables, and super-microcomputers.

Portables and Transportables

The smallest microcomputers available are **portables.** Portables are light enough to be carried and do not need an external source of power. They are powered by either rechargeable or replaceable batteries. Portables usually need some form of direct-access mass storage medium, such as floppy disks.

Portables can be divided further by size into briefcase, notebook, and hand-held. The Hewlett-Packard 110 is a briefcase computer noted for being much faster than other portables (see Figure 8-9). Radio Shack's Model 100 and Model 200 are notebook computers used mostly for word processing (see Figure 8-10).

Portables should be distinguished from another class of small microcomputers, the **transportables.** Transportables are generally larger than portables but are still small enough to be carried. They differ from portables by requiring an external power source. Even though it weighs only 7½ pounds, the Apple IIc is a transportable because it does not contain its own power source (see Figure 8-11).

Some portables are capable of performance almost equal to that of small desktop microcomputers, and their prices reflect it, from around

● **FIGURE 8–9**
Hewlett-Packard 110 Portable Computer.
This computer can fit into a briefcase, which makes carrying it on business trips easy.

$3,000 to $5,000. Other portables are dedicated to certain functions and carry a much lower price tag, between $800 and $2,000.

Each portable has different features, so users must evaluate their particular needs before selecting a portable. Some useful features include built-in modems and telecommunications software for transmitting and receiving data by telephone. Some portables have ports for connecting floppy disk drives, cassette recorders, or bar code readers. Most portables have built-in software such as a word processor, spreadsheet, or data-

● **FIGURE 8–10**
Radio Shack Model 100 Portable Computer.
This lower-priced portable is used mostly for special functions such as word processing.

● **FIGURE 8–11**
Apple IIc.
The Apple IIc is a transportable micro-
computer that requires an external
power source and a separate display.
It weighs only 7½ pounds.

base manager (see the section on software later in this chapter). Built-in
programming languages such as BASIC are also included with some
portable computers.

Three technologies are responsible for the sophistication of portables:
(1) microprocessors give portables the power of some full-sized computers
in a single chip. (2) Flat display panels allow portables to be slim and
therefore easy to carry. (3) Finally, battery power frees portables from
dependency on external power sources.

Portables have been found to be especially useful for reporters, businesspeople, and students. For example, a salesperson might use a portable to compose reports that are sent to the main office via telephone
lines. Journalists use portables in similar ways. A reporter can cover a
presidential news conference two thousand miles from the newspaper's
headquarters, write the story using a word processor and a portable
computer, and use a modem to send the finished product over telephone
lines to the editor's desk. Students carry briefcase or notebook computers
to classes and type notes into the computers from lectures. The typed
notes are easy to decipher and hard copies can be printed out for studying
at a later time.

Supermicrocomputers

Some microcomputers are so powerful that they can compete with low-
end minicomputers. These **supermicrocomputers** are usually built around
powerful thirty-two-bit microprocessors (see Figure 8–12). Because microprocessors are very inexpensive compared to the CPUs of minicomputers, supermicrocomputers offer a significant price edge over minicomputers. The low cost of microprocessors also makes it possible to build
supermicrocomputers with several microprocessors, each dedicated to a
particular task. For example, individual microprocessors can be dedicated to each user workstation, disk drive, or printer.

Supermicrocomputers must be able to store large amounts of data. Hard disks can store much more data than the traditional floppy disks used with microcomputers. Fortunately, the prices of hard disk drives are falling, making them ideal storage devices for supermicrocomputers.

One problem hindering full-scale implementation of supermicrocomputers is the limited amount of available software. But as they gain in popularity, there will be more interest in developing software for these machines just as a great deal of software was developed for traditional microcomputers.

Another problem is the loyalty of minicomputer users to their machines. Many users are skeptical of the power a supermicrocomputer has and would not readily choose a supermicrocomputer over a minicomputer system. Time will remedy this problem as the power of the small super-machines increases and as more uses are found for them. In fact, the minicomputer market is already weakening as more customers upgrade their systems by linking microcomputers to existing minicomputers or mainframes. Several developments, including lower prices, networking capabilities, better software packages, and increased storage capacity, help explain the market's preference for microcomputers in the mid- to late 1980s.

● Understanding The Microchips

Earlier we stated that a computer's power is derived from its speed and memory and the accuracy of electronic circuits. This section explains two of those factors, speed and memory, as related to microprocessors. It also

CONCEPT
SUMMARY 8–2
Microcomputer Sizes

DESKTOP MODELS	PORTABLES	TRANSPORTABLES	SUPER-MICROCOMPUTERS
Small enough to put on a desk	Small enough to be called briefcase, notebook, and hand-held computers	Require external power source	Overlap power of minicomputers
Large and bulky to carry		Easy to carry	Hold large amounts of data

discusses the software that integrates the workings of a microcomputer's circuitry.

THE MICROPROCESSOR'S SPEED

The power behind a microcomputer comes from the microprocessor, a silicon chip only fractions of an inch wide. Microprocessors can be categorized by their speed and the amount of primary storage they can directly access. The speed with which the microprocessor can execute instructions affects the speed of the microcomputer. Speed depends on two factors: word size and clock speed.

Word size is the number of bits that can be manipulated at one time. An eight-bit microprocessor, for example, can manipulate eight bits, or one byte, of data at a time. A sixteen-bit microprocessor can handle sixteen bits—two eight-bit bytes of data—at a time. Therefore, a sixteen-bit microprocessor can manipulate twice as much data as an eight-bit microprocessor in approximately the same amount of time. This does not mean, however, that there is a direct relationship between word size and speed. A sixteen-bit microprocessor is not necessarily twice as fast as an eight-bit microprocessor. It may be more than twice as fast in performing some operations but less than twice as fast in performing others. Generally, though, a sixty-four-bit microprocessor is faster than a thirty-two-bit microprocessor and the thirty-two-bit microprocessor is faster than either a sixteen-bit or an eight-bit microprocessor.

Regardless of the advances in microcomputer technology, many eight-bit machines will still be used. Applications and operating systems (see section on operating systems below) for eight-bit systems are proven, and most users do not require a lot of speed. In addition, eight-bit machines are cheaper. The sixteen- and thirty-two-bit microprocessors are more appropriate for business users for two reasons. First, in business, several users may use the same software and data in a system of linked microcomputers. Second, business users often work on several programs at one time and need increased primary memory, which can be handled by the sixteen- and thirty-two-bit microprocessors.

The **clock speed** of a microprocessor is the number of electronic pulses the chip can produce each second. Clock speed is built into a microprocessor and is measured in **megahertz (MHz).** *Mega* means million and *hertz* means times per second; one megahertz is one million times per second. The electronic pulses affect the speed with which program instructions are executed because instructions are executed at predetermined intervals, which are timed by the electronic pulses. To illustrate this concept, assume that one instruction is executed every 100 pulses. A 4 MHz microprocessor, then, could process 40,000 instructions per second (4 million pulses divided by 100 pulses). An 8 MHz microprocessor could process 80,000 instructions, or twice as many as a 4 MHz microprocessor. Thus, the more pulses produced per second, the faster the instructions can be executed. Most microcomputers have clock speeds ranging between 2 MHz and 8 MHz.

The amount of data that can be directly accessed in primary storage also affects the speed with which instructions can be executed. Each microprocessor can directly access only a certain amount of data in primary storage. This means that the microprocessor can manipulate a certain number of bytes of data without switching from primary storage to a supplementary storage bank. (A supplementary storage bank is part of primary storage and should not be confused with secondary storage such as floppy disks.) Typically, an eight-bit microprocessor can directly access 64K bytes of data and a sixteen-bit microprocessor can directly access 256K.

PRIMARY MEMORY

Primary memory is important in microcomputer speed because the more data directly accessible by the CPU, the faster the machine. In addition, the computer can use more complex programs. Primary memory consists of thousands of on/off devices. Each holds one bit. Common types of primary memory are RAM and ROM.

RAM

The primary storage that holds the data and programs for immediate processing is a form of semiconductor memory called random-access memory (RAM). RAM is the working area of the computer. Since RAM is volatile or nonpermanent, data or programs will be erased when the electric power to a computer is turned off or disrupted in some other way. When any changes or results are to be saved, they must be saved on an external form of storage; on magnetic disks or tapes, for example.

The size of RAM memory is stated in bytes. The most common sizes in microcomputers are 64K (kilobytes), 128K, 256K, and 512K. The sizes are related to the word sizes of microprocessors in that microcomputers with smaller word sizes can handle directly only a small amount of RAM. As the word size increases, so does the amount of RAM that can be handled. Just as sixteen-bit and thirty-two-bit microcomputers are appropriate for business uses, so are 256K and 512K RAMs appropriate for holding the increased data and programs that a business user needs to access.

ROM

When functions are built into the hardware of a microcomputer, they are placed in read-only memory (ROM). Read-only memory instructions cannot be changed or deleted by other stored-program instructions. Since ROM is permanent, it cannot be occupied by instructions or data read from a disk or tape. The various versions of ROM—PROM, EPROM, and EEPROM—are available for microcomputers. See Chapter 2 for a complete discussion of these chips.

RAM Disks

Accessing data on disks is a relatively slow process compared to the speed at which a microprocessor can manipulate data. Random-access memory (RAM) disks are currently the only type of storage device that can approximate the speed of a microprocessor. A RAM disk is an add-on card that contains RAM chips. It plugs into the computer in the same slot as the disk drive card, and is indistinguishable from a disk drive to the computer. A RAM disk functions like a storage diskette, but is not actually a separate physical disk. It is simply storage space in RAM that has been given the job of functioning like a disk. A typical RAM disk used with a microcomputer adds 256K to 512K of storage and has a retrieval rate fifty times faster than a floppy disk.

THE INSTRUCTION SET

Instructions are designed into a microcomputer's circuitry for performing the arithmetic and logic operations and storage and retrieval functions. These instructions are called the **instruction set.** The number of instructions in a set is often quite limited, ranging from 100 to 300. By manipulating the instruction set, programmers produce software that harnesses the computer's power in order to achieve the desired results.

Instruction sets approaching 300 instructions on thirty-two-bit microprocessors occupy a lot of space on the chip, leaving less room for other components and slowing processing speeds. A new development, the Reduced Instruction Set Computer (RISC), does fewer things in hardware and shifts more functions to the operating systems and application software. The implementation of RISC is still controversial, because the benefits of using RISC do not yet justify the costs. Even though RISC may not be widely used, it will encourage the more efficient use of space on microprocessors. Companies trying the RISC chips are Hewlett-Packard and IBM.

OPERATING SYSTEMS

An operating system is a collection of programs used by the computer to manage its operation and provide an interface between the user or application program and the computer hardware. A number of operating systems have been designed for use with microcomputers.

Most operating systems are loaded into a computer's RAM from floppy disks, a process called **booting.** The word *boot* derives from the expression "to lift yourself up by your own bootstraps," which is essentially what a computer does. In order to read and write data on a disk, the disk operating system must be in memory. The disk operating system, however, is kept on the disk. Therefore, it seems impossible for the computer to load its operating system when it must have the operating system in memory in order to read from a disk. In actuality, the computer already has a small program built into ROM that starts the process of reading the operating system code from a disk. Some systems require you to turn on the computer before inserting the operating system diskette; others require you to insert the diskette into the disk drive first. Care should be taken that the proper procedure is followed for the computer you are using so that operating system code will not be lost or scrambled.

Another word commonly used in discussing operating systems is the term *transparent*. The more transparent an operating system, the less the user needs to concern himself or herself with it and the less the operating system is noticed. Among the most transparent operating systems today is the Macintosh Finder. While a transparent operating system may be less confusing than other operating systems, it may offer less flexibility in customizing a computer system.

Several popular operating systems including the Macintosh Finder are discussed in the following sections.

CP/M

The first operating system developed for use with microcomputers was Digital Research's CP/M (Control Program for Microprocessors). CP/M was stored on a floppy disk so that it could be loaded into any microcomputer, provided the computer used the Intel 8080 or 8085 or the Zilog Z-80 eight-bit microprocessor. Microcomputer manufacturers could license CP/M from Digital Research. This was less expensive than developing their own operating systems.

CP/M became very popular and much software was written to be used with it. Consequently, many computer manufacturers adapted their machines for CP/M. Today, most machines using an eight-bit microprocessor are capable of running software under CP/M. These include Kaypro, the Apple II series, Radio Shack Model III and 4, Osborne, and Commodore 64.

CP/M was originally written for programmers and is not easy for a beginner to use. The user must know how the computer functions. Still, CP/M is very powerful and about 15,000 application programs have been written for it.

MS-DOS

Microsoft introduced its operating system, called MS-DOS, for sixteen-bit microprocessors in 1981, and licensed it to IBM to be used in the IBM PC. MS-DOS (also called PC-DOS) quickly became the most popular sixteen-bit operating system as IBM PC sales increased. More than 100 different computers use MS-DOS, and many application programs have been written to run on it. MS-DOS is designed to run on the Intel 8088 and 8086 sixteen-bit microprocessors and subsequent updates of those, such as the 80286.

MS-DOS is similar to CP/M with many of the same commands. Like CP/M, MS-DOS requires the user to have knowledge of the computer itself, making it difficult for a beginner to use. MS-DOS has many improvements over CP/M, however. For example, files stored on disk can be found much more quickly. MS-DOS can be adapted for different disks or other hardware the user wants to add.

Apple DOS and Apple ProDOS

Because the first Apple computer used the MOS 6502 microprocessor, CP/M could not be used as the operating system. In 1978, Apple developed the Apple DOS for its computers. Apple DOS is a simple operating system designed to be used by nonprofessional computer users; in other words, it is a transparent system. It is easy to learn and easy to use. Unfortunately, Apple DOS's simplicity does have some disadvantages. It has limited utilities compared to CP/M and MS-DOS and does not work well when using more than two floppy disks. Apple DOS allows its directory to fill only two screens. If many short files are created, the directory fills up before disk space does.

ProDOS is an updated version of Apple DOS that overcomes some of its problems. ProDOS can handle more files in disk storage and provides a better directory system. It also provides faster disk access.

These two systems will remain popular as long as Apple computers are sold, for thousands of application programs have been developed for them.

Unix

Unix is an operating system that Bell Laboratories developed for minicomputers in the late 1960s. It was first implemented on a microcomputer in 1978. Unix may become the industry standard over CP/M and MS-DOS because it was not designed for a specific microprocessor and it is written in a high-level language called C. It can be run on microcomputers, minicomputers, and mainframes and can be easily adapted for a new computer. This adaptability is important because of the significant number of new computers and microprocessors introduced each year.

Unix lets the user perform several tasks at one time from the same terminal. It also can handle multiple users tied to the same computer directly or via telephone lines. Unlike the other popular operating systems, its file structure allows files to be manipulated in many ways, and it has more than 200 utility programs. Unix is available on many computers and is preferred by many programmers.

Unix, too, has some disadvantages. There are many versions of the system, and they are not all compatible. Also, most application programs written for Unix are for scientific or engineering tasks. There are few application programs written for home users.

Other Operating Systems

Pick, an operating system similar to Unix in the number of utilities and features it offers, is a powerful system designed especially for business environments. Although Pick is powerful and has complex capabilities, it is simple to learn and easy to use. The user needs no extensive knowledge of how the computer works. But Pick is difficult to maintain and few people have experience with it.

A simple, uncomplicated operating system designed for home and small business use is TRS-DOS (Tandy/Radio Shack Disk Operating System). It is used with Radio Shack TRS-80 Models I, II, III, and 4. (Other Tandy/Radio Shack computers such as the TRS-80 Models 1000, 1200, and 2000 use MS-DOS. The Model 6000 uses a Microsoft version of Unix, the Xenix.) There are many good application programs written for TRS-DOS. The Model 4 was made to be CP/M-compatible, which may indicate the phasing out of TRS-DOS.

One operating system that has little in common with the operating systems discussed earlier is Apple's advanced operating system. The system is both complex and easy to use. It is a very transparent operating system. Instead of memorizing system commands, a user points to **icons** and pull-down menus on the screen with the help of a mouse (see Figure 8–13). An icon is a picture representation or graphic image that appears on the computer screen. Icons represent commands or menu choices. On the Apple Macintosh, for example, an icon of a trash can is used with the mouse to delete a file instead of a delete command.

Apple introduced the advanced operating system in 1983 in the Lisa microcomputer, which used the Motorola 68000 microprocessor. Lisa's operating system was easy to use, but it was slow and too expensive to sell well. Apple discontinued the computer in 1984 but tried the operating system, called the Finder, again in the Macintosh. The Macintosh has met with more success than Lisa, but lack of application software hurt sales when the Macintosh was first introduced. Apple has copyrighted the system, so there will be no compatible operating systems in the near future.

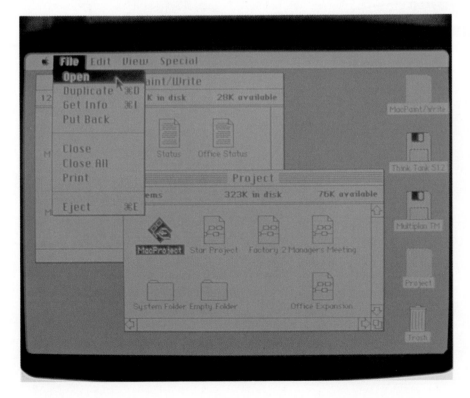

● **FIGURE 8–13**
The icons (graphic images) on the screen are used with a mouse to enter commands on the Macintosh. Icons and pull-down menus make the Macintosh one of the most user-friendly microcomputers on the market.

⊙ Enhancing Everyday Life

As encountered in our personal lives, computers help make everyday tasks easier. They have revolutionized everything from the way we bank and shop to the way we receive information. In only a few short years, microcomputers, due to their small size and relatively low price, have become almost as common in American households as televisions or stereos. Still, the number of uses for computers grows daily and is limited only by the imagination of the people who use them.

Some new cars are equipped with an electronic instrument panel that displays the car's precise speed and warns the driver of engine problems. Another new feature is the electronic navigation system. Pressing a button calls up a map that pinpoints the car's location—a much easier process than pulling a cumbersome map from the glove compartment.

The Shopping Machine store, located in the Park Center, Lancaster, PA, enables consumers to compare price and product information, as well as purchase merchandise at savings of up to 40%.

Thousands of wagers per minute, generated by the New Jersey Lottery System, are handled by Perkin-Elmer multi-processing computers.

Today, home computers support many applications such as word processing, financial planning, and data management. Sales representatives, consultants, freelance artists, and other independent businesspersons find microcomputers to be particularly useful for calculating expenses, preparing income statements, and storing client customer files.

CONCEPT
SUMMARY 8-3

Operating Systems

OPERATING SYSTEM	MANUFACTURER	COMPARISONS
CP/M	Digital Research	First developed for microcomputers Popular; much software written to be used with it Not easy for beginners to use
MS-DOS	Microsoft	First licensed for use on IBM PC Quickly became most popular 16-bit operating system Not easy for beginners to use
Apple DOS	Apple Computer	Designed to be used by nonprofessional computer users Easy to learn and easy to use Limited utilities and file usage Apple ProDOS overcomes some problems
Unix	Bell Laboratories	First used on minicomputers Can be easily adapted for a different computer Handles multiple users Handles several tasks from one terminal Many utility programs Not all versions are compatible Few applications for home users

COMPATIBILITY

When a microcomputer does not perform a desired task, the owner may solve the problem by adding peripheral equipment to the system, such as disk drives, color monitors, printers, and modems. Internal circuitry can even be added to expand the memory, increase the speed, or change the text windows of most computers. It is not always necessary to choose peripherals from the manufacturer of the microcomputer. Another manufacturer's equipment may have the same or better capabilities at a better price. The peripherals do have to be **compatible,** however. The word *compatible* describes the ability to use one manufacturer's equipment or software with another manufacturer's equipment.

Software also must be compatible. Programs designed for one operating system cannot be used on computers with different operating systems. Compatibility in software includes the ability to read and write data on the same diskette and to use common data files.

Compatibility can be extended by adding a **coprocessor** to a computer. The coprocessor makes the computer compatible with another operating system. It is a microprocessor that can be plugged into the original computer to replace or work with the original microprocessor. It allows software written for its operating system to be run on a machine that could not run the software otherwise.

● COMPUTERS AND INFORMATION PROCESSING

The coprocessor usually comes on a plug-in board or card along with other chips necessary for it to run. For example, adding a Z-80 board to the main system board will make an Apple IIe compatible with the CP/M operating system. The original microprocessor and the coprocessor share the computer's disk drives, keyboard, and other peripherals.

● Using Microcomputers

Microcomputers are general-purpose machines; that is, they are designed to perform a variety of tasks. The people who buy and use microcomputers are a diverse group—businesspeople, teachers, students, doctors, lawyers, and farmers—and their computing needs are just as diverse. They may need different types of peripheral equipment. They may need various types of services, such as information services and users groups. The following section describes some of the many options available for microcomputers.

PERIPHERALS

Certain peripheral devices work especially well in a microcomputer environment despite some limitations. The first limitation is cost; users of small systems often have limited budgets. The second limitation is ease of use. The devices must be easy to use because microcomputer users are generally not experienced programmers. Business users in particular may find it easier to pick up a telephone to locate information essential in making decisions if the microcomputer and its peripherals are difficult to use.

Input Devices

The increased use of microcomputers has promoted the popularity of a variety of input and output devices, many of which have become essential for easy use of the microcomputers.

The most common, in fact indispensable, input device is the keyboard. Most computer keyboards resemble typewriter keyboards in the layout of keys for letters, numbers, and symbols. They also include computer-specific keys such as control keys, arrow keys, and function keys. Typing combinations of these keys sends commands to the CPU for performing specific tasks, such as moving the **cursor,** printing a document, inserting a sentence, or removing some numerical data. (The cursor is a character on a computer display screen that shows where the next typed character will appear). A frequent addition to a keyboard is a numeric keypad, which enables the user to enter numbers in a manner similar to using an adding machine (see Figure 8–14).

Keyboard entry may be too slow or inconvenient for some applications. Other devices allow the user to bypass the keyboard in moving the cursor and in entering data or commands. They include joysticks, game paddles, the mouse, graphics tablets, and light pens.

Joysticks and **game paddles** are input devices generally used with game applications. Both devices are used for positioning the cursor or

● **FIGURE 8–14**
Numeric Keypad.

other symbol on the monitor screen. Game paddles are used for positioning a figure that moves vertically or horizontally on the monitor screen for a particular video game (see Figure 8–15). The joystick may be used for applications other than games, primarily graphics packages for creating on-screen art (see Figure 8–16).

The **mouse** is a hand-movable input device about the size of a Jell-O box that controls the position of the cursor on the screen. On the bottom is a small ball like a roller bearing. On top is a pushbutton or two for activating a command. When the mouse is rolled across a flat surface, it sends electronic signals through an input cord to the computer and the cursor moves accordingly. Using the mouse eliminates a considerable amount of typing (see Figure 8–17).

Graphics tablets are flat, boardlike surfaces directly connected to the microcomputer screen (see Figure 8–18). The user draws on the tablet

● **FIGURE 8–15**
Game paddles.

● **FIGURE 8–16**
Joysticks.

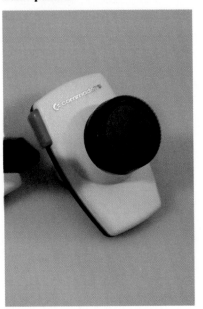

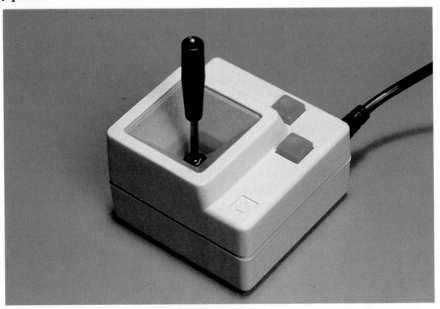

● **COMPUTERS AND INFORMATION PROCESSING**

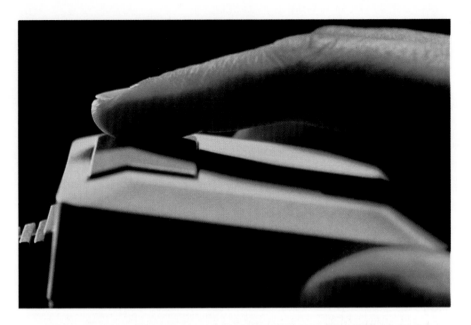

Some microcomputers allow the user to bypass the keyboard by using a mouse to enter data. The mouse is similar also to a track ball: in the mouse, the roller is on the underneath surface of the device and in the track ball, the roller is on the upper surface. The user rolls the mouse around on the desk and a cursor on the screen moves according to the movements of the mouse. A click of the button on the mouse commands the computer.

using a pencil-like device and the image is transmitted to the screen. Graphics tablets enable the user to employ colors, textures, and patterns when creating images.

A **light pen** is a pen-shaped object with a light-sensitive cell at its end. Users can select from a list of choices displayed on the screen by touching a light pen to the proper item. Light pens may also be used in highly technical fields for altering graphs and other drawings.

Other input devices once used with minicomputers and mainframes are being adapted for use with microcomputers. They include the voice input devices and scanning equipment discussed in Chapter 7.

Output Devices

The most common output device is the monitor. Monitors allow users to view information before sending it to the microprocessor for processing, as well as to view information sent from the microprocessor. The information displayed on the monitor can be in either character or graphic form.

A monitor can be considered one of the essential peripherals of a microcomputer system; without one, a microcomputer is almost useless. Many computers, such as the Macintosh and AT&T Unix PC, simply incorporate a monitor. Others, such as the Compaq portable and Apple IIe, arrive with the needed circuitry for plugging in monitors—that is, they are video-ready. However, an unadorned IBM PC contains no display circuitry. A display card must be added for either text-only or text and color graphics. This display card is often part of the hardware package included in the purchase of an IBM PC.

Monitors are generally divided into three categories: (1) monochrome, (2) composite color, and (3) RGB (red-green-blue). **Monochrome monitors** display a single color, such as white, green, or amber, against a black background. They display text clearly and are inexpensive, ranging from

● FIGURE 8–18
Graphics Tablet.
Macintizer allows the user to enter data by writing on a flat pad that transfers impulses of the movements of the writing to the proper positions on the screen.

$100 to $300. Most monochrome monitors are composite monitors, so called for their single video signal. They usually require no additional video circuitry in the computer.

Composite color monitors display a composite of colors received in a single video signal and are slightly more expensive than monochrome monitors (see Figure 8–19). They do deliver less clarity in displaying text, however, than monochrome monitors. In fact, on some, text is almost unreadable in the eighty-column form. Images on a composite color monitor are also less crisp than images on RGB monitors.

RGB monitors receive three separate color signals, one for each of three colors, red, green, and blue. Commonly used for high-quality graphics displays, they display sharper images than the composite color monitors, but produce fuzzier text than monochrome monitors. They are more expensive than composite color monitors, generally from $500 to $900. An add-on display card is necessary for using RGB monitors with most computers.

Also available are RF modulators for driving television sets, although television sets deliver less resolution than any of the other types of monitors.

Flat panel displays are available for portable computers. They are less bulky and require less power than the cathode ray tubes used in most monitors. They also show the image less clearly; looking at a flat panel display from an angle or in direct lighting makes the image faint or even invisible. Two common types of flat panel displays are liquid crystal display (LCD) and electroluminescence. LCDs generally show poor contrast and visibility, although new technology is improving the LCD dis-

● **FIGURE 8–19**
RGB Color Monitor.

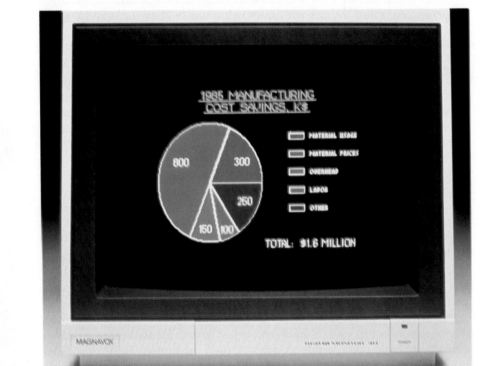

● COMPUTERS AND INFORMATION PROCESSING

play. The electroluminescent panel shows a better display and a wider viewing angle, but also costs more than the LCD. In the future, it is expected that electroluminescent panels will show full color and high-contrast designs that make the displays readable even in sunlight.

Common output devices for microcomputers besides monitors are printers and plotters, discussed in greater detail in Chapter 3. Both impact and nonimpact printers are used with microcomputers. Dot-matrix printers are usually used for rough drafts or cases when the quality of the print is not an important factor. Some dot-matrix printers produce more dots per letter and are used for good-quality textual output as well as for printing graphics such as bar graphs, varying sizes and fonts of type, and logos. Letter-quality printers, such as the daisy wheel or laser printers, are used when output must have the quality of typewritten pages.

Online Storage

The storage media commonly used with microcomputers are cartridge tapes, cassette tapes, and floppy disks. They were discussed in Chapter 6, but their features are reviewed here with respect to microcomputers. The tapes and disks are inexpensive and small, which makes them ideal for microcomputer data storage. They are not suitable for storing large amounts of data, however. Hard disks are more expensive than floppy disks, but they can hold more than ten times more data.

Cartridge tapes are best suited for storing short programs and data files. They allow only sequential access of data, which is very slow. The main advantage of cartridge tapes is their low cost. They are accessed by a tape drive.

Cassette tapes are popular with microcomputer users because, in most instances, they can be used with a regular cassette player, and they are easy to store. They are also inexpensive. Like cartridge tapes, data access with cassette tapes is sequential and very slow.

Floppy disks offer direct access of data, which makes them much faster than cassette tape. The disks come in three sizes and are reusable, lightweight, easy to store, and safe to mail. They are accessed by disk drives, which may be built into the computer or be separate units attached to the computer. A 5¼-inch floppy disk can hold as much as 1.2 Mb (megabytes) of data.

● **FIGURE 8–20**
Hard Disk Unit

Hard magnetic disks hold more data than cassette tapes and floppy disks (see Figure 8–20). Common capacities are from 5 Mb to 80 Mb, although some very expensive hard disks for special purposes hold more than 400 Mb. Data access is also faster with hard disks than with floppy disks. Actually, hard disks act more like RAM than secondary storage.

There are two varieties of hard disks: fixed and removable. A fixed disk is a sealed unit the user cannot open and is better protected from dust and other environmental factors. Often the disk drive unit comes installed in the computer. It may contain one or more polished aluminum platters covered with a high-quality magnetic coating. Fixed disks are reliable and hold a large amount of data. A removable disk allows the user to change disks. The disk is enclosed in a cartridge, which is simply inserted in the hard disk drive. This feature provides security because the disks can be removed and locked away from the computer. Remov-

A Twinkling of an Eye

With all the wonderful microcomputer equipment available for today's businesspeople, who's watching out for people who are disabled? Many disabled people cannot move their fingers to type on a keyboard or use their eyes to see the computer keyboard or read the printouts. Well, keyboard and printer, make way for the new electronic gadgets.

New sensing devices allow paraplegics and victims of stroke, muscular dystrophy, and cerebral palsy to control a computer by twitching a cheek or blinking an eye. The sensing device sends electrical signals generated by the body to the computer in order to perform a given task.

Voice synthesis makes it possible for a computer to talk to a person, and the person can likewise give oral commands to a computer. Optical scanners give computers the ability to read printed text and produce output in braille.

Perhaps the most famous of these machines is the Kurzweil Reading Machine (KRM) marketed by Kurzweil Computer Products, Cambridge, Massachusetts. The KRM merges optical scanning, microcomputers, and voice synthesis to read text out loud to the user. It also can print text in standard print, large print, or braille and can send output to other computers.

Combined with existing legal and economic incentives, the many new technologies are helping to open the workplace to the disabled. With computer technology, people who are confined to their homes can bring the workplace into their living rooms with a twinkling of an eye.

able disks are not as popular as fixed disks because most have less capacity than fixed disks. No matter what type of hard disk is used, a backup system such as floppy disks or tape is necessary.

Optical disks will change the way microcomputers are used in the future. With such tremendous storage capacity (550 Mb on a single 5¼-inch disk), they make possible a wide range of training and instructional capabilities for businesses. The great storage capacity of the optical disk makes it possible to store video images, which take up a great deal of storage space. Combined with computer data, the video images stored on one optical disk can provide instruction similar to that given in films, yet allow the user to interact through the computer rather than watch passively. Today's optical disks cannot be erased or recorded on, but that is expected to change by 1987 or 1988.

SOFTWARE PACKAGES

A **software package** is a set of standardized computer programs, procedures, and related documentation necessary for solving problems of a specific application. Many packages available for business use are discussed in the following sections and later in Chapter 13.

The Big Four

Software for business use often fills the needs of four basic tasks: doing word processing jobs, analyzing financial data, filing data, and producing pictures that summarize data.

Word processing software allows the user to handle text in four basic ways: writing, editing, formatting, and printing. What is written appears on a screen during the first three stages (the soft copy) and on paper during the printing process (the hard copy). During the writing and editing stages, text can be entered, moved, deleted, or searched. When text is formatted, it is designed for appearance on paper. Formatting may entail spacing between lines, setting margins, adding page numbers, underlining or boldfacing text, merging two or more documents, or centering headings. Printing may involve producing a rough draft or a final copy of the text on paper.

Electronic spreadsheets are used in preparing financial data for summaries (see Figure 8–21). Many are prepared like tables with data arranged in columns and rows. Each column and row has a heading. The user looks across the desired row and down the desired column in order to find the needed data. Some parts of the spreadsheet contain formulas using data from other parts of the spreadsheet. As the data is changed, the results of the calculations in the formulas change.

Data can be filed using data-management software. One type is the file handler, which copies traditional filing methods. Material is filed by category and data can appear in several files. The other type is the database manager, which allows entry of thousands of records that can be accessed in many types of ways.

Graphics software packages are designed for displaying data in chart form. Depending upon the hardware, the charts are displayed on the monitor screen or are printed using dot-matrix printers or plotters. Common charts drawn by graphics software are bar charts, line graphs, and pie charts.

Integrated Software

Integration suggests the blending of two or more parts into a whole. When the term *integration* is used in conjunction with software, it means that two or more types of software are blended into one application package. Integrated software generally conforms to three standards:

1. The software consists of what are usually separate application packages.
2. The software provides easy movement of data among the applications.
3. A common group of commands is used for all the applications in the package.

Integration may occur when several applications are combined into one, such as a data manager, spreadsheet, and graphics package, which can share data and pass data to another application. Integration can also occur when one type of software is enhanced. An example would be the addition of a spelling program, thesaurus, or grammar program to a word processing program.

Utilities and Other Functions

Software can be used for many other functions that a typical office employee or businessperson might encounter every day. Some software provides a calendar for entering appointments and business functions. Others set alarm clocks, dial telephone numbers, or act like calculators and notepads. Some programs provide the mechanism for writing outlines in preparation for a paper or presentation. Other programs check

Nosing Around in Other People's Business

Part of competition is knowing what the competition is doing. Traditionally, business professionals follow trends in their fields by reading the *Wall Street Journal*, *Barron's*, corporate annual reports, and other business journals. Another faster—and more effective—way to track the competition is available through information services. Information services are electronic libraries that contain just about any kind of information desired.

Information provided by these online data bases helps you assess another company's ability to defend or enlarge its market position. This information includes recognized business barometers such as cash flow, advertising budget, profits, revenues and market share, and corporate profiles that highlight a company's growth strategies, advertising approach, and market determination.

As many as 1,500 of the 2,900 online data bases worldwide provide business-related information. Much of this information is numerical and comes from the Securities and Exchange Commission (SEC) filings, quarterly and annual reports, analysts' reports, sales and earnings figures and forecasts, reports on market share and market trends, and stock and bond quotes. Information services that offer business data bases are ADP Data Services, CompuServe Information Service, Data Resources Inc., Dialog Information Services, Dow Jones News/Retrieval Service, Dun & Bradstreet Inc., In-Fact, Mead Data Central, Inc., SDC Information Services, Inc., The Source, and VU/TEXT Information Services, Inc.

spelling and grammar, offer alternate word choices, and allow you to program functions into one or two keys in order to save you time while typing.

TELECOMMUNICATIONS

Telecommunication is the electronic transmission of data from one location to another. Microcomputers can be hooked to telephones and modems so that data can be sent and received over telephone lines. The **modems** are necessary for transmitting computer signals over telephone lines that contain a different type of signal. Telecommunication is discussed fully in Chapter 9.

Telecommunication makes possible several new ways for using microcomputers.

Information Services

One advantage of owning a microcomputer is having the ability to keep up with the changing world without leaving the home, school, or office. **Information services,** also called commercial data bases, information utilities, or information networks, offer many types of general information to their subscribers.

Information services charge customers either a flat fee or a connect-time fee. Connect time refers to the actual time a customer is using the data base. If a customer does not use the data base at all one month, there is no charge. If a customer is being charged a flat fee, the monthly charge remains the same no matter how much or how little the customer uses the data base. Some services charge extra for use of particular data bases or services offered.

Customers of information services must also pay for any long-distance telephone charges, if a long-distance call is required to access the data base. Some telephone companies also charge an extra fee (separate from the long-distance charges) for customers who use modems.

Passwords are often used to ensure that only paying customers can access the service. Once connected to a data base, the user can access a variety of information including daily national and international news, sports news, gourmet recipes, foreign language drills, real estate information, and movie and book reviews. Businesspeople can access data about stock markets, money, and commodities. Popular information services are The Source, CompuServe, B.R.S., Dialog, and the Dow Jones/News Retrieval Service.

Electronic Bulletin Boards

Microcomputers can also be used to access **electronic bulletin boards,** which are operated by computer enthusiasts and can be accessed at little or no cost. Electronic bulletin boards are often set up for the users of a particular computer system, for example, the owners of Apple computers. Bulletin boards can be started by practically anyone who has a telephone, a microcomputer, a modem, and communications software. There are thousands of bulletin boards in operation in the United States. Of course, an electronic bulletin board will not contain as much information as an information service, but a well-constructed one can provide much information on specific topics. The value of a bulletin board increases as members contribute programs they have written to its library of programs. Users may need to contact the bulletin board operator (commonly called the system operator or sysop) before **downloading** or **uploading** a program from or to the bulletin board. The sysop may then assign the user a password that allows the program to be copied.

Some bulletin boards are set up for users with special interests rather than owners of particular computers. For example, there are bulletin boards for writers, lawyers, and pilots. Others have been created to help users research events or conduct informal polls on political issues.

Local Area Networks

Local area networks (LANs) link microcomputers in the same general area for the purpose of sharing information and hardware. Usually, the microcomputers are within a thousand feet of each other since they must be connected by a cable hookup.

Distributed Processing

An important development triggered by the use of microcomputers is the use of **distributed processing** (see Chapter 9). Microcomputers can be linked by communication lines so that processing can be done at different locations. The portability of microcomputers makes them ideal for distributed processing because they can be placed wherever users of the system are located.

Organizations that can benefit from distributed processing include manufacturing firms with factories located around the country, department stores with branches in different cities, and law firms with offices in many places. For example, plant managers at remote factories could handle inquiries and produce reports using microcomputers linked to the main corporate computer. Then plant managers and executives in other locations would have access to each factory's reports.

Distributed processing may change how an organization functions, especially if operating units in different locations do not have much interaction. At first, managers and executives might now know how to use the new information available to them and might be disturbed by top management's increased control over their units. If a distributed processing system is to be successful, users of the system will have to accept the changes that will occur.

USERS GROUPS

Where can a new microcomputer owner go for help in getting the machine to operate? When a $150 software package will not run on the machine, who can identify the problem? Which word-processing package priced under $200 works best on a certain microcomputer? Questions such as these often baffle the proud new owner of a microcomputer. One answer is a **users group.** A users group is a relatively informal group of owners of a particular microcomputer model or software package who exchange information about hardware, software, service, and support. Users groups may also form around applications and related topics, such as real estate, medicine, telecommunications, education, and computer-aided publishing.

The value of users groups comes from the accumulation of knowledge and experience ready to be shared by members. The best evaluation of hardware and software comes from one who has actually purchased and tried it. As software becomes more sophisticated and more hardware becomes available for enhancing microcomputers, users groups will become even more valuable.

Users groups may be beneficial to small companies because their internal computing experience is limited. Top management may join users groups to learn about new technology and how it can be used in maintaining a competitive position in a particular business field. Individual businesspeople may be interested in improving personal productivity.

Since users groups do not normally have telephones or office space, finding a local group is not always easy. However, dealers who sell microcomputers usually know how to contact users groups, and groups often post notices and flyers in computer stores. Information on national groups is sometimes included in the microcomputer package when it is sold. Contacting the manufacturer directly may also yield the name of the person to contact about a local group.

● Summary Points

● Microcomputers are the smallest and least expensive computers; they differ from minicomputers, mainframes, and supercomputers in capability, price, and size. The distinctions between microcomputers and larger systems are fading as microcomputers become more powerful.

● The increased power and miniaturization of microprocessors paved the way for the development of microcomputers.

● The first microprocessors could manipulate four bits of data at a time. Most microcomputers today can manipulate eight, sixteen, or thirty-two bits of data.

● Some early microcomputer pioneers include Ed Roberts of MITS, Stephen Wozniak and Steven Jobs of Apple, Jack Tramiel of Commodore Business Machines, John Roach of Tandy, and John Opel of IBM. Though their contributions vary, they all played important roles in making microcomputers available to the general public.

● Portable computers can be classified by size as briefcase, notebook, or hand-held. They are light enough to be carried and do not need an external power source. Transportables are larger than portables but are still light enough to be carried. They require an external power source.

- Supermicrocomputers are less expensive than minicomputers and provide users with high performance at a relatively low cost.
- The speed of microcomputers depends on word size and clock speed. Word size refers to the number of bits that can be manipulated at one time. Clock speed is the number of electronic pulses the microprocessor can produce each second.
- Primary memory consists of random-access memory (RAM) and read-only memory (ROM). A RAM disk is an add-on card that contains RAM chips and acts like a disk, providing speeds that approximate the microprocessor.
- Instructions for basic computer functions such as arithmetic and logic operations and storage and retrieval functions constitute the instruction set of the computer.
- An operating system is a collection of programs used by the computer to manage its operation and provide an interface between the user or application program and the computer hardware. Popular operating systems include CP/M, MS-DOS, Apple DOS, Apple ProDOS, and Unix. Since there is no single standard operating system for microcomputers, microcomputers with different operating systems are not compatible.
- Some input and output devices popular for use with microcomputers include joysticks, game paddles, the mouse, graphics tablets, light pens, printers, and plotters. Keyboards and monitors are among the essential peripherals for microcomputers.
- Cartridge tapes, cassette tapes, and floppy disks are the storage media commonly used with microcomputers. Hard magnetic disks are being used in some situations where large amounts of data must be stored. Optical disks are also becoming a popular storage medium for use with microcomputers, although they cannot yet be erased and reused.
- Popular software includes programs for word processing, electronic spreadsheets, data management, and graphics. Combinations of programs—such as a data manager, spreadsheet, and graphics package, or a word processor and spelling program—are called integrated software.
- Information services provide many types of information to microcomputer users.
- Electronic bulletin boards operated by sysops are generally set up for users of a particular computer system. The more people who contribute to the bulletin board, the more useful it becomes to users.
- Users groups offer owners advice and information from other microcomputer users about machines, programs, and topics of special interest such as electronic publishing or telecommunications.

● Review Questions

1. What differentiates microcomputers from larger computers?

2. Describe the development of the microprocessor and explain how it contributed to the development of the microcomputer.

3. Discuss why a closed system microcomputer might be less flexible than a system that you can open easily. Gain access to a microcomputer at home or at school and tell which type it is.

4. Differentiate between portables, supermicrocomputers, and the desktop models of microcomputers.

5. Explain how word size and clock speed affect the speed of a microcomputer.

6. Explain two words introduced in this chapter about operating systems: *booting* and *transparent*.

7. What is meant by microcomputer compatibility? What determines microcomputer compatibility?

8. Name some input devices that allow you to bypass the keyboard, reducing the amount of typing needed.

9. Name two disk technologies that allow greater computer capabilities than floppy disks. What is special about each?

10. How does a users group differ from an electronic bulletin board?

Apple

EARLY DEVELOPMENTS

When examining the growth and development of microcomputers, one name stands out from the rest—Apple. One reason Apple computers have distinguished themselves among other microcomputers is because they were one of the first small machines on the market. But in addition to its early entry in the field, Apple Computer Inc. developed a reputation for producing reliable, high-quality computing machines.

The origin of Apple computers is a story of ingenuity and risk taking. The company began in early 1976 when two young engineers collaborated on a small computing board for personal use. Steven P. Jobs, then aged twenty-one, and Stephen G. Wozniak, aged twenty-six, took six months to design a prototype and forty hours to build it. They soon had an order for fifty of their small machines.

With the first order in hand, the men raised about $1,350 by selling a used Volkswagen van and a programmable calculator. They set up shop in Jobs's garage and soon were doing well enough to form Apple Computer Company. Jobs was the business manager and Wozniak the engineer. There are many stories about why they choose the name "Apple." One of the better known is that an apple represents the simplicity that the men were trying to achieve in the design and use of their computers.

The first Apple computer was sold in kit form to electronics hobbyists. It was so successful that the demand for the kits soon outstripped the capacity of Jobs's garage and overtaxed their capital. Jobs and Wozniak believed their computer had great commercial and social value, so they dedicated themselves to finding the people and resources that would make their young company a success.

Their first recruit was A. C. "Mike" Markkula, Jr. Markkula, whom Jobs and Wozniak met through a mutual friend, was no stranger to the electronics business.

He had successfully managed marketing in two semiconductor companies that had experienced dynamic growth—Intel Corporation and Fairchild Semiconductor. Markkula's marketing background served Apple well. As the company grew, so did Markkula's importance; he acted for Apple in a number of different capacities, including president.

When Markkula joined the company, he worked closely with Jobs and Wozniak researching the microcomputer market and assessing Apple's chances of becoming an industry leader. The three men developed plans for acquiring the necessary capital, management expertise, technical innovation, software development, and marketing skills to make the company a leader. Initial financing to implement the plans came from Markkula and a group of venture capitalists that included Benrock Associates and Arthur Rock and Associates. Apple Computer, Inc. was incorporated on January 3, 1977.

Apple has grown from a two-man operation to an international corporation of more than 5,500 employees. The company remained a private corporation until December 1980, when it made an initial public offering of 4.6 million shares of common stock. In 1983, Apple became the youngest company to enter the ranks of the

Fortune 500 index of U.S. industrial corporations. Stephen Wozniak left the company to pursue academic and other interests in 1984. In 1985, Steven Jobs also left Apple to explore new interests.

APPLE TODAY

Since April 1983, Apple's growth has been directed by John Sculley, president and chief executive officer. Sculley, former president of Pepsi-Cola Co., has refined Apple's product line strategy and is beginning a transition period that it is hoped will make Apple a multiproduct, multibillion-dollar company.

Apple has two major product lines: The Apple® II family of computers, which includes the Apple® IIe, and the Apple® IIC; the Macintosh family of computers, which includes the Macintosh™ 128K, Macintosh™ 512K, and the Macintosh™ Plus. Apple also manufactures accessory products for these computers including printers, monitors, modems, and so on.

A manufacturing plant in Carrollton, Texas, produces the Apple II family for the United States market, and a facility in Cork, Ireland, serves the European market. The Macintosh product line is manufactured in Fremont, California, in one of the most highly automated manufacturing facilities in the nation. Peripherals for both product lines are manufactured in Garden Grove, California. In addition, Apple maintains a facility in Singapore for the production of logic boards used in its computers.

The Apple II family of products has become popular in homes and schools because of the enormous amount of software written for the machines. The Macintosh family, known for its sophisticated, high-resolution graphics and ease of use, is finding a market in small- and medium-sized businesses and on college campuses.

Because of their low cost, small size, and ease of use, microcomputers are being widely applied. Apple has helped define the microcomputer market by educating people about the potential of these machines and developing systems and software in direct response to customer needs. Apple was one of the first microcomputer companies to recognize the importance of product availability and fast, complete service. Today, the company has one of the most extensive microcomputer sales and service networks in the world. In slightly more than a decade, Apple has grown from a two-man operation in a garage in northern California to an international corporation.

DISCUSSION POINTS

1. What are the two major product lines manufactured by Apple today?
2. Why have the Apple II computers become so popular for use in homes and schools?

9

TELECOM-MUNICATIONS AND DISTRIBUTED COMPUTING

Steven Shapiro
Science Digest

All your life you've had to take tests: to be accepted into school, to remain there, to graduate and to get a job. How many times have you wondered whether the tests you've taken were truly accurate measures of your abilities? With the advent of computer adaptive testing, your curiosity may finally be put to rest.

Computer adaptive testing uses computer technology to tailor exams to a person's ability. Unlike pencil-and-paper tests, which generally ask all takers the same questions, computer adaptive tests choose new questions according to how well a test taker responded to previous ones. It is this homing in on each person's level of aptitude that distinguishes the testing, says David Weiss, a University of Minnesota psychology professor and one of the system's developers.

The testing software works with an item pool, a collection of questions that have been pretested, assigned a level of difficulty and ordered on a continuous scale from easiest to hardest. The test taker begins by answering the first question displayed on the monitor. If he answers correctly, the computer moves to a more difficult question. If he answers incorrectly, the computer chooses an easier question. This process continues until the examinee correctly answers questions consistently around a given level of difficulty, at which point the test is concluded and the computer tells the examinee how well he has done. For example, in one such test offered by the College Board, only about 17 questions out of a pool of 120 need be answered to establish an accurate final score of the examinee's aptitude. In this manner, the test quickly focuses on the test taker's ability. "It cuts testing time by about half," Weiss says.

The technology behind these features is not entirely new. Weiss and others have been developing the method since 1970. But with heightened concerns over the reliability and scope of exams such as the Scholastic Aptitude Test (SAT), computer adaptive testing is just now beginning to come on strong.

The Portland, Oregon, school district uses the MicroCAT software system produced by Assessment Systems Corporation of St. Paul, Minnesota. Ron Houser, a district official, has helped direct a pilot program for six schools. "The Assessment Systems program is extremely versatile and allows us to tailor tests to an individual school's needs," he says.

One of the school district's MicroCAT applications is as the graduation-standards test that all high school students must pass if they are to receive their diplomas, Houser says. If they don't pass the exam, the computer presents one or more subtests to help determine in what areas students are deficient.

On a grander scale, Educational Testing Service (ETS) in Princeton, New Jersey, which produces the SAT and other tests administered by the College Board, has begun a $30-million, 15-year program to create a number of advanced tests that use computer adaptive and other innovative testing methods.

According to William Ward, director of measurement technology research for the testing service, ETS and the College Board recently introduced their first computer adaptive system, which determines whether students just entering college are prepared for college-level courses or need more developmental work. "Because of the large scale of the SAT," he says, "lo-gistics, politics and legal reasons hinder implementing such testing for the SAT. But I fully expect it to come sooner or later."

Other organizations as well are making use of the technology. The armed forces are implementing a program to computerize the battery of tests they give recruits. And beginning in 1988, physicians across the nation will be taking licensing exams with the National Board of Medical Examiners' own approach to computerized testing: It presents simulations of illnesses or injuries, such as profuse bleeding, that the physician must correct with appropriate treatment.

But computer adaptive testing is not without its drawbacks and its critics. Large amounts of data are needed to create accurate item pools. Some educators contend that it discriminates by not asking everyone the same questions. And some fear that these tests will appear more objective than they really are.

Even with these concerns, the tests' accuracy, speed, simplicity of operation and flexibility may one day lead to the eclipse of older methods. Says Houser, "It's a real breakthrough in the way testing will take place in the future."

First appeared in SCIENCE DIGEST, a Hearst Publication.

● **Telecommunications equipment and software add flexibility to many tasks, allowing people to do work that otherwise would have to be done in an office, at home, or while traveling. Computerized testing combined with telecommunications technology might also mean that students cannot avoid taking tests by staying home from school anymore.**

● Introduction

Earlier chapters have presented information on both large and small computer systems. Discussions have focused on the physical components of computers (hardware, storage, input, and output) and on file organization and data design. This chapter focuses on data communications and how computer systems of all sizes are used in data communications.

Managing today's diverse businesses is a complex task, and management information needs extend beyond routine summary reports. A manager must have current knowledge of company operations in order to control business activities and to ensure that effective customer service is provided. Decisions must be made on short notice and on the basis of data gathered and analyzed from geographically remote locations. An efficient, fast way to capture, process, and distribute large amounts of data is needed. Data communication systems developed to meet this need help reduce delays in the collection and dissemination of data.

This chapter explains how communication systems allow users at remote locations to gain fast, easy access to computer resources. Included are discussions on the concepts and techniques involved in message transmission and the types of equipment that make data communication possible. Alternative methods of using communications technology to implement management information systems are also explored.

● Data Communications

Data communication is the electronic transmission of data from one location to another, usually over communication channels such as telephone or telegraph lines or microwaves. In a data communication system, data are transmitted between terminals and a central computer or between two or more computers. As people and equipment become geographically dispersed, the computer and input and output devices, or **terminals,** are hooked into a communication network. The communication network provides the means for the input and output devices to communicate with both themselves and the computer(s) tied into the network. The combined use of communication facilities, such as telephone systems, and data-processing equipment is called **telecommunication.**

Data communication using communication channels can take place between terminals that are in the same room or separated by an ocean. The difference between these two situations is the type of communication channel through which the data flows.

MESSAGE TRANSMISSION

Data can be transmitted over communication lines in one of two forms: analog or digital. Transmission of data in continuous wave form is referred to as **analog transmission.** An analog transmission can be compared to the waves created in a pan of still water by a stick. By sending "waves" down a wire electronically messages are sent and received. In the past, analog transmission was the major means of relaying data over long distances. This was due largely to the type of communication lines provided by American Telephone and Telegraph (AT&T). **Digital transmission,** on the other hand, involves the transmission of data as distinct on and off pulses. Digital communications tend to be faster and more accurate than analog transmission. Figure 9–1 illustrates the concepts of digital and analog transmission.

Analog transmission requires that the sender convert the data from the pulse form in which it is stored to wave form before transmitting it. This conversion process is called **modulation.** The opposite conversion—from wave to pulse form—is required at the receiving end before the data is entered into the computer. This conversion is called **demodulation.** Both modulation and demodulation are accomplished by devices called **modems** or **data sets.** The term *modem* is derived from the terms *modulation* and *demodulation.*

There are three types of modems: (1) acoustic coupler, (2) direct connect, and (3) internal. An **acoustic-coupler modem** is linked to a terminal and has a special cradle that holds a standard telephone handset (see Figure 9–2a). The modem processes audible analog tones that pass through the receiver, thus the term *acoustic* coupler. A **direct-connect modem** is connected to a computer terminal by a cable. The modem has another cable that plugs directly into a standard telephone jack (see Figure 9–

● **FIGURE 9–1**
Analog and Digital Transmission

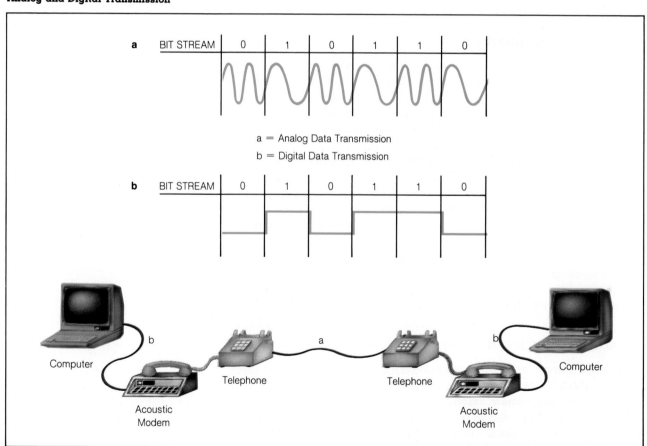

● **COMPUTERS AND INFORMATION PROCESSING**

2b). An **internal modem** consists of a circuit board that is plugged into the internal circuitry of the computer terminal, eliminating the need for a connection directly to a telephone (see Figure 9–2c).

Since the computer stores data in pulse form, when digital transmission is used, there is no need to convert data from wave to digital form. This reduces the time required to send messages and eliminates the data errors that frequently occur in the conversion process. Users can transmit large amounts of data faster and more reliably with digital transmission.

INPUT/OUTPUT OPERATIONS

One of the key functions of the input/output (IO) devices of a computer system is the conversion of data into machine-readable code. For instance, data on punched cards must be converted from Hollerith code into machine code (such as ASCII or BCD). Code conversion must be performed when data are entered from devices such as remote terminals and magnetic-ink character recognition devices. Code conversion is performed by the **input/output (I/O) control unit.** This unit is different from the control unit of the CPU. It is located between one or more I/O devices and the CPU and is used only to facilitate I/O operations.

Besides code conversion, I/O control units perform another important function, **data buffering.** A **buffer** is a separate storage unit (normally contained in the I/O control unit) for a particular input or output device. It is used as a temporary holding area for data being transferred to or from the CPU.

When data are read by an input device, they are converted to machine code and stored in a buffer. Once a specific amount of data has been collected in the buffer, it is transferred to the CPU. The buffer allows a large quantity of data to be transferred much faster than if the data items were transferred individually. For example, a buffer is used to temporarily hold data being entered from a remote terminal; this allows an entire record to be keyed on the terminal, held, and transferred all at once to the CPU. While the record is being keyed, the CPU processes other data (see Figure 9–3). The buffer serves a similar purpose when information is transferred from the computer to a printer or terminal as output.

● **FIGURE 9–2a**
Acoustic-Coupler Modem

● **FIGURE 9–2b**
Direct-Connect Modem

● **FIGURE 9–2c**
Internal Modem

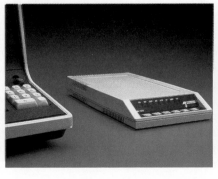

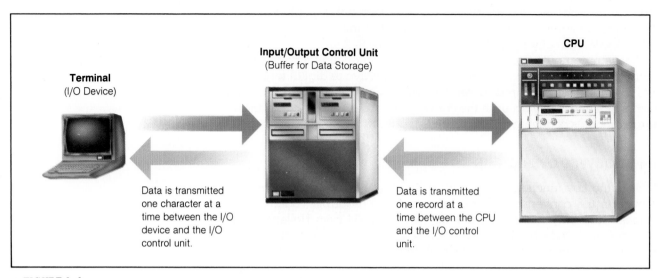

Terminal
(I/O Device)

Input/Output Control Unit
(Buffer for Data Storage)

CPU

Data is transmitted one character at a time between the I/O device and the I/O control unit.

Data is transmitted one record at a time between the CPU and the I/O control unit.

● **FIGURE 9–3**
Data Buffering

Although the CPU is very fast and accurate, it can execute only one instruction at a time. If it executes an instruction that requires input or output, it must wait while data are retrieved from or sent to an input/output device. Compared with the CPU's internal processing speeds, I/O speeds are extremely slow. Even high-speed I/O devices often work only one-tenth as fast as the CPU. When the CPU slows down to wait for input/output operations to take place, it is **input/output bound.**

● **TABLE 9–1**
Input/Output Bound

	TIME 1	TIME 2	TIME 3
Input	Item 1		
Process		Item 1	
Output			Item 1

The CPU is input/output–bound—it can operate only one item at a time.

The flow of data shown in Table 9–1 indicates that in this system the CPU does the process step when it has the necessary data but sits idle while input and output occur. To increase use of the CPU, **channels** have been developed to take over the task of transferring data to and from the CPU (see Table 9–2). Each channel is a small, limited-capacity computer that serves as a data roadway. The channel may be within the CPU or a separate piece of equipment connected to it. During processing, when the CPU encounters an instruction requiring input or output, the CPU indicates to the channel what is needed. The channel then goes to the required input device for data or sends information to the appropriate output device. The CPU, meanwhile, is free to execute other instructions; it is relieved of its responsibility to transfer data and can process the data more efficiently.

● COMPUTERS AND INFORMATION PROCESSING

Processing with Channels

	TIME 1	TIME 2	TIME 3
Input	Item 1	Item 2	Item 3
Process		Item 1	Item 2
Output			Item 1

With the aid of channels, the CPU can be active a greater percentage of the time.

There are two types of channels: selector and multiplexor. A **selector channel** can accept input from only one device at a time and is used with high-speed I/O devices such as a magnetic-tape or magnetic-disk unit. A **multiplexor channel** can handle more than one I/O device at a time. A byte multiplexor channel is normally associated with multiple high-speed devices but is less frequently encountered.

● Communication Channels

A **communication channel** is the link that permits transmission of electrical signals between **distributed data processing (DDP)** locations. The purpose of a communication channel is to carry data from one location to another. Communication channels can be classified in a number of different ways. The following discussion classifies channels by type, grade, and mode.

TYPES OF CHANNELS

Several types of media are used as communication channels for data transfer, the most common of which are telephone lines, coaxial cables, fiber-optic cables, and microwaves.

Telephone lines are one of the most widely used communication channels for the transmission of both data and voices. Ordinary telephone lines are composed of strands of copper wire that are twisted into pairs. Copper is an excellent conductor of electrical signals and data travels along the wire from one location to another.

Coaxial cable is composed of groups of both copper and aluminum wires. The wires are insulated to reduce the distortion that interferes with signal transmission (see Figure 9–4). Coaxial cables are buried underground and also lie at the bottom of the ocean. They permit high-speed transmission of data and are replacing ordinary telephone lines.

Fiber optics is a relatively new form of technology that permits digital transmission. In fiber-optic cables, light impulses (laser beams) are sent along clear, flexible tubing approximately half the diameter of a human hair (see Figure 9–5). A fiber-optic cable is about one-tenth the diameter of a wire cable. Because fiber-optic cables permit data to be transmitted without conversion to analog form, there are few errors in data transmission. The small tubing makes the cables easy to install. One drawback of fiber-optic cables, however, is that the light impulses lose signal strength over distance.

Making Movies

Peter Hyams was commissioned to write the screenplay and produce the film *2010: Odyssey Two*. The movie was to be based on a story by Arthur C. Clarke. Hyams was a great admirer of Clarke's work and wanted the screenplay to retain the "Clarke touch." This meant that Hyams and Clarke would have to be in almost constant communication while the screenplay was being written. Unfortunately Clarke lives on Colombo, an island in the Indian Ocean that is part of Sri Lanka, while Hyams has an office in Culver City, California.

The thirteen time zones separating the two locations made frequent conventional telephone conversations impractical, and regular mail was too slow for the type of communication the two men needed. The problem was solved with a most unusual communication system. Hyams chose two Kaypro computers, modems, and communication software to assist in the completion of the screenplay. The participants had daily discussions about the status of the screenplay while living literally on opposite sides of the globe. At the end of each workday, Hyams would leave his work in a file in the answer mode of his computer. Clarke would begin his workday by calling Hyams's Kaypro and reviewing the file. Clarke then made the appropriate changes to the file and sent it back to California.

The daily communication system between the two men was so successful that a book was published from the transcripts of their correspondence! The screenplay was successful, too; the movie was a hit. Data communication broke new ground in the movie business.

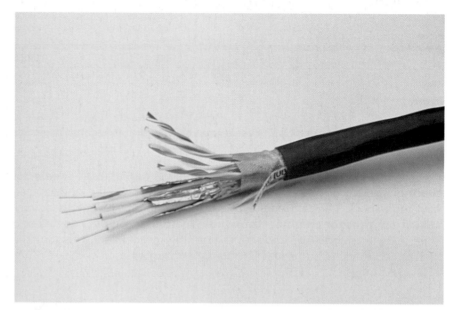

● **FIGURE 9–4**
Coaxial Cable

Microwave communication channels transmit data in analog form. Microwaves are sent through the atmosphere at high speeds in a way that is similar to radio or television transmission. Microwaves are transmitted from one ground station to another or from earth to satellite or vice versa. Unlike other communication channels, however, microwaves cannot bend. Since they must be transmitted in a straight line between two points, microwave transmission is frequently used in conjunction with satellites. Communication satellites rotate about the earth at ap-

● **FIGURE 9–5**
Fiber-Optic Cable

proximately the same speed that the earth rotates about the sun. Microwaves are sent in a straight line from an earth station to the satellite and redirected from the receiving satellite to another satellite or earth station (see Figure 9–6).

Microwave transmission is relatively error free and offers a great deal of flexibility because there is no need for a physical link between transmission points. On the negative side, microwave transmission is expensive because of the high cost of constructing ground stations and launching satellites.

GRADES OF CHANNELS

Communication channels can also be classified by grade. The **grade** or **bandwidth** of a channel determines the range of frequency at which it can transmit data. The rate at which data can be transmitted across the

● **FIGURE 9–6**
Satellite Communication System Using Microwaves

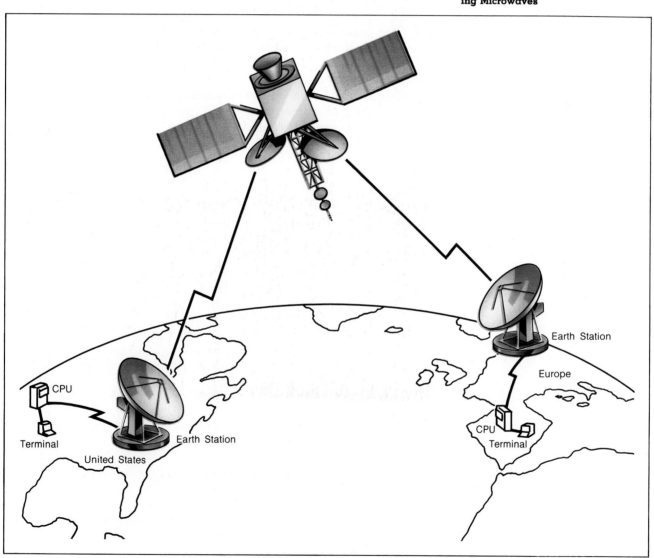

channel is directly proportional to the width of the frequency band. **Narrow bandwidth channels,** such as telegraph lines, can transmit data at rates between forty-five and ninety bits per second.

Voice-grade channels have wider frequency ranges. They can transmit at rates between 300 and 9,600 bits per second. Voice-grade channels such as telephone lines are used by AT&T for the Wide Area Telephone Service (WATS) line.

For applications that require high-speed transmission of large volumes of data, **broad-band channels** are most suitable. Coaxial cables, microwaves, and fiber-optic cables fall into this category. Broad-band transmission services can be leased from both Western Union and AT&T. Broad-band channels can transmit data at a rate of up to 120,000 bits per second.

MODES OF CHANNELS

Communication channels operate in one of three basic transmission modes: simplex, half-duplex, or full-duplex. The mode of transmission is dependent upon the application and the terminal equipment used. A simplex transmission is unidirectional, or one-way. A simplex modem can either send or receive data; it cannot do both. Half-duplex transmission permits data to flow in two directions but only one way at a time. Modems capable of half-duplex transmission are commonly used in telephone services and networks. Full-duplex transmission permits data to flow in both directions simultaneously. A modem capable of full-duplex transmission is the most versatile type available. Figure 9–7 illustrates the channel transmission modes.

CONCEPT SUMMARY 9–1

Communication Channels

TYPE OF CHANNEL	CHARACTERISTICS OF CHANNEL	GRADE OF CHANNEL
Telephone line	Twisted copper strands Excellent conductor of electricity Most widely used media Analog transmission	Voice-grade
Coaxial cable	Copper and aluminum wires insulated to reduce distortion High-speed analog transmission	Broad-band
Fiber-optic cable	Flexible, narrow tubing Uses laser beams to transmit data Digital transmission	Broad-band
Microwave	Similar to radio or television transmission Transmission must be in a straight line Used with satellites Analog transmission	Broad-band

● **COMPUTERS AND INFORMATION PROCESSING**

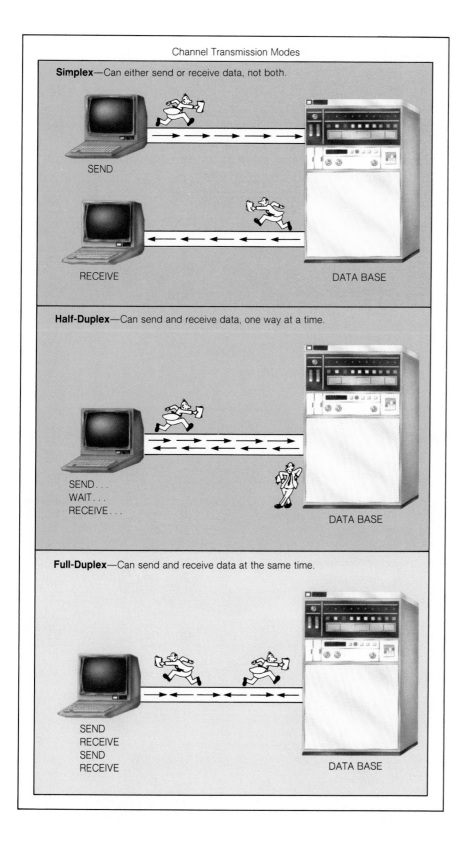

Channel Transmission Modes

Simplex—Can either send or receive data, not both.

SEND

RECEIVE

DATA BASE

Half-Duplex—Can send and receive data, one way at a time.

SEND...
WAIT...
RECEIVE...

DATA BASE

Full-Duplex—Can send and receive data at the same time.

SEND
RECEIVE
SEND
RECEIVE

DATA BASE

● **FIGURE 9–7**
Channel Transmission Modes

◯ Enhancing Communications

In 1957 the world watched in awe as the Soviet Union launched Sputnik, the first satellite to orbit earth. Computers, primitive by today's standards, were used to control and monitor the satellite as it whirled in its orbit. The launching of Sputnik, perhaps more than any other single event, marked the beginning of the change in the way we use computers for communication. The same technology that enabled scientists to communicate with Sputnik has been used to help us communicate faster and more efficiently on earth and in space.

Communications traffic and spacecraft tracking are monitored at RCA Americom's earth station in Vernon Valley, NJ.

● COMPUTERS AND INFORMATION PROCESSING

Satellite transmissions originate in offices and homes throughout the world and are brought over land to satellite antennas, called earth stations, from which they are then transmitted to an INTELSAT satellite. In the United States, COMSAT operates six major earth stations, such as this one in Andover, Maine.

The InfoMaster computer center in Middleton, VA, among the world's largest communications centers, is a key component of Western Union's consumer message network. The center, and another one like it in Missouri, provides automatic switching and storage for more than 300,000 messages daily and can transmit more than 100 million messages a year.

Land-based communication systems are changing the way people from diverse occupations send and receive information. An IBM information network provides up-to-the-minute market information to over 24,000 cotton farmers in Texas and Oklahoma. The service offers grain and livestock market prices, extension reports, and weather information.

● Communication Hardware

Data communication involves the use of computer terminals or microcomputers acting as computer terminals with input/output devices. Often data communication requires the use of special hardware to speed the transfer of data.

MULTIPLEXERS AND CONCENTRATORS

Multiplexers and **concentrators,** also known as **datacom handlers,** increase the number of input/output devices that can use a communication channel. It is advantageous to increase this number because terminals operate at much lower speeds (100 to 150 bits per second) than communication channels (300 to 9,600 bits per second for voice-grade channels). Thus, a channel is not used to full capacity by a single terminal.

Multiplexing can promote more economical use of a communication channel; it acts as a communication interface, combining the input streams from several devices into a single input stream that can be sent over a single channel to the computer system. This allows a single communication channel (typically voice-grade) to substitute for many slower subvoice channels that might otherwise have been operating at less than full capacity. Once the computer system has completed processing, the output message is sent to the multiplexer, which then routes the message to the appropriate device.

A concentrator differs from a multiplexer in that it allows data to be transmitted from only one terminal at a time over a communication channel. The concentrator **polls** the terminals one at a time to see if they have any messages to send. When a communication channel is free, the first terminal ready to send or receive data will get control of the channel and continue to control it for the length of the transaction. The use of a concentrator relies on the assumption that not all terminals will be ready to send or receive data at a given time. Figure 9–8 shows examples of communication systems with and without multiplexers and concentrators.

PROGRAMMABLE COMMUNICATIONS PROCESSORS

A **programmable communications processor** is a device that relieves the CPU of many of the tasks typically required in a communication system. When the volume of data transmission surpasses a certain level, a programmable communications processor can handle these tasks more economically than the CPU. Examples of such tasks include handling messages and priorities, terminating transmission after messages have been received, requesting retransmission of incomplete messages, and verifying successfully transmitted messages.

The two most frequent uses of communications processors are message switching and front-end processing. The principal task of the processor used for **message switching** is to receive messages and route them to appropriate destinations. A **front-end processor** performs message switching as well as more sophisticated operations, such as validating transmitted data and processing data before it is transmitted to the central computer.

● **COMPUTERS AND INFORMATION PROCESSING**

● **FIGURE 9–8**
**Communication Systems with and
without Multiplexers and Concentrators**

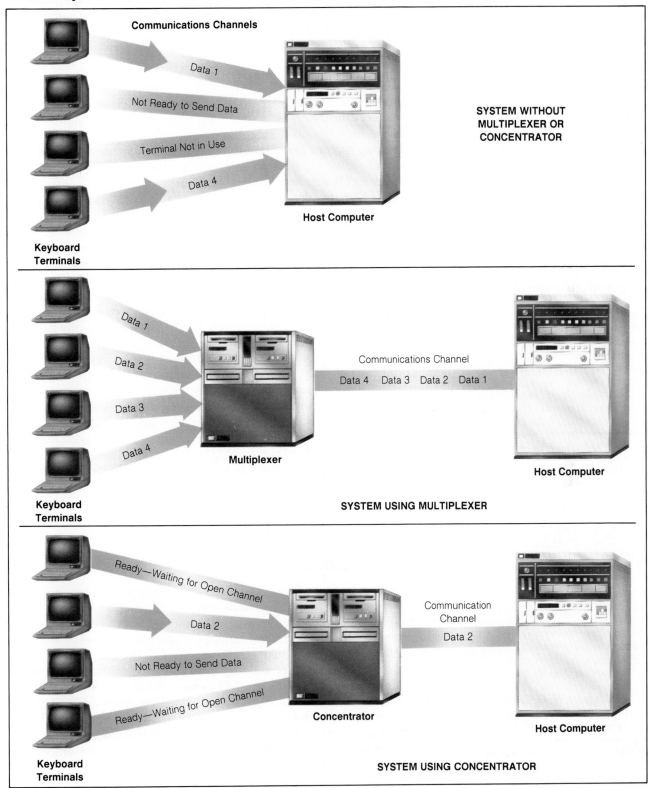

Communications Channels

Data 1

Not Ready to Send Data

Terminal Not in Use

Data 4

Host Computer

**SYSTEM WITHOUT
MULTIPLEXER OR
CONCENTRATOR**

**Keyboard
Terminals**

Data 1

Data 2

Data 3

Data 4

Multiplexer

Communications Channel

Data 4   Data 3   Data 2   Data 1

Host Computer

**Keyboard
Terminals**

SYSTEM USING MULTIPLEXER

Ready—Waiting for Open Channel

Data 2

Not Ready to Send Data

Ready—Waiting for Open Channel

Concentrator

Communication
Channel

Data 2

Host Computer

**Keyboard
Terminals**

SYSTEM USING CONCENTRATOR

◯ Data Communication Applications

The technology used to facilitate data communications is being used in a number of practical applications. In the following sections some of the more popular applications are described.

LOCAL-AREA NETWORKS (LANS)

A local-area network (LAN) operates within a well-defined and generally self-enclosed area, such as a small office building. The communication stations are usually linked by cable and are generally within 1,000 feet of each other. Distance among terminals in a LAN is limited by the time required for the signal to travel from one workstation to the next and by the decrease in the strength of the signal as it travels.

In local-area networks, microcomputers can be linked together to share peripheral devices and information and also to provide the ability to communicate between members of the network. Sharing peripheral devices such as printers and mass storage devices can reduce costs on a per-computer basis. For example, four or five microcomputers may share a high-speed, high-quality letter-perfect printer and a hard-disk unit. The ability to share information is very important; information contained at a central location provides greater data integrity (accuracy and timeliness) and is accessed or updated in a timely fashion from any number of locations within the network.

The ability to communicate among members of the network is also an important consideration. **Electronic mail** is one means of network communication. It allows one member of the network to send a message to another member. If the member receiving the message is not currently connected to the network, the message will be saved until the next time he or she makes the connection. Electronic mail can eliminate many of the unnecessary calls and return calls of a telephone message process.

There are many advantages to implementing a local-area network. Among other things, a LAN permits users to share hardware, software, and data. This sharing of resources reduces costs for the users and helps provide a more direct means of communicating.

ELECTRONIC BANKING

Banks process huge amounts of paper in the form of checks, loan records, deposits, savings clubs, investment information, and so forth. The account balance of every customer must be kept up to date and funds and data must be exchanged among banks. Computers are used to facilitate these activities in every banking institution across the country.

Data communication is now being used by banks in the form of **electronic funds transfer (EFT).** In an EFT system, the accounts of a party or parties involved in a transaction are adjusted by electronic communication between computers and/or computer terminals. No cash or checks actually change hands. Many banks now offer automated services such as direct deposit of checks into customers' accounts by their employers and automatic payment of bills.

One popular form of EFT is the **automatic teller machine (ATM).** ATMs are unattended remote devices that communicate with a bank's computer (see Figure 9–9). Many banks have installed the machines in the outside walls of bank buildings. The machines are also located at supermarkets, airports, college campuses, and shopping malls. Bank customers can use them twenty-four hours a day to check their account balances, transfer funds, make deposits or withdrawals, and draw out cash from a credit card account. Customers identify themselves by inserting plastic cards (often their credit cards) and entering identification codes. The cards contain account numbers and credit limits encoded on strips of magnetic tape. Once identification is approved, the customers select transactions by pushing a series of buttons.

Another application of EFT involves home banking. Using a telephone or a microcomputer and a modem a customer can perform banking transactions by entering account numbers and transaction codes through the keypad of the telephone or the keyboard of the microcomputer. A voice synthesizer, which is programmed to give transaction instructions and information, may respond to the customer. The same tasks can be performed if a customer has a keypad device attached to a television set and two-way cable television lines.

Some institutions accept the use of the "smart" card. A customer obtains from the bank a plastic card about the size of a normal credit card. Embedded in the thin plastic is a microcomputer—a chip that has programmable functions and a memory. Rather than operating on the basis of a credit limit, the card functions on a debit basis. To use the card, the customer transfers money from a savings account to the card account. When a purchase is made, the card is inserted into the reader at the store. The amount of a purchase is deducted from the customer's account and added to the store's account. Fraud is less likely than with an ordinary charge card since this card is personalized by a sequence of four digits, which make up the personal identity number (PIN). After three incorrect PINs are entered, part of the codes on the card self-destruct, rendering the card useless. An unauthorized user can almost never guess the correct PIN in three tries.

● **FIGURE 9–9**
Automated Teller Machine

Banks also perform transactions with each other by computers. The Federal Reserve System, for example, operates the Fed Wire transfer network for use by member banks. Another EFT network, BankWire, serves several hundred banks in the United States. EFT facilitates international banking through a system called SWIFT (Society for Worldwide Interbank Financial Telecommunications).

TELECOMMUTING

Perhaps one of the most interesting aspects of data communication to contemporary office workers is **telecommuting**—commuting to the office by computer rather than in person (see Figure 9–10). The system offers advantages in cities where office rent is high and mass transit systems or parking facilities are inadequate, and in businesses that do not require frequent face-to-face meetings among office workers. Telecommuting also provides greater flexibility for disabled employees and working parents.

Salespeople and journalists, who are often away from their offices, have successfully used a kind of telecommuting by taking portable computers and tiny printers with them on assignments. The portable computer is used to type memos, letters, stories, or reports. Using a modem, the person sends information over telephone lines to the office. Once the information has been received at the office, phone messages, edited copy, or other information can be sent back to the original writer.

Telecommuting does have disadvantages, however. Some employees may not have the discipline to work away from the office. They may fear that "out of sight is out of mind," particularly when promotions and raises are considered. In addition, managers may be uneasy about the amount of control they have over employees who work away from the office.

● Distributed Computing

The concept of **distributed computing** involves processing that to some degree is done at a site independent of a central computer system. The amount and type of processing that takes place at a distributed site varies from company to company, depending on the structure and the management philosophy of the company. Figure 9-11 illustrates a distributed system in which three dispersed minicomputers are connected by communication links to a large central computer. The three minicomputers may be located in three different functional areas of the organization; for example, finance, marketing, and production.

This type of approach to distributed processing gives the various functional areas the ability to process data independently of the central computer as well as to communicate data required by the entire organization to the central computer. Thus, some of the information generated in the functional areas can be communicated to the central computer to be used in corporate-wide planning and control.

The increase in popularity of microcomputers has led to their inclusion in distributed computing systems. Use of microcomputers by managers

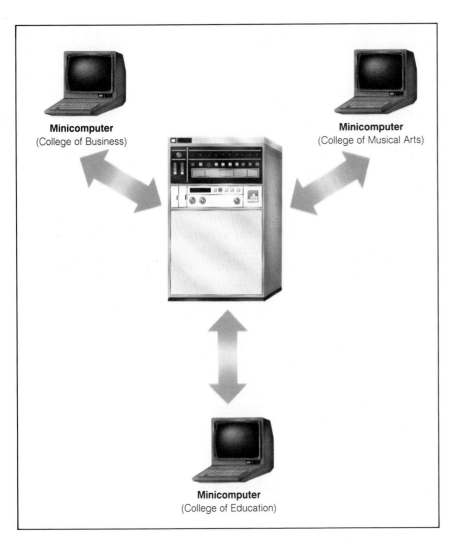

Minicomputer
(College of Business)

Minicomputer
(College of Musical Arts)

Minicomputer
(College of Education)

for planning and control in a distributed system has seen a dramatic increase.

A company's managerial philosophy normally determines the type of system and the amount of processing done at a distributed site. A company with a strong centralized managerial philosophy will do a large amount of processing at distributed sites, with the central computer serving primarily as a communication link among various sites. As the technology in data communication improves and computers become more widely used at dispersed locations, the importance and use of distributed computing will undoubtedly grow.

● Distributed Computing Networks

Distributed computing systems can encompass a number of different configurations designed to meet the varying needs of users. The development of the communication channels discussed earlier made possible the development and widespread use of computer networks. A computer **network** is the linking together of CPUs and terminals via a communication system. A network allows users at different locations to share files, devices, and programs. Many terminals may share the resources of one CPU, or multiple CPUs may be linked together. Terminals and CPUs may be geographically dispersed or situated within the physical constraints of a single office or building.

SINGLE CPU NETWORKS

A typical computer system consists of a single mainframe linked to a variety of peripherals. When peripherals are connected directly to the CPU, the system is called a **local system.** Advancements in computer technology have made it possible to place terminals (or other devices) in locations removed from the mainframe and connect them to the central computer by a communication channel. The resulting system is called a **remote system.**

Many businesses could benefit from a computer facility but find the costs prohibitive. For organizations that only infrequently need the power of a large computer system **time-sharing systems** have been developed. Under time sharing, multiple users with diverse tasks can access the same central computer and receive what seems to be simultaneous responses. Each user seems to have total control of the computer, but in reality the computer divides its time among the users. Each user is charged only for the computer resources actually used. This time-sharing system may be accessed by remote users via I/O devices and telephone lines or by local users whose I/O devices are connected directly to the system.

A system that supports time sharing must allocate computing time to users. The purpose of the time-sharing system would be defeated if one user had to wait a long time while another monopolized the CPU's processing facilities. A technique called **time slicing** can solve this problem. Each user is allocated a small portion of processing time. If the user's program is completely executed during this time, or if the programmer reaches a point at which input or output activity must occur before the allotted time is used up, the CPU begins (or resumes) execution of another user's program. If execution of the program is not completed during that allocated time, control of the CPU is transferred to another user's program and the first program is placed at the end of a waiting list. Once the program returns to the top of the list, execution is resumed at the point where it was stopped when control of the CPU was transferred to another user's program. This switching of programs occurs at such a rapid rate that users are generally unaware of it.

There are two methods of establishing time-sharing capability. One is to set up a time-sharing system **in-house** to obtain quick answers to such problems as production and cost analysis, forecasting, and accounts receivable. The other is to purchase time-sharing capability from a service company that owns and maintains one or more computer systems. The latter approach is often taken by small organizations that cannot afford to purchase their own computers. Because of the intense competition in this area, many service companies have expanded to provide not only time-sharing capability but also specialized programs and technical assistance.

The major advantages of time-sharing systems include the following:

- They provide an economical means for small users to access the resources of a large computer system.
- They allow each user to seem to possess a private computer.
- They offer the advantage of quick response capabilities.
- Through resource poolings, they provide access to greater numbers of application programs at a lower unit cost than privately owned and maintained computers.
- They relieve worry about equipment obsolescence.

Time sharing also has some inherent problems:

- Users connected to the system by telephone lines must worry about breakdowns in the lines or increases in amount of communication; these lines are not the best medium for transmission of data. Thus, applications involving extensive I/O operations may not be suited to time sharing.
- Because data can be accessed quickly and easily in a time-sharing system, concern for security must be increased. All programs and data must be safeguarded from unauthorized persons or use.
- When quick response is not a necessity, time-sharing capability may be a needless expense.
- System reliability may be lower than in non-time-sharing systems. The additional equipment and communication channels are possible areas for both mechanical and system-related problems.

MULTIPLE CPU NETWORKS

As with a single CPU and its terminals, a network's CPUs can be hooked together to form either local or remote systems. All networks are comprised of two basic structures: nodes and links. A **node** refers to the end points of a network and consists of CPUs, printers, terminals, and other physical devices. **Links** are the transmission channels that connect the nodes.

Nodes and links can be arranged in a number of different types of network configurations. Some of the more common are star, ring, hierarchical, bus, and fully distributed. Figure 9–12 illustrates these configurations.

In a **star configuration,** all transactions must go through a central computer before being routed to the appropriate network computer. This creates a central decision point, which facilitates workload distribution and resource sharing but exposes the system to single-point vulnerability. When the central computer breaks down, all the nodes in the network are disabled. An alternative approach uses a number of computers connected to a single transmission line in a **ring configuration.** This type of system can bypass a malfunctioning unit without disrupting operations throughout the network.

A more sophisticated approach is the **hierarchical configuration,** which consists of a group of small computers tied into a large central computing

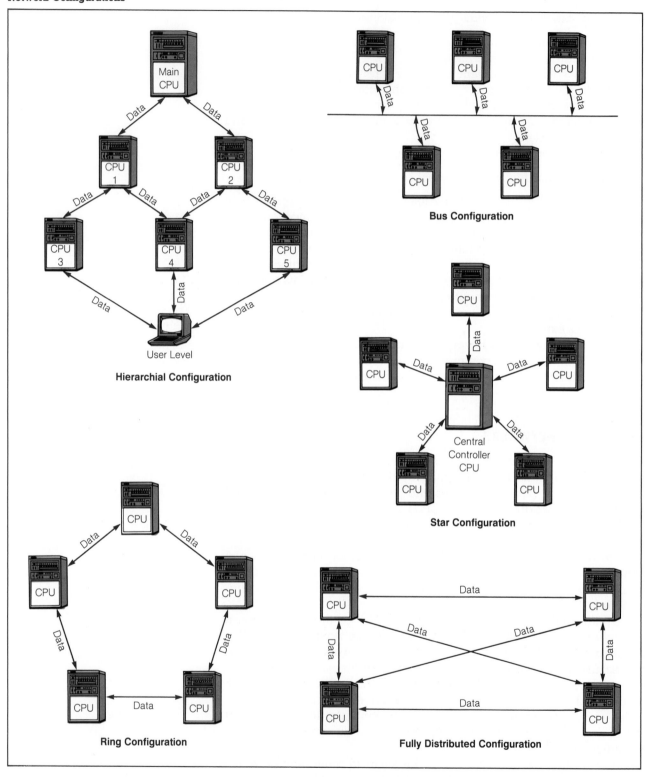

Hierarchial Configuration

Bus Configuration

Star Configuration

Ring Configuration

Fully Distributed Configuration

● COMPUTERS AND INFORMATION PROCESSING

complex. Under this approach, an organization's needs are divided into multiple levels, which are controlled by the single computer at the top of the hierarchy. The lowest level is the user level, where only routine transaction-processing power is supplied. This level is connected to the next higher level and its associated information system. At each level, the machine size increases while the need for distribution decreases. In a **bus configuration,** each computer plugs into a single bus cable that runs from workstation to workstation. Each computer must have its own interface that connects it to the network. As messages travel along the bus cable, stations monitor the cable and retrieve their own messages. If one node in a bus configuration breaks down, the system can still function effectively.

A **fully distributed configuration** is one in which every set of nodes in the network can communicate with every other set of nodes through a single communication link. Each local system has its own processing capabilities.

Network Configurations

STRUCTURE	FEATURE
Star	All transactions go through a central computer; single-point vulnerability
Ring	All computers connected to a single transmission line, but malfunctioning units are bypassed
Hierarchical	Organizational needs are divided into multiple levels; a single computer controls the hierarchy
Bus	Used primarily with local area networks; each computer must have an interface to connect to the bus cable that links the machines
Fully Distributed	Every set of nodes can communicate directly with every other set of nodes; local systems have their own processing capabilities

● Summary Points

● Data communication is the electronic transmission of data from one location to another, usually over communication channels such as telephone, telegraph, or microwaves. The combined use of data-processing equipment and communication facilities such as telephone systems is called telecommunication.

● Modulation is the process of converting data from the pulse form used by the computer to a wave form used for message transmission over communication lines. Demodulation is the process of converting the received message from wave form back to pulse form. These functions are performed by devices called modems, or data sets.

● Digital transmission involves transmitting data as distinct on and off pulses rather than as waves. This mode of transmission eliminates the specialized steps of conversion from pulse to wave form and subsequent reconversion from wave to pulse form at the destination.

• I/O control units and channels are used in an I/O subsystem to increase the efficiency of the CPU. A control unit converts input data into machine code, and vice versa. It is also used in data buffering.

• Channels control I/O operations and free the CPU to do other processing; this allows input, output, and processing to overlap. Selector channels can accommodate only one I/O device at a time and are used with high-speed devices; multiplexor channels can accommodate multiple I/O devices and are often used with low-speed devices.

• A communication channel is the link permitting transmission of electrical signals from one location to another. Types of communication channels include telegraph lines, telephone lines, coaxial cables, and microwaves. Communication channels can also be classified by grade, or bandwidth, and mode of transmission (simplex, half-duplex, and full-duplex).

• Multiplexers, concentrators, and programmable communications processors are hardware devices that reduce the costs associated with data transmission in a communication system.

• Local-area networks involve interconnecting computers in a single building or a complex of buildings. Electronic mail is a means of network communication in which one member of the network sends a message to another member.

• Distributed computing involves processing that, to some degree, is done at a site independent of the central computer system.

• Communication networks may have single or multiple CPUs and may be either local or remote. A time-sharing system allows several users to access the same computer at the same time. An in-house time-sharing system can be installed, or time-sharing capability can be purchased from a service company.

• Multiple CPU networks are characterized by several computers linked together to form either local or remote systems. Five common multiple CPU configurations are star, ring, hierarchical, bus, and fully distributed.

• The star configuration directs all transactions through a central computer. A ring configuration uses a number of computers connected to a single transmission line. A malfunctioning unit can be bypassed without disrupting operations throughout the network. A hierarchical configuration consists of a group of small computers tied into a large central computing complex.

• In a bus configuration, each computer plugs into a single bus cable that runs from workstation to workstation. A fully distributed network is one in which every set of nodes can communicate directly with every other set of nodes through a single communications link.

● Review Questions

1. What is telecommunication?
2. Explain the difference between digital and analog transmission.
3. What are modems and what purpose do they serve in data communication systems?

4. How does a data buffer help speed up data communication?

5. Distinguish among simplex, half-duplex, and full-duplex transmission modes.

6. How does the manner in which a concentrator communicates with an I/O device differ from the way in which a multiplexer performs the same function?

7. What is a programmable communications processor?

8. Which configuration for multiple CPU networks has the disadvantage of single-point vulnerability? Why?

9. What are some advantages of a time-sharing system?

10. What is meant by distributed computing?

Bank of America

EARLY DEVELOPMENTS

In October 1904, a small neighborhood bank opened for business in a remodeled tavern in the North Beach area of San Francisco. It assets at the end of 1904 were $285,000. The founder of this bank, Amadeo Peter Giannini, had decided that small wage earners and small businesses should be offered the same banking services heretofore reserved for wealthy individuals and large companies.

Giannini's Bank of Italy (so named until 1930) was completely destroyed by the San Francisco earthquake of 1906, but Giannini was able to load $80,000 in cash on wagons and move the money to his home for safekeeping. Before the larger banks could reopen, he was lending money from a plank-and-barrel counter at the waterfront. Surviving the bank-closing Panic of 1907, by 1918 the Bank of Italy had twenty-four branches in California—the leader in branch banking despite opposition from competitors and state officials. During the Great Depression, Giannini's newly named Bank of America survived while 8,000 other banks were liquidated, went bankrupt, or were forced to merge in order to stay afloat.

Today, Bank of America is one of the foremost banks in the world, with more than $119 billion in assets and approximately 1,700 branches and offices in the United States and seventy-three other countries. Its data-processing activities center around financial transactions and services such as check processing, savings services, Visa transactions, travelers' check services, and funds transfers. Two major data-processing centers handle the very large volumes of activity; one is located in San Francisco and the other in Los Angeles.

The most significant data-processing work is balancing the bank's books and determining its assets each night. Each day, paper records (in the form of checks and transaction records) and electronic records (in the

form of magnetic tape and storage disks) are sent to the data centers from the approximately 900 branches, from internal bank departments, and from other banks with whom the Bank of America does business. Bank of America has its own air and auto fleet to pick up and deliver the input and computer work from its branches and departments. Just to service the San Francisco data center, the fleets cover about 42,000 miles a day.

Once the balancing is completed, a multitude of reports are prepared to be used by the bank's branches and internal departments and by other banks with which it has direct correspondence. In addition, from the posted account information, numerous data bases (savings, checking, Visa, Versateller, student loans, travelers' checks, and many more) are updated with current customer information for the next processing day.

VERSATELLER

Bank of America uses many on-line applications of data communication technology. One is the Automated Teller Machine (ATM), known as the Versateller service (Figure 9–13). More than 1,300 Versateller machines throughout California are connected with the mainframe computers in Los Angeles and San Francisco. (In addition, the system is linked with a nationwide PLUS System, accessing about 9,500 ATMs belonging to other member institutions in the consortium.)

Versateller Machines

Control Unit

Branch

Terminals
Versateller Customer
Service Center

Control Unit

Control Unit

Programmable Communications Processor

Los Angeles Host Computer

Programmable Communications Processor

Modem

Modem

Control Unit

Programmable Communications Processor

San Francisco Host Processor

Control Unit

Programmable Communications Processor

Versateller Machines

Control Unit

Branch

Terminals
Versateller Customer
Service Center

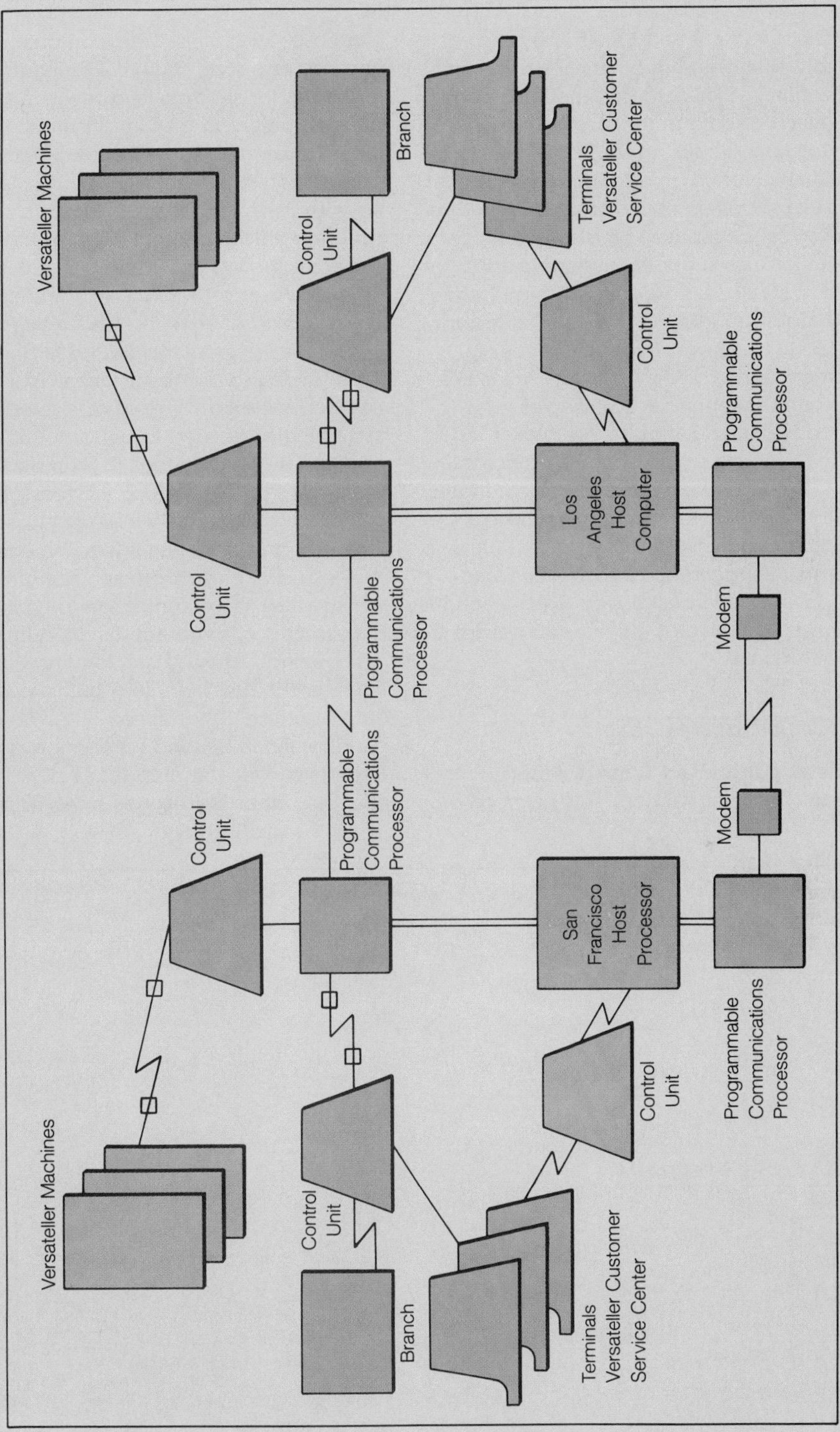

The two host computers are tied together by a communication link that uses telephone facilities. Programmable communications processors and modems at each end of the link covert the data in the form of signals from digital to analog and back again. Along the link, signals are sometimes carried on telephone lines, other times via microwave receivers or a combination of telephone and microwave, depending on distance.

Each host computer also supports a subnetwork of terminals used by its Versateller Customer Service Center for updating and inquiring into the customer data base; communication takes place over telephone circuitry. Within the customer service center, coaxial cables link the control units with the terminals themselves.

Each host supports a subnetwork of Versateller machines as well. In this subnetwork, the programmable control units are located in the data center; from there, telephone circuitry provides the communication link between the Versateller machines and the control units. A single control unit can support up to eighteen Versateller machines. As with all transmission over telephone circuitry, modems at each end of the line must make the digital/analog conversions.

MONEY TRANSFER SERVICE

Another major network handling Bank of America's activities is the Money Transfer Service. This network, composed of multiple minicomputers, uses telegraph lines, fiber optics, multiplexers, and satellites. It is responsible for sending and receiving messages between minicomputers in the San Francisco data center and those throughout the world. For example, the bank's private network links its San Francisco processing center with its subsidiary in New York and with Bank of America offices in other U.S. and overseas locations. In addition, the system interfaces with several external funds transfer or financial communications networks. These include FedWire, and New York Clearing House Interbank Payment System (CHIPS), and the Society for Worldwide Interbank Financial Transactions (SWIFT). Bank of America's system also interfaces with Telex. The technologies needed to perform this message switching depend on the countries to which the messages are being sent or from which the messages are being received. For example, messages to and from South America primarily use telegraph interfaces provided by Western Union; messages to Hong Kong are transmitted via satellite. Communication to London is furnished by a wide variety of communication links (Figure 9–14).

The London-bound line leaving a money transfer minicomputer is first fed into a multiplexer. Here it is combined onto a higher-speed line with other Bank of America lines headed for London. This line in turn is fed into a concentrating modem, where it is combined with two other high-speed lines. This single line travels

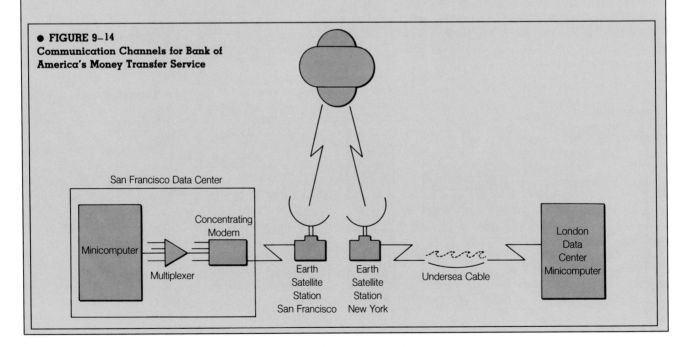

● **FIGURE 9–14**
Communication Channels for Bank of America's Money Transfer Service

San Francisco Data Center

Minicomputer

Multiplexer

Concentrating Modem

Earth Satellite Station San Francisco

Earth Satellite Station New York

Undersea Cable

London Data Center Minicomputer

.via telephone circuitry to a satellite earth station servicing the San Francisco Bay area. The signal is passed via satellite to New York where it is carried by telephone circuitry to Western Union International's undersea cable. Through this cable, it crosses the Atlantic to London, where it is dispersed through additional multiplexing equipment onto telephone circuits for its final journey to the bank's London data center's message-switching minicomputers. A reverse procedure is used in sending messages to San Francisco from London. Fiber optics are now being widely used as the primary local area network tool for the Money Transfer Service.

These networks, only a few of the many communication networks at Bank of America, show how greatly data communication technologies have increased the capabilities and efficiency of data processing in the banking industry. Bank of America's next stage of systems architecture development, called International Banking System and scheduled for completion in 1988, will change its technological environment from a series of stand-alone systems to a common data-base system.

DISCUSSION POINTS

1. Explain how Bank of America's data processing system provides up-to-the-minute account balances for its customers. Why is this operation important?

2. What other industries besides banking might benefit from a service similar to the money transfer service?

10 SYSTEM SOFTWARE

A Threat From Malicious Software

Jamie Murphy
TIME

Early this year a bomb went off in a computer at the Los Angeles department of water and power. The device did not explode; it was a "logic bomb," a smidgen of spurious software coding that had been secretly inserted into the giant IBM machine. At a preassigned time, the logic bomb suddenly went off and maliciously froze the utility's internal files. Work came to a standstill until a team of experts, including the Los Angeles police department's newly formed computer crime unit, was able to uncover the subversive coding. The unknown criminal, who could face five years in the California state penitentiary and a $10,000 fine, is still at large.

Los Angeles water and power got off lightly. The logic bomb had not disrupted the intricate systems that control the flow of water and electricity to the service's 1.2 million customers. Says Lieut. Fred Reno, the officer in charge of the case: "A lot of customers in the city of Los Angeles could have been affected. That really would have been a disaster."

While companies are reluctant to admit that they have been targets of dirty tricks, experts say that such crimes are on the increase. The potential for disaster is frightening. Software sabotage could alter data in computers at banks and stock brokerages or send false signals to air traffic controllers. That could mean the loss of millions of dollars or hundreds of lives.

Programs called "worms" are capable of altering a system's fundamental operations or shutting it down entirely. They delete specific portions of a computer's memory, thus creating a hole of missing information. Another type of software demon, called a "virus," instructs the host machine to summon its stored files. Each time the machine does so, the program copies itself onto the software. The computer's memory can soon turn into a mass of confusion.

Both of these destructive mini-programs occupy only a few hundred bytes of memory and are therefore virtually invisible among the millions of lines of code contained in a large computer. Worse still, they are ominously easy to create. Says Security Consultant Ian Murphy, 28: "Any decent programmer can write a virus in six hours. A novice can write one in 20 hours with assistance and 30 hours without assistance." The perpetrators are frequently disaffected engineers and computer technicians. Says Security Consultant Sanford Sherizen of Natick, Mass.: "A lot of people grew up in data processing, spent years holding computers together with Scotch tape, putting in extra hours, and in recent years of the industry's growth they don't feel they have got an adequate reward."

Two years ago, using an ordinary modem and telephone, a young software saboteur penetrated the system at Manhattan's Memorial Sloan-Kettering Cancer Center with another kind of subversive programming, called a "trapdoor." The program collected users' passwords as they logged on. No matter how often legitimate users changed their sign-on codes, the hacker was able to gain unauthorized access to the hospital's records by summoning the intervening trapdoor and reading off the newly accumulated list of passwords. The culprit was later apprehended. He pleaded guilty and faced a maximum penalty of six months in jail and a $500 fine.

In a case that hit an individual computer user, Technical Engineer Dick Streeter, 55, last June called in to a computer bulletin board based on Long Island, N.Y., hoping to upgrade the graphics capabilities of his IBM PC with a free program called EGA-BTR. After he transferred the software into his machine, Streeter's screen went blank. Soon after, a message flashed: "Arf, arf! Got you!" This so-called Trojan-horse program had erased nearly 900 accounting, word processing and game files that Streeter had stored in his machine. Said the dismayed engineer: "Had I logged on to the bulletin board while at work and it destroyed some work programs, I would have been cooked. Now I just feel stupid."

A few of the destructive hackers have some wit, albeit menacing. In a program called the Cookie Monster, the screen suddenly goes blank. Seconds later, the words "I want a cookie" appear. If the user types "cookie," the machine returns to normal. A few years ago, Richard Skrenta Jr., an 18-year-old Northwestern University student, wrote a virus program called Cloner. Every 30th time a disk containing the program is used, the virus harmlessly flashes a few verses across the screen; then the interrupted task resumes where it left off. "I wrote it as a joke to see how far it would spread," says Skrenta. "But it's easy for a malicious mind to change or add a few lines and turn a harmless toy into a vicious tool."

What can be done to stop the sabotage? The Pentagon, which spends $50 million a year on computer-safeguard research alone, protects its systems from hackers by transmitting classified data on private telephone lines. These are usually encased in metal tubes and filled with high-pressure gas. A break in the tube resulting from an unauthorized tap causes a telltale loss of pressure. Furthermore, all classified files are in codes that are changed daily, even hourly for acutely sensitive information.

Most business systems or private users, of course, cannot be so carefully protected. Researchers at AT&T's Bell Labs are prohibited from running programs that have been acquired over the phone until they have been tested for sabotage. Other companies use call-back boxes that phone would-be users at pre-authorized numbers only. The practice prevents intrusion by hackers who have learned the tele-

phone numbers that give access to the system. They may call in, but unless they are reachable at a cleared phone number, they will not be able to log on. But all security measures, including the Pentagon's, are vulnerable to users who have legitimate access to computer systems. "We have buttoned up. Nobody is going to browse through our classified files," says a senior Defense Department official. But even he admits the possibility of a break-in: "If anyone gets in, it will have to be an inside job."

● **The proliferation of microcomputers, which can easily enter remote computer systems using telecommunications equipment, has exposed system software across the country to crime: unauthorized access, theft of services, and vandalism.**

○ Introduction

The computer is a powerful machine that can be used to solve a variety of problems. Previous chapters have covered the major hardware components of a computer system and have shown how these components are used to store and process data and generate information. However, the computer cannot solve problems without using programs. Programming is a critical step in data processing. If the computer is not correctly programmed, it cannot deliver the needed information. This chapter explains the differences between system programs and application programs and discusses the various functions performed by operating system software. The chapter also describes some of the more advanced software developments that have been made in recent years. The concepts of multiprogramming and multiprocessing are introduced, and the use of virtual storage to overcome primary storage limitations is discussed.

○ Categories of Programs

Despite the apparent complexity and power of the computer, it is merely a tool manipulated by an individual. It requires step-by-step instructions to reach a solution to a problem. As stated earlier, this series of instructions is known as a program, and the individual who creates the program is the programmer. There are two basic categories of programs: (1) **system programs,** which coordinate the operation of computer circuitry and assist in the development of application programs; and (2) **application programs,** which solve particular user problems.

SYSTEM PROGRAMS

System programs directly affect the operation of the computer. They are designed to facilitate the efficient use of the computer's resources and aid in the development and execution of application programs. For example, one system program allocates storage for data being entered into the system; another system program instructs output to be sent to the appropriate device such as a line printer. We have already seen that computers differ in primary storage capacity, in the methods used to store and code data, and in the number of instructions they can perform. Consequently, system programs are written specifically for a particular type of computer and cannot be used (without modification) on different machines.

A system programmer maintains the system programs in good running order and tailors them, when necessary, to meet organizational requirements. Because system programmers serve as a bridge between the computer and application programmers, they must have the technical background needed to understand the complex internal operations of the computer. Because each organization uses a different set of application programs, system programs must be modified to execute the needed application programs in the most efficient manner and obtain the resulting information in an appropriate form.

System programs are normally provided by the computer manufacturer or a specialized programming firm. Thus, they are initially written in a general fashion to meet as many user requirements as possible. However, they can be modified, or tailored, to meet a particular organization's specific needs.

APPLICATION PROGRAMS

Application programs perform specific data-processing or computational tasks to solve an organization's information needs. They can be developed within the organization or purchased from software firms. Typical examples of application programs are those used in inventory control and accounting; in banks, application programs update checking and savings account balances.

The job of the application programmer is to use the capabilities of the computer to solve specific problems. A programmer need not have an in-depth knowledge of the computer to write application programs. Instead, the programmer concentrates on the particular problem to be solved. If the problem is clearly defined and understood, the task of writing a program to solve it is greatly simplified. Application software will be discussed in greater detail in Chapter 13.

○ Operating Systems

In early computer systems, human operators monitored computer operations, determined the order (or priority) in which submitted programs were run and readied input and output devices. While early electronic development increased the processing speeds of CPUs, the speed of human operators remained constant. Time delays and errors caused by human operator intervention became a serious problem.

DEVELOPMENT OF OPERATING SYSTEMS

In the 1960s, operating systems were developed to help overcome this problem. An **operating system** consists of an integrated collection of system programs that control the functions of the CPU, input and output, and storage facilities of the system. It also provides resources necessary for the development of application programs. By performing these tasks, the operating system provides an interface between the user or the application program and the computer hardware. Concept Summary 10–1 shows the relationship among the user, operating system, and computer hardware.

FUNCTIONS OF OPERATING SYSTEMS

The functions of an operating system are geared toward attaining maximum efficiency in processing operations. As already mentioned, elim-

Relationships Among User, Operating System, and Computer Hardware

CONCEPT SUMMARY 10–1

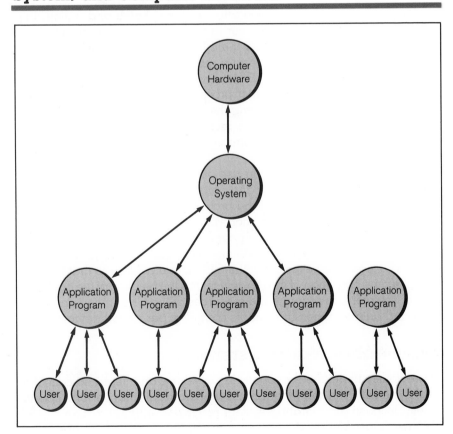

inating human intervention is one method. Allowing several programs to share computer resources is another; the operating system allocates these resources to the programs requesting them and resolves conflicts that occur when, for example, two or three programs request the use of the same tape drive or primary storage locations. In addition, the operating system performs an accounting function; it keeps track of all resource usage so that user fees can be determined and the efficiency of CPU utilization evaluated.

Another important function performed by the operating system is scheduling jobs on a priority basis. Although it may seem logical to run programs in the order in which they are submitted, this is not always the most practical approach. For instance, assume that five programs are submitted for processing within a short period of time. Suppose one program requires one minute of CPU time and the other four require one hour each. It may be reasonable to process the short program first. Or suppose one program will produce a vital report and the output of the others is less important. The more important program should probably be processed first. A system of priorities can be established based on considerations such as the required processing time and the need for the expected output.

TYPES OF PROCESSING HANDLED BY OPERATING SYSTEMS

There are two basic types of operating systems: batch and online. In a batch operating system several user programs ("jobs") are grouped into a batch and processed one after the other in a continuous stream. For example, in the morning an operator may load all jobs to be processed during the day onto a tape and begin entering them into the system. The batch operating system will direct processing without interruption until all jobs are completed, thus freeing the operator to perform other tasks.

An online operating system can respond to spontaneous requests for system resources, such as management inquiries entered from online terminals.

Operating systems currently in use on mainframe and minicomputer systems can handle both batch and online applications simultaneously. These operating systems direct the processing of a job but also respond to **interrupts** from I/O devices such as online terminals, printers, and secondary storage devices which communicate with the CPU through the operating system. When an I/O device sends a message to the CPU, normal processing is suspended (the CPU is interrupted) so that the CPU may direct the operation of the I/O device. It is the function of the operating system, therefore, to manage the resources of the CPU in its handling of batch and online processing and its control of peripheral devices.

COMPONENTS OF OPERATING SYSTEMS

As previously mentioned an operating system is an integrated collection of subsystems. Each subsystem consists of programs that perform specific duties. Because all operating system programs work as a "team," CPU idle time is avoided and utilization of computer facilities is increased.

Operating system programs are kept online in a secondary storage device known as the **system residence device.** The secondary storage media most commonly used are magnetic tape drives (TOS—tape operating system) and magnetic disk drives (DOS—disk operating system). Magnetic-drum technology has the fastest processing time, but many existing operating systems use magnetic-disk technology.

Two types of programs make up the operating system: **control programs** and **processing programs.** Control programs oversee system operations and perform tasks such as input/output, scheduling, handling interrupts, and communicating with the computer operator or programmer. They make certain that computer resources are used efficiently. Processing programs are executed under the supervision of control programs and are used by the programmer to aid in the development of application programs.

Control Programs

The **supervisor program** (also called the **monitor** or **executive**), the major component of the operating system, coordinates the activities of all other parts of the operating system. When the computer is first put into use the supervisor is the first program to be transferred into primary storage from the system residence device. Only the most frequently used components of the supervisor are initially loaded into primary storage. These components are referred to as **resident routines,** because they remain in primary storage as long as the computer is running. Certain other supervisor routines known as **transient routines** remain in secondary storage with the remainder of the operating system. Supervisor routines call for these nonresident system programs as needed and load them into primary storage. The supervisor schedules I/O operations and allocates channels to various I/O devices. It also sends messages to the computer operator indicating the status of particular jobs, error conditions, and so forth. Figure 10–1 illustrates how supervisor routines control the accessing of the system residence device programs.

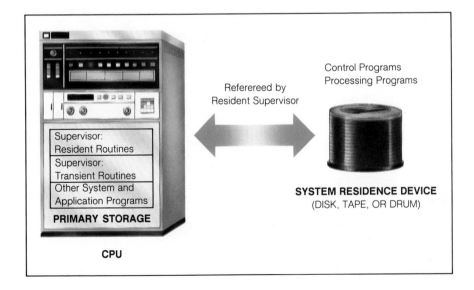

● **FIGURE 10–1**
Operating System in Primary Storage and System Residence Device

The operating system requires job-control information in order to instruct it as to how a particular job is to be carried out. (A *job* is a task to be processed by the CPU.) A **job-control language (JCL)** serves as the communication link between the programmer and the operating system. The term JCL was introduced by IBM for use on their systems. JCL is a very complex language with a large number of commands. Although other manufacturers have different names for their job-control languages, the term JCL has become so widely accepted that programmers generally use it to refer to any type of job-control language, regardless of the system.

In a batch operating system, job-control statements must be placed at the beginning of the job. These statements identify the beginning of the job, the user, and the specific program to be executed, describe the work to be done, and indicate the I/O devices required. The **job-control program** translates the job-control statements written by a programmer into machine-language instructions that can be executed by the computer.

In most computer systems, the data to be processed is kept on storage media such as magnetic tape or disk. On these systems, job-control statements and programs often are entered from a source other than that on which the data files are stored. For example, the JCL and program may be entered as a series of statements from magnetic tape, as shown in Figure 10–2a. Among other things, these JCL statements must specify which data files and I/O devices are required by the program.

● **FIGURE 10–2**
Continuous Job Streams for a Batch Processing System

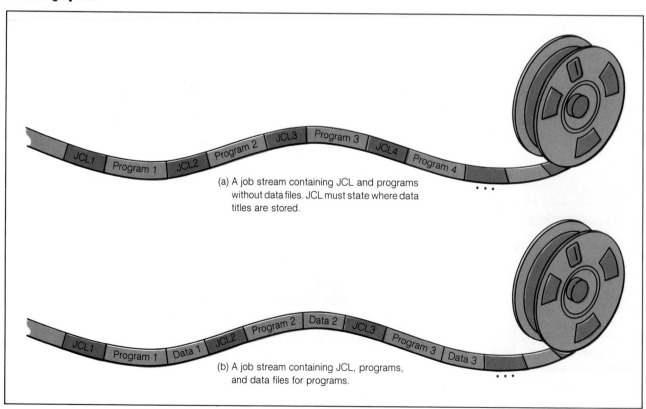

(a) A job stream containing JCL and programs without data files. JCL must state where data titles are stored.

(b) A job stream containing JCL, programs, and data files for programs.

On other systems, programs and data are read into storage from the same device used to submit the JCL (see Figure 10–2b). No additional I/O devices are required, but this is not an efficient method for processing large programs or data files. It is most often used when programs are being tested, before they are stored on a secondary-storage medium. Figure 10–3 shows a sample JCL used to translate a COBOL program into machine-readable form (that is, the 1s and 0s that the computer is capable of executing), which reads program data, processes the data, and then sends the results to a line printer.

The first statement uniquely identifies the job and indicates what system message will be displayed concerning the translation. The second statement identifies the particular step of the overall job and invokes the COBOL language translator (the program being executed is written in the COBOL language). Although this JCL contains only one step, multiple steps can be contained in a single job, as demonstrated in Figure 10–2. The third statement identifies the beginning of the COBOL source program, and the fourth statement identifies the beginning of the program data. The source program would be placed between statements three and four and the data between statements four and five. Statement five defines the master file to be used, which in this case is a disk file. The final statement simply identifies the line printer as the output device.

A job is often thought of as a single program entered by a user into the computer. In fact, most data-processing jobs require the execution of many related programs. For example, processing a weekly payroll job may require performing the following tasks:

1. Entering the payroll data at a keyboard. This data could then be transferred to tape.
2. Sorting the records into some order, such as by employee number.
3. Matching the resultant transaction file with the master payroll file.
4. Processing the matched data to produce payroll checks, a payroll check register, and various payroll reports.

Thus, several job-control statements are needed to indicate which operations are to be performed and the devices needed to perform them.

The control programs of the operating system must be able to control and coordinate the CPU while receiving input from channels, executing instructions of programs in storage, and regulating output. I/O devices must be assigned to specific programs and data must be moved between them and specific memory locations. The **input/output management system** oversees and coordinates these processes.

```
//PAY JOB ACCT, '***PAYROLL***', MSGLEVEL=(1,1)
//STEP1 EXEC COBVCG
//COB. SYSIN DD *

//GO. SYSIN DD *

//GO.FILE1 DD DSN=MASTER.FILE , DISP = SHR
//GO.OUTPUT DD SYSOUT=A
```

● **FIGURE 10–3**
Sample JCL

Processing Programs

The operating system contains several processing programs that facilitate efficient processing operations by simplifying program preparation and execution for users. The major processing programs contained in the operating system are the language translators, linkage editor, library programs, and utility programs.

Application programs are seldom (if ever) written in machine language because of the complexity and time that would be required to write them. Instead, most programs are written in a language closely resembling English. These are referred to as *high-level languages*, and will be discussed in Chapter 12. A **language-translator program,** as its name implies, translates these high-level language programs written by programmers into the machine-language instructions (1s and 0s) that the computer is able to execute.

A number of application programming languages are available: common examples include FORTRAN, COBOL, Pascal, and BASIC (all of which are discussed in Chapter 12). The programmer must specify (in a job-control statement) the language in which a program is written. When the program is to be executed, the job-control program interprets that job-control statement and informs the supervisor which language translator is needed. The supervisor then calls the appropriate language translator from the system residence device. The language translator converts the program (called the **source program**) into machine language so it can be executed.

The translated application program (called the **object program**) is usually placed on the system residence device until the supervisor calls for it to be loaded into primary storage for execution. It is the task of the **linkage editor** to "link" the object program from the system residence device to primary storage. It does this by assigning appropriate primary storage addresses to each byte of the object program. This object program, referred to as the load module, is then executed by the CPU. The process is illustrated in Figure 10–4.

Library programs are user-written or manufacturer-supplied programs and subroutines that are frequently used in other programs. So that these routines will not have to be rewritten every time they are needed, they are stored in a **system library** (usually on magnetic disk or tape) and called into primary storage when needed. They are then linked together with other programs to perform specific tasks. A **librarian program** manages the storage and use of library programs by maintaining a directory of programs in the system library; it also contains appropriate procedures for adding and deleting programs.

Operating systems also include a set of **utility programs** that perform specialized functions. One such program transfers data from file to file, or from one I/O device to another. For example, a utility program can be used to transfer data from tape to tape, tape to disk, card to tape, or tape to printer. Other utility programs known as **sort/merge programs** are used to sort records into a particular sequence to facilitate the updating of files. Once sorted, several files can be merged to form a single, updated file. Job-control statements are used to specify the sort/merge program to be accessed; these programs or routines are then called into primary storage when needed. See Concept Summary 10–2 for a summary of the types and purposes of operating system programs.

Additional Software

As mentioned at the beginning of the chapter, system programs are available from a variety of sources. Each data-processing department must decide which subsystems to include in its operating system. The original operating system is usually obtained from the manufacturer of the CPU. However, in some cases alternative operating systems can be purchased from software vendors.

Once the essential operating system has been purchased, optional subsystems may be obtained. These subsystems either improve an existing subsystem or provide additional capabilities to the operating system. For example, the operating system for a bank's computer might be

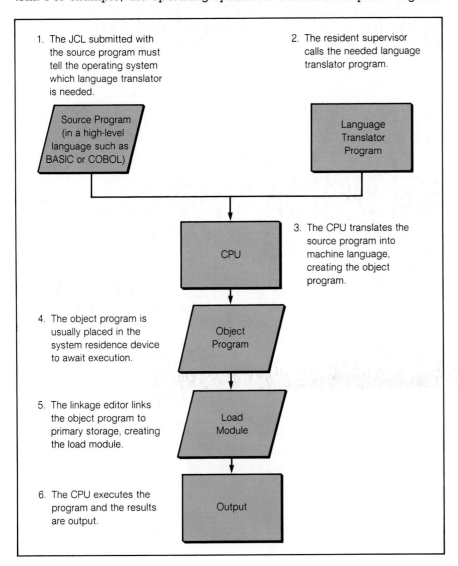

1. The JCL submitted with the source program must tell the operating system which language translator is needed.

2. The resident supervisor calls the needed language translator program.

Source Program (in a high-level language such as BASIC or COBOL)

Language Translator Program

CPU

3. The CPU translates the source program into machine language, creating the object program.

4. The object program is usually placed in the system residence device to await execution.

Object Program

5. The linkage editor links the object program to primary storage, creating the load module.

Load Module

6. The CPU executes the program and the results are output.

Output

● **FIGURE 10–4**
Translating and Executing a Program in a High-Level Language

Types of Operating System Programs

CONTROL PROGRAMS	PURPOSE
Supervisor program	Coordinates activities of all other parts of the operating system
Job-control program	Translates job-control statements into machine language
I/O management system	Coordinates the CPU while receiving input, executing instructions, and regulating output

PROCESSING PROGRAMS	PURPOSE
Language translator programs	Translate programs in high-level languages into machine language
Linkage editor	Links the object program from the system residence device to primary storage
Library programs	Contain subroutines frequently used by other programs
Librarian program	Manages the storage and use of library programs
Utility programs	Perform specialized functions such as transferring data from one file to another
Sort/merge programs	Perform tasks such as sorting files into a particular order and merging several files into a single file

supplemented with a subsystem to interface with MICR equipment (discussed in Chapter 4). Applications requiring the use of light pens with display terminals also demand special subsystems.

○ Multiprogramming

When the CPU is very active, the system as a whole is more efficient. However, the CPU frequently must remain idle because I/O devices are not fast enough. The CPU can operate on only one instruction at a time; furthermore, it cannot operate on data that is not in primary storage. If an input device is slow in providing data or instructions, the CPU must wait until I/O operations have been completed before executing a program.

In the earliest computer systems with simple operating systems, most programs were executed using **serial processing:** one at a time, one after the other. Serial processing was highly inefficient because the high-speed CPU was idle for long periods of time as slow input devices loaded data or output devices printed or stored the results.

Multiprogramming increases CPU active time by effectively allocating computer resources and offsetting low I/O speeds. Under multiprogramming, several programs reside in the primary storage unit at the same time. Although the CPU still can execute only one instruction at a time, it can execute instructions from one program, then another, then another, and back to the first again. Instructions from one program are executed until an interrupt for either input or output is generated. The I/O operation is handled by a channel, and the CPU can shift its attention to another program in memory until the program requires input or output. This rotation occurs so quickly that the execution of the programs in storage appears to be simultaneous. More precisely, the CPU executes the different programs **concurrently** which, in this context, is used to mean "within the same time interval." Figure 10–5 illustrates this process.

Although multiprogramming increases the system's flexibility and efficiency, it also creates some problems. First, the programs in primary storage must be kept separate. This is accomplished through the use of **regions** or **partitions.** Keeping programs in the correct region or partition is known as **memory management** or **memory protection.** A similar situation exists with I/O devices—two programs cannot access the same tape or disk drive at the same time. These problems are handled by operating system control programs.

A second problem that arises with multiprogramming is the need to schedule programs to determine which will receive service first. This requires that each program be assigned a priority. The highest-priority programs are loaded into **foreground partitions** and are called **foreground programs.** Programs of lowest priority are loaded into **background partitions** and are called **background programs** (see Figure 10–6). Background programs are typically executed in batch mode. When a foreground program is interrupted for input or output, control is transferred to another foreground program of equal or lower priority or to a background program.

For large systems with several foreground and background programs, scheduling is not a simple task. Two programs of the same priority may request CPU resources at the same time. The method deciding which program gets control first may be arbitrary; for example, the program that has been in primary storage longer may receive control first. Fortunately, the operating system is capable of handling such problems as they occur and in most instances makes the process of multiprogramming invisible to the user.

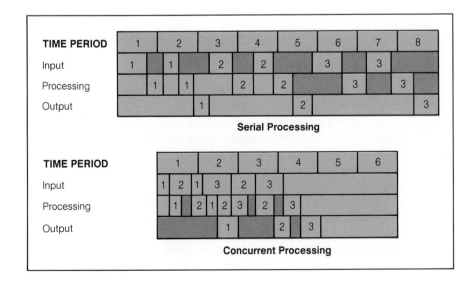

● **FIGURE 10–5**
Comparison of Serial Processing and Concurrent Processing

○ Virtual Storage

Multiprogramming increases system efficiency because the CPU can execute programs concurrently instead of waiting for I/O operations to occur. A limitation of multiprogramming, however, is that each partition must be large enough to hold an entire program; the program remains in memory until its execution is completed. Therefore, all the instructions of a program are kept in primary storage throughout its execution, whether they are needed or not. Yet a large program may contain many sequences of instructions that are executed infrequently. For example, the program may consist of several logical sections, but most of the processing may be done by only one or two of them. While this processing occurs, those sections not being used are occupying primary storage that could otherwise be used more efficiently. As processing requirements increase, the physical limitations of memory become a critical constraint and the productive use of memory becomes increasingly important.

For many years, the space limitations of primary storage have been a barrier to applications. Programmers have spent much time trying to find ways to trim the size of programs so that they could fit into the available primary storage space. In some cases, attempts have been made to segment programs (break them into separate modules) so that they could be executed in separate job steps; but doing this manually is both tedious and time consuming. While hardware costs have decreased and storage capacities have increased, this storage problem still exists in high-volume processing systems that require large programs.

To alleviate the problem an extension of multiprogramming called **virtual storage** (sometimes called **virtual memory**) has been developed. Virtual storage is based on the principle that only the immediately needed portion of a program must be in primary storage at any given time; the rest of the program and data can be kept in secondary storage. Since only part of a program is in primary storage at one time, more programs can reside in primary storage simultaneously, allowing more programs to be executed within a given time period. Using virtual memory gives the system the ability to treat secondary storage as if it were merely an extension of primary storage. This technique gives the "virtual" illusion that primary storage is unlimited.

To implement virtual storage, a direct-access secondary storage device such as a magnetic-disk drive is used to augment primary storage. The term **real storage** is usually given to primary storage within the CPU, while virtual storage refers to the direct-access storage (see Figure 10–7). Both real and virtual storage locations are given addresses by the operating system. If data or instructions needed are not in the real storage area, the portion of the program containing them is transferred from virtual storage into real storage, while another portion currently in real storage may be written back to virtual storage. This process is known as **swapping.** If the portion of the program in real storage has not been modified during execution, the portion from virtual storage may be simply

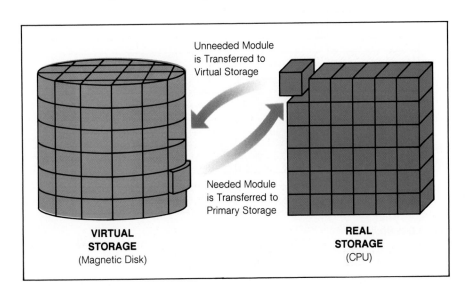

● **FIGURE 10–7**
Schematic Drawing of Virtual Storage and Swapping

Unneeded Module is Transferred to Virtual Storage

Needed Module is Transferred to Primary Storage

VIRTUAL STORAGE
(Magnetic Disk)

REAL STORAGE
(CPU)

laid over it, because copies of all parts of the program are kept in virtual storage.

There are two main methods of implementing virtual-storage systems, both of which use a combination of hardware and software to accomplish the task. The first method is called **segmentation.** Each program is broken into variable-sized blocks called **segments,** which are logical parts of the program. For example, one segment may contain data used by the program; another segment may contain a **subroutine** of the program; and so on. The operating system software allocates storage space according to the size of these logical segments.

A second method of implementing virtual storage is called **paging.** Here, primary storage is divided into physical areas of fixed size called **page frames.** All page frames for all programs are the same size, and this size depends on the characteristics of the particular computer. In contrast to segmentation, paging does not consider the logical portions of the programs. Instead, the programs are broken into equal-sized blocks called **pages.** One page can fit in one page frame of primary storage (see Figure 10–8).

In both paging and segmentation, the operating system handles the swapping of pages or segments whenever a portion of the program that is not in real storage is needed during processing.

Virtual storage offers tremendous flexibility to programmers and system analysts designing new applications; they can devote their time to solving the problem at hand rather than fitting programs into storage. Moreover, as already explained, the use of primary storage is optimized, because only needed portions of programs are in primary storage at any given time.

One of the major limitations of virtual storage is the requirement for extensive online secondary storage. Also, the virtual-storage operating

● **FIGURE 10–8**
Paging

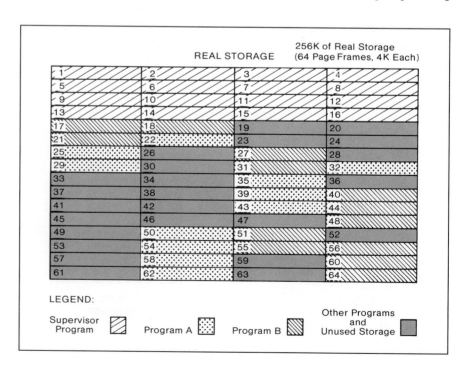

● **COMPUTERS AND INFORMATION PROCESSING**

system is highly sophisticated and requires significant amounts of internal storage. If virtual storage is not used wisely, much time can be spent locating and changing program pages or segments; in some programs, little actual processing occurs compared with the amount of swapping. (This is known as **thrashing.**)

○ Multiprocessing

Multiprocessing involves the use of two or more CPUs linked together for coordinated operation. Stored-program instructions are executed simultaneously, but by different CPUs. The CPUs may execute different instructions from the same program, or they may execute totally different programs. (In contrast, under multiprogramming, the computer appears to be processing different jobs simultaneously but is actually processing them concurrently, or within a given time interval.)

Multiprocessing systems are designed to achieve a particular objective. One common objective is to relieve a large CPU of tasks such as scheduling, editing data, and maintaining files so that it can continue high-priority or complex processing without interruption. To achieve this goal, a small CPU (often a minicomputer) is linked to the large CPU. All work coming into the system from remote terminals or other peripheral devices is first channeled through the small CPU, which coordinates the activities of the large one. Generally, the small CPU handles all I/O interrupts and so on, while the large CPU handles the "number crunching" (large mathematical calculations). A schematic diagram of this type of multiprocessing system is shown in Figure 10–9. The small CPU in Figure 10–9 is commonly referred to as a **front-end processor.** It is an interface between the large CPU and peripheral devices such as online terminals.

A small CPU may also be used as an interface between a large CPU and a large data base stored on direct-access storage devices. In this case, the small CPU, often termed a **back-end processor,** is solely responsible for maintaining the data base. Accessing data and updating specific data fields are typical functions that a small CPU performs in this type of multiprocessing system.

Many large multiprocessing systems have two or more large CPUs. These large CPUs are no different from those used in single-CPU (stand-alone) configurations. Each may have its own separate memory, or a single memory may be shared by all of them. The activities of each CPU can be controlled in whole or in part by a common supervisor program. This type of system is used by organizations with extremely large and complex data-processing needs. Each large CPU may be dedicated to a specific task such as I/O processing or arithmetic processing. One CPU can be set up to handle online processing while another handles only batch processing. Alternately, two CPUs may be used together on the same task to provide rapid responses in the most demanding applications. Many multiprocessing systems are designed so that one or more of the CPUs can provide backup if another malfunctions. A configuration that uses multiple large CPUs is depicted in Figure 10–10. This system also uses a small CPU to control communications with peripheral devices and perform "housekeeping chores" (input editing, validation, and the like).

Coordinating the efforts of several CPUs requires highly sophisticated software and careful planning. The scheduling of workloads for the CPUs involves making the most efficient use of computer resources. Implementing such a system is a time-consuming endeavor that may require the services of outside consultants as well as those provided by the equipment manufacturers. The payoff from this effort is a system with capa-

● FIGURE 10–9
Multiprocessing System with Small Front-End Processor and Large Mainframe

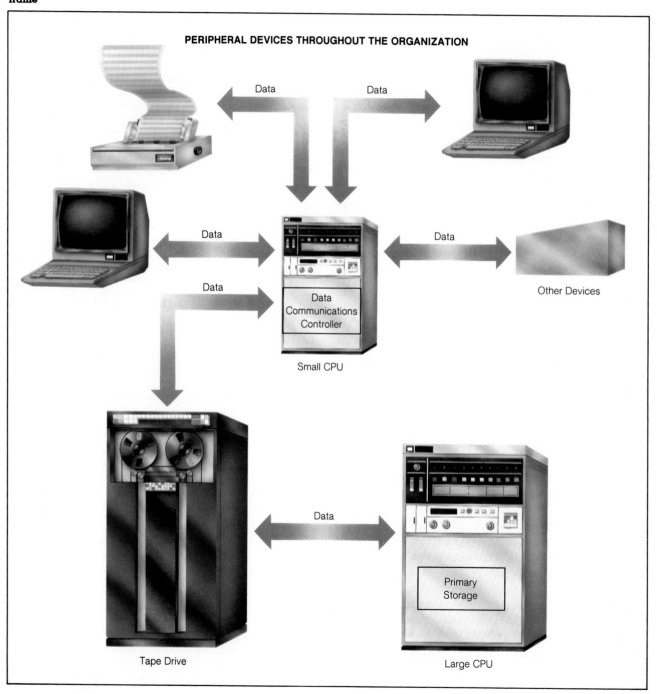

PERIPHERAL DEVICES THROUGHOUT THE ORGANIZATION

Data   Data

Data   Data   Other Devices

Data

Data
Communications
Controller

Small CPU

Data

Primary
Storage

Tape Drive   Large CPU

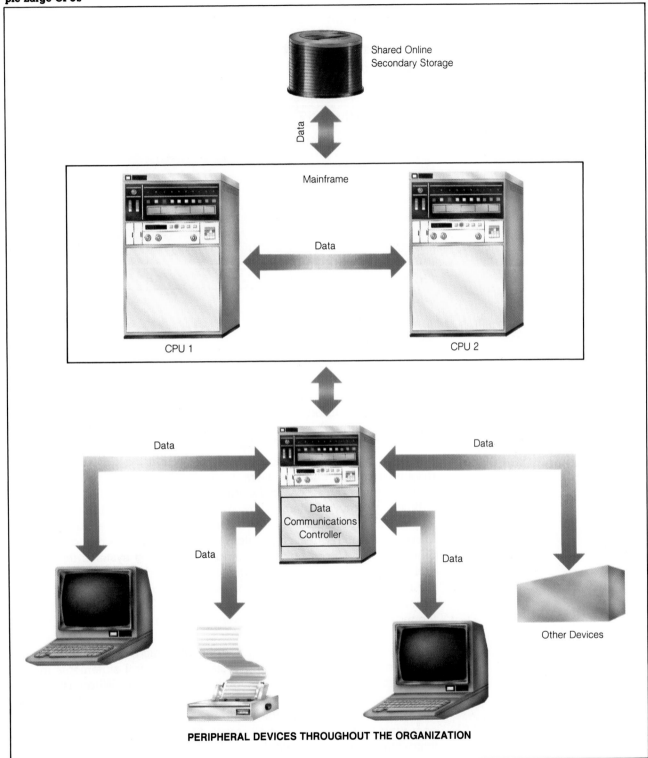

Shared Online
Secondary Storage

Data

Mainframe

Data

CPU 1

CPU 2

Data

Data

Data
Communications
Controller

Data

Data

Other Devices

PERIPHERAL DEVICES THROUGHOUT THE ORGANIZATION

bilities extending far beyond those of a single-CPU system. See Concept Summary 10–3 for a review of multiprogramming, virtual storage, and multiprocessing.

CONCEPT
SUMMARY 10–3

**Developments that
Improved
Computer Efficiency**

MULTIPROGRAMMING	VIRTUAL STORAGE	MULTIPROCESSING
• Involves storing several programs in primary storage at one time • Processes programs concurrently (that is, within a given time interval) by shifting back and forth among programs	• Involves use of pages or segments of a program • Only needed portions of program reside in primary storage, giving illusion that primary storage is unlimited	• Involves use of two or more CPUs linked together • Stored-program instructions are executed simultaneously

○ **Summary Points**

• A program is a series of step-by-step instructions that a computer can use to solve a problem.

• System programs are generally provided by the computer manufacturer or a specialized programming firm. Application programs can be developed within the organization or purchased from a software firm.

• An operating system is a collection of programs designed to permit a computer system to manage its own operations. It allocates computer resources among multiple users, keeps track of all information required for accounting purposes, and establishes job priorities.

• Batch operating systems allow uninterrupted processing of a batch of jobs without operator intervention. Online operating systems can respond to spontaneous requests for system resources, such as management inquiries entered from online terminals. Operating systems that handle both batch and online applications are standard.

• An operating system consists of control programs and processing programs stored on the system residence device. The supervisor program, the major component of the operating system, controls the other subsystems.

• A job-control language (JCL) is the communication link between the programmer and the operating system. Job-control statements instruct the operating system in how the job is to be executed. When using batch processing, each instruction that the operating system needs to execute the job must be stated at the beginning of the job. When using online operating systems, the user is prompted to enter the correct operating instruction when it is needed.

• The input/output management system is part of the operating system control programs. It receives input from channels, regulates output, assigns I/O devices to specific programs, and coordinates all I/O activities.

● Language translators convert English-like programs into the machine-language instructions that the computer is able to execute.

● Library programs consist of programs and subroutines frequently used in other programs; they are stored in a system library (usually on magnetic tape or disk) and called into primary storage when needed.

● The linkage editor links the object program on the system residence device to primary storage by assigning appropriate primary storage addresses to each byte of the object program.

● Utility programs perform specialized functions like sorting and merging and transferring data from one I/O device to another.

● Operating systems can be developed in a modular fashion by the addition of components to the original operating system.

● The CPU may be idle for a significant amount of time because of the speed disparity between the CPU and the I/O devices. Multiprogramming is used to increase the efficiency of CPU utilization.

● With multiprogramming several programs reside in the primary storage unit at the same time. Instructions from one program are executed until an interrupt for either input or output is generated. Then the CPU shifts its attention to another program in memory until that program requires input or output.

● When multiprogramming is used, the programs in primary storage are kept separate by use of partitions or regions. Memory protection and a method of assigning priorities to programs are required. High-priority programs are loaded into foreground partitions and low-primary programs are loaded into background partitions.

● Multiprogramming is limited by primary storage space limitations. A complete program may not fit into a partition; segments of some programs may take up space but be executed infrequently. These problems are alleviated by the use of virtual storage.

● Virtual storage involves loading only the part of a program needed in primary storage, while keeping the remainder of the program in secondary storage. This technique gives the illusion that primary storage is unlimited.

● Segmentation is a method of implementing virtual storage whereby each program is broken into segments of variable size. Each segment is a logical subunit of the complete program. Paging, another method of implementing virtual storage, uses equal-sized blocks called pages without considering logical parts of the program.

● Multiprocessing involves the use of two or more CPUs linked together for coordinated operation. Separate programs or separate parts of the same program can be processed simultaneously by different CPUs.

● Small computers can be linked to mainframes as either front-end processors or back-end processors. The former act as interfaces between the CPU and the I/O devices; the latter act as interfaces between large CPUs and data bases stored on direct-access storage devices.

● Large CPUs can be linked together to handle extremely large and complex data-processing needs. Each CPU may be assigned to a specific task, or it may be used with other CPUs on the same task to provide rapid response.

○ Review Questions

1. Distinguish between application programs and system programs. Give examples of each and explain why they belong in that particular category.

2. What are the major functions performed by an operating system? Is an operating system that can handle batch processing more complex and sophisticated than one that allows online processing? Explain.

3. Into what two categories can operating system programs be divided? List some programs under each category.

4. What is the function of the supervisor program?

5. Explain the steps in translating and executing a high-level language program.

6. What are some of the functions performed by the job-control language?

7. What is the purpose of the system residence device?

8. What is a utility program?

9. Distinguish between multiprogramming and multiprocessing. What are some of the problems that must be solved in a multiprogramming environment?

10. What is the purpose of placing programs in either foreground or background partitions of memory?

11. Why were virtual-storage systems developed? Compare and contrast the two techniques—segmentation and paging—used to implement virtual-storage capabilities.

12. What is a major limitation of virtual storage?

NCR Corporation

NCR

COMPANY HISTORY

The cash register was invented in 1879 by a Dayton cafe owner, James Ritty, and his brother John. By 1883, the National Manufacturing Company had been formed to manufacture the new device. John H. Patterson, who was using two cash registers in his small store in Coalton, Ohio, found they proved to be the difference between operating at a loss and making a profit. Patterson bought twenty-five shares of stock in the National Manufacturing Company. He became its secretary and a member of the board of directors; and in 1884, he purchased a controlling interest and changed the company's name to the National Cash Register Company.

Patterson's first factory employed 13 people and produced as many as five cash registers a week. By 1900, the company's registers were widely used throughout the United States and overseas. Today, almost a hundred years later, the corporation employs 65,000 people and has sales and service facilities in more than a hundred countries.

To more accurately reflect the corporation's expanded activities, the board of directors changed the company's name in 1974 from the National Cash Register Company to the NCR Corporation. Although NCR still designs and manufactures retail systems, its market has expanded to encompass many other types of products.

NCR TODAY

NCR Corporation today is a multinational organization engaged in developing, producing, marketing, and servicing business equipment and computer systems. Its product line includes electronic data-processing systems; electronic point-of-sale terminals for retail stores and financial institutions; a variety of data-entry and retrieval terminals; communication equipment such as modems, adapters, concentrators, and the like; individual free-standing business equipment; business forms; supplies; and related accessories. In addition, NCR acquired a communications firm in St. Paul, Minnesota, called COMTEN; a firm named ADDS (Applied Digital Data Systems) that specializes in general-purpose CRTs;

and a firm called DPI (Data Pathing Inc.) that specializes in manufacturing control terminals and systems.

To support its equipment, NCR develops application software as well as system software. A major new application is NCR MISSION (Manufacturing Information System Support Integrated On-Line). One of the largest applications ever undertaken by the company, MISSION can be used as a single- or multiple-plant system for the complete control of an industrial company's manufacturing operations. This application requires the use of a data-base management system and a transaction processor. The DBMS used is CINCOM's TOTAL. The transaction processor (communications monitor) was developed by the MCS organization and is called TRAN-PRO.

Numerous NCR plants across the nation and abroad design and manufacture hardware and software for NCR products. The plants are decentralized; each has a separate management information system (MIS) department to support it and produce the systems it needs. In an attempt to incorporate all common manufacturing systems used by the plants, a group called the manufacturing control system (MCS) was formed to oversee all the MIS departments. This overall MIS function was staffed with application programmers from outside the company to bring ideas to NCR. The group interviewed the plant managers to determine their individual needs and found these needs to be not only common among NCR management but also similar to those found in any type of manufacturing plant. The MCS group broke the system into subunits and assigned these subunits to sep-

arate plants for development. This required the design of system files, transaction processing, and I/O interfaces.

A design review committee of user personnel from three plants was established to evaluate the design and documentation produced by the various developing plants and to ensure that the systems satisfied user specifications. After the final design was agreed on, the MIS department within each plant proceeded with application programming.

The total system design includes many application modules that work together and draw on common resources. Eight of these modules, or subsystems, have been completed: the Bill of Material, Material Management, Inventory Management, Cost, Routing, Order Processing, Capacity Requirements Planning, and Material Requirements Planning.

Because MISSION was originally designed for use in NCR's own manufacturing plants, the system had to go through the tests given to systems designed for sale to customers before it was approved for customer use. The first of these tests is known as BETA test. For MISSION, it was a complete in-house system test of the completed application subsystems. This was followed by GAMMA test, which ensures the quality of the application. The final procedure was the Customer Verification Test (CVT). Normally, the system is installed in a user site for this test; in the case of MISSION, the system was installed in one of NCR's plants.

MISSION's debut was successful, and the completed subsystems have been made available to NCR customers. Each application subsystem is made up of 25 to 200 separate programs; for example, the Bill of Materials application contains 100 separate programs, half of which accept input from on-line terminals.

Since its debut, MISSION has been converted to run under VRX (Virtual Resource Executive). VRX is a group of software modules making up an operating system that allows multiprogramming, virtual storage, and multiple virtual machine capabilities.

In a multiprogramming environment, VRX schedules and runs up to thirty-five jobs concurrently. Real memory, processor time, and peripheral use are automatically allocated, and the user can exercise as much or as little control over job processing as needed.

The VRX handles a virtual storage environment by assigning currently active portions of virtual storage to real memory. The virtual memory, which is stored on a high-speed, random-access peripheral device, is divided into pages. The entire virtual storage operation is transparent to the application running in the system; that is, the programs are totally unaware of the environments created for them.

The virtual machine capabilities make it possible to tailor a system to operate on a specific programming language. The language compiler translates the source code into an intermediate, object-level code that is interpreted by firmware (small hardware chips that contain complete programs). In most cases, one source-code instruction (which usually requires many object-level commands) translates to one object-level command. Therefore, programs are compiled and executed much faster and far more efficiently than on machines that are not language oriented.

DISCUSSION POINTS

1. What are the advantages of purchasing an applications package such as MISSION instead of developing it in house?
2. What are the disadvantages of purchasing a package such as MISSION?

11 SOFTWARE DEVELOPMENT

● ARTICLE
Droids for Sale

Eleanor Johnson Tracy
Fortune

Famous for spacey androids like Artoo Detoo and See Threepio, *Star Wars* creator George Lucas has come up with a couple of friendly new machines to help earthlings. They are EditDroid and SoundDroid, programmed to come to the aid of Hollywood craftsmen. Lucas has spun off their production to Droid Works, a new joint venture of his privately held Lucasfilm Ltd. of San Rafael, California, and Convergence Corp. of Irvine, a small manufacturer of video-editing equipment that helped perfect the EditDroid. He also plans to spin off a second company later this year. It will be called Pixar, after the Pixar image computer, the new graphics machine it will produce.

The first product out of the Lucasfilm lab to go commercial, EditDroid automates the craft of film editing. Film is first converted to videotape, then to laser disk. Each disk stores the equivalent of 30 minutes of film. An editor cuts, splices, and manipulates the frames electronically on one of several screens in front of him. The technological advance lies in the software, which makes the editing console as simple to use as the traditional flatbed editing table. It's also a lot faster. Had the new machine been available when Lucas and his editors were compressing 90 hours of *Return of the Jedi* footage into a two-hour feature, it would have cut editing time by at least a third. Says Andy Zall, vice president of Complete Post Inc., a Hollywood editing studio that bought the first commercial model, "EditDroid is a brick-wall breaker that will revolutionize the industry."

Droid Works' Chief Executive Robert Doris describes SoundDroid as "a sound studio in a box." It allows a sound editor to edit the original sound track while adding new audio material, such as a musical score. Using a computer, SoundDroid records, stores, edits, mixes, and processes a myriad of different sounds—*Return of the Jedi* had some 130 separate sound tracks. The secret lies in a patented high-speed audio-signal processor that stores the sound on large magnetic disks and retrieves them when called for. Doris estimates that 800 companies are potential customers for the $175,000 SoundDroid, which will go on sale late this year, and 300 for the $93,000 EditDroid.

The appeal of the third new product, Pixar, might reach well beyond Hollywood. Pixar software can be manipulated to produce high-resolution, three-dimensional color pictures of just about anything the imagination can conjure, from trees and mountains to alien creatures. Pixar can also manipulate images from a nuclear magnetic resonance machine to help a doctor diagnose a disease, or from hundreds of seismic soundings to guide a prospector drilling for oil. It does the job 200 times faster than the advanced minicomputers now used for such tasks. The first commercial Pixar will be ready in September and will sell for $105,000.

Both Droid Works and Pixar plan public offerings, if Lucas's Midas touch with movies extends to technology. Lucasfilm intends to keep an equity interest in both. The parent, which already uses the Pixar, also plans to buy plenty of Droids. The new companies' executives plan to maintain their headquarters within a 20-minute drive of Skywalker Ranch, the $30-million-plus film complex Lucas is building on 2,500 acres north of San Francisco. Call it insurance that the force of George Lucas's imagination will be with them.

● **Software advancements are responsible for making the computer useful for such a wide range of applications. Advanced software packages are becoming more and more responsible for our work productivity, our health, and even our entertainment.**

● Introduction

Augusta Ada, Countess of Lovelace, made the following statement concerning the analytical engine which she helped Charles Babbage to develop, "The Analytical Engine has no pretensions whatever to originate anything. It can do whatever we know how to order it to perform. It can follow analysis; but it has no power of anticipating any analytical relations or truths. Its province is to assist us in making available what we are already acquainted with."

This statement briefly explains the basic problem in programming: the programmer must know how to instruct the computer, in an ordered way, in the exact steps it must take to solve a programming problem. People often solve problems intuitively, without identifying each step they perform. Computers lack this human capability. Therefore, using a computer to help solve a problem requires planning. In the early days of the computer, the most significant changes came in the area of improvements to the hardware. Changes in the methodology of software development did not keep pace with these hardware advances. Only in recent years have the methods used to develop software become the object of intensive research. It has been determined that to efficiently develop a well-designed solution to a programming problem, four steps, collectively referred to as the **software development process,** should be followed: (1) Define and document the problem. (2) Design and document a solution. (3) Write and document the program. (4) Debug and test the program and revise the documentation if necessary. Each of these steps will be discussed in detail in this chapter. See Concept Summary 11–1 for a review of the steps in the software development process.

● Defining and Documenting the Problem

It is virtually impossible to get somewhere if you do not know where you are going. Likewise, in programming, a clear and concise statement of the problem must be given before anything else is done. Despite this fact, many programming disasters have occurred because this step was glossed over. Often this situation occurs because the person who writes the program is not the same person who will be using it. Communication between these two people (or groups) can be inadequate, leading to misunderstandings concerning the desired results of the program and ultimately to programs that do not meet the user's needs. Therefore, before the project proceeds, the problem must be clearly defined and documented in writing and agreed upon by all parties involved. Because such analysis skills often differ from the skills required of a programmer, many corporations use **system analysts** to define and design a solution to the programming problem. The tasks of actually writing, debugging, and testing the program are then performed by members of the corporation's programming staff.

The documentation of the problem definition should include a description of:

● The desired output. All output and the manner in which it is to be formatted should be described here. Formatting refers to the way in which the output is to be displayed or printed to make it easy for the user to read and use. For example, placing output in table form with appropriate headings is one way of formatting it.

CONCEPT
SUMMARY 11–1

The Steps in the Software Development Process

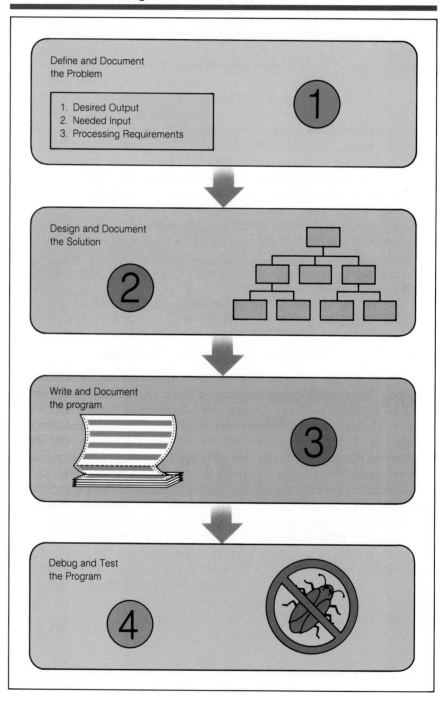

● COMPUTERS AND INFORMATION PROCESSING

• The input. What data is needed to obtain the desired output? From where will this data be obtained? How will this data be formatted? The programmer should make it as easy as possible for the user to enter the data that a program needs.

• The processing requirements. Given the stated output specifications and the required input, the processing requirements can be determined.

The documentation for these three items, the input, output, and processing steps, is referred to as the **program specifications.**

As an example of this process, let's define and document a specific programming problem. The accounting department's payroll section is not functioning properly. Checks are issued late, and many are incorrect. Most of the reports to management, local and state governments, and union officials are woefully inadequate. The payroll section's personnel often work overtime to process the previous week's payroll checks.

The problem is fairly obvious—company expansion and new reporting requirements have strained the accounting department beyond its capacity. A new computerized payroll system has been suggested. Management has agreed with this assessment and has contacted the computer services department for help in solving the problem. The accounting department and computer services department, working together, have defined the problem as shown below.

Problem Definition: Write a program to process the company's payroll. This program will generate not only individual paychecks but appropriate summary reports.

Desired Output: First of all, the payroll program must issue the paychecks. It also must send a statement of weekly and monthly payroll expenses to management and an updated list of changes in employee salaries and positions to the personnel department. The local, state, and federal governments require a monthly report of income taxes withheld, and the union receives payment of employee dues deducted by the payroll section. Not only the checks but all of these reports must be printed by the program.

Needed Input: The next step in defining the problem is to determine the input needed to generate the output listed above. This input includes each employee's time card, which contains the employee number and the hours worked each day of the week. Another input, dealing with new employees and changes in pay scales, is sent by the personnel department. Supervisors provide a special form regarding employee promotions. The tax section sends updates of tax tables used to calculate local, state, and federal withholdings. The union provides information about the withholding of union dues.

Processing Requirements: Given the needed output and input, the processing required of the new computerized payroll system is illustrated in Figure 11–1. First, each employee's gross pay must be calculated from the employee's time card and pay scale. Second, each deduction regarding taxes and union dues must be determined from the tax rates provided by the tax department and the information regarding union dues provided by the union, and these deductions must be subtracted from the gross pay to arrive at the net, or take-home, pay. Third, each employee's paycheck must be printed. Totals must be kept of all em-

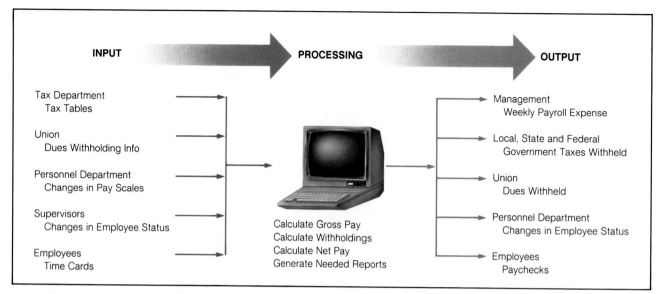

INPUT   PROCESSING   OUTPUT

Tax Department
   Tax Tables

Union
   Dues Withholding Info

Personnel Department
   Changes in Pay Scales

Supervisors
   Changes in Employee Status

Employees
   Time Cards

Calculate Gross Pay
Calculate Withholdings
Calculate Net Pay
Generate Needed Reports

Management
   Weekly Payroll Expense

Local, State and Federal
   Government Taxes Withheld

Union
   Dues Withheld

Personnel Department
   Changes in Employee Status

Employees
   Paychecks

● **FIGURE 11–1**
Problem Definition Step for Payroll Example

ployees' gross pay and net pay values as well as of taxes and union dues withheld. These totals are used to generate reports to management, government, and union officials. In addition, changes in any employee's work status must be reported to the personnel department.

The system analyst must not only thoroughly understand the problem, but also must write the statement of the problem in a clear, concise style. By documenting the problem, it becomes apparent whether or not it is clearly understood. This written documentation should be shown to the potential user(s) of the program to determine if the analyst's understanding of the problem is the same as that of the user(s). Making certain of this early in the programming process will save time and increase the probability that everyone involved will be satisfied with the end product.

● Designing and Documenting a Solution

Once the necessary program input, output, and processing requirements have been determined, it is time to design a solution. It is not necessary to know what programming language will be used in order to develop the logic of a tentative solution. (In fact, knowing the processing requirements first helps the programmer to select the language best suited to those requirements.)

THE FOUR BASIC LOGIC PATTERNS

After the processing requirements are known, the actual logic of the solution can be determined. In order to do this, it is necessary to know the basic logic patterns that the computer is able to execute. The power of the computer comes in large part through the programmer's ability to specify the sequence in which statements in a program are to be executed. However, the computer can execute only four basic logic patterns: the simple sequence, the selection pattern, the loop, and the branch. Programming languages may have more complicated statements, but they all are based on various combinations of these four patterns.

Simple Sequence

In a **simple sequence** the computer executes one statement after another in the order in which they are listed in the program. It is the easiest pattern to understand. Figure 11–2 demonstrates the simple sequence pattern as it relates to the payroll example.

Selection

The **selection** pattern requires that the computer make a choice. The choice it makes, however, is based not on personal preference but on

● **FIGURE 11–2**
Simple Sequence Logic Pattern

pure logic. Each selection is made on the basis of the results of a comparison. The computer can determine if a given value is greater than, equal to, or less than another value; these are the only comparisons the computer is capable of making. Complex comparisons are made by combining two or more simple comparisons. Figure 11–3 illustrates the selection pattern by demonstrating how the logic of the payroll example would consider overtime pay.

Loop

The **loop** pattern enables the programmer to instruct the computer to alter the normal next-sequential-instruction process and loop back to a previous statement in the program, so that a given sequence of statements can be performed as many times as needed. This is especially useful if the same sequence of statements is to be executed, say, for each

● **FIGURE 11–3**
Selection Logic Pattern

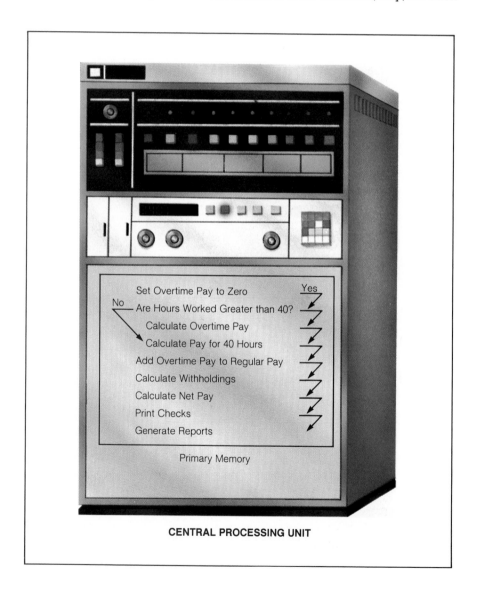

Set Overtime Pay to Zero   Yes

No — Are Hours Worked Greater than 40?

Calculate Overtime Pay

Calculate Pay for 40 Hours

Add Overtime Pay to Regular Pay

Calculate Withholdings

Calculate Net Pay

Print Checks

Generate Reports

Primary Memory

CENTRAL PROCESSING UNIT

● **COMPUTERS AND INFORMATION PROCESSING**

employee in a payroll program; the programmer need not duplicate the sequence of statements for each set of employee data processed. The looping pattern is illustrated in Figure 11–4.

Branch

The last and most controversial pattern is the **branch** (also called the GOTO), which is often used in combination with selection or looping (see Figure 11–5). This pattern allows the programmer to skip past statements in a program, leaving them unexecuted.

Branching is controversial for several reasons. If a program uses branches too often, the logic of the program becomes very difficult to follow. Such programs are difficult and time consuming for programmers to maintain and modify. Therefore, the use of the branch statement is strongly discouraged in most situations. When using most of the newer programming

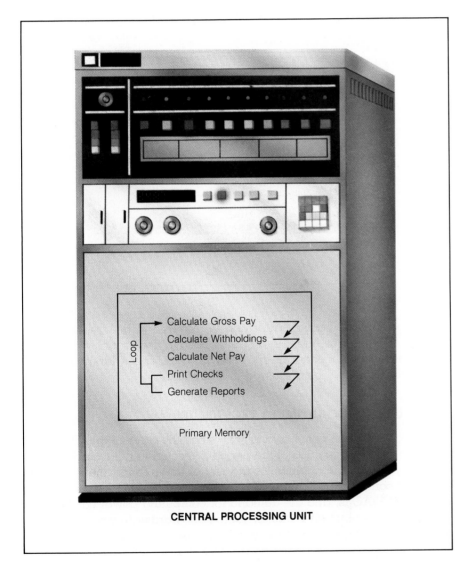

● **FIGURE 11–4**
Loop Logic Pattern

CENTRAL PROCESSING UNIT

CENTRAL PROCESSING UNIT

languages such as Pascal, Ada, and C, referred to as structured programming languages, there is very little need to use branch statements. Loops and selection patterns are used instead. These languages and their advantages will be discussed in Chapter 12.

STRUCTURED PROGRAMMING TECHNIQUES

Data processing has come a long way since the days of the UNIVAC I, when the leading scientists of the period projected that the world would need only ten such machines for the rest of time. Today the world has millions of computers with processing capabilities billions of times greater than ten UNIVAC Is, and the demand for computing power continues to increase. In the first generation of computers, hardware was expensive, accounting for 80 percent of the total cost, whereas software accounted for approximately 20 percent. Today those figures are reversed, and it appears this trend will continue for some time. Figure 11–6 graphically depicts this situation.

As the sophistication of hardware increased rapidly, the needed software technology did not keep pace. In the early days of software development, programming was very much an art. There were no standards or concrete rules. Many programmers approached their work haphazardly. Their main objective was to develop a program that executed properly but they were not concerned about how this was accomplished. This situation created the following problems:

- Programmer productivity was low. Developing a usable program of any significant size was a long, tedious process.
- The programs often were not reliable. **Reliability** refers to the ability of a program to always obtain correct results. These early programs often worked correctly at some times and incorrectly at others.
- The programs could not always correctly handle invalid input. A well-written program should be able to handle any type of input. For example, if the user types in a letter of the alphabet when a real number should have been entered, the program should be able to handle the situation appropriately by, for example, printing an error message.
- The programs were not easy to maintain (that is, keep in working order). The original programmers did not concern themselves with making the logic of the program easy for others to understand. Therefore, if a different programmer had to modify an existing program at a later date (a situation that happens continually in industry), it was a difficult task.

As programmers became aware of these difficulties, their attention was turned to developing methods of improving programming techniques. One of the earliest developments was the discovery by two mathematicians, Guiseppe Jacopini and Corrado Bohm, that any programming problem could be solved using a combination of three basic logic patterns: the simple sequence, the selection pattern, and the loop. Therefore, the fourth pattern, the branch, was unnecessary. Until this point, branches were used often, leading to programs with convoluted, difficult-to-follow logic.

Another event in the development of structured programming occurred in 1968 when E. W. Dijkstra published a letter in the Communications of the ACM (Association for Computer Machinists) titled "Go To Statements Considered Harmful." Dijkstra stated in this now-famous letter that using the GOTO statement (which uses the branch logic pattern) made the logic of a program virtually impossible to follow because execution skipped haphazardly from one part of the program to another. At this stage computer scientists began to realize that it was important to develop programming languages that allowed programs to be written without the use of the GOTO statement.

At about this time, computer scientists also determined that program structure could be obtained by breaking a program into more manageable subprograms or **modules,** each designed to perform a specific task. These subprograms can be compared to the chapters in a textbook; each chapter deals with a specific topic and has specific goals. The chapters are combined to present a unified whole. Dividing a program into sub-

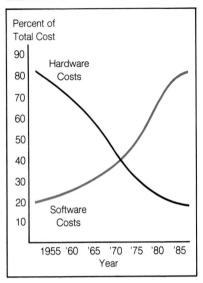

An Experiment in Structure

In 1972, structured programming theory was still not generally known or used by programmers in industry. Most of the articles on the subject were written for academic journals. However, several of these ideas, including those presented by Dijkstra, were of great interest to Dr. Harlan Mills and F. Terry Baker, both of whom worked for IBM. Mills and Baker encouraged IBM to try using structured programming techniques.

As a result of the efforts of Mills and Baker, IBM's "New York Times project" is generally considered to be the first time structured programming techniques were used in developing a large program in industry. The purpose of the project was to develop an on-line information system for the New York Times to access past newspaper articles. The entire project contained more than 80,000 lines of codes and only 21 errors were detected. This was an amazing record, particularly when compared to that of unstructured programs that had been written before this time. As an added bonus, the normal productivity of the production group was doubled. This first experiment in structured programming on a large scale set the trend for future software development practices in industry.

programs makes the program's logic easier to follow just as dividing a book into chapters (and subsections within those chapters) makes the facts and concepts presented easier to comprehend. The ability to easily divide a large program into fairly independent subprograms is an important characteristic of structured programming languages. Languages with this characteristic will be discussed in Chapter 12. Programs developed in this manner tend to have fewer errors than unstructured programs because the logic is readily apparent.

These events led to the development of a set of techniques, referred to as a group as **structured programming.** Structured programming encourages programmers to think about the problem first and thoroughly design a solution before actually beginning to write the program in a programming language. Using structured programming encourages the development of well-written programs that have easy-to-follow logic and tend to be more error-free than other programs. There are many characteristics that distinguish structured programming. These characteristics can be divided into two broad categories: those that affect the manner in which the program solution is designed (structured design techniques) and those that affect the style in which the actual program is written (structured coding). Structured coding will be discussed in the section on writing programs (step 3 of the software development process). Structured design techniques will be presented next.

TOP-DOWN DESIGN

Using a computer to solve a problem is considerably different than most people think. The programmer needs to know only a little about the computer and how it works, but he or she must know a programming language. The most difficult aspect of programming is learning to organize solutions in a clear, concise way. One method of organizing a solution is to define the major steps or functions first, then expand the functions into more detailed steps later. This method, which proceeds from the general to the specific, is called **top-down design.** Top-down design employs the **modular approach,** which consists of breaking a problem into smaller and smaller subproblems. Sometimes this is referred to as the "divide-and-conquer" method, because it is easier to deal with a large job by completing it a small step at a time. When the actual program is written, these subprograms can be written as separate modules, each of which performs a specific task. These modules are then joined together to form the entire program.

Structure Charts

Structure charts are used to document the results of the top-down design process by graphically illustrating the various modules and their relationship to one another. The most general level of organization is the main control module; this overall definition of the solution is the most critical to the success of the program. Modules at the next level contain broad descriptions of the steps in the solution process. These steps are further detailed in lower-level modules. The lowest-level modules contain the specific individual tasks the program must perform.

Figure 11–7 contains a structure chart that was developed to solve the payroll processing problem. Note that this structure chart has a total of

FIGURE 11–7
Structure Chart for Payroll Processing Problem

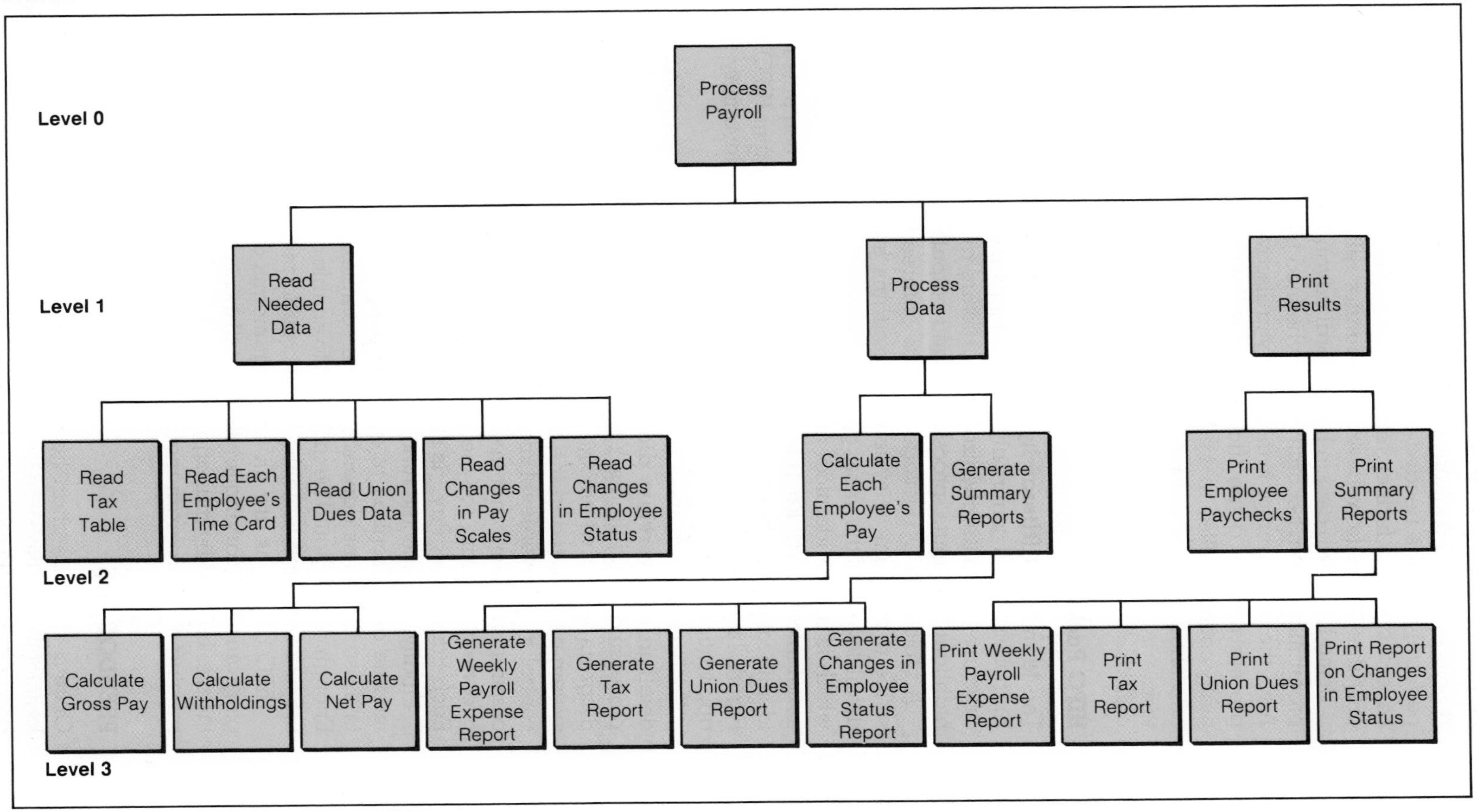

four levels. The topmost level, Level 0, contains a statement of the general problem. Level 1 contains three basic processing steps the program must perform: read the needed data, process that data, and print the results. Level 2 contains further refinements of the steps in Level 1. In Level 3, only three steps from Level 2 are further refined.

Using top-down design has several advantages. It helps to prevent the programmer from becoming overwhelmed by the size of the job at hand. Also, the programmer is more likely to discover early in the programming process whether a specific solution will work. When the program is actually coded (written in a programming language), each box in the structure chart can be written as a separate module performing a specific task.

HIPO Packages

The term **HIPO (Hierarchy plus Input-Process-Output)** is applied to a kind of visual aid commonly used to supplement structure charts. Whereas structure charts emphasize only structure and function, HIPO packages highlight the inputs, processing, and outputs of program modules.

A typical HIPO package consists of three types of diagrams that describe a program or system of programs from the general level to the detail level. At the most general level is the **visual table of contents,** which is almost identical to the structure chart but includes some additional information. Each block in the visual table of contents is given an identification number that is used as a reference in other HIPO diagrams. Figure 11–8 shows a visual table of contents for an inventory-processing application.

Each module in the visual table of contents is described in greater detail in an **overview diagram,** which includes the module's inputs, processing, and outputs. The reference number assigned to the overview diagram shows where the module fits into the overall structure of the system as depicted in the visual table of contents. If the module passes control to a lower-level module in the hierarchy for some specific processing operation, that operation is also given a reference number. An overview diagram for the payroll processing module (2.1), "Calculate Each Employee's Pay," is shown in Figure 11–9.

Finally, the specific functions performed and data items used in each module are described in a **detail diagram.** The amount of detail used in these diagrams depends on the complexity of the problem involved. Enough detail should be included to enable a programmer to understand the functions and write the code to perform them.

HIPO diagrams are an excellent means of documenting systems and programs. The varying levels of detail incorporated in the diagrams allow them to be used by managers, analysts, and programmers to meet needs ranging from program maintenance to the overhaul of entire systems.

PSEUDOCODE

Once a structure chart has been developed for a program, the actual logic of the solution can be documented; one method often used is pseudocode. **Pseudocode** consists of a narrative, English-like description of

● **FIGURE 11–8**
Visual Table of Contents for Payroll Processing Example

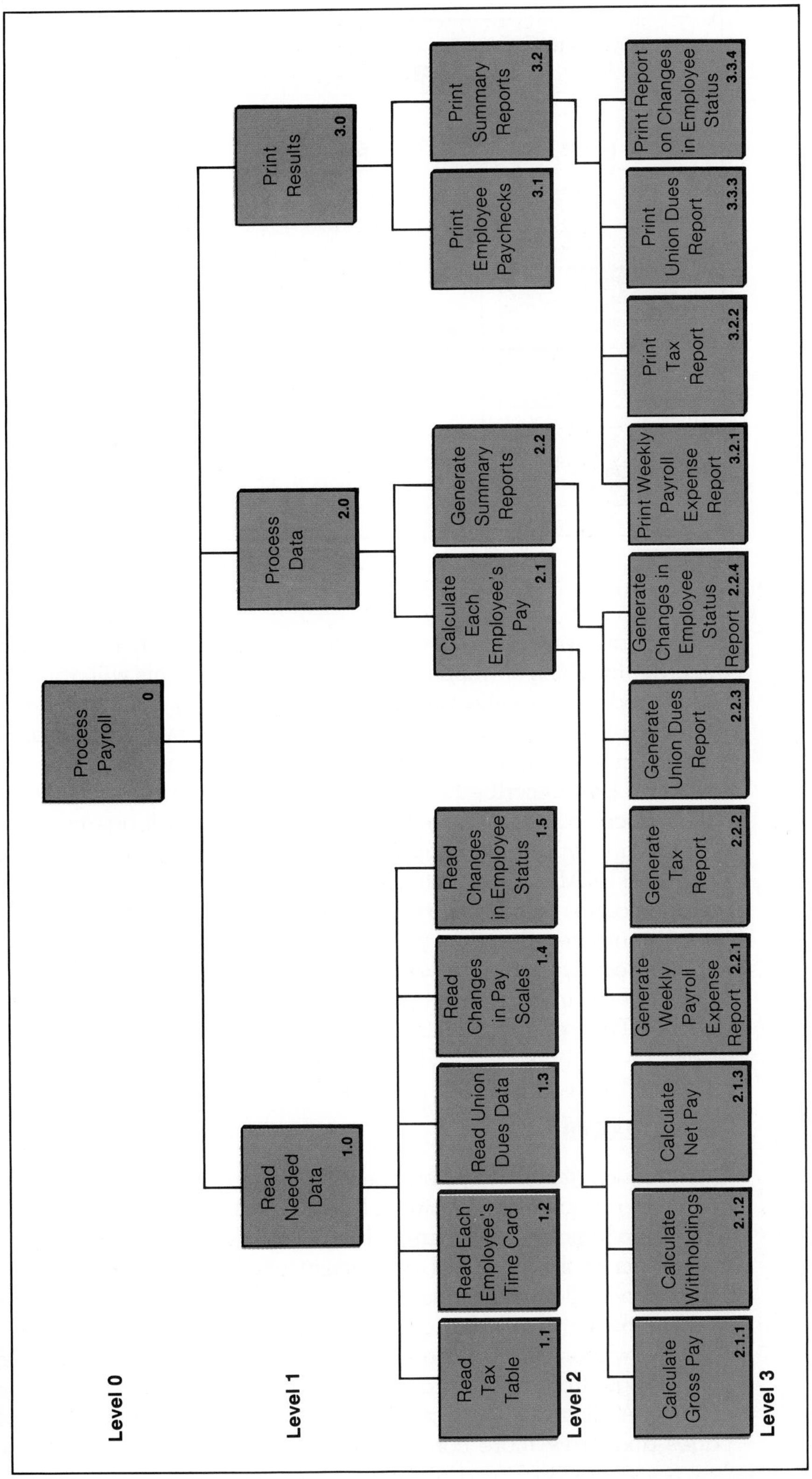

Level 0

Level 1

Level 2

Level 3

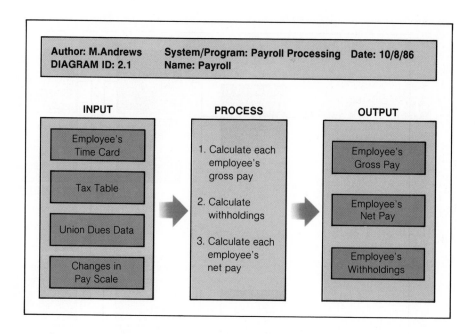

the logic of a program. The programmer arranges these descriptions in the order in which corresponding program statements will appear. Using pseudocode allows the programmer to focus on the steps required to perform a particular process, rather than on the syntax (or grammatical rules) of a particular programming language. Each pseudocode statement can be transcribed into one or more program statements.

Pseudocode is easy to learn and use. Although it has no rigid rules, several key words often appear. They include PRINT, IF/THEN/ELSE, END, and READ. Some statements are indented to set off repeated steps or conditions to be met. The statements cannot be translated for execution by the computer, therefore *pseudo-* is an appropriate prefix for this type of code because it means fake. Figure 11-10 shows how the three basic logic patterns used in structured programming could be written in pseudocode. The pseudocode for the payroll program is shown in Figure 11-11.

FLOWCHARTS

One way of graphically representing the logic of a solution to a programming problem is by using a **flowchart.** A flowchart shows the actual flow of the logic of a program, whereas a structure chart simply contains statements of the levels of refinement used to reach a solution. Each symbol in a flowchart has a specific meaning, as shown in Figure 11-12. Flowchart symbols are arranged from top to bottom and left to right. Flowlines connect the symbols and visually represent the implied flow of logic from symbol to symbol. Arrowheads indicate the direction of flow. A disadvantage of flowcharts is that they can take up many pages and grow more confusing as programs become more complex.

1. Simple Sequence Pattern

Read name
Read hours worked
Read hourly rate
Multiply hours worked by hourly rate
  to obtain gross pay

2. Selection Pattern

If hours worked is greater than 40
  Then subtract 40 from hours worked to
    obtain overtime hours

3. Loop Pattern

Begin loop; perform until no more records
  Read name
  Read hours worked
  Read hourly rate
  Multiply hours worked by hourly rate
    to obtain gross pay
End loop

● **FIGURE 11–10**
Pseudocode Illustrating Three Logic Patterns

Figure 11–13 shows examples of how the four basic logic structures could be flowcharted.

USING STRUCTURED DESIGN TECHNIQUES IN INDUSTRY

The program to generate a company's payroll would be long and complex, having many subprograms. In large corporations, programs such as this are developed by programmers working in teams. These programmers would use the structured design methods such as top-down design that we discussed earlier. They also would generally employ other methods to develop the software in an organized manner. Two commonly used methods, the chief programmer team and the structured walkthrough, are discussed below.

```
Begin
Begin loop; perform until no more records
  Read employee's name, hours worked, and hourly wage
  Calculate gross pay
  Calculate withholdings
  Calculate net pay
  Printcheck
End loop
Generate summary reports
End
```

● **FIGURE 11–11**
Pseudocode for Payroll Processing Example

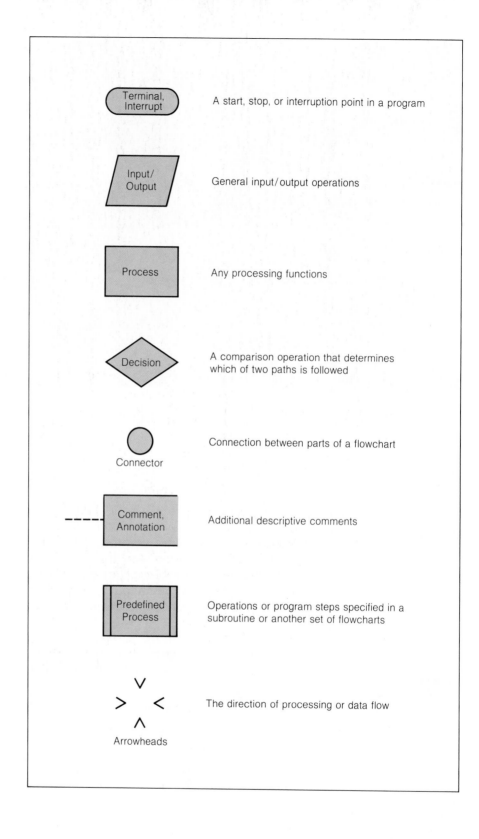

1. **Simple sequence pattern**
   One statement after another, executed in order as stored (A then B).

2. **Selection Pattern**
   Requires a test; depending on the result of the test, one of two paths is taken. For instance, IF A is true THEN do B; ELSE do C.

3. **Loop pattern**
   Execution of E and F continues in a loop fashion as long as D is true. If D is false, the loop is exited; E and F are not executed. The logic is DO E and F WHILE D is true.

4. **Branch pattern**
   Control is transferred from the simple sequence flow to another portion of the program. For instance, if G is false, GO TO J. The flow of the program continues with execution of J (rather than H) whenever G is false.

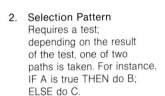
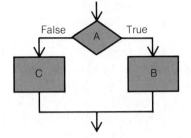
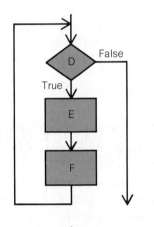
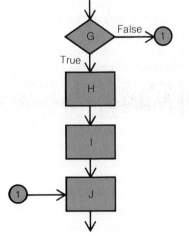

Chief Programmer Team

An important first step in coordinating a programming effort involves the formation of a **Chief Programmer Team (CPT),** which is a group of programmers under the supervision of a chief programmer. The number of team members varies with the complexity of the project. The purpose of this approach is to use each team member's time and abilities as efficiently as possible.

The chief programmer primarily is responsible for the overall coordination, development, and success of the programming project. He or she meets with the user(s) to determine the exact software specifications. Usually, a backup programmer is assigned as an assistant to the chief programmer to help design, test, and evaluate the software. Separate modules (that is, sections within a larger program, each performing a specific task) of the software are written and tested by programmers on the team. These modules are then integrated into a complete system.

The CPT also includes a librarian to help maintain complete, up-to-date documentation on the project and to relieve the team programmers of many clerical tasks. A librarian enhances communication among team members because he or she makes all program description, coding, and test results readily available to everyone involved in the effort. Figure 11–14 shows the organization of the chief programmer team.

The CPT approach facilitates top-down design and ongoing documentation of programs because each team member's tasks are clearly defined and coordinated with the entire team effort. This approach also helps with the testing of programs.

Structured Review and Evaluation

An important goal of a programming effort is to produce an error-free program in the shortest possible time. Meeting this goal requires the early detection of errors in order to prevent costly modifications later. One approach used to try to detect program errors at an early stage is an **informal design review.** The system design documentation is studied by selected management, analysts, and programmers, usually before the actual coding of program modules. After a brief review period, each person responds with suggestions for additions, deletions, and modifications to the system design.

A **formal design review** is sometimes used after the detailed parts of the system have been sufficiently documented. The documentation at this point may consist of structure charts, flowcharts, pseudocode, or any combination of these methods. Sometimes called a **structured walkthrough,** the formal design review involves distributing the documentation to a review team of two to four members, which studies the documentation and then meets with the program designers to discuss the overall completeness, accuracy, and quality of the design. The reviewers and program designers often trace through the programs checking for errors. In large ongoing projects, formal design reviews are often held at various points in the software development process. Because other programmers have a fresh outlook on the program, they can often identify problem areas that the original programmer is not able to recognize.

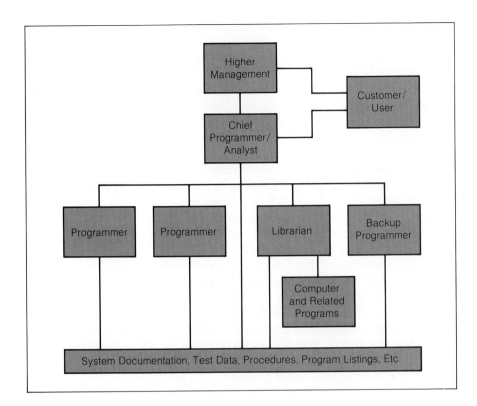

● Writing and Documenting the Program

After the programming problem has been defined and a solution designed, the program is written in a specific programming language; this process is referred to as **coding.** Sometimes the proposed solution will limit the choice of languages that can be used in coding the program. Other constraints outside the scope of the problem and its solution may also affect the choice of a programming language. A programmer may have no choice in the selection of a language for a particular application; for instance, a business may require the use of COBOL because of its readability and because it is used in the company's existing software.

Once the programming language is chosen, the programmer should proceed to code the program according to the **syntax** (the grammatical rules) of the particular language and the rules of structured programming.

STRUCTURED CODING

When structured programming techniques are used to create a program, certain rules are followed during coding. Four major rules concern the use of GOTO statements, the size of program modules, the definition of a proper program, and thorough documentation.

As previously discussed, one characteristic of structured programming is the lack of GOTO statements. The programmer generally writes the program within the confines of three logic patterns: the simple sequence, selection, and the loop. This discipline limits the use of the branch to jump from one program statement to another in a random fashion. Since a GOTO statement signals a jump, the programmer uses as few GOTO statements as possible.

When GOTO statements are avoided, the programmer can code each module as an independent segment. Each module should be relatively small (generally no more than 50 or 60 lines) to facilitate the translation of modules into program statements. When module size is limited in this manner, the coding for each module fits on a single page of computer printout paper, which simplifies program testing and debugging.

Yet another rule of structured coding dictates that modules should have only one entrance and one exit. A program segment that has only one entrance and one exit is called a **proper program** (see Figure 11–15). Following this rule makes the basic logic flow easy to follow and simplifies modification of a program at a later date.

A final rule to follow in writing structured programs is to include documentation, or comment statements, liberally throughout the program. The comments should explain the data items being used and the main module and document each of the lower-level modules. Documentation aids in testing and debugging programs, which should occur at intervals throughout the coding phase. Documentation is also helpful when the program needs to be modified at a later date. See Concept Summary 11–2 for a review of structured programming techniques.

TYPES OF STATEMENTS

Certain types of programming statements are common to most high-level programming languages; they are comments, declarations, input/output statements, computations, comparisons, and loops.

COMMENTS.   The type of statement known as the remark or comment has no effect on program execution; the computer simply ignores these statements. Comments are inserted at key points in the program as doc-

● **FIGURE 11–15**
A Proper Program
Each program segment, or module, has only one entrance and one exit.

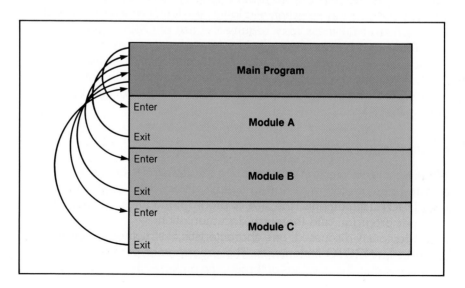

● **COMPUTERS AND INFORMATION PROCESSING**

Structured Design Techniques	
Top-Down Design	Reaches a problem solution by dividing a problem into more and more specific subproblems
Chief Programmer Teams	Uses a team approach to develop software wherein a group of programmers work under the supervision of a chief programmer
Structured Review and Evaluation	A formal review of the design of a program to locate errors and problem areas as efficiently as possible

Structured Coding	
Avoidance of GOTO statements	GOTO statements are discouraged so that program logic is easy to follow
Short program modules	The ideal length of a module is generally considered to be 50 to 60 lines
Proper program modules are used	Each program module has a single entrance and a single exit
Programs are well documented	The program is thoroughly documented to aid in testing, debugging, and later modification, if required

umentation—notes to anyone reading the program to explain the purpose of program segments. For example, if a series of statements sorts a list of names into alphabetical order, the programmer may want to include a remark to the effect: "This segment sorts names in ascending alphabetical order."

DECLARATIONS. The programmer uses declarations to define items used in the program. Examples include definitions of files, records, modules, functions, and the like.

INPUT/OUTPUT STATEMENTS. Input statements bring data into primary storage for use by the program. Output statements transfer data from primary storage to output media such as hard-copy printouts or displays on terminal screens. These statements differ considerably in form (though not so much in function) from one programming language to another.

COMPUTATIONS. Computational instructions perform arithmetic operations such as addition, subtraction, multiplication, division, and exponentiation.

COMPARISONS. This type of statement allows two items to be compared to determine if one is less than, equal to, or greater than the other. The action taken next depends on the result of this comparison.

LOOPS. The final type of statement is the loop, which allows a specified section of a program to be repeated as long as stated conditions remain constant.

● Debugging and Testing the Program

Using structured programming techniques encourages the development of programs with easy-to-follow logic, thus making them much less error-prone than unstructured programs. Nonetheless, programs of any significant length virtually always contain some errors and correcting them can account for a large portion of the time spent in developing software. Therefore, numerous techniques have been developed to make this process easier and more reliable.

The language translator can detect grammatical or syntax errors such as misspellings and incorrect punctuation. Such errors often occur because the programmer does not fully know the programming language being used. Errors in programs are called **bugs,** and the process of locating, isolating, and eliminating bugs is called **debugging.** The amount of time that must be spent in debugging depends on the quality of the program. However, a newly completed program rarely executes successfully the first time it is run. In fact, one-third to one-half of a programmer's time is spent in debugging.

After all of the syntax errors are located and corrected the program can be **tested.** This involves executing the program with input data that is either a representative sample of actual data or a facsimile of it. Often, sample data that can be manipulated easily by the programmer is used so that the computer-determined output can be compared with the programmer-determined correct results.

A complex program is frequently tested in separate modules so that errors can be isolated to specific sections, helping to narrow the search for the cause of an error. The programmer must correct all mistakes; running and rerunning a specific module may be necessary before the cause of an error can be found. The programmer then rewrites the part in error and resubmits it for another test. Care must be taken that correction of one error does not give rise to several others.

Each section of the program must be tested (even sections that will be used infrequently). The programmer often finds **desk checking** helpful. With this method, the programmer pretends to be the computer and, reading each instruction and simulating how the computer would process a data item, attempts to catch any flaws in the program logic.

After a programmer has worked for a long time to correct the logic of a program, he or she may tend to overlook errors. For this reason, programmers sometimes trade their partially debugged programs among themselves. The programmer tracing through a "fresh" program may uncover mistakes in logic that were hidden to the original programmer.

In many cases, program errors prove especially difficult to locate. Two

292   ● COMPUTERS AND INFORMATION PROCESSING

commonly used diagnostic procedures usually available to the programmer in such cases are dump programs and trace programs.

A dump lists the contents of registers and primary storage locations. The dump is often useful in locating an error because the values that were in the registers and primary storage at the time the error occurred can be checked for correctness. If an incorrect value is found, it can be used to help locate the error.

A trace, produced by a trace program, is apt to be easier to use than a dump. The trace lists the steps followed during program execution in the order in which they occurred. The programmer can specify that all or portions of a program be traced. The trace is often used in combination with the desk-checking procedure described above to see if the correct flow of execution has occurred. The values of selected variables (memory locations in primary storage) can also be displayed in the trace; this can be helpful in determining whether the necessary calculations have been performed correctly.

Although program testing, if conducted properly, will uncover most of the errors in a program, it is no guarantee that a program is completely correct. There may be errors that were overlooked in the testing process because of the extremely large number of execution paths a program can take. Therefore, the area of program **verification** is receiving increasing attention in the software development field. Verification involves the process of mathematically proving the correctness of a program through the use of predicate calculus. Although this area of study is still not refined to the level of commercial use, it is likely that it will be widely used in the near future.

It is important to remember that each time a program is modified, the documentation must also be modified to reflect any changes that were made to the program. This updating of documentation when changes are made is critical in industry because programs are continually being altered and expanded. If the documentation no longer matches the program, program maintenance can become very difficult.

● Summary Points

● A sequence of steps, collectively referred to as the software development process, is used to efficiently develop a programming problem solution. The steps are: (1) Define and document the problem. (2) Design and document a solution. (3) Write and document the program. (4) Debug and test the program and revise the documentation as necessary.

● When a programming problem is defined, it is necessary to state the desired output, the needed input, and the processing requirements. These three items collectively are referred to as the program specifications.

● After the problem is defined, a solution can be designed. When designing a solution, the programmer must realize that the computer is capable of executing only four basic logic patterns: a simple sequence (in which statements are executed in the order in which they occur), a selection pattern (in which a comparison is made), a loop (which allows for the repetition of a sequence of statements), and a branch (which allows for program execution to skip over statements). The branch pattern is controversial because its overuse can lead to programs with difficult-to-follow logic.

- Numerous problems were encountered in the early days of software development. Some of these problems were that programmer productivity was low, programs often were not reliable and did not correctly handle invalid input, and programs were not easy to maintain. Consequently, structured programming techniques were developed. Structured programming can be divided into two categories: structured design techniques and structured coding.
- When using structured design, top-down design is used to break a problem into smaller and smaller subproblems. Structure charts are used to graphically illustrate the result of the top-down design process. Each box in the structure chart can be written as a separate subprogram or module when the program is coded.
- HIPO packages are visual aids that supplement structure charts. Typically, an HIPO package consists of three types of diagrams: a visual table of contents, an overview diagram, and a detail diagram.
- Pseudocode consists of an English-like description of the logic of a program.
- Flowcharts graphically represent the logic of a programming problem solution. Each symbol has a specific meaning; flowlines and arrows indicate the direction of flow.
- In business and industry, typically a number of programmers work together on programming projects. Several structured design techniques are often used in developing these large projects. Two of these are chief programmer teams and structured review and evaluation.
- The chief programmer team (CPT) concept involves organizing a small group of programmers under the supervision of a chief programmer. Usually the chief programmer is assisted by a highly qualified backup programmer. A librarian is responsible for maintaining up-to-date documentation on the project. Other programmers are included on the team according to the needs of the particular project.
- Software designs must be reviewed before they are implemented. In an informal design review, the design documentation is reviewed before coding takes place. Later, a formal design review may be held to discuss the overall completeness, accuracy, and quality of the design.
- The process of writing the program in a programming language is referred to as coding. In structured coding, a number of rules are followed, including avoiding branch (GOTO) statements, dividing the program into independent modules each working together to form the entire program, writing each module so that it is a proper program (that is, containing only one entrance and one exit), and fully documenting the program.
- Some of the general types of statements in a program are: comments, declarations, input/output statements, computations, comparison, and loops.
- Although using structured programming techniques encourages the development of programs that are less error-prone than unstructured programs, programs of any length nearly always contain some bugs, or errors. Debugging is the process of locating and correcting these errors.

● Testing programs involves running them with a variety of data to determine if they always obtain correct results. It is difficult to locate all program errors through testing. Therefore, program verification, which involves mathematically proving the correctness of a program, is an area of increasing interest in the software development field. Although program verification is not yet practical on a large scale, it is likely to prove useful in the near future.

● Review Questions

1. What are the four steps in the software development process? Identify which steps could be performed by a system analyst and which by a programmer.

2. Why should the system analyst consult with the potential program user(s) when developing software?

3. What is included in the program specifications?

4. Is it important for a system analyst to have a specific programming language in mind when performing the first two steps of the software development process? Why or why not?

5. What are the four basic logic patterns that the computer is capable of executing? Which of these patterns is avoided in structured programming? Why?

6. List four early problems in software development that led to the development of structured programming techniques.

7. What is meant by the term top-down design and how are structure charts used in this design methodology?

8. Explain each of the three types of diagrams that are usually included in an HIPO package.

9. Draw a flowchart that depicts the steps necessary to convert a Fahrenheit temperature to a Celsius temperature and print both temperatures. Then write the pseudocode for this problem.

10. Explain the chief programmer team concept. What is the role of the librarian in this approach to software development?

11. List four rules that are followed in structured coding.

12. List and describe the different types of statements used in most high-level programming languages.

13. Explain the difference between program testing and program verification.

Eli Lilly and Company

COMPANY HISTORY

On May 10, 1876, Colonel Eli Lilly, a Civil War veteran, began operating a small laboratory in downtown Indianapolis, Indiana, to manufacture medications. With total assets of $1,400 in fluid extracts and cash, Lilly began producing pills and other medicines. In 1881, the firm, which had since incorporated as Eli Lilly and Company, moved to the location just south of downtown Indianapolis that today continues to house its principal offices and research headquarters.

Two of the best-known medical discoveries to which Lilly made substantial contributions are insulin and the Salk polio vaccine. More recently, the company has developed a number of important antibiotics, cancer treatment agents, and human insulin, the first human health product from recombinant DNA technology. Besides manufacturing pharmaceutical products, Lilly has diversified into agricultural products, cosmetics, medical instrument systems, and diagnostic products through its subsidiaries.

Products are manufactured and distributed through the company's own facilities in the United States, Puerto Rico, and 28 other countries. In 18 countries, the company owns or has an interest in manufacturing facilities. Its products are sold in approximately 130 countries.

LILLY TODAY

With interests in business and research scattered across the globe, Eli Lilly and Company has developed an extensive data-processing operation to support every department of the corporation. The Scientific Information Systems Division handles activities related to research and development. Corporate Information Systems and Services supports the firm's business data-processing needs. The Corporate Computer Center consists of five large IBM computers and three Digital Equipment Corporation computers that receive and process data trans-

mitted to the center via on-line teleprocessing, remote job entry (RJE), and time-sharing terminals located in user departments of the corporation in U.S. and overseas locations. The Corporate Computer Center supports more than 300 time-sharing terminals, more than 2,000 teleprocessing devices, and at least 100 RJE stations. In a typical business day, more than 12,000 programs are executed and about 600,000 teleprocessing transactions are processed. More than 300 personal computer work stations for professionals have been acquired, and about 500 secretarial workers now use office terminals.

The Information Systems Development Division, which employs approximately 400 people, is responsible for the design, development, and maintenance of business information systems. The division is composed of functional development groups; each group works with line management and staff groups to develop application programs designed to reduce operating expenses and furnish information for more effective management. Marketing activities, manufacturing departments, financial systems, all phases of engineering, patent and general legal affairs, corporate affairs, and industrial relations are supported by this organization.

When a user department requests a major new application, a project is initiated to begin a multiphase process called PLAD (Process for Lilly Application Development). The first phase of the process requires the department to document the objectives and requirements of the requested system. Some projects warrant the review and approval of a separate objectives document before the detailed requirements are studied. These documents are carefully prepared to serve several purposes:

—User and management sign-off helps assure that the system will meet the business need.

—Technical reviews provide the opportunity for computer operations, system programming, data management, and other support groups to verify feasibility and resource availability.

—Cost/benefit analysis supplies the basis for management approval.

After systems and user management have approved the objectives/requirements documents, the design phase begins.

In the external design phase, the users are given a detailed understanding of how the system will work, so they can verify that the system as planned by the designer will meet their specific needs. Logical system structure charts explain the flow and the transactions for each part of the system. Users participate in designing reports, screen formats, and inquiries. The external design report documents the architecture of the system and furnishes plans for the following phases.

The next phase, internal design, produces the blueprints for the construction of the system. The user language of the external design phase is translated into technical terms. The system structure is divided into subsystems and programs. Specifications describe the functions performed by each program. All data elements are defined in the data element dictionary. Data files used for communications between programs are specified. Experienced designers, not a part of the project team, conduct the design walk-through. The internal design report includes plans for the coding, testing, and installation phases to follow.

During the coding and unit test phase, additional members often join the project team. With the information from internal design and firm staffing plans, the project leader is able to project a fairly reliable finish date. Each team member begins detailed design and coding of assigned programs. When coding is completed, the program is submitted for compilation. Any clerical errors should be detected during the compilation process. This step is repeated until an error-free compilation is achieved.

The programmer then conducts a walk-through, explaining the purpose of the program to a previously uninvolved third party. This person, usually a fellow programmer, can provide fresh insights into areas where the purpose of the program is unclear (and thus requires additional comments). The person can also desk-check the program to identify logic errors that the programmer has overlooked.

At this point, before the actual testing, the program is usually recompiled according to a compiler program that optimizes the machine language code (builds instruction sequences that will be most efficient for repetitive processing purposes). It may also give diagnostic messages indicating possible logic problems.

The program is now ready to be executed using real, or "live," test data that represent what may be processed in real-life situations. If the data are processed correctly, the program is ready for use. However, cor-

rect processing seldom occurs on the first run. To identify the causes of errors, the programmer may submit trial runs with abnormal terminations that produce core dumps at the end of execution. Occasionally, an error is so subtle that the programmer cannot determine its cause by analyzing a dump. In this case, a trace program can be used to indicate the execution flow through the entire sequence of instructions. The programmer can then determine if the flow has mistakenly entered a wrong section of the program.

The system test phase includes heavy user participation and is actually the beginning of user training. Each subsystem is thoroughly tested with user-supplied input data. Finally, the entire system is tested, usually running in parallel with the old system.

After the system has been thoroughly tested, members of the staff who will be involved in its operation make a final review of the application. This review includes a check to see that (1) the system conforms to established standards; (2) user and system development documentation requirements have been satisfied; and (3) the system is ready to be assigned to "production" status. If the total application is found to be acceptable, it is released for implementation.

The application is allowed to operate for two to three months following implementation. After this period, the user area and operations staff review the application and either document their acceptance or suggest revisions.

The complexity of activities in developing a new application, from the objectives document through completion of the system test, is justified by the financial and business needs of such an undertaking. Failure to properly perform any of the steps in the process can result in at best considerable difficulty and at worst a complete failure of the application. For this reason, Eli Lilly and Company has adopted the stringent standards described here.

DISCUSSION POINTS

1. Why does Lilly involve users so heavily in designing a new application?

2. What procedures are used to test the applications prior to their implementation?

12 PROGRAMMING LANGUAGES

●ARTICLE
Simpler Writing for Complex Software

John Paul Newport Jr.
Fortune

While computers have grown exponentially faster and more powerful in recent years, programming has lagged behind; many experts think software is now the main barrier to greater performance. The authors of very complex programs may soon be able to make up some lost ground thanks to Rational, a small company with a big, bold name. Rational's R1000 computer system could boost the productivity of programmers writing complex software by a factor of ten—and make software more reliable.

The production model of the R1000 will not be ready until late this year, but four test machines are in the hands of customers, including Lockheed and Rockwell International. Lockheed estimates that the R1000 should reduce the final design stage of a very large software project from 15 months to three, and is so enamored of the system that it plans to invest $10 million in Rational. Says Walter Le-Berge, Lockheed's senior vice president for research and development: "We expect Rational to be an important part of our ability to compete for future contracts like the space station and the Strategic Defense Inititative."

The R1000 is the brainchild of Paul Levy, 29, and Michael Devlin, 30, who were classmates at the U.S. Air Force Academy. In 1979 the two were in charge of maintaining a massive computer program that tracked satellites for the Air Force in Sunnyvale, California. "We saw that these programs already were so complex that making changes in them was almost impossible," says Levy. Devlin came up with several new techniques for improving software development while working on his master's degree in computer science at Stanford University, and the pair decided to start a company to exploit his ideas. With the help of Arthur Rock, the venture capitalist behind Intel and Apple, Rational raised $30 million.

Levy and Devlin based their system on a powerful language called Ada, which Honeywell's French affiliate developed for the Pentagon in the 1970s. The Pentagon wants to make Ada its standard language for all weapons and communications systems, but contractors have balked because Ada is complicated to use. The R1000 makes Ada more lovable. It checks for errors and in many cases completes lines of instructions a programmer has started. It then translates the Ada program into the binary code that other computers understand. It can accommodate up to 30 programmers working at individual terminals. The R1000 monitors them and sends out warnings when one programmer's work seems incompatible with the rest.

Rational's first targets for the R1000 are the 20 largest aerospace companies, which should find it irresistible for coping with Ada. Most other companies may blanch at the $595,000 price (terminals and printers are extra). But Levy figures potential buyers of the R1000 also include automated manufacturers and software companies. With $17 million in cash and little debt, Rational's expectation of turning a profit next year may indeed be rational.

● **The R1000 will probably make the difficult Ada a more popular programming language. Someday devices may be able to receive simple spoken natural-language instructions and write, in turn, complex Ada programs.**

● Introduction

Languages are systems of communication. Programming languages are communication systems that people can use to communicate with computers. The earliest computers were programmed by arranging various wires and switches within the computer components. Up to 6,000 switches could be set on the ENIAC to execute one program. However, when a new program was to be run, all the switches had to be reset. This was clearly inefficient. The EDSAC, the first stored-program computer, allowed instructions to be entered into primary storage without rewiring or resetting switches. Codes that correspond to the required on/off electrical states were needed to enter these instructions. These codes were called **machine language**. Later, **assembly language** (which uses simple codes to represent machine-language instructions) was developed to offset the tedium of writing machine-language programs. A disadvantage of both machine and assembly languages is that they are dependent on the type of computer system being used; the programmer must be familiar with the hardware for which the program is being written.

The development of FORTRAN in the mid-1950s signaled the beginning of a trend toward high-level languages that were more oriented toward the programmer rather than the computer. Since that time, a wide variety of high-level languages has been developed. At the present time there are more than two hundred distinct computer programming languages.

This chapter discusses some of the programming languages most commonly used today. As with natural languages such as English and German, each of these programming languages has a history of development, specific characteristics, and so forth. The unique features, characteristics, advantages, and disadvantages of each language are explained in this chapter along with typical applications.

● Standardization of Languages

One of the advantages of using high-level languages is the potential for these programs to be **portable**; that is, to be able to be executed on a wide variety of systems with minimal changes. The problem with this idea is that the language must be standardized; that is, rules must be developed so that all of the compilers for a particular language will be able to translate the same program. Therefore, it is necessary that standards be established for programming languages. A number of agencies authorize these standards. The most influential is the American National Standards Institute (ANSI), which has developed or adopted widely used standards for many languages including FORTRAN, Pascal, BASIC, and COBOL (all of which will be discussed in this chapter). One difficulty is that many manufacturers do not entirely adhere to these standards. They often add extra features (referred to as "enhancements") to their compilers to make them more useful. This means that a program that will run on one computer system will not necessarily run on another system without modification.

● Categorizing Languages

Computer scientists have long tried to categorize programming languages. This categorization helps the programmer in determining which language might be most useful in a particular situation. Some different ways in which it is possible to categorize languages are listed below:

● **Low-level or high-level.** This refers to the degree to which the language is oriented toward the hardware as compared to the programmer. Low-level languages are oriented toward the computer whereas high-level languages are oriented more toward the programmer. Therefore, low-level languages are easier for the computer to execute but high-level languages are easier for people to use and understand.

● **Structured or unstructured.** The characteristics of structured programming languages were discussed in Chapter 11. Briefly, these languages allow programmers to easily divide programs into modules, each performing a specific task. Also, structured programming languages provide a wide variety of control structures such as loops (to perform repetitive tasks) and decision statements (to make comparisons). These features result in programs with easy-to-follow logic that are easy to modify and maintain. Many languages that were developed before the widespread acceptance of structured programming have since been modified to include structured techniques (COBOL is an example).

● **Procedure-oriented or problem-oriented.** Procedure-oriented languages place programming emphasis on describing the computational and logical procedures required to solve a problem. Commonly used procedure-oriented languages include COBOL, FORTRAN, and Pascal. A problem-oriented language is one in which the problem and solution are described without the necessary procedures being specified, therefore requiring little programming skill. RPG is the only problem-oriented language discussed in this chapter.

● **General purpose or special purpose.** General-purpose languages are those languages that can be used to solve a wide variety of programming problems. BASIC and Pascal are examples of general-purpose languages. Some examples of categories of special-purpose languages might be educational languages, business languages, and scientific languages. For example, FORTRAN, a language used mostly for mathematical and scientific applications, is an example of a scientific language.

Although it would be nice to be able to neatly categorize each language, many languages fall somewhere in between one extreme or the other in any specific category. For example, C, a programming language that we will discuss in more detail later, is often considered to be neither a low-level nor a high-level language, but somewhere in between. Nonetheless, these categories can prove useful in making generalized statements about languages and their appropriate uses. Therefore, where appropriate we will attempt to categorize the languages discussed in this chapter.

Special-Purpose Languages

CATE-GORY	CHARACTERISTICS	EXAMPLES
Education	Should teach good programming concepts and be fairly easy to learn; should be able to be used to write a variety of programs to give the beginner a range of experiences	Pascal Logo BASIC
Scientific	Able to perform complex mathematical operations with a high degree of accuracy	FORTRAN FORTH
Business	Able to handle large data files efficiently and to perform the types of data processing necessary in business	COBOL

● Low-Level Languages

MACHINE LANGUAGE

Machine language is the language of the computer; it is the only language that the computer is able to execute directly. Programs written in any other language must be translated into machine language before the computer is able to execute them.

Remember from Chapter 3 that all data in digital computers is stored as either on or off electrical states which we represent through the use of 1s and 0s. Machine language must take the form of 1s and 0s to be understood by the computer. But coding a program in this binary form is very tedious; therefore machine language is often coded in either octal (base 8) or hexadecimal (base 16) codes.

The programmer using machine language must specify everything to the computer. Every step the computer must take to execute a program must be coded; therefore, the programmer must know exactly how the computer works. The actual numerical addresses of the storage locations containing instructions and data must be specified.

In order to accomplish the necessary specificity, each machine-language instruction has two parts. The **op code** (short for operation code) tells the computer what function to perform, such as adding two values. The **operand** tells the computer what data to use when performing that function. The operand takes the form of the specific storage address where the data is located. Figure 12–1 shows some examples of machine-language instructions.

The greatest advantages of machine language are that the computer can execute it efficiently and that generally it uses less storage space than high-level languages. It also allows the programmer to fully utilize the computer's potential because the programmer is interacting directly with the computer hardware.

On the other hand, this type of programming is extremely tedious, time consuming, and error prone. The instructions are difficult to remember and to use. In addition, programs written in machine language will

● **FIGURE 12–1**
Machine-Language Instructions Expressed in the Hexadecimal (Base 16) Number System

48	00	23C0	
4C	00	23C2	
40	00	2310	
D2	01	2310	2310
48	00	2310	
4E	00	2028	
F3	17	3002	2028
9G	F0	3003	

execute only on the specific type of system for which they were written. Therefore, machine language is used only in rare instances today.

ASSEMBLY LANGUAGE

Assembly languages were developed to alleviate many of the disadvantages of machine-language programming. When programming in an assembly language, the programmer uses **mnemonics** (symbolic names) to specify machine operations; thus, coding in 0s and 1s is no longer required. Mnemonics are alphabetic abbreviations for the machine-language op codes. Table 12–1 shows some common arithmetic operations coded in assembly language and in machine language. Assembly-language instructions differ depending on the type and model of computer being programmed. Thus, assembly-language programs, like machine-language programs, can be written only for the type of computer that will execute them.

There are three basic parts to an assembly-language instruction: an op code and an operand, as in machine language, and a label. Table 12–2 shows a section of an assembly-language program with the parts of the instructions labeled. The **label** is a programmer-supplied name that represents the location in which a particular instruction will be stored. When the programmer wishes to refer to that instruction, he or she can simply specify the label, without regard to the actual address of the storage location.

The op code, as in machine language, tells the computer what operation to perform, but it is in mnemonic form. The operand, also in mnemonic form, represents the address of the item that is to be manipulated. Each instruction may contain one or two operands. The remainder of the line can be used for remarks that explain to humans the operation being

● **TABLE 12–1**
Examples of Assembly-Language Mnemonic Code

OPERATION	TYPICAL ASSEMBLY-LANGUAGE OP CODE	TYPICAL BINARY (MACHINE LANGUAGE) OP CODE
Add memory to register	A	01011010
Add (decimal) memory to register	AP	11111010
Multiply register by memory	M	01011100
Multiply (decimal) register by memory	MP	11111100
Subtract memory from register	S	01011011
Subtract (decimal) memory from register	SP	11111011
Move (numeric) from register to memory	MVN	11010001
Compare memory to register	C	01011001
Compare (decimal) memory to register	CP	11111001
Zero register and add (decimal) memory to register	ZAP	11111000

LABEL	OP CODE	OPERANDS A AND B	REMARKS
OVERTIME	AP	OVERTIME, FORTY	BEGIN OVERTIME COMPUTATION
	MP	OVERTIME, WKRATE	
	AP	GROSS, WKRATE	
	SP	WKHRS, FORTY	COMPUTE OVERTIME PAY
	MP	WKHRS, ONEHLF	
	MP	GROSS, WKHRS	
	MVN	GROSS +5(1), GROSS +6	
	ZAP	GROSS(7), GROSS (6)	
	AP	GROSS, OVERTIME	
TAXRATE	CP	GROSS, = P'25000'	BEGIN TAX COMPUTATION

performed (the remarks are optional and are simply ignored by the computer).

There are several advantages to using assembly language. The main advantage is that it can be used to develop programs that use storage space and processing time efficiently. As with machine language, the programmer is able to fully utilize the computer's processing capabilities. Second, the assembler program (the operating system that translates the assembly program into machine language) performs certain error-checking functions and generates error messages, if appropriate, that are useful to the programmer when debugging the program.

The main disadvantage of assembly language is that it is more cumbersome to use than high-level languages. Generally, one assembly-language instruction is translated into one machine-language instruction; this one-for-one relationship leads to long program preparation time. However, this feature makes it easier for the computer to translate the program into machine language than to translate a high-level language into machine language. Another disadvantage of assembly language is the high level of skill required to use it effectively. As with machine language, the programmer must know the computer to be used and must be able to work with binary or hexadecimal numbers. Finally, assembly language, like machine language, is machine-dependent; a program written for one computer generally cannot be executed on another.

Assembly language is often used for writing operating systems. Because operating systems are designed for particular computers, they are machine-dependent. The potential efficiency of assembly language also makes it well suited for operating-system programming.

● High-Level Languages

In this section we will discuss a cross-section of high-level languages. High-level languages are much easier to understand than low-level lan-

Levels of Programming Languages

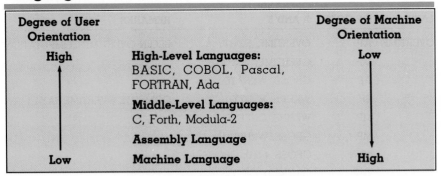

Degree of User Orientation		Degree of Machine Orientation
High	**High-Level Languages:** BASIC, COBOL, Pascal, FORTRAN, Ada	Low
	Middle-Level Languages: C, Forth, Modula-2	
	Assembly Language	
Low	**Machine Language**	High

guages because they use meaningful words such as READ and PRINT in their instructions. However, they must be translated into machine language for execution. This translation is performed by one of two types of system programs: an interpreter or a compiler. Interpreters and compilers will be discussed later in this chapter. Also, one high-level statement may generate several machine-language statements. Therefore, high-level language programs are more difficult to translate into machine language than are assembly-language programs. Traditionally, high-level languages have not made as efficient use of computer resources as machine and assembly languages. However, with the ever-increasing sophistication of compilers, this is no longer necessarily true.

FORTRAN

FORTRAN (FORmula TRANslator) is the oldest high-level programming language. It originated in the mid-1950s, when most programs were written in either assembly language or machine language. Efforts were made to develop a programming language that resembled English but could be translated into machine language by the computer. This effort, backed by IBM, produced FORTRAN—the first commercially available high-level language.

Early FORTRAN compilers contained many errors and were not always efficient in their use of computer resources. Moreover, several manufacturers offered variations of FORTRAN that could be used only on their particular computers. Although many improvements were made, early implementations of FORTRAN continued to suffer from this lack of standardization. In response to this problem, the American National Standards Institute laid the groundwork for a standardized FORTRAN. In 1966, two standard versions of FORTRAN were recognized, ANSI FORTRAN and Basic FORTRAN. A more recent version, FORTRAN 77, provides more enhancements to the language. In spite of the attempts to standardize FORTRAN, however, most computer manufacturers have continued to offer their own extensions of the language. Therefore, compatibility of FORTRAN programs remains a problem today.

In 1957, when the language was first released, computers were used primarily by engineers, scientists, and mathematicians. Consequently,

FORTRAN was developed to suit their needs and its purpose has remained unchanged. FORTRAN is a procedure-oriented language with extraordinary mathematical capabilities. It is especially applicable when numerous complex arithmetic calculations are necessary. In general, FORTRAN is not a good business language. Its capabilities are not well suited to programs involving file maintenance, data editing, or document production. However, use of FORTRAN is increasing for certain types of business applications, such as feasibility studies, forecasting, and production scheduling. Another disadvantage of FORTRAN is that it does not resemble English as closely as many high-level languages; therefore, the programs must be well documented so that they are understandable. Figure 12–2 contains a simple FORTRAN program that calculates a payroll.

BASIC

BASIC, an acronym for Beginner's All-purpose Symbolic Instruction Code, was developed in the mid-1960s at Dartmouth College by Professors John Kemeny and Thomas Kurtz. It was originally developed for use on time-

● FIGURE 12–2
Payroll Program in FORTRAN

```
FORTRAN IV G LEVEL 21      MAIN              DATE = 81214

      WRITE (6,1)
1     FORMAT('1','EMPLOYEENAME',5X,'NETPAY'/'')
2     READ (5,3) NA,NB,NC,ND,NHOURS,WAGE,IEND
3     FORMAT (4A4, I2, 2X, F4.2, 54X, I2)
      IF (IEND.EQ.99) STOP
      IF (NHOURS.GT.40) GO TO 10
      GROSS = FLOAT(NHOURS)*WAGE
      GO TO 15
10    REG = 40.*WAGE
      OVERTM=FLOAT(NHOURS-40)*(1.5*WAGE)
      GROSS=REG+OVERTM
15    IF (GROSS.GT.250.) GO TO 20
      RATE = .14
      GO TO 25
20    RATE = .20
25    TAX=RATE*GROSS
      PAY = GROSS - TAX
      WRITE (6,50) NA,NB,NC,ND,PAY
50    FORMAT ('  ', ,4A4, 3X, F6.2)
      GO TO 2
      END
```

Output

EMPLOYEE NAME	NET PAY
LYNN MANGINO	224.00
THOMAS RITTER	212.42
MARIE OLSON	209.00
LORI DUNLEVY	172.00
WILLIAM WILSON	308.00

BASIC or Pascal?

When microcomputers were born, the language they used was BASIC. Early microcomputers had little memory, and a programmer was forced to use condensed versions of the original BASIC written by Kemeny and Kurtz for the time-sharing mainframe system at Dartmouth College. Although microcomputer technology became more advanced, BASIC remained the most popular microcomputer language and soon became the standard beginning computer language in high schools.

A small group of programming wizards began to campaign against the use of BASIC in schools, claiming that BASIC encouraged poor programming and logic habits. They offered Pascal as an alternative, and the great BASIC/Pascal debate began: which language is best suited to be the beginning language for high school students?

The issue is important because the first language students learn sets up programming patterns that may continue throughout the students' careers. The argument between the proponents of BASIC and the gurus of Pascal focuses on such programming patterns. Most implementations of BASIC build bad habits such as transferring control within a program using the GOTO statement. However, with more structured versions of BASIC such as True BASIC becoming available, this is no longer a completely valid complaint. Nonetheless, Pascal is widely accepted as the introductory language at universities. Therefore, those high schools that aim to prepare their students for college programming courses will need to provide them with the necessary tools. A working knowledge of the Pascal language is a good starting point.

sharing systems to help students learn to program. Inspired by FORTRAN, BASIC is a simplified version of that first high-level language.

The growth in the use of time-sharing systems has been accompanied by an increase in the use of BASIC. Although BASIC was originally intended to be used by colleges and universities for instructional purposes, many companies have adopted it for their data-processing needs. In addition, the increased popularity of microcomputers in homes is furthering the use of BASIC, since it is the language most often implemented on these computers.

Among BASIC's most attractive features are its simplicity and flexibility. Because it is easy to learn, it can be used by people with little or no programming experience; a novice programmer can write fairly complex programs in BASIC in a matter of a few hours. It is a general-purpose language that can be used to write programs to solve a wide variety of problems. A BASIC program is shown in Figure 12–3.

The simplicity of BASIC has led many manufacturers to offer different versions of the language. Although there is an established standard (American National Standards Institute BASIC), few manufacturers adhere to this standard and virtually all of them have added their own quirks to the language. Therefore, BASIC programs written for one system often need substantial modification before being used on another.

The main criticism of BASIC focuses on the fact that traditionally it has not been a structured programming language. This means that many popular versions of BASIC do not encourage dividing the program into modules nor do they contain adequate control statements. In many implementations of BASIC it is often necessary to use unconditional branches (commonly referred to as GOTO statements) that can cause program logic to be convoluted and difficult to follow.

Some newer versions of BASIC do encourage the development of structured programs. One of these is True BASIC, which was developed by the original developers of BASIC, Kemeny and Kurtz, and was put on the market in 1984. True BASIC retains many of the strengths of the first version produced twenty years ago; it is an economical language, using English-like commands. Yet it provides extensions and options that allow programmers to develop properly structured programs and sophisticated graphics and perform text processing. In addition, ANSI is in the process of adopting new standards for a structured BASIC. It will be interesting to see how widely implemented these new standards will be.

PASCAL

Pascal was the first major programming language to implement the ideas and methodology of structured programming. Niklaus Wirth, a Swiss computer scientist, developed Pascal between 1968 and 1970; in 1971 the first compiler became available. Wirth named the language after the French mathematician and philosopher Blaise Pascal, who invented the first mechanical adding machine. In 1982, ANSI adopted a standard for Pascal.

Like BASIC, Pascal was first developed to teach programming concepts to students, but it rapidly expanded beyond its initial purpose and has found increasing acceptance in business and scientific applications.

```
10 REM ***                PAYROLL PROGRAM            ***
20 REM ***    THIS PROGRAM CALCULATES A WEEKLY       ***
30 REM ***    PAYROLL.                               ***
40 REM
50 PRINT "EMPLOYEE NAME",,"NET PAY"
60 PRINT
70 READ NME$,HRS,WAGE
80 WHILE NME$ <> "END OF DATA"
90     IF HRS <=40 THEN GROSS = HRS * WAGE ELSE GOSUB 1000
100    IF GROSS > 250 THEN LET TAX = .2 ELSE LET TAX = .14
110    LET TAX2 = TAX * GROSS
120    LET PAY = GROSS - TAX2
130    PRINT NME$,,PAY
140    READ NME$,HRS,WAGE
150 WEND
999 END
1000 REM
1010 REM *******************************************
1020 REM ***           SUBROUTINE OVERTIME        ***
1030 REM *******************************************
1040 REM
1050 LET REG = 40 * WAGE
1060 LET OVRTIME = (HRS - 40) * (1.5 * WAGE)
1070 LET GROSS = REG + OVRTIME
1080 RETURN
1090 REM *******************************************
2000 DATA "LYNN MANGINO",35,8.00
2010 DATA "THOMAS RITTER",48,4.75
2020 DATA "MARIE OLSON",45,5.50
2030 DATA "LORI DUNLEVY",40,5.00
2040 DATA "ERIC WILSON",50,7.00
2050 DATA "END OF DATA",0,0
```

Output

EMPLOYEE NAME	NET PAY
LYNN MANGINO	224
THOMAS RITTER	212.42
MARIE OLSON	209
LORI DUNLEVY	172
ERIC WILSON	308

Pascal increasingly is becoming the first programming language taught to students at the college level; at present, it is the introductory programming course for computer science students at 80 percent of all universities. It is relatively easy to learn, like BASIC; in addition, it is a powerful language capable of performing a wide variety of tasks including sophisticated mathematical operations. The main reason for the widespread use of Pascal as a teaching tool is that it is a structured language. Each Pascal program is made up of modules called procedures that can be nested within one another. Pascal contains a wide variety of useful control structures such as the IF/THEN/ELSE decision statement and the WHILE/DO loop. These features encourage students to develop good programming habits. Figure 12–4 contains a short program written in Pascal.

```
program payroll (emplfile, output);

(* This program calculates a weekly payroll. *)

type
   array20 = array[1..20] of char;

var
   emplfile : text;
   name : array20;
   wage, hours, grosspay, tax, netpay : real;

(********************************************************)

procedure readname (var name : array20);

var
   i : integer;
   count : integer;

begin   (* readname *)

   i := 1;
   while not eoln (emplfile) and (i <= 20) do
   begin   (* while *)
      read (emplfile, name[i]);
      i := i + 1
   end;   (* while *)
   readln (emplfile);

   for count := i to 20 do
      name[count] := ' '

end;   (* readname *)

(********************************************************)
```

At first Pascal's availability was limited, but more computer manufacturers are now offering Pascal compilers for their machines. Some compilers developed for microcomputers, such as the popular TURBO Pascal
implementation, are surprisingly inexpensive and versatile. Many of these
compilers have good graphics capabilities. Programmers can create intricate, detailed objects using properly equipped display terminals. This
feature is attractive to scientists and increasingly to business personnel
as well. A disadvantage of Pascal is that many people believe it has
poor input/output capabilities. Therefore, it is not particularly well suited
to applications involving manipulation of large data files.

COBOL

COBOL (COmmon Business-Oriented Language) is the most frequently
used business programming language. Before 1960 no language was
well suited to solving business problems. Recognizing this inadequacy,
the Department of Defense met with representatives of computer users,
manufacturers, and government installations to examine the feasibility
of developing a common business programming language. That was the

```
            begin   (* payroll *)

                reset (emplfile);
                writeln;
                writeln ('EMPLOYEE NAME':13, 'NET PpcAY':27);

                while not eof (emplfile) do
                begin   (* while *)
                    readname (name);
                    readln (emplfile, wage, hours);

                    (* Calculate gross pay *)
                    if hours <= 40
                        then grosspay := hours * wage
                        else grosspay := hours * wage + (hours - 40) * wage * 0.5;

                    (* Calculate net pay *)
                    if grosspay > 250
                        then tax := 0.2 * grosspay
                        else tax := 0.14 * grosspay; temp1.p
                    netpay := grosspay - tax;
                    writeln (name:20, netpay:20:2)

                end   (* while *)

            end.   (* payroll *)
```

Output

```
O  |                                                        | O
   |       EMPLOYEE NAME                    NET PAY          |
   |       LYNN MANGINO                     224.00          |
   |       THOMAS RITTER                    212.42          |
O  |       MARIE OLSON                      209.00          | O
   |       LORI SANCHEZ                     172.00          |
   |       WILLIAM LUOMA                    308.00          |
O  |                                                        | O
```

beginning of the CODASYL (Conference Of DAta SYstems Languages) Committee. By 1960 the committee had established the specifications for COBOL and the first commercial versions of the language were offered later that year. The government furthered its cause in the mid-1960s by refusing to buy or lease any computer that could not process a program written in COBOL.

One of the objectives of the CODASYL group was to design a machine-independent language—that is, a language that could be used on any computer with any COBOL compiler, regardless of who manufactured it. Thus, when several manufacturers began offering their own modifications and extensions of COBOL, the need for standardization became apparent. In 1968 ANSI published guidelines for a standardized COBOL that became known as ANSI COBOL. In 1974 ANSI expanded the language definition in a revised version of the standard. These standards have been widely accepted in industry. After many years of difficult analysis and compromise, a new set of ANSI standards for COBOL was published in 1985. These new standards made many changes to the language including adding structured programming facilities. It will be several years before it is known how widely accepted and implemented this new COBOL standard will be.

A key objective of the designers of COBOL was to make the language similar to English. Their intent was that a program written in COBOL should be understandable even to casual readers, and hence self-documenting. You can judge how successful they were by looking at Figure 12–5, which shows a payroll application program written in COBOL.

● **FIGURE 12–5**
Payroll Program in COBOL
(Continued Facing Page)

```
IDENTIFICATION DIVISION.
PROGRAM-ID. PAYROLL.
INPUT-OUTPUT SECTION.
FILE-CONTROL.
    SELECT CARD-FILE ASSIGN TO UR-S-SYSIN.
    SELECT PRINT-FILE ASSIGN TO UR-S-OUTPUT.

DATA DIVISION.
FILE SECTION.
FD   CARD-FILE
     LABEL RECORDS ARE OMITTED
     RECORD CONTAINS 80 CHARACTERS
     DATA RECORD IS PAY-RECORD.
01   PAY-RECORD.
     03   EMPLOYEE-NAME        PIC A(16).
     03   HOURS-WORKED         PIC 99.
     03   WAGE-PER-HOUR        PIC 99V99.
     03   FILLER               PIC X(58).

FD   PRINT-FILE
     LABEL RECORDS ARE OMITTED
     RECORD CONTAINS 132 CHARACTERS
     DATA RECORD IS PRINT-RECORD.
01   PRINT-RECORD             PIC X(132).

WORKING-STORAGE SECTION.
77   GROSS-PAY               PIC 9(3)V99.
77   REGULAR-PAY             PIC 9(3)V99.
77   OVERTIME-PAY            PIC 9(3)V99.
77   NET-PAY                 PIC 9(3)V99.
77   TAX                     PIC 9(3)V99.
77   OVERTIME-HOURS          PIC 99.
77   OVERTIME-RATE           PIC 9(3)V999.
77   EOF-FLAG                PIC X(3)        VALUE 'NO'.
01   HEADING-LINE.
     03   FILLER             PIC X           VALUE SPACES.
     03   FILLER             PIC X(21)       VALUE
          'EMPLOYEE NAME'.
     03   FILLER             PIC X(7)        VALUE
          'NET PAY'.

01   OUTPUT-RECORD.
     03   FILLER             PIC X           VALUE SPACES.
     03   NAME               PIC A(16).
     03   FILLER             PIC X(5)        VALUE SPACES.
     03   AMOUNT             PIC $$$$.99.
     03   FILLER             PIC X(103)      VALUE SPACES.

PROCEDURE DIVISION.
MAIN-LOGIC.
    OPEN INPUT CARD-FILE
         OUTPUT PRINT-FILE.
    PERFORM HEADING-ROUTINE.
    READ CARD-FILE
         AT END MOVE 'YES' TO EOF-FLAG.
    PERFORM WORK-LOOP UNTIL EOF-FLAG = 'YES'.
    CLOSE CARD-FILE
          PRINT-FILE.
    STOP RUN.
```

● **COMPUTERS AND INFORMATION PROCESSING**

COBOL programs have a formal, uniform structure. Many types of statements must appear in the same form and the same position in every COBOL program. The basic unit of a COBOL program is the sentence. Sentences are combined to form paragraphs; paragraphs are joined into sections; and sections are contained within divisions. COBOL programs

```
HEADING-ROUTINE.
     WRITE PRINT-RECORD FROM HEADING-LINE
          BEFORE ADVANCING 2 LINES.
WORK-LOOP.
     IF HOURS-WORKED IS GREATER THAN 40
          THEN
               PERFORM OVERTIME-ROUTINE
          ELSE
               MULTIPLY HOURS-WORKED BY WAGE-PER-HOUR
                    GIVING GROSS-PAY.
     PERFORM TAX-COMPUTATION.
     PERFORM OUTPUT-ROUTINE.
     READ CARD-FILE AT END MOVE 'YES' TO EOF-FLAG.

OVERTIME-ROUTINE.
     MULTIPLY WAGE-PER-HOUR BY 40 GIVING REGULAR-PAY.
     SUBTRACT 40 FROM HOURS-WORKED GIVING OVERTIME-HOURS.
     MULTIPLY REGULAR-PAY BY 1.5 GIVING OVERTIME-RATE.
     MULTIPLY OVERTIME-HOURS BY OVERTIME-RATE
          GIVING OVERTIME-PAY.
     ADD REGULAR-PAY, OVERTIME-PAY GIVING GROSS-PAY.

TAX-COMPUTATION.
     IF GROSS-PAY IS GREATER THAN 250
          THEN
               MULTIPLY GROSS-PAY BY 0.20 GIVING TAX
          ELSE
               MULTIPLY GROSS-PAY BY 0.14 GIVING TAX.
     SUBTRACT TAX FROM GROSS PAY GIVING NET-PAY.

OUTPUT-ROUTINE.
     MOVE EMPLOYEE-NAME TO NAME.
     MOVE NET-PAY TO AMOUNT.
     WRITE PRINT-RECORD FROM OUTPUT-RECORD
          BEFORE ADVANCING 1 LINES.
```

Output

EMPLOYEE NAME	NET PAY
LYNN MANGINO	$224.00
THOMAS RITTER	$212.42
MARIE OLSON	$209.00
LORI DUNLEVY	$172.00
WILLIAM LUOMA	$308.00

must have four divisions: IDENTIFICATION, ENVIRONMENT, DATA, and PROCEDURE. The divisions appear in the program in this order and are identified by headings, as shown in Figure 12–5.

COBOL offers many advantages for business users. Because of its English-like nature, programs require very little additional documentation; well-written COBOL programs tend to be self-explanatory. This feature makes programs easier to maintain and modify. This is very important because large business programs are always being altered, expanded, and so forth. Since the logic of the program is easy to follow, testing and debugging procedures are simplified. In addition, programmers other than the original ones can read the program and quickly discern what the program does and how it does it. COBOL also has strong file-handling capabilities; it supports sequential, indexed, and direct-access files (see Chapter 6). This feature is very important to large corporations that must deal with enormous quantities of data stored in files.

Because COBOL is standardized, a firm can switch computer systems with little or no rewriting of existing programs. Its standardization also has implications for programmers: once programmers learn COBOL through college training or previous experience, they can transfer their learning with little adjustment to various computer systems and organizations.

However, the effort to make COBOL as English-like and self-explanatory as possible has created two disadvantages. First, COBOL programs tend to be wordy and rather long. Using COBOL usually requires more statements to solve a problem than using a more compact language such as Pascal. Second, a large, sophisticated compiler program is needed to translate a COBOL source program into machine language. Such a compiler occupies a large portion of main memory. For this reason, COBOL compilers are only just becoming available on microcomputers and tend to be expensive.

Regardless of COBOL's disadvantages, it is likely to remain a popular language for many years. Polls indicate that more than 80 percent of business application programs are written in COBOL. Converting these hundreds of thousands of COBOL programs to other languages and retraining thousands of programmers and users would not be inexpensive or easy.

LOGO

Logo is a procedure-oriented, interactive programming language developed initially by Seymour Papert and the MIT Logo group in the late 1960s. Like BASIC and Pascal, it was originally designed as a teaching tool. Logo's main attraction is that it allows children and adults of all ages to begin to program and communicate with the computer in a very short period of time. Logo allows the user to draw images, animate them, and color them using very simple instructions.

Logo accomplishes this interactive programming of graphics through a triangular object called a turtle, which leaves a graphic trail in its path. The user can easily command the turtle to draw straight lines, squares, or other objects as his or her skill level increases. Figure 12–6 contains

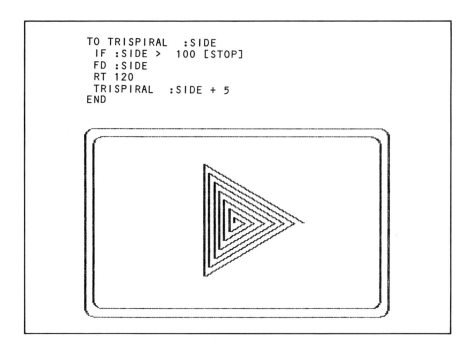

```
TO TRISPIRAL    :SIDE
 IF :SIDE >   100 [STOP]
 FD :SIDE
 RT 120
 TRISPIRAL   :SIDE + 5
END
```

a Logo program that illustrates statements that can be used to draw a triangular figure.

Logo was developed as an education-oriented language; its strengths lie in its ability to help the inexperienced user learn logic and programming. Because it is a structured language, it encourages the beginning programmer to develop good programming habits. Logo helps the user to determine and develop the procedures required to solve a given problem using the computer. It also helps the user learn to communicate with the computer and to develop an understanding of what programming is all about, including how to debug programs.

The word and list processing capabilities of Logo add more power to an already powerful programming language that is used in teaching geometry, language, physics, art, music, and architecture, to name only a few subject areas.

APL

APL (A Programming Language), conceived in 1962 by Kenneth Iverson, became available to the public through IBM in 1968. Over the years it has been expanded and has gained many enthusiastic supporters. Many businesses now use APL to write application programs.

The full power of APL is best realized when it is used for interactive processing via a terminal. A programmer can use APL in two modes. In the execution mode, the terminal can be used much like a desk calculator. An instruction is keyed in on one line and the response is returned immediately on the following line. In the definition mode, a series of instructions is entered into memory and the entire program is executed on command from the programmer. The APL programmer enters statements to create a source program, system commands to communicate with the operating system, and editing commands to modify the source program.

However, APL bears little resemblance to any other high-level language we will discuss.

Both character-string data and numeric data can be manipulated when APL is used. It is especially well suited for handling tables of related numbers, which are referred to as arrays. To simplify the programmer's task, a number of operations (up to fifty or more) are provided for array manipulation, logical comparisons, mathematical functions, branching operations, and so forth. The operators are represented by symbols on a special APL keyboard (see Figure 12–7). Some examples of APL coding are shown in Table 12–3. Figure 12–8 contains an interactive APL session.

APL operators can be combined to perform some very complex operations with a minimum of coding. APL's lack of formal restrictions on input and output and its free-format style make it a very powerful language. It is especially suited to handling tables of related numbers. It contains functions such as random-number generation, index generation, and matrix formation, making it very popular among statisticians. However, since it can be used for applications such as document production, graphics analysis, data retrieval, and financial analysis, APL also fills many business needs. APL is available through time-sharing networks for organizations that need only a limited amount of data processing.

APL has several disadvantages; one is that it is very difficult to read. A special keyboard is required to enter APL statements because of the number of unique symbols used; fortunately, the larger offering of new, low-cost terminals capable of handling several type fonts has greatly reduced this problem. Many people do not believe that APL is suitable for handling large data files. Another limitation of APL is the large amount of primary storage required by its compiler. Finally, APL is not available on as many different computer systems as are COBOL and Pascal.

● **FIGURE 12–7**
APL Keyboard

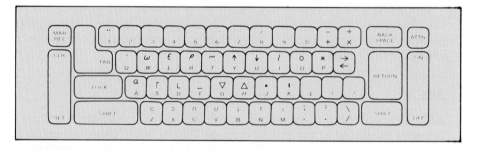

● **TABLE 12–3**
APL Coding

APL CODING	ENGLISH TRANSLATION
A + B	A plus B
A ← 25	A = 25
A⌊B	Finds the smaller of A and B
V1 ← 2 5 11 17	Creates a vector of 4 components and assigns this vector to V1
⌈/V1	Finds the maximum value in the vector V1

● COMPUTERS AND INFORMATION PROCESSING

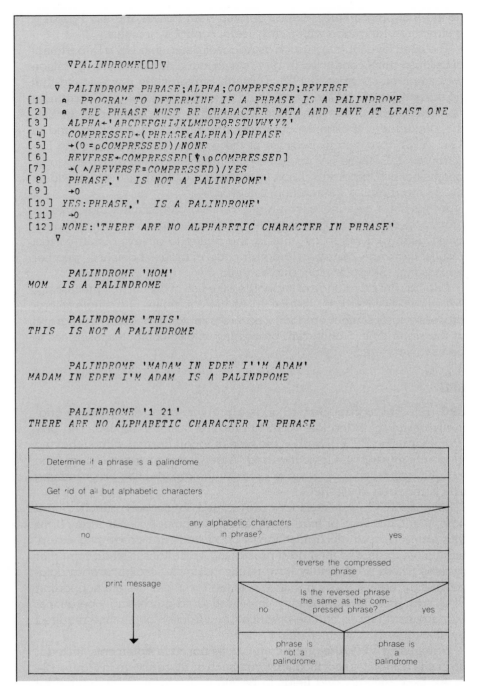

```
       ∇PALINDROME[□]∇

     ∇ PALINDROME PHRASE;ALPHA;COMPRESSED;REVERSE
[1]    ⍝   PROGRAM TO DETERMINE IF A PHRASE IS A PALINDROME
[2]    ⍝   THE PHRASE MUST BE CHARACTER DATA AND HAVE AT LEAST ONE
[3]    ALPHA←'ABCDEFGHIJKLMNOPQRSTUVWXYZ'
[4]    COMPRESSED←(PHRASE∈ALPHA)/PHRASE
[5]    →(0 =ρCOMPRESSED)/NONE
[6]    REVERSE←COMPRESSED[⍒⍳ρCOMPRESSED]
[7]    →( ∧/REVERSE=COMPRESSED)/YES
[8]    PHRASE,'  IS NOT A PALINDROME'
[9]    →0
[10] YES:PHRASE,'  IS A PALINDROME'
[11]   →0
[12] NONE:'THERE ARE NO ALPHABETIC CHARACTER IN PHRASE'
     ∇


       PALINDROME 'MOM'
MOM  IS A PALINDROME


       PALINDROME 'THIS'
THIS  IS NOT A PALINDROME


       PALINDROME 'MADAM IN EDEN I''M ADAM'
MADAM IN EDEN I'M ADAM  IS A PALINDROME


       PALINDROME '1 21 '
THERE ARE NO ALPHABETIC CHARACTER IN PHRASE
```

ADA

Ada is a relatively new, state-of-the-art programming language developed by the Department of Defense. Ada is named after Augusta Ada Byron, Countess of Lovelace and daughter of the poet Lord Byron. Augusta Ada Byron worked with Charles Babbage, programming his difference engine (see Chapter 2), and for this reason is often referred to as the first programmer. Ada is derived from Pascal and like Pascal is a structured language with many useful control statements.

The need for a language such as Ada was determined by a Department of Defense study conducted in 1974, which found that more than $7 billion was spent on software in 1973. Through further study it was found that no current high-level language could meet the needs of the Department of Defense and a new language would have to be developed. In 1980 the Department of Defense approved the initial Ada standard, and in 1983 ANSI approved it. Because of the considerable influence the Department of Defense has had and continues to have in this area, some people believe that Ada will someday replace COBOL as the most widely used programming language in business.

Ada is not a beginner's language; a skilled programmer may take six months to become proficient in the language. However, it has the sophistication and reliability (that is, the ability to always obtain correct results) that is necessary for programming in areas of defense, weather forecasting, oil exploration, and so forth.

Ada has the advantage of supporting the use of concurrent processing, which, as discussed in Chapter 10, is the capability of a single microprocessor to execute more than one program (or subpart of a program) at the same time. Concurrent processing allows computer resources to be used very efficiently.

RPG

RPG (Report Program Generator) is a problem-oriented language originally designed in the late 1960s to produce business reports. The programmer using RPG describes the type of report desired without having to specify much of the logic involved. A generator program is then used to build (generate) a program to produce the report. Little programming skill is required to use RPG.

Because RPG was originally developed to support punched-card equipment, it is used primarily with small computer systems. Many firms that formerly used electromechanical punched-card processing equipment have upgraded their data-processing operations to small computer systems. These firms usually have relatively simple, straightforward data-processing needs. In such cases, a small computer system supporting RPG can provide significantly improved data-processing operations. Management reports can be produced in a fraction of the time required by electromechanical methods.

When using RPG, the programmer does not code statements; instead, he or she completes specification forms such as those shown in Figure 12–9. All files, records, and fields to be manipulated must be defined by entries in specific columns on the specification forms. The operations to be performed and the content and format of output files are described similarly. The entries on the RPG forms are keypunched, combined with job-control cards, and submitted to the computer. The RPG program builds an object program from the source program, and the object program is executed by the computer (see Figure 12–10).

Like other programming languages, RPG is constantly being improved. IBM introduced a new version named RPGII in the early 1970s

• FIGURE 12–9
RPG Program Specification Forms

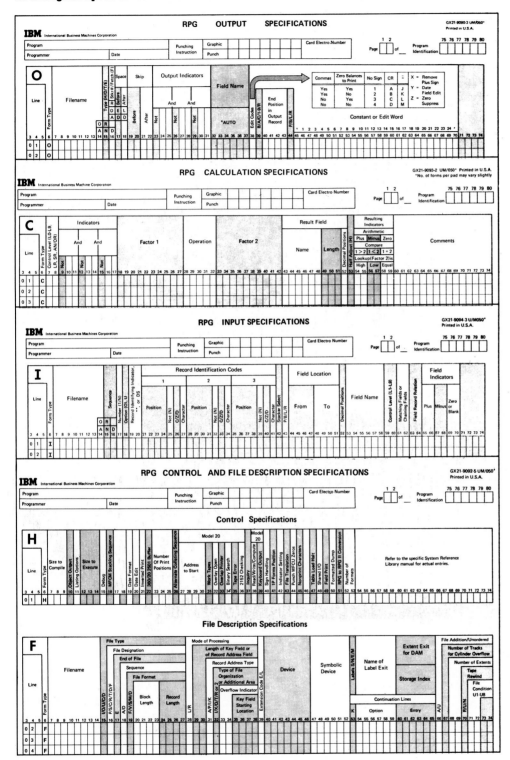

```
00010H        0003         132
00020F*                        PAYROLL EXAMPLE
00030FCDIN    IP F 80  80            READO1
00040FPRINTR  O  F 132 132     OF   PRINTER
000501* DEFINES INPUT
00060ICDIN    ZZ 01 80  CD
000701                              1     6 DATE
000801        ZZ 02
000901                              1    10DEPT   L1
001008                              2     5 EMPNO
001101                              6    92HRS
001201                             10   133RATE
001301                             14   140EXEMP
00510C*TO FIND GROSS PAY, NET PAY
00511C    40            SETOF                  30
00512C    N40 02        SETON                3040
00520C    02      HRS   COMP 40.00          100909
00530C    02 09   RATE  MULT HRS      GROSS 52H
00540C    02 10   HRS   SUB  40.00    OTHRS 42
00550C    02 10   RATE  MULT 40.00    REG   52
00560C    02 10   RATE  MULT 1.5      OTRT  43
00570C    02 10   OTHRS MULT OTRT     OVER  52
00580C    02 10   REG   ADD  OVER     GROSS 52
00590C    02      EXEMP MULT 14.40    EXAMT 52H      EXEMPT AMT
00600C    02      GROSS SUB  EXAMT    BASE  52
00610C    02      BASE  MULT .12      INCTX 52HN     INCOME TAX DED
00620C    02      GROSS SUB  INCTX    NET   52
00630C    02      GROSS ADD  DGROSS   DGROSS 62
00640C    02      HRS   ADD  DHRS     DHRS  52
00650C    02      GROSS ADD  GGROSS   GGROSS 72
00660C    02      HRS   ADD  GHRS     GHRS  62
001400* DEFINES HEADINGS AND OUTPUT
001500OPRINTR   H 0201    01
001600       OR         OF
001700                              10'DATE'
001800                   DATE       19' /  / '
002100                              67'PAYROLL'
002200                             120'PAGE'
002300                   PAGE      125'  0'
002400       H 02       L1
002500       OR         OF
002600                              10'DEPT'
002700                              24'EMP NO'
002800                              37'HOURS'
002900                              49'RATE'
003000                              63'GROSS'
003100                              81'EXEMPTIONS'
003200                             100'INCOME TAX'
003300                             115'NET PAY'
003400       D 02       02
003500                   L1 DEPT
003510                   30 DEPT      8
003600                   EMPNO       23
003700                   HRS         37'  .  '
003800                   RATE        49'  .  '
003900                   GROSS       63'  0.  '
004000                   EXEMP       76
004100                   INCTX       97'  0.  '
004200                   NET        114'  0.  '
004300       T 33       L1
004400                              27'DEPARTMENT
004500                   DGROSS  B   63'  , $0.  '
004600                   DHRS    B   37'  0.  '
004700       T 30       LR
004800                              29'GRAND TOTALS
004900                   GGROSS  B   63'  , $0.  '
005000                   GHRS    B   39'  0.  '
```

```
//GO.PRINTR DD SYSOUT=A
//GO.CDIN   DD =
052775
10029400031753
10087410029002
10141420044401
10160400026754
10387445049954
10401510037502
10403400029003
20037300024502
20098400029701
20201400044501
20221440041503
20485478541705
/*EOF
```

Output

```
                                    PAYROLL
  DEPT     EMP NO     HOURS     RATE      GROSS     EXEMPTIONS     INCOME TAX     NET PAY

  1        0029       40.00     3.175     127.00         3           10.06       116.94
           0087       41.00     2.900     120.35         2           10.99       109.36
           0141       42.00     4.440     190.92         1           21.18       169.74
           0160       40.00     2.675     107.00         4            5.93       101.07
           0387       44.50     4.995     233.51         4           21.11       212.40
           0401       51.00     3.750     211.87         2           21.97       189.90
           0403       40.00     2.900     116.00         3            8.74       107.26

  DEPARTMENT
  TOTALS              298.50             $1,106.65

  DEPT     EMP NO     HOURS     RATE      GROSS     EXEMPTIONS     INCOME TAX     NET PAY

  2        0037       40.00     2.450      98.00         2            8.30        89.70
           0098       40.00     2.970     118.80         1           12.53       106.27
           0201       40.00     4.450     178.00         1           19.63       158.37
           0221       44.00     4.150     190.90         3           17.72       173.18
           0485       47.85     4.170     215.90         5           17.27       198.63

  DEPARTMENT
  TOTALS              211.85              $801.60

  GRAND TOTALS        510.35             $1,908.25
```

for use on its IBM System/3 computers. This new version has been widely accepted and is now supported by many computer manufacturers; in fact, it has essentially replaced the original RPG. A third version introduced in 1979, RPGIII, features the ability to process data stored in a data base.

RPG is easy to learn and use because the basic pattern of execution is fixed. Because it does not require large amounts of primary storage, it is one of the primary languages of small computers and minicomputers. RPG provides an efficient means for generating reports requiring simple logic and calculations; it is commonly used to process files for accounts receivable, accounts payable, general ledgers, and inventory.

Unfortunately, the computational capabilities of RPG are limited. Some RPG compilers can generate machine-language instructions for up to thirty different operations. However, compared with COBOL, FORTRAN, and Pascal, RPG's looping, branching, and comparison-making capabilities are restricted. It is not a standardized language; therefore RPG programs may require a significant degree of modification if they are to be executed on a computer other than the one for which they were initially written. This is especially true if a firm changes computer manufacturers. However, if a firm stays with a particular manufacturer's equipment its RPG programs can generally be run on a similar but more powerful computer with only slight modifications.

C

Developed in 1972, **C** is rapidly becoming popular for both system and application programming. It has some capabilities similar to those of assembly languages, such as the capability to manipulate individual bits and bytes in storage locations. Yet it also offers many high-level language features, such as a wide variety of useful control structures. Therefore, sometimes it is referred to as a *middle-level language*.

C is popular for several reasons. First, it is independent of machine architecture, so that C programs are portable. That is, the same program can be run on different computers. Second, C can be implemented on a wide variety of systems, from eight-bit microcomputers to supercomputers such as the Cray-1. Third, it includes many structured programming features found in languages like Pascal. Figure 12–11 contains a payroll program written in C.

C was designed by Dennis Ritchie at Bell Laboratories. One of the first uses was in the rewriting of Bell Laboratories' UNIX operating system. UNIX and its utilities include more than 300,000 lines of C source code, a very ambitious programming project. Today, many major microcomputer manufacturers and software developers use C for system programs, utility programs, and graphics applications. Digital Research, for example, is using C for all its newer products, including CP/M-68K for the 68000 microprocessor and the new Personal BASIC. Both Microsoft and VisiCorp have used C in products ranging from Multiplan and Xenix to Visiword and Visi On.

C is a general-purpose language that features economy of expression, modern data structures, and a rich set of operators. Although it is considered a system programming language, it is also useful for numerical, text-processing, and data-base programs. It is a "small" language, using many built-in functions. Therefore, the compilers are simple and compact. Unlike Pascal, which assumes that the programmer is often wrong and thus limits the chances for the programmer to write incorrect statements, C assumes that the programmer is always right and allows the programmer a freer programming style. Therefore, truly spectacular errors are easier to make in C. C is a compiled language and also contains rather cryptic error messages that can confuse a novice programmer. For these reasons, C is clearly intended for the professional programmer.

MODULA-2

Modula-2 is a descendant of Pascal. Designed by the creator of Pascal, Niklaus Wirth, Modula-2 contains all aspects of Pascal as well as features drawn from Modula, a language developed from experiments with concurrent processing. Like Ada, Modula-2 allows for the use of concurrent processing, thereby encouraging the efficient use of the microprocessor. Because Modula-2 is similar to Pascal, it is easy for programmers who already know Pascal to learn it.

As Pascal became widely implemented during the 1970s, it became evident that certain improvements to the language were possible. Wirth proposed to create a single, high-level language that also had low-level capabilities to interact more closely with its given hardware. In this respect, Modula-2 is similar to C and FORTH (FORTH is discussed in the next section).

The most outstanding feature of Modula-2 is its use of the module, a concept drawn from its parent Modula. Each of these modules performs a specific task. It is a structured language that is easy to modularize and has a wide variety of useful control structures. Because Modula-2 is a

● **FIGURE 12–11**
Payroll Program in C

```
main()
{
/*****************************************************
     This program calculates a weekly payroll.
*****************************************************/

    double atof();
    float wage, hours, grosspay, tax, netpay;
    char *chwage, *chhours, *name;

    flag = 0;
    printf ("EMPLOYEE NAME                 NETPAY \n");
    emplfile = fopen("payroll","r");
    while (1) {
/*****************************************************
             procedure read data
*****************************************************/
        readname(name);
        if (flag)
             break;
        readname(chhours);
        readname(chwage);

/*****************************************************
             Calculate gross pay
*****************************************************/
        wage = atof(chwage);                  /* convert the string  */
        hours = atof(chhours);                /* to a float value    */
        if (hours <= 40)
             grosspay = hours * wage;
        else
             grosspay = hours * wage + (hours - 40.0) * wage * 0.5;

/*****************************************************
             Calculate net pay
*****************************************************/
        if (grosspay > 250)
            tax = 0.2 * grosspay;
        else
            tax = 0.14 * grosspay;
        netpay = grosspay - tax;
```

(Continued on Next Page)

```
/****************************************************
              Print the results
 ****************************************************/
        printf("%-24s  %7.2f\n",name,netpay);
        }  /* while loop closing bracket */
        fclose(emplfile);
} /* main closing bracket */

/****************************************************
              Subroutine readname
 ****************************************************/
readname(ts)
char *ts;
{
        int cc;
        char *cs;

        cs = ts;
        while ((cc = getc(emplfile)) != EOF)    /*look for EOF */
                {
                if (cc == 13)                   /* return if CR is seen */
                        break;
                if (cc != 10)                   /* do not process LF */
                        *cs++ = cc;             /* build the string */
                }
        if (cc == EOF) flag = 1;                /* IF EOF we are done */
        *cs = '\0';                             /* make sure we terminate
                                                   a string value */

}
```

Output

```
  EMPLOYEE NAME              NETPAY
  LYNN MANGIN                224.00
  THOMAS RITTER              212.42
  MARIE OLSON                209.00
  LORI SANCHEZ               172.00
  WILLIAM LUOMA              308.00
```

● **FIGURE 12–11**
Continued

new programming language, it remains to be seen how widely implemented it will be.

FORTH

Working at Kitt Peak National Observatory, Charles Moore developed **FORTH** in response to what he saw as a need for an adequate programming language to use in tracking satellites and studying the universe. Like C and Modula-2, FORTH is often categorized as a middle-level language. By using the many library commands to define new special-purpose commands, FORTH can be modeled to meet the programmer's particular needs.

A FORTH program consists of the definitions of many words (commonly called procedures or subroutines in other languages). A program is a list of words, with simple words defining more complex ones. The notation

● COMPUTERS AND INFORMATION PROCESSING

looks strange; the mathematical expression 8 + 4 * 5 would appear as 4 5 * 8 + in FORTH. The reason for this is that FORTH operates on the principle of a stack—a pile of objects from which you add or remove only the topmost element, just as you would from a stack of dishes. Other programming languages use stacks internally, but FORTH makes the stacks available to the programmer. Let's see how the idea of stacks works on the expression 4 5 * 8 +. If FORTH sees a number, it pushes that number onto the top of the stack. If it sees an operator such as * or +, it removes the top two numbers off the stack and applies the operation, then puts the result back onto the top of the stack. Therefore, 4 and 5 would be multiplied, leaving 20 on top of the stack. Then FORTH removes the 20 and the 8 from the stack and sees the symbol +. It adds 20 and 8, the next two numbers on the stack. The result is 28.

FORTH has become the standard language for astronomical observatories around the world. It also is used to guide automated movie cameras, run portable heart monitors, and simulate radar for the air force. In addition, it is being used increasingly for the less glamorous tasks involved in data base management and word processing.

The simplicity of FORTH makes it fast and efficient. Adding new features to FORTH is also possible. Because FORTH systems are interpreted, the programmer can write one word (procedure) at a time and test it thoroughly before writing the next word. However, this strange-looking language is hard to read, and sometimes strange names are given to the words. In the name of speed, FORTH lacks many of the safety features built into other languages, so it is difficult to debug.

LISP

LISP (or LISt Processing) is the language commonly associated with artificial intelligence (AI). Using concepts of lambda-calculus (a branch of mathematics) and a new idea in computing called list processing, John McCarthy developed the language in 1960 at Massachusetts Institute of Technology. LISP aids in the manipulation of nonnumeric data that change considerably in length and structure during execution of a program. Essentially, LISP involves performing built-in or user-defined functions on lists.

In LISP, a list is a group of elements in a particular order. The following example contains seven elements, A, LIST, IS, A, GROUP, OF, ELEMENTS.

(A LIST IS A GROUP OF ELEMENTS)

Using parentheses can separate elements of a list, as follows:

(A LIST IS A GROUP OF ELEMENTS (IN A PARTICULAR ORDER))

The elements of this list are A, LIST, IS, A, GROUP, OF, ELEMENTS, and IN A PARTICULAR ORDER.

To beginning programmers in LISP, the tangle of parentheses can be confusing. However, the lists can contain collections of functions, such as finding the square or cube of a number; sentences; mathematical formulas; logic theorems; or even complete computer programs. This capability makes LISP a powerful tool in applications such as the generation of mathematical proofs, algebraic manipulation, and simulations of human problem-solving techniques.

Although LISP dominates AI research, a new language, PROLOG, is beginning to be recognized by the academic community as a useful language in AI. Part of the reason for interest in PROLOG is that the Japanese have chosen it to be the standard language for their fifth-generation project, a project that could make Japan the world leader in advanced computer applications and expert systems.

● Natural Languages

Computer scientists have always realized that computers can't achieve their full potential if only a few people know how to use them. Programmers have helped to make software "user friendly" by using menus and other devices to make the machines interact in humanlike ways. One way in which people's interaction with these machines could be greatly improved would be if data bases could be queried in plain English.

Natural languages, or **query languages** as they are sometimes called, are programming languages that attempt to allow the user to state queries in English-like sentences. The question is then translated into a form that the computer can understand. A sentence such as "HOW MANY WOMEN HOLD A POSITION AT LEVEL 10 OR ABOVE?" may be entered by a member of the personnel department to gain information for reporting purposes. In some cases, if the natural language processor does not fully understand the inquiry, it may request further information from the user in order to process the given inquiry.

Natural languages have been designed primarily for the novice computer user for use as online, data-base, query languages. Natural-language processors normally are designed to be used with a vocabulary of words and definitions that allows the processor to translate the English-like sentences to machine-executable form. Currently, natural-language sentences are typed at the keyboard; however, in the future the combination of voice recognition technology and natural languages could result in a very powerful tool for computer users. The ability to interface natural-language systems with graphics software also provides a valuable tool for managers in decision making. Although limited to mainframe computers in the past, natural-language systems are being developed for minicomputer and microcomputer systems as well.

● Programming Languages—A Comparison

Implementing an information system involves making an important decision concerning the type of programming language to use. Some questions must be asked:

● What languages does the selected (or available) computer system support?
● Does the company require that the system be written in a particular

language? For example, in some businesses, all application programs must be written in COBOL.

● Will the application require mostly complex computations, file processing, or report generation?

● Are equipment changes planned for the future? If so, is it important that the chosen language be implemented on a wide variety of computer systems?

● How frequently will programs need modification?

● What languages do the programmers who will program and maintain the system know?

The size of the computer system is an obvious constraint on language choice. The size of the primary storage of microcomputers limits the use of languages such as APL and ADA. But languages such as Pascal, C, and BASIC are widely available on microcomputers. Although the computational capabilities of RPG are limited, it can still supply sufficient information for the management of small firms.

For large systems, the type of processing is the key consideration in choosing a language. Business applications typically involve large amounts of data on which relatively few calculations are performed. Substantial file processing (requiring many I/O operations) is required; thus, many business applications are **input/output-bound.** In such cases, COBOL is the language generally chosen, although Ada is growing in popularity.

Scientific programming applications usually require many complex calculations on relatively small amounts of data. Therefore, they tend to be **process-bound.** The computational capabilities of FORTRAN make it ideal for such applications although Pascal also is often used because it is structured better than FORTRAN.

Because of the diversity of programming languages, many firms choose to use several. For example, a firm can write scientific programs in FORTRAN and file-updating programs in COBOL. It is also possible to write part of a program in one language and another part in a different language; this involves compiling the various portions of the program in separate steps and linking together the resultant object programs. These steps can be specified in job-control statements. For example, a program written in COBOL may call up an assembly-language program to perform extensive sorting of alphanumeric data, because assembly language can perform sorting tasks more efficiently than COBOL and thus save processing time.

Nevertheless, there has been a definite trend away from programming in assembly language. Because of the one-to-one relationship between assembly-language instructions and machine-language instructions, programming in assembly language is very time consuming. Assembly-language programs may be efficient, but writing them is laborious. In contrast, high-level languages shift the programming emphasis away from detailed computer functions toward procedures for solving problems. If it is necessary to use low-level language commands such as those involving bit and byte manipulation, one of the so-called "middle-level" languages such as C or Modula-2 should be considered. These languages incorporate the advantages of both high-level and low-level languages.

◉ Enhancing Space Exploration

Not surprisingly, computers have found a place in the exploration of space. Without computers, human beings would not have been able to orbit the earth or walk on the moon. The vastness of our universe makes its exploration a never-ending endeavor. Yet, increasingly more powerful computers continue to support such exploration. Computers also play an increasingly important role in astronomical research.

Before participating in an actual Space Shuttle flight, astronauts must go through rigorous training. Scientist-Astronaut Anna L. Fisher learns how to operate the computerized flight equipment in a shuttle mockup at Johnson Space Center. The equipment is the same as that on board the shuttle.

The Kitt Peak National Observatory near Tuscon, Arizona is the national research center for ground-based optical astronomy in the Northern Hemisphere. It is the site of the 4-meter Mayall Telescope, the third largest reflector in the United States. The telescope is under computer control for locating and tracking objects. As data is gathered by the telescope, another computer analyzes it. The telescope often uses CCD (Charged Coupled Device) cameras, which are light-sensitive electronic devices. CCD cameras are more sensitive than photographic plates and they provide an image that can be processed immediately at the telescope.

The DIGISTAR installation at the Hansen Planetarium in Salt Lake City, Utah, is the world's first digitally-driven planetarium projection system. The DIGISTAR console serves as the operator interface to the Host Computer and Graphics Processor.

On earth, activity in the mission control center at Johnson Space Center revolves around monitoring the progress of the Space Shuttle. Scientists and technicians closely watch CRT screens displaying information about the shuttle's flight. The large screen on the wall displays computer-generated paths of the shuttle as it passes over the earth.

Translating High-Level Language Programs

Assembly and high-level languages are much more widely used by programmers than machine language. Since these languages cannot be executed directly by computers, they are converted into machine-executable form by language-translator programs. As discussed in Chapter 10, these translator programs are part of the computer's operating system. The language-translator program translates the source program (that is, the sequence of instructions written by the programmer) into machine language. The translator program for assembly language programs is called an **assembler program.** A high-level language translator can be either a **compiler program** or an **interpreter program.** Assemblers, compilers, and interpreters are designed for specific machines and languages. For example, a compiler that translates a source program written in FORTRAN into a machine-language program can only translate FORTRAN programs.

During the compilation or assembly (the translation process), an object program is generated which consists of the source program in machine language. To help the programmer, the compiler can provide a listing of all compiler-detected errors. Only after all errors preventing compilation have been corrected can the object program be created and submitted to the computer for execution. Several attempts at successful compilation or assembly may be needed before the programmer is able to locate and correct all errors.

An interpreter, a language translator that is used extensively on microcomputer systems, unlike assemblers and compilers, evaluates and translates a program one statement at a time. The interpreter reads each program statement checking for syntax errors, such as typing mistakes; if errors are found, an appropriate error message is generated. If there are no errors, the interpreter translates the statement into machine language and executes it before proceeding to the next statement. This is in contrast to an assembler or a compiler, which first check the entire program for syntax errors and then translate the entire program into an object program that is executed. An interpreter program is typically smaller than an assembler or compiler program. For this reason and because there is no need to store an object program in the computer, interpreters are popular on microcomputer systems. An interpreter, however, can be inefficient. Program statements that are used more than once during a program's execution must be evaluated, translated, and executed each time the statement is used.

Batch Versus Interactive Processing

There are two basic types of processing: **batch** and **interactive.** In batch processing, programs are grouped together (or "batched") over time and then processed one after another, in a continuous stream. The user does not interact directly with the computer during program execution. In a bank, all transactions—deposits, withdrawals, loans, or loan payments—are entered into the computer system as they occur. However, a summary of the number and dollar amounts of all transactions for a day may not be processed until night, when the bank is closed. Then the computer processes all the data and reports the day's business in summary form.

Sometimes a large computer can process data very quickly and provide the user with results by batch processing in a short time. However, batch processing is usually slow, because the programs must wait for their turn to be executed. Nonetheless, batch processing can make good use of computer time because the programs are executed efficiently and can be run at times when the system is less busy, such as at night.

In many cases, the user needs to see the results of processing as quickly as possible. Interactive processing provides this kind of feedback; therefore it is often used for individual transactions. A person making a plane reservation wants to know immediately what's available and at what cost. Not only that, the computer system must record the transaction immediately, or a travel agent in another office may sell the same seat to another customer. A bank customer putting money in a savings account wants the result entered in a bankbook now, not tomorrow or next week. Often individual transactions are completed by interactive processing but summarized by batch. Although the bank customer has an immediate record of a deposit, the summary of a day's similar transactions will not be produced until the bank is closed. Figure 12–12 illustrates batch and interactive processing.

◉ Summary Points

● Machine language and assembly language, which are low-level languages, require extensive knowledge of the computer system being used.
● Machine language, consisting of 1s and 0s, is the only language that the computer is capable of executing directly. It is different for each type of computer.

A Comparison of Batch and Interactive Processing		CONCEPT SUMMARY 12–3
	BATCH PROCESSING	**INTERACTIVE PROCESSING**
Characteristics	Programs wait in line to be executed in a continuous stream, without user intervention	User interacts directly with the computer during program execution
Advantages	Makes efficient use of computer resources; programs can be processed at times when the computer is less busy, such as at night	Input can be entered at the keyboard and results quickly displayed on the terminal screen, thereby allowing the user to obtain fast results; files are updated immediately
Disadvantages	Is generally slower than interactive processing; user cannot interact with computer during execution	Does not use computer resources as efficiently as batch processing

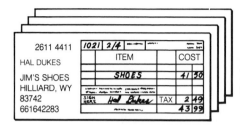

Data entered from
source documents

BATCH PROCESSING
Data is entered at the keyboard
and saved on disk. It can then
be submitted to the computer
at a later time.

Update
stored
on tape

Data
processed
all at
once
from
tape

Data
stored
on tape

● **FIGURE 12–12**
Continued

An architect prepares
presentation graphics
to show clients samples
of his firm's work.

Interactive processing
is widely used in
developing business
reports and tables.

INTERACTIVE PROCESSING
The user interacts directly
with the computer during
execution.

Using a light pen with
her computer, this woman
modifies the compuer
program that produced
the woven design.

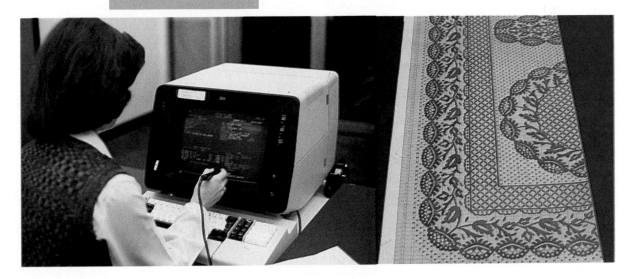

- Assembly-language statements use symbolic names (called mnemonics) to represent machine operations, making assembly-language programming less tedious and time-consuming than machine-language programming. Before assembly-language programs are executed they must be translated into machine language. Because there is generally a one-to-one correspondence between assembly- and machine-language statements, this translation is easier to make than when a high-level language is used.

- Programming languages can be divided into various categories, such as high level or low level, structured or unstructured, procedure-oriented or problem-oriented, and general or special purpose. Dividing programming languages into categories helps programmers in making generalizations about languages and in choosing the right language to meet a specific need.

- High-level language statements contain English-like words such as READ and PRINT; these statements must be translated into machine language before execution. High-level languages are more oriented toward the user whereas low-level languages are more oriented toward the computer hardware. A single high-level language statement may translate into many machine-language statements.

- FORTRAN is the oldest high-level language and commonly is used for scientific applications because of its ability to perform mathematical calculations with a great deal of accuracy.

- BASIC is an easy-to-learn language that is widely implemented on microcomputers and is often taught to beginning programmers.

- Pascal is a structured language that was developed as an instructional language. It is relatively easy to learn and is useful in both business and scientific applications.

- COBOL is the most popular business programming language. It was designed to be English-like and self-documenting. The main disadvantage of COBOL is that a large and sophisticated compiler is required to translate programs. A main advantage of COBOL is its ability to handle large data files efficiently.

- Logo is an interactive, education-oriented language that uses an object called a turtle to help beginners become familiar with the computer and computer graphics.

- APL is a powerful interactive language that can be used in execution mode or definition mode. Both character-string data and numeric data can be manipulated easily. Because APL includes a large number of unique symbols as operators, it requires a special keyboard. The APL compiler needs a large amount of primary storage; this restricts its use of medium-sized and large computers.

- Ada is a relatively new, structured high-level language that was developed for use by the Department of Defense. It allows for the use of concurrent processing and is a sophisticated language that obtains the level of accuracy necessary for programming in the areas of defense, weather forecasting, oil exploration, and so forth.

- RPG is a problem-oriented language designed to produce business reports. Because the RPG generator can build a program to provide specified output, little programming skill is required to use this language.

- C is a structured high-level language that also includes low-level language instructions; therefore it is sometimes referred to as a middle-level language. It is a general-purpose language that features economy of expression, modern data structures, and a wide variety of operators. C is used for both system and application programming.

- Modula-2, a descendant of Pascal, is based on the idea of structured subprograms, or modules, which are nested within one another. Like C, Modula-2 is a high-level language that includes low-level language instructions. Modula-2 also allows for concurrent processing, thereby helping the programmer make efficient use of the microprocessor.

- FORTH is another high-level language that contains low-level language instructions, thereby allowing the programmer to interact closely with the computer's hardware. FORTH is used in astronomical observatories around the world.

- LISP is the language commonly used in artificial intelligence programming and research. It involves performing built-in or user-defined functions on lists.

- Natural languages (or query languages) are designed to allow the novice computer user to access the computer's capabilities more easily. For example, easy to write and understand English-like sentences allow the user to access information in a data base.

- Factors to consider when selecting an appropriate programming language include: What languages can the computer support? Does the company require that application programs be written in a particular language? Are computations simple? Does the application require a great deal of handling of large data files? Are equipment changes planned in the future? How often will programs be modified? What languages do the programmers who will work on the project know?

- Assembly-language programs are translated into machine language by an assembler. There are two types of translator programs for high-level language programs—compilers and interpreters. Compilers translate the entire source program into machine code, thereby creating an object program, which is then executed. Interpreters translate the source program one statement at a time. In general, interpreters are smaller than compilers and therefore take up less space in primary storage. However, interpreters can be less efficient than compilers because statements that are used more than once in a program must be retranslated each time.

- The two basic types of processing are batch and interactive. Batch processing provides for a better utilization of computer resources because the programs are "batched" and processed one after the other in a continuous stream. Batch programs can be run at times when the system is less busy, such as at night. When batch processing is used, the user cannot interact with the computer during program execution.

- Interactive processing allows the user to communicate directly with the computer in a conversational mode. Response time usually is almost immediate.

● Review Questions

1. Distinguish between machine languages and assembly languages. What are the advantages and disadvantages of each?

2. Why were high-level languages developed? Name an advantage and a disadvantage high-level languages have over low-level languages.

3. Why is it desirable to attempt to standardize high-level languages? How does language standardization aid portability?

4. List four ways in which languages can be categorized. How is this categorization process helpful to programmers?

5. List three categories of special-purpose languages and name a language that fits into each category.

6. Give at least two reasons why Pascal has become a widely taught language for introductory programming students.

7. What are some common characteristics of scientific-oriented programming languages? How do these characteristics differ from business-oriented programming languages?

8. Describe some of the key advantages associated with COBOL language.

9. List and discuss some of the factors that should be considered when a programming language is to be chosen for a particular application program.

10. What is the purpose of natural languages? For what type of user are they best suited?

11. How does a procedure-oriented language differ from a problem-oriented language? List some common procedure-oriented languages and a problem-oriented language.

12. How does batch processing differ from interactive processing? If you were developing a hotel reservation system, would you choose batch processing or interactive processing? Explain your choice.

Sperry UNIVAC

THE COMPANY HISTORY

The foundation of one of the oldest ongoing manufacturers of computer equipment, Sperry Corporation, is closely tied to the world's first all-electronic digital computer, ENIAC (Electronic Numerical Integrator and Automatic Computer). ENIAC was designed at the University of Pennsylvania's Moore School of Electrical Engineering in 1946. The ENIAC project, under the direction of John W. Mauchly and J. Presper Eckert, was completed for the U.S. Army.

Mauchly's and Eckert's success with ENIAC encouraged the two men to form their own computer company, the Electronic Control Company. Over the years, the company underwent many name changes, probably the most well known of which is Sperry Univac. The first general-purpose commercial computer produced by the new company was the Universal Automatic Computer, or UNIVAC® I. UNIVAC I made extensive use of peripheral equipment and could simultaneously read new information, perform calculations on the information, and record the output results. Perhaps the most famous use for UNIVAC I was predicting the outcome of the 1952 presidential election, the first time a computer was ever used for such a purpose. UNIVAC I predicted that Eisenhower would defeat Stevenson and suggested that the electoral votes would be 438 to 93. The actual electoral count was 442 to 89 in favor of Eisenhower.

Remington Rand bought out Eckert and Mauchly in 1950. A second acquisition by Rand brought together a contingent of mathematicians and engineers that developed a more sophisticated version of UNIVAC called UNIVAC 1101. The 1101 is believed to be the first electronic computer that was used in a real-time, on-line mode. Real time means being able to find information or answers to inquiries virtually instantaneously. UNIVAC 1101 was connected to a wind tunnel at Wright Patterson U.S. Air Force Base in Dayton, Ohio. Sensors recorded information in the wind tunnel and transmitted the information to the computer for processing. Real-time responses made it possible for technicians to evaluate the computer feedback and quickly make needed adjustments to the wind tunnel.

Sperry has pioneered many computer advances and improved on major technological developments in data processing in every computer generation from the first to the fourth. From vacuum tubes to semiconductor circuitry, Sperry has made its mark. In more recent years, the company has developed hardware to facilitate data communications and continued work in developing real-time computers.

SPERRY TODAY

Another focus at Sperry is to make programs and systems easier for the nonprofessional data-processing person to operate. The Mapper® System is a fourth-generation language system designed by Sperry's Information Systems Group for the nonprofessional computer user. It is designed for use in the fields of business, government, and education, and can support large numbers of end users. Mapper allows end users to draw on their own experiences in manipulating data and generating reports without having to rely on help from data-processing departments. In the past, data-processing personnel have often underestimated the ability of end users to access data and process information. The Mapper System gives end users the flexibility to create information-processing systems that are tailored to meet

specific information needs and to access the data for decision making.

The user-friendly design of Mapper increases productivity while reducing processing costs. The system has an on-line tutorial for self-learning. If a user runs into difficulty, the system automatically displays the exact point of the on-line documentation that deals with the problem situation. This eliminates the frustration users face when flipping through manuals that often contain only cryptic message codes about the problem.

Mapper is available to users in a broad range of equipment choices. The system can be installed on Sperry or IBM personal computers. It is also offered for use with minicomputers and mainframes. Small businesses with limited budgets can take advantage of Sperry's time-sharing system and buy time on a Sperry mainframe equipped with the Mapper System. Other features of Mapper that make it a popular choice by many users include the following:

● It can support a large network of both remote and local terminals, printers, disks, and other devices.
● It has extensive security features to control user access.

● It is fully recoverable.
● It can interface with other systems.
● It is highly efficient and gives users fast response.

Technological advances, such as those used to develop Mapper, have helped Sperry succeed in a highly competitive industry. In the spring of 1986, Sperry took another step to continue its successful pattern of growth and development. A merger with Burroughs Corporation has helped Sperry become the second largest computer manufacturer in the country. A solid base of technological development combined with good business judgment ensure that Sperry will serve the growing need of electronic systems markets throughout the world.

DISCUSSION POINTS

1. How does Mapper's user friendliness help increase productivity?
2. Name some of the features of Mapper that make it popular with users.

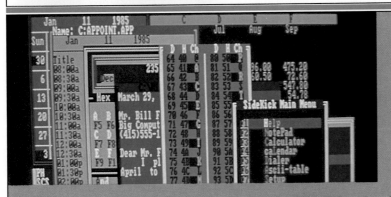

13 APPLICATION SOFTWARE

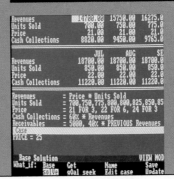

A Convert to the Write Stuff

Jamie Murphy
TIME

Conservative Pundit William F. Buckley Jr. has long had an unbridled passion for writing machines. He once mailed an unsolicited testimonial to the president of Smith-Corona, praising the company's $170 portable as "the most wonderful electric typewriter" he had ever used. Now the syndicated columnist, author of 24 books and editor of the *National Review*, has found a new object for his techno-literary affections. Buckley has shifted his allegiance to word processors, demonstrating his loyalty by accumulating eight of the machines and scattering them among his offices in New York City, Connecticut and Rougemont, Switzerland. "I don't compose anything on a typewriter if I can help it," says the irrepressible author. "Now I do all my editing on the screen."

One obvious reason for Buckley's conversion is speed. "Writing on the word processor takes less time," he declares. So much less, in fact, that even his professional friends are impressed. "It takes Bill 20 minutes to write a column," says Peter McWilliams, an acquaintance and the author of several best-selling, how-to computer books *(The Word Processing Book, The Personal Computer Book.)* "Word processors were really made for him."

Buckley provided evidence of that earlier this year while vacationing aboard a chartered yacht off the Pacific island of Bora-Bora. With the help of an Epson PX-8 lap-size machine, he fired off a 7,500-word draft of a children's book in two hours, a feat that can be compared with writing a college term paper during lunch break and getting it published. *The Temptation of Wilfred Malachey* (Workman, $10.95) is a morality tale for children from ages eight to 13, in which a demonical IBM 4341 mainframe teaches a New England prep-school student that computing can be more profitable

than petty theft. Says Buckley, referring obliquely to an ancient Roman philosophy of virtue: "There is a tug in the story toward right reason." The book shows no sign of having been tossed off in half a sweltering Pacific afternoon. "I think it's a lot of twaddle that using a word processor affects the quality of writing for the worse," says the author, who claims a touch-typing speed of 110 words per minute on the computer keyboard.

Buckley's microelectronic baptism took place late in the winter of 1982 while he was visiting the Baltimore home of Critic Hugh Kenner. There, Kenner introduced him to the workings of a vintage Heathkit/Zenith model Z-89 computer. The next month Buckley purchased his first system: a second-hand Z-89 with a Diablo printer and a copy of the pioneering Pie word processing program. Buckley took the gear along on his annual winter pilgrimage to Switzerland where, guided by 16 pages of careful instructions prepared by Kenner, he turned out in only five weeks his 20th book, *Overdrive* (Doubleday, $16.95).

Buckley has since abandoned the Heathkit. Aside from the seagoing Epson, he has four Kaypro portables, two IBM PCs (an AT and an XT), and a TeleVideo terminal. The IBM AT, which he keeps at his home in Connecticut, is able to store an entire novel in its customized internal memory. All the computers run the best-selling WordStar program. "I'm told there are better programs," says Buckley. "But I'm also told there are better alphabets." Despite owning all this equipment, he has never played a computer game, tapped into a data base or run numbers through an electronic accounting program, and has only just learned how to use software to alphabetize his list of phone numbers.

Like many other computer converts, Buckley has drawn a number of his friends into the fold, and the roster of his recruits reads like a literary *Who's Who.* He bought one of the first editions of McWilliams' *The Word Processing Book* and dispatched copies to TV News Commentator John Chancellor and former New York *Times* Editor Harrison Salisbury. He advised Knopf Editor Sophie Wilkins to buy a Heath for her work as a translator. He regularly corresponds with an elite user group, which includes New York *Times* Book Reviewer Christopher Lehmann-Haupt and Pulitzer-Prizewinning Author David Halberstam. But Buckley tries hard not to sound overzealous. Unlike his friend Halberstam, whom he once described as "impossibly evangelistic," Buckley takes pains not to be 100% boring on the subject. "I'm about 75% boring," he estimates. Nonetheless, when he is home for dinner with Wife Pat and Son Christopher, 32, talk frequently turns to smart keys and modems. Says Buckley: "My wife has asked me if, some time before she dies, we couldn't have a meal where the topic of conversation is not computers."

● **Computers are slowly winning over individuals who have resisted using them for one reason or another. Corporations have been less hesitant. With the available commercial software, all text processing, number manipulating, and graphics work, as well as the actual designing and manufacturing of products, can be handled much more efficiently using computers.**

● Introduction

In Chapter 11 we examined the software development process. This process is used when a company develops an application software package for in-house use from scratch. In recent years, however, the use of commercially written application software packages has increased dramatically. There are commercial packages available for everything from running a doctor's office to performing sophisticated statistical analysis of research data. This chapter focuses on application software for large computer systems. We will discuss some of the advantages and disadvantages of using commercially developed application software. Included in the chapter are discussions of different kinds of application packages—productivity tools, functional tools, and end-user development tools. The chapter concludes with some guidelines for choosing an application software package.

● Advantages and Disadvantages of Commercial Application Software

Many factors have contributed to the increase in commercially developed software packages. You may recall from Chapter 2 that a court decision forcing IBM to "unbundle" its software had a major impact on the growth of the software industry. During that period companies also began to realize that developing programs in-house required a staff of highly talented and skilled programmers. Many found the cost of in-house software development prohibitive, so they began using commercially developed packages. Other factors contributing to the increased use of commercial packages include, first, the speed at which commercial packages can be implemented. Usually less time is needed to implement a commercial application package than to develop software in-house. Second, the quality and sophistication of commercial packages means that often a commercial package will contain more features than could realistically be included in a package developed in-house. Third, the reliability of the packages can be assumed. Because the package is already on the market, presumably it will work properly (or at least well enough to be usable). The reputation of the commercial developer is on the line; therefore, the developer is eager to market a package that will work properly. Because of the strong competition in the field, commercial software developers also have an incentive to provide good quality support for the user. Software support involves a variety of user services such as providing on-site staff training and "hot-line" phone numbers that allow the user to talk directly with experts on their software. On the other hand, it may take long periods of time to isolate and correct errors in packages developed in-house.

While there are benefits to using commercially developed software, there are also disadvantages. A commercially developed package may not meet the user's exact needs and therefore may require extensive modification. In industry, a general rule of thumb is that about 85 percent of an application package can be used exactly as it is written. The other 15 percent of the package must be modified according to user needs. In addition, the customer usually depends on the vendor from whom the package was purchased to provide support. In the early days of commercial application packages, there were considerable problems in this area. Software developers did not have the personnel or the facilities to provide the needed support. Vendors would make impossible promises concerning the capabilities of their software, leaving many users highly dissatisfied. However, word quickly spread concerning unreliable software, developers, and vendors. Today most developers and vendors are extremely concerned about their reputations and produce and market high-quality products. Therefore, for many companies, buying and using commercial application software has become a way of life. For most companies, developing and maintaining application software has become costly; this cost can be reduced by purchasing commercial application software.

● General Categories of Application Software Packages

The computer industry has grown at a rate unmatched by any other industry. Because of this rapid growth, some areas of the industry are not clearly defined or are the subject of disagreement among industry professionals. Commercial application software development is one area in which some confusion exists. There is a lack of consensus among professionals about how to label or categorize software packages. In this chapter we will divide application software into three broad categories: productivity tools, functional tools, and end-user development tools. Although these categories overlap to some extent, they do provide a useful method of making generalized statements about the different types of application software currently available.

● Productivity Tools

Productivity tools are software packages that can increase user productivity. Common examples of productivity tools are text processors, graphics packages, spreadsheets, and file managers. These tools can be used for a wide variety of tasks. Productivity tools are simply aids in achieving a goal; the exact goal may vary depending on the particular situation.

TEXT PROCESSORS

Software packages that allow the user to manipulate documents consisting of text, such as reports and tables, are referred to as **text** or **word processors.** Anyone who has ever used a text processor knows how helpful they are when creating and editing reports, tables, and so on. No longer are typing mistakes and organizational problems a major difficulty. Portions of the text can be easily deleted, inserted, or moved. Other features often included in text processors are the ability to justify the left and right margins and center headings. Footnotes can be inserted

Categories of Application Software Packages

CATEGORY	EXPLANATION	EXAMPLES
Productivity tools	Used to increase user productivity	Text processor Graphics package Spreadsheet File Manager
Functional tools	Perform a specific purpose	Payroll Billing Accounts receivable Inventory control Manufacturing resource planning
End-user development tools	Allow the end-user to develop software tailored to a specific situation, often through the use of a fourth-generation programming language	Decision support system (DSS) Data-base management system (DBMS)

at the bottom of pages and pages can be numbered automatically. Most text processors allow the user to specify options such as italics, underlining, or boldface type. An example of a text processor containing all of the features mentioned above is DIGITAL's Standard Runoff.

Often text processors will include extensions such as **spelling checkers,** which compare each word in a specified document with the contents of an online dictionary. If a particular word does not appear in the dictionary, it is flagged so that the user can check it for correct spelling. Most spelling checkers allow the user to add words to the dictionary so that it can be customized to meet the user's needs and vocabulary.

GRAPHICS PACKAGES

Graphics packages allow the user to create bar graphs, line graphs, pie charts, and so forth. Figure 13–1 shows examples of the different types of graphs that might be created with this type of application software. Normally, the user need only specify the type of graph desired and the size of each field within the graph. Different parts of the graph can be appropriately labeled. When using color monitors, the user can determine the colors of various parts of the graph, creating an attractive, professional-looking product in minimal time. Graphics packages are very useful for managers who must prepare reports summarizing complex information.

There are many specialized graphics packages available. Some allow geologists to create color-coded graphics of the earth's surface; these

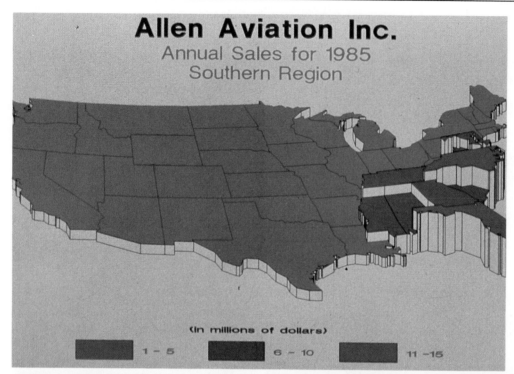

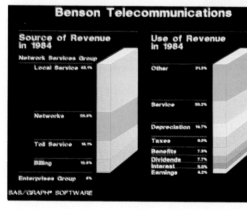

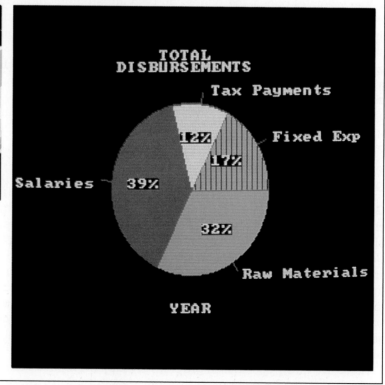

graphics are based on aerial photographs. Presentation graphics packages are especially designed for managers and educators to use when preparing presentations of slidelike shows for groups. The packages allow figures and graphs to be pulled easily from other sources. Composite screens can be created and a wide range of display and dissolve techniques are generally available. Special cameras can create slides from images on terminal screens. In addition, special projectors designed to be attached to computer terminals can be used to project the images onto a screen.

SPREADSHEETS

A spreadsheet, or ledger sheet, is primarily used in business by accountants for performing financial calculations and recording transactions. An **electronic spreadsheet** is simply a computerized version of a traditional spreadsheet. Electronic spreadsheets, however, are being used for more than just doing financial calculations and recording transactions. An electronic spreadsheet consists of a table of rows and columns used to store and manipulate any kind of numerical data. The point in a spreadsheet where a particular row and column meet is called a **cell.** Each cell is a unique location within the spreadsheet. Cells can contain labels, values, and formulas.

The use of formulas is what makes spreadsheets powerful. A formula can be applied to the contents of specified cells to obtain a result. For example, a user could calculate the amount of monthly payments on a loan, depending on the interest rate being charged. It would also be a simple matter to determine how much monthly payments would be if the length of payment time varied, say for thirty-six, forty-eight or sixty months. The ability to alter variables within the spreadsheet makes such calculations a simple matter. Figure 13–2 shows the variety of functions that are often available with spreadsheets that are part of integrated packages.

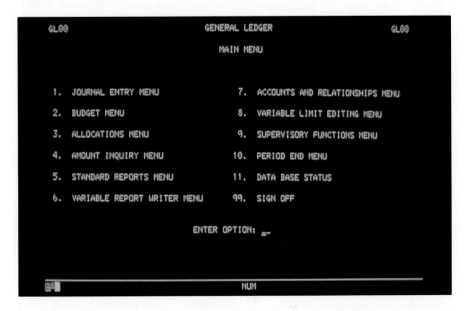

● **FIGURE 13–2**
Integrated accounting packages, such as this one from Software International Corporation, allow the user to select from a menu of available functions.

FILE MANAGERS

File managers are designed to duplicate the traditional manual methods of filing. Before the use of computers for filing, sections or departments in a business generally kept records that pertained only to their particular area of interest. The payroll department, for example, might keep an employee's name, number, address, salary, and number of deductions to facilitate the writing of paychecks. The personnel department might keep each employee's name, employee number, salary, job title, address, employment history, and spouse's name. Each department would keep its own information independently for its own use.

Computers and computerized record keeping made it possible for the procedures and methods of recording, filing, and updating data to be converted from paper file folders and file cabinets to computer software and storage devices. These computerized files can be updated easily and also can be accessed by more than one person at a time. Project Management is an example of a file manager produced by the SAS Institute, Inc.

● Functional Tools

Functional tools are software packages that perform a specific function. For example, an inventory program used by a grocery store has only one purpose: to keep track of the inventory. An enormous variety of functional tools are currently available and the number increases daily.

Businesses are the most common users of these commercial application packages. Uses for the packages include accounting, manufacturing, sales, and marketing. We will discuss some commonly used types of packages here.

ACCOUNTING PACKAGES

Most functional packages are built-in modules. For example, in accounting, a particular package might have payroll, billing, accounts receivable, and accounts payable modules. When a company purchases a particular package, only those modules needed are obtained. Others can be added on later, if desired. Therefore, the package is tailored to individual needs. Because these modules are then integrated into an entire package, they can interact with one another, passing data between them. These packages can be customized to generate well-designed reports that meet the needs of a specific company. Balance sheets and income statements can be produced, as well as other reports. Figure 13–3 shows a screen for an accounts payable package. Such packages can generate a wide variety of output (see Figure 13–4).

MANUFACTURING PACKAGES

Manufacturing application packages, like other functional packages, tend to be composed of a number of integrated modules. The modules used depend on the needs of the particular company. In manufacturing, application packages are used to determine material requirements so that inventory needs can be projected to maintain a steady inventory of items on hand. This is important because keeping excess inventory on hand is expensive and ties up capital that could be used elsewhere. If a company maintains multiple warehouses, application packages can track down needed material, making operations run more smoothly overall and making efficient use of stock on hand.

Manufacturing resource planning (MRP) packages have been developed to meet these needs. MRP joins a variety of functions in the areas of business planning and production planning and scheduling. Such a system can maximize resources by helping to route materials efficiently; in addition, overhead is kept at a minimum because only needed inventory is kept on hand. Another important aspect of manufacturing is the scheduling of equipment and people. Often, equipment must be carefully scheduled so that it can be used in the most efficient way possible. A large amount of manufacturing time is used in setting up equipment. For example, if a lathe must be set up in a special way to turn the arms for a certain type of chair, all of the arms that will be needed over an established period of time should be cut at once.

MRP software has become popular and indeed essential because, if implemented correctly, it can save a company large amounts of money; the average return on the investment varies from 50 to 200 percent. In addition, the average MRP user reduces inventory by 17 percent, increases manufacturing productivity by 10 percent, and realizes cost reductions of approximately 7 percent.

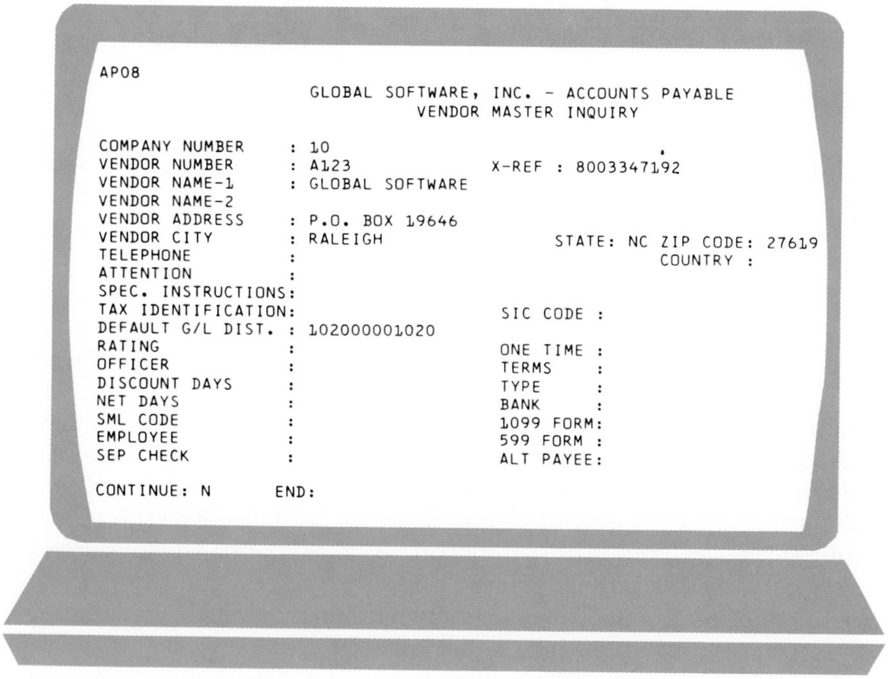

● **FIGURE 13–3**
This screen demonstrates Global Software, Inc.'s Accounts Payable Ledger Inquiry.

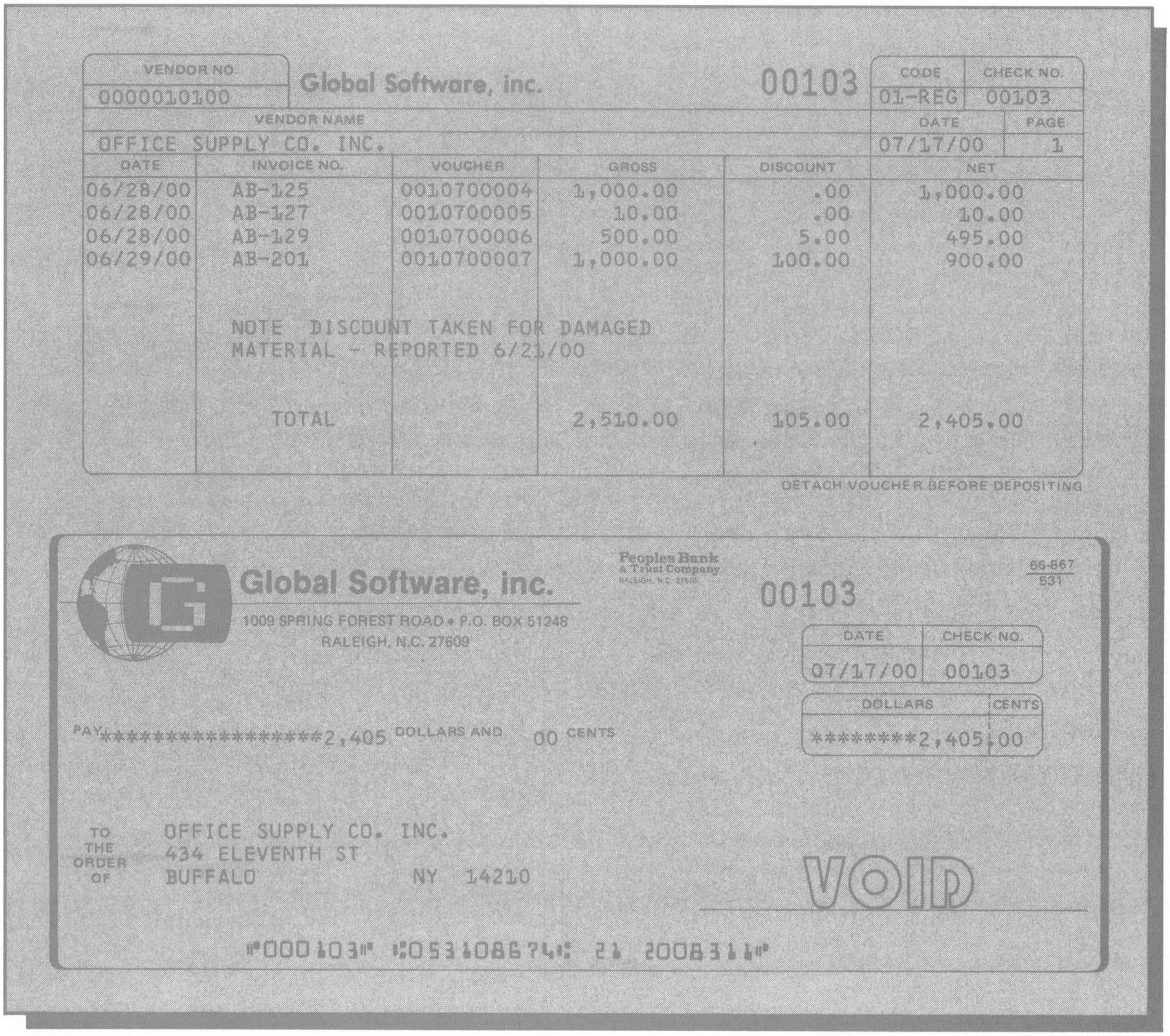

VENDOR NO.					CODE	CHECK NO.
0000010100	Global Software, inc.			00103	01-REG	00103

VENDOR NAME	DATE	PAGE
OFFICE SUPPLY CO. INC.	07/17/00	1

DATE	INVOICE NO.	VOUCHER	GROSS	DISCOUNT	NET
06/28/00	AB-125	0010700004	1,000.00	.00	1,000.00
06/28/00	AB-127	0010700005	10.00	.00	10.00
06/28/00	AB-129	0010700006	500.00	5.00	495.00
06/29/00	AB-201	0010700007	1,000.00	100.00	900.00
	NOTE DISCOUNT TAKEN FOR DAMAGED MATERIAL - REPORTED 6/21/00				
	TOTAL		2,510.00	105.00	2,405.00

DETACH VOUCHER BEFORE DEPOSITING

Global Software, inc.
1009 SPRING FOREST ROAD • P.O. BOX 51248
RALEIGH, N.C. 27609

Peoples Bank & Trust Company

00103

66-867
531

DATE	CHECK NO.
07/17/00	00103

DOLLARS	CENTS
********2,405	00

PAY*****************2,405 DOLLARS AND 00 CENTS

TO THE ORDER OF
OFFICE SUPPLY CO. INC.
434 ELEVENTH ST
BUFFALO NY 14210

VOID

⑈000103⑈ ⑆053108674⑆ 21 2008311⑈

● **FIGURE 13–4**
Global Software, Inc.'s Accounts Payable System can perform a variety of tasks such as generating correctly formatted checks.

SALES AND MARKETING PACKAGES

Sales analysis software is used to analyze data on sales transactions over a given period of time. The software generates reports stating sales made by each salesperson, quantity of sales of a particular item or in a particular region, profits, and so forth.

Another area in which sales departments commonly use application software is ordering. Excellent software packages are available to maintain order records. New orders are entered, the status of existing orders can be updated, and filled orders can be deleted. This type of package can be integrated with inventory and billing operations. For example, when an order is filled, the data concerning how much the customer owes can then be passed on to the software that performs the billing. When an order is shipped, the inventory package could be instructed to update the inventory.

TURNKEY SYSTEMS

Functional tools can be aimed at either horizontal markets or vertical markets. A tool for the horizontal market would be an accounting package that was designed for general use and could therefore be used by any type of accounting department that needed to perform general accounting tasks. Such a package would not be customized for a particular business. On the other hand, a set of application software packages to run a doctor's office is an example of a functional tool aimed at the vertical market. Such a group of packages has a very specific market, doctors' offices, and a specific purpose, helping to perform those tasks that can be computerized. Therefore, the package can be tailored in ways that a more general package cannot.

Developing functional tools for the vertical market is a rapidly expanding field. Some software companies not only set up a complete system of integrated packages designed to meet the user's needs but also supply the necessary software. These packages, in which everything is provided for the user, are referred to as **turnkey systems.** They are very popular with small businesses that do not have the in-house expertise to locate and implement the appropriate hardware and software.

For example, a company that implements turnkey systems for dentists' offices might first determine the exact needs of a particular office and then set up a minicomputer system that will be capable of efficiently running the needed application packages such as scheduling, billing, storing patient records, and generating needed reports. This provides a single integrated system that is designed to meet a variety of needs in a specific situation.

Ortho-Track is one company that has designed a specific system for use in orthodontists' offices. Not only does Ortho-Track provide the hardware and software for the business, it also provides on-site training when the system is first implemented and a telephone hotline to handle later questions or problems. The software used by this system, like that for other systems, is modularized. Therefore, the office personnel can choose only those modules that are suited to their needs. The user can also customize the way in which output is displayed on the screen. The Ortho-Track system is typical of many of the systems aimed at the vertical market. The number of companies providing this type of specialized service is growing daily.

● End-User Development Tools

End-user development tools (also referred to as **fourth-generation software development tools**) are software packages with which the end-user (the person actually using the software) can develop a package addressing the specific needs of the particular situation. There are several reasons why end-users may choose to develop their own package rather than to buy a commercial package. Sometimes the user's needs are highly specialized; therefore the market for such a package is small and an appropriate one may not be available. In addition, by developing its own package, a company can tailor the software to the exact needs of

Simulation software is used regularly in business and training. Interestingly, such software can also be applied to the development of a wide variety of fascinating objects. Alan Adler, a lecturer in engineering at Stanford, has developed a better flying disk. Called the Aerobie, it is capable of flying 1,125 feet—a considerably longer distance than the farthest Frisbee throw on record. This makes the Aerobie the world's farthest-thrown object.

Adler created a formula to use in a simulation program that was capable of designing an object that could attain perfect balance at all speeds. The simulation was capable of determining the "lift slope" of the two airfoils. The resulting object, the Aerobie, is a wide flat ring currently being sold for $8.95. The company, Superflight, is offering a $1,000 reward to the first person who throws the Aerobie at least 1,200 feet.

the particular situation. There is a wide variety of end-user development tools on the market, including simulation software, statistical packages, decision support systems, and data-base management systems.

Creating a software package using these tools requires little skill. Often development tools allow users to solve problems that ordinarily would require the attention of data processing departments. This frees users from dependency upon data processing departments and is an important advantage in many companies where the data processing department may have a backlog of months' worth of projects.

Fourth-generation programming languages, or query languages as they are often called, are used with these end-user development tools. The end-user can quickly learn to use these languages because they are similar to English. These languages allow managers to manipulate corporate data in a fast, friendly, flexible way. The user must learn the necessary commands and syntax, but because the statements are similar to English, they require little time or skill to learn.

SIMULATION SOFTWARE

People establish theories based on what they observe and measure in reality. Models are then built to test the theory to see if it is correct. If the model works properly, it can be used for **simulation,** which is the use of a model to project what will happen in a particular situation. A simple example of this process would be the development of a formula for converting Fahrenheit temperatures to Celsius. The reality is that any given temperature can be stated in terms of both the Fahrenheit and the Celsius scales. Therefore, a theory could be proposed that because these two scales are based on an absolute value (temperature), it should be possible to come up with a formula to convert a temperature stated in one scale to the other. Once a theory has been created, a model can be developed. One way of developing a model is to take a range of Fahrenheit and Celsius temperatures and determine the relationship. From this a model could be stated:

Celsius = 5/9 × Fahrenheit + 32

If this model consistently yields correct results when used in simulation, it can be assumed to be reasonably accurate; if not, the model will have to be altered accordingly. After it has been shown that using the model in simulation consistently yields correct results, it is no longer necessary to check the results against reality. Therefore, results are considered accurate simply by using the model. Concept Summary 13–2 explains the relationship between reality and simulation.

Simulation is particularly useful in making business decisions. For example, if a manager needs to know how cost-effective building a new plant would be, a simulation package can help in making such a decision. Usually such software makes use of a wide variety of information stored in the company's data base to arrive at a conclusion.

An example of a general-purpose simulation software package is GPSS (General Purpose Simulation System), developed by IBM. This package allows the user to establish variables and then alter the relationships

Illustration of Relationship between Reality and Simulation

REALITY	The temperature of a given entity can be determined using either the Fahrenheit or Celsius scales
THEORY	A specific, consistent correlation exists between these two scales; therefore, it should be possible to convert a temperature stated in one scale to its corresponding temperature in the other scale
MODEL	The proposed formula: Celsius = 5/9 × Fahrenheit + 32
SIMULATION	Convert a temperature in one scale to its equivalent in the other scale; after extensive testing, if these conversions are continually consistent with reality, the simulation can be assumed to be accurate

between the variables. The software package will determine how these alterations will affect output.

Decision Support Systems

Decision support systems (DSS) help managers to make and implement decisions. They are fully integrated, obtaining data from a wide variety of sources such as different departments within a company; they allow the user to analyze this data on an interactive basis. These systems also generally include a number of productivity tools that were previously discussed, such as graphics packages and spreadsheets. What makes the decision support system unique is the way in which these tools are integrated into a highly sophisticated package. Such systems are widely used by financial institutions, oil companies, automobile manufacturers, and other similar industries. The theory behind decision support systems will be discussed in detail in Chapter 15; our emphasis here is on the software used to implement these systems. Decision support systems use fourth-generation languages to query data bases to obtain necessary information; in addition they can be used to simulate specified conditions to determine the output of a particular situation. An example of such a system is the SAS System, developed by SAS, Inc. It is an integrated decision support system that includes 125 procedures including spreadsheets, statistical analysis, and decision support. Sophisticated graphics and report-generating features allow the output to be attractively displayed or printed. Figure 13–5 demonstrates this package.

There are a number of application software packages available that allow the manager to interactively probe a computerized model for results concerning various decision alternatives. These packages include MARKETPLAN and BRANDAID, which help in preparing marketing plans; CALLPLAN and DETAILER, which aid in the allocation of a sales force; and MEDIAC, which helps to prepare advertising media schedules.

Another package is the Interactive Financial Planning System (IFPS). IFPS is an interactive planning package that centers around a model

The results generated by the SAS decision support system can be displayed
in a variety of ways, including easy-to-
understand graphs.

based on a manager's perception of the real-world system. Marketed by
EXECUCOM Systems Corporation, IFPS can be considered a generalized
planning or modeling system. As a generalized system, IFPS can be used
for such applications as balance sheet and income statement preparation, operating budgets, forecasting, strategic planning, risk analysis,
and capital budgeting. Because IFPS does not incorporate a specific
model, it offers management a great deal of flexibility. See Figure 13–6
as an illustration of the decision support aspect of IFPS.

● Expert Systems

Expert Systems are built using what is known of the human thought
processes to mimic the decision-making processes of human experts in
narrowly defined fields. Software designers try to program the computer
to follow the same path of thinking as top experts in the specified field.
Expert systems are different from decision support systems in that they
only cover very small fields of knowledge; decision support systems attempt to allow managers to make decisions based on a wide range of
data and factors (see Figure 13–7).

The heart of the system is a knowledge base that contains facts and
rules used by experts. The user asks questions of the system through the
use of fourth-generation programming languages. When responding to
these questions, the expert system draws on its knowledge base.

Although the quality of these systems is growing rapidly, as yet they
are unable to make the type of sophisticated inferences that a human

● **COMPUTERS AND INFORMATION PROCESSING**

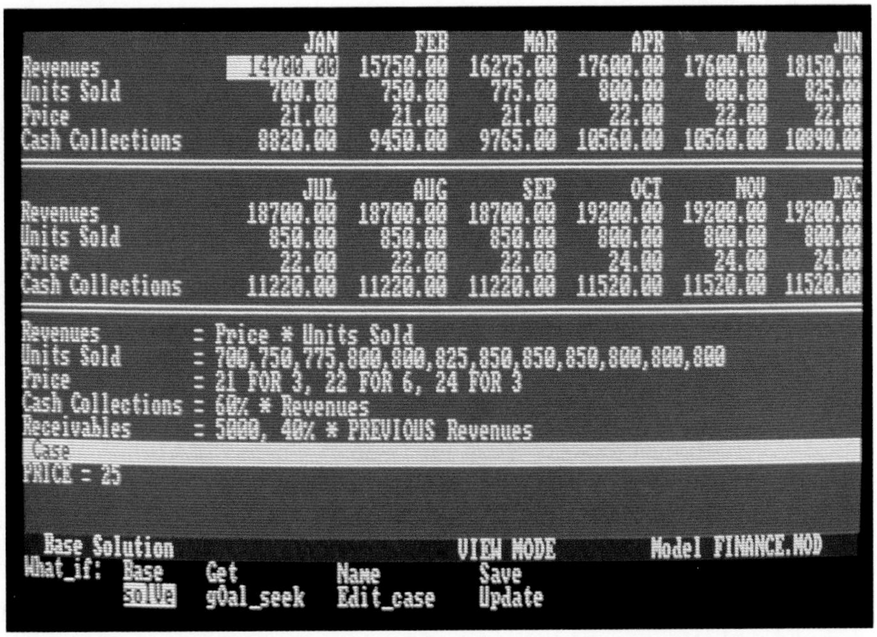

● **FIGURE 13–6**
The What-If? feature of IFPS enables the user to calculate the effect of changes on selected values to the remaining values with a single menu selection.

expert can make. Nonetheless, expert systems offer a number of advantages over human experts. For example, knowledge is not lost as it may be when a human expert dies or moves to another job.

One expert system is MYCIN, which is used to diagnose infectious diseases and recommend appropriate drugs. Another interesting expert system is RI, developed by J. McDermott, at Carnegie-Mellon University, which is used to determine the best configuration of the VAX-11/780 computer system for a particular user. PROSPECTOR is an expert system that helps geologists in locating mineral deposits. Taxadvisor, developed by R. Michaelsen at the University of Illinois, helps users with estate

IRA MASTER MENU

ENTER TRAN ID ■

IMAS	LOGON/LOGOFF/CH DATE	IPOS	POST TRANSACTIONS
IEDP	EDIT PARTICIPANT REC	IPNA	ADD REPEATING TRANS
IEDI	EDIT INVESTMENT REC	IPNI	REPEATING INQUIRY
IEDT	EDIT TRANSACTION REC	IPNR	REPEATING RELEASE
IEDA	ADD INVESTMENT	IPRT	POST REPEATING
INQP	PARTICIPANT INQUIRY	IPRE	PROFILE EDIT
INQI	INVESTMENT INQUIRY	IPRO	PROFILE INQUIRY
INQT	TRANSACTION INQUIRY	I002	DAILY SUMMARY REPORT
IFND	FIND SS# BY NAME	INAC	ADD NEW PARTICIPANT
ICSS	CHANGE SOCIAL SEC #	IPNE	EDIT REPEATING TRANS

● **FIGURE 13–7**
IRA Master from Fogle Computing Corp. is an expert system used for investment purposes.

planning. It determines ways in which the client can minimize income and death taxes and also makes investment and insurance recommendations. More expert systems in every conceivable field are being designed all the time.

STATISTICAL PACKAGES

An interesting application of prewritten software packages is in the area of statistics. Before the advent of these packages, scientists and statisticians spent many hours analyzing data, using calculators and complex mathematical formulas. Today, elaborate statistical procedures can be performed accurately and quickly with the aid of **statistical packages.** The user must write a simple program that then generates the needed statistics, but because the program is written in a fourth-generation language, these packages are easy for people with no programming experience to use. Three commonly used statistical packages are SAS (Statistical Analysis System), SPSS (Statistical Package for the Social Sciences), and Minitab. These packages can provide a wide variety of arithmetic and trigonometric functions. In addition, statistical functions calculating means, ranges, variances, and standard deviations, as well as more complicated statistics, are easily performed.

To use a statistical package, the user must write a program in a fourth-generation programming language designed specifically for that package. Figure 13–8 shows a sample SAS program and its output. In addition to performing a wide variety of statistical operations, SAS also allows the user to determine how the output will be printed. Statistical packages are often included as part of a decision support system, thereby allowing managers to analyze data as desired.

DATA-BASE MANAGEMENT SYSTEMS

Data-base management systems (DBMS) consist of a series of programs that are used to design and maintain data bases. A data-base management system is more complex than a file manager because programs can be developed to access the data base in a variety of ways.

For example, if the accounting department accessed employee records contained in a data base, the records could be displayed in a way that was most convenient for their needs. Also, only the record fields needed by the accounting department would be displayed. On the other hand, a different program could be written to access the same data base for the personnel department. This program would display only the information needed by personnel.

Data-base management systems are divided into three categories depending on the way in which data contained in them is stored. The categories, which were explained in Chapter 7, are hierarchical, network, and relational. The oldest data-base structure is the hierarchical structure. An example of a hierarchical data base is IMS, which was developed by IBM and has been widely used for some time. A commonly used network data base is DBMS-20.

When using hierarchical or network systems, programs called **schemas** are written that determine the manner in which the records stored

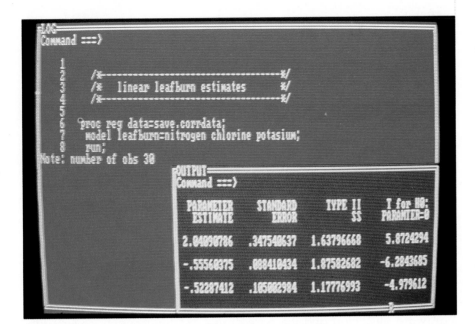

in the data base will be related to one another. These schemas are written in a **data definition language (DDL).** Once this is accomplished, a program written in a **data manipulation language (DML)** determines how users can access the data base. In these programs, data manipulation language statements are embedded in another language, such as COBOL. Therefore, writing a program to access a hierarchial or network data base requires a significant amount of programming skill.

On the other hand, when using a relational data base, the user simply accesses the data base directly through the use of a fourth-generation language. The American National Standards Institute (ANSI) has approved SQL (Structured Query Language) as the standard fourth-generation language to query relational data bases. Three relational data bases currently available are DB2, developed by IBM; ORACLE, developed by Oracle Corporation; and INGRES, developed by Relational Technology. Both of these data bases can be queried by using the fourth-generation language SQL. Data bases provide an enormous amount of flexibility in allowing users to access data in a wide variety of ways.

● Choosing An Application Software Package

The user who needs to decide whether to buy a commercial application package or to develop the needed software system in-house is facing a difficult decision. Some of the questions that should be asked are:

● Does the data processing department have the needed system analysts and/or programmers who have the needed skills to develop the package in-house?

● Is there commercial application software that can meet the stated needs (or at least be easily modified to meet these needs)?

Theoretically, decision support systems can be a tremendous help in management decision-making. But how useful have they been in actual corporate settings? Several years ago, market analysts at Parke-Davis, a pharmaceutical company, started using Easytrac, which consists of a collection of decision support software specifically designed for marketing. The system allows the company to keep track of the amount of money competitors are spending on advertising and the quantities and types of drugs that are shipped to drugstores, hospitals, and supermarkets. With this data in hand, the market analysts can generate reports on consumer responses to various advertising campaigns and promotions. Data on which factors made a doctor prescribe a specific product is also tabulated. For example, was it word-of-mouth from a colleague, an advertisement in a medical journal, or information and samples given to the doctor by a salesperson? Having this information readily available helps Parke-Davis determine how to spend its advertising money most effectively.

In addition, Easytrac has components that are useful when generating reports, including graphics applications that allow the user to create pie charts, bar graphs, and so forth. Because of the variety and quality of the tools it provides, Easytrac has proved an invaluable marketing tool that allows Parke-Davis to operate efficiently in a highly competitive field.

● Will the appropriate commercial software run on the available computer system?
● Is there adequate documentation?
● Will the vendor or manufacturer provide the needed support?
● Is there time available to write the software in-house or is obtaining a package that can be quickly implemented a critical factor?

If after carefully considering the above factors it has been decided to purchase a commercial application package, it then must be determined which package will best meet the user's needs. If possible, the user should arrange to try the package on a trial basis to determine how well it will work day in, day out. Another source of information on the quality of application software is user surveys. Several publications conduct such surveys on a regular basis. For example, *DATAMATION* conducts a yearly survey of data processing managers called the Applications Software Survey, asking them to evaluate packages they are using. The results of this survey can be a very helpful guide in choosing software. According to *DATAMATION*, there are four areas of primary concern in evaluating these packages: performance, operations, I/O functionality, and vendor support. Performance is concerned with such factors as the efficiency of hardware utilization and the ease of use. I/O functionality covers data entry provisions and how quickly and easily output format changes can be made. The applications software packages covered in the survey fall into business categories such as general accounting, payroll and personnel, and business management and forecasting.

When choosing application software packages, customers often turn to resources within their specific field. Another method of evaluating application packages is simply word-of-mouth. Company management within a specific industry often has frequent contact with management in similar companies and can ask these people what types of packages they are using and how they would evaluate the performance of the software.

Probably the best method of choosing a package is to try a number of them on a trial basis to determine how each will actually perform on the job. Because the application package will probably be used for some time to come, the time spent in making an informed choice is well spent.

● Summary Points

● The use of commercially written application software packages has increased dramatically in recent years. Such packages have a number of advantages over software written in-house, including generally lower cost, faster implementation, better quality, and reliability. There are some disadvantages, however, including the fact that a commercial package may not meet the user's needs as precisely as one developed in-house. Also, the user is dependent upon the vendor or the developer for support.

● Application software can be divided into three broad categories: productivity tools, functional tools, and end-user development tools.

- Productivity tools are packages that can be used in a wide variety of ways to increase the productivity of the user. Examples are text processors, graphics packages, spreadsheets, and file managers.

- Functional tools perform a specific function or purpose. Functional packages are generally built from modules so that they can be customized to meet the user's needs. Accounting packages produce payrolls, balance sheets, and income statements. Manufacturing resource planning (MRP) packages are commonly used in manufacturing to handle inventory and schedule employees and equipment efficiently. In sales and marketing, software packages keep track of order status and generate sales reports.

- Turnkey systems are popular with small businesses. Companies specializing in these systems supply the user with a complete package, including hardware, software, training of staff, and on-going support. Because the software is usually modularized, it can be customized easily to meet the user's needs.

- End-user development tools allow the end-user to use fourth-generation programming languages to develop an application package to exact specifications. Fourth-generation programming languages are more English-like than high-level languages such as COBOL and require only a short period of time to learn.

- Simulation software uses a model to project what will happen in a particular situation. Decision support systems help managers to make and implement decisions. They obtain data from a wide variety of sources, most commonly data bases. In addition, they incorporate a wide variety of packages such as graphics and spreadsheets. IFPS is a decision support system that allows the user to manipulate variables to determine how various results will be affected.

- Expert systems attempt to mimic the decision-making processes of experts in narrowly-defined fields. These systems use a knowledge base to answer questions posed by the user.

- Statistical packages quickly and accurately perform statistical analysis of data. SAS, SPSS, and Minitab are three examples of statistical packages.

- Data-base management systems consist of a series of programs that are used to design and maintain data bases. When using hierarchical or network data bases, a data definition language must be used to write a program that determines how the data base is organized. Then programs are written in data manipulation languages that allow the user to access the data base. The end-user can then access the data base through the use of a fourth-generation language. Relational data bases do not require the use of data definition languages or data manipulation languages. These data bases can be accessed directly by using fourth-generation languages.

- When choosing an application package, many factors must be taken into account. Some of them are: (1) Can the package be written by the company's data processing department? Are the needed analysts and programmers available? (2) Is there a commercial package available that can meet the stated need and will this package run on the available computer system? (3) Is there adequate documentation for the commercial software and will the vendor or manufacturer supply the needed support? (4) Is there time to develop the package in-house?

● If a company decides to buy a commercial package, a particular package must be chosen. User surveys conducted by magazines and journals are one helpful method of determining if current users are satisfied with their software. Another method is to ask other companies in the same field how happy they are with the software they are using. But using the software on a trial basis is the best test of how well it will perform in a particular setting.

● Review Questions

1. What are some advantages of using commercially written application software? What are some disadvantages?

2. Into what three categories can application software be placed?

3. Explain what is meant by the term *productivity tool* and give three examples.

4. What is the difference between functional tools aimed at the vertical market and those aimed at the horizontal market?

5. List some functional tools commonly used in business.

6. Give a definition of simulation software.

7. What is an expert system? Why might such a system be preferable to a human expert? Why not?

8. What is the purpose of statistical packages? Name two commonly used statistical packages.

9. What is a data definition language?

10. Name some factors that should be considered when choosing an application software package.

Microsoft Corporation

MICROSOFT.

EARLY DEVELOPMENTS

The microcomputer industry began in the mid-1970s and since then has experienced rapid growth. Most visible have been the successes of various hardware suppliers—Apple Computer, Tandy Corporation, and IBM, to name a few. It was the marked achievements of these suppliers that stimulated the development of a number of related businesses—most notably companies that designed and manufactured software to run on the new machines.

Founded in 1974, Microsoft Corporation has quickly become the largest developer of software for microcomputers in the United States, establishing itself as a pioneer in an industry teeming with pioneers. Since 1977, sales have doubled every year, staffing has jumped from 5 to more than 500, and the company outgrew its new quarters in less than one year. Microsoft has given new meaning to the concept of rapid expansion.

Beginning with Microsoft's initial product, the first BASIC language for microcomputers (still an industry standard), the company established a reputation for developing innovative, state-of-the-art products. One of the most notable features of Microsoft's design standards is that each new generation of software is compatible with the software of the previous generation.

Microsoft began as a partnership between William H. Gates and Paul G. Allen. It was recognized as a privately held corporation in 1981 with Gates as executive vice president and chairman of the board and Allen as executive vice president. Jon Shirley joined the company as president in August 1983. Today, Microsoft is the leading independent software supplier of easy-to-learn and well-supported productivity tools, languages, and operating systems. With dealers nationwide, three offices in Europe, and branches in Japan, Australia, and Korea, Microsoft is growing and changing to meet the needs of the worldwide software industry.

PRODUCT LINE

Microsoft has the most comprehensive range of microcomputer software products of any company in the world, maintaining a full line of language compilers, interpreters, operating systems, business tools, and even entertainment packages.

In 1980, Microsoft licensed the UNIX operating system from Bell Labs and began to develop its own enhanced version for microcomputers, which is called XENIX. UNIX is a powerful, multiuser operating system designed for microcomputers, and Microsoft successfully adapted it, with a number of improvements, to run on the 16-bit microprocessor. With the release of the XENIX operating system, Microsoft began providing maintenance, support, and even application assistance to original equipment manufacturers (OEMs) and end users. As a result, Microsoft rapidly became the main supplier of a popular, standardized, high-level 16-bit operating system that was powerful and also accessible to almost every microprocessor on the market. The XENIX operating system was developed to run on multiuser computers with 16-bit microprocessors and on DEC's PDP-11 series. To date, forty companies in eight different countries have licensed XENIX.

Also in 1980, Microsoft developed and introduced the Microsoft SoftCard, a plug-in board that allows Apple II owners access to both Microsoft BASIC and the CP/M operating system for the Zilog Z-80 microprocessor, and thereby tens of thousands of software packages. The first year on the market, Microsoft sold 25,000 units; since then SoftCard has been installed in more than 100,000 Apple systems.

Approached by IBM and working closely with them, Microsoft developed a new 16-bit operating system. When IBM introduced its personal computer in August 1981, Microsoft MS-DOS was the only operating system for which IBM provided additional software. Within a year, IBM had announced full support of twelve Microsoft products, and by June 1982, thirty other companies had released software designed to run on Microsoft MS-DOS. Microsoft also adapted a number of 8-bit languages to the 16-bit microprocessor. Those languages include Microsoft BASIC interpreter and compiler, as well as Business BASIC, Pascal, COBOL, C, and FORTRAN compilers.

Microsoft has developed a number of second-

generation software packages and tools, such as Multiplan electronic worksheet, a sophisticated electronic planning and modeling tool designed to be the friendliest and most powerful on the market. By the end of 1982, Multiplan was offered by thirty-six different microcomputer manufacturers and was available in seven languages. According to recent surveys, Multiplan has become the leading program for business, displacing the original electronic spreadsheet, VisiCalc®.

Microsoft also offers productivity tools that help consumers to design and quickly build customized Multiplan electronic worksheets. The Budget expert system for budget planning and control and the Financial Statement expert system for performing financial statement ratio analysis were both released in the spring of 1983 and have received overwhelming acceptance from business managers and professionals.

In March 1983, Microsoft introduced SystemCard, designed for the IBM Personal Computer to integrate serial and parallel interface with additional memory (up to 256K bytes of RAM) and a clock/calendar, all on one card. This card saves space in the expansion-limited IBM PC system unit.

Following the release of SystemCard, Microsoft introduced a low-cost, hand-held input device called the Microsoft Mouse. Mouse is small and lightweight and is used to quickly insert, delete, and reposition the cursor or blocks of text within a document without having to use the keyboard. Microsoft Mouse has been developed for use with the IBM Personal Computer and other systems that run on the MS-DOS operating system.

With the release of the Microsoft Mouse, Microsoft also introduced a highly sophisticated word processing software package, Microsoft Word. Features like style sheets, footnotes, glossaries, columnar formatting, and multiple windows have helped make Word an industry leader. Typical of Microsoft's careful planning, Word was designed to take advantage of anticipated developments in computer printers by allowing users to specify not only paper and type sizes but also special character sizes, ink colors, and up to sixty-four different type fonts. Word has become a best seller among users of the Apple's Macintosh computer and Laserwriter printer.

Marketing best-selling software is a way of life at Microsoft. Another of the company's best-selling application programs, Excel, is a spreadsheet also designed for the Macintosh. Excel offers integrated business graphics and data-base modules with the spreadsheet. Windows, a graphical operating environment, runs on the MS-DOS operating system.

In the area of entertainment, the most significant software package released by Microsoft is Flight Simulator, which has become one of the biggest selling programs for the IBM Personal Computer. With Flight Simulator, the players "pilot" an aircraft (similar to a Cessna Skylane) through takeoff and landings at more than twenty airports. They may alter the environment to simulate various weather conditions, as well as daytime or nighttime flight.

Microsoft, while continuing to develop other consumer applications and tools, is committed to the philosophy of constantly improving software and developing upwardly compatible versions of all established products for the new generation of 16-bit computers.

DISCUSSION POINTS

1. What key issues does microsoft consider critical to software developers in the future, and why are these issues important?
2. Why is the development of standards for user interface an important consideration for a software developer?

14

SYSTEM ANALYSIS AND DESIGN

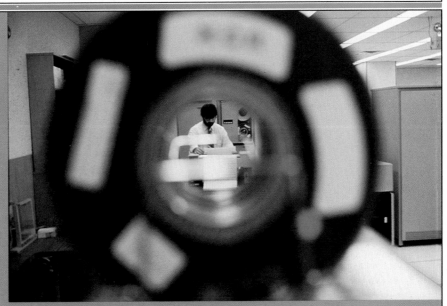

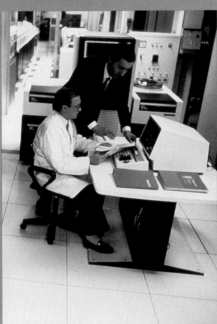

○ARTICLE
Here Comes the Erasable Laser Disk

Brian Dumaine

Fortune

New Computer Disks that use laser technology have tremendous capacity to store information, but up till now the so-called optical disks have been one-way streets. Once data were entered, they couldn't be changed, limiting optical disks to such uses as storing company archives. Now 3M says it has developed an optical disk on which data can be moved, changed, and erased just as it can on magnetic disks. The company, already one of the largest U.S. manufacturers of floppy magnetic disks, will begin producing the new disks in relatively small quantities in April. Says James N. Porter, publisher of *Disk Trend Report*, an annual survey of the disk drive business: "3M's disk is a milestone for the industry."

One of 3M's 5¼-inch disks can hold 250,000 pages of text; 25 magnetic hard disks of the same size are needed to hold that amount. The compact disks are designed especially for personal computers. Edward S. Rothchild, a San Francisco-based optical disk consultant, says that the new disks will enable microcomputers to do many tasks that must now be done on a mainframe or a minicomputer. A doctor, for instance, could keep all his patients' records, the contents of many of his medical textbooks, and a pharmaceutical database on one disk. A naval architect could conceivably use his desktop computer to design a supertanker, instead of using a computer-aided-system costing well over $100,000.

With 3M's system, a laser hits a layer of metallic material spread over the surface of the disk. When data are being entered, heat from the laser produces tiny spots with differing magnetic polarity on the disk's surface. To read the data, the laser scans the disk and a lens picks up different light reflections from the various spots. To erase, the laser heats the magnetized spots again, changing them back to their original polarity.

There is no erasable optical disk drive on the market yet—and 3M's disk will be useless without one. Japanese manufacturers Sony, Hitachi, Matsushita, and Sharp have announced prototypes, and others—including IBM and Xerox—have products in the works. So initially 3M's production of a few hundred optical disks a month will be sold to the manufacturers that are developing the drives. The first of these should hit the market next year. Though 3M does not intend to make an optical disk drive of its own, it has been working with several manufacturers—which it won't name—in developing the process.

In time, optical disks will do battle head-on with magnetic disks. But magnetic disks still have a few things going for them. They're faster at recording and finding data, for example, and there's a lot of software around that cannot be used in optical disk systems without alteration.

The new systems, however, will have an impressive cost advantage. Some industry experts believe drives for optical disks capable of storing about 250,000 pages of text should cost around $1,500 at retail in a few years. Today's hard disk magnetic-drive systems cost about the same but can store only about 10,000 pages. Rothchild predicts that the market for erasable optical disks and drives will exceed $11 billion by 1990, a little more than half of the magnetic disk and drive market last year.

● **The erasable optical laser disk, first being produced for use with microcomputers, should become a valuable part of large computer systems requiring the storage of enormous amounts of data that might need to be updated.**

● Introduction

In computer-based information systems, the hardware and software technologies discussed in earlier chapters are applied as tools for the collection, storage, and retrieval of information that is either helpful to management or required for routine business practices. Information that is helpful to management might include sales analyses, while information that is required for normal business practices might include payroll processing or income tax reporting. It is necessary to understand the hardware and software technologies in order to develop an effective management information system.

This chapter focuses on how hardware and software technologies are used in the development of computer-based information systems and explains the various phases involved in designing and implementing such systems. Topics covered include system analysis, design, programming, implementation, and audit and review.

● System Analysis

The first step of **system analysis** is to formulate a statement of overall business objectives—the goals of the system. Identifying these objectives is essential to the identification of information the system will require. The next step is for the analyst to acquire a general understanding of the scope of the analysis.

By viewing the system from the top down, the analyst determines on what level the analysis should be conducted (see Figure 14–1). This level should be agreed upon with management and reviewed in the form of a proposal to conduct a system analysis. The proposal should provide management with the following:

● A clear and concise statement of the problem or reason for the system analysis.
● A statement clearly defining the level of the system analysis and its objectives.
● An identification of the information that must be collected and the potential sources of this information.
● A preliminary schedule for conducting the analysis.

The proposal ensures that management knows what resources will be required during the system analysis. It also helps the system user to make sure the analyst has identified the problems correctly and understands what the analysis should accomplish. Because system analysis is costly and time consuming, the scope of the analysis should be clarified in this way before the analyst continues.

Once the proposal has been accepted, the analysis can proceed. Data relevant to decision makers' information needs is gathered and analyzed. When the analysis is completed, the analyst communicates the findings to management in the **system analysis report.** On the basis of this report, management decides whether or not to continue with the next step in system development—system design.

● FIGURE 14–1
Top-Down View of an Organization's Information System

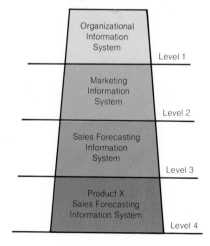

REASONS FOR CONDUCTING SYSTEM ANALYSIS

System analysis is performed for various reasons, which determine its scope or magnitude. An analysis may be required because of a need to solve a problem, as a response to new information requirements, as a method of incorporating new technology into a system, or as a means of making broad system improvements. The gathering and analyzing of data occur at different levels of intensity, depending upon the scope of the analysis. The reasons for conducting system analysis are discussed in the following sections.

Solving a Problem

Sometimes information systems do not function properly and require adjustment. Perhaps a particular manager is not getting a report at the time when it is needed, or an insufficient number of copies of a certain report are being printed, or the information a report provides is incorrect.

In attempting to solve problems like these, the analyst may find that the effort expands into broad system improvements. One problem may lead to another, which may then lead to another, and so forth. Because this snowball effect frequently occurs it is important for the analyst to determine the scope of the system analysis at the outset of the project, as described earlier. Analysts must use discretion and discipline in solving the problem at hand.

Responding to New Requirements

Information systems should be designed to be flexible so changes can be made easily. Unfortunately, it is often difficult to anticipate future information needs; new requirements more often than not cause changes that require a new system analysis. For example, oil companies have experienced a series of changes in government regulations in recent years. Passage of the windfall profits tax followed by the earlier-than-expected deregulation of domestic oil prices created instant headaches for the companies and instant projects for system analysts. Information systems, especially for the accounting departments, had to be updated very rapidly in order to comply with new laws.

There are other areas in which government regulations have affected business information systems. Personnel is one of those areas; regulations governing hiring and firing practices are constantly changing. Another area affected by government regulations is privacy. New laws designed to protect the rights of citizens mandate that more and more information must be kept confidential.

New requirements also originate from nongovernment sources. A company may add a new product line, necessitating a whole new series of reports. A new labor agreement may require additional benefits and deductions or a different way of calculating base pay.

Implementing New Technology

The introduction of new data-processing technology can cause major changes in information systems. Many companies started with punched-card, batch-processing environments. When magnetic tape became available, larger files could be processed and more information could be stored. The introduction of magnetic-disk technology opened up direct-access processing, causing major changes to information systems in the late 1960s. New input devices such as visual display terminals began to replace paper forms and punched cards for data entry.

In banking alone, the introduction of MICR (magnetic-ink character recognition) technology eliminated thousands of bookkeeping jobs because it allowed electronic posting of entries to accounts instead of manual posting. In grocery stores and other retail stores, bar-code readers and optical-character readers are being combined with point-of-sale devices to dramatically change internal accounting and checkout procedures. There are dozens of other ways in which new technology has led to changes in information systems. We could list many other examples, but the important thing to remember is that changes in technology often lead to changes in information systems.

Making Broad System Improvements

There may be times when an organization wants to update its entire information system. An increase in size or sales volume may make such a change necessary. Competition from a rival may provide an incentive to improve efficiency.

One example of a broad system improvement is the introduction and use of online ticketing by major airlines. As soon as the first company converted to this new method, other airlines had to follow suit to remain competitive. The new method forced changes in the airlines' entire accounting and reservations systems.

During the boom years of the 1950s and 1960s numerous companies discovered that their information systems were out of date because of mergers and acquisitions. Many companies found that it was advantageous to update their entire information systems rather than to just keep patching them.

A broad system improvement normally requires an extensive system analysis because it has a very broad scope.

DATA GATHERING

After the proposal to conduct system analysis has been accepted, the analyst sets out to gather data. The type and amount of data gathered depends upon the scope and goal of the system analysis. Data can be supplied by internal and external sources.

Internal Sources

Four common sources of internal information are interviews, system flowcharts, questionnaires, and formal reports. A brief description of each source follows.

INTERVIEWS.   Personal interviews can be a very important source of data. Preliminary interviews provide data about current operations and procedures as well as the users' perception of what the system should do. The analyst must be diplomatic yet probing. Often during an interview the analyst discovers informal information in the form of reports, personal notes, and phone numbers that indicates how the current information system really works. Without interviews, these "extras" might never appear.

SYSTEM FLOWCHARTS.   After gathering the documents that provide the system input, the analyst turns to the system flowchart to identify the processing steps used in the system. Devices and files used in the system, the resulting output, and the departments that use the output are identified. (A more detailed discussion of system flowcharts will appear later in this chapter.)

QUESTIONNAIRES.   Questionnaires are used to collect details about system operations. By keying questions to specific steps in a system flowchart, the analyst can obtain detailed data on the volume of input and output. Information such as the frequency of processing, the time required for various processing steps, and the personnel used can also be identified.

Questionnaires are useful only if they are properly constructed. Further, the analyst must be careful to take note of who filled out a particular questionnaire; a manager might respond differently from an employee. The analyst must also be sure to follow up if a questionnaire is not returned (see Figure 14–2).

FORMAL REPORTS.   Formal reports, the major output of many systems, should be studied carefully by the analyst (see Figure 14–3). The processing steps taken to convert data to information usually become apparent when these reports are examined. The number of copies of each report made and the people who receive them helps to identify the flow of information within an organization. Where and how a report is stored may indicate the degree of sensitivity and the importance of the information it contains. The advent of inexpensive paper copiers makes the task of determining all users of a particular report extremely difficult. The ease with which copies are made can be a disadvantage.

External Sources

Systems analysts should examine external sources of information during the data-gathering stage. Standard external sources are books, periodicals, brochures, and product specifications from manufacturers. Customers and suppliers are sometimes good sources. For example, asking customers what information they would like to see on an invoice might aid in the analysis of an accounts receivable system. Analysts should also attempt to contact other companies that have developed or implemented similar information systems.

DATA ANALYSIS

After data has been collected, it must be organized so that it can be seen in proper perspective. While the focus during data collection is on *what*

Types of
Data Gathering

INTERNAL SOURCES	EXTERNAL SOURCES
Interviews	Books
System flowcharts	Periodicals
Questionnaires	Brochures
Formal reports	Manufacturers' product specifications
	Customers and suppliers

● **FIGURE 14–2**
Sample Questionnaire

TITLE   *Report Analysis—Batch Payroll Report*
NUMBER   *378-Batch-Pay*
PURPOSE   *To determine demand for and timing of Batch Payroll Report*

1. Do you currently receive, or would you like to receive, the Payroll Report?
   ☐Yes   If yes, please answer the remaining questions.
   ☐No   If no, please go to the end of the questionnaire.

2. How often would you like to receive the Payroll Report?
   ☐Weekly   ☐Quarterly   ☐Annually
   ☐Monthly   ☐Semiannually

3. What would you be using the report for?
   ☐Department budgeting of payroll expenses
   ☐General information only
   ☐Other _____

4. How do you rank this report in relation to other reports you receive?
   ☐Above average   ☐Average   ☐Below average

5. Do you require more payroll information than is contained on the report?
   ☐Yes   ☐No
   If yes, please list the additional information you require:

6. Please indicate any other information that would be useful in revising or updating
   the Payroll Report.

   _____

   _____

                              Thank you for your cooperation.

Signed _____ Title _____

Department _____ Date _____

Example of a Formal Report

● COMPUTERS AND INFORMATION PROCESSING

is being done, the focus during data analysis is on *why* certain operations and procedures are being used. The analyst looks for ways to improve these operations.

Information Needs

An analysis should be conducted to determine both management's information needs and the data that will be required to meet those needs. This will have a great impact later when input/output requirements are being determined.

Determining information needs requires that the analyst use a system approach. In a file-processing environment, it is relatively easy to create and manipulate files. But many companies are rapidly moving into database environments. Creating and maintaining an effective data base requires that data items be independent. This means that the data must be analyzed and organized from a corporate-wide perspective. A file can no longer be created for use by a single department; data must be accessible to many other departments as well. The goal is to properly relate each data item to all other data items, ignoring departmental boundaries.

Some techniques used to analyze data and determine information needs are grid charts, system flowcharts, and decision logic tables. While these techniques are some of the most frequently used, there are many others. Analysts should use the tools and techniques that are best suited for analyzing gathered data. In the following paragraphs grid charts, system flowcharts, and decision logic tables are explained.

GRID CHARTS.   The **tabular** or **grid chart** is used to summarize the relationships among the components of a system. Relationships among components such as inputs, outputs, and files are often depicted on grid charts. Figure 14–4 is a grid chart indicating which department used which documents of an order-writing, billing, and inventory-control sys-

● **FIGURE 14–4**
Grid Chart

Document \ Department	Order Writing	Shipping	Billing	Inventory	Marketing	Accounts Receivable
Sales Order	X				X	
Shipping Order	X	X	X	X		
Invoice			X		X	X
Credit Authorization					X	X
Monthly Report					X	X

tem. For example, the billing department uses shipping and invoice documents while accounts receivable uses invoices, credit authorization, and monthly reports.

SYSTEM FLOWCHARTS.   In Chapter 11, program flowcharts were concerned with operations on data. In contrast, **system flowcharts** emphasize the flow of data through the entire data-processing system, without describing details of internal computer operations. A system flowchart represents the interrelationships among various system elements.

The general input/output symbol used in program flowcharting is not specific enough for system flowcharting. A variety of specialized input/output symbols are needed to identify the wide variety of media used in input/output activities. The symbols are miniature outlines of the actual media (see Figure 14–5).

Similarly, specialized process symbols are used instead of the general process symbol ( ) to represent specific processing operations. For example, a trapezoid is used to indicate a manual operation such as key-to-tape data entry (see Figure 14–6).

The difference in emphasis in the two forms of flowcharting is due to the differences in the purposes they serve. A program flowchart aids the programmer by providing details necessary to the coding of the program. In contrast, system flowcharts are designed to represent the general information flow; often one process symbol is used to represent many operations.

Figure 14–7 is a sample system flowchart that shows the updating of an inventory master file. The **online storage** symbol ( ) indicates that

● **FIGURE 14–5**
Specialized Input/Output Symbols for System Flowcharting

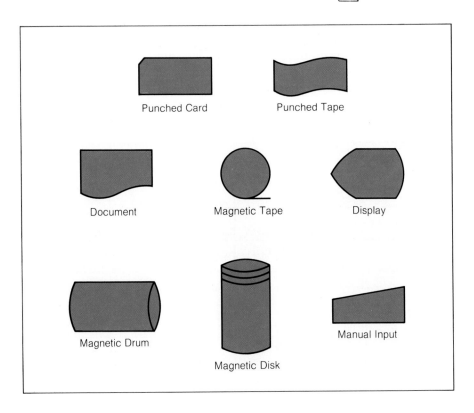

Punched Card   Punched Tape

Document   Magnetic Tape   Display

Magnetic Drum   Manual Input

Magnetic Disk

Merge   Extract   Collate

Auxiliary Operation   Manual Operation   Sort

the file is kept on an online external storage medium such as disk or tape. The file is used to keep track of the raw materials and finished products of the organization. Whether or not this information is current depends on how often the master file is updated. If it is updated as soon as a product is shipped or a raw material supply depleted, then the information it provides is up-to-date. Usually, however, the updating is done on a periodic basis. All changes that occur during a specific time period are batched and then processed together to update the inventory master file. Reports from the shipping, receiving, and production departments are collected. The data from this set of documents are entered into the computer via a CRT. The data entered on the CRT and the inventory master file then serve as input for the updating process.

The flowchart in Figure 14–7 outlines the steps in this process. In addition to updating the inventory master file, the system generates three reports, which give management information about inventory, order shipments, and production. Notice that in the system flowchart one process symbol encompasses the entire updating process. A program flowchart must be created to detail the specific operations to be performed within this process.

DECISION LOGIC TABLES.   A **decision logic table (DLT)** is a tabular representation of the actions to be taken under various sets of conditions. The decision table expresses the logic for arriving at a particular decision under a given set of circumstances. The structure within the table is based on the proposition "if this condition is met, then do this."

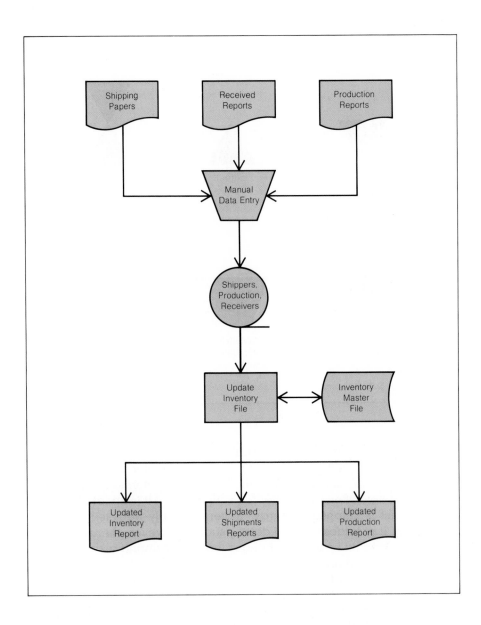

The basic elements of a decision logic table are shown in Figure 14–8. The upper half lists conditions to be met and the lower half shows actions to be taken. That is, the **condition stub** describes the various conditions; the **action stub** describes the possible actions. **Condition entries** are made in the top right section. **Action entries** are made in the bottom right section.

A decision table is not needed when conditions can be communicated and understood easily. However, where multiple conditions exist, a decision table serves as a valuable tool in analyzing the decision logic involved. Figure 14–9 shows a decision table for selecting applicants for an assembly-line job.

The rules for selecting applicants are based on the age, education, and experience of the candidates. The applicants must be at least eigh-

● FIGURE 14-8
Decision Logic Table

HEADING	Rule Numbers							
	1	2	3	4	5	6	7	8
CONDITION STUB	Condition Entries							
ACTION STUB	Action Entries							

teen years old to be considered for the position. They must have at least a high school education or a year's experience to be interviewed for further evaluation. If they meet both requirements, they are hired directly. The Ys in the table mean yes, the Ns mean no, and the Xs indicate what actions are to be taken. The decision table is read as follows:

● Rule 1: If the applicant's age is less than eighteen years, then reject him or her.
● Rule 2: If the applicant is at least eighteen years old but has no high school education and less than one year's experience, then reject him or her.
● Rule 3: If the applicant is at least eighteen years old, has no high school education, but has experience of more than one year, then call him or her for an interview. Once a candidate has been selected for an interview, another decision table may be needed to evaluate the interview.
● Rule 4: If the applicant is at least eighteen years old, has a high school education, but has less than one year's experience, then call him or her for an interview. Again, another decision table might be used to evaluate the interview.

● FIGURE 14-9
Decision Logic Table for Selecting Applicants

SELECTING APPLICANTS		Rules				
		1	2	3	4	5
CONDITIONS	Age < 18 Years?	Y	N	N	N	N
	High School Education?		N	N	Y	Y
	Experience > 1 Year?		N	Y	N	Y
ACTIONS	Reject	X	X			
	Interview			X	X	
	Hire					X

- Rule 5: If the applicant is at least eighteen years old, has a high school education, and has more than one year's experience, then hire him or her.

A more detailed decision logic table is shown in Figure 14–10. The first step in constructing such a table is to determine which conditions must be considered. In this case, the conditions are: (1) Is the customer's credit rating AAA? (2) Is the quantity ordered above or equal to the minimum quantity for a discount? (3) Is there enough stock on hand to fill the order? The conditions are listed in the condition stub section of the decision table.

The next step is to determine what actions can take place. These are: Either (1) bill at a discount price or (2) bill at a regular price; and either (3) ship the total quantity ordered or (4) ship a partial order and back-order the rest. These possibilities go in the action stub section.

Once the conditions and possible courses of action have been identified, the conditions can be related to corresponding action entries to indicate the appropriate decision. Thus, Rule 4 could be interpreted as follows: "If the customer has a credit rating of AAA and the quantity ordered is equal to or above the minimum discount quantity and there is enough stock on hand, then the customer is to be billed at the discount price and the total order is to be shipped."

Decision tables summarize the logic required to make a decision in a form that is easy to understand. They are used to record facts collected during the investigation of the old system and can also be used to summarize aspects of the new system. In the latter case, they guide programmers in writing programs for the new system.

SYSTEM ANALYSIS REPORT

After collecting and analyzing the data, the system analyst must communicate the findings to management. The system analysis report should include the following items:

● FIGURE 14–10
Decision Logic Table for Order Processing

ORDER PROCESSING	Rules							
	1	2	3	4	5	6	7	8
Credit Rating of AAA	Y	Y	Y	Y	N	N	N	N
Quantity Order >= Minimum Discount Quantity	Y	N	N	Y	Y	N	Y	N
Quantity Ordered <= Stock on Hand	N	Y	N	Y	N	Y	Y	N
Bill at Discount Price	X			X				
Bill at Regular Price		X	X		X	X	X	X
Ship Total Quantity Ordered		X		X		X	X	
Ship Partial and Back-Order Remaining Amount	X		X		X			X

- A restatement of the scope and objectives of the system analysis.
- An explanation of the present system, the procedures used, and any problems identified.
- A statement of all constraints on the present system and any assumptions made by the analyst during this phase.
- A preliminary report of alternatives that currently seem feasible.
- An estimate of the resources and capital required to either modify the present system or design a new one. This estimate should include costs of a feasibility study.

The system analyst proceeds to the detailed system design only if management approves this report.

● System Design

If, after reviewing the system analysis report, management decides to continue the project, the system design stage begins. Designing an information system demands a great deal of creativity and planning. It is also very costly and time consuming. In system analysis, the analyst has focused on what the current system does and on what it should be doing according to the requirements discovered in the analysis. In the design phase, the analysis changes focus and concentrates on how a system can be developed to meet information requirements.

Several steps are useful during the design phase of system development:

- Reviewing goals and objectives.
- Developing a system model.
- Evaluating organizational constraints.
- Developing alternative designs.
- Performing feasibility analysis.
- Performing cost/benefit analysis.
- Preparing a system design report and recommendation.

REVIEWING GOALS AND OBJECTIVES

The objectives of the new or revised system were identified during system analysis and stated in the system analysis report. Before the analyst can proceed with system design, these objectives must be reviewed, for any system design offered must conform to them.

In order to maintain a broad approach and flexibility in the system design phase, the analyst may restate users' information requirements to reflect the needs of the majority of users. For example, the finance department may want a report of customers who have been delinquent in payments. Since this department may be only one subsystem in a larger accounts-receivable system, the analyst may restate this requirement more generally. It might more appropriately be stated as follows: (1) maintain an accurate and timely record of the amounts owed by customers, (2) provide control procedures that ensure detection of abnormal accounts and report them on an exception basis, and (3) provide, on a timely basis, information regarding accounts receivable to different levels of management to help achieve overall company goals.

A well-designed system can meet the current goals and objectives of the organization and adapt to changes within the organization. In discussions with managers, the analyst may be able to determine organizational trends that help to pinpoint which subsystems require more flexibility. For instance, if the analyst is developing a system for an electric company, strong consideration should be given to providing flexibility in the reporting subsystem in order to respond to changing regulatory reporting requirements.

DEVELOPING A SYSTEM MODEL

The analyst next attempts to represent symbolically the system's major components to verify understanding of the various components and their interactions. The analyst may use flowcharts to help in the development of a system model or may simply be creative in the use of diagrammatic representations.

In reviewing the model, the analyst refers to system theory to discover any possible omissions of important subsystems. Are the major interactions among subsystems shown? Are the inputs, processes, and outputs appropriately identified? Does the model provide for appropriate feedback to each of the subsystems? Are too many functions included within one subsystem?

Once a satisfactory system model has been developed, the analyst has an appropriate tool for evaluating alternative designs (discussed later in this section). Each alternative can be evaluated on the basis of how well it matches the requirements of the model. Figure 14–11 is an example of a conceptual model of an accounts-receivable system.

● **FIGURE 14–11**
Model of an Accounts-Receivable System

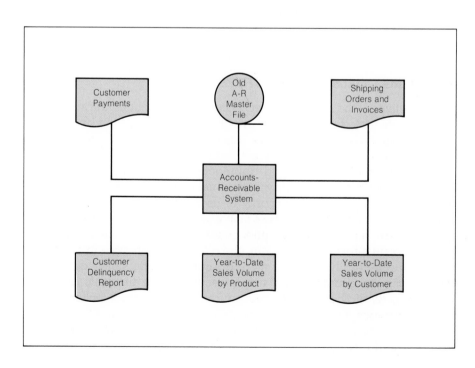

EVALUATING ORGANIZATIONAL CONSTRAINTS

No organization has unlimited resources; most have limitations on financial budgets, personnel, and computer facilities and time constraints for system development. The system analyst must recognize the constraints on system design imposed by this limited availability of resources.

Few organizations request the optimal design for their information requirements. Businesses are profit-seeking organizations. Only in an extremely rare case does an organization request an all-out system development with no cost constraints. (Competition or technological developments, for example, may make such an uncharacteristic decision mandatory.)

The structure of the organization also affects subsequent designs developed by the analyst. A highly centralized management may reject a proposal for distributed processing. Similarly, an organization with geographically dispersed, highly autonomous decision centers may find designs that require routing reports throughout the central office unsatisfactory.

Human factors are also an organizational constraint that must be evaluated during the system design phase. Special consideration must be given to the users of the system. A proposed system design should be **user friendly.** In other words, the system must be designed not only to meet the needs of the user, but also to meet those needs through an easy-to-use, understandable design.

A **menu-driven** system design, for example, guides the user through the computerized system helping him or her attain the needed information. A menu-driven system displays menus (lists of available choices or actions) to the user (see Figure 14–12). With the menu-driven system, the user can be guided through the process of using the system.

Technological advances such as a mouse, touch-sensitive screens, or a voice recognition system may also help make a system design more compatible for its human users. The human factors of system design are extremely important.

Before proceeding with system design, the analyst must be fully aware of the various organizational constraints and critically evaluate their impact on the system design.

DEVELOPING ALTERNATIVE DESIGNS

Systems can be either simple or complex. Simple systems require simple controls to keep processes working properly. Complex systems, on the other hand, require complex controls. A business is a complex system; it requires vast numbers of interactions among its many interrelated subsystems. It naturally follows that information systems developed for business use must be complex, since they model the actual business.

There is more than one way to design a complex information system, and system analysts are generally required to develop more than one design alternative. This requirement is useful because it forces the analyst to be creative. By designing several possible systems, the analyst may discover valuable parts in each that can be integrated into an entirely new system. The alternative systems may also be designed in ascending

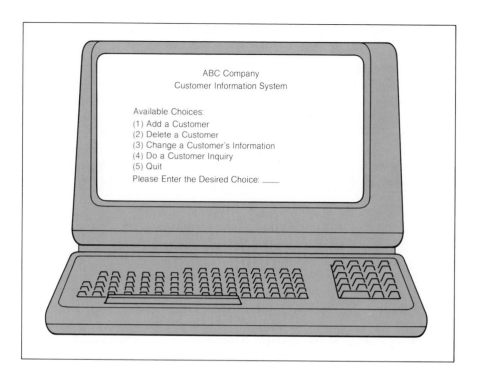

order of complexity and cost; since management often desires alternatives from which to choose, designing alternative systems in this fashion is quite appropriate.

The analyst must work with a number of elements in designing alternative systems. Computerized information systems have many components. Inputs, outputs, hardware, software, files, data bases, clerical procedures, and users interact in hundreds of different ways. Processing requirements may also differ in each alternative. For example, one may require batch processing and sequential organization of files; another may provide random-access processing using direct-access storage and online terminals. The data collection, processing, storage, retrieval, and update procedures vary, depending on the alternative selected.

Each alternative developed by the analyst must be technically feasible. In some instances, analysts try to design at least one noncomputerized alternative. Although this may be difficult, it often reveals unique methods of information processing that the analyst has not considered when developing the computerized systems.

In designing each alternative, the analyst should include tentative input forms, the structures and formats of output reports, the program specifications needed to guide programmers in code preparation, the files or data base required, the clerical procedures to be used, and the process-control measures that should be instituted.

With the increasing use of online systems, the input forms are often input screens. These screens must be designed in as much detail as their hard-copy counterparts. The analyst, in consultation with those who will be inputting the data, must design each screen to maximize efficiency in data input. The screen format must be easy for users to view and understand (see Figure 14–13).

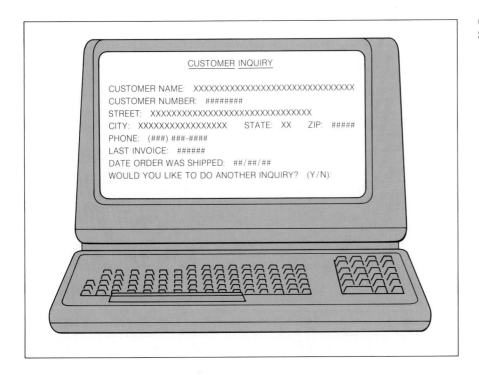

CUSTOMER INQUIRY

CUSTOMER NAME: XXXXXXXXXXXXXXXXXXXXXXXXXXXXXX
CUSTOMER NUMBER: ########
STREET: XXXXXXXXXXXXXXXXXXXXXXXXXXXXXX
CITY: XXXXXXXXXXXXXXXX   STATE: XX   ZIP: #####
PHONE: (###) ###-####
LAST INVOICE: ######
DATE ORDER WAS SHIPPED: ##/##/##
WOULD YOU LIKE TO DO ANOTHER INQUIRY?   (Y/N):

Output reports must be designed so that users can quickly and easily view the information they require. The analyst often prepares mock-up reports that approximate how the actual computer-generated report will look (see Figure 14–14). Most contain sample data. It is easier for users to relate their needs to such sample reports than to discuss them in abstract form with the analyst in an interview. Mock-up reports also allow the analyst to verify once again what is required of the system.

Once the input forms or screens and output reports have been designed, a detailed set of programming specifications for each alternative must be prepared. The analyst must determine what kind of processing is to occur in each of the system designs. The analyst often works in conjunction with the programming staff to determine these requirements and to develop cost estimates for program coding.

File and data-base specification is particularly important. The analyst must be aware of the physical layout of data on a file. The storage media and keys used to access data on the files need to be determined (see Chapter 7 for details on file design). The analyst should also determine the potential size of each file, the number of accesses and updates that may take place during a particular time period, and the length of time for which users may wish to retain each file. Since each of these specifications requires the use of computer facilities, the estimates help the analyst determine the potential cost of each design alternative.

The analyst must carefully examine each clerical procedure required in a particular system alternative. In a sense, the analyst must imagine himself or herself actually performing the steps required. From the receipt of data through the processing steps to the final output, the analyst must determine the most efficient methods for users to perform their required tasks.

● FIGURE 14-14
Output Report Format

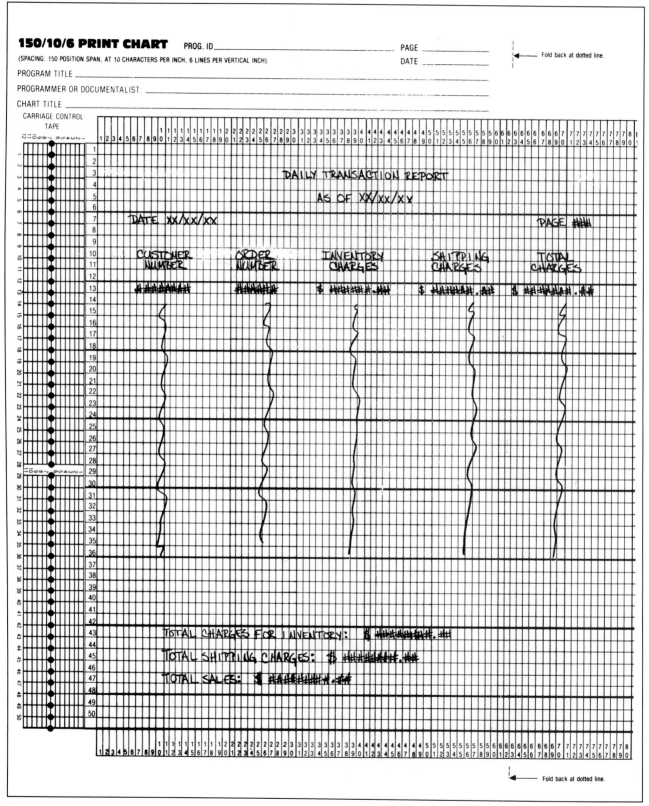

150/10/6 PRINT CHART PROG. ID _____ PAGE _____
(SPACING: 150 POSITION SPAN, AT 10 CHARACTERS PER INCH, 6 LINES PER VERTICAL INCH) DATE _____

◄— Fold back at dotted line.

PROGRAM TITLE _____
PROGRAMMER OR DOCUMENTALIST: _____
CHART TITLE _____

DAILY TRANSACTION REPORT

AS OF XX/XX/XX

DATE XX/XX/XX   PAGE ###

CUSTOMER   ORDER   INVENTORY   SHIPPING   TOTAL
NUMBER   NUMBER   CHARGES   CHARGES   CHARGES

###-###-##   ###-#### $ ###,###.## $ ##,###.## $ ###,###.##

TOTAL CHARGES FOR INVENTORY: $ ###,###,###.##
TOTAL SHIPPING CHARGES: $ ##,###,###.##
TOTAL SALES: $ ###,###,###.##

◄— Fold back at dotted line.

Process-control measures were easier in the days of batch processing. With online systems, however, changes made to files and data bases are instantaneous. If the changes are made on the basis of incorrect data, incorrect values will be stored, accessed, and reported. The analyst must institute controls from initial data capture and entry through processing and storage to final reporting. Methods to restore data bases when errors in data entry occur should be developed. Security procedures should be instituted to prevent unauthorized access to stored data. Since the advent of privacy legislation (discussed in Chapter 17), the development of control procedures has become increasingly important.

PERFORMING FEASIBILITY ANALYSIS

While developing each alternative system, the analyst must keep asking the question, "Is this feasible?" A design may require certain procedures that the organization is not staffed to handle; the design, therefore, must be discarded, or the appropriate staff acquired. The analyst may discover an alternative with great potential for reducing processing costs but may find that the company does not own the hardware required to implement it. The analyst may choose to present this alternative to management rather than disregard it. The analyst must use personal judgment and experience to eliminate unfeasible alternatives.

The users' educational backgrounds and organizational positions must be taken into consideration. The lack of familiarity of some employees with computer-based information systems may prohibit the use of a complex system. Highly educated managers may resist a simple information system because they feel uneasy working with it. Companies in rural locations may be unable to properly staff data-processing departments.

Analysts must also determine whether there are legal constraints that affect the design of the system. For example, several presidents have proposed to Congress that a massive, integrated data base be created containing data about citizens receiving benefits from the government. The objective is to reduce fraud, inefficiency, and multiple payments. It is possible, however, that such a data base might violate privacy laws (see Chapter 17). Although the system is feasible from a technical standpoint, the controls that would have to be incorporated to conform with legal constraints have hindered its development.

When performing a feasibility analysis, time is frequently a limiting factor. A time constraint may appear before system development begins, during the development process, or during implementation. The required completion date may preclude the selection of a complex alternative, necessitate changing the selected design to one less complex, or require that the system be developed in stages different from those suggested by the analyst.

The economic feasibility of a project is paramount. Many systems have fallen by the wayside because of budgetary constraints. The system's economic feasibility is determined by cost/benefit analysis, which is discussed in the next section. In performing this analysis, the analyst must be extremely careful. Costs that at first appear to exceed the budget may in fact give rise to greater benefits. The expression "you have to spend money to make money" is often applicable here. It is up to the analyst to foresee such possibilities.

PERFORMING COST/BENEFIT ANALYSIS

Cost/benefit analysis is a procedure commonly used in business decision making. A firm has limited financial resources. They must be allocated to projects that appear to offer the greatest return on the costs of initial development. In order for cost/benefit analysis to be performed, both costs and benefits must be quantified. Costs are easier to determine than benefits. Some benefits are tangible (or realizable as cash savings). Others are intangible (not necessarily obvious reductions in costs). Naturally, intangible benefits are especially difficult to determine. How does one estimate the benefit from an improved information system that provides better customer service?

An analyst might approach the cost/benefit analysis of an accounts-receivable system in the following fashion. A company is unable to respond to 20 percent of customer orders because of inefficiencies in its current information system. A proposed new system will reduce lost sales by increasing the customer service level so that only 5 percent of orders remain unprocessed. By observing the current sales level and predicting how much sales will increase if the new system is implemented, the analyst can approximate the cash benefits of the alternative.

The costs of an alternative include direct costs like the initial investment required for materials and equipment; setup costs required to create computer files from old manual systems, install data-processing equipment, and hire personnel; and educational costs to educate the users of the new system. Ongoing expenses resulting from employees' salaries, computer operations, insurance, taxes, and rent must also be identified.

It is not always necessary for positive economic benefits to exist for an alternative to be considered feasible. For example, environmental impact statements are required by law from some companies. Design alternatives for a system that must produce these reports need to provide accurate and timely information in spite of the cost/benefit relationship involved. Careful planning, however, will minimize the resources required to develop such a system.

The analyst can also use statistics in determining costs and benefits of large system designs. Sampling and modeling enable the analyst to provide cost/benefit figures not readily apparent from available information. By modeling the complex interactions of accounts-receivable, inventory, and service levels, the analyst may be able to determine how savings in one area affects costs in another. Other techniques, ranging from judgment to common sense to experience, are useful to the analyst attempting to choose the best alternative.

The design alternative that management selects often depends on the results of the cost/benefit analysis. The analyst must ensure that a comprehensive cost/benefit study has been performed on all alternatives.

PREPARING THE DESIGN REPORT

Once the analyst has completed all of the steps described earlier, a report is prepared to communicate findings to management. The **system design report** should explain in general terms how the various designs will satisfy the information requirements determined in the analysis phase.

The report should also review the information requirements uncovered in the system analysis, explain in both flowchart and narrative form the proposed designs, detail the corporate resources required to implement each alternative, and make a recommendation.

Since many organizational personnel may not have participated actively in the analysis stage of system development, the analyst restates information requirements in the design report to tell these decision makers the constraints considered in creating alternative designs. The restatement also shows that the analyst understands what information the new system should provide.

Each of the proposed alternatives should be explained in easy-to-understand narrative form. Technical jargon should be avoided. The purpose of the design report is to communicate; using words unfamiliar to the reader will hinder this communication process. Flowcharts for each alternative should be provided as well.

From the detailed design work performed on each alternative, the analyst should glean the important costs, benefits, and resources required for its implementation. This, more than any other portion of the report, will be analyzed carefully by those empowered to make a design selection. Their decisions will be based on the projected benefits of each design versus the corporate resources required to implement it.

Finally, the analyst should make a design recommendation. Due to familiarity with both the current system and each of the alternative designs, the analyst is in the best position to make a recommendation for implementing a successful alternative design. If the analyst has been thorough in analyzing resource costs and potential benefits, as well as objective in viewing corporate goals, this recommendation is apt to be adopted by management.

After evaluating the system design report, management can do one of three things: (1) approve the recommendation, (2) approve the recommendation with changes (this may include selecting another alternative), or (3) select none of the alternatives. The "do nothing" alternative is always feasible but will not solve any of the problems that led to the system analysis in the first place. If the design of the system is approved, the analyst proceeds with implementation.

● System Programming

PROGRAMMING

A computerized information system depends on computer programs for converting data into information. Programs may be produced in-house or purchased in the form of commercially prepared software packages. If the programs are written in-house, the system analyst should help decide which language must be chosen. To make the system easier to maintain and change, programs should be developed in independent modules (see Chapter 11).

The analyst, in conjunction with the programming department, may wish to evaluate software packages designed to perform tasks similar to those required of the selected design as an alternative to in-house programming. These software evaluations should be made on the basis of system compatibility and adaptability.

TESTING

Before a system becomes operational, it must be tested and debugged. Testing should take place at all levels of operation. Programs are tested by dividing them into logical modules. Each module should be tested to ensure that input is accounted for, files are updated, and reports are correctly printed. Once all program testing is complete, system testing takes place. System testing involves checking all application programs that support the system. All clerical procedures used in data collection, data processing, and data storage and retrieval are included in system testing.

DOCUMENTATION

Creating documentation involves taking an overview of the entire system including subsystems and their functions. Generally documentation falls into one of three classifications: system documentation, program documentation, and procedure documentation. System documentation usually includes system flowcharts, forms and files input to the system's subsystems, and reports and files output from the subsystems. Program documentation includes program flowcharts, explanations of the program's logic patterns, and explanations of the data elements on computer files. Procedure documentation instructs users on how to perform particular functions in each subsystem. These instructions are designed to help users obtain the information they need quickly and easily.

SPECIAL CONSIDERATIONS

In designing solutions to business problems, analysts and programmers must be aware of other considerations besides developing the programs required to help solve a particular problem. Since system analysis and design concentrate on inputs, processing, and outputs, the following issues must be considered: (1) The form of input to the program determines how the program should ask for data. (2) Processing steps should verify the accuracy of data and identify potential errors. (3) The program may be required to produce output that is not in hard-copy form.

Today's computer systems give users a variety of ways to communicate with programs. The programmer must know in advance which input devices will be used to put data into the program. Different input devices require different input considerations. The input devices and forms of data input must be precisely defined before solution design begins, or considerable time may be required to rework programs designed to accept input in an inappropriate format.

Businesses are naturally concerned with the accuracy of data used to provide the information managers use to make decisions. Programmers must do their part to help keep data error free; merely designing a program with logically correct processing statements providing the required output may not be enough. Most programmers are required to include extensive edit checks on the data before storing it in data files. **Edit checks** are processing statements designed to identify potential errors in the input data.

Several broad types of edit checks can be incorporated into the solution design. In some situations combinations of these edit checks are required. The determination of how many and what kinds of edit checks should be performed on input data is usually made by all personnel involved in the solution design. Users, management, system analyst, and programmers should all be involved in ensuring the integrity of input data.

In modern systems, not all data is entered directly into a program by users nor output fed directly to hard-copy reports. Many systems require the use of interdependent programs in which the output from one program is used as input to another. Programmers need to ensure that output from one program is in a form acceptable as input to another.

● System Implementation

In the implementation stage of the system methodology, the analyst is able to see the transformation of ideas, flowcharts, and narratives into actual processes, flows, and information. This transition is not performed easily, however. Personnel must be trained to use the new system procedures, and a conversion must be made from the old system to the new one.

PERSONNEL TRAINING

Two groups of people interface with a system. The first group includes the people who develop, operate, and maintain the system. The second group includes the people who use the information generated by the system to support their decision making. Both groups must be aware of their responsibilities regarding the system's operation and of what they can and cannot expect from it. One of the primary responsibilities of the system analyst is to see that education and training are provided to both groups.

The user group includes general management, staff personnel, line managers, and other operating personnel. It may also include the organization's customers and suppliers. These users must be educated as to what functions they are to perform and what, in turn, the system will do for them.

The personnel who operate the system must be trained to prepare input data, load and unload files on secondary storage devices, handle problems that occur during processing, and so on.

Education and training can be provided in large group seminars or in smaller tutorial sessions. The latter approach, though fairly costly, is more personal and more appropriate for complex tasks. Another approach, used almost universally, is on-the-job training. As the name implies, the employee learns while actually performing the tasks required.

Personnel training and education are expensive, but they are essential to successful system implementation.

CONVERSION

The switch from an old system to a new one is referred to as a conversion. Conversion involves not only changes in the mode of processing data but also changes in equipment and clerical procedures.

Several approaches can be used to accomplish the conversion process. The most important ones are explained below:

- *Parallel conversion.* When **parallel conversion** is used, the new system is operated side by side with the old one for some period of time. An advantage of this approach is that no data is lost if the new system fails. Also, it gives the user an opportunity to compare and reconcile the outputs from both systems. However, this method can be costly.
- *Pilot conversion.* **Pilot conversion** involves converting only a small portion of the organization to the new system. For example, a new system may be implemented on one production line. This approach minimizes the risk to the organization as a whole in case unforeseen problems occur, and enables the organization to identify problems and correct them before implementing the system throughout the organization. A disadvantage of this method is that the total conversion process usually takes a long time.
- *Phased conversion.* With **phased conversion,** the old system is gradually replaced by the new one over a period of time. The difference between this method and pilot conversion is that in phased conversion the new system is segmented and only one segment is implemented at a time. Thus, the organization can adapt to the new system gradually over an extended period while the old system is gradually being phased out. One drawback is that an interface between the new system and the old system must be developed for use during the conversion process.
- *Crash conversion.* **Crash** (or **direct**) **conversion** takes place all at once. This approach can be used to advantage if the old system is not operational or if the new system is completely different in structure and design. Since the old system is discontinued immediately upon implementation of the new one, the organization has nothing to fall back on if problems arise. Because of the high risk involved, this approach requires extreme care in planning and extensive testing of all system components.

○ System Audit and Review

EVALUATING SYSTEM PERFORMANCE

After the conversion process is complete, the analyst must obtain feedback on the system's performance. This can be done by conducting an audit to evaluate the system's performance in terms of the initial objectives established for it. The evaluation should address the following questions:

1. Does the system perform as planned and deliver the anticipated benefits? How do the operating results compare with the initial objectives? If the benefits are below expectation, what can be done to improve the cost/benefit tradeoff?

2. Was the system completed on schedule and with the resources estimated?

3. Is all output from the system used?

4. Have old system procedures been eliminated and new ones implemented?

5. What controls have been established for input, processing, and output of data? Are these controls adequate?

6. Have users been educated about the new system? Is the system accepted by users? Do they have confidence in the reports generated?

7. Is the processing turnaround time satisfactory, or are delays frequent?

All persons involved in developing the system should be aware that a thorough audit will be performed. The anticipated audit acts as a strong incentive; it helps to ensure that a good system is designed and delivered

The Purposes and Steps of System Development Stages

STAGE	PURPOSE	STEPS
Analysis	To formulate overall objectives To determine focus of analysis	Gather data from internal and external sources Analyze data Prepare system analysis report
Design	To determine how a system can meet information requirements	Review goals and objectives Develop system model Evaluate organizational constraints Develop alternative designs Perform feasibility analysis Perform cost/benefit analysis Perform system design report
Programming	To write programs that perform information tasks according to system requirements	Test system programs Document all parts of system
Implementation	To bring the new system into use	Train personnel Switch from old system to new
Audit and review	To obtain feedback on system's performance	Compare actual performance with objectives Direct and correct errors Make changes as necessary

on schedule. As a result of the audit or of user requests, some modification or improvements of the new system may be required.

MAKING MODIFICATIONS AND IMPROVEMENTS

A common belief among system users is that after a system has been installed, nothing more has to be done. On the contrary, all systems must be continually maintained. System maintenance detects and corrects errors, meets new information needs of management, and responds to changes in the environment.

One of the important tasks of the analyst during the system audit is to ensure that all system controls are working correctly. All procedures and programs related to the old system should have been eliminated. Many of the problems that the system analyst deals with during system maintenance and follow-up are problems that were identified during the system audit. A well-planned approach to system maintenance and follow-up is essential to the continued effectiveness of an information system.

RESPONDING TO CHANGE

A well-designed information system is flexible and adaptable. Minor changes should be easily accommodated without large amounts of reprogramming. This is one of the reasons why structured programming was emphasized in Chapter 12; if each program module is independent, a minor change in one module will not snowball into other changes.

No matter how flexible or adaptable a system is, however, major changes become necessary over time. When the system has to be redesigned, the entire system cycle—analysis, design, programming, implementation, and audit and review—must be performed again. Keeping information systems responsive to information needs is a never-ending process.

● Summary Points

● System analysis is conducted for any of four reasons: to solve a problem, to respond to a new requirement, to implement new technology, or to make broad system improvements.

● Problem solving is an attempt to correct or adjust a currently malfunctioning information system. The analyst must balance the desire to solve just the problem at hand with an attempt to get at the most fundamental causes of the problem. The latter could snowball into a major project.

● A new requirement is caused by either internal or external change. A typical example is a new law or a change in government regulations.

● New technology can force system analysis by making formerly infeasible alternatives feasible.

● The most comprehensive system analysis is conducted for a broad system improvement, which can be necessitated by rapid sales or rapid internal growth or by a desire to redesign the present system.

- Data is gathered during system analysis from internal and external sources. Interviews are an excellent way of collecting data and often lead to unexpected discoveries. System flowcharts help the analyst get a better understanding of how the components in a system interrelate. Questionnaires can be helpful, but they are sometimes difficult to design, administer, and interpret. Formal reports tell the analyst much about the present workings of the system.

- An analyst should also collect data from external sources such as customers, suppliers, software vendors, hardware manufacturers, books, and periodicals.

- Data should be analyzed in any manner that helps the analyst understand the system. Grid charts, system flowcharts, and decision logic tables are three of the tools analysts use to accomplish this task.

- The final result of the system analysis stage is the system analysis report, a report to management reviewing the results of the analysis and the feasibility of proceeding with system design and implementation.

- If the system analysis report is approved, the analyst begins the design stage. Goals and objectives of the new or revised system are reviewed. system model is developed and organizational constraints are evaluated.

- Alternative designs should always be generated in the design phase. There is always more than one way to design a system, and management likes to have alternatives from which to select.

- When developing the various alternatives, the analyst must include tentative input forms or screens, output report formats, program specifications, file or data-base designs, clerical procedures, and process-control measures for each alternative.

- Each alternative should undergo a feasibility analysis. This involves looking at constraints such as those imposed by hardware, software, human resources, legal matters, time, and economics.

- A cost/benefit analysis should be conducted to determine which alternative is most viable economically. While tangible costs and benefits are easy to determine, intangible benefits are difficult to quantify.

- The final step in system design is preparing a design report to present to management. This report should explain the various alternatives and the costs, benefits, and resources associated with each. The report includes the analyst's recommendation.

- The next stage of the system methodology is system programming. Programming is one of the most time-consuming parts of the system methodology and begins almost immediately after management has approved a design.

- Testing is performed when each program module is completed. When all program testing is done, system testing commences.

- Documentation is a necessary part of system and program development. System documentation provides an overview of the entire system and its subsystems and includes system flowcharts and narratives describing the input forms and computer files as well as the output reports and computer files.

- During implementation, converting to the new system can be done in several ways. In parallel conversion, the old and the new system operate together for a period of time. In pilot conversion, the new system is first implemented in only a part of the organization to determine its adequacies and inadequacies; the latter are corrected before full-scale implementation. In phased conversion, the old system is gradually replaced with the new system one portion at a time. In crash conversion, the new system is implemented all at once.

● Once a new system is operational, it must be audited to ascertain that the initial objectives of the system are being met and to find any problems occurring in the new system. System maintenance is the continued surveillance of system operations to determine what modifications are needed to meet the changing needs of management and to respond to changes in the environment.

● Review Questions

1. What is the purpose of the proposal to conduct system analysis? How will the definition of the scope of the analysis affect the overall system analysis?

2. Identify and briefly describe the possible reasons for conducting a system analysis.

3. Which four internal sources of data do analysts frequently use? Which one appears to be most effective?

4. Briefly describe what a decision logic table is and how it can be used by a system analyst and a programmer.

5. What type of information should be contained in the system analysis report?

6. How does the focus of system design differ from that of system analysis?

7. Why is it difficult to design a perfect information system?

8. What information should be contained in the system design report? Whom is the report to be presented to, and how should it be presented?

9. What are some of the methods used to train personnel in new system procedures? What groups of individuals must undergo training?

10. Explain why the documentation of both systems and programs is important to the long-term success of a system.

11. List and briefly explain the types of conversion available for a system implementation. Given a situation in which a new computer-based information system is replacing a manual system, which method of conversion might be best?

12. Why is a system audit important? What is the difference between system audit and system maintenance?

GENERAL COMPUTER USE

Marathon Oil Company, a wholly owned subsidiary of U.S. Steel, is a fully integrated oil company; exploration, production, transportation, and marketing of crude oil and natural gas, as well as refining, transporting, and marketing of petroleum products, are its primary activities. The pursuit of these activities has led to the establishment of significant international operations extending to six continents and involving more than 22,000 employees.

Four distinct computer centers are maintained by the Marathon Oil Company. One is the Computing and Information Technology Department at its Exploration and Production Technology Support facility in Littleton, Colorado. The primary function of this department is support of petroleum engineering and geophysical research conducted at the research center. The computer system itself is a dual processor Burroughs B7900 mainframe and the necessary tape and disk drives. Several pieces of on-line equipment directly associated with research activities are also used.

A second computer facility is located at Marathon's international office in London, England. This computer facility consists of one IBM 3081 and a variety of peripherals that support the BRAE project, which is concerned primarily with the construction and operation of large offshore drilling and production platforms.

The remaining two computer facilities are primarily devoted to business-related computing. An IBM 3084 and an IBM 3081 located at Marathon's corporate headquarters in Findlay, Ohio, and an IBM 3081 located in its Houston, Texas, office are connected in a multiprocessor arrangement with a variety of peripheral devices. One processor in Findlay is used mainly for batch processing, whereas the second processor is used for data-base on-line application. The processor located in Houston is used as a test and backup machine.

The Computer Services Organization at Findlay encompasses three functional areas: Systems Development, Technical and Telecommunications Planning, and Computer Division. The applications developed and operated at Marathon range from a simple payroll procedure to computer control of refining operations. It is not unusual to find one project development group updating an existing billing system while another group is formulating a highly sophisticated engineering application. Thousands of programs have been developed to handle user requests. An average of 6,100 jobs (29,000 programs) are processed each day.

SYSTEM DEVELOPMENT

The Systems Development Division of the Computer Services Organization employs approximately 260 analysts and programmers who maintain current systems and develop new systems arising from user requests. Marathon uses PRIDE, a standard methodology for system development marketed by M. Bryce & Associates. In all, seven phases of system analysis and design are outlined in the PRIDE methodology.

Phase I is essentially a feasibility study comprising the following steps:

1. Project Scope. The overall nature of the project is defined; emphasis is placed on what the study intends to accomplish.

2. Information Requirements. Data are collected during extensive interviews with individuals who will interface with the new system and become its primary users.

3. Recommendations and Concepts. A general flowchart of the proposed system is developed; it depicts the flow of key documents through the system. A narrative is included to explain the flow.

4. Economics. The projected costs of developing the proposed system and the annual costs associated with its operation are determined. Savings generated by the system, as well as a payout schedule, are included.

5. Project Plan. A calendar schedule outlining the time required to complete the proposed system is set up.

Several alternatives are usually generated during Phase I. These alternatives are presented to management, which selects the one it considers most feasible. The chosen alternative is then carried forward into Phase II.

During Phase II, all major functions of the system are identified. The total system is divided into logical subsystems. Each subsystem is thoroughly documented through the use of flowcharts. Included in the flowcharts are subsystem identification, the inputs and outputs associated with the subsystem, and the files to be accessed, referenced, or updated by the subsystem. Any output report generated by the subsystem is also formatted at this time. A narrative is included to clarify any points not represented by the flowcharts. The entire package is then presented to management for final approval. Once the design has been approved by management (at the end of Phase II), no other formal presentation of the entire system is made, although the final details of each subsystem are reviewed.

Phase III entails subsystem design and focuses directly on the project plan for each subsystem. Administrative procedures and computer procedures are thoroughly documented in a subsystem design manual. Flowcharts and narratives are again used as documentation tolls. During this phase, it is unusual to discover overlooked outputs, such as control totals, that the system should provide. These changes are incorporated, and the final formats for all output reports are developed.

Phase IV separates the activities of analysts and programmers. The analysts begin work on the administrative procedure design, which is denoted as Phase IV–1. The key activity here is the development of a user's manual. The system design manual generated during Phase II generally becomes the first chapter of this manual; the remaining chapters are devoted to the component subsystems. Necessary input documents are designed and added to each subsystem definition. The previously designed output documents are usually carried forward. The procedures or methods to be used in inputting data are defined.

While the analysts are developing the user's manual, programmers are busy with program design, Phase IV–2. Programmers make extensive use of HIPO techniques during this phase, which eventually leads into Phase V. During Phase V, the actual programs are produced. This phase tends to overlap with Phase VI, during which each program module is tested.

The activities of the analysts and programmers are carefully coordinated so that the user's manual and the programs are completed at approximately the same

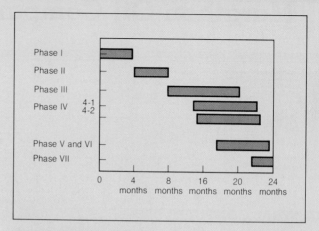

● **FIGURE 14–A**
Medical Claims System Time-Phased Development Chart

time. The entire system is now ready to begin the final phase outlined in the PRIDE methodology—a complete systems test. Phase VII involves extensive volume tests and comprehensive training of the system users.

An example of a system developed internally by this method is the Medical Claims System, designed to speed the processing of medical claims submitted by Marathon employees. Before this system was developed, each claim was processed manually. First, a medical claims processor thoroughly checked the claim's validity. After all the medical bills associated with the claim had been received, the processor filled out a worksheet to complete the claim. The processor was then able to prepare a check for the employee.

The new system greatly simplifies and speeds this processing. Once the entire claim has been collected, it is entered into the system via a CRT. This is the last human interface with the claim; the system handles all subsequent processing, including generation of the check.

The bar chart in Figure 14–A indicates the time involved in each phase of the development of this system. More than 4,600 hours were required for development. This means that if one person were to devote 40 hours a week to this task, more than two years would be required to finish it.

Marathon's Systems Development Division is very active in developing new systems as well as in maintaining systems already in operation. (Despite their continual efforts to satisfy users' demands, a sizable backlog of requests remains.) As users continue to become more comfortable with computer interaction, the demands on this division will undoubtedly grow.

DISCUSSION POINTS

1. The structured approach outlined in PRIDE methodology is effective, but should such a detailed approach be followed in system analysis, design, and implementation?

2. What types of documentation are included in the PRIDE methodology?

15 MANAGEMENT INFORMATION SYSTEMS AND DECISION SUPPORT SYSTEMS

○ ARTICLE
Life Support for Your Computer

Anthony Ramirez

Fortune

Mainframe computers are swaddled in specialized computer rooms where heat, humidity, smoke, dust, and static electricity are eliminated or controlled. Excess heat can lead to microprocessor burnout, smoke and dust to garbled data, and low humidity and static electricity to loss of memory. Personal computers are prey to the same ills, but few would buy $3,000 machines if they had to hermetically seal the family garage as a computer sanctum. Fortunately, PCs don't have to be treated that tenderly. Says Jack Hodgson, an official with the Boston Computer Society, the largest U.S. computer club, a user can't do much to hurt his machine "short of beating it with a stick." Still, elementary caution is due.

Put the computer system away from open windows, heat vents, radiators, and air conditioners. This helps reduce dust, smoke, and other airborne particles as well as control variations in temperature and humidity. A good rule of thumb: if the room is uncomfortable for humans, it will probably also discomfit computers.

Leave the computer on for the entire day, even if it will be used only briefly a few times. Continually heating up and cooling down circuits can widen undetected hairline fractures in chips, leading to the kinds of glitches that disappear at the repair shop but reappear when you're composing the great American novel. Computers are designed to use little electricity, so power bills from all-day operation aren't high. A good reason for keeping a brand-new computer on: most electronic parts, if they are going to fail, will do so within the first ten hours of operation, well within the typical 90 days covered by the warranty. When you leave your computer on, lower the density of the monitor so as not to burn an image onto the screen.

Don't smoke, eat, or drink around the computer system. Smoke is especially insidious because tobacco tar can jam between the disk head, which reads and stores data, thus leading to misreads. Dust has the same vandalistic propensities, so use a dust cover when the equipment isn't on.

To guard against too much electricity, which can burn the system's insides, buy a surge suppressor, which can cost $50 to $100. These devices absorb most power surges that come from utilities or electrical storms. During severe lightning storms, however, surges are so powerful they can bust through telephone lines and electrical cords even when a computer system is turned off.

To guard against brownouts, or power drops, which can wipe out data stored in memory, consider buying a constant power generator, which lifts the power flow to an acceptable level for 15 minutes. Since these devices cost several hundred dollars, however, you might prefer to make copies of all valuable data. Don't hook up the computer to a line shared by another appliance: turning on the Cuisinart creates a mini-brownout. Since magnetism can distort or erase data, don't put telephones, stereo speakers, tape recorders, or other devices with motors or magnets next to the computer.

Place an antistatic mat on the floor to eliminate static electricity, which can cause gaps in the data.

If all fails and the computer system does break down, document precisely what happened. It will help the repairman figure out what went wrong and may reduce the likelihood that the gremlin will return.

● **An individual's investment in a personal computer is comparable, relatively, to the investment a corporation might make in a computer system. The care required by microcomputers is less than that required by mainframes but just as necessary for optimum performance.**

● COMPUTERS AND INFORMATION PROCESSING

○ Introduction

For many years, computers have been used to perform routine and repetitive operations formerly done manually. When functions such as payroll preparation and order writing are computerized, many hours of human labor are saved. Each organization has specific needs that must be met by its computer system. The types of information that can be provided by a system are as diverse as the organization and the information. Since no two organizations are exactly alike, their computer systems are also different. Large hospitals, corporations, universities, or research laboratories usually need mainframe computers to handle their information needs while a microcomputer and peripherals might easily handle the data processing requirements for a small retail store or restaurant. Once the information is processed, it may or may not be helpful to management. This chapter explains how a management information system (MIS) ensures that the information that has been processed is useful to a company by focusing on the information needs of the organization rather than on the hardware needs.

○ Definition of a Management Information System (MIS)

Information is data that has been processed and is useful in decision making. It helps decision makers by increasing knowledge and reducing uncertainty. Modern businesses cannot be run without information; it is the lifeblood of an organization. An information system can supply many types of information. Originally, information systems provided standard reports such as accounting statements, sales summaries, payroll reports, and personnel reports. More recently, information systems have been designed to provide information to support decision making. This application is called a **management information system (MIS).**

In Chapter 1, you learned how data processing takes raw facts called data and organizes them into information. Data processing is concerned with the immediate task of data organization. The emphasis in data processing is on the short-term or daily operations of an organization; it provides detailed kinds of information. An MIS is a formal information network using computers to provide management information for decision making. The emphasis in an MIS is on intermediate and long-range planning; therefore, less detailed and more summarized information is necessary. The goal of an MIS is to get the correct information to the appropriate manager at the right time and in a useful form. This is not always an easy task. See Concept Summary 15–1 for a review of the characteristics of data processing and management information systems.

○ Levels of Management

In order for an MIS to be successful, it is important to determine the kinds of information each manager needs. To do this, one must understand the various levels of management that exist and the kinds of decisions

Data Processing vs. Management Information Systems

CHARACTERISTICS OF DP	CHARACTERISTICS OF MIS
Changes data into information	Provides correct and timely information to appropriate manager
Emphasis on short-term daily operations	Emphasis on intermediate and long-range operations
Provides detailed information	Provides summarized information

that are made at each level. Three levels of management generally exist within an organization, and managers at each of these levels make different types of decisions that require different types of information. Figure 15–1 depicts the three management levels.

TOP-LEVEL MANAGEMENT

Top-level managers are concerned with strategic decision making. Activities at this level are future-oriented and involve a great deal of uncertainty. Examples include establishing goals and determining strategies to achieve the goals. These strategies may involve introducing new product lines, determining new markets, acquiring physical facilities, setting financial policies, generating capital, and so forth.

MIDDLE-LEVEL MANAGEMENT

Middle-level managers are concerned with tactical decision making. The emphasis in middle level is on activities required to implement the strat-

● **FIGURE 15–1**
Levels of Management and the Decisions Made at Each Level

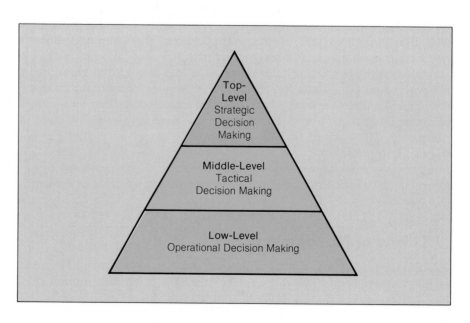

egies determined at the top level; thus, most middle-management decision making is tactical. Activities include planning working capital, scheduling production, formulating budgets, making short-term forecasts, and administering personnel. Much of the decision making at this level pertains to control and short-run planning.

LOWER-LEVEL MANAGEMENT

Members of the lowest level in the management hierarchy (first-line supervisors and foremen) make operating decisions to ensure that specific jobs are done. Activities at this level include maintaining inventory records, preparing sales invoices, determining raw material requirements, shipping orders, and assigning jobs to workers. Most of these operations are structured and the decisions are deterministic—they follow specific rules and patterns established at higher levels of management. The major function of lower-level management is controlling company results— keeping the results in line with plans and taking corrective actions if necessary.

PROBLEMS AND DIFFERENCES

Managers at all levels must be provided with decision-oriented information. The fact that the nature of decisions differs at the three levels creates a major difficulty for those attempting to develop an MIS: the information must be tailored to provide appropriate information to all levels (see Figure 15–2).

Decisions made at the lower level are generally routine and well defined. The needs of first-level supervisors can be met by normal administrative data-processing activities such as preparation of financial statements and routine record keeping. Although this level of decision making is fairly basic, it provides the data-processing foundation for the entire organization. If the information system is faulty at this level, the organization faces an immediate crisis.

Tactical decision making is characterized by an intermediate time horizon, a high use of internal information, and significant dependence on rapid processing and retrieval of data. Many middle-level decisions are badly structured. The major focus of tactical decisions is how to make efficient use of organizational resources.

The main problems in MIS design arise when planners attempt to define and meet information requirements of top-level management. Delineating these information needs clearly is extremely difficult, if not impossible. Most problems are nonrepetitive, have great impact on the organization, and involve a great deal of uncertainty. Most information systems serve the needs of the two lower levels but are not adequately designed to cope with the variety of problems encountered by top management.

Since the information needs at the three levels differ, data has to be structured differently at each level. For routine operating decisions such as payroll preparation and inventory stocking, separate employee and inventory files are adequate. To serve the middle and top levels, the data should be organized to provide inquiry capabilities across functional lines and to handle routine information reports. Concept Summary 15–2 summarizes the differences among the decision-making levels.

○ Types of Reports

Management information systems typically generate several types of reports containing information that may be used in decision making. Reports generated include scheduled listings, exception reports, predictive reports, and demand reports.

● **FIGURE 15–2**
Functional Information Flow
Information at the lowest level contains the most detail. As information flows upward, details are weeded out; only important facts are presented to top management.

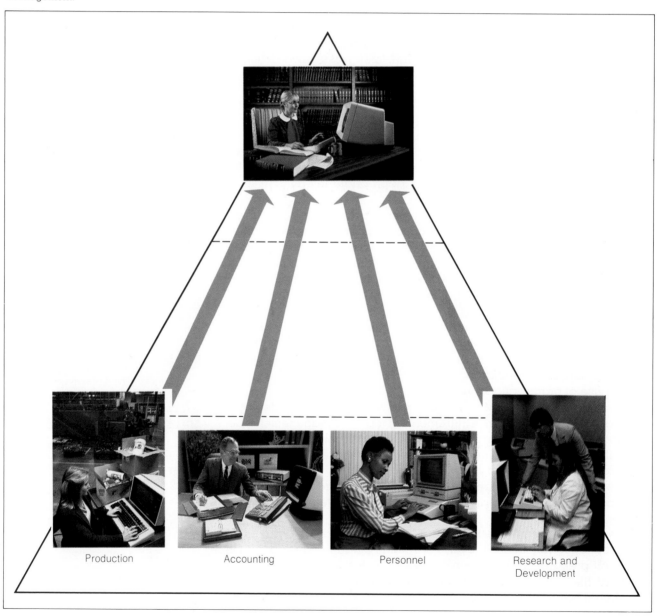

Production   Accounting   Personnel   Research and Development

Differences among Decision-Making Levels

Characteristics	LEVELS OF DECISION MAKING		
	Operational	Tactical	Strategic
Time horizon	Daily	Weekly/monthly	Yearly
Degree of structure	High	Moderate	Low
Use of external information	Low	Moderate	Very high
Use of internal information	Very high	High	Moderate
Degree of judgment	Low	Moderate	Very high
Information online	Very high	High	Moderate
Level of complexity	Low	Moderate	Very high
Information in real time	High	High	High

SCHEDULED LISTINGS

Scheduled listings are produced at regular intervals and provide routine information to a wide variety of users. Since they are designed to provide information to many users, they tend to contain an overabundance of data. Much of the data may not be relevant to a particular user. Such listings constitute most of the output of current computer-based information systems.

EXCEPTION REPORTS

Exception reports are action-oriented management reports. The performance of business systems is monitored, and any deviation from expected results triggers the generation of a report. These reports can also be produced during processing, when items are collected and forwarded to the computer in a group. Exception reports are useful because they ignore all normal events and focus management's attention on abnormal situations that require special handling.

PREDICTIVE REPORTS

Predictive reports are used for planning. Future results are projected on the basis of decision models that can be either simple or highly complex. The usefulness of these reports depends on how well they can predict future events. Management can manipulate the variables included in a model to get responses to "what if" kinds of queries. Predictive reports are especially suited to the tactical and strategic decision making performed in the middle and upper levels of management.

DEMAND REPORTS

As the name implies, demand reports are produced only on request. Since these reports are not required on a continuing basis, they are often requested and displayed on a computer terminal. The MIS must have an extensive and appropriately structured data base to provide responses to unanticipated queries. No single data base can meet all the needs of the user, but a data base in a well-designed MIS should include data that may be needed to respond to possible user queries. Because it requires a sophisticated data base, demand reporting can be expensive, but it permits decision makers to obtain relevant and specific information at the moment it is needed.

○ Management and MIS

Although an MIS can help management make decisions, it cannot guarantee that the decisions will be successful. One problem that frequently arises is determining what information is needed by management. To many, decision making is an individual art. Experience, intuition, and chance affect the decision-making process. These inputs are all but impossible to quantify. In designing a system, the analyst relies on the user to determine information requirements. Frequently lacking precise ideas of what they need, managers request everything the computer can provide. The result is an overload of information. Instead of helping the manager, this information overload creates another problem: how to distinguish what is relevant from what is irrelevant.

After the MIS has been installed, management does not always consider the change beneficial. In some cases, however, the people who must use the system were not involved in the analysis and design; therefore their expectations are unrealistic. Managers frequently expect that decision making will be totally automatic after implementation of an MIS. They fail to recognize that unstructured tasks are difficult to program. Even though routine decisions (such as ordering materials when inventory stock goes below a certain point) can be programmed easily, decisions that depend on more than quantitative data require human evaluation, because the computer system has no intuitive capability.

Other problems may arise. As the computer takes over routine decisions, managers may resist further changes. They may fear that their responsibility for decision making will be reduced or that the computer will make their positions obsolete. They may fail to realize that the availability of good information can enhance their managerial performance.

The success of an MIS depends largely on the attitude and involvement of management. An MIS is most apt to be successful when it is implemented in an organization already operating on a sound basis, rather than in an organization seeking a miracle.

○ Design Methodology

As the pace of technological innovation accelerates, data-processing departments must try to keep current with the changes. Software development is far behind existing technology, because software development is extremely labor-intensive. As a result, data-processing departments today face a productivity problem; they must obtain greater software development for each dollar invested. The basic ways of increasing productivity are: (1) to automate the software development process; (2) to require employees to work harder, or longer, or both; or (3) to change the way things are done. Structured design attempts to achieve greater productivity by focusing on the third method.

TOP-DOWN DESIGN

Top-down design is a structured approach to designing an MIS. The approach attempts to simplify a system by breaking it down into logical functions, or modules. These, in turn, are further divided. The system is first defined in terms of the functions it must perform. Each of these functions is then translated into a module. The correct system design may require several of these modules to perform all the required tasks.

In top-down design, the most general level of organization is the main module; this overall view of the organization is most critical to the success of the system design. Modules at this level contain only broad descriptions of functions in the system. These functions are further broken down into lower-level modules that contain more detail about the specific steps to be performed. Depending on the complexity of the system, several levels of modules may be required, with the lowest-level modules containing the greatest amount of detail.

The modules of the system design are related to each other in a hierarchical manner. These relationships can be depicted graphically in a structure chart. Figure 15–3 shows a portion of such a chart for the application process at a university. Using top-down design, the application process is broken down into its main modules: reviewing the applications, notifying applicants, and considering applicants for financial aid. Each of these functions can be broken down into more specific tasks. For example, the review process consists of checking the application form, obtaining transcripts to verify the grade-point average, obtaining official SAT or ACT scores, and reading the essays submitted by the applicant. These tasks may be broken down even further, if necessary.

DESIGN ALTERNATIVES

The development of an MIS is an integrated approach to organizing a company's activities. The company's MIS must be structured in a way that will allow it to realize the full benefits of integration. When considering alternative organizational structures, the analyst faces virtually unlimited possibilities. This section describes four basic design structures: centralized, hierarchical, distributed, and decentralized. These structures should be viewed as checkpoints along a continuous range of design alternatives rather than as separate, mutually exclusive options. For example, a system design may incorporate characteristics from both the distributed system and the decentralized system.

The **centralized design** is the most traditional approach. It involves the centralization of computer power. A separate electronic data-processing (EDP) department is set up to provide data-processing facilities for the organization. This department's personnel, like other staff personnel, support the operating units of the organization. All program develop-

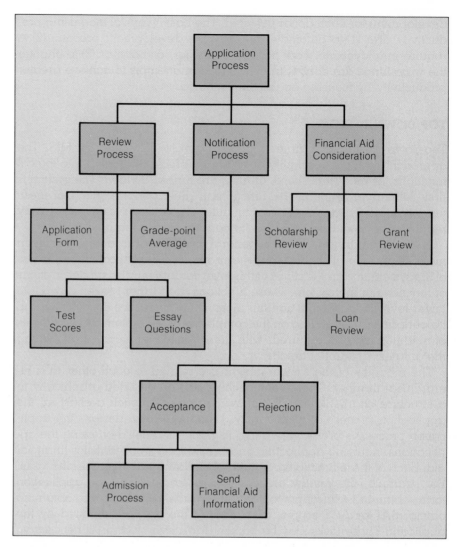

ment, as well as all equipment acquisition, is controlled by the EDP group. Standard regulations and procedures are employed. Distant units use the centralized equipment by a remote access communication network. A common data base exists, permitting authorized users to access information (see Figure 15–4a).

When **hierarchical design** is used, the organization consists of multiple levels with varying degrees of responsibility and decision-making authority. In hierarchical design, each management level is given the computer power necessary to support its task objectives. At the lowest level, limited support is required, because the work is considered technical in nature. Middle-level support is more extensive, because managerial decisions at this level require more complicated analysis (hence, more information processing). Finally, top-level executives require little detailed information since they work with general issues requiring information that can be obtained only with greater processing and storage capabilities. An example of this design approach is shown in Figure 15–4b.

The **distributed design** approach identifies the existence of independent operating units but recognizes the benefits of central coordination and control. The organization is broken into the smallest activity centers requiring computer support. These centers may be based on organiza-

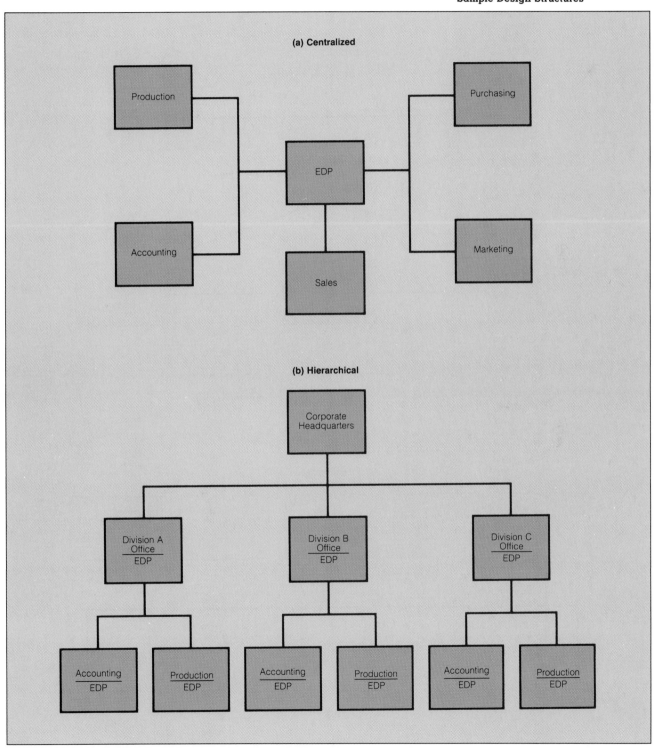

(a) Centralized

Production

Purchasing

EDP

Accounting

Sales

Marketing

(b) Hierarchical

Corporate
Headquarters

Division A
Office
___
EDP

Division B
Office
___
EDP

Division C
Office
___
EDP

Accounting
___
EDP

Production
___
EDP

Accounting
___
EDP

Production
___
EDP

Accounting
___
EDP

Production
___
EDP

tional structure, geographical location, functions, operations, or a combination of these factors. Hardware (and often people) are placed within these activity centers to support their tasks. Total organizationwide control is often evidenced by the existence of standardized classes of hardware,

● **FIGURE 15–4**
Continued

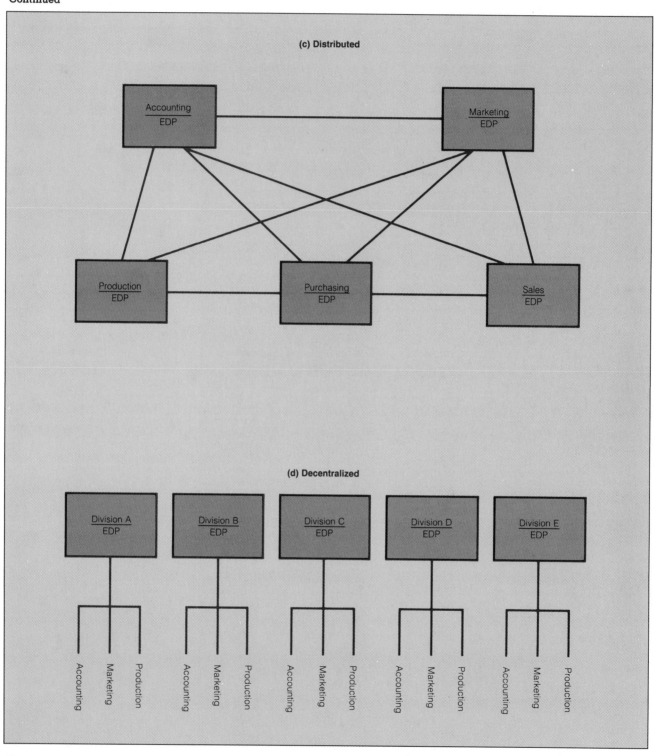

(c) Distributed

(d) Decentralized

common data bases, and coordinated system development. The distributed computer sites may or may not share data elements, workloads, and resources, depending on whether they are in communication with each other. An example of the distributed design approach is given in Figure 15-4c.

In a **decentralized design,** authority and responsibility for computer support are placed in relatively autonomous organizational operating units. These units usually parallel the management decision-making structure. Normally, no central control point exists; the authority for computer operations goes directly to the managers in charge of the operating units. Since there is no central control, each unit is free to acquire hardware, develop software, and make personnel decisions independently. Responsiveness to user needs is normally high because close working relationships are reinforced by the proximity of the system to its users. Communication among units is limited or nonexistent, thereby ruling out the possibility of common or shared applications. This design approach can only be used where an existing organizational structure supports decentralized management. Furthermore, it is not highly compatible with the MIS concept. An example of the decentralized design approach is shown in Figure 15-4d.

○ Decision Support Systems

Closely related to the MIS is the decision support system. Whereas an MIS supplies managers with information to support structured decisions, a **decision support system (DSS)** provides managers with information to support relatively unstructured decisions. For example, an MIS may provide information about sales trends, changes in productivity from one quarter to the next, or fluctuation in inventory levels. Information such as this tells the manager what has already happened. A DSS, on the other hand, may provide financial planning models or optimal production schedules that information managers can use to determine what *might* happen.

Essentially, a DSS and an MIS do the same thing—they process data to get information that is useful to managers. What, then, is the difference between them? Some professionals in the information field believe the difference is that an MIS supports only structured or operational decisions whereas a DSS supports unstructured or strategic decisions. The distinction is based on the type of decision supported. Others believe DSSs are merely subsystems of a larger MIS, capable of processing different types of data as a result of technological advances in hardware and software.

THE PURPOSE AND SCOPE OF A DSS

DSS separates structured (or operational) decision making from unstructured (or strategic) decision making. For example, a purchase order for a certain product may be generated automatically if an inventory stock level falls below a certain amount. Such a structured decision can be handled easily by a computer.

A decision support system, on the other hand, places more emphasis on semistructured or unstructured decisions. While the computer is used as an analytical aid to decision making, the DSS does not attempt to automate the manager's decision making or to impose solutions. For example, an investment manager must make recommendations to a client concerning the client's investments. The manager's decision is based on stock performance and requires a certain amount of judgment. The computer can be used to aid the decision but cannot make the actual recommendation to the client.

The primary use of computer technology within a DSS has been to speed the processing of the large amounts of data needed for the manager to consider the full effects of a possible decision. It also permits managers to consider a greater number of alternatives—alternatives that otherwise might not have been considered due to time constraints. But as previously stated, a DSS, and within it the use of computers, must be a normal and comfortable extension of the manager's overall method of problem solving and decision making.

Advocates of DSS, therefore, claim that its emphasis is toward improving the effectiveness and quality of decision making. The purpose of the DSS is not to replace management information systems but to enhance them. Because advances are being made in applying computer technology to the areas of tactical and strategic decision making, the rewards that can be realized are even greater than those that have occurred in the area of operational decision making. Computer applications in the areas of tactical and strategic decision making are a logical step forward in the application of computer technology to management science and a logical addition to and advancement in the area of management information systems.

A MODEL: THE HEART OF A DSS

As stated in the section on decision-oriented reports, predictive reports use decision models to project future results. Such models are suited to tactical and strategic decision making, which is the focus of a DSS.

A **model** is a mathematical representation of an actual system. The model contains independent variables that influence the value of a dependent variable. Think of the independent variables as the input and the dependent variable as the output.

In the real world, many relationships are based on the effect of an independent variable on a dependent variable. For example, the price of a sofa depends on the costs of the materials needed to make it. Sales of a new brand of toothpaste depend, in part, on the amount of money spent advertising it. The number of microwave ovens sold depends on, or is a function of, the price of the oven. This relationship between price and sales could be represented by the following mathematical model:

Microwave oven sales = f(Price of the oven)

The relationship could be expressed as a mathematical equation. Then a manager could plug different prices into the equation and get some idea of how many microwave ovens would be sold at each price.

The fact that each manager must have a decision model based on his or her perception of the system is what has made the implementation of DSS so difficult. Managerial styles, as well as the environments in which people manage, are unique to each manager. In order for the DSS to be useful, it must be designed to aid a manager in his or her particular decision-making style.

THE FUTURE OF DSS

One of the key factors, if not the key factor, in the acceptance of decision support systems within business is management. How the management of a company views modeling and decision support systems is the critical factor that determines whether or not they are successfully implemented and used. Although decision modeling is used in a large number of firms, if its full potential is to be realized, obstacles such as management resistance, a lack of management sophistication, and interdepartmental communication problems must be overcome.

Many people feel that the acceptance and use of decision modeling and decision support systems in business is being slowed by the resistance of top management, which often has a skeptical attitude toward scientific management techniques and an unwillingness to accept and have confidence in these techniques. In addition, management is also sensitive to a situation in which the promise of what can be done with computers is far different from that which is finally accomplished. Before management will fully accept the use of computers and decision support systems, promises of what can be accomplished must be realistic. Until these promises are realized, management's willingness to accept new decision-making aids will be hindered.

Until now, decision support systems have been discussed in a functional context. Each functional area of an organization may have its own DSS. The current trend, however, is the use of **simultaneous decision support systems,** or **corporate planning models.** The primary goal of simultaneous decision support systems is to combine into one system the various functional areas of an organization that affect the performance and output of other functional areas. The marketing areas of a firm, for instance, must coordinate advertising and sales efforts with production to insure that the demand generated for a product can be met.

Organizations realize that consistent, overall strategic planning is required if the organization is to survive in a dynamic environment. For this reason, firms are attempting to develop simultaneous decision support systems that can coordinate the functional areas of a corporation as well as aid the organization's strategic and tactical planners. Figure 15–5 illustrates a possible structure for a simultaneous decision support system.

The number of organizations using simultaneous decision support systems or corporate planning models is growing. There is little doubt that the future of decision support systems lies in this direction. Advances in the areas of decision model development and applying computer technology to managerial decision making are helping simultaneous decision support systems gain widespread acceptance and use.

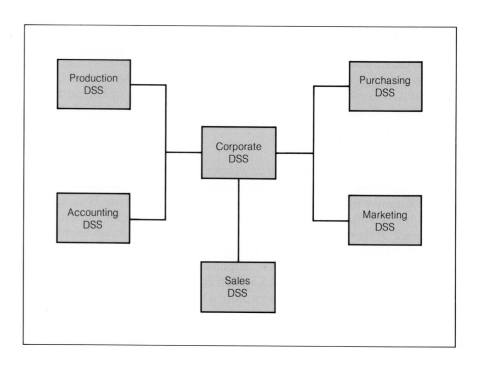

○ Summary Points

● A management information system (MIS) is a formal information network that uses computer capabilities to provide management with the information necessary for decision making. The goal of an MIS is to get the correct information to the appropriate manager at the right time.

● There are three levels of management: top-level management makes strategic and future-oriented decisions, middle-level management makes tactical decisions (implementing the strategies developed by top-level managers), and lower-level management makes the day-to-day decisions that keep the organization operating efficiently.

● Managers at all levels must be provided with decision-oriented information. Since the information needs at the three management levels differ, data has to be structured differently at each level.

● Decision-oriented reporting identifies various types of reports required by management. Scheduled reports are produced at regular intervals and provide routine information. Exception reports are action-oriented and monitor performance—they indicate when a particular operation is not behaving as expected. Predictive reports use models to project possible outcomes of different decisions. Demand reports are usually one-time-only requests that cover unanticipated information needs.

● Structured design is a method of breaking down a problem into logical segments, or modules. Each module performs a logical function. These modules, in turn, may be broken down further. Modules are related to one another in a hierarchical fashion, but each module is independent of the others.

- The ways in which an MIS can be designed within the structure of an organization are virtually unlimited. Common approaches are centralized, hierarchical, distributed, and decentralized structures.
- The centralized approach generally uses a single computer department to provide data processing for the entire organization.
- The hierarchical approach gives each management level the computer power needed to support its task objectives.
- The distributed approach places computer support in key activity centers, and information is shared among the various functions.
- The decentralized approach places authority and responsibility for computer support in relatively autonomous organizational units.
- Decision support systems emphasize effective decision making. Managers in strategic areas are provided with relevant information to help them make decisions. Support is provided for tasks that are not routine or structured. To be most useful, the decision support system should be compatible with the manager's decision-making processes.
- The use of computers within decision support systems has primarily been to help speed the manager's analysis of decision alternatives.
- A decision model acts as the heart of a decision support system. It is a mathematical representation of an actual system. The model should be developed by the manager who will use it so that it represents his or her perception of the actual system.
- The future of DSS may lie in simultaneous decision support systems or corporate planning models, which are decision support systems designed to coordinate decision making within an entire organization.

○ Review Questions

1. Describe the type of information that should be provided by decision-oriented reports. What level(s) of management benefit most from this type of information?

2. What levels of management exist in a typical organization? What are the information requirements at each level? What are some difficulties for the MIS attempting to supply needed information to each level?

3. Briefly explain how tactical decision making differs from strategic decision making, and how operational decision making differs from strategic decision making.

4. Identify the types of reports an MIS generates. Describe the uses of each type of report and show, by examples, where each could be utilized.

5. Contrast the distributed and centralized MIS design alternative. Which of them is likely to be more responsive to user needs?

6. Explain how "garbage in–garbage out" can affect the decision-making process in a negative way.

7. Explain the progression of the details presented in the top-down design approach of designing an MIS.

8. What is a decision support system? How does it differ from an MIS?

9. What is the purpose of a DSS? How should it interact with the manager who is using it?

10. What is a decision model? Is a model an exact replication of an actual system? Why or why not?

EXECUCOM

COMPANY HISTORY

EXECUCOM Systems Corporation, headquartered in Austin, Texas, is the world's leading developer and marketer of business planning and analysis software for corporations, governments, and universities.

Founded in 1974, Execucom pioneered the field of designing financial planning languages for executive and management use. Since the first release of its premiere product, IFPS®, Execucom has been the major supplier of corporate decision support software to Fortune 500 companies. Today, Execucom's products are used at more than 1,500 installations in more than 1,000 leading organizations worldwide and are available in more than 30 operating environments.

Execucom has established many "firsts" in the field of decision support. It was one of the first companies with a nonprocedural language, first with integrated full-scale optimization, and first with a broad base of support for customers, ranging from consulting and education services to sponsorship of international conferences to further the DSS movement.

Throughout its history, Execucom has been recognized internationally both for its products and services. IFPS is the only DSS product to receive the coveted ICP 100 Million Dollar Award and was recently named the first choice of planning languages among corporate information centers. In addition, Execucom has been rated number one in customer service and product support and is the number one choice of university business schools that teach financial modeling.

In February 1986, Execucom was acquired by Travelers/Diebold Technology Company, Inc., a venture of the Travelers Corporation of Hartford, Connecticut, and John Diebold.

The company markets its product through its ten domestic and Canadian sales offices, subsidiaries, dealers, and distributors around the world.

IFPS

IFPS, Execucom's first decision support product, combines all the necessary tools of corporate decision support in one complete system. The product, now in its tenth release, includes a descriptive and nonprocedural modeling language, independent models and data, sophisticated interrogation and analysis, extensive functions and subroutines, complex business consolidations, ad hoc and customized reporting, and a powerful command language for automating applications. IFPS is available in more than thirty operating environments including IBM, DEC, Hewlett Packard, Honeywell, Prime, Burroughs, and UNIVAC.

The Marine Midland Bank of New York uses IFPS to help the bank make long-range plans. The bank relies on IFPS to reduce the guesswork in decision making. One measure of organizational profitability at Marine Midland is called the Contributing Margin Report (CMR). IFPS is used to produce monthly CMRs. The bank began using IFPS with an IBM 4341 in the late 1970s after it decided that the time-sharing system previously in operation was too expensive. IFPS has helped Marine Midland increase the scope of monthly CMRs

while reducing the cost of producing the reports. The system has also increased the speed with which the reports are generated.

Marine Midland Bank is just one example of the successful use of IFPS in the business world. With the growing need for timely decision-making, the company predicts that reliance on Execucom's decision support package by a wide array of companies will also grow.

DISCUSSION POINTS

1. What are some of the features incorporated into the design of IFPS?

2. Describe how the Marine Midland Bank uses IFPS to make long-range plans.

16

THE IMPACT OF COMPUTERS ON PEOPLE AND ORGANIZATIONS

○ ARTICLE
VDT Issues
Demand Sensitivity

Mel Mandell

Computer Decisions

To what extent are all of us who work with crt screens in particular and video display terminals (VDTs) in general at risk? As indicated by the research cited in the cover article by Associate Editor David Roman, the risk of health problems is probably low. However, the emotional tide is high concerning at least one aspect of the perceived threat from high-voltage VDTs: the effects of low-frequency radiation.

For some, the absence of proof that VDTs expose them to harmful radiation only adds to their concern. This supposedly unresolved question is a big part of what makes the VDT health issue such an emotional one for users. Knowing that something is a source of danger gives one a measure of control because one can take protective steps to minimize risks. But to merely suspect that something presents a hazard—a hazard as nebulous as "subtle biochemical effects"—doesn't allow for decisive action. One doesn't know what not to do first.

We know how to cope with and eliminate the VDT-related problems of eyestrain, musculoskeletal symptoms, and stress. The big problem is that most offices were not designed to accommodate VDTs. All the externals in these offices are wrong: lighting, seating, work-surface height, and temperature. Managers intent on souping up productivity impose VDTs on these of-fices, promising or hoping that any discomforts they cause would soon go away.

Some managers, though confined by tight budgets, have found solutions for their stressed employees. One manager who took part in our round-table countered VDT glare by placing an incandescent light at each opera-tor's copy stand. Another manager, acknowledging that a repetitious work pattern is a detriment to both produc-tivity and employee morale, condones frequent breaks for the clericals in his office.

Productivity is a VDT-related issue that causes users to bristle. Managers often expect a much higher rate of productivity from employees almost as soon as the machines are uncrated. Although VDTs and their supporting machinery are capable of great speed, the humans who run them are not, nor is it advisable for them to strive toward automatonlike work habits.

VDTs got off on the wrong foot with users in many organizations due to insensitive management, not because of any proven evil inherent in the technology. VDT users have had good reasons to resent a technology that has caused them stress and dehumanized their contributions to organizational successes. Happily, some managers have developed an ergonomic state of mind—that is, they have "adjusted" their attitudes to reflect humanistic as well as corporate realities. Such thinking is both sensitive and productive.

● **Computers are often seen by managers as miracle cures for productivity problems, and often they are. But they can create problems as well as solving them. Ergonomically sound workplaces and humanistic attitudes on the part of managers serve to maximize the technology's potential.**

● Introduction

Computers, although incapable of conventional thought and feeling, greatly affect our personal lives and the world in which we live. Because of computer technology, the way in which we live has changed drastically in recent history. The computer revolution has had an impact on individuals and organizations alike. While most people agree that computers benefit our society, the computer revolution has had some negative effects on people and organizations.

This chapter discusses the impact the computer has had on both our individual lives and on organizations and their struggle to survive in an ever-changing environment. The behavioral aspects of the impact of computers is discussed, as is the nature of their impact on organizations in business, industry, and government. The chapter also reviews some of the effects the computer has had on the office environment by exploring office automation.

● Behavioral Aspects of Computer Use

COMPUTER ANXIETY

The rapid pace at which computers have been integrated into our society has created a group of people who fear the effects computers have on their lives and society in general. People who have this fear are said to be suffering from **computer anxiety** or **computerphobia.** In many cases these individuals are intimidated by computers. Some people not familiar with computers are afraid that if they make a mistake and press the wrong button, valuable information will be destroyed. Another common fear experienced by many people is the threat of job loss due to computerization. The overwhelming use of jargon associated with computers also leads to computer anxiety. Terms such as bits, bytes, 256K ROM, CPU, disk drives, emulators, and networks can be confusing and intimidating to the computer novice.

Age, too, is a factor that contributes to computerphobia. People who grew up in an environment largely unaffected by computer technology tend to resist using the machines while young people are much quicker to accept the new technology. The fear of the continuing advancement of computers into our lives—a fear of the unfamiliar—is often referred to as *high-tech anxiety*. High-tech anxiety is predominant among older people, who have had limited contact with the computer in general.

Another type of computer anxiety is thought to be gender related. Recent studies involving women in computer fields, however, have shown that women in computer-related jobs perform their duties with the skill and confidence equal to that of males. Genevieve Cerf, an instructor in electrical engineering at Columbia University, feels that women make better programmers than men. Many studies have found that women are more organized, more verbal, and more likely to consider the end user when writing computer programs. Studies by biologists and psychologists suggest that women are better than men at skills that depend on the left hemisphere of the brain—communication and logic skills. Logic skills, in particular, are essential to computer programming.

⬤ Enhancing Productivity

Both the quality and quantity of work can be improved when computers are used to change or simplify a process. Clerical and manufacturing tasks that have been manually performed for centuries change radically in character when computers are used to accomplish them. Computers speed up the chores of preparing letters and reports, keeping track of sales and inventory, and performing dirty and dull assembly processes. They also allow errors to occur in simulations rather than in the actual products. Although corporations once bought computers more for prestige than for convenience, today companies analyze their needs and try to purchase computer equipment that helps them realize their long-term productivity goals.

The Floor of the New York Stock Exchange, where orders are routed, executed in the auction market, and reported via SuperDot 250. SuperDot 250 is the electronic pathway linking member firms all over the United States directly to the trading floor.

Computers are used by the more than 600 editorial staff at the Chicago Tribune to perform a variety of functions.

Rockwell International Graphic Systems Division in Reading, PA, which manufactures newspaper printing presses, monitors factory time and attendance and labor productivity with a Honeywell factory data collection system. Terminals on the factory floor and in managers' offices supply the factory's 1200 employees with timely information on job status, job cost, and payroll.

To automate its domestic distributors, Parlamat, the Italian food-processing firm, turned to HIS Italia for 120 micro-System 6/20 computers. Honeywell and Parlamat developed a network that handles the administrative and accounting needs of its distributors and communicates with Honeywell's DPS 8 large computers at Parlamat headquarters.

One benefit for women who obtain a computer science degree and enter the field is pay. According to a National Science Foundation study, women with computer science degrees earn nearly 100 percent of the salary that men holding a similar position earn. This fact may seem trivial; however, in some occupations women earn as little as 59 cents for every dollar earned by a man in a similar position. The equal pay issue draws much attention and may be one reason why women account for 26 percent of computer professionals.

Still another type of computer anxiety stems from a fear of depersonalization. To many people, the use of a computer for things such as record keeping and billing often leads to a feeling of being treated as a number rather than as a person. This factor of impersonalization has led many people to develop negative attitudes concerning computers.

COMPUTER LITERACY

There is currently no standard definition of **computer literacy.** Most people, however, feel that being comfortable using computers to solve problems of both an academic and a personal nature is important. This implies that students need some knowledge of basic programming techniques and the functions of various hardware components. Computer literacy courses have been designed to teach these subjects.

One goal of high school computer literacy courses is to give students an understanding of how computers work. Students learn to identify the parts of a computer; they also learn to follow the path that electricity takes and see firsthand the practical need for and use of the binary number system. Computer literacy courses also examine the effect of computers on society. Knowing the history of computers, examples of current uses, and projected future trends is important to understanding how computers are changing our lives.

The importance of computer literacy was evidenced by the proposal introduced by the Federal Commission on Excellence in Education in May 1983 to implement new guidelines to stem the "rising tide of mediocrity" in our society. Among these guidelines was a suggestion that all students be required to take a half-year of computer science in high school. Despite all the controversial opinions generated by the report, that particular suggestion was questioned by very few people. Why? The most likely answer is that parents and other adults realize there is no way to stop the growing use of computers. Schools cannot be allowed the option of ignoring computers, because these machines alter jobs, entertainment, and home life so radically. It is becoming evident that people who learn about computers are advancing in their jobs, while people who avoid the use of computers may be forfeiting promotions and even job security. Although computer literacy is vital in the education of younger generations, members of the adult work force should also take steps to gain computer literacy.

JOB DISPLACEMENT AND RETRAINING

Ever since the Industrial Revolution, automation has been a source of concern to people. Technology has automated processes leading to greater efficiency and lower costs but it has also eliminated many jobs. The growing use of computers has led to the growing fear of unemployment and depersonalization. Whether or not this fear is justified is yet to be seen. Evidence of the past three decades does not indicate that increased automation leads to increased unemployment. To be sure, workers have been displaced; but each new technology has created new employment opportunities that more than compensate for the jobs eliminated. For example, the invention of the automatic weaving machine eliminated many jobs in the garment industry; but this effect was offset by the creation of a whole new industry involved in the manufacture and marketing of the new equipment.

Several studies have been conducted to determine the effects of computer automation on jobs. While the results have not been conclusive, in general they indicate that a certain amount of job displacement can be expected because the computers take over many routine clerical jobs. The extent to which such displacement occurs depends on several factors, including the following:

● The goals that are sought from the use of the computer. Is the objective to be able to handle an increasing workload with the same personnel, or is it to reduce costs by eliminating jobs?

● The growth rate of the organization. If the organization is expanding, it can more easily absorb workers whose jobs are being eliminated since many new jobs are created to cope with the increasing business.

● The planning that has gone into the acquisition and use of the computer. With careful preparation, an organization can anticipate the personnel changes a computer system will bring about and make plans either to reassign the affected people or to help them to find new jobs with other organizations. First-time use of a computer-based system will definitely create new jobs in the areas of computer operations, data entry, programming, and system analysis and design. Usually, however, the skills and education required for these jobs differ from those required for the eliminated jobs. Displaced employees can be trained, however, to handle jobs such as operating computer equipment and keying in data. Employees can also be sent to schools for more formal training.

The current task of retraining displaced and unemployed workers has been assumed by groups such as businesses (which provide internal retraining), colleges, vocational schools, private training centers, and the federal government (through aid to states). Some of the more popular programs for retraining include robotics maintenance, computer programming, numerical control machinery programming and operation, word processing, computer maintenance, and electronics (see Figure 16-1).

CHANGES IN THE WORKPLACE

Computers have made changes in the workplace common. Farmers, secretaries, and business managers alike have experienced the effects computers can have on their jobs. The office is one area that offers great potential for automation. Office automation is discussed in the following

● **FIGURE 16–1**
Retraining can help workers whose
jobs are eliminated by the introduction
of computers into the workplace.

section, while the impact the computer has had on workers and workstations will be discussed here.

Worker interaction with computers has led to new concerns. Perhaps the concerns that have received the most publicity have been those regarding worker health. The biggest complaint of office workers in automated offices is that of eyestrain, followed closely by complaints of backstrain. The issue of whether the small amount of radiation given off by the CRT screen is hazardous has not been resolved satisfactorily. It is recognized, though, that with prolonged contact CRTs cause eyestrain, loss of visual acuity, changes in color perception, back and neck pain, stomachaches, and nausea.

To help alleviate some of the health concerns associated with the automated workplace, a new science has emerged. **Ergonomics,** the method of researching and designing computer hardware and software to enhance employee productivity and comfort, promises a better, more productive workplace. Major areas of research include the different elements of the workstation and software.

To reduce such physical problems as eyestrain and backstrain, it is recommended that the time spent at a CRT be reduced to a maximum of two hours per day of continuous screen work, that periodic rest breaks be granted, and that pregnant women be permitted to transfer to a different working environment upon request. Recommendations have also been made regarding the design of the CRT and of the keyboard. Suggestions have been made regarding their slope, layout, adjustability, and use of numeric keypads and function keys (see Figure 16–2).

Other problems with the workstation include poor lighting and noise generated by printers. Sound-dampening covers and internal sound dampening are recommended but still do not reduce the noise sufficiently. The best solution to date is to put the printers in a separate room or at least away from the workers' area. Along with these suggestions,

recommendations have been made regarding the tables and chairs used for data-processing work.

The application of ergonomics to workstations has resulted in a 10 to 15 percent improvement in performance in some offices (see Figure 16–3).

● Office Automation

As computer technology enters the workplace, the office environment is experiencing changes. Businesses are realizing that automating office

● FIGURE 16–3
An ergonomically designed workstation can help improve worker health and productivity.

procedures is efficient, cost effective, and, in fact, necessary to deal with the exploding information revolution. **Office automation,** the generalized and comprehensive term applied to this transition, refers to all processes that integrate computer and communication technology with the traditional manual processes. Virtually every office function—typing, filing, and communications—can be automated.

This section will discuss the characteristics of the elements that comprise office automation: word processing, communications, and local area networks.

WORD PROCESSING

Word processing is often considered the first building block in automating the workplace. It is the most widely adopted office automation technology; an estimated 75 percent of U.S. companies employ some type of word processing. Word processing, the manipulation of written text to achieve a desired output, bypasses the difficulties and shortcomings associated with traditional writing and typing. Word processors offer many functions to increase efficiency in the text-manipulation process. You may recall from Chapter 13 that standard features include automatic centering, pagination (page numbering), alphabetizing, justification of type, and reformatting of paragraphs; word processors also usually have features enabling them to boldface, search and find, and move blocks of text.

Special function keys and codes are used to format the document being typed. The user may create, edit, rearrange, insert, and delete material— all electronically—until the text is exactly as desired. Then the text can be printed as well as stored on tape or disk for later use. Each copy of the text printed is an original; thus the output of a word-processing system is of a consistently high quality.

Word processing can be used for a variety of tasks. Some popular uses include editing lengthy documents (this eliminates the need to have a document completely retyped every time it is edited), producing original form letters, and completing lengthy forms where tab stops can be automatically generated to increase the typist's speed. Some other functions that can be performed on many word-processing systems are merging data with text, processing files, performing mathematical functions, generating the output of photocomposition devices, facilitating electronic filing, and distributing text after it has been created, which allows documents prepared in one location to be printed in others.

A typical word-processing system consists of a keyboard for data input, a CRT or LED display screen for viewing text material, a secondary storage unit (disk or tape), and a printer for generating output (see Figure 16–4). Word processing is available in a variety of configurations, including electronic typewriters, dedicated word processors, dedicated data processors, and small business computers.

The major advantages of word processing over traditional text preparation are increased productivity and reduction in preparation time. Word processing, like data processing, relieves workers of time-consuming and routine tasks, thereby increasing standards of productivity and quality. It is estimated that a secretary's productivity can be increased

25 to 200 percent using word processing. Because a document does not have to be retyped every time a change is made, the preparation time is reduced dramatically.

One disadvantage of word processing is the increase in the number of times a document is revised. Because it is so easy to change a document, personnel make changes more often than when documents are prepared manually. To a point this can be useful; however, there is a limit to the number of time a revision improves a document. Another disadvantage in the past has been the cost of purchasing and implementing a word-processing system. Decreasing equipment costs, however, are making word processing more affordable for companies of all sizes.

Only a fraction of computer capabilities were applied to current word-processing techniques in the past. Currently, many systems offer such features as spelling checkers that handle personal names, built-in dictionaries of definitions to provide the user with the meaning of an unfamiliar word, and thesauruses that provide the user with alternative words to be used. Word processors may eventually automatically and correctly hyphenate words (they only guess now) and check for correctness of standardized abbreviations, commas around dates, and written-out numbers compared to numerals. In case the user's grammar is not up to par, some word processors may check and correct grammar and try to anticipate the next character to be typed. The user will be able to override the computer in case it does not select the correct character; however, this feature could save the user a considerable amount of time when lengthy words or phrases are duplicated throughout a document.

Color word processing should be available in the future. With this feature, each revision could be shown in a different color so that a distinction could be made as to the most recent revision. Also, different levels of management could have color codes so that informed decisions could be made as to what should be changed and what should not. Word processors have become much more portable; they are used on airplanes and in cars. A few offer voice-input capabilities, eliminating the initial typing requirement. Word processing is in its infancy, with many future capabilities not even thought of yet.

COMMUNICATIONS

An important benefit of office automation is the communication capabilities it makes possible. Such capabilities allow the electronic exchange of information between employees. Communications may be accomplished through forms such as electronic mail, teleconferencing, and telecomputing.

Electronic Mail

Electronic mail is the transmission of messages at high speeds over telecommunication facilities (see Figure 16–5). It is used primarily for internal, routine communications; however, with the development of new technology, it is beginning to replace the traditional postal service. The concept behind these computer-based mail systems involves the storage of messages in a special area until the recipient can access them. People using electronic systems can be in remote locations. Receivers are notified of waiting mail when they log on to their computer. They can then

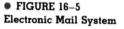
● **FIGURE 16–5**
Electronic Mail System

view the incoming mail items on a CRT screen or can have the items printed on their terminal. The mail can be revised, incorporated into other documents, passed along to new recipients, or filed like any other document in the system. Some electronic mail systems allow the sender to cancel the message if it has not yet been read by the recipient. The sender may also check to see if the messages he or she has sent have been read yet by the recipient by including a "receipt required" message with the document. Some systems also provide a delayed sending option, allowing the sender to create a message and have it sent at a set time in the future.

There are two basic forms of electronic mail: teletypewriter systems and facsimile systems. **Teletypewriter systems** transmit messages as strings of characters. **Facsimile systems,** sometimes called **telecopier systems,** produce a picture of a page by scanning it, as a television camera scans a scene or a copier scans a printed page. The image is then transmitted to a receiver, where it is printed.

Another type of electronic message system on which much work is currently being done is the **voice message system (VMS),** or **voice mail.** In VMS, the sender presses a special "message" key on the telephone, dials the receiver's number, and speaks the message. The spoken message is converted by the VMS into digital form and stored in the computer's memory. A button lights on the receiver's phone. When the user presses the "listen" key, the message is reconverted into voice form. Unlike standard answering machines, with VMS recipients can fast-scan the messages. Voice mail also allows for longer messages than answering machines.

Teleconferencing

In an effort to reduce travel time and expenses associated with out-of-town travel, businesses are turning to teleconferencing. **Teleconferencing,** permitting two or more locations to communicate via electronic and image-producing facilities, offers businesses a viable alternative to long-distance, face-to-face communications.

Five forms of teleconferencing exist. The most basic form of conducting electronic meetings, **audio conferencing,** is simply a conference call linking three or more people. Ideal for impromptu conversations, audio conferencing requires no major equipment investments but is limited to voice only.

The next level, **augmented audio conferencing,** combines graphics with audio conferencing. In this situation, visual information accompanies the conversation in the form of facsimile, electronic blackboards or freeze-frame slide shows. Augmented audio conferencing is frequently used for technical discussions that require supplemental graphics to explain concepts.

Computer conferencing is well suited for ongoing meetings among a number of people. Information is exchanged at the participants' convenience using computer terminals; participants need not attend at the same time. New material can be added or previously submitted ideas can be critiqued. This differs from electronic mail in that discrete messages are not transmitted; instead comments are input in reference to specific issues. Computer conferencing has been found to reduce decision-making time considerably.

Video seminars represent the next level of sophistication. They employ one-way, full-motion video with two-way audio. The most common application of video seminars is for formal presentations that involve a question-and-answer session such as a press conference. Individuals from the audience communicate with the presentation headquarters via a separate two-way phone link. The entire audience can hear the question and view the official response. Special facilities with television equipment are needed for this type of conferencing.

Finally, there is **videoconferencing**—the technology currently receiving the most attention. Videoconferencing, employing a two-way, full-motion video plus a two-way audio system, provides the most effective simulation of face-to-face communication (see Figure 16–6). It is the only form that meets the need for full interaction; the participants are able to see and hear each other's responses. Videoconferencing is best suited for planning groups, project teams, and other groups that want a full sense of participation. It is not suitable for all situations, however. It does not seem to be effective when a participant is trying to persuade an audience or to sell something.

The cost effectiveness of videoconferences depends upon the geographic dispersion of the company, the number of intracompany meetings, and the management structure of the company. If the company does not have major offices throughout the country, videoconferencing may not be cost effective. Also, because different types of videoconferencing equipment are not compatible, it can only be used for conferences within the company, not with other companies.

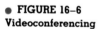
● **FIGURE 16–6**
Videoconferencing

Telecomputing

Companies as well as individuals may subscribe to online information services—services that offer access to one or more data bases. This is often referred to as **telecomputing.** By accessing the online data bases, workers receive additional information and save considerable research time. There are many information services available that provide information on a wide variety of topics. Three of the more popular services are The Source, CompuServe, and Dow Jones News/Retrieval. Some of the services offered include: news stories; potentially news-making events; up-to-the-minute stock, bond, and commodity information; sports information; information on alcohol problems; and law libraries (see Figures 16–7 and 16–8).

Usually, a membership fee is assessed from the user, and a password and account number are issued. The online service then usually charges the user for service time or connect time. Depending upon the network accessed and the time of day, service time costs $5 to $25 per hour. The only equipment needed is a computer, a modem, and a communications software package to instruct the user's computer how to talk to the computer at the other end. For such a small expense, employees can receive up-to-the-minute information with a minimal amount of effort and time.

● Computers in Business and Industry

As computers have entered American society, nowhere have they had more impact than in business and industry. Part of this is due to the fact that using computers speeds operations, reduces mistakes in calcula-

● **FIGURE 16–7**
CompuServe offers users access to a number of online data bases.

CONCEPT SUMMARY 16–1

Forms of Electronic Communication

FORM	CHARACTERISTIC
Electronic mail	Used primarily for internal communication
Teleconferencing	Used to reduce travel time and expenses
Telecomputing	Offers computer access to online data bases

tions, and gives companies efficient, cost-effective analyses that would be nearly impossible with manual operations. Another major reason for the great impact of computers is the domino effect. If Business A speeds up its operations through the use of computers, then Business B must also computerize to compete. The same applies to the use of automation in industry. Once one factory incorporates automation, it sets a standard to be imitated and repeated.

These factors have caused a phenomenal increase in the number and types of computer applications in business and industry. Some experts even claim that these computer applications are helping to trigger a new type of industrial revolution.

COMPUTERS IN BUSINESS

Because businesses are so varied in purpose and structure, it is nearly impossible to examine all business uses of computers. However, it is possible to look at how computers are used in many businesses. Businesses have special uses of computers. For example, a retail store might be interested in computerizing inventory, whereas a stock brokerage would be more interested in computerizing its customer files. In general, though, there are three areas in which computers are used in most businesses: (1) accounting and finance, (2) management, and (3) marketing and sales.

Accounting and Finance

In the past, financial transactions were tediously calculated, either by hand or by calculator, and recorded using pencil and paper. This method has rapidly become obsolete as computers have moved into virtually every area of accounting and finance. To illustrate this point, let us examine how computers are being used in the areas of general accounting, financial analysis, and information management.

General accounting software is a very popular type of business software. In fact, it was the first business software to be offered for personal computers. Some of the most common uses of general accounting software are for preparing checks, reports, and forms. Forms, because of their repetitive nature, are well suited to computer processing. General accounting packages that produce reports keep users informed of everything from inventory on hand to monthly credit account balances. Checks are a frequent form of output from general accounting software.

Today, the most common use of the computer in financial analysis is the electronic spreadsheet. Spreadsheets are used to design budgets, record sales, produce profit-and-loss statements, and aid in financial analysis. Refer to Chapter 13 for more information regarding spreadsheets.

Data management software for business computers gives them the capability of an electronic filing system. Data entered into selected categories can be retrieved by specifying, for example, files on employees receiving a certain salary or employees hired on a certain date. Systems like these make file retrieval faster and more flexible and decrease the amount of storage space required.

Data management software packages designed for microcomputers enable a manager's appointments to be recorded and recalled as necessary. Some systems in this category also maintain expense account records. Chapter 13 also contains a discussion on data management software for large computer systems.

Management

Communication is an important part of business management, and computer graphics are becoming an essential part of business communication. In the average business, computers are used to produce graphs that keep management informed and up-to-date on company statistics, sale records, and the like.

It is well known in business that executives make 80 percent of their decisions based on 20 percent of the data—that 20 percent representing the core data necessary to run their businesses. Finding that data can be difficult for managers if they are presented with pages upon pages of data. Graphically displayed data makes the task much easier. It is widely agreed that such displays can help managers to make better decisions. Also, comparisons, relationships and trends, and essential points can be clarified more easily with graphics (see Figure 16–9). Finally, computer graphics are the most cost-effective means of presenting the manager with that 20 percent of core data.

Marketing and Sales

Businesses use computers in a variety of ways to facilitate sales, record sales, update inventories after sales, and make projections based on expected sales (see Figure 16–10). In addition to these standard functions, some computers are also being used in customer contact.

The Helena Rubenstein cosmetic firm was instrumental in the movement of computers onto the sales floor. The cosmetic computer assisted customers in their decisions about perfumes, makeup, and colorings. The firm's effort was very successful and inspired similar applications by other companies.

COMPUTERS IN INDUSTRY

The financial and bookkeeping uses of computers apply to both business and industry. However, industry also uses computers in designing and manufacturing products. In this chapter, we will discuss four of those ways: (1) with the use of CAD/CAM, (2) with the use of CIM, (3) with the use or nondestructive testing, and (4) with the use of robotics.

CAD/CAM

One of the fastest growing areas of computer use in industry is **computer-aided design (CAD).** CAD allows the engineer to design, draft, and

● **FIGURE 16–9**
Graphically displayed data helps make decision making easier for managers.

● **FIGURE 16–10**
Salespeople use computers to keep track of sales data.

analyze a prospective product using computer graphics on a video terminal (see Figure 16–11). The designer, working with full-color graphics, can easily make changes, so he or she can test many versions of a product before the first prototype is ever built. CAD can also analyze designs for poor tolerance between parts and for stress points. This can save companies a great deal of money by eliminating defective designs before the money is spent to build a product.

Computer-aided design is often coupled with **computer-aided manufacturing (CAM).** The combination is referred to as **CAD/CAM.** Using CAD/CAM, the engineer can analyze not only the product but also the manufacturing process.

Once the rough design of the product has been entered into the computer, the engineer can have the computer simulate any manufacturing step (see Figure 16–12). For example, if the product must be drilled, the engineer can create a computerized drill that can be guided, either by the engineer or the computer, to simulate the drilling process. This simulation can be very helpful in two ways. First, it indicates any major problems that may be encountered on the assembly line—before it is even set up. Second, the computer will record exactly how the tool moved and will store that information on magnetic tape. If that factory uses robotics and **numerically controlled machinery,** those tapes can be used

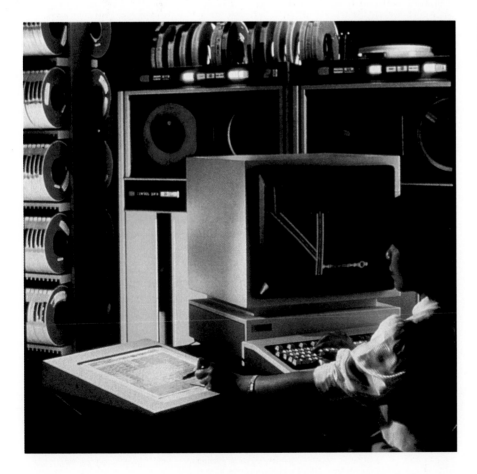

● **FIGURE 16–11**
Computer-aided design is used by engineers to design products.

● **FIGURE 16–12**
Computer-aided manufacturing is often
coupled with computer-aided design in
the manufacturing process.

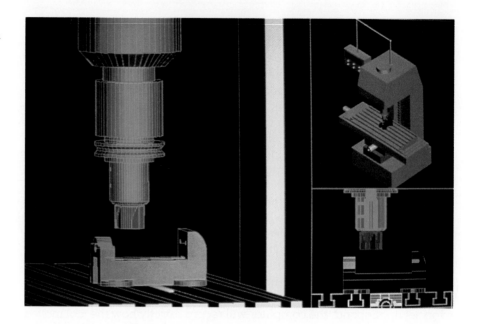

to drive the actual machines in manufacturing the product. In this way,
CAD/CAM can take the engineer from idea to final product.

Computer Integrated Manufacturing (CIM)

For even greater savings and more efficient operation, manufacturers
can tie CAD and CAM processes together with **computer-integrated
manufacturing (CIM).** CIM is an attempt to link various departments of
a company into a central data base. The CIM data base can help management run a more coordinated, efficient operation. The ideal CIM
system would control the design and manufacture of a company's products without disruption. From raw materials to finished product, the operation would run smoothly. The CIM system would control scheduling
and monitoring of operations.

In the United States no fully functional plants combine CAD/CAM and
CIM. Some operations do employ the CIM concept in certain areas, though.
Boeing, General Motors, and General Electric are experimenting with
CIM. Boeing has saved $2.8 million annually by using CIM to link certain
design and manufacturing operations.

To be successful, CIM requires a long-term commitment from management. General Electric found that CIM was most successful when
implemented in a step-by-step plan. As the uses of CAD and CAM increase, CIM will become more common, too.

Nondestructive Testing (NDT)

Quality control has long been a problem for industry. Finding flaws or
weaknesses in products is an important aspect of the successful operation
of a company and is necessary for long-term growth. Until recently, most
companies had to be content spotting flaws with a visual inspection or

a physical stress test of their products. A visual inspection is effective only if the flaw is easily seen, and a stress test often destroys the object being tested.

Some manufacturers are relying on a new technology to test new and old products for flaws created during manufacturing or for weaknesses caused by wear and deterioration. The technology is called **nondestructive testing (NDT).** This process combines X rays, high-frequency sound waves, or laser beams with powerful microcomputers to inspect the interior of a product. Use of NDT locates the likely trouble while leaving the product intact. The process can detect the difference between dangerous flaws and harmless nicks.

Nondestructive testing is used to examine the interior of aircraft engines and to check welds in gas pipelines. Airplane mechanics may soon rely on NDT for early detection of metal deterioration. The growth in NDT is based on the increasing use of machines designed to operate near the limits of physical tolerance. Flaws that are not identified early could cause a disaster. Another reason for the growth of NDT is the increasing use of new, unpredictable materials. New construction materials may contain hard-to-discern flaws that could mean failure for a manufacturer.

Powerful new data-processing capabilities have made it possible for workers to determine the difference between serious and minor flaws. Being able to tell the difference between the two could save a company a great deal of money.

The use of computers in NDT to process data from radiology and ultrasound tests is growing in popularity. Radiology involves passing X rays or gamma rays through a product or structure. Flaws in the material appear as shadows on an X ray. Ultrasound testing uses high-frequency sound waves that are beamed into the test material. Flaws stop the sound beam, deflecting it to a source that collects and processes data about such things as the size and precise location of the defect.

Robotics

Almost everyone is familiar with the terminology given workers: those who perform management-level jobs are referred to as white-collar workers; those performing unskilled tasks or factory jobs are called blue-collar workers. However, the influx of computers into the working world of the factories has created another category: the steel-collar worker. The steel-collar workers are nonhuman—robots.

Science fiction writer Isaac Asimov popularized the term *robotics*. **Robotics** is the science that deals with robots, their construction, capabilities, and applications.

Currently, American factories have tens of thousands of robots hard at work (see Figure 16–13). By 1990 this figure is expected to reach nearly 150,000. General Motors, General Electric, and Westinghouse are the three leading users of industrial robots. These steel-collar workers perform standard jobs, such as spot welding and spray painting, as well as more complex jobs like fitting light bulbs into the dashboards of cars. The automobile industry is the leading user of robots in the United States.

The steel-collar worker is not always as efficient as one may think. Robots perform well on the factory floor, but they have been known to

● **FIGURE 16–13**
Robots are used on the assembly line
to manufacture cars.

go berserk. Swinging its powerful steel arm, a robot can deliver blows to anything within its reach. The problem—a crossed wire. Also, robots lack common sense and intelligence. For example, consider the case of a robot that drills holes in the doors of cars as they pass on the assembly line. If the car is not in the right position, the robot will drill holes in whatever is there.

Two generations of robots have appeared so far. The first generation possesses mechanical dexterity but no external sensory ability. The robots cannot see, hear, touch, or smell. Second-generation robots, however, possess more humanlike capabilities, including tactile sense or crude vision; they can "feel" how tightly they are gripping an object or "see" whether there are obstacles in their path.

Robots are appearing in places other than the factory, such as the area of sales. In Aurora, Colorado, an office supply store has robots for salespersons. For example, they will tell customers about the specials within the store while pointing to the wares displayed.

CONCEPT
SUMMARY 16–2

Computers in Industry

CAD	CAM	CIM	NDT
Computer-aided design	Computer-aided manufacturing	Computer-Integrated manufacturing	Nondestructive testing
Using computers to design, draft and analyze prospective products	Using computers to simulate manufacturing steps	Using computers to link the departments of a company into a central data base	Using computers to identify hidden flaws in products

● Summary Points

● Computer anxiety is the fear people feel about computers and the effects computers may have on individual's lives and society.

● In order to prepare students for the future, computer literacy courses are beginning to be taught throughout elementary and secondary education systems.

● Studies conducted by Genevieve Cerf at Columbia University have found that, overall, women may make better programmers than men.

● Computer-related fields pay women and men equally for similar positions and work.

● Job displacement and retraining are issues that must be dealt with as computer technology continues to automate more and more jobs and processes.

● Ergonomics is the method of researching and designing computer hardware and software to enhance employee productivity and comfort. It has focused on recommendations for the workstation environment and for making software more user friendly.

● Office automation refers to all processes that integrate computer and communications technology with traditional manual office processes.

● The manipulation of written text to achieve a desired output is referred to as word processing; word processing is the most widely adopted office automation technology.

● Word processing is available on four major types of configurations: (1) electronic typewriters, (2) dedicated word processors, (3) dedicated data processors, and (4) small business computers.

● Communication capabilities derived from office automation allow the exchange of information electronically between employees.

● Electronic mail is the transmission of messages at high speeds over telecommunications facilities and can be in the form of a teletypewriter system, a facsimile system, or a voice message system.

● The method of two or more remote locations communicating via electronic and image producing facilities is called teleconferencing. Five forms of teleconferencing exist: (1) audio conferencing, (2) augmented audio conferencing, (3) computer conferencing, (4) video seminars, and (5) videoconferencing.

● Accessing online information services, referred to as telecomputing, can provide a vast amount of information for a minimal amount of time and money.

● Computerization in business has taken place primarily in three functional areas: (1) accounting and finance, (2) management, and (3) marketing and sales.

● General accounting software, electronic spreadsheets, and data management software have been heavily used in the area of finance.

● Computer graphics have become a very important factor in business communication and decision making.

● Computer-aided design (CAD) allows an engineer to design, draft, and analyze a potential product without leaving the computer terminal.

● The combination of computer-aided design and computer-aided manufacturing (CAD/CAM) allows the engineer to analyze both the design and manufacturing process.

- Computer-integrated manufacturing (CIM) is an attempt to link various departments of a company into a central data base. The CIM data base can help management run a more coordinated, efficient operation.
- Nondestructive testing (NDT) combines X rays, high-frequency sound-waves, or laser beams with powerful microcomputers to inspect the interior of a product. Use of NDT locates the flaws while leaving the product intact.
- Robots are being used in factories, primarily in the manufacture of automobiles, for tasks such as spot welding, spray painting, and fitting lightbulbs into dashboards.

● Review Questions

1. What is computer anxiety? List some reasons why you feel computer anxiety is important to those who design, implement, and maintain computer applications.

2. What is ergonomics? What are some recommendations that have been made as a result of ergonomics?

3. What are some of the advantages of office automation?

4. Differentiate among the five forms of teleconferencing.

5. What is the difference between telecommuting and telecomputing?

6. Define a local area network and list some of its advantages.

7. Why have computer graphics become an important aspect of business management?

8. Explain how CAD/CAM is used in product development.

9. Define NDT and explain how it is used in product inspection.

10. In your opinion, what is the most identifiable effect computers have had on society?

11. Do you feel that we, as humans, will permit our society to be as automated as possible, or will there be some point in the future at which we will limit what computers can do? Briefly explain your answer.

Decision Support Software

EARLY DEVELOPMENTS

Decision Support Software was established in 1981 and incorporated in 1982. The company is dedicated to producing quality software that supports the decision-making process. These decision-making tools are sophisticated enough for business and yet simple enough for personal use.

Within the company, computers are used for product development and maintenance, consulting services, and research and development. Computers are also used for general business office applications, which include accounting and financial analyses, word processing, and list management.

To produce innovative decision-making tools that are functional, user friendly, and reliable, DSS has incorporated techniques from the fields of computer science, operations research, business administration, and psychology. DSS currently produces and markets three software packages: Expert Choice®, The Accountant, and The Business Accountant. The company offers educational training and seminars for software and related areas. The focus at DSS is on decision support systems and expert support systems.

PRODUCTS

One expert support system created by DSS, Expert Choice, is currently being used by government organizations, business, industry, and institutions of higher education. Expert Choice is used by these organizations for a number of applications including strategic planning, capital acquisitions, advertising and marketing, employee evaluation, research and development, budget allocation, and resource allocation. Individuals have used the system for personal decision making, such as determining where to live, what car to buy, and which career to pursue.

Expert Choice is a structured approach to addressing, communicating, and organizing the decision-making process. It accommodates quantitative data and subjective judgments, both of which are pertinent to every high-level decision. The program differs from conventional decision analysis techniques by not requiring numerical guesses. Expert Choice lets the decision maker graphically portray a complex problem in the form of a hierarchy, which is a natural way of organizing information for the human mind. Establishing a hierarchy helps focus attention on each part of the problem, amplifying the decision maker's capabilities. Expert Choice uses three principles of analytic thinking: hierarchical organization, establishing priorities, and logical consistency.

Expert Choice makes it possible to focus on each element of a complex problem: one element compared with another on each criterion. This is the decision process reduced to its simplest terms—pairwise comparisons. Expert Choice helps the user structure the problem, prompts the user for judgments, and combines or synthesizes judgments into a unified whole in which alternatives are prioritized.

The Accountant is an easy-to-use decision support system that offers a systematic approach to organizing financial records. While The Accountant uses a double-entry system, it does not require that the user have a knowledge of accounting. The program helps the user make informed financial decisions. It provides valuable

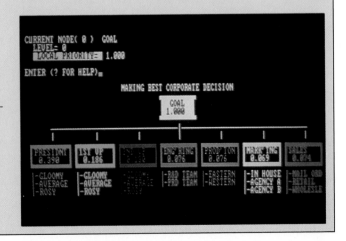

---

reports to help examine complete financial activity for a current month or previous months. Reports generated by the program include net worth, budget versus actuals, end of month balances, and periodic reports.

Another decision support system developed by Decision Support Software, The Business Accountant, is designed for use by consultants, small business owners, and entrepreneurs. It provides a powerful and flexible bookkeeping system for the nonaccountant. The Business Accountant offers a systematic approach to organizing financial records, making complete financial information available to the user at all times. The program generates valuable reports to help keep track of financial activity for a current or previous month. Re-

ports include profit and loss statements, balance sheets, budget versus actual analysis, end of month balances, and departmental accounting.

At Decision Support Software, both decision support systems and expert support systems are helping the young company make its mark on the world.

DISCUSSION POINTS

1. How does Expert Choice differ from conventional decision analysis techniques?
2. What are some of the features of the Business Accountant?

17 COMPUTER SECURITY, CRIME, ETHICS, AND THE LAW

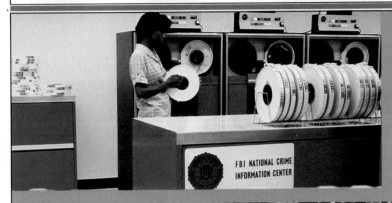

FBI NATIONAL CRIME INFORMATION CENTER

Breaches of Confidence

Andrew C. Revkin
Science Digest

Just a few years ago, electronic eavesdropping meant planting a bug in a flowerpot or tapping a phone wire. Not anymore: Leaks are now showing up in the fast-growing system of data and communications channels that crisscrosses the globe, from electronic mail to cordless phones to satellites. As fast as this network is expanding, so too is the potential for unseen surveillance—from within and without, for purposes of justice or crime.

New potential abuses stem from the increasing availability of "high-performance technology and computer literacy," says Michael Nye, president of Marketing Consultants International Inc. in Hagerstown, Maryland, and author of *Who, What & Where in Communications Security.* "Intercepting information used to be a needle-in-a-haystack problem," he says. "Computer technology now allows for the rapid and automatic sifting out of information of interest to the interceptor."

The latest stir was created by a demonstration conducted by Wim van Eck, an electrical engineer with the Dutch postal, telephone and telegraph service. He combined a portable television, an antenna and some electronic circuitry, stuck the gear in a van and proceeded to eavesdrop on institutions across Europe. According to Harold Joseph Highland, editor of *Computers & Security,* which published the first American accounts of Van Eck's feat, the engineer was able to pick out signals from a computer eight floors up in an office complex and from terminals in a bank across a wide boulevard. Scotland Yard was electronically invaded for a report produced by the BBC.

Van Eck relied on a phenomenon that has long been both feared and exploited by American and Soviet intelligence agencies: Computers and their cables, circuits and peripheral attachments emit electromagnetic radiation that can be picked up through walls, floors and windows and translated into TV images.

More than a decade ago, the National Security Agency (NSA)—the huge, secret bureaucracy that monitors Soviet communications, breaks codes and prevents our own codes from being broken or our communications monitored—created the top-secret program called Tempest. The program developed a standard for shielding computer communications hardware so that no stray signals would be leaked. Many federal agencies were equipped with Tempest-class electronics.

Last fall the NSA was given the task of maintaining communications security for every federal agency. It is also receiving many inquiries from outside the government. In the private sector, however, the NSA is encouraging the use of scramblers or encryptors.

Some of the weakest spots in the electronic network, according to several consultants, are the various communication links between any two points. Interception is possible at almost every step along the transmission path of voices, pictures or data—from phone line to microwave to satellite to terminal. Reports indicate that even fiber-optic cables, in which signals are sent via laser beam, may be tappable.

One example is satellite communications. "The network structures, both land and extraterrestrial, were not built to be secure," says Belden Menkus, a computer security consultant in Middleville, New Jersey. "They were built to move stuff, quickly and in large quantities. A hacker publication recently provided detailed instructions on how to break into and manipulate the teleconferencing service of AT&T." When that company was informed, "the feathers flew," Menkus says.

Cellular phones also have security problems. According to Nye, a simple radio scanner, which searches frequencies until a signal is picked up, can make private phone conversations excruciatingly public. "People who use cellular telephones are out of their mind," he says. "You'd be amazed at what we hear."

According to Menkus, you can't assume that a communication line is "inherently secure unless you secure it yourself." There are several types of scramblers available for cellular phones, but they are expensive and in limited use. For companies sending data rather than voices over phone lines, electronic mail or airwaves, there are encryption programs available. Norton-Lambert Corporation has developed a communications program called LYNC 5.0, which has an optional encryption function that scrambles files sent via electronic mail or bulletin boards.

Yet because of haste, cost or inconvenience, scramblers and encryptors are often neglected, says Priscilla Regan, principal author of a recent OTA report on electronic surveillance: "It's easy to forget you're broadcasting over the airwaves."

Andrew C. Revkin is a staff writer for the Los Angeles Times.

● **The security of data being processed and stored is a problem growing as fast as the computer industry itself. In the end, personal ethics provides the only real security, and a person can only be sure of his or her own.**

● Introduction

There is no doubt that computers have had a very significant impact on our lives and our society. By the same token, extensive use of computers has created new problems that must be dealt with. Just as the computer's success is attributed to people's imagination, many of the problematic situations that must be dealt with result from human nature. Computer crime and security, for example, are two issues that have created considerable concern among individuals who use computers for personal and business purposes. With computers being used as the main means of storage of personal information on credit, employment, taxes, and other aspects of a person's life, privacy is becoming a growing concern.

This chapter reviews some of the human issues associated with the use of computers. Computer crime and security as well as ethics and privacy are discussed. The chapter concludes with a discussion of warranties and copyright law.

● Computer Crime and Security

Computer crime is a greater problem than most people realize. Americans are losing billions of dollars to high-technology criminals whose crimes go undetected and unpunished; estimates of losses range from at least $2 billion to more than $40 billion a year. While no one really knows how much is being stolen, the total appears to be growing fast.

The earliest known instance of electronic embezzlement occurred in 1958, just a few years after IBM began marketing its first line of business computers. By the mid-1970s, scores of such crimes were being reported every year, and yearly losses were estimated to be as high as $300 million.

Many more problems appear to be ahead. Home computers and electronic funds transfer (EFT) systems pose a new threat to the billions of dollars in data banks accessible through telephone lines (see Figure 17-1). Already, criminals have made illegal switches of money over the phone, and more cases can be expected as EFT systems become widespread. Furthermore, the trend to distributed systems presents many opportunities for security and privacy violations.

COMPUTER CRIME DEFINED

What is meant by the term *computer crime*? The legal community has been focusing on answering this question through legislation and court opinions. Taking a broad but practical view, computer crime can be defined as a criminal act that poses a greater threat to a computer user than it would to a non-computer user, or a criminal act that is accomplished through the use of a computer.

Computer crime, therefore, consists of two kinds of activity: (1) the use of a computer to perpetrate acts of deceit, theft, or concealment that are intended to provide financial, business-related, property, or service advantages; and (2) threats to the computer itself, such as theft of hardware or software, sabotage, and demands for ransom. Because computer crimes

Electronic funds transfer made possible with a home computer and telephone lines poses a threat to billions of dollars in data banks.

seldom involve acts of physical violence, they are generally classified as white-collar crimes. While there is no single type that commits computer crimes, computer criminals are often young and ambitious with impressive educational credentials. They tend to be technically competent and come from all employee levels, including technicians, programmers, managers, and high-ranking executives.

TYPES OF COMPUTER CRIME

Computer crimes can be classified into four broad categories: (1) sabotage, (2) theft of services, (3) property crimes, and (4) financial crimes. This section examines each of these categories and gives examples drawn from actual crimes.

Sabotage

Sabotage of computers results in destruction or damage of computer hardware. This type of computer crime often resembles traditional sabotage because the computer itself is not used to carry out the destruction. Sabotage may require some sophistication if computer-assisted security systems must be thwarted or if the system is manipulated to do harm to itself.

Computers are targets of sabotage and vandalism especially during times of political activism. Dissident political groups during the 1960s, for instance, conducted assaults on computer installations, often causing extensive damage. Other forms of physical violence have included flooding the computer room and shooting a computer with a revolver. One fired employee simply walked through the data storage area with an electromagnet, thereby erasing valuable company records.

Obviously, these acts of violence do not require any special expertise on the part of the criminal. Sabotage may, however, be conducted by dissatisfied former employees who put to use some of their knowledge of company operations to gain access to and destroy hardware and software.

Theft of Services

Computer services may be abused in a variety of ways. Some examples of theft of computer services have involved politicians using a city's computer to conduct campaign mailings and employees conducting unauthorized free-lance services on a company computer after working hours.

Time-sharing systems have been exposed to abuse due to inadequate or nonexistent security precautions. It is much easier to gain unauthorized access to a time-sharing system than to a closed system. Though most systems require the user to have a password to gain access, a system is only as good as the common sense and caution of its users. A time-sharing system that does not require regular changing of access codes is inviting the theft of valuable computer time. The amazing lack of care exercised by supposedly sophisticated users made national headlines when a group of high school computer buffs in Milwaukee were discovered accessing numerous information systems, including banks, hospitals, and the defense research center in Los Alamos, New Mexico. The students reportedly gained access by using each system's password. Some of the passwords had not been changed for years, while others were obtained from public sources.

Wiretapping is another technique used to gain unauthorized access to a time-sharing system. By tapping into a legitimate user's line, one can have free access to the system whenever the line is not being used by the authorized party.

One of the prime examples of computer services theft took place at the University of Alberta. In 1976, a student at the university began an independent study under the supervision of a professor. The purpose of the study was to investigate the security of the university's computer system, a time-sharing system with more than 5,000 users, some as far away as England. After discovering several gaps in the system's security, the student was able to develop a program that reduced the possibility of unauthorized use and tampering. The student brought this program to the attention of the computer center, which took no action on the student's recommendations. It was assumed that planned changes in the system would remove security shortcomings. However, the changes were not implemented for another nine months. During that period, the program, which was capable of displaying passwords, was leaked to several students on campus. "Code Green," as the program was nicknamed, was eventually run several thousand times.

The university attempted to crack down on the unauthorized users and revoked several students' access privileges. Two of the students involved could get the computer to display the complete listing of all user passwords, including those at the highest privilege levels. In essence, this gave them unlimited access to the computer's files and programs. These students retaliated against the university administration by occasionally rendering the system inoperable or periodically inserting an obscenity into the payroll file. With an unlimited supply of IDs, they were able to escape detection, compiling a library of the computer's programs and monitoring the implementation of the new security system. The desperate university computer personnel focused exclusively on this situation, keeping a detailed log of all terminal dialogues. This effort led them to a terminal in the geology department one evening, and the students were apprehended.

Theft of Property

The most obvious computer crime that comes to mind in crimes of property is the theft of computer equipment itself. Thefts have become more common with the increasing miniaturization of computer components and the advent of home computers. These crimes are easily absorbed into traditional concepts of crime and present no unique legal problems. More intriguing is the issue of what actually constitutes property in the context of computer crimes. Different courts have come to very different conclusions on this issue.

Computer crimes of property theft frequently involve merchandise from a company whose orders are processed by computers. These crimes are usually committed by internal personnel who have a thorough knowledge of the operation. By record manipulation, dummy accounts can be created, directing a product order to be shipped to an accomplice outside the organization. Similarly, one can cause checks to be paid out for receipt of nonexistent merchandise.

Theft of property need not be limited to actual merchandise but may also extend to software. People with access to a system's program library can easily obtain copies for personal use or, more frequently, for resale to a competitor. Technical security measures in a computer installation are of little use when dishonest personnel take advantage of their positions of responsibility.

This kind of theft is by no means limited to those within the company structure, however. A computer service having specialized programs but poor security may open itself up to unauthorized access by a competitor. All that is necessary is that the outsider gain access to proper codes. This is accomplished in a number of ways, including clandestine observation of a legitimate user logging on from a remote terminal or use of a remote minicomputer to test for possible access codes.

Financial Crimes

Although not the most common type, financial computer crimes are perhaps the most serious in terms of monetary loss. With the projected increasing dependence on electronic fund transfers, implications for the future are serious.

A common method of committing this kind of crime involves checks. Mass-produced, negotiable instruments can be manipulated in a number of ways. An employee familiar with a firm's operations can direct that multiple checks be made out to the same person. Checks can also be rerouted to a false address. These crimes do not seem so incredible when one realizes the scope of *unintentional* mistakes that have been made with computerized checks. For example, the Social Security Administration once accidentally sent out 100,000 checks to the wrong addresses while the system's files were being consolidated.

Another form of a financial computer crime is known as the "round-off fraud." In this crime, the thief, perhaps a bank employee, collects the fractions of cents in customers' accounts that are created when the applicable interest rates are applied. These fractions are then stored in an account created by the thief. The theory is that fractions of cents collected from thousands of accounts on a regular basis will yield a substantial amount of money.

Still another crime involves juggling confidential information, both personal and corporate, within a computer. Once appropriate access is gained to records, the ability to alter them can be highly marketable. One group operating in California engaged in the business of creating favorable credit histories to clients seeking loans.

These cases exemplify the types of electronic crime being committed: manipulating input to the computer; changing computer programs; and stealing data, computer time, and computer programs. The possibilities for computer crime seem endless. It has been suggested that computers are used extensively by organized crime and that a computer-aided murder may already have taken place.

The unique threat of computer crime is that criminals often use computers to conceal not only their own identities but also the existence of the crimes. Law officers worry because solving computer crimes seems to depend on luck. Many such crimes are never discovered because company executives do not know enough about computers to detect them. Others go unreported to avoid scaring customers and stockholders. Many reported crimes do not result in convictions and jail terms because the complexities of data processing mystify most police officials, prosecutors, judges, and jurors.

CRIME PREVENTION AND DETECTION

The computer's ability to make statistical analyses is used in New York City to help authorities pinpoint buildings that are likely targets for arson. Several agencies contribute information to the computer about fires. Further data are available on fires that have occurred in the recent past. The computer constructs profiles of the most probable targets of arsonists. The city can keep a watch on the likely buildings and tell their owners

Types of Computer Crime

CONCEPT SUMMARY 17–1

TYPE OF CRIME	DESCRIPTION OF CRIME
Sabotage	Destruction or damage of computer hardware
Theft of service	Unauthorized use of computer time
Theft of property	Stealing computer equipment
Financial crime	Using a computer to steal money from an individual or organization

◉ HIGHLIGHT

Trusted Employee or Computer "Criminal?"

Contrary to popular belief, the average computer criminal is not a "hacker" or computer expert. As a matter of fact, many have gained their computer knowledge through on-the-job training. According to a survey done by the National Center for Computer Crime Data (NCCCD), the typical computer criminal is usually a disgruntled employee exacting revenge on an employer.

NCCCD discovered that the average age of the criminal in their sample was 27, and a total of 43 persons had been charged. Of the 43, 13 were computer programmers, 7 were bank tellers, and another 7 were data-entry clerks. Banks are the most common victims, and theft of money the most common crime.

In addition to theft, dissatisfied employees have used company computers for extortion and sabotage. Sabotage usually takes the form of a "logic bomb." A logic bomb is a software program that is set to go "off" at a particular time. When it is automatically activated, it destroys, replaces, removes, or rearranges data in an operating system.

In one case in Los Angeles, someone who was evidently very familiar with the central computer at the city's Department of Water and Power managed to set a logic bomb that shut down the system for five days. It took 20 people nearly a week to find the problem and get the system working again. This particular bomb did not destroy data, but rearranged it. Obviously, this cost the city a great deal in lost production time as well as manpower hours.

how to lessen the risk of fires. The program is also intended to decrease the owners' incentive to burn the buildings to collect the insurance proceeds. Part of the data mix fed into the computer is the names of landlords who are behind in their taxes or who have been cited for safety or occupancy violations.

Another computerized crime predictor maintained by the FBI has drawn a good deal of criticism—some of it from members of Congress. No complaints are heard about the system as it pertains to tracking known criminals. But people are worried that the Justice Department may use the system to monitor people who are considered a threat to officials but who have never been convicted of a crime. Under the plan, the Secret Service can place in the FBI's National Crime Information Center computer (see Figure 17–2) the names of persons considered to be threats to the president, vice president, presidential candidates, visiting heads of

● **FIGURE 17–2**
Italcable, an intercontinental telecommunications service, utilizes a computer-assisted security system to meet its stringent security and building operation requirements.

state, or anyone else the Secret Service must protect. Among the most elaborate communication systems in the world, the National Crime Information Center is linked to 64,000 federal, state, and local justice agencies (see Figure 17–3).

The Secret Service receives about 9,000 reports a year about people who might constitute a danger to public figures. Of these, 300 to 400 are considered dangerous. By putting these names in the bureau's massive computer, the Secret Service is able to learn immediately if any of its suspects are arrested and can keep track of their movements. In addition, any local law enforcement agency can quickly determine if a person they are considering arresting or have arrested is a Secret Service suspect. Those concerned about civil liberties express fears that through this system anyone's name might find its way into the computer, possibly causing damage to an innocent person.

Not only have computers aided in crime prevention, they have also made some headlines in crime detection (see Figure 17–4). A far-ranging computer system helped put an end to the string of child killings in Atlanta. Using two IBM computers and several data bases, the Atlanta police department was able to pinpoint Wayne Williams as the prime suspect in the twenty-eight killings and ultimately convict him for the murder of two.

Because ten different law enforcement agencies were involved in the Atlanta cases, officials agreed early in the investigation that a system was needed for handling and cross-checking the great volume of investigative data and tips that poured in. The computer system was designed so that key words could be fed into it to generate a printout of all other data that contained those words. For example, if someone reported seeing a blue van in the area where a body was discovered, operators could ask the computer to bring up all other references to "blue" and "van." Through such repeated uses of the computer, Williams was finally apprehended. When Williams went to trial, the computer system was used

● **FIGURE 17–3**
The FBI's National Crime Information Center (NCIC) computer is linked to state and local law enforcement agencies.

● **FIGURE 17–4**
Computer technology has become an
important tool in police work.

to check defense testimony against prior statements, and the results were
factored into the cross-examination.

COMPUTER SECURITY

Computer security involves the technical and administrative safeguards
required to protect a computer-based system (hardware, personnel, and
data) against the major hazards to which most computer systems are
exposed and to control access to information.

Physical computer systems and data in storage are vulnerable to several hazards: fire, natural disaster, environmental problems, and sabotage.

Physical Threats to Security

● *Fire.* Fire is a problem because most computer installations use com-
bustible materials—punched cards, paper, and so on. If a fire starts,
water cannot be used to extinguish it, because water can damage magnetic storage media and hardware. Carbon-dioxide fire-extinguisher systems are hazardous because they would endanger employees, if any
were trapped in the computer room. Halon, a nonpoisonous chemical
gas, can be used in fire extinguishers, but such extinguishers are costly.
● *Natural disasters.* Many computer centers have been damaged or
destroyed by floods, cyclones, hurricanes, and earthquakes. Floods pose
a serious threat to the computer hardware and wiring. However, water
in the absence of heat will not destroy magnetic tapes unless the tapes
are allowed to retain moisture over an extended period of time. Protection
against natural disasters should be a consideration when the location
for the computer center is chosen; for example, the center should not be
located in an area prone to flooding.

● *Environmental problems.* Usually, computers are installed in buildings that were not originally planned to accommodate them. This practice may lead to environmental problems. For example, water and steam pipes may run through a computer room; bursting pipes could result in extensive damage. Pipes on floors above the computer room are also potentially hazardous; so all ceiling holes should be sealed. Data on magnetic media can be destroyed by magnetic fields created by electric motors in the vicinity of the computer room. Other environmental problems include power failures, brownouts (temporary surges or drops in power), and external radiation.

● *Sabotage.* Sabotage represents the greatest physical risk to computer installations. Saboteurs can do great damage to computer centers with little risk of apprehension. For example, magnets can be used to scramble code on tapes, bombs can be planted, and communication lines can be cut. Providing adequate security against such acts of sabotage is extremely difficult and expensive.

Data Security Measures

In addition to safeguarding their computer systems from these physical difficulties, companies must protect stored data against illegitimate use by controlling access to it. There is no simple solution to these security problems. Organizations such as government agencies and businesses have instituted various security measures—most to restrict access to computerized records, others to provide for reconstruction of destroyed data. Some examples are given below:

● Backup copies of data are stored outside the organization's location, and recovery procedures are established.

● Authorized users are given special passwords. Remote-terminal users have their own unique codes, and batch-processing users have specific job cards. Codes and passwords should be changed frequently.

● The scope of access to the computer system is proportionate to the user's security clearance and job responsibility. Access to specific portions of the data base can be gained only by those whose jobs necessitate it.

● Installations are guarded by internal security forces. For example, access to the data-processing department may be restricted to personnel with special badges and keys (see Figure 17–5).

● Data is **encrypted,** or translated into a secret code, by complex coding devices that scramble information before it is transmitted or stored. When data is transmitted to or from remote terminals, it is encrypted at one end and **decrypted,** or translated back into plain text, at the other. Files can also be protected by the data's being encrypted before it is stored and decrypted after it has been retrieved. Data is principally encrypted on its way out of the computer and decrypted on its way back in.

● Computer installations use detectors that identify legitimate individual computer users by fingerprints or voice patterns. For example, computer makers have developed attachments that grant access only to operators who put proper thumbprints on glass plates. Adoption of these expensive devices is slow, however, because they deter the main objectives of using computers: economy and convenience.

Enhancing the Quality of Life

Computers have enhanced the quality of our lives in many ways, from improving health care to enriching leisure time. Advances in medical research and treatment have been made possible through computer technology. Computerized equipment is used extensively in the health care field for laboratory testing and analysis, computer-assisted diagnosis, and monitoring and treatment of patients. Professionals in the fields of law enforcement and fire fighting use computers to help carry out their duties. Prison life can improve when computers are used to help prisoners learn new skills. Computers can even enhance the quality of our vacations and help bridge the generation gap.

Jennifer Smith, a paraplegic, demonstrates the new hybrid walking system under development at Wright State University's National Center for Rehabilitation Engineering in Dayton, Ohio. The experimental system includes the WSU computer-controlled walking system, a lightweight reciprocating brace from Louisiana State University, and a walker or canes.

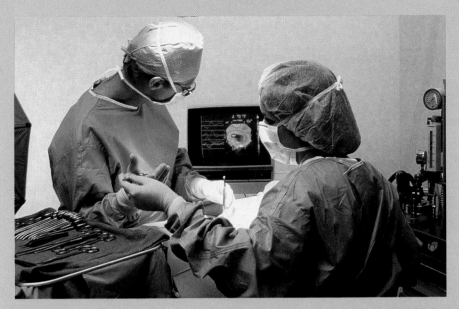

In hospitals, computers are used to assist doctors in the diagnosis and treatment of illnesses. Bio-Logic Systems produces microcomputer equipment that can help diagnose brain tumors. Electrodes from an electroencephalograph are connected to a patient's head and a color video map reveals brain activity. The electrical activity mapping capability also serves as an important intraoperative monitoring device.

At the Los Angeles District Attorney's office, Honeywell's DPS 6 System integrates powerful data processing, office automation, and communications capabilities to give prosecutors quick access to the department's felony and misdemeanor files, and criminal history records at other government offices.

The computer revolution has had an effect on people of all ages. The Playing To Win Computer Center in East Harlem offers learning opportunities to teenagers, parents, and grandparents.

 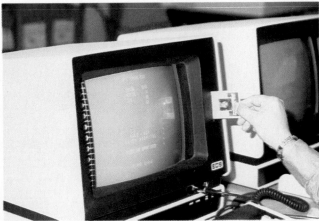

● **FIGURE 17-5**
Devices such as data keys (left) and identification cards (right) help protect stored data by limiting access to the data.

Establishing Computer Security

While these security measures help protect data, they are not complete. They may not prevent internal sabotage, fraud, or embezzlement. For example, an employee with a special access code may steal classified information. Banks and insurance companies are especially susceptible. Often, these companies do not wish to report the incidents because of the bad publicity and the difficulty in solving such crimes.

How, then, can organizations establish computer security? First, computer users must recognize their role in security. If a high-level priority is assigned to security in the company, employees must be made aware of it and of the security measures that are being taken.

Second, many organizations recognize the need to have a well-trained security force—a department of security guards who specialize in maintaining data security, conducting system audits, and asking the right kinds of questions on a daily basis. Computerized records should be scrutinized regularly to see that everything is in order.

Third, a company should exercise a great deal of care in the selection and screening of the people who will have access to computers, terminals, and computer-stored data. Companies should choose programmers as carefully as they select attorneys or accountants.

Last, companies must discharge employees who stray beyond legal and ethical boundaries. Whenever these incidents occur, it is imperative that it be shown that they will not be tolerated and that, however hard the necessary course of action, those responsible for security and protection have the integrity to follow through.

CONCEPT SUMMARY 17-2

Computer Security

PHYSICAL THREATS TO SECURITY	SECURITY MEASURES
Fire	Make backup copies
Natural disaster	Issue passwords to authorized users
Environmental problems	Encrypt data
Sabotage	Post security guards and identification detectors

● Computer Ethics

Another issue facing both organizations and individuals in relation to computer use is computer ethics. Computer ethics are also largely dependent on human nature.

The term **computer ethics** refers to the standard of moral conduct in computer use. Although some specific laws have been enacted in problem areas such as privacy invasion and crime, ethics are a way in which the "spirit" of some laws can be carried to other computer-related activities. Some of the topics currently being addressed under the ethics issue include hacking, the security and privacy of data, employee loyalty, and the copying of computer software. Security and privacy of data are discussed in other sections of the chapter, while discussions of hacking, employee loyalty and software copying follow.

Hacking

Hacking is a computer term used to describe the activity of computer enthusiasts who are challenged by the practice of breaking computer security measures. Hackers do this for a number of reasons including to gain access to confidential data or illegal computer time, or for fun. Computer users should be aware that seemingly innocent activities such as hacking are actually criminal acts. Regardless of the reason, hacking is the same as intentionally committing a crime. Gaining unauthorized access to another computer can be as serious as breaking into someone's home.

The case discussed earlier in which a group of Milwaukee high school students gained access to the defense research center's computer in Los Alamos, New Mexico is a prime example of hacking. The youths, after being caught, stated that they did not see any classified information, but that they did accidentally erase some files. The same group of students accessed another computer in a New York cancer center. The computer, which was used to monitor 250 cancer patients, failed for a short time due to the activity of these youths. When questioned about why they behaved this way, the group said they did not know it was a crime, and it gave them something to do in the evenings!

Employee Loyalty

Employee loyalty is another ethical issue that has surfaced in the area of data processing. Because the field of data processing is a dynamic environment with a shortage of qualified personnel, there are many job opportunities. There is also a great deal of job changing among data-processing personnel. Because an employee has some obligations to his or her current employer, there have been a number of court cases that address the issue of employee loyalty to employers as a duty.

In one particular case, a data-processing consultant employed by Firm A was seeking a similar job with Firm B. Firm B was in competition for consulting contracts with Firm A. Prior to being offered a position with Firm B, the consultant was asked to attend an interview with a potential

● HIGHLIGHT
Who Goes There?

Just like military bases, computer systems have sentries, and unless the correct password is used, access to data is denied. However, unless passwords and secret identification codes are used properly, they are virtually useless.

All too often passwords are easily guessed or discovered by unauthorized personnel. Many times the authorized user will keep the written password in an obvious spot or neglect to change it for months at a time.

Some computer systems have their own password security systems built in. Passwords are designated by the system that the user must *define* and change on a regular basis. Others automatically change the system password every week.

There are also ways the user can safeguard the password security system. Passwords should be kept completely secret. If possible, the screen should remain dark when the password is keyed in, and the password kept in the system should be in code and changed often. Individual passwords should also be changed often, anywhere from once a week to once a month. The written copy should be kept in a safe place, possibly the office safe or a locked file cabinet.

Passwords are probably the most common security system used in corporations and institutions, and great care should be taken in their use.

client on behalf of the firm. Unbeknownst to either the consultant or Firm B, Firm A was also seeking a contract from the client.

When Firm A became aware of the situation they sued the consultant, who at that time worked for Firm B. The suit alleged that the consultant breached his duty of loyalty to Firm A. The day the consultant attended the interview, he had called in sick to Firm A. The court criticized the consultant, finding that the illness excuse not only permitted him to aid himself but also aid the competitor on the employer's time. An appellate court disagreed. The court ruled that since neither Firm B nor the consultant knew Firm A was also competing for the contract, the employee had the right to seek alternate employment. The court believed that employees have the right to change jobs as long as they are not under contract for a definite term. That the right should be exercisable without the necessity of revealing the plans to the current employer.

Although the court opinions differed, it should be noted that the courts do recognize some degree of duty of loyalty to the employer on the part of the employee. For this reason, all employees in the area of data processing should be aware of their obligations and rights as employees and as potential employees. Actions taken in the process of changing positions should be conducted in an ethical fashion.

Software Copying

Another area of ethical concern is **software copying,** or **piracy.** Software piracy is the unauthorized copying of a computer program that has been written by someone else. Many software manufacturers write security measures into their programs so that they cannot be copied without authorization. However, some computer enthusiasts are challenged by trying to break this form of security as well. Whether done for personal use or to sell for profit, software piracy is a crime.

Computer ethics cannot be emphasized enough. It is the responsibility of each computer user to evaluate his or her own actions and determine the standard of morals to be followed. Only through ethical behavior will the ultimate security and privacy of computers and computer data be assured.

● Privacy

The widespread use of computers, information systems, and telecommunications systems has created a major concern in recent years—the invasion of individual privacy. **Privacy** involves an individual's ability to determine what, how, and when personal information is communicated to others. With computers becoming the main means of storing personal information relating to credit, employment, taxes, and other aspects of a person's life, the issue of privacy assumes great importance.

ISSUES

Before computerized record keeping became widespread, most business and government decisions about such benefits as credit, educational grants, and Medicare were based on personal knowledge of the individuals involved and the limited data obtained from a decentralized system of public records. Privacy was protected to some extent by the inefficiency of the sources and methods of collecting data. The details of people's lives were maintained in widely dispersed, manually maintained files and in the memories of people who knew them. It was difficult to compile from these sources a detailed dossier on any individual.

Because computers have made data both easier to obtain and easier to store, more data is collected and stored (see Figure 17–6). Often an individual's data stored in one main file can be accessed easily by entering his or her social security number. The increased ease of obtaining data tempts organizations to collect more data than necessary. People have less control over who has access to personal data when it becomes part of a huge data base. They are unaware of whether their personal data files are complete and accurate. They may not even be aware that certain information is being kept.

The major concerns about the issue of privacy can be summarized as follows:

- Too much personal data about individuals is collected and stored in computer files.
- Organizations are often making decisions solely on the basis of these files.
- Much of the personal data collected about individuals may not be relevant to the purpose for which it is to be used.
- The accuracy, completeness, and currency of the data may be unacceptably low.
- The security of stored data is a problem.

Of course, the same computer systems that erode individual privacy are also allowing private and public institutions to operate more efficiently. For example, a firm must control its risks when issuing credit and, therefore, needs enough information about individuals to make responsible decisions. The solution to the privacy issue must be an appropriate balance between the legitimate needs of organizations for information about people and the rights of individuals to maintain their privacy.

The data bases that are responsible for the privacy concerns are most prevalent within the federal government (see Figure 17–7). Much of the data is acquired from census returns filed each decade and income tax returns filed annually. The Department of Transportation records owners of boats and aircraft. This department also notes any drivers' licenses that are withdrawn, suspended, or revoked by any state. Data about veterans, social security or welfare recipients, aliens, minority businesses, and dealers in alcohol, firearms, and explosives are stored away in huge data bases. Some people fear that using debit cards and computers for making purchases will create new opportunities for compiled assumptions about their habits and personal lives. The government could glean statistics concerning everything from where and how often a family dines out to what kinds of magazines and books they read.

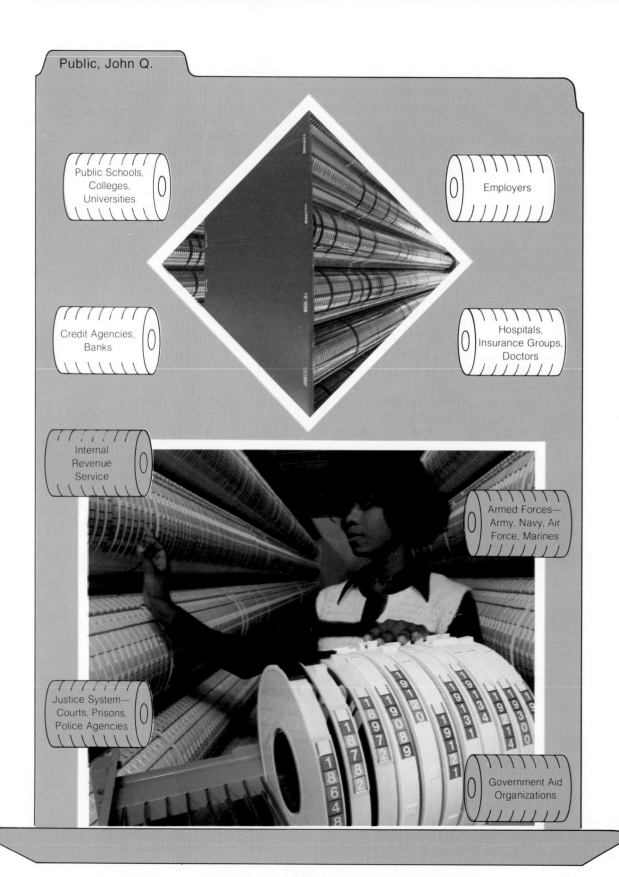

Public, John Q.

Public Schools, Colleges, Universities

Employers

Credit Agencies, Banks

Hospitals, Insurance Groups, Doctors

Internal Revenue Service

Armed Forces— Army, Navy, Air Force, Marines

Justice System— Courts, Prisons, Police Agencies

Government Aid Organizations

LEGISLATION

Since the early 1970s several laws have been enacted to protect privacy by controlling the collection, dissemination, and transmission of personal data. By far the most numerous have been passed by the federal government to protect against abuse of the government's own record-keeping agencies. But state legislatures are also beginning to recognize the widespread abuses that computer technology has created, and numerous states are taking action to stop the abuse.

Federal Legislation

One of the first federal laws to address the problem of abuse was passed in 1970 while a second was passed in 1973. The Freedom of Information Act of 1970 allows individuals access to data about themselves in files collected by federal agencies. The law was passed because of the potential for the government to conceal its proceedings from the public. The Crime Control Act of 1973 protects the privacy of data collected for state criminal systems that are developed with federal funds.

Perhaps the most sweeping federal legislation was the Privacy Act of 1974. Signed on January 1, 1975, this act is designed to protect the privacy of individuals about whom the federal government maintains data. Although the act was a step in the right direction, it was criticized for its failure to reach beyond the federal government to state and private institutions. The act contains these provisions:

- Individuals must be able to determine what information about themselves is being recorded and how it will be used.
- Individuals must be provided with a way to correct inaccurate information that is collected about themselves.

● FIGURE 17–6 (opposite page)
The stacks and rows of magnetic tapes show how easily just one corporation can accumulate and store huge amounts of data using computer systems. Multiply one corporation's data base by the many data bases kept by other organizations including the federal government, and you can see how John.Q. Public could be completely unaware of what data is recorded about him. The ease with which organizations can record, store, and access data has led to concerns about data privacy and correct use of data.

● FIGURE 17–7
Huge data bases such as the one maintained by the IRS lead many people to fear abuse of their privacy.

● Information collected for one purpose cannot be used for another purpose without the consent of the individual involved.

● Organizations creating, manipulating, using, or divulging personal information must ensure that the information is reliable and must take precautions to prevent misuse of the information.

Several other laws have been passed by the federal government in an attempt to control data-base misuse or protect the privacy of individuals. The Family Educational Rights and Privacy Act of 1974 is designed to protect privacy by regulating access to computer-stored records of grades and behavior evaluations in both private and public schools. The act provides that no federal funds will be made available to an educational agency that has a policy of denying parents and students access to the student's relevant educational records. The Tax Reform Act of 1976 was passed to safeguard the confidentiality of personal tax information. The Right to Financial Privacy Act of 1978 provides further protection by limiting government access to the customer records of financial institutions, protecting to some degree the confidentiality of personal financial data.

As computers use has continued to grow during the 1980s, the federal government has continued to enact legislation directed toward protecting the privacy of individuals. The increased use of electronic funds transfer led to the passage of the Electronic Funds Transfer Act of 1980. This law requires financial institutions to notify customers whenever a third party accesses a customer's account. The Comprehensive Crime Control Act of 1984 provides for protection from computer abuse in some areas that were overlooked in earlier legislation. In this act only a few limited categories of privacy abuse are defined. One provision of the law prohibits individuals without authorization from knowingly accessing a computer to obtain either information that is protected by the Right of Financial Privacy Act of 1978 or information contained in the file of a consumer reporting agency. Another provision prohibits individuals from knowingly accessing a government computer and using, modifying, destroying, or disclosing information stored in the computer or preventing the use of the computer. More recently, concern has focused on abuses of privacy during the actual transmission of data. This concern led to the drafting of the Electronic Communication Privacy Act of 1986 which prohibits the interception of data communications, for example, electronic mail. The act has undergone consideration by both houses of congress and is expected to become a law very soon.

State Legislation

Many state laws regarding government record-keeping practices are patterned after the Privacy Act of 1974. Most states have enacted some controls on such practices in the public sector and most of the laws have been passed since 1978. By the end of 1985 thirty-six state legislatures had passed laws regarding computer crime, and most states addressed the privacy issue in one form or another. Computer crime laws on the state level are generally quite similar to each other. Differences lie mainly in how each state defines a particular term or violation. For example, offenders may be considered to have "willfully," "knowingly," "intentionally," or "purposefully" committed a violation. In Florida, "willfully" is defined as acting with intent, and the term is equated with "knowingly," "intentionally," and "purposefully." The state of Utah, however, has separate definitions for "willfully," "knowingly," and "intentionally." When terms such as these are not clearly defined within the law, their meanings are determined by examining either general statutory definitions for criminal behavior or case law for the particular jurisdiction.

Some state laws address the unlawful access to data bases in more detail than the federal Comprehensive Crime Control Act of 1984. For instance, South Dakota has a provision that prohibits the disclosure of passwords. Kentucky makes it a felony to access a computer system for the purpose of attempting to alter information. In Hawaii, all unauthorized computer use is considered a felony, while Idaho makes a distinction between accessing information (a misdemeanor) and altering information (a felony).

Relatively few information privacy violation cases have been litigated, whether on the state or federal level. Since one problem of privacy violation is that data is transferred and disclosed without the knowledge or consent of the subjects, people are not likely to know how their personal data is used and probably will not realize they may have a claim to take to court. Furthermore, privacy litigation is something of a contradiction in terms: by taking claims to court, litigants may expose private aspects of their lives to a far greater extent than the initial intrusion did.

● Warranties, Copyright Law, Public-Domain Software, and Shareware

This portion of the chapter discusses two of the legal issues associated with owning a computer system—the warranties for hardware and software and the copyright law as it applies to computer software. A discussion of express and implied warranties will be followed by a review of copyright law and its application to the writing of computer programs. The section concludes with a brief discussion on public-domain software and shareware.

WARRANTIES

The **Uniform Commercial code (UCC)** is a set of provisions proposed by legal experts to promote uniformity among the state courts in their legal treatment of commercial transactions. By using Article Two of the UCC, the courts have a common basis for rendering decisions concerning the sale of computer hardware and software by vendors.

Common law, on the other hand. is based on customs and past judicial decisions in similar cases. If Article Two of the UCC does not apply to a transaction, then the common law of contracts will apply. The UCC is a far better system since it is more modern and basically abolishes the concept of *caveat emptor* (a Latin legal maxim meaning "let the buyer beware"). Under Article Two, for example, the computer user is given implied warranty protection, whereas under common law, buyer protection is not presumed or implied and must be negotiated and agreed upon in the final contract. Most computer vendors are reluctant to agree to such negotiations.

Two main conditions must be satisfied for the UCC to apply to computer acquisitions. First, the contract must be one for goods, not services. As a general rule, the UCC is not applicable to contracts for services. Second, the contract should be for the *sale* of goods. Article Two of the UCC does not normally apply to leases or licenses.

Express Warranties

Under Article Two of the UCC, **express warranties** are created when the seller makes any promise or statement of fact concerning the goods being sold which the purchaser uses as a basis for purchasing the goods. By doing so, the seller warrants, or guarantees, that the goods are those that will meet the purchaser's needs. An express warranty may be created by the supplier's use of a description, sample, or model in attempting to sell the goods, although the seller's contract terms will often attempt to limit or disclaim all such warranties. Express warranties are also found in the written contract, such as statements that defective equipment will be replaced or repaired for up to one year after delivery. A **breach of contract** occurs if the goods fail to conform to the express warranty, in which case the buyer is entitled to a reduction in the price of the goods as compensatory damages. One drawback of express warranties is that the purchaser must keep the defective equipment. Therefore, unless expressly stated in the contract, the computer hardware or software would not have to be replaced, only reduced in price.

Implied Warranties

Implied warranties were also created under Article Two of the Uniform Commercial Code. **Implied warranties** suggest that a contract for the sale of goods automatically contains certain warranties that exist by law. An implied warranty need not be verbally made nor included in the written warranties of a contract to be effective. Two major types of implied warranties include implied warranty of merchantability and implied warranty of fitness for a particular purpose.

The **implied warranty of merchantability** only exists if the seller is considered a merchant. Computer and software vendors are classified as merchants because they are in the business of selling computer-related products on a repetitive basis. In the case of a purchased computer system, an implied warranty of merchantability guarantees the user that the system will function properly for a reasonable period of time. As in the case of express warranties, however, the purchaser must keep the defective equipment.

To create an **implied warranty of fitness** for a particular purpose, the purchaser must communicate to the supplier the specific purpose for which the product will be used. The purchaser must then rely upon the supplier's judgment, skill, and expertise to select suitable computer hardware and software. If the computer hardware or software later fails to meet those needs, the supplier has breached this implied warranty and is liable for damages. The violation of this warranty permits the purchaser to recover only a certain amount of the sales price.

COPYRIGHT LAW

Computer software, or computer programs, have been accepted for copyright registration since 1964. In order for a program to be protected under the copyright law, it must contain a notice of copyright that is visible to the user. This notice of copyright must consist of three things: (1) the © symbol, the word *copyright*, or the abbreviation *copr.*, (2) the year of the work's first publication, and (3) the name of the copyright owner (see Figure 17–8). If these three items are not given, however, the copyright is not necessarily forfeited—but the duplicator of the program may not be liable for damages. Unpublished programs are also eligible for protection under the copyright law, and registration is not required since copyright protection exists from the moment of creation. Registration is only required to obtain the right to sue for copyright infringement.

Current copyright law only protects against unauthorized copying and not against unauthorized use. It is not against copyright law, however, to make a copy of a program that is in a magazine, for example, or for archival purposes. There is some question whether copyright law applies to a program in machine-readable form—such as object code—if a copyright was obtained on the source program. In some cases, the program output can also be copyrighted.

PUBLIC-DOMAIN SOFTWARE AND SHAREWARE

One area of growing use in the computer field is that of **public-domain software.** Public-domain software is software that is unprotected by copyright law and, therefore, falls into the "public domain" of unrestricted use. Public-domain software, frequently obtained from electronic bulletin

● **FIGURE 17–8**
Copyright information is often displayed prominently as part of the opening screen.

boards, is free to all users. The only cost associated with a public-domain program is the cost of the phone service needed to reach the bulletin board on which the program appears or the cost of the disk to which the program is copied.

Public domain-programs were originally written by computer hobbyists and amateurs to fill the void of commercial software available for microcomputers. The programs, which appeared on bulletin boards or were passed among members of user groups, were often undocumented and full of "bugs." Today there are fewer bugs in the programs, and many come with sophisticated documentation. Besides bulletin boards and user groups, public-domain software now can be obtained from online services such as CompuServ and The Source. Most public-domain programs include the source code for user convenience.

Closely related to public-domain software is **shareware.** Authors of shareware retain the copyright to their work. They make their programs available to the public with the idea that, if a user likes the program, he or she will make a donation to the author. Generally the source code is not distributed with a shareware program. Users of shareware are encouraged to copy and distribute the programs freely. The basic philosophy behind shareware is that users are in the best position to judge the value of a program and that authors, if they know their fees depend upon it, will produce a quality product. For this reason, the quality of shareware programs tends to surpass that of public-domain programs.

● Summary Points

● Taking a broad view, computer crime can be defined as any criminal act that poses a greater threat to a computer user than it would to a non–computer user, or a criminal act that is accomplished through the use of a computer.

● Computer crimes can be classified in four categories: sabotage, theft of services, theft of property, and financial crimes.

● Uses of computers in the prevention and detection of crimes include pinpointing likely arson targets, monitoring people who are potential threats to public officials, and handling and cross-checking data and tips in murder investigations.

● Physical threats to computer security exist in the forms of fire, natural disasters, environmental problems (such as power failures, brownouts, and external radiation), and sabotage.

● Data security is an issue that must also be addressed by organizations that store sensitive data on computers. Illegitimate use of data must be controlled through access security measures.

● Computer ethics refers to the standard of moral conduct for computer use. Computer ethics are largely dependent on human nature.

● Hacking is the practice of breaking computer security measures to gain unauthorized access to a computer system. Hacking is a criminal act.

● Employee duty or loyalty is an ethical issue that can pose a serious problem to companies in competition for both business and employees.

● Unauthorized software copying, or piracy, is a crime whether done for personal use or for profit.

- The Freedom of Information Act of 1970 allows individuals access to data about themselves in files collected by federal agencies. The Crime Control Act of 1973 protects the privacy of data collected for state criminal systems.

- The Privacy Act of 1974 is designed to protect the privacy of individuals about whom the federal government maintains data.

- The Family Educational Rights and Privacy Act of 1974 is designed to protect privacy by regulating access to computer-stored records of grades and behavior evaluations in both private and public schools. The Tax Reform Act of 1976 was passed to safeguard the confidentiality of personal tax information while the Right to Financial Privacy Act of 1978 limits government access to customer records in financial institutions.

- The Fair Credit Reporting Act of 1970 attempts to regulate the information practices of private organizations and is intended to deter privacy violations by lending institutions that use computers to store and manipulate data.

- As computer use has continued to grow during the 1980s, the federal government has continued to enact legislation directed toward protecting the privacy of individuals. The increased use of electronic funds transfer led to the passage of the Electronic Funds Transfer Act of 1980. The Comprehensive Crime Control Act of 1984 provides for protection from computer abuse in some areas that were overlooked in earlier legislation. The Electronic Communication Privacy Act of 1986 prohibits the interception of data communications, for example, electronic mail.

- By the end of 1985, thirty-six states had passed legislation regarding computer crime and most of these laws addressed the privacy issue in one form or another. Computer-crime laws on the state level are generally quite similar to each other, the differences being in the way terms or violations are defined.

- The Uniform Commercial Code (UCC) is a set of provisions established by legal experts to act as a uniform guide to state courts for resolving contract disputes.

- For the UCC to be applicable, the contract must be one for goods rather than services, and the contract should be for the sale of goods, not for leases or licenses.

- Under Article Two of the UCC, express warranties and implied warranties can be created on behalf of the purchaser.

- Copyright law is one method of protecting computer programs from being illegally copied. Copyright registration is not required but is necessary in order to seek damages for a copyright infringement.

- Public-domain software is software that is unprotected by copyright law and falls into the "public domain" of unrestricted use.

- Authors of shareware retain the copyright to their work. Programs are made available to the public with the idea that a user will make a donation to the author.

● Review Questions

1. What is computer crime? Do you feel computer crime is a serious problem in our society?

2. Describe some of the ways computers are being used in the detection and prevention of crimes.

3. Briefly explain some of the measures that can be taken by an organization to insure data security.

4. What is meant by the term *computer ethics*? Describe some instances, other than those discussed, in which computer ethics would be required.

5. Do you feel that computer ethics within an organization should be described through a formal company document that establishes what is ethical and what is not, or should computer ethics be a personal issue left to the discretion of each employee? Briefly explain your answer.

6. Why has the issue of privacy become so important? Do you feel that organizations that maintain information on individuals should be required to disclose this information to those people to verify its correctness? Why or why not?

7. What are the areas of privacy abuse addressed by the Comprehensive Crime Control Act of 1984?

8. What are the main differences among state laws addressing the privacy issue?

9. Distinguish between express warranties and implied warranties. What are the two types of implied warranties?

10. Why is the copyright law important to a computer software vendor? Would a vendor be protected even if he or she neglected to register the software?

11. Distinguish between public-domain software and shareware.

ALCOA

COMPANY HISTORY

Aluminum, which is the most plentiful metallic element in the earth's crust, occurs only as a chemical compound. For many years, the difficulty of reducing it to metallic aluminum made the metal too expensive for commercial use. In 1886, two young men—independently but simultaneously—unlocked the secret of a low-cost, electrolytic process for separating aluminum from its oxide. One of the men, Charles Martin Hall, a graduate of Oberlin College in Ohio, was able to bring his discovery to commercialization, and in 1888, six Pittsburgh industrialists financed the formation of the Pittsburgh Reduction Company, which later was renamed the Aluminum Company of America (ALCOA).

Once aluminum was available at low cost, uses for the metal grew steadily. An early successful application was cooking utensils. The steel industry was also an early customer as aluminum alloys became useful in the making of automobile parts. As the uses for aluminum grew, so did ALCOA. World War II was a major turning point for the company. Wartime needs required vast amounts of additional aluminum, and ALCOA built many plants for the government. After the war, antitrust regulations required ALCOA to sell all but one of its wartime plants. Despite this setback, post-World War II growth was strong, and ALCOA prospered. Today, ALCOA and affiliated companies sell aluminum throughout the world. The past decade has brought major changes in the worldwide environment for aluminum producers, and ALCOA is becoming a broader-based company with a research thrust toward chemicals, ceramics, polymers, laminates, and advanced manufacturing systems.

DATA SECURITY

As ALCOA has become a more complex organization with an emphasis on research and development, data security has become an important aspect of the company's success. At ALCOA, the focus of data security is on support and acceptance by the user community. To ensure the support of the thousands of computer users at many remote locations, ALCOA has decentralized the responsibility for data security administration to several middle-level managers throughout the company.

ALCOA's security policy, security software, and positive user attitudes are all equally important to the effec-

tiveness of the program. Of these, positive user attitudes are undoubtedly the most difficult to achieve. This is due partly to the logistics of creating security awareness among large numbers of users and partly to the inclination of people to adopt convenient data access practices rather than those intended to safeguard the corporation's data resources. Since people are more easily influenced by individuals whom they know well, local administrators are obviously in a better position to promote security than an unknown central administrator whose office may be three time zones away.

At ALCOA, the belief in positive user attitudes and local data security administrators is strong. According to national surveys, the odds that a computer criminal is a company insider are an astonishing 9 to 1. Central administrators are at a disadvantage in preventing crimes and abuses because they neither know nor are known by more than a few of the individuals who interface with the computer. ALCOA's local administrators, on the other hand, are likely to have job responsibilities that keep them in relatively close contact with the groups of computer users they control, either functionally or geographically. These administrators are more likely to know which users are high security risks. Traditionally, high security risks include employees who are disgruntled, are having money or drug problems, or are being transferred or terminated.

Local administrators can respond quickly to such situations by making direct on-line adjustments via security software. They are not deterred by the notion that security is someone else's problem, and they are not impeded by the phone calls and paperwork that are the bane of central administration. Also, potential violators are less likely to misuse the computer or commit a crime if they know and respect their local data security administrator.

One of the benefits of the decentralized security system at ALCOA has been increased productivity, as well as improved security and a decrease in costs. Decentralization has increased productivity by eliminating the need for central support personnel to process requests and the staff of central administrators to review and approve the requests. The task of processing requests for

user IDs and file accesses has been automated by a combination of purchased security software and programs written in house.

Decentralization has also increased user productivity by reducing the time users wait for computer change requests to be processed. Before decentralization, users had to fill out more specialized change request forms, have them approved and signed by an authorized individual, and mail them to the home office. At the home office, the signatures were validated, and the forms were reviewed, processed, and returned by mail to the individual who authorized them. This procedure took one to two weeks. Today, ALCOA's local security administrator makes these changes on-line with immediate confirmation of accuracy.

The success of a decentralized program depends upon a central individual to give direction to the overall program and ensure that all local administrators are observing certain standard rules. This may be one of the reasons that relatively few corporations (less than 20 percent) have adopted the decentralized approach to data security and accessing mainframe computers that has successfully been implemented at ALCOA. Also important to the success of a decentralized program are good naming conventions for data security programs, user-friendly security packages that spare local administrators from having to master a great deal of technical jargon, the coordinating of necessary changes to various data sets when user IDs are added or deleted, and the reporting of unauthorized access attempts to the administrators responsible for both the user and the data.

All of these measures and many more have helped make decentralization successful. From corporate headquarters to the grass roots level, decentralization has won the approval of the Aluminum Company of America.

DISCUSSION POINTS

1. Discuss how decentralization has improved data security at ALCOA.
2. Why is positive user attitude the most difficult aspect of data security to achieve.?

18 COMPUTERS IN OUR LIVES: TODAY AND TOMORROW

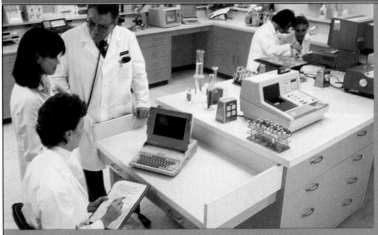

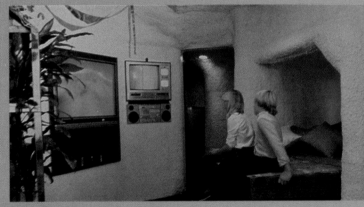

OUTLINE

What Will "Smart" Robots Mean to You?

Gordon Williams
Family Weekly

Are you ready for the day when your newest co-worker isn't a human being but a robot that has been programmed to do a job very much like yours? And are you looking forward to the day when you can surrender the household drudgery to a robot that has been programmed to wash the floors, vacuum, stand guard against burglars, and mix a perfect martini in response to your spoken command?

It isn't science fiction at all: Robots are here already in growing numbers. The Robotic Industries Association reckons that some 8,000 robots are in use in American industry. Peter Heytler, research associate at the University of Michigan's Industrial Development Division, says there could be 100,000 industrial robots in America by 1990.

Robots for the home are coming, too. George A. Cretecos Jr. is president of Robotland in Boca Raton, Fla.—one of the first retail stores to sell only robots. In its first nine months in business, it sold $100,000 worth of "personal" robots—at prices that start at $19.95 and run to $5,000 and more. They can do simple lifting operations, and the more expensive ones are linked to computers that can be programmed to "teach" the robots new tasks.

In fact, we're already well into what Dr. James L. Crowley calls the second generation of robots. Crowley, research scientist at the Robotics Institute of Carnegie-Mellon University in Pittsburgh, says first-generation "robots" could only perform one specific task, such as welding. The new robots can be programmed to perform a variety of tasks.

Third-generation robots will be intelligent machines. Crowley says. "Tell them what you want done, and they'll plan the necessary actions to accomplish it. They'll think it through."

We already use robots that have optical scanning devices, and we have computers that can recognize isolated words spoken by one person. Tomorrow's robots will have three-dimensional vision, close to what humans have, and they'll respond to normal, conversational speech from anyone who speaks to them. These robots will be in factories within a decade, Crowley says.

He adds that, by then, we'll have true household robots able to do all those chores that people don't like to do and priced low enough so that most families will be able to afford them.

As in so many things technological, Japan is the leader in robots, with two-thirds of the world's total. But the United States is doing the advanced work today, and not all of Japan's devices are true robots. To qualify as a robot, the device must be programmable so it can perform various jobs. If it does just a single job (welding, for instance), it isn't a true robot.

There are two obvious advantages to robots. One is that they can do work that humans don't want to do, jobs that are "3-D" (dull, dirty, and dangerous), or "3-H" (hot, heavy, and hazardous). And a robot costs a lot less than a human.

Lori Lachowicz, manager of the Robotic Industries Association, cites studies showing that in the auto industry, the cost of using a robot is around one-third the cost of a human worker. No wonder that one-third or more of all robots are in the auto industry.

So far, there haven't been many complaints from humans who work alongside robots. But that's mostly because robots do those jobs that human workers don't want to do, and because robots still haven't taken many jobs away from humans. It could be a different story once those third-generation robots appear. By then, we'll have whole factories that employ almost nothing but robots.

We need the cost savings that robots can bring in order to make and keep American industry competitive in world trade. That means that more of us will have to learn how to work alongside smart robots. It also means that we'll have to develop other jobs for American workers displaced by robots.

One positive sign is that the new United Autoworkers Union contracts with General Motors Corp. and the Ford Motor Co. created huge funds ($1 billion at GM and $330 million at Ford) to, among other things, compensate workers displaced by just such technical advances as robots.

● **From robots that can think to computers that are actually alive, the future of the computer age is rapidly approaching. Exactly where it will go is by no means certain. But, given the impact computers have had over the past decade, you can be sure its effects will be profound.**

● Introduction

Only forty-five years ago, vacuum tubes controlled the electrical circuits in computers. Today, scientists dream of "growing" electronic circuits from protein material. In the 1930s and 1940s, robots played important roles in science fiction. Today robots are no longer visions of the future. They are working in our factories and helping our young people learn in school. A February 1964 *U.S. News and World Report* article, "Is the Computer Running Wild?" announced that the first computers run by integrated circuits would make their debut that year. Today, Hewlett-Packard scientists have placed 450,000 transistors on a single, quarter-inch-square silicon chip. Computer technology has advanced so rapidly that computer scientists who grew up on vacuum tubes, transistors, and science fiction are performing research in biochips and gallium arsenide.

The gains in technology have benefited many areas: artificial intelligence, robotics, medicine and science, home use, and education. This chapter discusses some of the current directions and concerns in these fields as well as some trends in hardware technology.

● Trends in Hardware Technology

In 1958, Jack S. Kilby of Texas Instruments introduced the first integrated circuit. It was a crude little piece of metal with several fine wires and other components sandwiched with solder. Later, Robert N. Noyce of Fairchild Semiconductor designed another type of integrated circuit that better protected the circuits on the chip. Soon a single chip less than one-eighth of an inch square contained sixty-four complete circuits. The number of circuits etched on a single chip continued to increase until, in September 1984, IBM announced a defect-free prototype of a one million bit (megabit) chip. Circuits have become so miniaturized that writers describe them in terms of angels dancing on the head of a pin and house-by-house maps of large cities etched on postage stamps (see Figure 18-1).

Still scientists explore the building of very high speed, ultralarge-scale integrated circuits. Experts predict that by 1990 a single chip may contain as many as sixteen million transistors. Packing many components in such a small space reduces the distance that electricity travels and achieves extremely fast computer speeds.

When electronic components are crowded closer together to decrease these distances, however, two problems arise. The first problem is one that plagued the users of early computers: the generation of heat. The densely packed circuits in ultralarge-scale integrated circuits create enough heat and use enough power to burn out the chips. The second problem is an offshoot of the first. As circuits are crowded closer together, the chance increases that one circuit will receive unwanted signals from nearby circuits in what is often termed *cross talk*. (Cross talk resembles the problem you may experience when making a long-distance telephone call and hearing another conversation in the background.) The following sections discuss several ways in which scientists are solving these problems: the raw materials for making chips, laser technology,

A Computer Chip
This chip with 450,000 transistors provides as much computing power as yesterday's room-sized computer yet is only large enough to cover Lincoln's head on a penny.

and parallel processing. Many people feel the development of technologies that solve these problems is signaling a movement into the fifth computer generation.

CHIP TECHNOLOGY

As scientists address these problems, they try different materials to make chips. For example, silicon may have met its match in a material called gallium arsenide. Integrated circuits made with gallium arsenide achieve speeds five to seven times those of the fastest silicon computer chips. Gallium arsenide chips also require lower voltages to operate, generate less heat, and create less cross talk than silicon chips. Although expensive, the chips are being used in a variety of ways. Their speed makes them suitable for use in supercomputers. Because the chips resist radiation, they can be used effectively in missile guidance, electronic warfare, radar systems, and surveillance satellites.

Perhaps the most revolutionary idea in chip development is the **biochip,** which exists in theory only. Some scientists believe that tiny computer circuits can be grown from the proteins and enzymes of living material such as *E. coli* bacteria. Like other life forms, they would require oxygen and the signals they would send would be most like those sent and received by our brains. Since biochips would be made from a living material, they could repair and reproduce themselves. They would be ten million times as powerful as today's most advanced computers.

Biochips might first be used as "microscopic noses" that could sense odors indicating unusual or dangerous conditions. The chips could also be implanted in a person's brain and linked to a visual sensor like a miniature camera in order to help the blind see. Some biochips placed in the human bloodstream could monitor and correct chemical imbalances. Although the idea of biochips may seem farfetched, scientists are already experimenting with genetic engineering, altering or designing the genetic material of plants and animals. Examples include the manufacture of human insulin and the human growth hormone, interferon. Can biochips be far behind?

LASER TECHNOLOGY

Lasers aid computer technology in an important way: they carry signals through hair-thin fibers of the purest glass in a technology known as **fiber optics.** Optical fibers carry tiny staccato pulses of light that can turn on and off ninety million times per second. Fiber-optic cables are being used for linking computer terminals and mainframes in large industrial complexes (see Figure 18–2). They are also rapidly replacing conventional telephone lines in many cities, such as Fort Wayne, Indiana, and in long-distance lines across the United States. Fiber optics offers several advantages. Transmission of data by fiber optics is faster and more accurate than transmission by ordinary telephone lines. The actual cables are small: an optical cable one-half inch in diameter can carry as much data as a copper cable as thick as a person's arm. The fibers are immune to electromagnetic and noise interference and are difficult to tap. Finally, the raw material used to make the fibers is sand, a cheap and common resource. The advantages of fiber optics will increase the attractiveness of using telecommunications for banking, shopping, and medical purposes.

Manufacturers of computer chips may also benefit from the use of laser beams. An ultraprecise laser beam could be used as a tiny blowtorch in correcting defective chips, sometimes 50 to 65 percent of the total production. Eventually, researchers hope to use lasers, computers, and robots in building circuits on chips and automatically making all the interconnections between the circuits.

● **FIGURE 18–2**
A Fiber-Optic Cable

PARALLEL PROCESSING

Traditional processing occurs serially. A single channel carries all the data bit by bit, one by one, between primary storage and the control unit. The concepts of multiprogramming and virtual storage give the illusion to multiple users that a computer is performing many tasks at once. The computer is really processing several programs during the same period of time by rotating segments of the programs in quick succession.

The human brain, on the other hand, processes information in parallel sequence. It deals with large amounts of data and handles many different cognitive tasks effortlessly and *simultaneously*. Innovative forms of hardware architecture facilitate **parallel processing** by computer. Parallel processing imitates the brain's behavior by dividing a problem into several portions and processing the portions simultaneously. The architecture involves two or more CPUs or microprocessors.

Parallel processing increases computer speed without further miniaturizing the circuitry and encountering the problems associated with densely packed electronic components. Applications using parallel processing occur on supercomputers and include speech understanding, interpretation of data from many sensing devices, simulations, navigation uses, and artificial intelligence.

● Artificial Intelligence

The term *number crunching* was born in the vacuum tube era of computing when mathematicians, scientists, and engineers used the machines for manipulating huge amounts of numerical data. Even today number crunching is what most computers do best. As programmers and developers of computer languages become more proficient at designing advanced software, however, number crunching will give way to more conceptual applications. Scientists will need faster, more powerful computers for these applications, which include voice recognition, robotics, and the ability to understand natural language.

The new computers and languages only begin to imitate human intelligence at higher levels of abstraction. Humanlike thinking, common sense, self-teaching, and decision-making skills performed by machines are termed **artificial intelligence (AI).** Since human intelligence is not clearly understood, current AI programs incorporate just a few aspects of it. The most common AI applications are **expert systems.** These systems imitate an expert in a field, drawing conclusions and making recommendations based on huge data bases of information and on *heuristics*, guidelines that help reduce options or uncertainty.

An example of an expert system is Dr. Lawrence Weed's medical diagnosis program, Problem-Knowledge Coupler (PKC). The patient and doctor enter history, symptoms, and test results on the computer keyboard and, after making cross-references, the computer responds with a list of diseases or conditions that the patient might have. This helps the doctor decide on a diagnosis and treatment.

Expert systems also help people in business and industry. Financial Advisor from Palladian Software is used for analyzing financial data for an organization. It takes into account inflation, taxes, and other economic factors. Ford Motor Company has signed an agreement with Carnegie Group of Pittsburgh for the development of programs that can approve credit applications and diagnose brake systems. Westinghouse Electric Corp. uses an expert system for selecting materials for pressurized water-reactive steam generators used in nuclear energy plants.

Many of these expert systems are not prepared from scratch. Rather, they are programmed into software, such as KEE (Knowledge Engineering Environment by Intellicorp), a "shell" or frame on which to build a tailor-made expert system for a particular user.

Many experts in AI contend that expert systems do not qualify as true AI. Intelligence involves coping with change and incorporating new information for improving performance, and expert systems do neither. The country's top researchers have taken different approaches to the way the wealth of human knowledge must be organized inside the computer. John McCarthy, director of Stanford's Artificial Intelligence Laboratory, is optimistic about the use of **nonmonotonic logic** in building computer knowledge.

Monotonic logic allows conclusions to be drawn from assumptions, and if more assumptions are added, the new conclusions will not make the previous conclusions wrong. For example, "If X is a bird and birds can fly, then X can fly" is monotonic logic. But what if X is a dead bird or a penguin? As you can see, monotonic logic doesn't always hold true. Nonmonotonic logic adapts to this by saying "X can fly unless something prevents it." In other words, it allows for unusual situations.

Another approach is being taken by other researchers, primarily Marvin Minsky at Massachusetts Institute of Technology and Roger Schank at Yale University. It is based on the **script theory,** which says that in any particular situation, humans have an idea of how the thinking or dialogue would go. For instance, we each have a dentist's office script, a classroom script, and a restaurant script. Memories of past events are usually filed in our minds under keys associated with the structure of these scripts.

What these researchers want is to give the computer a way to use common sense and make inferences based on the situation at hand. They realize, though, that the inferences need some boundaries. It is defining and programming these boundaries that presents the challenge. If AI is to be developed further, experts need more accurate descriptions of human thought processes, improved programming for imitating those processes, large data bases, and improved hardware architecture.

Advances in AI will lead to natural English communication with computers. Intelligent computers could read books, newspapers, journals, and magazines and prepare summaries of the material. They could scan mail and sort all letters but those with the most illegible addresses. Used in education, AI could help students learn to read, remember, and think and also help researchers understand how people think. Among the current applications for advanced AI systems are voice recognition systems and robotics.

VOICE RECOGNITION

Although the simplest way to input data into a computer is to speak, voice recognition technology is still primitive. Today's systems may recognize many words but they are usually limited to one speaker or one pitch range. "Speaker-independent" systems—those that accept a variety of voices—cost more than $10,000 and have a vocabulary limited to one or two dozen words. More versatile systems must be trained by the user to understand a particular vocabulary and recognize the user's voice pitch, accent, and inflection (see Figure 18–3). Each word must be enunciated and spoken discretely, that is, not run together with other words in a phrase. And heaven forbid that the user catch a cold!

Because of these limitations, voice recognition is best used with short-answer data. Tomorrow's systems will improve with advancements in AI and computer memory. Research in voice recognition now focuses on the ability to accept larger vocabularies, different voices, and continuous, or flowing, speech.

Some experts believe that keyboardless systems based on voice recognition and AI will become popular in the future. Users could hook the systems to their telephone lines to access just about any data base, leave messages on electronic bulletin boards, and conduct transactions—all without a single keystroke. Such systems would need to recognize natural language and overcome the problems associated with syntax and ambiguity. Users would not need to type specific codes or speak according to a standard question format but could simply request information in the same way they might ask another person. They could also direct computers to write application programs from general descriptions of needs. Natural language would provide a simple yet precise way of stating these descriptions. (See Chapter 10 for a discussion of natural languages.)

● FIGURE 18–3
Voice Recognition System
A voice-data entry system in GE's Maryland appliance plant lets workers talk directly to a computer as they monitor the quality of parts moving past on a conveyor.

ROBOTICS

Robotics will change as AI develops, too. Scientists are working hard to develop robots that are more mobile and sophisticated. Existing robots are deficient in four areas: vision, touch, mobility, and methods of instruction.

Perhaps the most crucial problem to overcome is that of vision. Robots see in only two dimensions, length and width; unlike humans they do not judge depth. Some scientists are designing robots that use fiber-optic "eyes" as tiny cameras for relaying images to their computers. As AI becomes more sophisticated, engineers can program robots to "see" objects and rotate them until recognition is possible. Robots with this capability work as bin-pickers, sorting different parts from huge baskets of parts used in building machinery or other products. When special chips designed for processing and analyzing images are perfected, the robots can recognize objects much faster through parallel processing. With these advances, robots would be able to navigate throughout a person's home without bumping into objects. A robot could travel to the next room through a door, rather than being stopped by the wall. In addition, when confronted with an object in its path, the robot could decide whether to roll over it, move it out of the way, travel around it, or call for help.

A second difficulty, robot touch, has improved greatly with the development of sophisticated sensors. Some robots are equipped with several kinds of hands—after all, a robot does not really care what it looks like! Ichiro Kato has developed a robot hand dexterous enough to play a Schumann melody on the piano. Karen Hensley, a robot researcher, designed a hand that enables a robot to turn a doorknob. In a janitorial catalogue, she found a gripper that janitors use on the end of a long pole for changing light bulbs on high ceilings. Hensley's "hand" will be worn by Pluto, a robot developed by Hans Moravec, a professor at the Robotics Institute in Pittsburgh. Other robot hands can pick up a raw egg as easily as a heavy paperweight. Computer-driven robot arms can feed a bedridden patient and assist in nursing care.

Although most sensors are used to give robots skills in handling objects, scientists are experimenting with sensors that enable a robot to maintain balance while walking. Most of today's mobile robots travel on wheels, with the front two wheels providing the power to move and the back one or two wheels acting as balancers. Walking robots must maintain their own balance, and how do you program balance? Research in designing walking robots has been aided by a desk-high robot that bounces around on one leg, as if riding a pogo stick. The longer the robot can keep its balance, the more successful the engineers have been.

Finally, a robot is useless without an adequate way to receive instructions, learn new tasks, and even make rudimentary decisions. Most industrial robots are just one or two steps away from human-operated machines. The features that distinguish them are their typical crane, or arm, shape and their ability to operate by themselves once the instructions are completed. Although current software can guide a robot to perform welding jobs, drill holes, trim vinyl dashboards, paint fenders, sort parts for manufacturing processes, and assemble minute electronic components, robots cannot use a bank of programs in learning a new

A New Wave in Voice Recognition

A new discovery by Victor Zue, a scientist at MIT, may change the course of voice recognition research. While watching spectrograms (computer-enhanced versions of the electrical wave forms of speech), he noticed that the spectrograms contained common features for each sound. For example, no matter who was speaking, the spectrogram depicted the s sound in stop as a dark rectangular wedge. Zue identified hundreds of these common features. Speech scientists at Carnegie-Mellon University in Pittsburgh believed that if Zue could read the spectrograms, a computer could, too. They programmed a computer to recognize the shapes and patterns that Zue had catalogued as universal in certain words, no matter who spoke them.

An advanced system based on Zue's idea is already being used by the National Security Agency for monitoring overseas telephone calls. By recognizing key words, NSA's supercomputers can isolate and record suspicious calls. On a more commercial level, Kurzweil Applied Intelligence in Waltham, Massachusetts, is testing a typewriter that will print almost 10,000 spoken words. What a boon this machine would be to handicapped people! Quadriplegics could use such a machine for writing letters, making telephone calls, and communicating by radio. Advanced voice systems could also be used by elderly or handicapped people for instructing robots that would fetch things, help with chores, or call an emergency number if an accident happened.

job or making decisions. Software is only now enabling robots to distinguish shapes in three dimensions. In order to pass rigorous tests for home or hospital use, a mobile robot or robot arm must be able to distinguish between a glass of water and a cup of soup. It must recognize its master's voice and respond to natural language commands. It must recognize objects in its path and determine whether to proceed or stop. It must be able to sense how fast it is moving and how tightly it is clutching. And it must be able to synthesize existing programs so that the user can program it by simple English statements to do new tasks. All these abilities stem from research into human learning behavior and AI (see Figure 18–4). Researchers at the Veterans Administration Hospital in Palo Alto, California, are only beginning to realize the potential of such robots. At the hospital, a quadriplegic learns to work with a robot that will fetch objects, help him eat, and hold a book. Perhaps one day robots will help quadriplegics the way seeing-eye dogs help the blind.

CONCEPT SUMMARY 18–1

Improvements in Technology

IDEA	IMPROVEMENT
Gallium arsenide chips	These chips are five to seven times faster than silicon chips, and help avoid the problem of cross talk
Biochips	Although chips in theory only, biochips would be much smaller and more powerful than today's chips and could be used to improve the condition of the human body
Parallel processing	This concept would allow computers to use two or more CPUs to process data simultaneously rather than in sequence
Lasers	Lasers in fiber optics improve telecommunications, and lasers can be used in the manufacture of chips
Voice recognition	New voice-recognition systems would be able to accept larger vocabularies, different voices, and continuous or flowing speech
Robotics	Research in robots is geared toward improving robot vision, touch, mobility, and methods of receiving instruction

● Computers in Medicine

Medical personnel diagnose illnesses, provide treatments, and monitor patients. Computer technology is used in facilitating the timeliness and accuracy of these jobs, which in turn affects the quality of life.

COMPUTER-ASSISTED DIAGNOSIS

Computers are increasingly combined with testing equipment to provide diagnostic tools in hospitals and clinics (see Figure 18–5). Four common forms—multiphasic health testing, expert systems, computerized axial

● **FIGURE 18-4**
Synthesizing Concepts of AI into a Robot

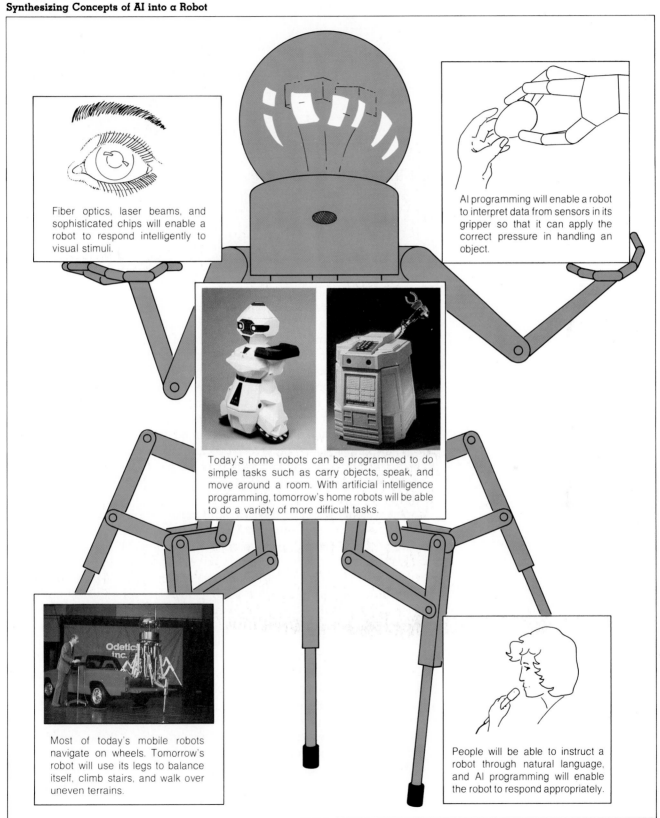

Fiber optics, laser beams, and sophisticated chips will enable a robot to respond intelligently to visual stimuli.

AI programming will enable a robot to interpret data from sensors in its gripper so that it can apply the correct pressure in handling an object.

Today's home robots can be programmed to do simple tasks such as carry objects, speak, and move around a room. With artificial intelligence programming, tomorrow's home robots will be able to do a variety of more difficult tasks.

Most of today's mobile robots navigate on wheels. Tomorrow's robot will use its legs to balance itself, climb stairs, and walk over uneven terrains.

People will be able to instruct a robot through natural language, and AI programming will enable the robot to respond appropriately.

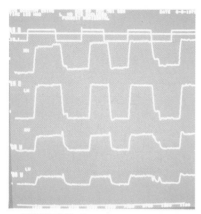

● **FIGURE 18–5**
Computers in Diagnosis
Graphic representation of a patient's eye motion is depicted by the CENOG on the screen (left). An operator at a computer terminal monitors the patient in the testing chamber (right).

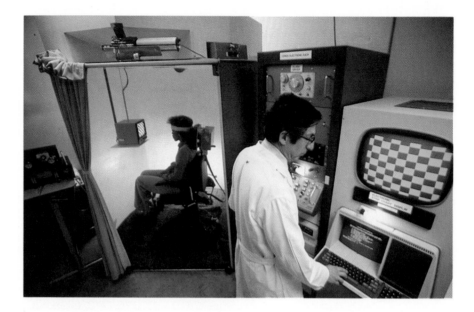

tomography, and nuclear magnetic resonance scanning—help with preventive health care and offer nonsurgical testing techniques. In **multiphasic health testing,** computer equipment aids in performing a series of tests, stores the results of the tests, and reports the results to doctors. Physical examinations are performed by trained technicians and paramedics using the computer equipment. Procedures include electrocardiograms, X-ray tests, blood tests, vision and hearing tests, blood pressure tests, and height and weight measurement. The computer system compares the results of the tests to predetermined standards of normal health. The patient's physician receives a report of the test results and meets with the patient. Multiphasic testing permits the doctor to spend more time on diagnosis and treatment, and can be valuable in preventive health care.

Expert systems also help physicians in making diagnoses. Among these systems are Mycin, developed at Stanford University for diagnosing blood diseases, and Chest Pain, developed by Dr. Evlin Kinney, a research cardiologist in Miami Beach, Florida, for analyzing chest pain. The latter program was built on an existing expert system shell, Expert Ease, from Human Edge Software in Palo Alto, California. Dr. Kinney cautions, however, that medical expert systems provide only one more factor for consideration in making a diagnosis. The physician may want to reason through his or her conclusions again if they differ from the diagnosis offered by the expert system.

Computerized axial tomography, commonly known as CAT scanning, is a diagnostic aid that joins two tools—X-rays and computerized evaluations of X-ray pictures. A CAT scan can do something that ordinary X-ray tests cannot: it can provide clear pictures of cross-sections of the body. Using many cross-sections together provides a three-dimensional composite of an organ or bone (see Figure 18–6).

Medical Data Systems of Ann Arbor, Michigan, has taken the CAT scan one step further. The company markets a computer system that

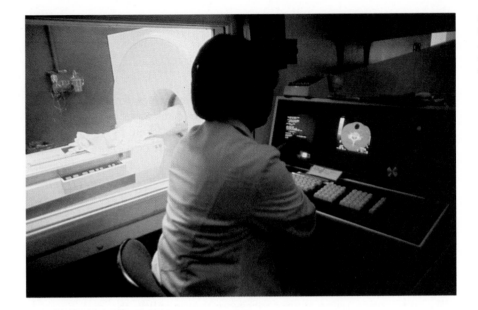

constructs a three-dimensional image of an organ on a video monitor and also recreates the actual movement of the organ in the simulated organ on the screen. Doctors are able to identify parts of the organ that are not functioning normally.

Nuclear magnetic resonance (NMR) scanning may soon replace the CAT scan in hospitals. Unlike X-ray tests or CAT scans, NMR can "see" through thick bones. Moreover, NMR works without radiation. Magnetic pulses sent through the body react differently when they come into contact with different parts of the body. A computer is used for collecting the results and creating a detailed picture of the inside of the body. Often NMR scanning is more successful in detecting problems than CAT scanning. Since the procedure does not use radiation, it can be used for testing children and pregnant women. There are some drawbacks to NMR scanning, however. For example, it does not produce clear images of bones or spot breast cancer.

Both CAT scans and NMR scans allow doctors to conduct tests without invading the body through surgery. This prevents the infections, blood clots, and fatigue associated with surgery.

Computers also help ensure the success of reconstructive surgery. Computer-generated pictures can predict the results of reconstructive surgery. In the case of a patient with a deformed skull, CAT scan cross-sections are used to produce three-dimensional pictures of the skull. The computer studies the results of the CAT scan and presents a picture of the skull after reconstruction. Models based on the computer picture help the doctor plan the proper surgical techniques. They also help the patient visualize the outcome of the surgery.

The applications of computers in medicine are almost limitless. Perhaps by the end of the 1980s computers will be used for testing the skills and efficiency of doctors. Computers may also be combined with robots for performing delicate surgery, sometimes from another location across the country. In addition, computers will be used increasingly in hospitals and doctors' offices in the everyday record-keeping and accounting procedures of any business.

COMPUTER-ASSISTED TREATMENT

New uses for computers in treatment are emerging daily, while other uses are being improved. For example, due to microprocessors, today's pacemakers are lighter in weight than earlier models. In addition, they can simulate the beating of a healthy heart: doctors can enter up to thirty separate functions, such as delay between pulses, pulse width, and energy output per pulse. In this way, a pacemaker can deal with each patient's particular heart problems.

Microprocessors also control the movements of artificial limbs. Electrical signals from muscles in an amputee's upper arms, for instance, can generate natural movements in an artificial arm and hand. These new artificial limbs are so sophisticated that they are powerful enough to open jars or crack walnuts, yet deft enough to pick up a tomato or a styrofoam cup full of coffee.

An application using microprocessors that is still in the experimental stages involves the controlled release of medication or other treatments by devices implanted in the body (see Figure 18–7). One device currently undergoing testing is called PIMS (Programmable Implantable Medicine System). PIMS is a three-inch computer that is programmed to release measured doses of a drug over time. When a drug is taken orally, once or twice a day, it is distributed throughout the whole body. Frequently, only a small amount of the drug reaches the correct organ. Also, the amount of the drug present in the bloodstream varies over time as each dose is administered. PIMS and other similar devices are designed to overcome these problems. One experimental device being tested by diabetic patients dispenses a forty-day supply of insulin from a refillable reservoir using a miniature pump. The reservoir is refilled with a hypo-

● **FIGURE 18–7**
The Itrel Spinal Cord Stimulation System
This implantable spinal cord stimulator is used for management of chronic, intractable pain. It produces electrical signals that block pain messages traveling to the brain. The stimulator can be programmed by either the console or the handheld programmer.

dermic needle. Radio telemetry and a desktop computer console allow doctors to monitor a diabetic's blood sugar level and reprogram the rate at which the pump dispenses medicine. The device has the potential of eliminating some of the life-threatening side effects of diabetes.

Another use of computers in the treatment of patients involves using computer-controlled lasers. During surgery, lasers are used to destroy tiny, hard-to-reach tumors once considered inoperable. X-ray films taken before surgery pinpoint the tumor's location. The surgeon uses a powerful microscope with a laser attached to it to locate the tumor. After correctly positioning a dot of light that indicates where the laser will strike when activated, the surgeon presses a foot pedal that fires the laser and destroys the tumor. Computer-controlled lasers are also being used in the treatment of kidney stones. A patient being treated for kidney stones is submerged in a tank of water and a computer-controlled laser is aimed at the stone, already located by use of X-rays and dye injections. When the laser strikes the kidney stone, it is dissolved into minute harmless particles. Conventional treatment of kidney stones involves major surgery. The laser technique does not require cutting into the body cavity, thereby eliminating the complications of surgery and reducing the recovery period for the patient.

● Computers in Science

Scientists perform calculations, simulate real situations, and observe equipment and conditions while doing their research. Because of the enormous volumes of data that must be stored and processed for some scientific tasks, scientists use large computers for handling the data and producing output in a form that is easy to read and interpret. Often the tasks that require large amounts of data involve monitoring the environment, chemical industries, nuclear power plants, and the weather. Immediate alert to problems in these areas is crucial. For example, the crisis that occurred at the Three Mile Island nuclear power plant when the temperature of the nuclear reactor exceeded safe limits and threatened to melt down the core may be avoided in the future with emergency management systems. The life-endangering gas leak at the Union Carbide plant in Bhopal, India, might have been prevented with computerized warning systems.

An emergency management system developed by Form & Substance in Westlake Village, California, was designed for the chemical industry and contains information such as the properties of the chemicals manufactured at the particular plant site, evaporation rates of the chemicals, the influence of the surrounding land on wind patterns and flow, and backup plans of any number of possible accident situations. The computerized data bank is constantly updated with information supplied by chemical sensors around the plant. These sensors keep track of temperature, toxin levels, and wind velocity and direction (see Figure 18–8).

In the event of an emergency, the system will supply instructions and appropriate emergency telephone numbers for notifying authorities and warning nearby residents. Similar emergency management systems are

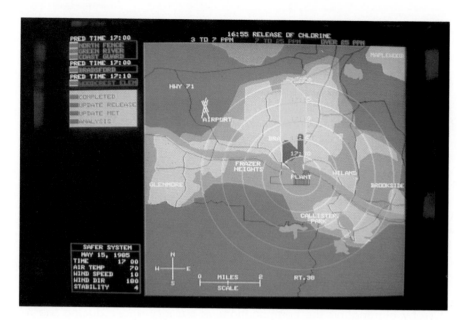

● **FIGURE 18-8**

Emergency Management System
The SAFER system (left) is an emergency response system that alerts industrial companies to toxic releases that could pose potential harm to the employees and the neighboring area. The system displays actions to take in a variety of emergency situations. The display frame (right) illustrates the essential graphic information helpful in an emergency.

required in nuclear power plants by the Federal Nuclear Regulatory Commission. Following the April 1986 core meltdown in a nuclear plant at Chernobyl in the Soviet Union, U.S. officials and citizens will be even more concerned about safety and warning systems in North American nuclear plants. Although an emergency management system will not guarantee that a crisis can be resolved, it will make emergency evacuation and response much more efficient.

The forecasting of weather is one of the most interesting applications of computers. Several variables, such as air pressure, wind velocity, humidity, and temperature are fed into huge computers for the processing of complex mathematical equations that describe the interaction of these variables. By combining the data with mathematical models, forecasters can predict the weather.

Although local forecasters use radar data directly, they also rely on national and international weather information. The world's weather information is collected by the National Weather Service in Maryland (see Figure 18-9) from a variety of locations: hundreds of data-collecting programs (DCPs) placed on buoys, ships, weather balloons, and airplanes; about seventy weather stations; and four satellites. Two of the satellites orbit the earth over the poles and send pictures revealing the movement and shape of clouds. The other two satellites are in stationary orbits above the equator.

The Weather Service's "brain" consists of fourteen computers housed at the meteorological center. These computers receive information from some of the DCPs whose data are beamed up to the two stationary satellites above the equator. The computers also receive information from other DCPs; the information travels from ground station to ground station. The fourteen computers use all of this incoming data to construct a mathematical description of the atmosphere. These weather reports—2,000 daily—are sent to local weather offices. Manual processing would take

● **COMPUTERS AND INFORMATION PROCESSING**

so much time that the results would not be available until the weather conditions had already occurred.

Another application of scientific monitoring involves volcano watching. The May 1980 prediction of the eruption of Mount St. Helens in the state of Washington was predicted by scientists with the help of data analyzed by computers. Devices such as tiltmeters, which show trends in the tilt of the crater floor, and seismometers, which measure harmonic tremors around the volcano, sent data to a laboratory in Vancouver, Washington, every ten minutes. In the laboratory, computers analyzed that data, helping scientists predict volcanic activity. Because instruments like these are located inside the volcano, volcanic eruptions can be predicted within thirty minutes; this allows time for scientists working near and on the volcano to be quickly evacuated by helicopter. One thing that cannot be predicted, however, is the fury of the eruption and the extent of the mudflow it creates. Mount St. Helens, one of the most heavily monitored volcanoes in the world, surprised the scientists monitoring it with the heavy mudflow that followed its eruption.

Computers can also control scientific instruments and devices. The use of computers in this area frees the scientists to spend valuable time conducting other experiments rather than overseeing the instruments. For example, computers reduce both the time and cost involved in the study of cells at the California Institute of Technology in Pasadena. Deoxyribonucleic acid (DNA) is a chemical that carries genetic information in human cells (see Figure 18–10). Strands of DNA once were synthesized (cloned) by a manual process that took weeks and sometimes months, and cost from $2,000 to $3,000. A computer can perform the same task in less than a day for only $2 to $3. Since the procedure involves much repetition, it was easy for technicians to make mistakes. By turning the tasks over to a computer, the mistakes were eliminated and the procedure became more economical.

● **FIGURE 18–10**
DNA Synthesis
This is a computer-generated reconstruction of DNA.

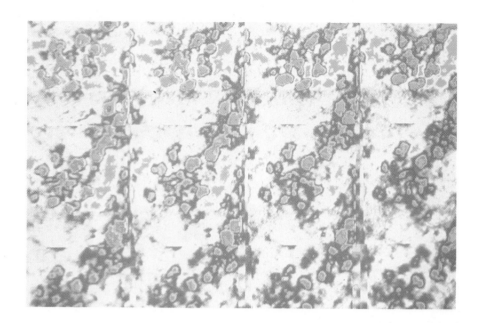

CONCEPT
SUMMARY 18–2

Computers in Medicine and Science

Diagnosis	Multiphasic health testing
	Expert systems
	Computerized axial tomography (CAT) scanning
	Nuclear magnetic resonance (NMR)
Monitoring	Emergency management systems (for chemical plants and nuclear plants)
	Weather
	Volcanic activity
Procedures	Pacemakers
	Artificial limbs
	PIMS (Programmable Implantable Medicine System)
	Laser surgery
	Synthetic DNA

◉ Computers for All of Us

Much of our discussion has centered on computer technology that benefits research and industry. Eventually, the technology will trickle down to the microcomputer user. In the meantime, what can we expect in the near future in the areas of personal computers, laser technology, and education? The following sections discuss ways in which we might use the new technologies at home and examine some issues involved with our increased dependence upon computers and related technologies.

MICROCOMPUTERS AT HOME

Despite the slump in sales of microcomputers for home use, many analysts predict sales will go up when new and faster computers are introduced. In addition, they believe that more people will get used to making transactions through home computers and trying out home control and robotic devices linked to microcomputers. People will try out these applications for fun, preferring human interaction for most transactions and believing that home control and robots cannot be cost-justified. As the technology becomes more prevalent, more families will become accustomed to these applications as routine. They will avoid the costs of driving and the irritation of traffic in running small errands, and they will find ways to decrease the responsibilities of chores in a two-income family. Homes of the future will not only be labor- and energy-saving for the homeowner, but also will help handicapped people in achieving independence.

The microcomputers that will be used at home in the future will have powerful graphics and computational capabilities. They will use less power than a 150-watt lightbulb. Screen displays will be larger and have a higher degree of resolution. The amount of primary storage will increase to handle many types of applications including artificial intelligence and intelligent tutors. And the prices will be affordable for most families.

Families will use their computers and telephones to conduct some banking and purchasing transactions and keep up with the status of their bank accounts, credit ratings, and store charges (see Figure 18–11). They will receive video versions of major newspapers, stock market reports, restaurant listings, computer graphic art, music, and movie reviews. They will be able to finish high school or take college courses for credit through their microcomputers. They will learn to program their computers

● **FIGURE 18–11**
A Home Information System

for customized tasks by inputting commands in English (or whatever language they speak naturally). Finally, they will use microcomputers increasingly in controlling the home environment and security. The center of the home may even move from the kitchen and fireplace to a new center, the electronic hearth where all these activities will take place.

In addition, more people will own personal robots that actually are useful rather than merely entertaining. The robots will perform household chores such as laundry and house cleaning.

In Arizona, a computer-controlled house has been built as a showcase of automated systems. Called Ahwatukee (a Crow Indian word meaning "house of dreams"), this house is described as the state of the art in technology, ecology, and sociology. Visitors come by the thousands each month to view the house in a half-hour tour. Five microcomputers are linked to run the five systems in the house. Heating, cooling, and the opening and shutting of doors and windows is the primary function of the environmental control system. The security system protects against intruders with the use of television cameras, sensors, and a password-controlled front door. The sensors also watch for fire and will sound a warning if necessary. An electrical switching system uses sensors to note people moving through the house and adjust lights appropriately. Cost-efficient use of electricity is assured with the energy management system, and an information storage and retrieval system is provided for personal or home business needs.

Another such house, called Xanadu, Home of the Future, is located in Kissimmee, Florida. This "intelligent home of the future" features such attractions as a robotic chess set, an electronic art gallery, a children's electronic learning center, and an automatic clothes retrieval system that stores and cleans all clothing (see Figure 18–12).

Less elaborate systems are available for just about any home user. These systems govern appliance use and regulate energy consumption and ventilation. Among them are TomorrowHouse from Compu-Home Systems International in Denver, Colorado; Waldo from Artra Corporation in Arlington, Virginia; and HomeBrain from HyperTek in Whitehouse, New Jersey.

INTERACTIVE VIDEO

The combination of optical disks and computer programming has created a promising tool called **interactive video.** Some educators believe it will replace the computer, the instructional film, and perhaps even textbooks in many fields. Interactive video merges graphics and sound with computer-generated text by linking an optical disk (videodisk), a videodisk player, a microcomputer with a color monitor and disk drive, and computer software. Using this equipment, a person can watch news footage of historical events, learn about the most current advances in science, and listen to the music of great composers or the speeches of famous people. The interactive process begins when the user responds to computer-generated questions and forms inquiries to input into the system. The videodisk can be accessed at a chosen point, and motion sequences can be shown in slow motion or still frame for observing critical details.

a. The kitchen/greenhouse produces its own fresh fruits and vegetables, while meals are planned, prepared, and served by computer-controlled devices.

b. The children's room is a private entertainment and education center.

● **FIGURE 18–12**
Xanadu, Home of the Future

c. Xanadu's Exterior.

Videodisk technology will change the way we share information. As a student, you may receive a homework package consisting of software on a floppy disk and graphics on a videodisk to play on your equipment at home. As an employee, you could use the technology for learning how to show new cars, trade shares on a stock exchange, or maintain and repair large earth-moving equipment. As a consumer, you will buy huge data bases of information on any topic ranging from medical subjects to career guidance or browse through videodisk catalogs of the latest merchandise. Interactive video has become so attractive that some people believe the videodisk player will become the most important peripheral device of this decade. The technology will become even more appealing when disks are developed that can be erased and reused. It will become one more technology to add to our electronic hearth.

Enhancing Research and Technology

Computers have made a major impact in laboratories around the world. They can simplify complex or time-consuming experiments and have opened up new areas of research never imagined until the advent of computers. Ironically, computers themselves have revolutionized the manufacturing of microchips, the miniature components that give all computers their power.

In the future, easy-to-use input and output devices may help large numbers of people become more comfortable with computers. This experimental touch tablet displays color blocks to indicate the position and force of multiple touches. Systems like this could let people use their fingers to communicate with machines quickly and precisely.

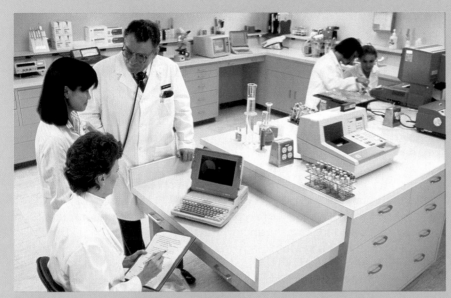

Scientists are using computers to record and analyze data in research laboratories. Calculations that once took hours to complete manually are now being completed in split seconds on computers.

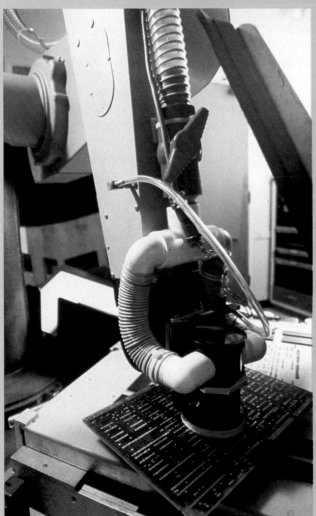

Circuit boards with complex wiring must be checked for errors. Computer-controlled robots are used by many companies to speed up this tedious checking process.

Once hand-drawn on huge pieces of paper and converted into computer memory by a process called digitizing, computer circuits are now planned by computer-aided design (CAD) technology. A designer enters data by drawing with a light pen at a graphics terminal.

THE CARD: WHO'S WATCHING WHOM?

If our lives do not become centered around an electronic hearth, another technology has the potential for governing our lives. It is "smart cards," plastic cards or keys with embedded information. So far, smart cards are used only for specialized functions. Blue Cross-Blue Shield is issuing the LifeCard, a wallet-sized card on which medical history is stored by laser beam (see Figure 18–13). In Japan, Nipponcoinco vending machines accept laser cards as payment for food. The machine reduces the card's value, originally $40, each time the user buys food. Other cards will be used for recording car repairs, guiding a student's learning, and reporting economic news. The cards act almost like credit cards, and the owner controls their use.

Why not have just one card containing a dedicated computer that performs all personal and financial transactions? Such a card may be more of a reality than we think, says George Morrow, founder and chairman of the board of Morrow, Inc., maker of personal computers and other computer equipment (see Figure 18–14). Banks and creditors face mounting piles of paper, bad checks, and unpaid bills. They have already begun to solve the first problem through automatic tellers and EFT, and people now accept the use of credit cards. The next step could be a card that would identify you, provide a personal audit, balance your checkbook, and pay your utility bills. You would use the card to buy food and clothing. You would never have to balance a checkbook, worry about money being lost in the mail, or face being mugged. Banks and stores would benefit because you could not buy goods without having sufficient funds to cover your purchases. Criminals and thieves could be easily tracked: in a cashless society, they could make no purchases without their cards. In addition, a remote computer could sense when a convicted

criminal travels more than two blocks from home. People with a drinking and driving violation or more than four speeding tickets could no longer buy gasoline because a remote computer would program their cards, denying them that privilege. Even governments would benefit. Cash-only deals would be eliminated, guaranteeing the federal government its income tax and state and local governments their sales taxes.

Although many benefits could be realized from using these cards, there are negative implications, too. Governments would have control of every-one's money and could thereby ensure "correct" behavior. The cards could monitor the kinds of things we buy. Our tastes in reading material might be recorded and categorized as "acceptable," "suspicious," or "criminal." People in marketing research could access our records and determine purchasing and travel habits. Our cards could not be used to purchase candy and pie if we were overweight. We might have to use the cards to take breaks at work. Our lives could revolve around the cards.

EDUCATION: THE NEWLY DISADVANTAGED?

Some futurists believe that one day almost every type of job will require employees to use computers. Education will certainly change through computer use and access to data bases. Most transactions will take place via computers and telecommunications. People with little computer ex-perience will be profoundly affected. They will not be able to access a data base, read the material on the screen, or hold a job that requires a great deal of computer use. Therefore, some educators are pressing for extensive computer education in schools.

Computer education includes computer literacy and computer pro-gramming. Computer literacy courses teach technical knowledge about computers, ability to use computers in solving problems, and awareness of how computers affect society. Programming classes often involve learning to program a computer in the popular languages BASIC and Pascal.

On the other hand, other researchers believe that computer education as a prerequisite for jobs is largely a myth. They say that only a small percentage of jobs will require actual knowledge of technical areas in-volving electronic circuits, computer programming, and hardware. Rather, they believe that reading and thinking skills and general knowledge will distinguish the haves from the have-nots. If computers are to be used, they must become tools in learning these skills. Educators group software packages meant for teaching into an all-encompassing category: **com-puter-assisted Instruction (CAI).** Through CAI, students encounter a pa-tient "teacher" that allows them to learn at their own rates, receive im-mediate feedback, and feel comfortable with both successes and mis-takes. Included in CAI is a wide selection of software:

- Drills for quizzing the student.
- Tutorials for introducing students to new material and skills and quiz-zing them on their understanding of the material.
- Simulations that imitate real-world situations, allowing students to learn through experience and induction without having to take actual risks.
- Games for learning new concepts and practicing new skills.

● Problem-solving software that encourages exploration and application of previous knowledge (see Figure 18–15).

Although a trend toward accountability in measuring how much a student learns may make the drills and tutorials attractive to teachers, educators realize the importance of computer use in developing thinking skills. Among the software packages that do more than drill and tutor are Rocky's Boots and Robot Odyssey I from The Learning Company, Menlo Park, California; Where in the World Is Carmen Sandiego? from Broderbund Software, San Rafael, California; and The Incredible Laboratory, The King's Rule, and The Puzzle Tank from Sunburst Communications, Pleasantville, New York. Adults as well as students use these packages.

Regardless of which computer skills are learned, people are realizing the many ways in which computers can help them learn, conduct business, take care of their health, and achieve competency at work. Although not everyone may learn how to write a computer program or how a computer works, most people can learn to use computers in accepting challenges of the future and enriching their lives.

● Summary Points

● Scientists are working on strategies to overcome two major problems with miniaturizing integrated circuits: heat generation and cross talk.
● Gallium arsenide can be used to make chips that are faster, require less power, generate less heat, and are more resistant to radiation than silicon chips.
● Biochips are chips in name only; no prototypes have been developed. If developed, these chips will be grown from the proteins and enzymes of living material such as *E. coli* bacteria. They could repair and reproduce themselves.

● **FIGURE 18–15**
Microcomputers in School
This student uses a computer as an aid in a chemistry experiment.

- Research in fiber optics aids telecommunication development because digital pulses can be sent through the glass fibers, which are immune to electromagnetic and noise interference, and are difficult to tap.
- Parallel processing will facilitate development of applications using forms of artificial intelligence because processing occurs simultaneously rather than serially.
- Today's artificial intelligence applications are called expert systems. These systems imitate an expert in a field, drawing conclusions and making recommendations based on a huge data base. Some scientists believe expert systems are not true artificial intelligence.
- Principles of AI can improve voice recognition systems. Research focuses on the ability to accept larger vocabularies, different voices, and continuous or flowing speech.
- Artificial intelligence will increase robot powers of sight and touch, help robots walk, and give them the ability to make decisions.
- Computers are increasingly combined with testing equipment to provide diagnostic tools in hospitals and clinics. In multiphasic health testing (MPHT), computer equipment aids in performing a series of tests, stores the results of the tests, and reports the results to doctors. Doctors also use expert systems that help diagnose various conditions, including blood diseases and chest pain, for example.
- Two noninvasive diagnostic aids used in hospitals and clinics are computerized axial tomography (CAT or CT), commonly known as a CAT scan, and nuclear magnetic resonance (NMR) scanning.
- Microprocessors help in treatments, for example, in pacemakers, artificial limbs, and PIMS (Programmable Implantable Medicine System).
- Laser surgery for such conditions as kidney stones allows a surgeon to destroy the offending body without cutting into a person.
- Scientists use computers for solving many problems including monitoring chemical plants, nuclear plants, the weather, and volcanoes. In addition, scientists can use computers for performing repetitious tasks such as creating synthetic DNA, thus freeing themselves for conducting valuable experiments.
- People will begin to use microcomputers for many tasks at home: monitoring energy consumption and security, accessing commercial data bases, performing business transactions; taking high school or college courses, and entertaining themselves.
- Because of the potential for interactive video (learning in an interactive way using a computer system), some experts believe the videodisk player will become the most important peripheral device for microcomputer systems in this decade.
- Electronic technology presents new challenges. One involves cards used for financial transactions, which could become monitoring devices of people's behavior.
- Some experts believe people who cannot use computers will be the newly disadvantaged. Others believe reading and thinking skills and general knowledge will determine the haves and have-nots of the future. Students can use computers for computer-assisted instruction (CAI) to learn such skills. CAI software includes drills, tutorials, simulations, games, and problem-solving software.

● Review Questions

1. Why is gallium arsenide a better material for building faster chips?

2. What tasks would biochips perform if they existed?

3. How are laser beams used with fiber optics?

4. How do expert systems compare with scientists' criteria for artificial intelligence?

5. What are some of the difficulties that must be overcome in voice recognition?

6. What are some of the difficulties that must be overcome before robots are useful in homes?

7. Explain how multiphasic health testing can help a physician in making a diagnosis.

8. What is the difference between a CAT scan and NMR scanning?

9. Name and explain three ways microprocessors are being used in the treatment of patients.

10. Briefly describe how computers are used for monitoring volcanic activity.

11. How might computers be used in homes in the next decade or two?

12. What are some of the objections people have to carrying one card that can be used for a multitude of financial purposes?

13. Name five ways that computers can be used in building reading and thinking skills and general knowledge in education.

Intel

COMPANY HISTORY

The information revolution, sparked by the introduction of the computer, is transforming the world just as the industrial revolution transformed the world two hundred years earlier. The technology needed to fuel the information revolution is a product of many minds and many companies, but Intel Corporation has clearly been one of the leaders in creating new technology. Intel is responsible for two of the major postwar innovations in microelectronics that have made today's electronic age possible—large-scale integrated (LSI) memory and the microprocessor. Starting in 1968 with 12 employees, revenues of $2,672, and a vision of the future, Intel has grown to a complex organization of more than 12,000 employees in locations around the world and revenues exceeding $1 billion.

One of the keys to Intel's success has been its founding team, Robert N. Noyce, Gordon E. Moore, and Andrew S. Grove. In addition to earning Ph.D.s from well-respected universities, all three men were scientific pioneers early in their careers. Noyce and Moore met while working at Shockley Semiconductor Laboratory and later became part of the team that founded Fairchild Semiconductor. Grove joined Fairchild in 1963 and worked closely with Noyce and Moore. When the three became dissatisfied with their roles at Fairchild, they left the company and formed their own electronics firm. A long search for a suitable company name brought the suggestion Integrated Electronics. The name was appropriate, for it described the field the new organization was about to tackle, but unfortunately, it was already taken. By combining the first syllables of the two words *integrated* and *electronics*, however, the team came up with Intel. The name Intel was similar to the name of another company, Intelco, so the team solved the con-

flict by purchasing the rights to use the name. Later, Moore claimed that purchasing the rights "was easier than thinking up another alternative."

The new company concentrated on finding ways to use emerging LSI technology (the placement of thousands of microminiature electronic devices on a tiny silicon chip) in computer memory. At that time, nearly all computer memories still used magnetic cores. Magnetic cores were cheaper than semiconductors, but the Intel team felt that declining integrated circuit (IC) prices would soon make ICs a viable option as a source for computer memory.

Although research and development was an important part of Intel, the company did not want to have a reputation as merely an R&D organization. Corporate policy required that useful products be delivered to the marketplace. The slogan "Intel Delivers" was adopted and is still in use today.

The early years at Intel were intense, and success was not immediate. In 1969, however, a microprocessor was developed using silicon gate and Schottky bipolar technology. The new technology produced a chip with greater density and performance than any integrated

circuit designs in the past and for a lower price. With this development, the company's future was guaranteed.

GENERAL COMPUTER USE

The same technology that Intel engineers developed for use in the marketplace found its way back into the company. Currently, all Intel facilities are equipped with state-of-the art computers from microcomputers to mainframes. As semiconductor chips have increased in complexity, there has been a corresponding need for computational tools that can support the design of those chips. Intel's computer-aided design (CAD) efforts have resulted in a highly sophisticated set of tools that are improving the product development cycle in the face of growing complexity.

At Intel, computing requirements have nearly doubled every year since the mid-seventies, and today computers are used in nearly every facet of work at the company. Computers are used to enter and track business orders, control the manufacturing process, assist in product design, control finances, and synchronize worldwide operations.

Intel maintains two large-scale computing centers that serve as a corporate nerve center for processing information. Access to these centers is provided through a worldwide communication network interconnecting local sales offices and major plants in the United States, Europe, Israel, the Caribbean, Japan, and other locations in the Far East. Data centers are also located in the United Kingdom, Israel, and Japan, where local requirements dictate additional local capacity. Throughout Intel locations around the world, computing intensive tasks such as design engineering and factory automation are supported with dedicated local computers. International administrative communications are facilitated by a worldwide electronic mail system that allows manufacturing headquarters in Arizona rapid access to management in other locations around the globe.

State-of-the art is the byword at Intel. Because the information revolution is constantly changing, Intel keeps its eye on the future as it strives to meet the needs of the marketplace.

DISCUSSION POINTS

1. For what two major post-war innovations in microelectronics is Intel responsible?
2. Describe some of the ways that computers are used at Intel.

● APPENDIX A
Career Opportunities

● People and Their Roles

Men and women with technical or managerial skills in data processing are employed in almost every industry. The need for data-processing personnel exists not only in business firms but also in hospitals, schools, government agencies, banks, and libraries. However, the major emphasis of this section is on computer-related career opportunities in a business environment.

A typical computer installation in a business organization is expected to perform at least three basic functions: system analysis and design, programming, and computer operation. Personnel with the education and experience required to work in these areas are needed. Data-base technology has created the need for specialists in data-base analysis and administration. An information system manager is needed to coordinate activities, set goals for the data-processing department, and establish procedures to control and evaluate both personnel and projects in progress.

INFORMATION SYSTEM MANAGERS

Historically, data-processing managers have been programmers or system analysts who worked their way up to management positions with little formal management training. But the increasing emphasis on information systems and information management has brought a change; professional managers with demonstrable leadership qualities and communication skills are being hired to manage information system departments.

The *management information system (MIS) manager* is responsible for planning and tying together all the information resources of a firm. The manager is responsible for organizing the physical and human resources of a department. He or she must devise effective control mechanisms to monitor progress toward company goals. The following knowledge and skills are useful assets for an MIS manager:

● A thorough understanding of an organization, its goals, and its business activities.
● Leadership qualities to motivate and control highly skilled people.
● Knowledge of data-processing methods and familiarity with available hardware and software.

A man or woman seeking a career in information system management should have a college degree. A degree in business administration with a concentration in the area of management information systems is desirable for managing business data-processing centers. Some employers prefer an individual with an MBA degree. To handle high-level management responsibilities, a candidate for a position as MIS director should have at least two years of extensive management experience, advanced knowledge of the industry in which the individual hopes to work, and competence in all technical, professional, and business skills.

SYSTEM DEVELOPMENT PERSONNEL

Programmers

Generally, three types of programming are done in an organization: *application programming*, *maintenance programming*, and *system programming*. Persons working in any of these areas should possess the following basic skills:

● Good command of the programming language or languages in which programs are written.
● A knowledge of general programming methodology and the relationships between programs and hardware.
● Analytical reasoning ability and attention to detail.
● Creativity and discipline for developing new problem-solving methods.
● Patience and persistence.

Application programs perform data-processing or computational tasks that solve specific problems facing an organization. This type of programming constitutes the bulk of all programming tasks. An application programmer must take a broad system design prepared by an analyst and convert it into instructions for the computer. Responsibilities of application programmers also include testing, debugging, documenting, and implementing programs.

An application programmer in business data processing must apply the capabilities of the computer to problems such as customer billing and inventory control. A business-oriented application programmer should know the objectives of an organization and have a basic understanding of accounting and management science in addition to the skills outlined earlier.

Scientific application programmers work on specific or engineering problems, which usually require complex mathematical solutions. Thus, scientific application programming usually requires a degree in computer science, information science, mathematics, engineering, or a physical science. Some jobs require graduate degrees. Few scientific organizations are interested in applicants with no college training.

Program maintenance is an important but often neglected activity. Many large programs are never completely debugged, and there is a continuing need to change and improve major programs. In some organizations, maintenance programming is done by application programmers. To be effective, a maintenance programmer needs extensive programming experience and a high level of analytical ability.

System programmers are responsible for creating and maintaining system software. System programmers do not write programs that solve day-to-day organizational problems. Instead, they develop utility programs; maintain operating systems, data-base packages, compilers, and assemblers; and are involved in decisions concerning additions and deletions of hardware and software. Because of their knowledge of operating systems, system programmers typically offer technical help to application programmers. To perform these duties effectively, a system programmer should have: (1) a background in the theory of computer language structure and syntax and (2) extensive and detailed knowledge of the hardware being used and the software that controls it.

Employers may look for specialized skills in system programmers. For example, the increasing impact of minicomputers and microcomputers is creating a demand for programmers with experience in real-time or interactive systems using mini and micro hardware. Also, the advanced technology of today's communication networks offers excellent opportunities for programmers skilled in designing, coding, testing, debugging, documenting, and implementing data communication software.

Educational requirements for programmers vary depending upon employers' needs. For a business-oriented application programming job, a college degree, though desirable, is usually not required. However, most employers prefer applicants who have had college courses in data processing, accounting, and business administration. Occasionally, workers experienced in computer operations or specific functional areas of business are promoted to programming jobs and, with additional data-processing courses, become fully qualified programmers.

People interested in becoming system programmers should have at least one year of assembly language programming experience or a college degree in computer science. In addition to a degree, work experience, although not essential for a job as a programmer, is extremely beneficial.

Computer programming is taught at a number of different schools. Technical and vocational schools, community and junior colleges, and universities all offer programming courses. Many high schools offer computer programming to adults in evening classes, as well as to regular day students.

Application and system programmers will continue to be in exceptionally high demand. Application programmers with exposure to data-base management and direct-access techniques, remote processing, conversational programming, structured design, and distributed processing will be in greatest demand. As the use of minicomputers and microcomputers increases, knowledge of Assembler, C, Pascal, and BASIC will become valuable. System programmers knowledgeable in data communications, network planning and analysis, data-base concepts, and terminal-oriented systems will be in demand. With these opportunities in mind, data processing, computer science, and business administration students may choose to direct their education toward some degree of specialization.

Programmers frequently advance into higher levels within an organization. A programmer who demonstrates his or her technical competence and the ability to handle responsibility may be promoted to head programmer and given supervisory responsibilities. Some application programmers become system programmers, and vice versa.

System Analysts

The *system analyst* plays a significant role in the analysis, design, and implementation of a formal information system. The analyst has the following responsibilities.

- Helping the user determine information needs.
- Gathering facts about existing systems and analyzing them to determine the effectiveness of current processing methods and procedures.
- Designing new systems, recommending changes to existing systems, and being involved in implementing these changes.

The analyst's role is critical to the success of any management information system. He or she acts as an interface between users of the system and technical personnel such as programmers, machine operators, and data-base specialists. This role becomes more important as the cost of designing, implementing, and maintaining information systems rises.

An effective system analyst should have:

- A general knowledge of the firm, including its goals, objectives, products, and services.
- Familiarity with the organizational structure of the company and management rationale for selecting that structure.
- Comprehensive knowledge of data-processing methods and current hardware and familiarity with available programming languages.
- The ability to plan and organize work and to cooperate and interact effectively with both technical and nontechnical personnel.
- A high level of creativity.
- The ability to communicate clearly and persuasively with technical personnel as well as with persons who have little or no computer background.

Minimum requirements for a job as a system analyst generally include work experience in system design and programming and specialized industry experience. System analysts seeking jobs in a business environment should be college graduates with backgrounds in business management, accounting, economics, computer science, information systems, or data processing. System analysts are often required to have an MBA or some graduate study. For work in a scientifically oriented organization, a college background in the physical sciences, mathematics, or engineering is preferred. Many universities offer majors in management information systems; their curricula are designed to train people to be system analysts.

Some organizations, particularly small ones, do not employ system analysts. Instead, *programmer/analysts* are responsible for system analysis and programming. In other companies, system analysts begin as programmers and are promoted to analyst positions after gaining experience. However, the qualities that make a good analyst are significantly different from those that characterize a good programmer. There is no clear career path *from* programming *to* analysis, though such movement is possible.

System analysis is a growing field. According to data from the United States Department of Labor, the need for system analysts will continue to increase throughout the 1980s; it is estimated to increase 37 percent by 1990. There is a continuing high demand for system professionals by computer manufacturers, and the increasing use of minicomputers and microcomputers will create an even greater need for analysts to design systems for small computers.

DATA-BASE SPECIALISTS

Data-base specialists are responsible for designing and controlling the use of data resources. A *data-base analyst*—the key person in the analysis, design, and implementation of data structures—must plan and coordinate data use within a system. A data-base analyst has the following responsibilities:

- Helping the system analyst or user analyze the interrelationships of data.
- Defining physical data structures and logical views of data.
- Designing new data-base systems, recommending changes to existing ones, and being involved in the implementation of these changes.
- Eliminating data redundancy.

A data-base analyst needs technical knowledge of programming and system methodologies. A background in system software is valuable for persons planning physical data-base structures. The job requires a college education and courses in computer science, business data processing, and data-base management system design. Many colleges offer courses in data-base management to train people to be data analysts.

A career path within the data-base specialty may lead to the position of corporate *data-base administrator (DBA).* This is a management-level position responsible for controlling all the data resources of an organization. The primary responsibilities of this position include:

- Developing a dictionary of standard data definitions so that all records are consistent.
- Designing data bases.
- Maintaining the accuracy, completeness, and timeliness of data bases.
- Designing procedures to ensure data security and data-base backup and recovery.
- Facilitating communications between analysts and users.

- Advising analysts, programmers, and system users about the best ways to use data bases.

To handle these responsibilities, a data-base administrator must have a high level of technical expertise, as well as an ability to communicate effectively with diverse groups of people. Supervisory and leadership skills developed through experience are also important.

Demand is strong for data-base specialists. With the increasing trend toward data-base management, the need for people with the technical knowledge to design data-base-oriented application systems is increasing.

DATA-PROCESSING OPERATIONS PERSONNEL

Data-processing operations personnel are responsible for entering data and instructions into the computer, operating the computer and attached devices, retrieving output, and ensuring the smooth operation of the computing center and associated libraries. An efficient operations staff is crucial to the effective use of an organization's computer resources.

The *librarian* is responsible for classifying, cataloging, and maintaining the files and programs stored on cards, tapes, disks, diskettes, and all other storage media in a computer library. The librarian's tasks include transferring backup files to alternate storage sites, purging old files, and supervising the periodic cleaning of magnetic tapes and disks.

The librarian's job is important because he or she controls access to stored master files and programs. Computer operators and programmers do not have access to tapes or disks without the librarian's approval. This prevents unauthorized changes or processing runs.

The educational background required for a computer librarian is not extensive. A high-school diploma along with knowledge of basic data-processing concepts and clerical record-keeping skills would qualify most people for this job.

A *computer operator's* duties include setting up equipment; mounting and removing tapes, disks, and diskettes; and monitoring the operation of the computer. A computer operator should be able to identify operational problems and take appropriate corrective actions. Most computers run under sophisticated operating systems that direct the operator through messages generated during processing. However, the operator is responsible for reviewing errors that occur during operation, determining their causes, and maintaining operating records.

People seeking jobs as computer operators should enjoy working with machines. They should also be able to read and understand technical literature. A computer operator has to act quickly without error. A good operator can prevent the loss of valuable computer time, as well as the loss or destruction of files. An operator must also possess the communication skills to explain to users why programs did or did not work.

Most operators receive apprentice training. Few have college degrees. Formal operator training is available through technical schools and junior colleges. To be effective, training should include several weeks of on-the-job experience.

A *data-entry operator's* job involves transcribing data into a form suitable for computer processing. A *keypunch operator* uses a keypunch machine to transfer data from source documents to punched cards. Operators of other key-entry devices transfer data to magnetic tape or magnetic disk for subsequent processing.

A *remote terminal operator* is involved with the preparation of input data. The operator is located at a remote site, probably some distance from the computer itself. The data is entered into the computer directly, from the location at which it is generated.

Data-entry jobs usually require manual dexterity, typing or keying skills, and alertness. No extensive formal education is required; a high-school diploma is usually sufficient. However, all personnel in this category should be trained carefully to minimize the incidence of errors. Usually several weeks of on-the-job training is provided. New operators must become familiar with the documents they will be reading and the data-entry devices they will be using.

Occupations in computer operations are affected by changes in data-processing technology. For example, the demand for keypunch operators has declined as new methods of data preparation, such as direct data-entry techniques, have been developed. However, the expanding use of computers, especially in small businesses, will require additional computer operating personnel.

● APPENDIX B
Microcomputer Buyers' Guide to Hardware and Software

● Introduction

For a number of reasons, buying a microcomputer and software can be a difficult and time-consuming task. As with stereo components and other appliances, there are many models of microcomputers. Choosing one out of 150 models can seem impossible. Add to that choice the hundreds of peripheral devices, add-ons, and worthwhile software packages from which to select and the task is indeed complex and confusing.

The purchase of a computer is a major investment for most people, so care must be taken not to make expensive mistakes. Spend time learning about the different systems on the market and analyzing what you want to do with a computer before making a decision. Otherwise, your computer purchase may end up in the closet gathering dust.

● Looking at the Big Picture

Experts often recommend that you choose the software and then match the hardware needs to the software. Although this is a good policy, there may be important hardware factors involved in a final decision. Use the following list as a general guide before considering specific requirements.

1. You should have a good idea of what you want to do with your computer and software. Do you want to write papers, analyze financial data, file data, create graphs and charts, publish a newsletter, or use the same data interchangeably among several programs?

2. Know about how much data you will be using at once—ten pages or fifty pages of text, a day's figures or a month's figures of financial data. Both software needs and data needs help define how much memory and speed you need in hardware.

3. Know the functions and names of basic hardware devices.

4. Know some basic functions of various software packages. (See Chapters 10, 11, 12, and the Applications Software Supplement for details about software, programming, and languages.)

5. Test computers and programs at the store. Test programs with data similar to what you will be entering. You may narrow your choice of software to two or three packages, then list a few machines that will run your software.

6. Find out whether the machines on your final list can be used for other purposes in the future.

7. Decide whether the hardware and software must be compatible with those used at work.

8. Be sure that all equipment and software is compatible within the system. Printers, for example, require certain types of connections. Be sure you have the proper connections.

9. Check with friends, computer magazines, and user groups for further information about the software and hardware you are considering.

10. Try different products at different stores.

11. Get firm prices. Find out how much is included in the basic package. The price may include the CPU only, or the CPU, monitor, and disk drive. You may need additional cash outlays for cards that drive a printer or produce graphics.

12. Find out about warranties, service, and exchange policies.

13. Set price limits, but don't be too price conscious. By identifying your intended uses, you already will have defined some price limits.

WHERE TO BUY

Once you have analyzed your needs and determined the appropriate software, you can purchase your computer from several sources: microcomputer vendors, retailers, and mail-order houses.

Computer vendors such as IBM, DEC, Burroughs, and NCR offer their line of microcomputers through a direct sales force. Buying through a computer manufacturer can have several benefits. Often, the salespeople are highly trained in the use of microcomputers in business and can assist you in determining which microcomputer system will meet your needs. Microcomputer vendors can also provide maintenance contracts for on-site repair and can offer replacement equipment if some part of your system should be down for a period of time.

Microcomputer manufacturers also market their products through department stores and computer specialty stores. The sales personnel at some outlets may lack the knowledge you need in making your choices. Be sure you feel comfortable with the salespeople. Computer specialty stores are often staffed with knowledgeable people and in most cases have an in-house service department.

Buying from a mail-order house can be to your advantage if you know exactly what you want to purchase. In many cases, mail-order houses offer products for less than computer specialty stores. Before you buy from a mail-order house, determine what you can expect in the way of services, and make sure you are dealing with a reputable dealer.

OTHER CONSIDERATIONS

You may wonder whether you should buy your system now or wait for newer technology. This question should always be considered before making a decision. Of course, advances will be made and prices will continue to fall. On the other hand, waiting could prevent you from realizing the benefits that technology has already provided.

If you do not have enough money for purchasing the system you want, you may be tempted to buy a cheaper system. Money spent on a cheaper system may be wasted if you do not like the software or hardware and do not use it. Under these circumstances, it may be better to wait a few months while you earn extra money or make alternative arrangements for purchasing the system you do want.

When you are considering various software and hardware for purchase, one of the most important factors should be the documentation. The importance of documentation can be overlooked by hardware and software vendors; however, you will undoubtedly refer to documentation for resolving questions you will have. Good documentation is complete, accurate, and easy to use. Documentation includes both the manuals that accompany hardware and software and on-screen help.

TRAINING

If you will require some training after purchasing your hardware and software, there are a number of options. Seminars offered by microcomputer software vendors and independent training firms are available for some of the more popular software packages. These seminars will guide you in using all the features of the packages. Local computer stores often offer similar classes and seminars (see Figure B-1).

Colleges and high schools also offer classes in computer use and programming through the normal program or adult education programs. User groups can help resolve questions you have about equipment or

● **FIGURE B–1**

Local computer stores frequently offer training seminars to new computer owners.

programs. A final form of training is through individual home study. Many hardware and software vendors provide tutorials on the use of their products. Tutorials may also be available from independent sources and can be purchased in many bookstores.

● Evaluating Software

You must know what you plan on doing with your software before you can evaluate the features of software packages. Consider the following specific factors in your final decision.

Learning

Gain knowledge about software by reading computer magazines, asking a knowledgeable friend, or joining a user group.

Testing

Test several programs of the type you are considering. Use data similar to what you plan to use after the purchase. Have a checklist of requirements.

Hardware Requirements

Check the hardware requirements for using the software. Be sure there are no problems with compatibility.

Flexibility

Be sure the software can grow as your needs expand. A good program will let you run the program using only the basic commands needed to accomplish the application, and then allow you to incorporate more sophisticated commands as you learn and need them.

Organization

Look for a clear and logical screen appearance. A screen that is cluttered and poorly organized will take more time to learn and will not be efficient to use. Some programs are so clear that they let you learn almost by instinct. Look at how the program handles movement between the program modes.

Error Handling

Determine how the program deals with errors. Error handling capability is an area that, if overlooked in the selection of a program, can spring up as one of the most annoying and disastrous aspects of the program. You should consciously try to make the program you are testing fail, in order to see how it handles the error conditions. A good program will let you recover from common errors. For example, if you are in the middle of a save operation and you get an error message that the disk is full, the program should allow you to replace the disk and then redo the save operation without losing any data.

Data Requirements

Be sure the program will handle the amount of data you will be entering. For example, check the number of records a data manager can support, the number of pages of text a word processor can work with, or the number of columns and rows that a spreadsheet can support.

Command Style

Check the type of command style used in the program. Command style refers to the approach used to command the program. Several approaches are the full menu with explanation, the menu alone, a single command with explanation, memorization of all commands with no menus available, or menus with alternative key command options. Although menus are helpful to beginners, experienced users may find that menus slow down the input and processing stages.

Help Screens

Make sure the help screens are really helpful. Help screens that you can call from any point in the program and that return you to where you left off are the most efficient and helpful.

Copy Protection

The question of copy protection can be important. Being able to copy a program allows a great deal of flexibility. If the software cannot be copied, you may not be able to use it with a hard disk, local area network, or electronic disk simulator because you cannot move the copy from a floppy disk. You should also be able to make backup copies of the program. Several software developers are now offering special versions of their software for use with hard disks.

Vendor Policies

Find out the policy of the vendor if the software is updated or if there are programming errors in the software.

Macros

Not essential, but very helpful, is the program's ability to use macro commands. A macro command allows you to string together several commands and define them as a single key. When that key is struck, the sequence of commands is executed automatically. For example, in a word processing program it may be necessary to search for a word or phrase, replace the word or phrase with another, and save the change. Performing operations such as this with a single keystroke increases the efficiency and ease of use of a program. Macros may be offered in a separate software package that is compatible with the one you will be using.

Defaults

Examine the program for default values. A default is a value that the computer assumes when you do not tell it what value to use. For example, many word processors are set up to produce a standard business letter on 8½ by 11 inch paper without your having to specify this size. Default values make the program more flexible. They should be easy to change, allowing you to set them so the most often used formats will automatically be used when the program is run. They should also be easy to override temporarily while you are using the program.

● Choosing the Hardware

The most important consideration in buying hardware is whether it can handle the software you have chosen. Other factors include ease of use, expected output, storage, and devices that can be added to expand the capabilities of your system.

THE MICROPROCESSOR

Early microcomputers had 8-bit microprocessors. These computers are still popular today and will remain so because software for them is proven, and many users do not need the speed and primary storage available with 16-bit and 32-bit microprocessors.

The 16-bit and 32-bit microprocessors have greater primary memories and allow the computer to process instructions at a much faster rate. If you intend to use your computer for jobs like financial analysis or want to run two or three programs at once, a larger microprocessor is necessary.

MONITORS

Some computers have a built-in video display. Most, however, require the purchase of a separate video display or monitor. There are several things to consider when purchasing a monitor. First, you must decide whether you want a color monitor or a monochrome monitor.

Second, decide on screen dimensions. Microcomputer monitors come in either 40-column or 80-column widths and 24- or 25-line displays. If you are going to use your system for word processing, an 80-column screen is more desirable. That is because the text that fits on one line of a standard 8½-inch piece of paper requires the entire width of an 80-column display. It may also be advisable to choose a display screen large enough to show several portions of one program or portions of two or three programs in case you want to exercise that option.

Third, consider the resolution of the characters displayed on the monitor. Resolution refers to the clarity of those characters. Characters are created using small dots called pixels (picture elements). The smaller the dots and the more closely packed they are, the clearer the images on the screen.

Fourth, make sure there is a way to control the brightness, contrast, and focus of the display. Controlling these factors permits you to adjust the display to suit the lighting conditions of the room in which you are working. Glare can be a stubborn nuisance, too. Most monitors now incorporate some kind of antiglare coating, either inside or outside the glass. Snap-on glare covers are available for most monitors as well. Tilt and swivel display stands, an extra for most monitors, can provide a better viewing angle for the elimination of glare and muscle tension in the neck.

Fifth, check whether the image leaves a ghostlike trail or flickers and blurs when text is scrolled or when you enter data.

KEYBOARDS

Keyboards for microcomputers can come in one of two forms. They can be attached to the computer enclosure or detached from it. Detached keyboards may be either connected to the computer by a cord or operated by batteries (see Figure B-2).

The angle of the keyboard is important. Keyboards that are part of the machine's enclosure cannot be adjusted, and typing for long periods on these can be tiresome. Detachable keyboards adjust to various angles.

Keyboard touch is another consideration. Most microcomputers have standard touch-sensitive keys that make a noise similar to typewriter keys. A few offer pressure-sensitive keyboards (membrane keyboards). These may be more suitable for use around small children or heavy industry because they protect the keyboard from dirt and spills. Pressure-sensitive keyboards are difficult for touch-typing and would not be a wise choice for word processing.

Some keyboards offer special features such as repeating keys, function keys, and numeric keypads. Numeric keypads are helpful when a considerable amount of numeric data is to be entered.

SECONDARY STORAGE

Secondary storage for microcomputers includes tape cassettes, tape cartridges, floppy disks, and hard disks. When selecting which type of secondary storage to buy, consider price, amount of storage, access time, and security.

Tape cassettes and cartridges are the lowest-priced form of storage, but accessing data is slow because all the data must be read in order to find the required data.

Floppy disks are fairly inexpensive and provide direct access to data, thereby making data retrieval faster than tape storage. Floppy disks come in three sizes: 8-inch, 5¼-inch, and 3½-inch. The 5¼-inch size is the most common. The 3½-inch disks are usually packaged in hard plastic for better protection in handling outside the disk drive.

Hard disks are the most expensive form of storage but allow very rapid access to data. They may be shared by more than one microcomputer,

● **FIGURE B–2**
Choosing the appropriate hardware is an important step in the computer buying process.

and offer more system flexibility. Some software cannot be placed on hard disks without also inserting the program disk in a regular disk drive.

Security is highest for tapes, floppy disks, and hard disks with removable cartridges because these items can be locked up.

PRINTERS

Printers can be one of the most expensive peripherals you purchase. There are a number of features that should be considered when shopping for a printer:

- The speed with which printing occurs.
- The amount of noise the printer makes. If the printer of your choice makes considerable noise, purchase a sound shield to cover the printer during operation.
- The availability of supplies such as ribbons, cartridges, or special paper required by the printer.
- The number of characters per inch (the pitch).
- The size of the platen (the carriage roller). (A larger size may be needed in printing spreadsheets, for example.)
- The type of paper feed—tractor feed, which uses tiny pins in pulling the paper through the printer, and friction feed, which is the type of paper feed used by typewriters.
- The quality of print. Letter-quality printers produce solid characters suitable for formal communication, and dot matrix printers produce characters made of tiny dots. Some dot matrix printers produce near-letter-quality characters and can be used for most purposes.
- The flexibility of different fonts and sizes of print. Letter-quality impact printers produce one size of print. The font can be changed by exchanging the removable print element. Dot-matrix printers allow flexibility in printing many fonts, or styles of type, and many sizes of type. These printers may be more suitable for newsletters. For a more expensive printer with high-quality output and a high degree of flexibility in fonts and sizes, consider the laser printer.
- The number of copies to be made. Dot-matrix printers do not print through multiple copies, so an impact printer is needed if carbon copies are to be made.

ADD-ONS

Add-ons are printed circuit boards or expansion boards that can increase the capabilities of your computer (see Figure B-3). They can be used for several purposes:

- Changing the number of characters displayed on the width of the screen.
- Adding graphics capabilities to the computer.
- Adding a coprocessor to the computer so that software for a different operating system can be run.
- Adding memory.
- Providing interfaces for input and output devices such as printers, joysticks, mice, and graphics tablets.

The software you choose may require the use of one or more expansion boards. Check the requirements carefully before purchasing equipment. Some computers are sold with interfaces for video displays and graphics, for example, while others need additional boards. Be careful that dealers have not installed poor-quality, low-priced expansion boards into PCs for sale at discount.

You can spot poor manufacturing in expansion boards by looking at the wires and soldering on both sides of the board. The soldering should be bright silver. You should not see wires poking through the solder, lumpy solder, or many areas where solder appears to have been scraped.

When buying an expansion board, test it at the dealer's, making sure all the functions work. If you are not knowledgeable about computers, it is best to have the board installed in your machine by the dealer. Power to the computer should be off and the cords removed from wall outlets before installation takes place. In addition, you should discharge static from your body before touching the components. The best way is to touch the metal chassis of any grounded appliance, like an office copier.

Again, be sure the expansion board is compatible with all the other elements of your computer system.

OTHER HARDWARE DEVICES

Depending on your intended uses and specific needs, your microcomputer system may require other specialized hardware devices. For example, a particular graphics package may require the use of a joystick for data input. Special hardware devices includes the following: joystick, Koala pad or other graphics tablet, game paddle, modem for using a telephone with your computer, track ball, light pen, mouse, digitizer, touch screen, voice recognition or voice synthesizer system, and music synthesizer. Descriptions of these items are found in this text and in popular computer literature such as magazines and paperback books.

● Buyers' Checklist

When selecting a microcomputer, a checklist is often helpful. The following checklist can help you identify the items you need.

1. List the expected uses of your computer.

2. List the software requirements for handling your intended uses.

3. List the application programs that can meet your designated needs.

4. Given the software requirements listed above, check the specific hardware requirement below.

THE MICROPROCESSOR
—— 8-bit
—— 16-bit
—— 32-bit
—— K internal memory needed

THE MONITOR
—— 40-column display
—— 80-column display
—— Monochrome display
    —— White
    —— Green
    —— Amber
—— Color display
    —— Composite
    —— RGB
—— Glare shield

THE KEYBOARD
—— Detachable
—— Upper- and lower-case letters
—— Repeating keys
—— Numeric keypad
—— Function keys

THE PRINTER
—— Dot-matrix
—— Letter-quality
—— Friction feed
—— Tractor feed
—— Individual sheet feed
—— Carriage width
    —— 80-column
    —— 132-column
—— Speed
—— Pitch
—— Noise shield

ADD-ONS (EXPANSION BOARDS)

— Graphic display
— Printer interface
— Interface for other devices such as joystick, graphics tablet, and so on
— Additional memory
— Coprocessor

OTHER HARDWARE DEVICES

— Joystick
— Graphics tablet
— Track ball
— Paddle
— Modem
— Light pen
— Mouse
— Touch screen
— Voice recognition
— Voice synthesis
— Music synthesis
— Digitizer

● APPENDIX C
A Guide to Networks

One of the benefits of buying a microcomputer is having the opportunity to access computer networks. Accessing a network can provide you with an opportunity to obtain resources and information as well as play computer games and communicate with other computer users.

This guide will introduce you to the world of computer networks. There are several ways in which networks can be utilized. One way is to link your computer via telephone lines to established information services or electronic bulletin boards. Another is to interconnect computers within a building or a complex, forming a local area network (LAN).

● Information Services

Information services, also known as commercial data bases, allow the personal computer user to gain access to vast storehouses of information. Although you access the information services via telephone lines, the initial procedure is not as simple as dialing the phone. You must first make sure you have the proper communication links on your computer. In general, you will need a modem and some type of communications software. The specifications for each may vary with the brand of computer you have and also the information services you plan to subscribe to. It is best to consult your computer store or the information service you are considering to find out exactly what you will need.

After installing your end of the communications link, you are ready to go—almost. Most services require payment of an initial fee. You are then issued a special user identification number and/or a password. This ensures that only paid subscribers have access to the service. All services also charge an hourly connect rate, which will vary with the time of the day you are connected and the type of information you wish to access. The information services will provide their rates to subscribers and all interested persons. The hours of availability of the services also vary; not all services can be accessed twenty-four hours a day. Another cost that may be associated with the services is telephone line charges by your local telephone company. There may be local phone numbers for you to use, but these are only available in areas where there are a lot of potential users. If local numbers exist, the services will provide them.

COMPUSERVE

CompuServe is the largest information service available to individual and family users. The initial fee includes a user's guide, a free first hour of connect-time, and a subscription to *Today* magazine (a CompuServe publication). Hourly connect rates vary depending on the day and time of day you use the service and the type of modem you have. Some of CompuServe's special services (such as stock price and dividend information) may have additional charges.

CompuServe uses a menu-choice and word-search approach. Menu-choice allows the user to access the desired information by selecting a topic and entering the numbers. Word-search allows the user to enter a word or topic into designated areas of CompuServe while the computer looks for the related information.

Some of the topics of information provided by CompuServe include: Public and Marine Weather, which provides information on conditions throughout the country; CB, which is a simulation of Citizen's Band radio; and Family Matters Forum, which offers subscribers helpful assistance on parenting and family-related topics. CompuServe also offers more than forty-five games and allows users to shop at home by browsing through an electronic catalog that contains more than 30,000 items (see Figure C–1).

You can send messages to other subscribers by using CompuServe's EMAIL. In addition to the Associated Press wire service, you can also access three newspapers: the *St. Louis Post-Dispatch*, the *Middlesex Daily*, and the *Washington Post*. CompuServe also has about sixty special-interest groups. Each group shares a common interest such as music or owning an IBM-PC. Subscribers can communicate directly with CompuServe, giving their comments and suggestions, which may be used to add new services. CompuServe is always changing and adding to its resources.

THE SOURCE

Like CompuServe, The Source is geared toward individual and family users. There is a one-time subscription fee plus a monthly minimum charge. Hourly connect rates vary. Again, some services may charge additional fees. The Source also uses a menu-choice approach.

When connected to The Source, you can consult the *Official Airline Guide, Electronic Edition*, to find the best route and fare for your next flight. If your destination is New York, Washington, or other major U.S. cities, you can even select restaurants before you go by using the restaurant guide. The Source also offers you the convenience of shopping at home. You can order more than 50,000 items listed in an electronic catalog, or play more than eighty games.

Through the EMPLOY option, you can look for job openings or potential employees in about forty different categories, ranging from accounting

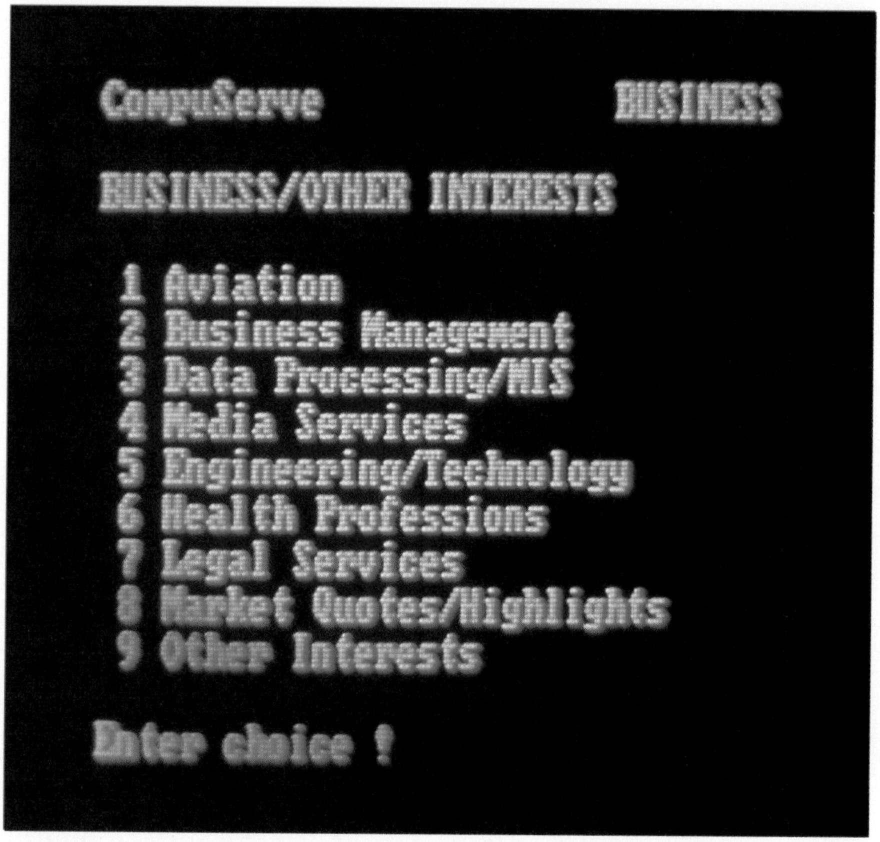

● **FIGURE C–1**
Users of CompuServe make menu selections from among a wide range of
topics.

to utilities. The Source also allows you to send messages to other subscribers through the Mailgram service. If you want to talk with others
who are connected to The Source at the same time, you can use the
CHAT option. Do you need help with finances? The Source offers programs that figure depreciation schedules, balance your checkbook, and
amortize a loan. As a Source subscriber, you can access the United Press
International (UPI) wire service.

The Source calls its special-interest groups Private Sector. There are
more than thirty groups, including groups for school administrators, public utilities, and radio stations. A group sponsor pays a service charge
for twenty-five membership account numbers and the ability to put data
bases on The Source. Like CompuServe, The Source is always updating
its services and keeps its users informed through its newsletter,
SourceWorld.

DOW JONES NEWS/RETRIEVAL

The Dow Jones News/Retrieval Service is designed with business information in mind and its primary users are business professionals and
individuals interested in business. There are various user levels available
with varying subscription fees. Connect rates per hour also vary. Dow
Jones News/Retrieval uses a menu-choice approach to its services.

The Dow Jones News/Retrieval system provides information on every company listed on the New York and American stock exchanges, as well as some selected companies whose stock is traded over the counter. You can get historical stock market quotes and current information that is only fifteen minutes behind the action on the exchange floors. The service also gives corporate earnings estimates and price/volume data.

With a Dow Jones News/Retrieval subscription, you can get UPI summaries of local and national news, news stories from various financial newspapers and magazines, and access to the *Academic American Encyclopedia.* The service also has movie reviews and weather information, and allows you to shop at home.

Three software packages are available with which you can record and manipulate information from the News/Retrieval data bases. The Market Analyzer performs seventeen analytical functions and charts the results. The Market Microscope ranks companies and industries by sixty-eight financial indicators. The Market Manager monitors and updates investment portfolios.

DIALOG INFORMATION SERVICES

DIALOG Information Services offers two different data base collections for the serious researcher (see Figure C–2). The Information Retrieval Service data base collection has no subscription or minimum fee; however, there is a charge for a user's manual. Online hourly fees vary, depending on the data base you wish to access. The Knowledge-Index data base has variable hourly rates and limited hours of access. DIALOG uses a word-search approach for both of these services.

DIALOG Information Retrieval Service has comprehensive coverage of virtually every area of study—history, science, arts and humanities, law, medicine, and current affairs. More than 60,000 journals have been referenced as well as books, dissertations, patents, and pamphlets. You

● **FIGURE C–2**
DIALOG offers users access to two different data base collections.

enter the word or words about which you want to gather information and DIALOG gives you a list of all references.

The Knowledge Index consists of about fifteen of the Information Retrieval data bases containing data from 10,000 journals. Some of the topics include computers, government publications, magazines, and psychology. Subscribers use a simplified word search to get the abstracts and references to the articles.

SPECIALTY SERVICES

In addition to the networks mentioned above, there are also many specialty services. BRS/After Dark, which operates evenings and weekends, is a bibliographic retrieval service. LEXIS is a service for the legal profession that includes cases, regulations, laws, and decisions in the United States, Britain, and France. AMA/NET has four different data bases that provide medical personnel with information on drugs, diagnosing, medical legislation, and public health issues. HORSE has information on the breeding and race records of more than one million racehorses in North America. The number of information services or commercial data bases is increasing daily and the variety of information available is always expanding (see Figure C–3).

● Bulletin Boards

Electronic bulletin boards provide a place for users to post notices of all kinds. Although information services such as CompuServe and The Source provide bulletin board space for their subscribers, all you need to access most boards is the phone number and the proper communications link on your computer. Bulletin boards are free to the users (unless long-distance phone calls are placed). There are hundreds of bulletin boards

● **FIGURE C–3**
Commodities-market information is updated daily, and these farmers make use of a specialty network to access quotes from the futures exchange.

throughout the country (some estimates are around 1,100) and the number is constantly rising.

Bulletin board users log onto a "host" computer. Once they are connected, users can send or receive data, messages, and information, copy programs from the board, and leave programs to be copied. The "host" computer is frequently another microcomputer whose owner decided to start the bulletin board. The flexibility of the board depends upon the host.

Bulletin boards are usually good sources for hardware and software reviews, new product information, and free programs. They also offer users the opportunity to meet other computer enthusiasts. Local computer dealers and user groups can provide information on bulletin boards in the areas near you.

● Local Area Networks

As discussed in Chapter 9, local area networks (LANs) help link computers to share peripherals and information. Most LANs operate in business or academia. Since dozens of microcomputers can be linked together, LANs eliminate the need for each computer to have its own printer and floppy disks containing the same general information. The microcomputers on the LAN can access the data stored on the others.

Because LAN technology is relatively new, it is expensive and somewhat complex to establish one. It is important to consider present and future needs and compare them with the capabilities of the LAN to avoid establishing one that is soon outdated. Professional consultants can aid with the LAN selection and provide custom software. Some microcomputer vendors such as Apple Computers, Digital Microsystems, and North Star Computers have developed networks for use with their own machines. These networks are called proprietary networks. Other vendors have developed LANs that were adopted by other companies, which are called nonproprietary networks.

PROPRIETARY NETWORKS

There are a number of proprietary networks from which users can choose. Applenet was introduced by Apple Computer in 1983. It can connect 128 workstations over a distance of 8,000 feet. Digital Microsystems (not to be confused with Digital Equipment Corporation) provides HiNet, which connects up to thirty-two stations over a distance of 1,000 feet. Users can share disks and printers. Proprietary networks also provide the capability for electronic mail.

NorthNet by North Star Computers was developed for use on their Advantage microcomputers. It allows the sharing of resources over 4,000 feet. Vector Graphic developed LINC (an acronym for Local Interactive Network Communications) for use on Vector-4 products. LINC can connect up to sixteen stations over a 2,000-foot distance.

NONPROPRIETARY NETWORKS

Nonproprietary networks include Omninet, Ethernet, PLAN, and ARC-net. Omninet, developed by Corvus Systems, can connect up to sixty-four workstations over a distance of up to 1,000 meters. The users can share a central hard disk unit and printer. Omninet is compatible with Apple IIs and IIIs, IBM Personal Computers, the DEC LSI-11, and Texas Instruments' Professional. It is a CSMA/CD access method.

Xerox Corporation provides Ethernet, which can support up to 1,024 workstations over a limited distance. Different distributors sell Ethernet-compatible products. The IBM-PC Ethernet connection is known as EtherSeries. EtherLink has software to allow the transferring of files and the sharing of printers. EtherShare offers a shared hard disk and several software packages including EtherMail, which provides the ability for all workstations to send and receive electronic mail.

PLAN (Personal Local Area Network) 4000 from Nestar Systems is compatible with Apple IIs and IBM-PCs. PLAN 4000 can link up to sixty-four microcomputers over a distance of up to four miles. This LAN uses the token-passing access method. Software is available for sharing disks and printers and for electronic mail.

Datapoint Corporation introduced ARCnet in 1977. It can link up to 255 stations as far as four miles apart. ARCnet uses a token-passing access method and can connect users to a hard disk drive. Tandy Corporation provides ARCnet for its Radio Shack Models II and 16. Tandy also provides a series of shared disk systems and software that is necessary for office use.

The LANs on the market combine the aspects of the technology in various ways. Each network is suited to slightly different environments. Since industry standards change with the development of LANs, it is best to find a consultant who can analyze your needs and match them to a LAN, or contact your vendor to see what is available for your equipment.

HOW TO REACH SOME LAN VENDORS

Apple Computer, Inc. (Applenet)
20525 Mariani Avenue
Cupertino, CA 95014
(408) 996-1010

Corvus Systems (Omninet)
2029 O'Toole Avenue
San Jose, CA 95131
(408) 946-7700

Datapoint Corporation (ARCnet)
9725 Datapoint Drive
San Antonio, TX 78284
(512) 699-7151

Digital Microsystems (HiNet)
1840 Embarcadero
Oakland, CA 94606
(415) 532-3686

Nestar Systems, Inc. (PLAN 4000)
2585 East Bayshore Road
Palo Alto, CA 94303
(415) 493-2223

NorthStar Computers, Inc. (NorthNet)
14440 Catalina Street
San Leandro, CA 94577
(415) 375-8500

Vector Graphics, Inc. (LINC)
500 N. Venter Park
Thousand Oaks, CA 91320
(805) 499-5831

Xerox Corporation (Ethernet)
Office Systems Division
1341 W. Mockingbird Lane
Dallas, TX 75247
(214) 689-6000

HOW TO REACH SOME POPULAR INFORMATION SERVICES

CompuServe, Consumer Information Service
5000 Arlington Center Blvd.
P.O. Box 20212
Columbus, OH 43220
(800) 848-8199 or (614) 457-0802 in Ohio

DIALOG Information Services, Inc.
3460 Hillview Ave.
Palo Alto, CA 94304
(800) 227-1927 or (800) 982-5838

Dow Jones News/Retrieval
P.O. Box 300
Princeton, NJ 08540
(800) 257-5114

The Source
Source Telecomputing Corp.
1616 Anderson Road
McLean, VA 22102
(800) 336-3366

APPLICATION SOFTWARE SUPPLEMENT

● SECTION I
Word Processors

● Introduction

First-time computer users are typically initiated into the world of computing on a word processor. Word processors are a daily necessity for large and small businesses. With such a wide variety of users, it is not surprising that word processors provide the largest software market.

Word processors have greatly improved the writing process, eliminating much of the drudgery involved in more traditional means of putting thoughts onto paper. A major advantage of word processing is that mistakes can be corrected on the computer screen before anything appears on paper. A person can change, move, or erase words, sentences, and paragraphs without retyping the whole document. The final version is printed when the writer is completely satisfied with it.

This section introduces you to word processing. It includes an explanation of word processing, its uses, and some of the common features of word-processing packages.

● Understanding Word Processors

A word processor is a program that lets you write, edit, format, and print text. Basically, the purpose of all word processors is the same: to help the user create a good-looking and well-written document. To familiarize you with word-processing concepts, Table I–1 provides a quick reference to terms frequently encountered when using a word processor.

● Table I-1
Frequently Encountered Word-Processing Terms

TERM	DEFINITION
Automatic pagination	A feature that enables a word processor to automatically number the pages of the printed copy.
Block	A group of characters, such as a sentence or paragraph.
Block movement	A feature that allows the user to define a block of text and then perform a specific operation on the entire block. Common block operations include block move, block copy, block save, and block delete.
Boldface	Heavy type, for example, this is **boldface**.
Character	A letter, number, or symbol.
Character enhancement	Underlining, boldfacing, subscripting, and superscripting.
Control character	A coded character that does not print but is part of the command sequence in a word processor.
Cursor	The marker on the display screen indicating where the next character can be displayed.
Default setting	A value used by the word processor when not instructed to use any other.
Deletion	A feature in which a character, word, sentence or larger block of text may be removed from the existing text.
Document-oriented word processor	A word processor that operates on a text file as one long document.
Editing	The act of changing or amending text.
Format	The layout of a page; for example, the number of lines, margin settings, and so on.
Global	An instruction that will be carried out throughout an entire document, for example, global search and replace.
Header	A piece of text that is stored separately from the text and printed at the top of each page.
Incremental spacing	A method in which the printer inserts spaces between words and letters to produce justified margins; also called *microspacing*.
Insertion	A feature in which a character, word, sentence, or larger block of text is added to the existing text.

Most word processors divide the computer screen into two areas. One area gives information about the status of the program and about the format of the document. The other area contains the text of the document being edited (Figure I–1).

The part of the screen that gives information about the status of the program often contains a **menu.** A menu is a list of commands or prompts on the display screen. For example, an editing menu in a word processor might include commands such as copy, move, delete, print, format, insert, and undo. A user could perform any of these commands on the

TERM	DEFINITION
Justification	A feature for making lines of text even at the margins.
Line editor	The type of editor that allows the user to edit only one line at a time.
Memory-only word processor	A word processor that cannot exchange text between internal memory and disk during the editing process.
Menu	A list of commands or prompts on the display screen.
Page-oriented word processor	A word processor that operates on a text file as a series of pages.
Print formatting	The function of a word processor that communicates with the printer to tell it how to print the text on paper.
Print preview	A feature that allows the user to view a general representation on the screen of how the document will look when printed.
Screen editor	The type of editor that allows the user to edit an entire screen at a time.
Screen formatting	A function of a word processor that controls how the text will appear on the screen.
Scrolling	Moving a line of text onto or off of the screen.
Search and find	A routine that searches for, and places the cursor at, a specified string of characters.
Search and replace	A routine that searches for a specified character string and replaces it with the specified replacement string.
Status line	A message line above or below the text area on a display screen that gives format and system information.
Subscript	A character that prints below the usual text baseline.
Superscript	A character that prints above the usual text baseline.
Text buffer	An area set aside in memory to temporarily hold text.
Text editing	The function of a word processor that enables the user to enter and edit text.
Text file	A file that contains text, as opposed to a program.
Virtual representation	An approach to screen formatting that allows the user to see on the screen exactly how the printed output will look.
Word wrap	The feature in which a word is automatically moved to the beginning of the next line if it goes past the right margin.

document being created. A **status line,** also found in this part of the screen, supplies format information about the document, such as the line and column number where the cursor is located, the page number of the text on the screen, and the number of words or characters in the document.

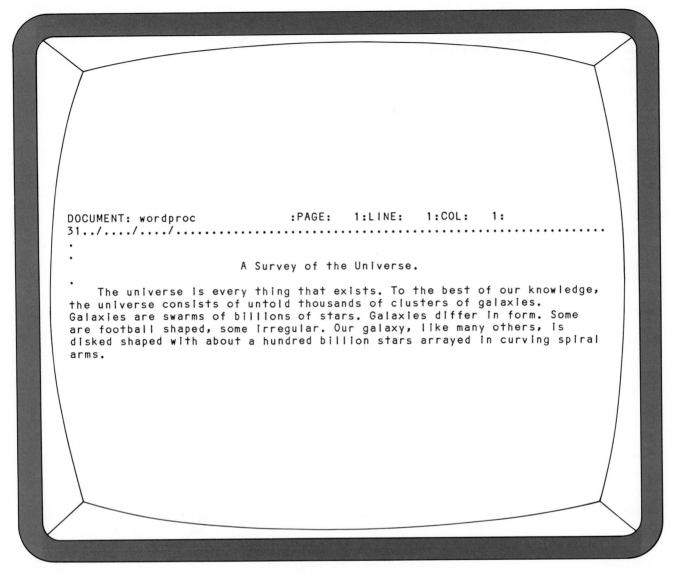

```
DOCUMENT: wordproc                  :PAGE:   1:LINE:   1:COL:   1:
31../..../..../.............................................................
  .
  .
                    A Survey of the Universe.
  .
    The universe is every thing that exists. To the best of our knowledge,
the universe consists of untold thousands of clusters of galaxies.
Galaxies are swarms of billions of stars. Galaxies differ in form. Some
are football shaped, some irregular. Our galaxy, like many others, is
disked shaped with about a hundred billion stars arrayed in curving spiral
arms.
```

● **FIGURE I–1**
Screen Display from Multimate.
The upper part of the screen displays the name of the document, the page and line number of the cursor's location, and the tabulations. The bottom part of the screen is the document being edited.

The remainder of the screen, which contains the words as they are typed, is often called the **editing window.** All editing of a document takes place in the editing window. When a mistake is made, it can easily be corrected in the editing window. Words, sentences, and even entire paragraphs can be moved, modified, or deleted by special commands.

The editing window displays twenty-five lines or less. There is also a limit as to how many characters will fit across the width of the screen. Some word processors display 40 characters across the screen; others display 80. Later in this section, you will learn about features that let you see an entire document one section at a time.

When you first enter text using a word processor, the computer's RAM (random-access memory) stores the text. For short documents, entire contents are kept in RAM. The storage method used for long documents depends on whether the word processor is memory based or disk based.

In a **memory-based word processor,** the entire document must fit into memory. Documents larger than available memory are divided into two or more documents and saved in separate files. AppleWriter II and PFS:WRITE are examples of memory-based word processors. Creating and editing a large document with a memory-based word processor is difficult if text must be moved frequently between separate files.

Creating and editing a large document with a **disk-based word processor** is much easier. A disk-based word processor loads into memory only the part of the document that is being edited, storing the remainder in temporary disk files. When you edit a different part of the document, text is automatically transferred between temporary disk files and RAM, usually without a significant delay. However, some operations, such as jumping from the first page to the last page of a large document, can cause noticeable delays of a minute or more. With a disk-based word processor, the size of a document is limited only by the amount of disk space that is available. Microsoft Word, Wordstar, and Multimate are examples of disk-based word processors.

To save a document, a text file must first be created on a disk. There are different ways to create a file on disk. Some word processors treat a text file as a series of pages. This type of word processor is referred to as a **page-oriented word processor.** This means that only one page of a document can be created or saved on disk at a time. Also, only one page of a document can be edited at a time. A **document-oriented word processor,** on the other hand, treats a document as a single continuous file, and the entire document can be saved with one command. Document-oriented word processors make editing a long document easier because pages do not have to be worked on separately. The bottom portion of one page and the top portion of the next page can appear on the screen at the same time.

Once the document is saved, it can be retrieved at any time either for printing or further editing. A document can be in perfect order before one word is committed to paper.

● Uses of Word Processors

Word processors are used in many places including homes, businesses, and schools. The features included in a word processor often depend on how it is going to be used.

At home, word processors can be used to write school reports, personal letters, or minutes from a meeting. Most word processors for home use are easier to operate than those designated for business use because they usually have fewer features than business word processors. For example, print-formatting capabilities, which control page breaks, page numbering, and character enhancements, are limited in a word-processing package for home use.

In offices, word processors are used to produce reports, formal correspondence, brochures, legal papers, and other important documents. They merge names and addresses into form letters to personalize the letters. Business-oriented word processors often include spelling checkers, on-line dictionaries, or on-line thesauruses.

Word processors have revolutionized the publishing industry. Books, newspapers, and magazines are produced faster with fewer mistakes. Sometimes, documents are not printed until they are ready for distribution. Writers enter text at computer terminals. Editors review the work at their terminals. Then, designers lay out the pages electronically. They choose the type style, size, and column width. Finally, the document is printed. With this electronic procedure, some documents are printed only once, eliminating some of the paper steps necessary in conventional publishing.

Schools are increasing their use of word processors. Students can write essays or reports on the computers in their classroom. Often, teachers can format tests and worksheets on a computer much faster than on a typewriter. Of course, school secretaries can use word processors to prepare school reports and letters.

No matter how word processors are used, they allow writers to think more about organizing ideas than about the mechanics of writing. Editing a document before it is printed is easier with a word processor.

CHECKPOINT I–1

1. Explain how a word processor makes it easy to correct mistakes made when you type a document.
2. Where is text stored when it is first entered on the computer?
3. Describe how a word processor can be used in a home.
4. Describe how a word processor can be used in an office.
5. How have word processors changed the publishing industry?

● Features of Word Processors

All word processors perform the same general tasks, but the programs differ in types and number of features. Generally, the more features included in a package, the more the package will cost.

The following section discusses four categories of features: writing and editing, screen formatting, print formatting, and additional features.

WRITING AND EDITING FEATURES

Writing and editing features make typing and changing text fast and easy. They remove many of the mechanics, such as cutting, pasting, and retyping, typically associated with the manual writing of documents (Figure I–2).

Cursor Movement

The cursor is the line or box on the screen that shows the point where text can next be entered on the screen. Some word-processing packages allow cursor movement anywhere on the screen, which speeds up typing and editing.

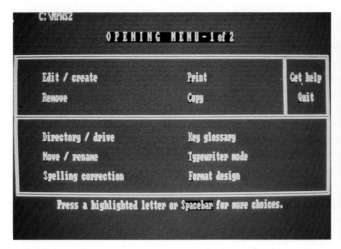

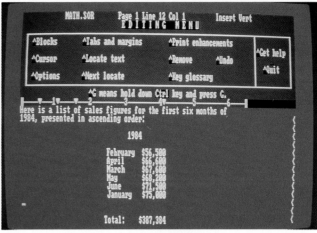

● **FIGURE I–2**
MicroPro's WordStar 2000.
a. This photograph of WordStar 2000's Opening Menu indicates some of the writing features the program performs.
b. This photograph from WordStar 2000's Editing Menu indicates some of the editing features the program performs.

Keys used to move the cursor are programmed in the software package. Many computers use arrow keys to move the cursor, and at least one computer, the Macintosh, relies on a mouse to control the cursor. Keys commonly used to move the cursor are the following:

- *Home:* Moves the cursor to the top left corner of the screen.
- *Top of page:* Moves the cursor to the first character on the screen.
- *End of page:* Moves the cursor to the last character on the screen.
- *Tab:* Moves the cursor to the right a set number of spaces.
- *Page up:* Displays the page that comes directly before the one shown.
- *Page down:* Displays the page that comes directly after the one shown.
- *Next word:* Moves the cursor to the first character of the next word.
- *Previous word:* Moves the cursor to the first character of the word before it.
- *Next page:* Shows the next page and places the cursor at the first character on that page.
- *Previous page:* Places the cursor at the first character on that page.
- *Goto:* Moves the cursor to a specified location.

Scrolling

If a document has twenty-five or more lines, all of the lines cannot be seen on the screen at once. **Scrolling** moves the lines of text on and off the screen. New lines move onto the screen as lines on the top of the screen scroll off. Scrolling can be visualized by imagining that the document is contained on a scroll and that the computer screen is a stationary window placed over the scroll. If we were to wind the scroll up, lines of text would disappear off the top of the screen and new lines would appear on the bottom. Word processors also allow you to scroll down. In this case, lines of text disappear off the bottom of the screen and new lines appear on the top. Some word processors also allow horizontal scrolling to handle lines longer than the display window.

Insert and Replace

The **insert and replace** features allow new characters to be entered into a document replacing old characters. They are commonly used features in any word processor. Insert lets you add characters, words, sentences, or larger blocks of text to the existing document. A new character or characters can be inserted in the middle of existing text. The characters that follow the inserted text move to the right to make room for it.

The replace feature lets you correct a spelling or typing mistake. By moving the cursor to the incorrect characters and typing over them, you replace the mistakes with the new characters.

Most programs give you a choice of being in insert mode, where new characters are added to the text without deleting any, or in replacement mode, where new characters take the place of those already in the text. Most word processors begin in the insert mode. To switch between the two modes, programs use a command that acts as a toggle switch to put the program in one mode or the other. When the command is executed again, it switches to the other mode. The command used to toggle between the two modes varies from word processor to word processor.

Word Wrap

When you have reached the end of a line using a typewriter, you press the <Return> key to go to the beginning of the next line. Most word processors have a feature called **word wrap.** At the end of a line, if a word goes past the margin, it automatically moves to the next line. This allows you to type faster since there is no need for you to be aware of where each line must stop.

Delete

Some word processors allow for **deletion** of a character, word, or larger block of text from the document. There are typically two forms of character deletion in most word processors. The first, backward deletion, deletes the character to the left of the cursor, moves the cursor to the blank position, and then shifts the rest of the line over to fill in the space left blank by the deleted character. Most delete features automatically adjust the rest of the text to fill in the space. Typically, the backspace key is used for reverse deletion. For example, each time the backspace key is pressed, it moves the cursor back one space, erases the character in that space, and closes up any remaining text.

Forward deletion is the second form of character deletion. The cursor is placed under or on the character to be deleted, and a delete command is executed erasing the selected character from the text. The remaining text shifts to the left filling the gap. This command is typically performed by pressing a single key, such as a <DEL> key. Continually executing this command, for example holding down the <DEL> key, continues the deleting and shifting. Entire words or phrases can be deleted using this method. Which method is more useful depends on the situation. Backward deletion is often used to correct typographical errors immediately after they are made. Forward deletion is more often used to edit an existing document for meaning or style. Methods for deleting large sections of text are discussed in the next section on block operations.

Block Operations

Block operations, which allow manipulation of large numbers of characters at the same time, are much more efficient than single-character operations. To begin block operations, mark the beginning and end of the block of characters you wish to manipulate. This is followed by the command to manipulate the block.

Marking a block of text typically requires that the cursor be moved to the beginning of the block, where a command is issued marking the beginning of the block. The cursor is then moved to the end of the block, and a similar command is issued marking the end of the block. The actual method for marking a block of text varies. Some programs have separate commands to mark the beginning and end of the block, whereas others use the same command for both. Some programs provide shortcuts for marking a word, sentence, paragraph, or even the entire document.

Word processing programs often display marked text differently from the rest of the text. Two common ways are inverse video and highlighting. Inverse video reverses the screen colors of the marked area of the text. Highlighting increases the intensity of the characters in the marked area.

Typical block operations include the following:

- Block-delete
- Block-move
- Block-copy
- Block-save
- Block-merge

Block-delete marks a block of text and then issues a single command to delete the entire block of text. In some programs, once you delete a block of text it is gone for good. Other, more "friendly" programs place the deleted block of text into a **buffer** (also called a clipboard). A buffer is a separate area of memory in which characters can be stored and retrieved. Typically, only one block of text can be stored in a buffer at a time. When another block of text is placed in the buffer, the previously stored block is erased. Some word processors allow you to view the contents of the buffer; others do not. The buffer is usually limited in size. If the delete operation exceeds the buffer size, then it must be performed in separate steps.

Block-move marks a block of text and then moves it from one location to another. This procedure is usually performed in one of two ways. The first way marks the block and places the cursor at the point to which you want to move the block. A command is issued to move the block of text. The second way, the cut and paste method, marks the block of text. Next, a command to cut the block is made. The text moves into the buffer and disappears from the display screen. Other operations that do not use the buffer may be performed next, or you can place the cursor where you want the text to be inserted and issue a paste command to place the block from the buffer back into the text.

Block-copy marks a block of text and duplicates it at a new location. Block-copies are accomplished in a similar fashion as block-moves, except the original marked text is copied rather than deleted.

Block-save marks a block of text and saves it as a new file on a disk.

Block-merge reads a file from disk and merges it with the document currently in memory.

Undo

An **undo** feature cancels a command, allowing you to undo what you have done. The text returns to the form it was in before the command. For example, if you delete a page when you only want to delete one word, the undo feature retrieves the page. But the undo feature will usually only work for the last action taken. If you delete a page by mistake and then type even one new character, you typically cannot retrieve the page.

Search

A **search** feature lets you look for a word or phrase in the document. This is helpful when you find a misspelled word in a long report. You can search for each time the word appears and then correct it.

Some word processors have a **search and replace** feature. This feature not only finds a certain word or phrase but also lets you replace it with another word or phrase. **Global search and replace** finds all occurrences of a word or words and automatically replaces the word with another word or words. For example, if a report uses the pronoun *he*, you could search for each time *he* appears and change it to *she*.

Some word processors only allow you to search forward from the point of the cursor. Others are more flexible and allow you to search backward or to request a global search no matter where the cursor is presently located. Several options for defining a match may also be available. Typical options are the following:

● *Upper/lower case match:* The case of the strings must match exactly. For example, the string "pizza" would not match the string "Pizza."
● *Whole word only match:* The string search must be for a separate word. For example, the string "good" would not be found in the word "goodness."
● *Wild card match:* Finds any word containing the specified characters in the specified location. For example, if "★" were a wild card character, "re★" would find report, retread, rehire, and so on.

Save

This feature saves the text stored in RAM onto a secondary storage device such as a floppy disk. When you type a long document, saving it often is a good idea. Then, if the power goes off or you accidentally erase a large block of text, most of it will be saved on disk.

With some word processors, you can save a document and continue typing. Others assume you are finished when you save a document. If you want to continue, you have to load the document into memory again.

SCREEN-FORMATTING FEATURES

Screen-formatting features control how the text appears on the screen and includes displays that give on-screen information about the document. Figure I–3 shows a typical screen display. A smaller area, typically located in the upper part of the screen, displays status information, menu/command selections, and help/error messages. The larger portion shows the text being edited. The number of lines allocated to each section depends on the individual program. Users with less experience generally want more information displayed, whereas more experienced users generally prefer to have less information and more of the text displayed. Many programs avoid this conflict by allowing users to decide how much information to display. The following are some of the more common screen-formatting features.

● **FIGURE I–3**
Screen Display from WordStar 2000.
The top line of the screen shows status information. The Editing Menu showing command selections is under the status line. A help message explaining the meaning of "^G" is under the Editing Menu. The rest of the screen shows the text being edited.

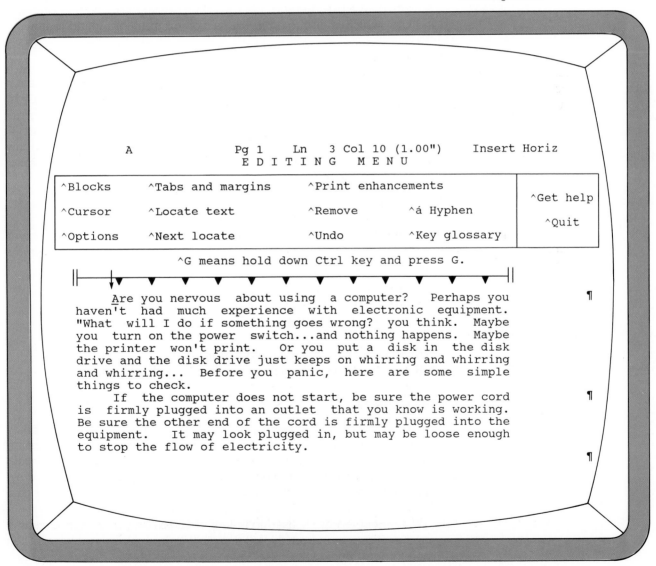

```
            A                 Pg 1    Ln   3 Col 10 (1.00")    Insert Horiz
                                E D I T I N G    M E N U

        ^Blocks        ^Tabs and margins    ^Print enhancements
                                                                    ^Get help
        ^Cursor        ^Locate text         ^Remove      ^á Hyphen
                                                                    ^Quit
        ^Options       ^Next locate         ^Undo        ^Key glossary

                    ^G means hold down Ctrl key and press G.
```

Are you nervous about using a computer? Perhaps you haven't had much experience with electronic equipment. "What will I do if something goes wrong? you think. Maybe you turn on the power switch...and nothing happens. Maybe the printer won't print. Or you put a disk in the disk drive and the disk drive just keeps on whirring and whirring and whirring... Before you panic, here are some simple things to check. ¶

If the computer does not start, be sure the power cord is firmly plugged into an outlet that you know is working. Be sure the other end of the cord is firmly plugged into the equipment. It may look plugged in, but may be loose enough to stop the flow of electricity. ¶

Screen-Oriented Word Processing

In any word processor, the relationship between what is on the screen and what is printed on paper is important. Ideally, what you see on the screen should exactly match what is printed on the paper. This is generally referred to as the what-you-see-is-what-you-get feature or **screen-oriented word processing.** Actually, most word processors will not match exactly. For example, you might choose to have the title of a paper centered on the page. With some word processors, the title may appear on the screen at the left margin, but when the paper is printed, the title will be centered. A more screen-oriented word processor centers the title on the screen. Some word processors may not show certain character enhancements on the screen, such as boldface or italics, but these character enhancements appear when the document is printed. The closer a particular software package comes to screen-oriented word processing, the easier it is to correctly format a document the first time it is printed. An alternative to screen-oriented word processing is off-screen print formatting, which is discussed in the section on print-formatting features.

Screen Size

Many word processors display 80 characters in a line. Some display even more if you scroll horizontally. Still other computers can display only 40 columns per line. There are several ways a word-processing program can work with a 40-column screen. One way is to let the text over 40 columns wrap around onto the next line. Another way is to horizontally scroll so that more than 40 columns can be displayed. With horizontal scrolling, however, reading the document is difficult.

Status Displays

Some word processors show a status line on the screen. This line gives format information about the document. Examples of items in the status line are the following:

- Line number where the cursor is located
- Column where the cursor is located
- Page number on the screen
- Amount of available memory
- Number of words or characters in the document
- Ruler line showing margins, tab stops, and indents

Tabs/Indents

The **tab** feature of most word processors works the same as the tab key on a typewriter. Set tabs in any column and activate them by pressing the TAB key. Options include tabs that place columns of words to the left, center, or right of the tab setting. With some word processors, you set tabs so that columns of numbers line up along their decimal points (see Figure I–4).

The **indent** feature is used to indent all lines of a paragraph the same number of spaces in from the left margin (Figure I–5). This feature is often used for long quotations.

Page Breaks

Some word processors display a mark indicating the end of one page and the beginning of another. This feature helps avoid bad breaks in the text. For example, you would not want the last word of a paragraph on a new page. Page breaks can be set to occur automatically after a certain number of lines, or they can be manually placed at any position in the document. Inserting manual page breaks can be tedious; however, relying on automatic page breaks can create such problems as orphan and widow lines. An orphan line occurs when the first line of a paragraph is the bottom line of a page. The remainder of the paragraph follows at the top of the next page. A widow line occurs when the last line of a paragraph falls at the top of a page. The preceding lines of the paragraph are located on the bottom of the page preceding the widow line.

● **FIGURE I–4**
An Example of Decimal Tabs from Multimate.
All columns of numbers line up along their decimal points. The symbols before the figures represent the decimal tabs.

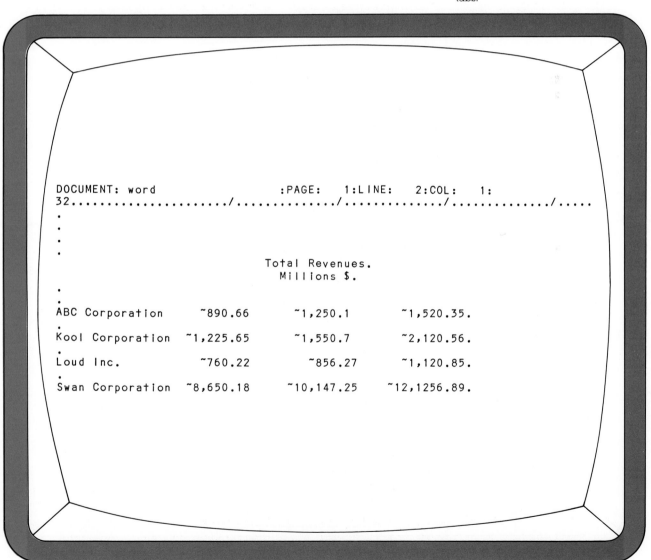

```
DOCUMENT: word                    :PAGE:  1:LINE:   2:COL:   1:
32......................./.................../.................../...../
 .
 .
 .
 .
                         Total Revenues.
                         Millions $.
 .
 .
ABC Corporation      ~890.66      ~1,250.1       ~1,520.35.
 .
Kool Corporation  ~1,225.65       ~1,550.7       ~2,120.56.
 .
Loud Inc.            ~760.22       ~856.27       ~1,120.85.
 .
Swan Corporation  ~8,650.18      ~10,147.25     ~12,1256.89.
```

PRINT-FORMATTING FEATURES

Print-formatting features determine how a document will look, such as the width of the margins and the amount of space between lines. Some word processors embed codes or print formatting commands within the text that direct the printer how to print the document. The exact commands may vary based on the particular word-processing program and/or type of printer being used. Printer commands are usually surrounded by a special character such as a period or backslash that identifies them as printer commands. The special character print-formatting commands in a document are not printed. A print-formatting program interprets these commands and sends the results to the printer. This makes it difficult to tell how a document will look when it is printed by looking at what is on the screen. Some programs offer a print-preview feature that allows

● **FIGURE I–5**
An Example of the Indent Feature from WordStar 2000.
Two long quotations, footnote 2 and footnote 3, were indented using the indent feature.

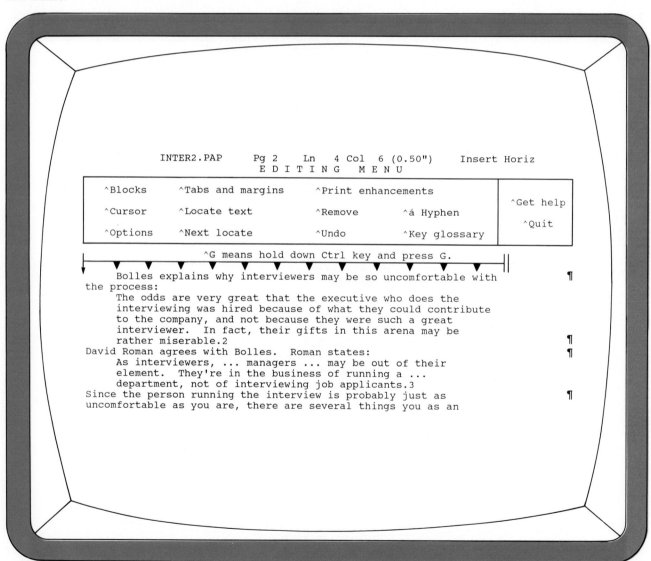

```
        INTER2.PAP     Pg 2   Ln  4 Col  6 (0.50")    Insert Horiz
                    E D I T I N G   M E N U

  ^Blocks      ^Tabs and margins   ^Print enhancements
                                                          ^Get help
  ^Cursor      ^Locate text        ^Remove    ^á Hyphen
                                                          ^Quit
  ^Options     ^Next locate        ^Undo      ^Key glossary

                 ^G means hold down Ctrl key and press G.

    Bolles explains why interviewers may be so uncomfortable with    ¶
the process:
    The odds are very great that the executive who does the
    interviewing was hired because of what they could contribute
    to the company, and not because they were such a great
    interviewer.  In fact, their gifts in this arena may be
    rather miserable.2                                               ¶
David Roman agrees with Bolles.  Roman states:                       ¶
    As interviewers, ... managers ... may be out of their
    element.  They're in the business of running a ...
    department, not of interviewing job applicants.3
Since the person running the interview is probably just as          ¶
uncomfortable as you are, there are several things you as an
```

● **COMPUTERS AND INFORMATION PROCESSING**

you to see on the display screen what the document will look like when it is printed. Most new programs use the screen-oriented formatting approach, which is much easier to use and understand.

Print-formatting can be divided into three processes: page design, paragraph layout, and character attributes.

Page design is the process of fitting the text on a page. Margins, headers and footers, and page lengths are all a part of page design. Figure I–6 shows a typical page design.

Margin Settings

Some word processors allow margins to be set on all four sides. Others allow only the left and right margins to be set. When the margins can be set by the user, many word processors have **default settings.** Default

● **FIGURE I–6**
An Example of Page Design from Multimate.
The print parameters shown here determine the design of a page.

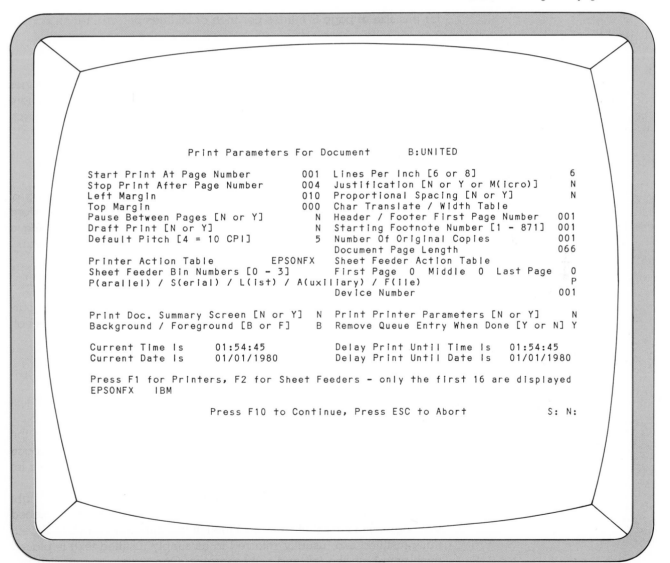

```
        Print Parameters For Document        B:UNITED

Start Print At Page Number        001   Lines Per Inch [6 or 8]              6
Stop Print After Page Number      004   Justification [N or Y or M(icro)]    N
Left Margin                       010   Proportional Spacing [N or Y]        N
Top Margin                        000   Char Translate / Width Table
Pause Between Pages [N or Y]         N   Header / Footer First Page Number  001
Draft Print [N or Y]                N   Starting Footnote Number [1 - 871] 001
Default Pitch [4 = 10 CPI]          5   Number Of Original Copies          001
                                        Document Page Length               066
Printer Action Table         EPSONFX    Sheet Feeder Action Table
Sheet Feeder Bin Numbers [0 - 3]        First Page  0  Middle  0  Last Page  0
P(arallel) / S(erial) / L(ist) / A(uxiliary) / F(ile)                       P
                                        Device Number                      001

Print Doc. Summary Screen [N or Y]  N   Print Printer Parameters [N or Y]    N
Background / Foreground [B or F]     B   Remove Queue Entry When Done [Y or N] Y

Current Time Is      01:54:45           Delay Print Until Time Is    01:54:45
Current Date Is      01/01/1980         Delay Print Until Date Is    01/01/1980

Press F1 for Printers, F2 for Sheet Feeders - only the first 16 are displayed
EPSONFX   IBM

              Press F10 to Continue, Press ESC to Abort          S: N:
```

settings are preset margins that are activated when the user does not state any others.

Headers and Footers

A header is a piece of text printed at the top of the page, such as a title for each page of text. A footer is a piece of text that is printed at the bottom of a page, such as a page number. Headers and footers are stored separately from the text. They are automatically printed at the appropriate place on every page in the document. There are usually options to place them to the left, right, or centered on a page.

Page Length

Page length is typically stated in terms of the number of lines per page. The standard page is 8 1/2-by-11 inches. One of the most common settings for this size of page is 6 lines per inch or 66 lines per an 11-inch page.

Automatic Page Numbering

A word processor that has **automatic page numbering** produces pages with printed page numbers. Some word processors let you choose where the page numbers appear. Others can print them only in one place, such as in the top right corner.

Paragraph Layout

On most word processors the ENTER or RETURN key ends a string of characters forming a paragraph. Paragraph length could be one word or many sentences long. Typical areas of concern when designing a paragraph layout include paragraph margins and justification of text.

Paragraph Margins

Most word processors allow control of margin settings for individual paragraphs, thereby overriding the page margins. This allows you to set off certain portions of the text.

Centered, Left-, Right-, and Fully Justified Text

Most word processors allow for centered, left-, right-, or fully justified text (Figure I–7 shows examples of each).

When you use a typewriter and **center** a line, you must count the characters in the line, divide this number by two, and then backspace that many times from the center of the page. Most word processors let you center a word of line by simply pressing one or two keys.

Left-justified text is placed flush against the left margin with the right margin allowed to be ragged or uneven. Right-justified text is placed flush against the right margin with the left margin allowed to be ragged. Fully justified text (usually referred to as simply justified text) is placed flush with both the left and right margins. One way to accomplish this

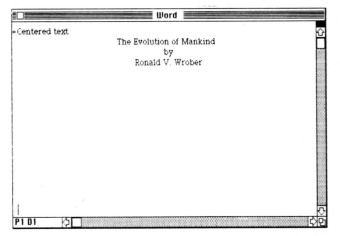

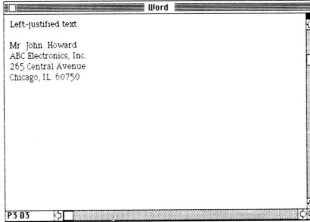

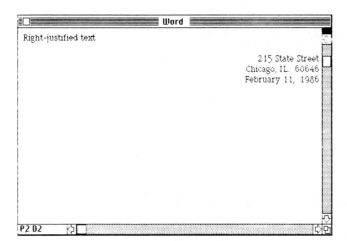

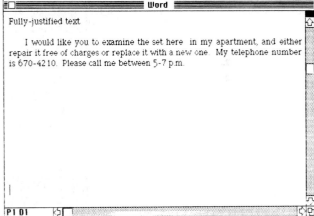

● **FIGURE I–7**
Examples of Justified Text from Microsoft Word.
a. Centered Text b. Left-justified Text
c. Right-justified Text d. Fully-justified Text

is by adding spaces between words. However, this method can give the document an awkward appearance when the spacing between words varies widely. Another, more precise method is to use microspacing or proportional spacing. This method automatically inserts very small spaces between letters and words to give the document a more professional appearance.

Line Spacing

A **line-spacing** feature lets the user choose the amount of space between lines. A document that is single spaced has no blank lines between printed lines. A double-spaced document has one blank line between printed lines. Some word processors allow for triple spacing. Many times, line spacing appears only in the printed document. The screen shows only single spacing.

Character Attributes

The appearance of an individual character is determined by its attributes. The attributes include character size, design, and enhancement. Character enhancements change the normal appearance of a character. They include such modifications as boldface, underline, italics, subscript, and superscript words. Boldface is type that is darker **(boldface)** (see Figure I–8). Underlined words have a line printed under them (underline). Italic words slant to the right *(italic)*. Subscript lowers the selected characters below the baseline of the text (sub$_{script}$). Superscript raises the selected characters above the baseline of the text (super^{script}). If the word processor has these features, the printer must have the capability to print them.

OTHER FEATURES

Help Facilities

On-line help are tips called up on the display screen that give information about a command or function. Help screens are presented through a menu or context-sensitive system. With a menu system, whenever the help function is activated, a menu of all the available help topics is displayed. The user chooses the topic about which information is needed. With a context-sensitive system, the program monitors the command or function being performed. When help is activated, the user immediately receives help information about the command or function being used.

Windows

In word processing, a window is an area of the screen that allows you to view a document or portions of a document. Early word processors

● **FIGURE I–8**
This photograph from Microsoft Word illustrates the use of boldface. The words "Too Tall Toys" and "Too Tall Toy Company" are bolded.

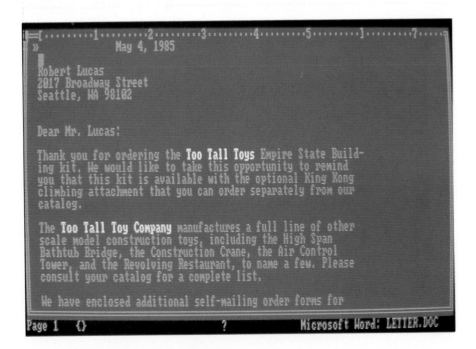

only had one window. With one window, only one portion of one document can be seen at a time. The trend today is toward multiple windows. With multiple windows, several portions of one document or portions of several documents can all be seen at the same time. There are advantages to using more than one document window. You can edit several documents at once to maintain consistency. While writing a document, you can go to other documents or to other places in the current document for information. You can easily copy and move text between documents or within the current document.

Dictionaries and Thesauruses

Two valuable tools for any writer are a dictionary and a thesaurus. Many programs incorporate one or both of these on disk. A dictionary program allows a user to check spelling quickly and efficiently (see Figure I–9). Most dictionaries on disk include between 20,000 and 80,000 words. Words spelled incorrectly or not contained in the dictionary are highlighted in some manner so that the user can check them and make the appropriate corrections. Many dictionaries allow you to add words to them. The electronic thesaurus allows you to request the synonyms of any word on the screen that is contained in the thesaurus. If the word is not in the thesaurus, a message stating this is usually displayed. Some programs may let you add the word with the appropriate synonyms.

Print Merge

Many programs have a print merge option that allows you to print multiple versions of a document or personalize a form letter. The option typically consists of two documents. The main document contains standard text that remains constant, with instructions and special fields that

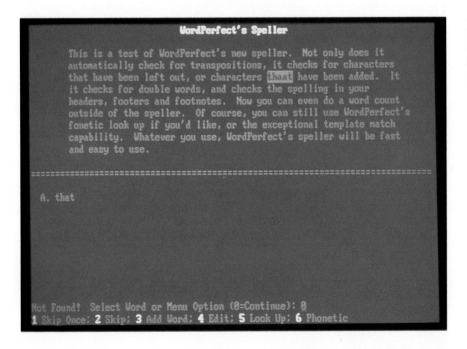

● **FIGURE I–9**
WordPerfect's speller, illustrated in this photograph, will check a word, a page, or a document for spelling errors and bring up a list of possible corrections.

are used to receive the text that varies from letter to letter. The merge document contains pieces of text that vary from letter to letter, such as names and addresses.

● Hardware Requirements

Certain minimum hardware requirements must be met before a word-processing system is functional. The exact hardware needed to run a package depends on the word processor.

The most fundamental piece of hardware needed to run a word processor is a computer with sufficient memory to run the program. Most word processors require a minimum of 64K of RAM. Many word processors, particularly those designated for business use, require more.

At least one disk drive is needed to operate a word processor. In most cases, two disk drives make operations much easier, and many word processors require two drives to operate.

Next, a monitor on which to view the text being entered is needed. Although color monitors will work, they are not well suited for word processing because the characters may not appear sharp and clear. A high-resolution monochrome monitor produces the best quality text on the screen.

Finally, a printer is needed. There are many types of printers on the market. Generally, a printer is selected based on how the word processor will be used. For example, an inexpensive, dot-matrix printer is adequate if the word processor is mostly being used for writing short letters and school reports. However, if the documents need to look as if they were typewritten, a more expensive letter-quality printer is necessary.

CHECKPOINT I-2

1. Name the three general groups of word-processing features.
2. Describe word wrap.
3. Why is the undo feature useful?
4. Describe information included in the status line on the screen.
5. Name three print-formatting features.

● Summary

● Word processors are used in homes, businesses, schools, and many other places.

● A word processor lets the user write, edit, format, and print text.

● Text entered on a word processor is stored in RAM. Some text using a secondary storage device, such as a floppy disk, can be retrieved later.

● The features of a word processor depend on the purpose for which it will be used.

● Common writing and editing features are cursor moving, word wrap, scrolling, insert and replace, delete, search, undo, and save.

● Common screen-formatting features include screen size, tabs, page breaks, and status displays.

- Common print-formatting features are margin settings, line spacing, centering, automatic page numbering, and special characters.
- The basic hardware needed to run a word processor includes the computer, disk drive, monitor, 80-column card, printer, and printer interface card.

● Review Questions

1. Describe a word processor.

2. What tasks do the writing and editing features of a word processor perform?

3. What is a cursor? Explain how controlling the movement of the cursor helps the user write and edit with a word processor.

4. What is the purpose of a scrolling feature?

5. What is meant by "search and replace"?

6. How could the page-breaks feature help?

7. When would you use a word processor's margin-default settings?

8. Why would you need a word processor that can display and print eighty columns?

9. List the basic hardware devices that you need for a computer to run a word-processor program.

10. Describe three jobs you can do with a word-processor program that you could not do with a typewriter.

● SECTION II
Data Managers

● Introduction

Schools, hospitals, restaurants, and in fact all types of businesses store data. The ability to quickly and efficiently retrieve, sort, and analyze data could easily make the difference between a company's success and failure. The types of data collected include employee records, bills, supplies, budgets, and insurance information. Before microcomputers became standard business equipment, the most common way to organize data was to store the records in folders in file cabinets. File cabinets, however, use a lot of space and sometimes several departments may keep the same data. This duplication of data is a waste of time, effort, and space and can lead to confusion or errors if one copy is changed.

Data managers are software packages that computerize record-keeping tasks. This section explains what a data manager is and how it works. It also describes how data managers are used and their most common features.

● What Is a Data Manager?

A data-manager software package is used to organize files. Data managers let you store and access data with your computer. Data kept in folders and envelopes in a manual filing system can be stored in secondary storage devices such as floppy disks.

Understanding how data is stored in a filing cabinet is easy. Folders with related data are kept in the drawers of the cabinet. Each folder has a label that identifies the contents. The contents of each drawer may be related to a certain topic. To find one data item, you would have to select the appropriate drawer and then search through the folders in that drawer to find the one with the data you needed.

With a data manager, data are recorded electronically on floppy disks or magnetic tapes. Instead of people looking through drawers and folders for a certain item, the computer searches the disk or tape for it.

Each data item, such as a student name, an insurance policy number, or the amount of a bill, is called a **field** (Figure II–1).

A group of related fields form a **record.** Your school may keep a record about each student. A student record might contain fields such as the student's name, home address, parents' names, class standing, courses taken, and grade-point average (Figure II–2).

A **file** is a group of related records. For example, all the student records in a school make up one file. The school may have other files, such as one for teacher records, another for financial records, and yet another for school board records.Data managers are useful because they perform many tasks faster and more easily than the tasks can be completed with a manual filing system. Most data managers can perform the following:

- Add or delete data within a file
- Search a file for certain data
- Update or change data in a file
- Sort data into some order
- Print all or part of the data in a file

● **FIGURE II–1**
An Example of Fields Stored on dBaseIII.
The cursor is positioned on field 1.

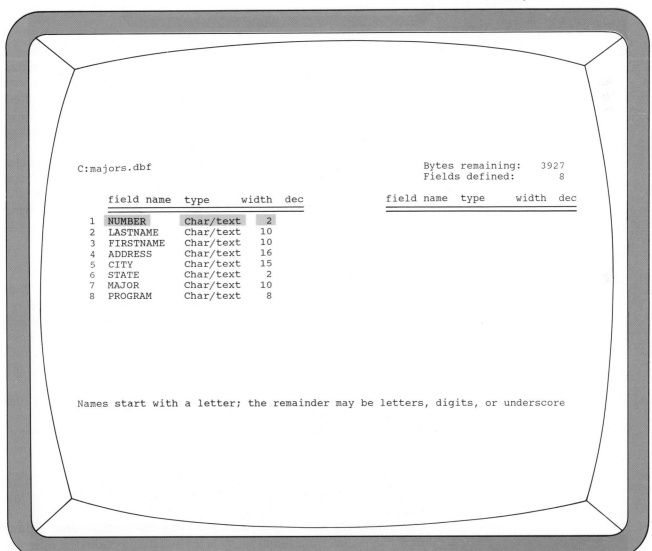

```
C:majors.dbf                                        Bytes remaining:   3927
                                                    Fields defined:       8

        field name   type      width  dec          field name   type      width  dec

    1   NUMBER       Char/text      2
    2   LASTNAME     Char/text     10
    3   FIRSTNAME    Char/text     10
    4   ADDRESS      Char/text     16
    5   CITY         Char/text     15
    6   STATE        Char/text      2
    7   MAJOR        Char/text     10
    8   PROGRAM      Char/text      8




Names start with a letter; the remainder may be letters, digits, or underscore
```

● **FIGURE II–2**
An Example of a Record Stored on dBase III.
The screen displays record number 24.

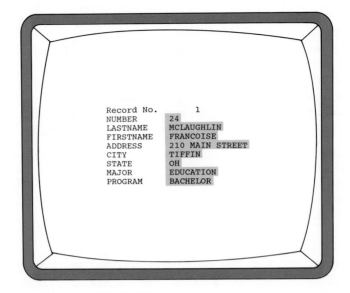

```
Record No.        1
NUMBER        24
LASTNAME      MCLAUGHLIN
FIRSTNAME     FRANCOISE
ADDRESS       210 MAIN STREET
CITY          TIFFIN
STATE         OH
MAJOR         EDUCATION
PROGRAM       BACHELOR
```

In addition to completing tasks quickly and easily, a computer seldom makes mistakes. With a computer, you can add, delete, or change data without retyping paper forms or making messy corrections. You can direct the computer to search a file for the records with the same field or fields. You can sort by any field and then place the records in their original order or sorted again in a different way.

There are two distinct types of data managers: file handlers and data-base packages. They differ mostly in the way they organize data, and because they organize data differently, they also access it differently. File handlers and data-base packages are discussed in the following sections.

FILE HANDLERS

File handlers were developed to replace traditional filing systems. With traditional filing systems, each office had records needed for that office. At a college or university, the admissions office might have kept records of student names, addresses, parent names, and standard test scores. The health center might have kept student names, addresses, parent names, and medical histories on file. Each file was used only by the office in which it was used.

With the advent of computers and computerized record keeping, the procedures and methods of recording and filing data were converted from paper, file folders, and file cabinets to computer software and storage devices. Each office or department still only had access to its own independent files.

File handlers, therefore, can access only one data file at a time. There is only one two-way path that data can travel between the data files and the file handler software (Figure II–3).

Since different files may contain the same information, **data redundancy** can occur. Data redundancy is the repeating of data in different files. In the university example, students' names, addresses, and parents'

● **COMPUTERS AND INFORMATION PROCESSING**

names are repeated in each file. When the same data are kept in many files, quickly updating or changing them in all the files is difficult.

File handlers are most useful in small organizations where some data redundancy is not a problem. They can be used effectively when information is not often shared among offices or departments. Because many software packages are available for microcomputers, file handlers are popular with home computer users.

DATA-BASE PACKAGES

File-handling software has some drawbacks for companies with enormous amounts of data. Because of the duplication of data and the difficulty of keeping one piece of information—such as an employee address—current in several files, large companies began to develop data bases. A **data base** consolidates various independent files into one integrated unit while allowing users access to the information they need. Data can be accessed from a number of paths (Figure II–4).

Each data item is stored once, making it easier to maintain. Users can still search for, update, add, or delete data, just as they do with a file handler, but they can perform these tasks on all the records at one time.

A data base can be compared to a room containing all the filing cabinets for an organization. Each department can go to the room to get information. Because unduplicated data are kept in one place, all departments can easily access and update information they require.

Data-base packages store data so they can be accessed in many ways. A university data base might be accessed by the admissions office, the registrar's office, the financial aid office, and the deans' offices. A college dean might request the names of students who will graduate with aca-

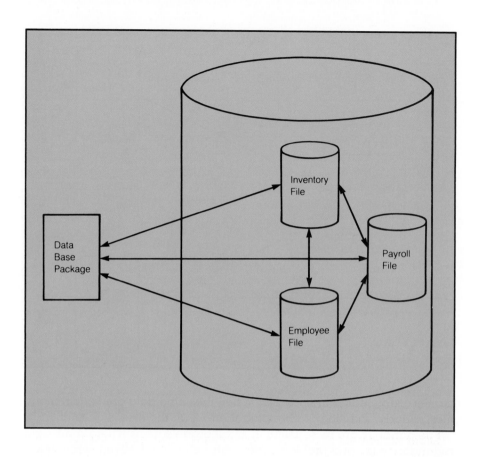

demic honors, whereas the financial aid director might need a listing of all students participating in a work-study program.

Data bases reduce data redundancy and make updating a file easier. New data are entered only once. Data-base packages also allow direct access to data. This means the computer can go directly to needed data without searching through data items in order.

Data bases are expensive to design and maintain. For example, pharmacies use data bases to store drug and patient information to help pharmacists avoid giving patients medicines that may be harmful. Police departments use data bases to track criminals or to find missing persons or stolen cars. In both cases, the computer checks the data base for cross-references.

CHECKPOINT II–1

1. Explain the uses of a data-manager software package.
2. How are data stored in a filing cabinet?
3. How are data stored by a data manager?
4. Name the five tasks most data managers can perform.
5. What is the main difference between a file handler and a data-base package?

Uses of Data Managers

Earlier, we stated that data managers are used in the home, in business, and for special purposes. The next two sections describe how data managers are used in homes and businesses. Following is a section on specialized uses of data managers.

HOME USES

Data managers are popular software packages for home use. They can be used to create and organize a computerized address book, Christmas card list, or recipe file. A data manager can be used for just about any type of record keeping. Collectors of coins, stamps, baseball cards, or any other items can keep an up-to-date file of their collections.

By computerizing recording and filing tasks in the home, you can keep records in a compact form. Instead of having numerous notebooks and folders that must be maintained manually, you enter new data into the computer. You can store files on several floppy disks or cassette tapes.

Besides storing files in a compact form, data managers can find the data much faster than by looking through folders and notebooks. For example, they can be used to prepare reports for the preparation of taxes. You could keep a record of financial transactions throughout the years and place a field labeled "Tax Deductible" in the data record to indicate whether a transaction was tax related. At tax time, the data manager could be used to pick out the tax-related transactions and print a report (Figure II–5).

Other home uses of data managers include keeping personal records, creating mailing lists, keeping appointment calendars, and indexing books in a personal library.

BUSINESS USES

In business, data managers can replace the traditional filing system of papers, folders, and filing cabinets. A data manager can maintain employee records, control inventory, and list suppliers and customers (Figure II–6). A small sporting goods retail store could computerize its inventory to improve sales through more efficient and timely record keeping. By recording daily sales, managers can see when the stock levels are low and they can reorder. The store can have an ample supply of items at all times.

Some data managers perform mathematical tasks. They can total the values of the same field in each record or find the average or find records with the lowest or highest value in the field. A data manager with mathematical capabilities can determine dollar sales of an item for a certain period. The mathematical features of a data manager can also be used for inventory control. Employees would not need to count the items in the store. The data manager can display subtotal and total inventory for tax reporting at the end of the year.

A major benefit of computerized record keeping is the savings in time in both updating data and searching for information. Data managers free employees to concentrate on tasks that can only be done by humans, such as talking to customers or planning new displays.

SPECIALIZED USES

Some data managers are designed for use in special or unique situations such as mass mailing.

Creating mailing lists is a popular application. A data manager can store data about people, such as names, addresses, interests, hobbies, and purchases. (People's interests and hobbies can be determined from studying the products they order or magazines they receive.) For example, the data manager can sort and print a list of people who order a sewing or craft item or who receive craft catalogs. The data manager can then print mailing labels for these people.

Data managers can be used with word processors to produce personalized form letters for individuals or organizations found on the mailing lists. They can supply the names and addresses to be inserted in the letter.

● **FIGURE II–5**

An example of how records might be used to store tax-related transactions on dBase III. "TD" means tax deductible.

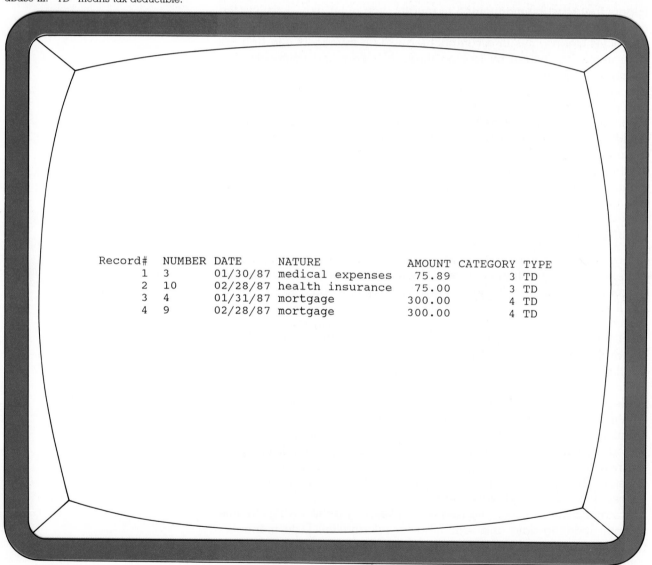

```
Record#   NUMBER  DATE        NATURE              AMOUNT  CATEGORY  TYPE
     1    3       01/30/87    medical expenses     75.89         3  TD
     2    10      02/28/87    health insurance     75.00         3  TD
     3    4       01/31/87    mortgage            300.00         4  TD
     4    9       02/28/87    mortgage            300.00         4  TD
```

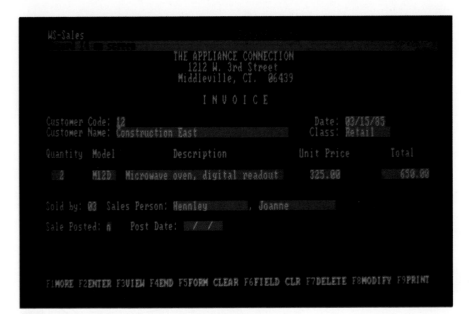

● **FIGURE II-6**
A computerized invoice on a screen
from DATAEASE by Software Solutions,
Inc.

● Features of Data Managers

Most data managers offer standard features (Figure II-7) selected from
a main menu and submenus by typing the number or letter of the option
or by moving the cursor to it (Figure II-8). The features include adding
and deleting records, searching for and updating records, sorting the
data file, indexing the data file, and printing. More specialized features
of a data manager include report generation and query facilities. Following is a brief overview of each of these features.

ADD AND DELETE

The **add** feature allows you to add a record on another person not yet
in your existing file. The **delete** feature allows you to remove or erase a
record you no longer want.

SEARCH AND UPDATE

The **search** feature searches for the record or records that contain specified data. You may want to know which of your friends and relatives
have birthdays in March. With a data manager, you can search the file
for the records with March in the birthday field.

The **update** feature lets you change data contained in a record. If your
aunt moves to a new city, you would want to change her address in
your file. First, you could search the file for your aunt's record. Then you
could change the data in the address field.

SORT

The **sort** feature is used to arrange the records in a file. Records are
usually stored in the order they are entered, but the computer can sort

the records in any order according to one data field. The most common ways to sort records are alphabetically and numerically.

You might want to sort your friends and relatives file in alphabetical order according to last name. The computer looks at the name field. Then it arranges the records in alphabetical order. You could also sort the records in order according to the years in which people were born, starting with the earliest year.

Before sorting records in a certain order, you must see whether the data fields are organized in a way that makes the sort possible. For example, to sort records according to last name, the name field needs to be arranged with the last name listed first (last name, first name). If names are entered as first name, last name, the computer sorts according to first name.

● FIGURE II–7
WestFile Main Menu

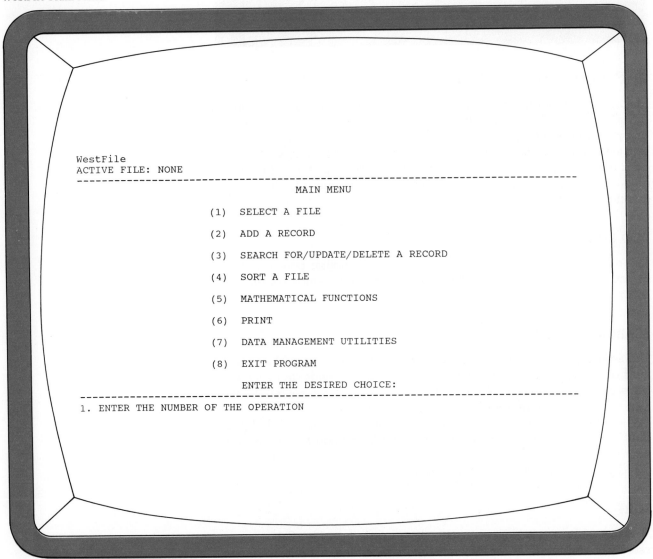

```
WestFile
ACTIVE FILE: NONE
-------------------------------------------------------------------------------
                              MAIN MENU

          (1)   SELECT A FILE

          (2)   ADD A RECORD

          (3)   SEARCH FOR/UPDATE/DELETE A RECORD

          (4)   SORT A FILE

          (5)   MATHEMATICAL FUNCTIONS

          (6)   PRINT

          (7)   DATA MANAGEMENT UTILITIES

          (8)   EXIT PROGRAM

                ENTER THE DESIRED CHOICE:
-------------------------------------------------------------------------------
1. ENTER THE NUMBER OF THE OPERATION
```

● COMPUTERS AND INFORMATION PROCESSING

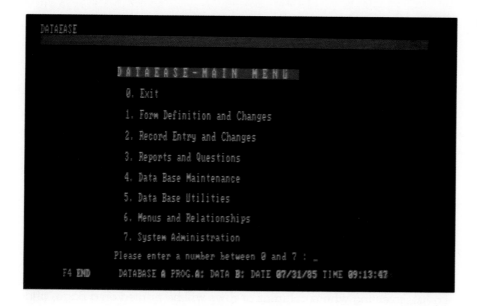

● **FIGURE II-8**
**The Main Menu from DATAEASE by
Software Solutions, Inc.**

INDEXING

An index is used to maintain ascending or descending order among a list of entries. An advantage to indexing over sorting is that with indexing, a list can be ordered by more than one **key** without holding redundant data. This is accomplished by creating separate indices for each order desired. With indices, a master list contains all information with each entry assigned a number. For example,

Master List

no.	name	position	salary
1.	smith	programmer	22,000
2.	wills	plumber	50,000
3.	jones	painter	18,000
4.	taylor	writer	20,000

When an index is created, it consists of only a list of keys in order and a pointer to the master list. For example,

name index		salary index	
key	master no.	key	master no.
jones	3	18,000	3
smith	1	20,000	4
taylor	4	22,000	1
wills	2	50,000	2

The name index is used to look up a name and the salary index used to look up a salary.

PRINT

The print feature lets you print a hard copy of your files. Some data managers can print reports. Others print simple lists of the records in a file. To print mailing lists or mailing labels, the data manager must have the print feature.

The most basic print feature allows records to be sorted and printed in the sorted order. Some data managers allow users to state which data fields from each record they want printed. Others can only print the entire record.

REPORT GENERATION

A report generator produces printed reports from lists stored in one or multiple files. The power and flexibility of report writers varies greatly from program to program. Some simply print lists in column format, others print in column and row formats and may perform mathematical operations (Figure II-9). Other options include selecting only a portion of a list, selecting where columns or rows will be printed on a page, and selecting which columns or rows should be totaled, averaged, or converted to percentages. Figure II-10a shows a data base listing the members of a museum. Figure II-10b shows a report generated from the files shown in Figure II-10a.

QUERY FACILITIES

In a data-base management system, data can be requested by using a query facility. Questions such as "How many," "What," and "Find" are common queries (Figure II-11). Some query facilities are complicated to use. However, many are easy enough to allow a nonprogrammer to process and update information stored in a data base. Some programs

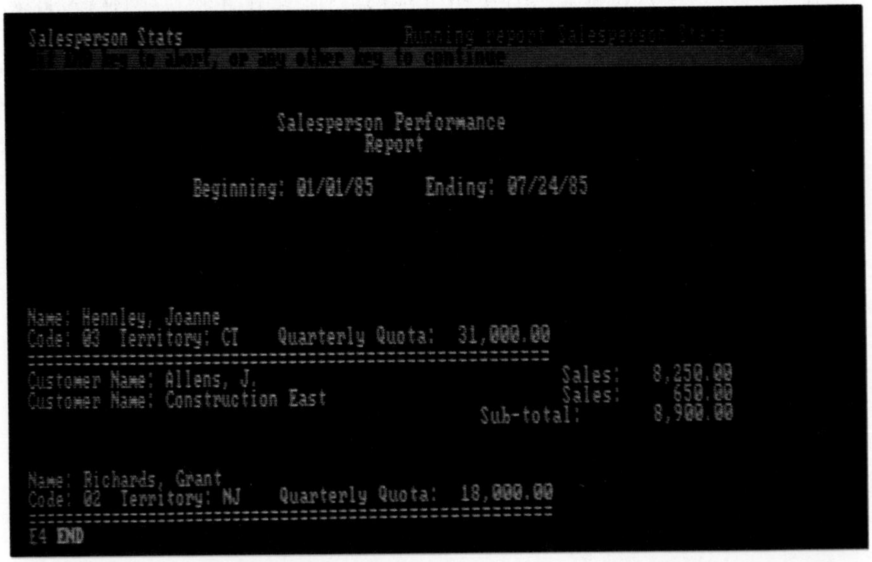

● **FIGURE II-9**
Sample Sales Report Created on DA-TAEASE by Software Solutions, Inc.

require a specific query language, whereas others allow use of natural language commands. In some data bases, it is important that you understand and use the query facility because relationships among fields are established by query commands.

● Hardware Requirements

Hardware requirements for data managers vary from package to package, depending largely on the capabilities of the particular package. However, some basic hardware requirements need to be considered for any data-manager package. Following is a brief discussion of each of these requirements.

● **FIGURE II–10a**
Example of Report Generation from dBase III
This screen shows a master list of members of a museum. Each record includes the last name, address and the date their membership expires for each member.

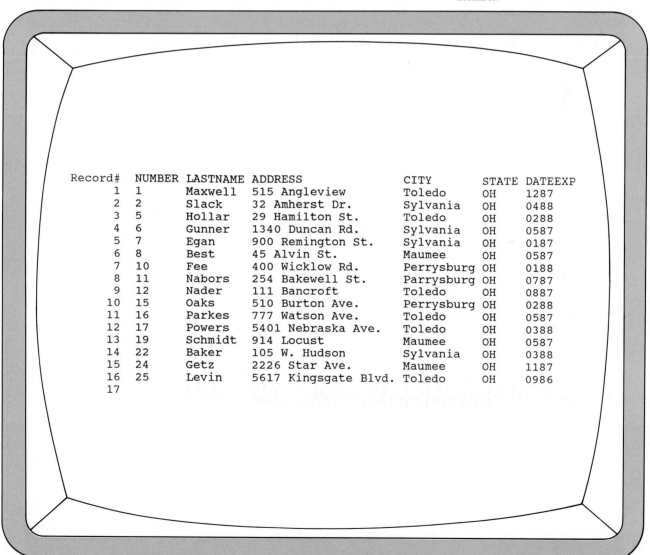

Record#	NUMBER	LASTNAME	ADDRESS	CITY	STATE	DATEEXP
1	1	Maxwell	515 Angleview	Toledo	OH	1287
2	2	Slack	32 Amherst Dr.	Sylvania	OH	0488
3	5	Hollar	29 Hamilton St.	Toledo	OH	0288
4	6	Gunner	1340 Duncan Rd.	Sylvania	OH	0587
5	7	Egan	900 Remington St.	Sylvania	OH	0187
6	8	Best	45 Alvin St.	Maumee	OH	0587
7	10	Fee	400 Wicklow Rd.	Perrysburg	OH	0188
8	11	Nabors	254 Bakewell St.	Parrysburg	OH	0787
9	12	Nader	111 Bancroft	Toledo	OH	0887
10	15	Oaks	510 Burton Ave.	Perrysburg	OH	0288
11	16	Parkes	777 Watson Ave.	Toledo	OH	0587
12	17	Powers	5401 Nebraska Ave.	Toledo	OH	0388
13	19	Schmidt	914 Locust	Maumee	OH	0587
14	22	Baker	105 W. Hudson	Sylvania	OH	0388
15	24	Getz	2226 Star Ave.	Maumee	OH	1187
16	25	Levin	5617 Kingsgate Blvd.	Toledo	OH	0986
17						

Internal memory size: Most data managers require a certain amount of internal memory, or RAM, ranging from 48K to 256K. As the RAM increases, so does the amount of data that can be stored in a file.

Secondary storage: Floppy disks are the most common type of secondary storage used with data managers. Some data managers store all files on separate floppy disks. Others have storage room for files on the same disk that contains the data manager.

If you use floppy disks as secondary storage, you will need either one or two disk drives. Some packages can handle more than two disk drives. The more disk drives you use, the more data you can access without switching disks.

Printer requirements need to be considered next. The type of printer needed depends on how you want to use the data manager. If you use

● **FIGURE II–10b.**
Example of Report Generation from dBASE III
This screen shows a report on the members whose membership expiration date is May, 1987.

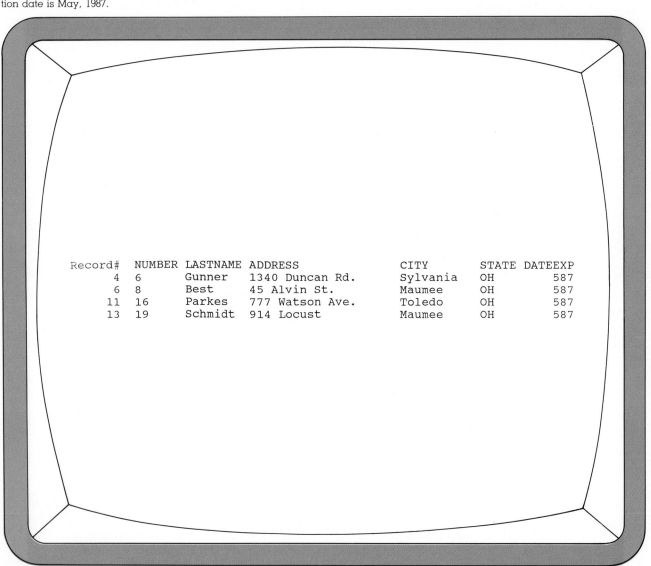

```
Record#   NUMBER LASTNAME ADDRESS           CITY      STATE DATEEXP
      4   6      Gunner   1340 Duncan Rd.   Sylvania  OH      587
      6   8      Best     45 Alvin St.      Maumee    OH      587
     11   16     Parkes   777 Watson Ave.   Toledo    OH      587
     13   19     Schmidt  914 Locust        Maumee    OH      587
```

● **COMPUTERS AND INFORMATION PROCESSING**

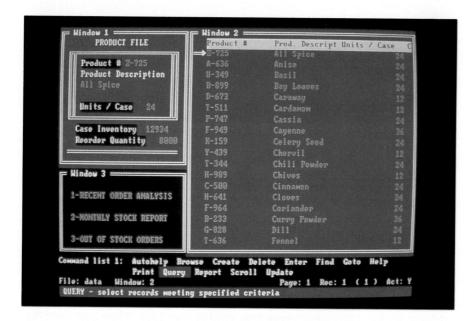

your data manager mostly for printing files for your own use, a dot-matrix printer will work well. But if you want to use it with a word processor to print letters and mailing labels, a letter-quality printer might be needed.

Monitor requirements: A monochrome monitor should work well for most purposes. If the data manager is going to be used with graphics software, a color monitor with graphics power might be needed.

If the computer and monitor do not automatically display 80 columns on the screen, then consider an 80-column card to increase the amount of text displayed to 80 columns. You may need 80 columns to see certain fields on the screen. Some data managers require an 80-column display.

These hardware requirements are only the basic requirements common to most data-management packages. Other requirements not listed here depend on the package chosen. Before using any data-management package, it is a good idea to review the hardware requirements listed on the software package and in the documentation.

CHECKPOINT II–2

1. Describe three ways a data manager can be used by a home computer user.
2. Explain how a data manager is used to create mailing lists.
3. Which data-manager features are used to find and change the address in one record in a file? Which feature is to be used to put the records in a file in a certain order according to one data field?
4. What kinds of math tasks can some data managers perform?
5. Name three hardware requirements to consider before using a data manager.

● Summary

● Data managers are software packages used to store data and keep records in a filing cabinet.

● Data stored by a data manager are recorded electronically on storage media such as floppy disks or cassette tapes.

● Each data item stored by a data manager is called a field. A group of related fields forms a record. The related records make up a file.

● Most data managers perform five basic tasks: add or delete data within a file, search a file for certain data, update or change data, sort data into some order, and print all or part of the data in a file.

● File handlers and data-base packages are two types of data managers.

● File handlers were developed to replace traditional filing systems. They access only one data file at a time. Data redundancy sometimes occurs with file handlers.

● A data base combines all organizational files. Data items are stored only once, so data redundancy is reduced.

● Data-base packages allow for direct access.

● Data managers are used in homes to create and organize computerized address books, Christmas card lists, and recipe files. They are used by collectors to keep track of coin, stamp, and baseball card collections.

● In business, data managers can replace the traditional filing system of papers, folders, and filing cabinets storing employee records, inventory records, and customer lists.

● A special use of data managers is to create mailing lists and labels.

● The hardware requirements to consider for a data manager are amount of internal memory, secondary storage, type of printer, and type of monitor.

● Review Questions

1. Explain how fields, records, and files differ.
2. How does a data manager perform filing tasks faster than a person?
3. Define file handler. Define data-base package.
4. Explain how a data base organizes data differently from a file handler.
5. What is data redundancy? Which type of data manager reduces data redundancy?
6. What type of organization uses a file handler? What type of organizations uses a data-base package?
7. How are data managers used in offices?
8. List three uses of a data manager not mentioned in the chapter. Describe each of these uses.
9. Name three common features of data managers. Explain the use of each feature.
10. What should you consider before choosing a printer to use with a data manager?

● SECTION III
Spreadsheets

● Introduction

Like most computer programs, a **spreadsheet** takes care of simple, commonly encountered manual tasks. Basically, a spreadsheet program is a calculator that uses a computer's memory capability to solve mathematically oriented problems. With a spreadsheet program, you can set up columns of numbers to keep track of money or objects.

Typically, a pencil, a piece of paper, and a calculator are the tools used to solve mathematical problems. With a spreadsheet program, computers can calculate at the speed of electricity. This capability is more useful with more complicated formulas. Imagine doing your tax returns and realizing after finishing that you forgot to include your new car as an expense. Every calculation following that part of the form would be incorrect. With a spreadsheet program, however, you simply insert the forgotten number and recalculate all the totals. This is only one example of what a spreadsheet can do. With the ability to recalculate, as well as store, print, merge, and sort numeric information, a spreadsheet is an extremely useful tool.

This chapter describes what a spreadsheet is, how it is used, and covers features common to most spreadsheet programs.

● What Is a Spreadsheet?

Ledger sheets are primarily used in the business environment by accountants and managers for financial calculations and the recording of transactions. A spreadsheet is actually a ledger sheet like the one shown in Figure III–1. To keep the numbers in line, ledger sheets have columns in which the numbers are written.

An **electronic spreadsheet** is a grid of columns and rows used to store and manipulate numeric information. The grid appears on the display screen and data are stored in the computer's memory. Probably the most significant advantage of an electronic spreadsheet over the traditional spreadsheet is the ability not only to store numbers but also to store formulas for calculating numbers. One number in a formula can easily

		HOME BUDGET			
		Expenses:			
		Rent	235 00		
		Food	100 00		
		Gas	97 00		
		Electric	75 00		
		Phone	25 00		
		Car	100 00		
		TOTAL EXPENSES	632 00		

● FIGURE III–1
Traditional Paper Spreadsheet

be changed without reentering the entire formula. Table III–1 is a quick reference to terms frequently encountered when using an electronic spreadsheet.

A spreadsheet program enables a computer to perform complex mathematical calculations. Numbers, or **values,** are entered into the **cells** formed by the columns and rows. Each cell relates to a certain storage location in the computer's memory. **Labels** can be entered to identify what the numbers mean (Figure III–2).

Formulas as well as values can be entered into cells. A formula is a mathematical expression that can contain numbers from other cells and constant numbers. If you change one number in a cell used in a formula, the program automatically recalculates using the new number.

Since electronic spreadsheets can instantaneously recalculate a formula, they can be used to ask "what if" questions when you want to

● Table III-1
Terms Associated with Electronic Spreadsheets

TERM	DEFINITION
Cell	A storage location within a spreadsheet used to store a single piece of information relevant to the spreadsheet.
Coordinate	The location of a cell within a spreadsheet; a combination of the column letter and row number that intersect at a specific cell.
Formula	A mathematical equation used in a spreadsheet.
Label	Information used for describing some aspect of a spreadsheet. A label can be made up of alphabetic or numeric information, but no arithmetic may be performed on a label.
Value	A single piece of numeric information used in the calculations of a spreadsheet.
Window	The portion of a worksheet that can be seen on the computer display screen.

know what will happen to certain numbers in a spreadsheet if other numbers change. The following are examples of "what if" questions:

- What if I spend $50 more at the grocery store each month?
- What if the interest earned by my savings account goes up 0.5 percent?
- What if I take a job working on commission rather than salary?

With a spreadsheet program, the computer instantly adjusts the numbers affected by the changed number. If a person calculated the numbers by hand or with a calculator, all the numbers would have to be recopied on a new paper spreadsheet. A spreadsheet program calculates in seconds what it would take a person several hours to do by hand. The new spreadsheet appears almost immediately on the screen.

● **FIGURE III–2**
From Lotus 1-2-3
Columns A, B, D, and F contain labels.
Columns C, E, and G contain values.

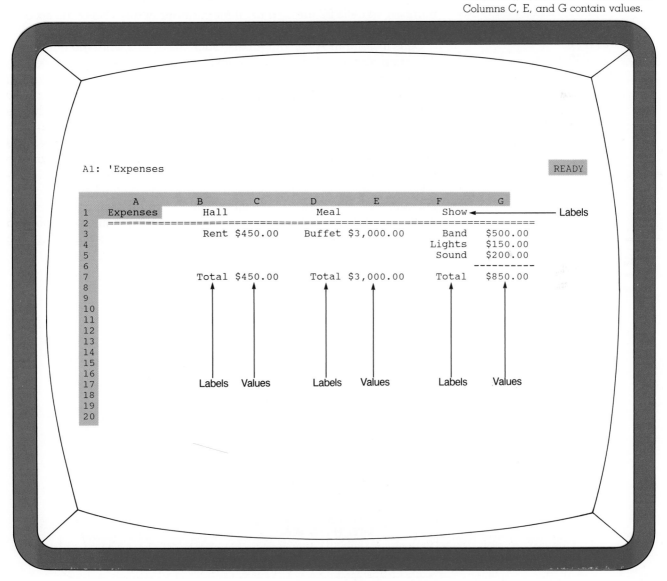

● How a Spreadsheet Works

When a new spreadsheet is loaded into the computer, a screen similar to the one shown in Figure III–3 appears. The numbers listed down the left side of the grid represent the rows. The letters listed across the top of the grid represent the columns.

Each cell in the spreadsheet has a name, or **coordinate.** The coordinate of a cell consists of a letter for its column and a number for its row. For example, the cursor is at cell A1 in Figure III–3. Cell position C4 is in column C and row 4. Cell position D16 is in column D and row 16, the last cell shown on the screen.

You enter data into the spreadsheet by typing on the keyboard. The data enters the cell where the cursor is located. In Figure III–4, the formula B2 + B3 + B4 + B5 + B6 + B7 enters cell B9. Notice that the number 632.00 appears on the screen in cell B9. That number is the sum of the numbers in cells B2 through B7. If the number in any one of the six cells in the formula changes, the entire spreadsheet will be recalculated.

Cells in column A contain labels. Each label tells what the number in the same row in column B represents. For example, the label FOOD in cell A3 indicates that the number in cell B3 stands for the amount of money spent on food.

Although the size of the spreadsheet—how many rows and columns it contains—depends on the program, most spreadsheets contain at least 64 columns and 256 rows. Other programs contain hundreds of rows and thousands of columns. The part of the spreadsheet that appears on the screen at one time is the **window.**

On most spreadsheet programs, the arrow keys on the keyboard move the cursor so other parts of the spreadsheet can be seen on the screen. If the cursor is moved outside the window, the spreadsheet scrolls to

● **FIGURE III–3**
A New Spreadsheet When First Loaded

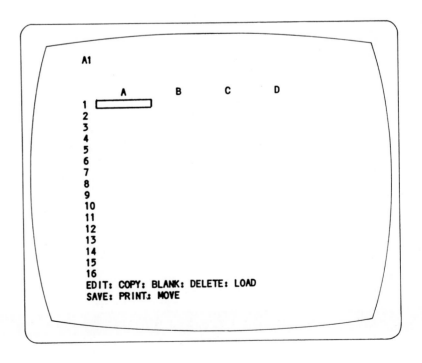

● COMPUTERS AND INFORMATION PROCESSING

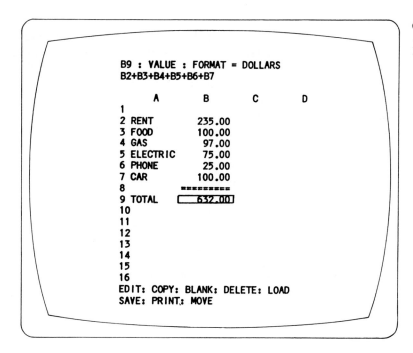

```
B9 : VALUE : FORMAT = DOLLARS
B2+B3+B4+B5+B6+B7

          A          B          C          D
 1
 2  RENT         235.00
 3  FOOD         100.00
 4  GAS           97.00
 5  ELECTRIC      75.00
 6  PHONE         25.00
 7  CAR          100.00
 8              =========
 9  TOTAL       [  632.00]
10
11
12
13
14
15
16
EDIT: COPY: BLANK: DELETE: LOAD
SAVE: PRINT: MOVE
```

reveal the part of the spreadsheet where the cursor is currently located. If you try to scroll past a border of a spreadsheet, most programs will beep or provide a message telling you that this cannot be done.

Another way to move the cursor is with a GOTO command. A GOTO command jumps the cursor to a specified cell coordinate. For example, if the cursor is located in cell A1, you can command it to go to cell R130. GOTO command allows the cursor to move quickly to another location in the spreadsheet.

The cell identified by the cursor is the active cell available for immediate use or modification. Cell A1 is always the active cell when a spreadsheet program is first started. Moving the cursor changes the active cell.

On most spreadsheets, the lines at the top of the screen make up the **status area,** which provides information about the cell at the cursor's position. In Figure III–4, the first item, B9, tells us that the cursor is currently located in cell B9. The next item, value, indicates that a value, or number, is stored in cell B9. If the cell contained a label, the word "label" would have been displayed here. The next item tells the format of the cell. In this example, it shows that the cell is set up to display dollar amounts. The next line of the status area shows what was actually entered into the cell. In this example, the formula B2 + B3 + B4 + B5 + B6 + B7 is entered in cell B9.

Most spreadsheets also have a **command area.** The command area in Figure III–4 appears at the bottom of the screen and displays the available commands.

There are several modes of operation in a spreadsheet with which you should become familiar. These modes may have slightly different names among different programs, but the functions are similar. We will refer to these modes as the ready mode, entry mode, and command mode.

When a spreadsheet program starts, it is always in the ready mode. This is the mode that enables the cursor to be moved around the spreadsheet. Typing any valid character or command will activate one of the other modes. For example, typing a slash (/) in Lotus 1-2-3 puts you into the command mode. When the command mode is activated, the command area, a menu of the available commands, appears on the screen. Many spreadsheets have more than one command level, that is, by selecting one command, a menu showing additional available commands appears. Some commands can be executed without entering the command mode by entering the commands directly at the keyboard.

New information is entered into the active cell when the program is in the entry mode. The entry mode is activated by typing a letter, number, or symbol (for example, a plus, minus, left parenthesis, at-sign, or quotation mark). While in entry mode, the cursor cannot be moved. The entry mode is typically terminated by pressing the <Enter> key. This causes whatever was in the cell before to be erased and replaced with the contents just entered. Pressing the <Esc> key also terminates the entry mode but leaves the old contents of the cell intact.

● Uses of Spreadsheets

Managers in decision-making positions frequently use spreadsheets. These people are responsible for making sure their companies run smoothly. Since an important part of running any business is managing money, a spreadsheet helps people manage money, goods, and employees.

Business data, such as sales figures, expenses, payroll amounts, prices, and other numbers, are stored in the spreadsheet (Figure III–5). A man-

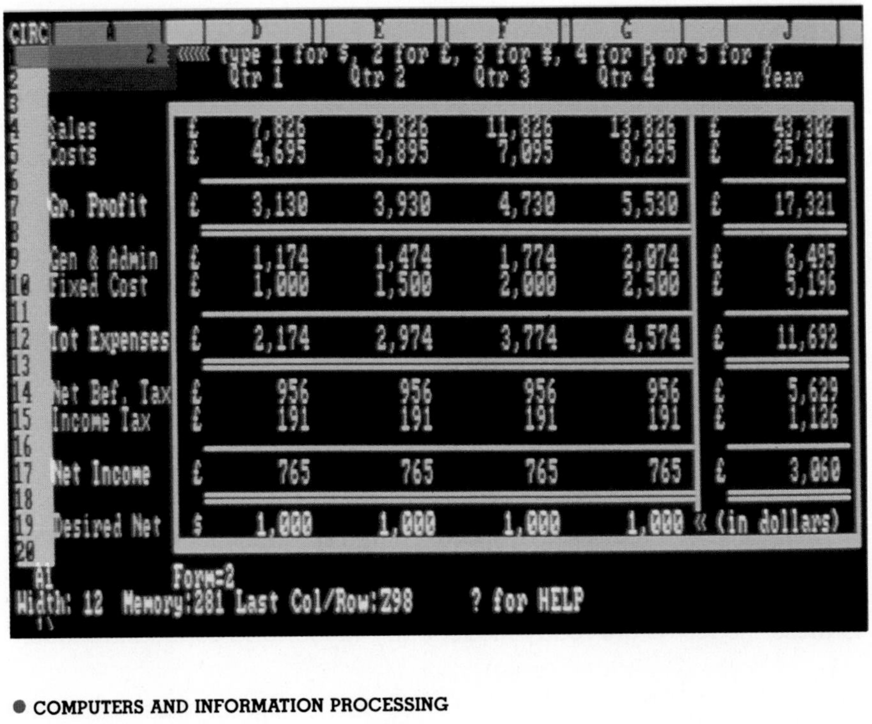

● FIGURE III–5
Spreadsheet Showing Business Data
from SuperCalc 3

● COMPUTERS AND INFORMATION PROCESSING

ager can enter formulas to calculate profits and losses. Other formulas compute the percentage of profits paid in taxes. Any calculation a manager would normally figure by hand can be included in the spreadsheet.

A number in a spreadsheet can be changed to show how that change affects the other numbers. For example, an increase in the cost of a material used in manufacturing can be entered into a spreadsheet to show that the increase affects the profits gained from selling the item. The spreadsheet program automatically recalculates formulas when the numbers in cells change. This feature is a time-saver.

By using a spreadsheet instead of a calculator, pencil, and paper, a manager can spend more time thinking about how to run the business. The answers to "what if" questions are quickly calculated. This ability has made electronic spreadsheets a popular business tool.

Owners of home computers can also benefit from using spreadsheets. Spreadsheets simplify any task that requires calculating numbers. One common use of a spreadsheet program is to keep track of household expenses. The program can figure the percentage of each paycheck that goes to rent, electricity, and food. You can then see which expenses increase and decrease each month. You can also find out how much should be saved each month for a family vacation or a new appliance.

A spreadsheet program can keep track of a team's weekly bowling scores. It can record and tally church donations. It can keep track of your grades at school and determine the marks you need to get the grades you want.

Complex spreadsheets are used in science and engineering. Scientists can use spreadsheets to calculate the outcomes of their experiments under different conditions.

CHECKPOINT III–1

1. How is a spreadsheet used?
2. What is the use of labels in a spreadsheet?
3. How is each cell in a spreadsheet named?
4. Suppose cell B4 contains the value 56. The formula B4/2 was entered into cell B9. What value will be shown in cell B9? Explain what the spreadsheet program does when the value in cell B4 is changed to 70.
5. How are spreadsheets used in businesses? How are they used in homes?

● Features of Spreadsheets

More than two hundred spreadsheet programs are on the market today. Two of the most commonly used spreadsheet programs are Lotus 1-2-3 and SuperCalc 3 (Figure III–6). Spreadsheet programs have features to fit certain needs. Many are easy to use. Others help the user solve a specific type of problem. Still others have features to give them speed during processing.

The purpose of most spreadsheet features is to make the program flexible. This means that the user can adapt the spreadsheet to individual

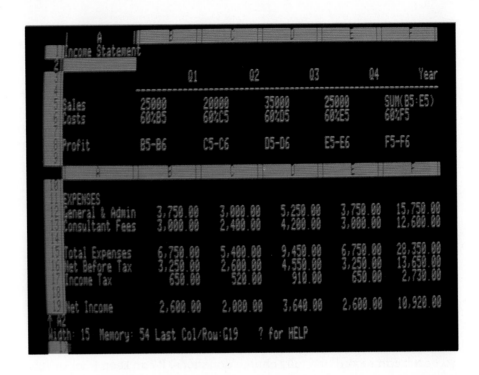

needs. The following common features are found in most spreadsheets today.

VARIABLE COLUMN WIDTH

Some simple spreadsheets have set column widths. This means only a certain number of characters can be entered into a cell. A set width causes problems if you want to enter data with more characters than allowed.

Variable column width is a feature that allows the user to set the width of columns. This feature is particularly useful when entering long descriptive labels.

For example, if names of people are used as labels with a column width of twelve characters, some names might not fit in a cell. Shortening the names might be confusing. If the spreadsheet has a variable column width feature, you can set the column to hold as many characters as needed. That way, each name fits in the cell, avoiding confusion. Figure III–7 shows a spreadsheet that has variable column width.

AUTOMATIC SPILLOVER

The **automatic spillover** feature allows labels that are too long for one cell to spill over into the next cell. This feature solves the same problem as a variable column width feature. What if the columns in a spreadsheet are set for 12 characters? If you have a label with 16 characters in cell B3, the first 12 characters will be placed in cell B3. The last 4 characters will run over into cell B4. Figure III–8 illustrates automatic spillover of labels.

TITLES

A **title** feature shows the labels in a spreadsheet on the screen at all times. This feature is useful when the spreadsheet has data in many columns and rows. If labels are entered in the first column, they cannot be seen if the cursor is positioned in column 30. The title feature freezes labels on the screen so they can be seen at all times, regardless of which columns appear on the screen. Figure III–9a shows the top portion of a large spreadsheet. Figure III–9b shows what the screen would look like without a title feature when scrolling to column Q. As shown in Figure III–9c, making sense out of the numbers is much easier when the titles are still visible.

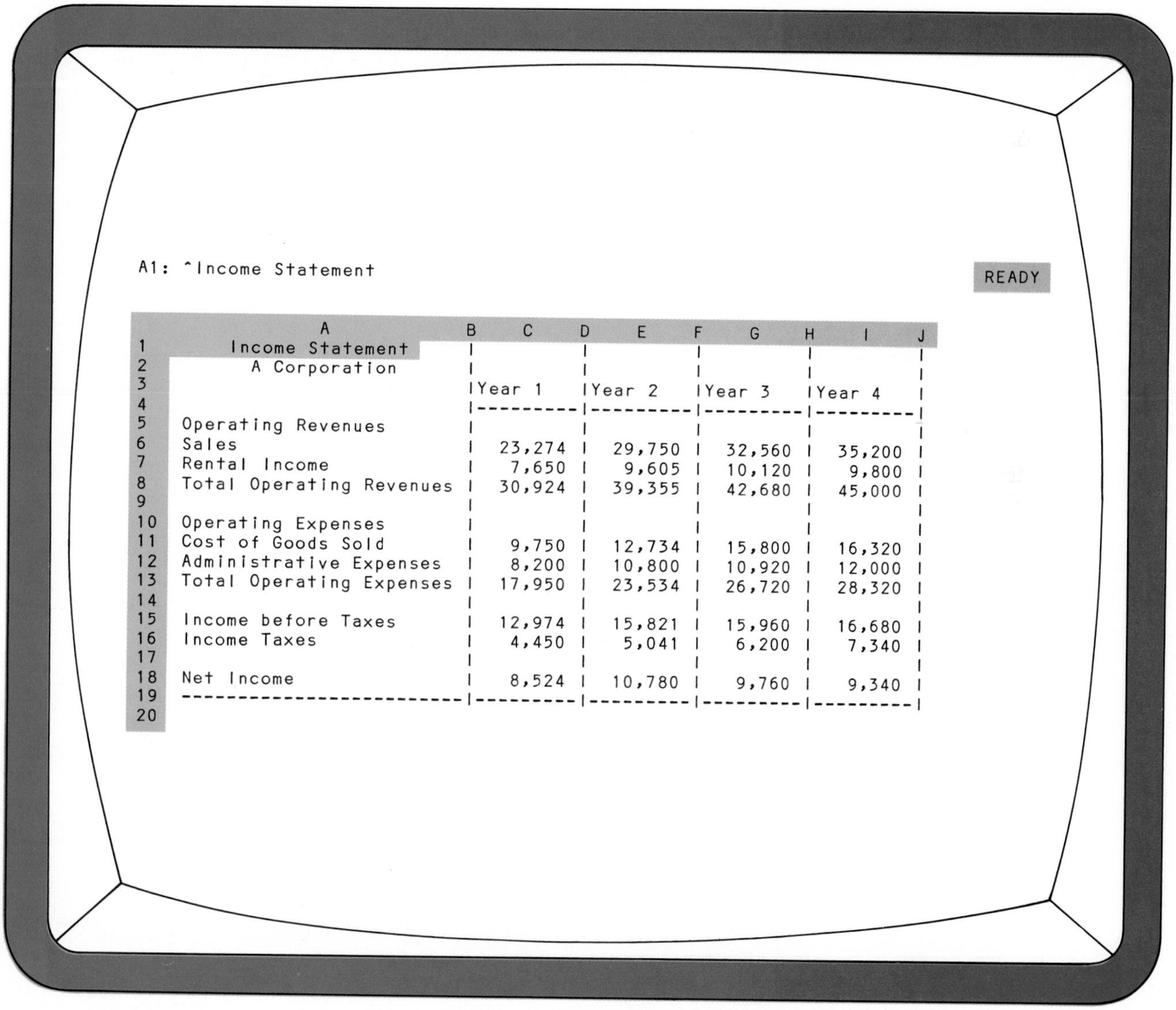

● **FIGURE III–7**
Variable Column Width on Lotus 1-2-3
Column A has 25 characters, columns B, D, F, H, and J have only 1 character, and columns C, E, G, and I have 9 characters.

```
A1:  ^Income Statement                                                    READY

                        A     B   C    D   E    F   G    H   I    J
 1              Income Statement  |       |        |        |
 2                 A Corporation  |       |        |        |
 3                                |Year 1 |Year 2  |Year 3  |Year 4  |
 4                                |-------|--------|--------|--------|
 5      Operating Revenues        |       |        |        |
 6      Sales                     | 23,274| 29,750 | 32,560 | 35,200 |
 7      Rental Income             |  7,650|  9,605 | 10,120 |  9,800 |
 8      Total Operating Revenues  | 30,924| 39,355 | 42,680 | 45,000 |
 9                                |       |        |        |
10      Operating Expenses        |       |        |        |
11      Cost of Goods Sold        |  9,750| 12,734 | 15,800 | 16,320 |
12      Administrative Expenses   |  8,200| 10,800 | 10,920 | 12,000 |
13      Total Operating Expenses  | 17,950| 23,534 | 26,720 | 28,320 |
14                                |       |        |        |
15      Income before Taxes       | 12,974| 15,821 | 15,960 | 16,680 |
16      Income Taxes              |  4,450|  5,041 |  6,200 |  7,340 |
17                                |       |        |        |
18      Net Income                |  8,524| 10,780 |  9,760 |  9,340 |
19      --------------------------|-------|--------|--------|--------|
20
```

WINDOWS

Since a spreadsheet has more columns and rows than can be shown on the computer screen at one time, a **window** feature lets you divide the screen into miniscreens or windows. Each window shows a different part of the spreadsheet independently of the others (Figure III–10). The window feature helps you keep track of what is happening in other parts of the spreadsheet. Most spreadsheets are capable of displaying only two windows at the same time; however, some programs allow more. Figure III–11 shows a spreadsheet that uses windows.

● **FIGURE III–8**
Automatic Spillover from Lotus 1-2-3
The title "Income Statement" is shown in columns A and B.

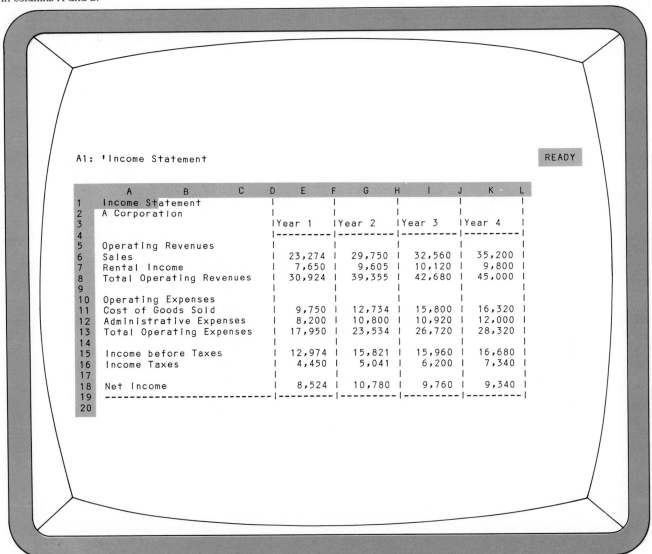

A1: 'Income Statement   READY

	A	B	C	D	E	F	G	H	I	J	K	L
1	Income Statement											
2	A Corporation											
3					Year 1		Year 2		Year 3		Year 4	
4					---------	---------	---------	---------				
5	Operating Revenues											
6	Sales				23,274		29,750		32,560		35,200	
7	Rental Income				7,650		9,605		10,120		9,800	
8	Total Operating Revenues				30,924		39,355		42,680		45,000	
9												
10	Operating Expenses											
11	Cost of Goods Sold				9,750		12,734		15,800		16,320	
12	Administrative Expenses				8,200		10,800		10,920		12,000	
13	Total Operating Expenses				17,950		23,534		26,720		28,320	
14												
15	Income before Taxes				12,974		15,821		15,960		16,680	
16	Income Taxes				4,450		5,041		6,200		7,340	
17												
18	Net Income				8,524		10,780		9,760		9,340	
19												
20												

INSERTING AND DELETING ROWS AND COLUMNS

Some spreadsheets allow you to add new columns or rows to the spreadsheet as needed. You can also remove a column or row, even if it contains data.

This feature can be dangerous if the spreadsheet does not adjust formulas that contain cells affected by the inserted or deleted column or row. For example, if you add a new row 6, the old row 6 becomes row 7. All the remaining rows in the spreadsheet are renumbered too. If a formula somewhere in the spreadsheet uses cells from the old row 6, it

● **FIGURE III–9a**
Title Feature from Lotus 1-2-3
The first few columns of a large spreadsheet.

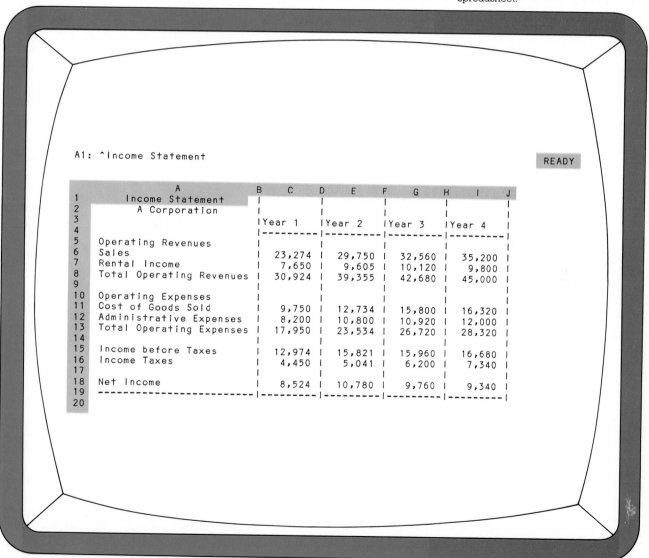

```
A1:  ^Income Statement                                                    READY

              A          B    C    D    E    F    G    H    I    J
   1     Income Statement    |         |         |         |         |
   2       A Corporation     |         |         |         |         |
   3                         |Year 1   |Year 2   |Year 3   |Year 4   |
   4                         |---------|---------|---------|---------|
   5     Operating Revenues  |         |         |         |         |
   6     Sales               |  23,274 |  29,750 |  32,560 |  35,200 |
   7     Rental Income       |   7,650 |   9,605 |  10,120 |   9,800 |
   8     Total Operating Revenues | 30,924 | 39,355 | 42,680 | 45,000 |
   9                         |         |         |         |         |
  10     Operating Expenses  |         |         |         |         |
  11     Cost of Goods Sold  |   9,750 |  12,734 |  15,800 |  16,320 |
  12     Administrative Expenses | 8,200 | 10,800 | 10,920 | 12,000 |
  13     Total Operating Expenses | 17,950 | 23,534 | 26,720 | 28,320 |
  14                         |         |         |         |         |
  15     Income before Taxes |  12,974 |  15,821 |  15,960 |  16,680 |
  16     Income Taxes        |   4,450 |   5,041 |   6,200 |   7,340 |
  17                         |         |         |         |         |
  18     Net Income          |   8,524 |  10,780 |   9,760 |   9,340 |
  19     --------------------|---------|---------|---------|---------|
  20
```

will have to be changed so it uses the cells from the new row 7. If the formula is not changed, it will be wrong.

Some spreadsheets automatically adjust the formulas. If a row or column is added that affects cells used in formulas, the program changes the cells in the formulas to correspond to their new location in the spreadsheet.

GRAPHICS

Many spreadsheets can create graphs using data from the spreadsheet (Figure III–12). These may be bar or line graphs or pie charts.

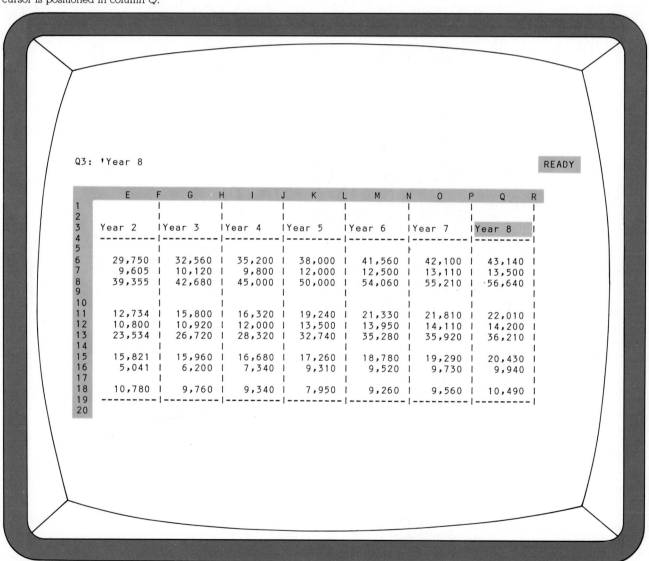

```
Q3: 'Year 8                                                              READY

        E     F     G     H     I     J     K     L     M     N     O     P     Q     R
 1             |           |           |           |           |           |           |
 2             |           |           |           |           |           |           |
 3  Year 2   |Year 3     |Year 4     |Year 5     |Year 6     |Year 7     |Year 8     |
 4  -------- |---------  |---------  |---------  |---------  |---------  |---------  |
 5             |           |           |           |           |           |           |
 6   29,750  |  32,560   |  35,200   |  38,000   |  41,560   |  42,100   |  43,140   |
 7    9,605  |  10,120   |   9,800   |  12,000   |  12,500   |  13,110   |  13,500   |
 8   39,355  |  42,680   |  45,000   |  50,000   |  54,060   |  55,210   | ·56,640   |
 9             |           |           |           |           |           |           |
10             |           |           |           |           |           |           |
11   12,734  |  15,800   |  16,320   |  19,240   |  21,330   |  21,810   |  22,010   |
12   10,800  |  10,920   |  12,000   |  13,500   |  13,950   |  14,110   |  14,200   |
13   23,534  |  26,720   |  28,320   |  32,740   |  35,280   |  35,920   |  36,210   |
14             |           |           |           |           |           |           |
15   15,821  |  15,960   |  16,680   |  17,260   |  18,780   |  19,290   |  20,430   |
16    5,041  |   6,200   |   7,340   |   9,310   |   9,520   |   9,730   |   9,940   |
17             |           |           |           |           |           |           |
18   10,780  |   9,760   |   9,340   |   7,950   |   9,260   |   9,560   |  10,490   |
19  -------- |---------  |---------  |---------  |---------  |---------  |---------  |
20
```

PREDEFINED FORMULAS

Most spreadsheet programs allow a user to save frequently used formulas. If a spreadsheet is used frequently for the same purpose, you may want to set up a **template.** A template saves time by using a set of predefined formulas already entered into a spreadsheet. For example, a template could be prepared for weekly bowling scores. Then each week, the new figures could be entered without having to reenter the formulas. Templates are time-savers.

Some spreadsheets come with predefined formulas already stored in the program. These ready-to-use templates are for specific purposes such as real estate management or investment tracking.

● **FIGURE III–9c**
Title Feature from Lotus 1-2-3
If the title feature is used, the titles from column A will appear on the screen when the cursor is positioned in column Q.

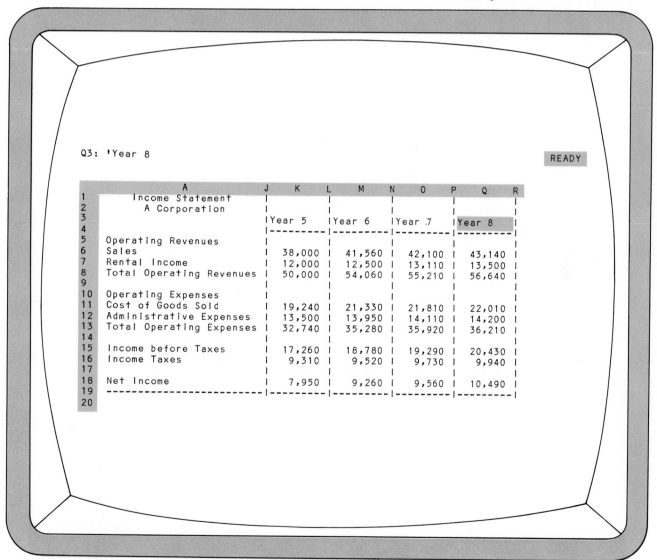

```
Q3: 'Year 8                                                              READY

              A           J    K       L    M       N    O       P    Q    R
 1      Income Statement  I       I          I          I             I
 2        A Corporation   I       I          I          I             I
 3                        IYear 5 I    IYear 6    IYear 7     IYear 8  I
 4                        I----------I----------I----------I----------I
 5   Operating Revenues   I          I          I             I
 6   Sales                I    38,000 I    41,560 I    42,100 I    43,140 I
 7   Rental Income        I    12,000 I    12,500 I    13,110 I    13,500 I
 8   Total Operating Revenues I 50,000 I  54,060 I    55,210 I    56,640 I
 9                        I          I          I             I
10   Operating Expenses   I          I          I             I
11   Cost of Goods Sold   I    19,240 I    21,330 I    21,810 I    22,010 I
12   Administrative Expenses I 13,500 I    13,950 I    14,110 I    14,200 I
13   Total Operating Expenses I 32,740 I 35,280 I    35,920 I    36,210 I
14                        I          I          I             I
15   Income before Taxes  I    17,260 I    18,780 I    19,290 I    20,430 I
16   Income Taxes         I     9,310 I     9,520 I     9,730 I     9,940 I
17                        I          I          I             I
18   Net Income           I     7,950 I     9,260 I     9,560 I    10,490 I
19   -------------------------I----------I----------I----------I----------I
20
```

Three windows on a screen from The
Smart Spreadsheet by Innovative Software, Inc.

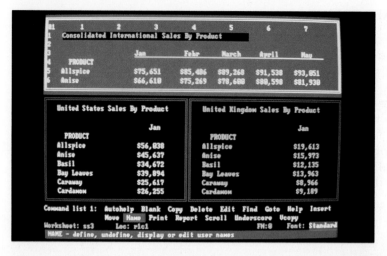

● **FIGURE III–11**
Window Display from SuperCalc 3

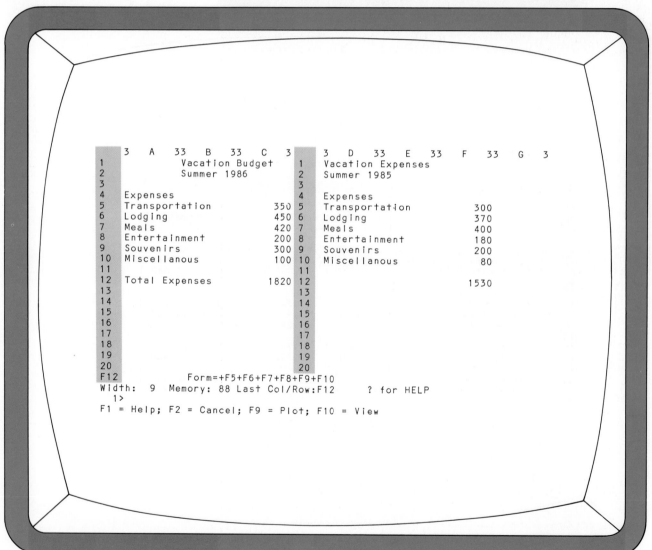

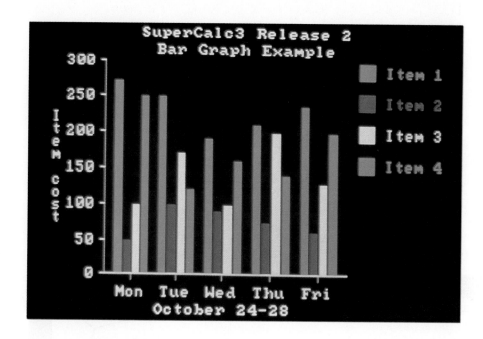

LOCKING CELLS

To prevent a user from altering or destroying a template, cells containing formulas can be **locked.** Once a cell is locked, no one (without the correct password) can change it. Cells are locked by using a special command supplied by the spreadsheet program.

HIDING CELLS

Some spreadsheets can hide the contents of a cell, so they are not shown on the screen. This feature is useful when a company enters data employees are not supposed to see. When a person uses the spreadsheet, the contents of **hidden cells** remain secret.

FORMATTING CELLS

Formatting commands control how the contents of a cell are displayed. Options for formatting the contents of a cell include embedded commas, leading dollar signs, trailing percent signs, and the number of places included after the decimal point. Once you decide how you want a cell formatted, you issue the appropriate formatting command and the format rule for that cell is created. The format rule is stored for each cell along with the cell's value. Most programs display the formatting rule for the active cell in the status area. In Figure III–13, the formatting rule and the formula for cell D6 are both displayed in the status area.

Format rules can be assigned to an individual cell, a group of cells or globally for the entire spreadsheet. In many spreadsheets, issuing a global format command does not override individual or previously given group format commands.

RANGES

A range of cells is a rectangular group of cells that is treated as a unit for some operation. A range may be a single cell, part of a column, part of a row, or a larger rectangle of cells from both rows and columns. Methods used to identify a cell range vary from program to program. Some programs use cursor movement keys, some use a mouse, and others have the user specify the coordinates of the upper-left- and lower-right-hand corners of the range. For example, Figure III–14 shows a spreadsheet with the range B4 through D16 marked.

Once a range of cells has been marked, several different operations can be performed. For example, a specific range of cells can be printed, copied, moved, or deleted.

● **FIGURE III–13**
Formatting Rule for Cell D6 from Lotus 1-2-3

The status line displays the current format of cell D6. P2 means percentage with two decimal places.

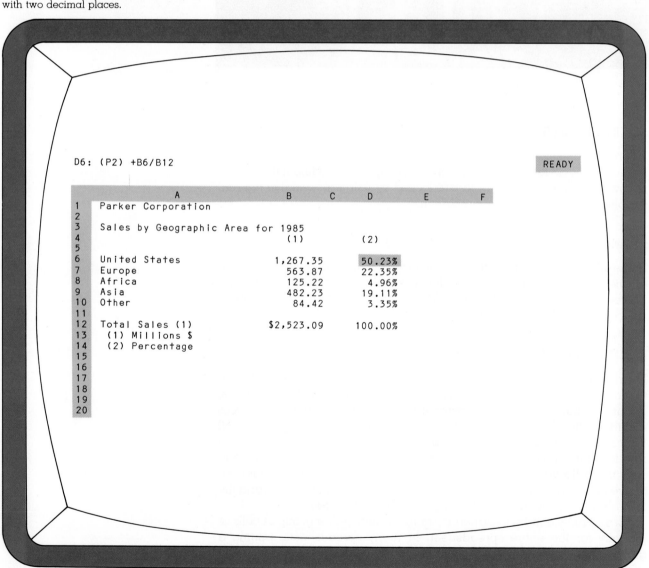

```
D6:  (P2) +B6/B12                                              READY

             A                B      C      D        E        F
 1   Parker Corporation
 2
 3   Sales by Geographic Area for 1985
 4                            (1)            (2)
 5
 6   United States          1,267.35       50.23%
 7   Europe                   563.87       22.35%
 8   Africa                   125.22        4.96%
 9   Asia                     482.23       19.11%
10   Other                     84.42        3.35%
11
12   Total Sales (1)       $2,523.09      100.00%
13    (1) Millions $
14    (2) Percentage
15
16
17
18
19
20
```

COPY

The **copy** feature is a frequently used spreadsheet feature. Copy allows the user to copy a cell or group of cells to another part of the spreadsheet. For example, if you use the same data several times in one spreadsheet, you can continually copy the cell containing that data throughout the spreadsheet. With the copy feature, the same data only has to be entered once.

Most spreadsheets allow you to copy cells from one spreadsheet to another. Some spreadsheet programs use windows and a temporary storage area (often called a buffer or clipboard) to copy from one spreadsheet to another. Other spreadsheet programs allow the user to specify a range of cells in another spreadsheet stored on disk and then directly read that information from the disk into the active spreadsheet.

● **FIGURE III–14**
A Range of Cells on Lotus 1-2-3

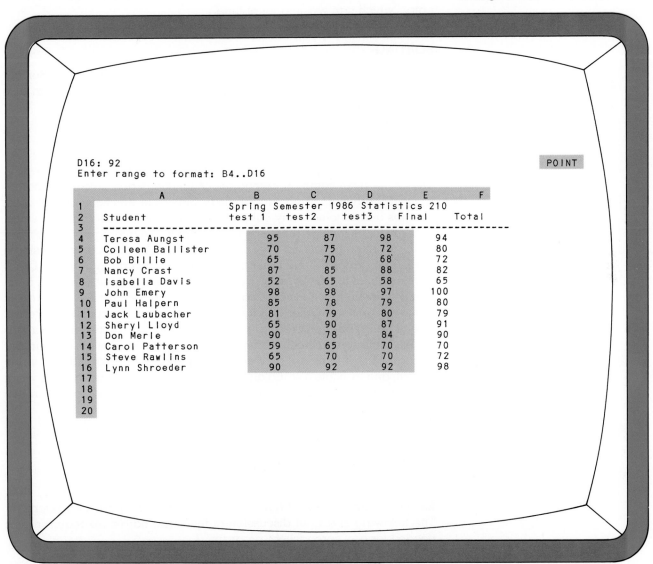

RECALCULATION

The **recalculation** feature automatically adjusts the result of a formula when a cell used in the formula changes. In some programs, you can turn the recalculation feature on and off. You might want to turn it off if you are changing several cells. When the recalculation feature is off, only the value for the cell just entered is recalculated. The computer will not process changes in any formula that result from changing the contents of the cell until you request them. To bring the entire spreadsheet up to date, the user has to tell the spreadsheet program to recalculate the formulas. When the user tells the program to recalculate all the formulas (rather than having the program automatically recalculate formulas as soon as a cell is changed), it is called manual recalculation. In the manual recalculation mode, the program waits until given the appropriate command before recalculating the spreadsheet. When the automatic recalculation mode is on, the computer recalculates all formulas after each entry, which can waste a lot of time.

SORTING

Some spreadsheet programs sort data within the spreadsheet. **Sorting** can be done alphabetically if the cells contain labels. Sorting can also be done numerically if the cells contain numbers or formulas.

FUNCTIONS

Most spreadsheets provide functions as a shortcut to accomplish certain tasks. The most common categories of functions are statistical, mathematical, financial, string, and logical. Statistical functions accept a list of items and automatically calculate the statistics. Some common statistical functions include functions that compute the average and the standard deviation of a list of items. Mathematical functions accept a single value and perform a mathematical transformation on that value. Other mathematical functions include a sine function and an exponential function. Financial functions calculate the effect of interest rates on sums of money over time. Other common financial functions compute internal rate of return and net present value. String functions perform operations on text in the spreadsheet. Common string functions calculate the number of characters in a string, convert a string from a label format to a value format, and truncate a string after a certain number of characters. Logical functions test the condition of cells or compare the values between two cells.

● Hardware Requirements

Minimum hardware requirements must be met to make a spreadsheet functional, and the exact hardware depends on the particular package. The following is a brief discussion of the basic hardware requirements needed for any spreadsheet program.

- *Internal memory:* All software packages require that the computer have a minimum amount of internal RAM memory. With a spreadsheet program, memory is used to store program instructions and the data entered into the spreadsheet. The more internal memory the computer has, the more data can be stored in a spreadsheet.
- *Secondary storage:* Floppy disks are the most common type of secondary storage used with spreadsheets. Some spreadsheets store all files on separate floppy disks. Others use the same disk as the spreadsheet program.

If floppy disks are your secondary storage, one or two disk drives are needed. Some packages can handle more than two disk drives. The more disk drives you use, the more data you can access without switching disks.

- *Printers:* The type of printer needed depends on how the spreadsheets will be used. If spreadsheets are mostly for your personal use, a dot-matrix printer is adequate. But if the spreadsheets are to be used for business purposes, a letter-quality printer is more appropriate.
- *Monitor display:* The number of characters displayed on the monitor is important. A monitor that displays 40 columns (or characters) across will only let you see about 4 columns on most spreadsheets. An 80-column card displays 8 spreadsheet columns. A spreadsheet is easier to understand when you can see more columns on the screen.

A special circuit board for displaying spreadsheets can be installed in the computer. The circuit board shows 12 spreadsheet columns on the screen at one time.

CHECKPOINT III-2

1. What problem does a variable column width feature solve?
2. Explain the danger of adding or removing a column from a spreadsheet when the column contains data.
3. What is a template?
4. Why would you want to hide the contents of a cell?
5. Explain how a recalculation feature works.

● Summary

- Spreadsheet programs help solve math problems. They let you set up columns of numbers to keep track of numeric data.
- An electronic spreadsheet is a program that displays data on a grid of columns and rows.
- Values (numbers) are entered into cells formed by the columns and rows. Labels can be entered to tell you what the numbers mean.
- Formulas are mathematical expressions that can be entered into the cells of a spreadsheet.
- Spreadsheets help answer "what if" questions. "What if" questions are formed when you want to know what will happen to certain numbers in a spreadsheet if other numbers change.

- A cell's coordinate tells the cell's location in the spreadsheet. It is made up of a letter or letters for its column and a number for its row.
- The part of the spreadsheet that you can see on the screen at one time is called the window. The status area shows information about the cell at the cursor's position. The command area displays usable commands.
- Spreadsheets are used by people in business to help them make decisions about running their companies. In homes, spreadsheets are used to simplify any task that requires calculating numbers.
- Spreadsheet programs have different features to fit certain needs.
- The variable column width feature lets you set the width of columns.
- The automatic spillover feature allows labels that are too long for one cell to spill over into the next cell.
- An insert feature lets you add new columns or rows to the spreadsheet after data have been entered. A delete feature lets you remove a column or row.
- A template is a set of predefined formulas already entered into a spreadsheet.
- A locking cell feature lets you lock a cell so data cannot be changed or erased unless you use a special command. Another feature lets you hide the contents of a cell.
- A title feature shows spreadsheet labels on the screen at all times.
- A copy feature lets you copy a cell or group of cells to another part of the spreadsheet.
- The recalculation feature automatically adjusts the result of a formula when one of the cells used in it is changed.
- The hardware requirements to consider with a spreadsheet program are internal memory size, secondary storage, type of printer, and monitor display.

● Review Questions

1. Define the following terms: value, cell, label, and formula.
2. When are "what if" questions used?
3. Where would cell E10 be located in a spreadsheet? Where would cell H7 be located?
4. What is the window of a spreadsheet?
5. What type of information is found in the status area of a spreadsheet?
6. Think of two ways you could use a spreadsheet program. Explain these uses.
7. Why is an automatic spillover feature helpful when you enter labels in a spreadsheet?
8. Why would you want to store predefined formulas in a spreadsheet?
9. What is the purpose of locking cells?
10. How does a title feature help you in a spreadsheet program?

● SECTION IV
Integrated Software

● Introduction

By the late 1970s, microcomputers had become a standard piece of office equipment. Managers' jobs had become more productive and efficient through the use of application software such as word processors, data managers, and spreadsheets. Application software had become so fundamental to their work that managers looked for ways to use more than one application at a time. A company's comptroller, for example, might use a spreadsheet to compute a monthly profit and loss statement, a word processor to write a report about the profit and loss statement, and a graphics program to translate some of the figures in the statement into a pie chart. With an individual software package for each application, the comptroller would have to save the current file, shut down the current program, change disks, load a new program, and open a new file each time applications were switched. This process was frustrating and contributed to the development of a single program that could perform more than one function. The result of this effort was integrated software.

In a conventional sense, integration suggests blending two or more parts into a unified whole. Integrated software makes several applications available to a user at one time and makes it possible to move data between applications. Users generally expect that integrated software will conform to these three standards:

1. The software consists of what are usually separate application programs.
2. The software provides easy movement of data among the separate applications.
3. A common group of commands is used for all the applications in the software package.

This section introduces you to integrated software. It explains what integrated software is, how it is used, and some different types of integrated software on the market today.

● Understanding Integrated Software

When working with individual application packages, sometimes referred to as stand-alone software, the user finds that each program has its own way of presenting itself. For example, pressing the keys <Ctrl>-<Q>, <S> is the command to save a document in WordStar, but in Word-Perfect, the <F10> key is pressed. This difference in commands is frustrating. If you want to run several different programs, you have to have the time and patience to master each program's commands, menus, and other conventions.

Not only is there command incompatibility among stand-alone software, but there is data incompatibility as well. A word-processing program can write a financial report, but it may not be able to generate a graph to be included in the report. A spreadsheet program may be able to analyze an incredible amount of financial data, but it may not be able to incorporate that same data into a graph.

Integrated software attempts to maximize both command and data compatibility. Basically, integrated software is two or more application programs that work together allowing easy movement of data between the applications. In addition, integrated software uses a common group of commands among all the applications. For example, the command used to block off a section of text in a word processor is the same command used to block off a section of rows and columns in a spreadsheet.

For data to be compatible, programs must use the same data format. A data format determines how a program reads information. For example, data items in one program may be separated by a comma; in another program, data items may be separated by a space. If data formats match, the same data can be used in different programs. For example, a mailing list in a data manager can be used by a word processor. Financial data in a spreadsheet can be turned into a graph by a graphics program, and the graph can be embedded into a report produced on a word processor.

Applications often included in an integrated software package are data managers, spreadsheet analysis, word processing, and graphics (Figure IV–1). Another application found in some integrated packages is communications. Even though an integrated software package includes several applications, it is generally based on one predominant application. The other applications in the package usually support the predominant one. For example, the word processor is predominant in Jack 2, Symphony is based on a spreadsheet (Figure IV–2), and Metafile is based on a data base. In general, the abilities of the leading application are greater than those of the other applications in the package.

● Uses of Integrated Software

The cost of integrated software and the hardware required to run it are two reasons why integrated software is rarely used in homes. Prices for integrated software packages range from $300 to $1,500, but most packages cost over $400. Few people are willing to invest that much money

a. The arrows indicate the ways in which the different applications can integrate with one another.

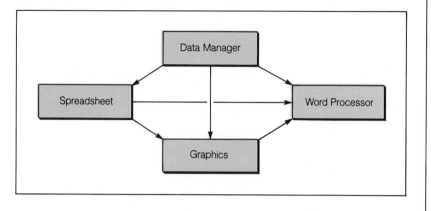

b. This chart shows one way the applications might be integrated in order to complete a personnel cost report.

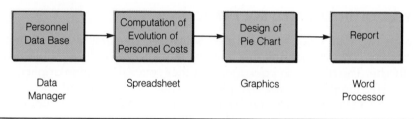

● **FIGURE IV–1**
Integrated Software Package Structure
a. The arrows indicate the ways in which the different applications can be integrated with one another. b. This chart shows one way the applications might be integrated to complete a personnel cost report.

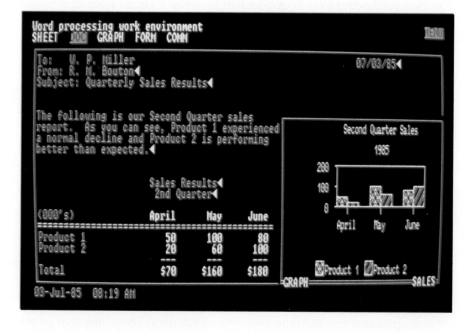

● **FIGURE IV–2**
Spreadsheet, Graphics, and Text Integrated on a Screen from Symphony by Lotus Development Corporation

in software that will just be used in the home, and few need the sophistication of an integrated package for their personal computing needs.

In business, however, integrated software is extremely useful. Any business already using stand-alone word processing, spreadsheet analysis, data management, or graphics packages probably could benefit from an integrated package. For example, a securities analyst may primarily use an electronic spreadsheet to keep track of financial records. Periodically, however, the analyst may want to use a modem to retrieve data from Dow Jones News/Retrieval service. Or she may want the use of a data base for client information. Occasionally, she may need to write a report with a word processor, and in that report she may want to include a pie chart representing percentages from spreadsheet figures. With stand-alone software, the securities analyst would have to learn how to completely run four to five different programs. Every time she wanted to switch applications, she would have to go through the process of quitting one program and loading another. An integrated software package would certainly make this securities analyst's work a lot easier by eliminating the complexities of moving from one application to another.

TYPES OF INTEGRATED SOFTWARE

There are four types of integrated software. The first is the all-in-one package. This is perhaps the most widely known and used integrated software. The all-in-one package combines several common applications to make a single program. Symphony by Lotus Development and Framework by Ashton-Tate are two of the more popular all-in-one packages. Symphony combines a spreadsheet with graphics, word-processing, and data-base functions (Figure IV–3). Framework contains these four applications along with outlining and communications capabilities. These packages make moving from one application to another very convenient for the user because each application is really a component of a single program.

All-in-one packages also offer the user the benefit of a common command set. For example, the delete command would be the same whether the user was deleting from the spreadsheet or the word processor. Consistency of command is especially valuable to a person who may use some applications on a limited basis. The user does not have to memorize a lot of seldom-used commands.

There are some drawbacks to all-in-one packages. The functions represented in all-in-one packages are generally not as complete as the functions offered in single application programs. An all-in-one package with complex word-processing capabilities may be weak in the spreadsheet or graphics area. Therefore, a user with highly sophisticated graphics requirements may find a package lacking in graphics capabilities and would want to use a stand-alone package for graphics needs. Power requirements are another drawback of all-in-one packages. The integrated package Jazz (by Lotus) (Figure IV–4) was developed for the 512K "Fat Mac" and requires 256K of RAM to operate. Obviously, Jazz would be useless on the smaller 128K Macintosh.

. The second type of integrated software is called the integrated series. These programs are actually separate application programs that share

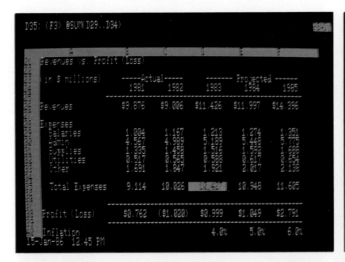

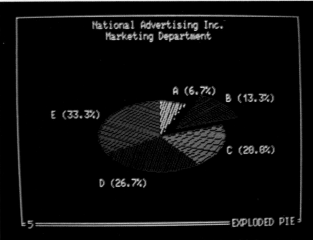

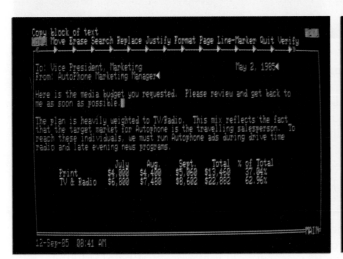

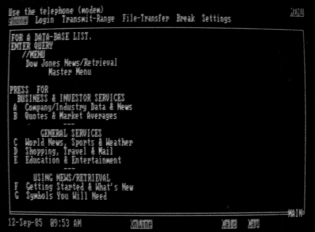

● **FIGURE IV–3**
Four Screens from Symphony by Lotus Development Corporation.
a. Spreadsheet. b. Graphics. c. Word Processing. d. Data base communications.

a common command set. The command set allows data to be transferred from one application to another quickly and easily. Smart Software by Innovative Software is one example of an integrated series. Programs in an integrated series offer the varied functions and ease of transfer of stand-alone programs without using the memory requirements of all-in-one packages.

The systems integrator is the third type of integrated software. The systems integrator makes moving data between stand-alone packages residing in memory possible. The integrator also permits simultaneous operation of stand-alone packages. IBM produces a systems integrator called Topview. One advantage of this type of integration is that it allows the user to select the stand-alone application that is best suited for the user's needs. A drawback, however, is that the stand-alone packages do not usually offer common command sets, so the user must memorize

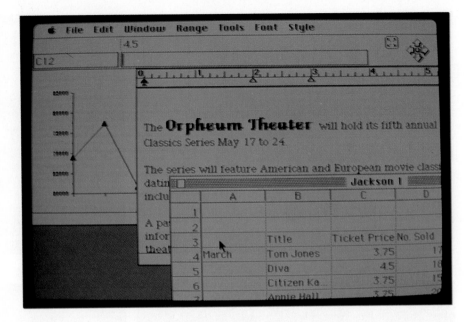

dissimilar commands. Systems integrators also use large amounts of RAM, which makes them unsuitable for use with small microcomputers.

The last type of software integration, the background utility approach, offers limited integration capabilities. This method permits the user to load a type of utility software commonly called "desk accessories" into RAM. Calculators, calendars, telephone dialers, and notepads are all types of desk accessories. Once the utility software is loaded, a stand-alone application program is also loaded into RAM. The user can then select the desk accessory needed to accompany the application program (Figure IV-5). Many microcomputer users feel that background utilities more than meet their software needs. A background utility is useful with stand-alone programs, but the utility programs use so much RAM that some application programs will not load.

Needs of the individual user vary greatly. Each user must evaluate his or her software needs before selecting an integrated package. Determining whether each application has enough features to produce the quality of output desired is an important consideration when selecting an integrated software package.

● Hardware Requirements

Generally, the hardware requirements for an integrated software package are far greater than the hardware requirements for stand-alone software. As is true of all software, the exact hardware needed to run a package depends on that particular integrated software package.

Most integrated software packages require a computer with a lot of internal memory. Some packages may only require 128K of RAM, but most require 512K or more.

A minimum of two disk drives is necessary for most integrated software packages. Some packages even require a hard disk.

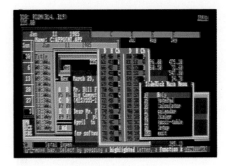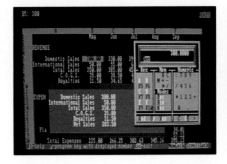

● **FIGURE IV–5**
SideKick Desk Accessories on Top of Lotus 1-2-3

Since one primary purpose of integrated software is to be able to integrate graphics with spreadsheets and word processors, having an integrated package without a graphics monitor does not make much sense. Some integrated packages even require a monitor with a color graphics board.

The final hardware consideration is a printer. Letter-quality printers are generally used with integrated software since the software is most often used in business. Another consideration is the graphics capability of the printer. The printer should be able to print a quality reproduction of whatever graph the integrated package is capable of generating.

● Summary

● An integrated software package consists of separate application programs.
● The major characteristics of an integrated software package are the ability to move data easily among the separate applications and use of a common group of commands.
● Data management, word processing, spreadsheet analysis, and graphics are the applications usually incorporated in an integrated software package.
● Integrated software packages are usually based on a major application, with the other applications supporting the major one.
● Integrated software packages were developed as microcomputers began to be used for powerful and complex computing applications.
● There are four types of integrated software packages. They are all-in-one packages, integrated series packages, systems integration packages, and background utility approach packages.

● Review Questions

1. Define integration as it is used in conjunction with software.
2. What applications are commonly used in integrated software?
3. What is an all-in-one package?
4. What are the drawbacks to all-in-one packages?
5. What is a systems integrator?
6. What is the background utility approach?

BASIC SUPPLEMENT

● Section I
Introduction to BASIC

● Preface

BASIC has traditionally been accepted as the most effective programming language for instructional purposes. In recent years, business and computer manufacturers have recognized the vast potential for the BASIC language beyond education. Therefore, the availability and usage of BASIC has increased dramatically. Today most small business computer systems and home computer systems rely exclusively on BASIC programming support.

One major problem associated with such tremendous growth has been the lack of controls on the implementation of the language. Although there is a national standard (ANSI) version of BASIC, it is normally not followed by computer designers. Thus there are differences in the BASIC language found on various computers. The material in this book not only presents BASIC found on a typical large time-shared computer system (Digital Equipment Corp.), but also includes coverage of microcomputer implementations (Apple, Macintosh/Microsoft, IBM/Microsoft, TRS-80).

Color coding has been used extensively throughout the material to assist the reader. The following legend should prove valuable:

BLUE	Computer Output
BROWN SHADING	Statements Referenced in Text
RED	User Response

● Background on BASIC

BASIC, an acronym for Beginner's All-purpose Symbolic Instruction Code, was developed in the mid-1960s at Dartmouth College by Professors John Kemeny and Thomas Kurtz. It is a high-level language that uses English-like words and statements such as LET, READ, and PRINT. It is easy to learn and is considered a general-purpose programming language, because it is useful for a wide variety of tasks.

BASIC, like English and other languages used for communication, includes rules for spelling, grammar, and punctuation. In BASIC, however, these rules are very precise and allow no exceptions. They enable the programmer to tell the computer what to do in such a way that the computer is able to carry out the instructions.

BASIC was originally developed for use in a large, interactive computer environment: one or more BASIC users could communicate with the computer *during* processing and feel as though they had the computer all to themselves. As the demand for minicomputers and microcomputers increased, manufacturers of such computers felt pressure to develop simple but effective languages for them. Rather than create entirely new languages, most opted to offer BASIC because of its interactive capability—the user can communicate directly with the computer in a conversational fashion. Many altered the original BASIC, however, to suit their equipment. The result is that although the BASIC language has a universally accepted set of standard rules called **ANSI BASIC,** each manufacturer adds its enhancements, or extensions, to this standard to make use of the special features of its machines.

This supplement discusses BASIC commands common to most computer systems but will note the language variations among the different versions. The main implementation used in this text is BASIC-PLUS-2 as implemented on the DECsystem 20/60. All programming examples have been run on this system. In addition, differences between this implementation and the IBM Personal Computer, the Apple, the TRS-80, and the Macintosh have been noted. Although there are a variety of BASIC implementations available for these microcomputers, this supplement discusses only the Apple II Plus, the Apple IIe, and the Apple IIc with Applesoft, the IBM PC and Macintosh with Microsoft BASIC, and the TRS-80 Model 4 computer with Model 4 BASIC.

● Introduction to Programming

Programming is the process of writing instructions (a program) for a computer to use to solve a problem; these instructions must be written in a programming language. A program can be anything from a simple list of instructions that adds a series of numbers together, to a large, complex structure with many subsections, which calculates the payroll for a major corporation.

When computers were first developed, programming was extremely complex and programmers were happy simply to get their programs to work. There was little concern over writing programs in a style that was easy for other people to understand. Gradually, however, programmers began to realize that working with such programs was very difficult, particularly when someone other than the original programmer had to alter an existing program.

Because of this problem, programmers began developing ways to make programs easier to understand and modify. These techniques, which have been developed over the last twenty years, are referred to as **structured programming.** Structured programming has two basic characteristics: (1) the program logic is easy to follow, and (2) the programs are divided into smaller **subprograms** or **modules,** which in BASIC are referred to as subroutines. Thus, structured programming avoids large, complex programs in favor of more manageable subprograms, each designed to perform a specific task. Because the logic of structured programs is easier to follow than that of unstructured programs, they are more likely to be free of errors and are easier to modify at a later date.

This supplement will emphasize the concepts of structured programming. Because many versions of BASIC were developed before the concept of modularization was thoroughly understood, these older versions do not lend themselves to structured programming. We will try to present techniques for working around these difficulties whenever possible.

● The Programming Process

Software is a program or a series of programs that tells the computer hardware what to do. Since the computer must be able to read and interpret each instruction, the program must be precisely written. To know what instructions are required to solve a problem, the programmer follows five steps, commonly called the **programming process:**

1. Define and document the problem.
2. Design and document a solution.
3. Write and document the program.
4. Submit the program to the computer.
5. Test and debug the program and revise the documentation if necessary.

DEFINING AND DOCUMENTING THE PROBLEM

Misunderstandings concerning the desired results of a program can lead to programs that do not meet the user's needs. Therefore, before the programmer begins work, the problem must be clearly defined and documented in writing. **Documentation** consists of any comments, diagrams, or other information that explains the program to people. This documentation should include a description of program input and output:

1. What data is necessary to obtain the desired output? From where will this data be obtained? How will this data be entered? The programmer should make it as easy as possible for the user to enter the data that a program needs.
2. All output and the manner in which it is to be formatted must be described. Formatting here refers to the way in which the output is to be displayed or printed to make it easy for the user to read and use. For example, placing output in table form with appropriate headings is one way of formatting it.

Let's practice defining and documenting a simple problem. Suppose you need a program to convert a given number of feet to miles. The output is the number of miles in the stated number of feet. The input is the number of feet to be converted. You will also need to know the conversion formula (that is, how many feet there are in one mile). You now have all the information needed to solve the problem. This information could be documented as follows:

Problem Definition

Write a program to convert a given number of feet to miles.

Needed Input

The number of feet to be converted.

Needed Output

The number of miles in a given number of feet. The output will be formatted like this:

There are xxx.xx miles in xxxx.xx feet.

The programmer must understand the problem thoroughly, and must also write the statement of the problem in a clear, concise style. Documenting the problem makes it apparent whether or not the problem is clearly understood.

DESIGNING AND DOCUMENTING A SOLUTION

Once the programming problem is thoroughly understood and the necessary input and output have been determined, it is time to write the steps needed to obtain the correct output from the input. The sequence of steps needed to solve a problem is called an **algorithm.** In an algorithm, every step needed to solve a problem must be listed in the order in which it is to be performed. Developing an algorithm is an important step in all programming.

Computers, *cannot* make assumptions as humans can. Therefore, when developing an algorithm for a computer to follow, take care that no steps are left out.

Let's develop an algorithm for the problem of converting feet to miles. The steps could be stated like this:

1. Read the number of feet to be converted to miles.
2. Find the number of miles by dividing the number of feet by 5,280 (the number of feet in one mile).
3. Print the number of miles.

Top-Down Design

Using a computer to solve a problem is considerably different than most people think. The programmer needs to know only a little about the computer and how it works, but he or she must know a programming language. The most difficult aspect of programming is learning to organize solutions in a clear, concise way. This is where **top-down design** becomes helpful. The term "top-down design" means that the programmer proceeds from the general to the specific, attempting to solve the major problems first and worrying about the specific details later.

The process used in top-down design is called **stepwise refinement,** which is the gradual breaking down of a problem into smaller and smaller subproblems. Sometimes this is referred to as the "divide-and-conquer" method, because it is easier to deal with a large job by completing it a small step at a time. This approach prevents the programmer from becoming overwhelmed by the size of the job at hand.

Top-down design can be applied to solving all types of everyday jobs. For example, cleaning a room, which is a single job, is actually comprised of many smaller tasks, such as these:

- Pick up and organize small items.
- Clean floor surfaces.
- Clean walls and/or windows.
- Clean furniture.

Each of these tasks can be further divided; for example, the second one might be broken into smaller tasks like this:

● COMPUTERS AND INFORMATION PROCESSING

- Clear floors of all items.
- Vacuum all carpet.
- Shake rugs (outside).
- Sweep wood surfaces.
- Mop tile surfaces.

Of course, it would be possible to divide each of these tasks into even smaller subtasks.

The diagram in Figure I–1 is called a **structure chart.** This chart graphically represents the stepwise refinement process by connecting general tasks with their associated subtasks. Level 0 contains the general statement of the problem and Level 1 contains the first level of refinement. Note that the second step (clean floor surfaces) is the only task that has been further refined in this example, as shown in Level 2. A complete structure chart to clean a room would be much larger and have many more levels of refinement.

Flowcharting

Once a solution has been reached, it must be documented. One way is by using a structure chart as we did in the room-cleaning example. The structure chart graphically depicts the levels of refinement of the problem and demonstrates how the separate tasks (also referred to as modules) are related to one another. Two other commonly used ways to document solutions are flowcharts and pseudocode.

One way of graphically representing the steps necessary to solve a programming problem is by using a **flowchart.** A flowchart shows the actual flow of the logic of a program, whereas a structure chart simply contains statements of the levels of refinement used to reach a solution. The meanings of different flowchart symbols are stated in Figure I–2. At this point, do not worry if you do not understand them all.

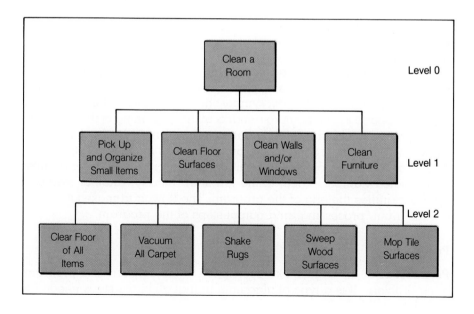

● **FIGURE I–1**
Structure Chart for Cleaning a Room

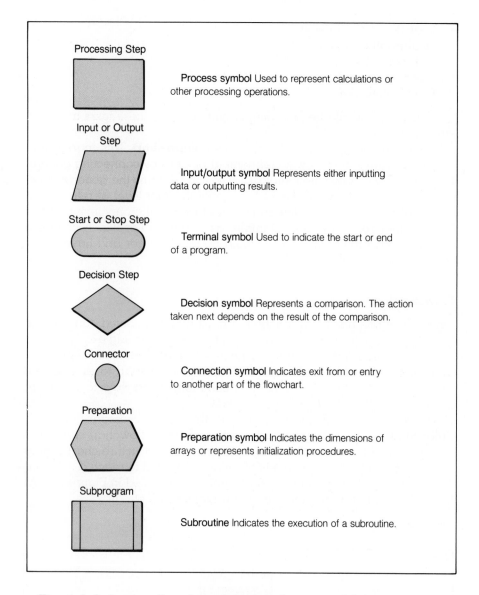

Figure I–3 shows a flowchart depicting the steps of the programming example. Notice how the symbols are shown in logical order, top down, connected by arrows. The first symbol shows the start of the program. It may correspond to one or more remarks at the beginning of the program. The second symbol shows an input step—we enter the feet. The third shows the processing done by the program—conversion of feet to miles. After that, we want to see the result, so we output the number of miles in the stated number of feet to the terminal. Finally, another start/stop symbol signifies the end of the program. The flowchart makes it easy to see the input, processing, and output steps of the program.

Pseudocode

Pseudocode is an English-like description of the solution to a programming problem. It is a type of algorithm in that all of the steps needed to solve the problem must be listed. However, algorithms can be written to solve all types of problems whereas pseudocode is developed specifically to solve programming problems. Unlike a flowchart, which is a graphic representation of the solution, pseudocode is similar to the actual program. It lets the programmer concentrate on a program's logic rather than the **syntax** or grammatical rules, of a programming language. All of the logical structures present in programs can be written in pseudocode. There are no rigid rules concerning the writing of pseudocode, but once you have developed a style, it is a good idea to follow it consistently.

The problem solution shown in the flowchart in Figure I–3 could be written in pseudocode like this:

Begin
Input the number of feet
Convert the feet to miles
Print the number of miles in the stated number of feet
End

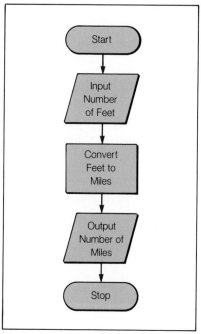

● FIGURE I–3
Flowchart for Conversion Program

WRITING AND DOCUMENTING THE PROGRAM

If the solution has been designed carefully, the third step—writing and documenting the program—should be relatively easy. All that is required is to translate the flowchart into BASIC statements. Figure I–4 shows this program written in BASIC. As you can see, many BASIC words, such as INPUT and PRINT, are easy to interpret. The symbol / means "divide." The REM statements in lines 10–80 are used to document the program. Compare the coded BASIC statements in Figure I–4 to the flowchart in Figure I–3; the correspondence between the two is obvious.

In the program in Figure I–4, each statement starts with a **line number.** Line numbers tell the computer the order in which to execute statements.

Lines 10–80 are comments describing the program. (We know this because they all start with the word REM.) During execution, the computer ignores all such statements; they are for documentation purposes. Line 90 tells the computer to print a statement (shown in quotes)—your cue to enter the number of feet—and then to accept the input after you type it in. Line 100 is an example of an assignment statement, which assigns a

● **FIGURE I–4**
Conversion Program

```
00010 REM ***                          CONVERSION                          ***
00020 REM ***
00030 REM ***   THIS PROGRAM CONVERTS FEET TO MILES GIVEN THAT THERE        ***
00040 REM ***   ARE 5280 FEET IN A MILE.                                    ***
00050 REM ***   MAJOR VARIABLES:                                            ***
00060 REM ***     FEET          NUMBER OF FEET                              ***
00070 REM ***     MILES         FEET CONVERTED TO MILES                     ***
00080 REM
00090 INPUT "ENTER THE NUMBER OF FEET";FEET
00100 LET MILES = FEET / 5280
00110 PRINT "THERE ARE";MILES;"MILES IN";FEET;"FEET."
00999 END
```

value on the right side of the equal sign to special variables on the left (this is discussed in Section 3). Line 110 instructs the computer to print the headings shown in quotes, along with the number of feet and miles. Finally line 999 tells the computer to stop processing.

SUBMITTING THE PROGRAM TO THE COMPUTER

When students first start programming, they tend to rush through solution development and coding. They want to enter their programs into the computer and see them run. This feedback is one of the most exciting aspects of programming; it is a good feeling to have mastery over such a complex, sophisticated machine. Nonetheless, the beginning student should not hurry the early steps of the programming process. A little time spent carefully developing a solution can help to avoid a lot of frustrating time in the computer lab attempting to correct program errors.

The method used to submit programs to the computer is highly dependent on the system being used. For more detailed instructions, consult your instructor, the documentation for your BASIC system, or some other appropriate source.

DEBUGGING AND TESTING THE PROGRAM

Structured programming techniques encourage the development of programs with easy-to-follow logic and fewer errors than unstructured programs. Nonetheless, programs of any significant length virtually always contain some errors, and correcting them can account for a large portion of time spent in program development.

Debugging is the process of locating and correcting program errors. The most common errors made by a beginning programmer are simple typing mistakes, referred to as **syntax errors.** Carefully proofreading program statements as they are typed can prevent the majority of these errors.

Once the computer is able to run your program, you will need to test it with a variety of data to determine if the results are always correct. A program may obtain correct results when it is run with one set of data, but incorrect results when run with different data. This type of error is referred to as a **logic error.** It is caused by a flaw in the program's algorithm.

How the programmer is able to determine that a program contains an error depends upon the type of error that has been made. If a typing error is made, the computer usually will not be able to execute the program and an error message will be printed. If the programmer makes a logic error, the program may stop executing prematurely or it may execute properly but obtain incorrect results. Once errors are corrected in a program, the programmer must remember to also revise any corresponding documentation.

Figure I–5 shows the output of the conversion program. The conversion example is relatively simple, but it shows each of the steps required to develop a program. Although other problems may be more complex, the steps involved are the same. Successful programming can only come about through application of the five steps in the programming process.

● COMPUTERS AND INFORMATION PROCESSING

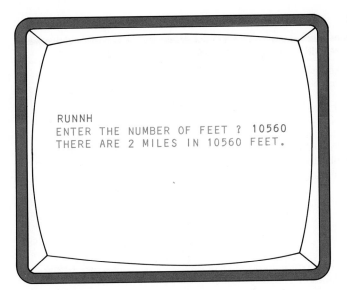

```
RUNNH
ENTER THE NUMBER OF FEET ? 10560
THERE ARE 2 MILES IN 10560 FEET.
```

● Interacting with the Computer

An important step in BASIC programming is learning to control the computer. Although this supplement cannot present the full operational details for each computer, we will discuss the principles of how to turn the computer on, make contact with BASIC, retrieve a program from external storage, display the program, alter the program, and save it for future use.

BASIC programming requires the use of different types of instructions; these instructions can be divided into two categories: BASIC statements and BASIC commands. Some of the instructions—for example, LET, READ, and INPUT—are BASIC statements. These statements are assembled into programs to solve specific business, scientific, engineering, and mathematical problems. This BASIC supplement describes their characteristics and how they are used.

BASIC commands (see Table I–1) are used by the programmer to communicate with the operating system of the computer in order to perform functions like saving programs for future reference and making changes in programs. Some commands—for example, LIST, RUN, and DELETE—are almost universally used but are not covered by ANSI standards. The rest of this section will describe such commands as they relate to the DECsystem 20, IBM Personal Computer (PC), Macintosh, Apple II, II Plus, and IIe, and Radio Shack's TRS-80 Model A microcomputer.

DECsystem 20/60

The computer used to run the program in this text is the DECsystem 20, Model 60, (DECsystem 20/60). The DECsystem 20/60 is a large minicomputer that can contain up to several million bytes of addressable internal storage for programs. The implementation of BASIC used in this textbook is BASIC-PLUS-2.

	DECsystem	APPLE	MACINTOSH	TRS-80	IBM
POWER SWITCH LOCATION	Left rear of terminal	Left rear of computer	Left rear of computer	Right front under keyboard	Right rear of computer
SIGN-ON PROCEDURES					
User	Control-C	No response	No response		No response
Computer response	TOPS-20 MONITOR	APPLE II*	Icon of disk with blinking question mark	TANDY CORPORATION LOGO DATE MM/DD/YY? (flashing cursor)	Enter today's date (m-d-y): time The IBM Personal Computer DOS Version 1.10 (C) Copyright IBM Corp. 1981, 1982 A >
User	LOG ACCT. # PASSWORD	No response	No response; insert appropriate disk	Enter date	Respond to date query
STARTING BASIC					
User	BASIC	Comes up in BASIC	Insert MS-BASIC disk	Type BASIC	Type BASIC or BASICA (For Advanced BASIC) after computer types A >
Computer response	READY	Flashing cursor**	Display directory of MS-BASIC disk	READY	OK
User	NEW	Begin typing program	Double-click MS-BASIC icon	Begin typing program	Begin typing program
Computer response	NEW FILENAME—		Command box appears		
User	Enter name of program; begin typing program		Begin typing program		
SYSTEM COMMANDS					
List	LIST	LIST	LIST	LIST	LIST
Execute a program	RUN	RUN	RUN	RUN	RUN
Store program on secondary storage	SAVE	SAVE name	SAVE "name"	SAVE "name"	SAVE "name"
Retrieve program from disk	OLD OLD FILENAME—	LOAD name or RUN name	Load "name" or LOAD "name", R	LOAD "name"	LOAD "name"
SIGN-OFF PROCEDURES					
User	GOODBYE or BYE	No response	Select QUIT from File Menu (see Appendix E)	No response	No response
Computer response	KILLED JOB	No response	Displays directory window	No response	No response
User	Power off	Power off	Select CLOSE, then EJECT from File Menu; Power off	Power off	Power off

* For APPLE IIe and APPLE IIc the computer response is (LOADING INTEGER BASIC)
** For APPLE IIc the computer response is **BE SURE CAPS LOCK IS DOWN,** then a flashing cursor

A description of hardware for this system depends heavily on which CRT terminal is used with this computer. A user's guide provided by the manufacturer of the specific model can provide further hardware information. The CRT discussed here is the standard VT-100 terminal.

Starting the Computer

The power switch (toggle variety) is on the lower left at the back of the terminal. Press the <CTRL> (control) and C keys at the same time to provide the link between the terminal and the computer. A header will appear, followed by the symbol @:

```
TOPS-20 Monitor 5.1(5622)

@
```

This is the prompt for the TOPS-20 monitor. (A *monitor* is the housekeeping program that controls the computer.) You must now type LOGIN, followed by an account identifier and a password. The password should be known only to those who need access to the programs in that particular account. For example, the programs for this book were kept in an account called IACCT.MANDELL. The screen looks like this after you have logged in:

```
@LOGIN IACCT.MANDELL
```

Notice that the password does not appear on the screen. The monitor knows that any characters following the blank after an identifier are not to be made public.

After you have logged in properly and pressed the <RETURN> key, the computer responds with a header giving the date and time. Then the monitor prompt @ is displayed. If you hear beeps as you attempt to log in, it is an indication that you forgot to press <CTRL> C or that the computer is down. Try pressing <CTRL> C once again.

To use the BASIC language, just type BASIC after the monitor prompt. When the computer is prepared to accept BASIC commands, it responds with the prompt READY. To display a summary of all the available BASIC commands, you can type HELP.

To create a program, type NEW. The computer then asks for a name for the program:

```
READY
NEW
New program name -- IRENE.1

READY
```

If you press <RETURN> without supplying a name, the computer will call the program NONAME. You can now proceed to type in your program.

Saving and Loading Programs

We assume this computer uses magnetic disks for secondary storage. To save a program named IRENE.1, type SAVE IRENE.1:

```
READY

SAVE IRENE.1
```

To load the program again, type OLD followed by the filename. If you do not specify a filename, the computer will ask for the old program's name. Type IRENE.1:

```
READY
OLD
Old file name -- IRENE.1

READY
```

After the computer again responds READY, you may run or list the program or perform editing operations on it.

IBM PERSONAL COMPUTER

The IBM Personal Computer runs an enhanced version of Microsoft BASIC. Although it is possible to use cassette storage with the IBM, we will be discussing the hardware configuration for disk storage only.

Starting the Computer

Place the disk operating system (DOS) diskette into Drive A, the left drive. Then turn on the computer. The power switch is located at the right rear of the machine. Remember to turn on the monitor and to turn up the brightness dial, too. As soon as the computer is turned on, it will attempt to load the DOS. (If there is no diskette in the disk drive, the computer will "come up" in Cassette BASIC.)

Once the DOS has been booted, or loaded, the computer asks for the date and time. If you do not wish to enter the date and/or time, merely press the <←> (return) key after the prompts, which appear as follows:

```
Current date is Tues 1-01-1986
Enter new date (mm-dd-yy):
Current time is  0:00:52.83
Enter new time:
```

After you have responded to the time prompt and pressed <←>, the computer responds with a display similar to the following:

```
The IBM Personal Computer DOS
Version 3.10 (C)Copyright International Business Machines Corp 1981, 1985
        (C)Copyright Microsoft Corp 1981, 1985
A>
```

The A> is the system prompt. Simply type BASIC and press the <←> to load the disk BASIC translator. Then you will see the BASIC prompt:

```
Ok
```

Now you are ready to type your program.

Saving and Loading Programs

The IBM DOS has a convenient file-by-name catalog system. To save a program (for example, one named TESTS), type the following:

```
SAVE "TESTS"
```

The length of the program file name should be less than or equal to eight characters. Do not embed any spaces within the program name. To load the program from a disk, type:

● COMPUTERS AND INFORMATION PROCESSING

```
LOAD "TESTS"
```
The ending quotation marks are optional.

MACINTOSH

The implementation of BASIC used on the Macintosh for this supplement is Microsoft 2.0.

Starting the Computer

Turn on the Macintosh power switch, which is located on the lower left side of the back of the terminal. Now place the Microsoft BASIC disk in the disk drive. When the screen comes on, you will be in the "Finder" or monitor mode. On the lower half of the screen you will see several icons, or symbols, representing the various forms of BASIC that are available for use; choose the one that best fills your needs. The "mouse," or control box, is a feature of the Macintosh that requires some explanation. It works like a remote control: you move the box in the direction you wish the screen's cursor arrow to go. Once you have maneuvered the cursor arrow over the appropriate icon, "double-click" the button on the mouse: press the button twice, rapidly. The computer will now load the chosen version of Microsoft BASIC. The Command window, appearing at the bottom of the screen, indicates that you are now in BASIC. Type the word NEW in the Command window as shown, then press <Return>:

You can then begin typing your BASIC program, which will appear in the list window in the right portion of the screen.

In addition to the Command window and the list window, the Microsoft BASIC screen displays two other regions: a menu bar at the top of the screen and an output window. Program manipulating commands can be performed either by using the Command window or by using the other features. Only the Command window method will be dealt with in this supplement; consult your system manual for details on the alternative methods for the operations described here.

Saving and Loading Programs

To save a program named "TESTS", for example, type SAVE "TESTS" (note that the filename must be in double quotation marks) in the Command window and press <Return>:

To load the program from a disk, type LOAD "TESTS" in the Command window, then press <RETURN>:

APPLE II, II PLUS, AND IIe

The Apple II initially contains INTEGER BASIC, which lacks many important features of ANSI BASIC. Therefore, our discussion is limited to the use of this computer after Applesoft floating-point BASIC has been loaded. The Apple II Plus and the Apple IIe computers automatically "come up" in Applesoft BASIC.

Starting the Computer

The power switch is located on the left rear portion of the computer. An external monitor or cathode-ray tube (CRT) is required, so you must remember to turn on power to this device also. If a disk drive is attached, it will whir and try to boot the disk operating system (DOS), so be sure that a diskette is placed in the disk drive before the computer is turned on. (When the disk drive boots the DOS, it loads from a diskette the instructions that tell the computer how to manage the disk. This must be done before the computer can perform any disk-related tasks.) The computer automatically "comes up" in Applesoft BASIC, as indicated by the prompt] character.

Saving and Loading Programs

Programs commonly are accessed from disk on this system. The Apple has a convenient file-by-name catalog system for the DOS. To save an Applesoft program—for example, one named TESTS—on disk, type the following:

```
SAVE TESTS
```
and press <Return>. To load the same program from disk, type this:

```
LOAD TESTS
```
and press <Return>. You can now run the program. Alternatively, you can type RUN TESTS without first loading the program; this causes the DOS both to load and to run the program.

TRS-80 MODEL 4

The following description of the TRS-80 computer refers to the Model 4, with Model 4 Disk BASIC.

Starting the Computer

Place the system diskette with Model 4 Disk BASIC into Drive 0 (zero), the bottom drive. Turn on the power switch, which is located under the right side of the keyboard. As soon as the computer is turned on, it will load

● COMPUTERS AND INFORMATION PROCESSING

the disk operating system (TRSDOS). You will see the TRSDOS start-up logo and a prompt to enter the date. Enter the date in MM/DD/YY format and press <ENTER>. For example, to enter the date December 16, 1987, type:

```
12/01/87
```

The computer converts these numbers to Mon., Dec. 16, 1987 and displays this information. Then the following system prompt message appears:

```
TRSDOS Ready
```

This message indicates that you are at the operating system level. To load BASIC into the system, type:

```
BASIC
```

A paragraph with copyright information appears on your screen, followed by:

```
Ready
```

You may now begin using BASIC.

Saving and Loading Programs

To save a program, you need to assign it a "filespace" or filename. For example, if you write a program concerning authors, you could assign it the filespec AUTHOR and type the following command:

```
SAVE "AUTHOR"
```

It takes a few seconds for the computer to write your program to the disk, but when this process is completed, the Ready prompt appears.

The filespec of the program can have a maximum of eight alphanumeric characters. It can also have an optional extension of up to three characters. A slash (/) must be included between the filespec and the extension. The first character of both the filespec and the extension must be a letter. If a file with this filespec already exists, its contents will be lost, because the file will be re-created. For example:

```
SAVE "AUTHOR/BOK"
```

You may also add a drive number to the filespec by typing a colon (:) and the drive number:

```
SAVE "AUTHOR:1"
```

The drive number tells the computer to save the program on the disk in Drive 1. If no drive number is specified, the computer defaults to Drive 0. If you specify a disk drive, make sure you have a disk in that drive.

If you want to use this program again, you must load it back into memory. To do this, type:

```
LOAD "filespec",R
```

The trailing R is optional; if it is included, the filespec will be loaded and run. If the R is not included, the filespec will simply be loaded.

As with SAVE, you can specify a disk drive by typing a colon and the drive number. For example:

```
LOAD "AUTHOR:1"
```

The drive number tells the computer to load the program from the disk in Drive 1. If no drive is specified, the computer defaults to Drive 0. If you specify a drive number, make sure that you have a disk in that drive and that the program you specified is on that disk; otherwise, an error will occur. BASIC will return to the command mode after the load and/or run has been completed.

● BASIC Commands

BASIC commands are **immediate-mode** (or **direct**) instructions; that is, they are executed as soon as the carriage control key (<Return> or <Enter>) is pressed. They differ from BASIC language statements, which are not executed until the program is run. The most commonly used commands are discussed here. Table I–1 summarizes these commands for the five computers.

NEW.   The NEW command tells the computer to erase any program currently in active memory. After typing this command, you can start entering a new program.

LIST.   After typing in a long program, you may want to admire the finished product. Type LIST to see the program statements displayed at the terminal. If you have a very short program, LIST can display the whole program on the screen. However, if the program has more lines than the screen does, only the last part of the program will remain on the screen.

Some screens permit only twenty-four lines to be displayed. You can display portions of programs by specifying the lines to be listed—LIST 250–400, for example. Most computers also allow you to suppress scrolling, that is, to freeze the listing temporarily (see "Controlling the Scroll" later in this section).

SAVE.   After you have typed many program lines, you will want to avoid losing them when the computer is turned off. To do this, you have to move a program from main memory to an auxiliary storage medium such as a magnetic tape or disk. This move is accomplished by the SAVE command. There are generally several options to this command; for example, you may supply a name that distinguishes this particular program from all others.

LOAD.   This command moves the designated program from auxiliary storage to main computer memory. Before moving the program, LOAD closes all open files and deletes all variables and program lines currently residing in memory. On the DECsystem, the OLD command is used instead of LOAD.

CONTROLLING THE SCROLL.   If your program's output consists of forty lines of information but your screen only has a twenty-four-line capacity, how will you see all your output? The forty lines will be displayed so quickly that you will not be able to read them until the listing is finished.

By then, however, the first sixteen lines will be gone—scrolled off the top of the screen.

Most computers have a means of controlling the scroll of the screen. The programmer can simply push one or two keys to freeze the display and then press the same keys to resume listing when desired. This method also can be used to freeze the output listing of a program during execution. Table I–2 summarizes the method of scroll freezing used on each of the five computers.

● Editing a Program

Everyone makes typing mistakes. You should quickly learn how to correct yours. You may find a mistake before you press the RETURN key, or you may find it later. These two conditions call for different methods of correction.

BEFORE RETURN HAS BEEN PRESSED. Suppose you type LOST when you wish to LIST a program. If you notice the error before pressing RE-TURN, you can move the computer's cursor back to the O in LOST by pressing the DELETE key (on the DEC), the ← key (on the Apple, IBM, and TRS-80), or the Backspace Key (on the Macintosh). Then you can retype LIST correctly.

AFTER RETURN HAS BEEN PRESSED*. If you notice an error after RE-TURN has been pressed, the simplest correction, in principle, is to retype the whole line. This may get tiresome for long lines, however—especially if you need to change only one character. Each computer has a means of correcting mistakes within a given line. There is not enough space

*The Macintosh has a variety of ways to edit, therefore we suggest you refer to your manual.

● Table I–2
Scroll Control

	SCROLL STOP	SCROLL START
DECsystem	No Scroll Key	No Scroll Key
IBM PC	Ctrl-NUMLOCK	Press any key
Macintosh	*	*
Apple II, II Plus, IIe	Ctrl-S	Press any key
TRS-80 Model III	Shift-@	Press any key

1. Ctrl-S means to hold down the control (<Ctrl>) key and the S key at the same time.
2. Shift-@ means to hold down the Shift key and the @ key at the same time.

* When a program is listed, scrolling is controlled by clicking the vertical and horizontal scroll arrows and boxes on the right side and bottom of the List window.

To stop scrolling output, click the Run menu at the top of the screen, and then click Suspend, which is found in the Run menu. To continue processing, click the Run menu again. Then click Continue, found in the Run menu.

here for a full explanation of these methods, but there are two general kinds—the screen editor and the line editor.

To use the screen editor, list the portion of the program containing the error. Then move the cursor to the position of the error—typically by pressing four keys with arrows that move the cursor up, down, left, or right. The incorrect characters then can be typed over or deleted, or new characters can be inserted between existing characters.

The line editor works on individual lines. The user specifies the line containing the error and uses commands such as REPLACE, INSERT, and DELETE instead of moving the cursor to the error.

● Summary Points

● BASIC (Beginners All-purpose Symbolic Instruction Code) was developed in the mid-1960s by Professors John G. Kemeny and Thomas E. Kurtz.

● Structured programming languages were developed to encourage the writing of easy-to-understand, more error-free programs. They have two basic characteristics: the logic of the program is easy to follow, and the program is divided into subprograms, each performing a specific task.

● The following are the five steps in the programming process: (1) define and document the problem; (2) design and document a solution; (3) write and document a program; (4) enter it into the computer; and (5) test and debug the program, and revise the documentation if necessary.

● Programs are best designed by using a top-down approach, in which a large task is divided into smaller and smaller subtasks, moving from the general to the specific.

● Program design can be documented by structure charts to show top-down design and by flowcharts to display the order and type of program steps to be performed.

● BASIC has rules of grammar (syntax) to which programmers must adhere.

● BASIC commands are used by the programmer to communicate with the operating system of the computer. Some commonly used ones are NEW, LIST, RUN, and SAVE.

● Editing commands help the programmer correct mistakes.

● Review Questions

1. What is BASIC?
2. What is software?
3. What are characteristics of structured programs?
4. What is an algorithm and how is it used in the programming process?
5. Name the five steps of the programming process.
6. What is documentation, and why is it important?
7. What is a syntax error?
8. Explain the function of the system command NEW.
9. Explain the function of the system command LIST.
10. Explain the function of the system command SAVE.

● Section II
BASIC Fundamentals

● Introduction

One of the best ways to learn any programming language is to examine sample programs. This and the remaining sections in this text will intersperse discussions of the language's general characteristics with program examples and practice problems to promote the learning process.

This section discusses some BASIC fundamentals: line numbers, BASIC statements, constants, character strings, and variables. All are demonstrated so that you can use them properly when you write programs.

● Fundamentals of the BASIC Language

A program is a sequence of instructions which tells the computer how to solve a problem. Figure II–1 is an example of a BASIC program that calculates the gross pay of an employee who worked 40 hours at $4.50 per hour.

Each line in a BASIC program is called a BASIC statement. All BASIC statements are composed of special programming commands (key words recognized by the BASIC system) and elements of the language: constants, variables, and operators. BASIC statements are divided into two general categories: executable statements and nonexecutable statements. Whether or not a line is executable is determined by the command used in the statement. In the example in Figure II–1, the first two lines of the program are nonexecutable. The computer simply ignores these statements, skipping over them and moving on to the next statement. All of the remaining lines of the program in Figure II–1 are executable. This means that the computer does something when these lines are encountered.

On the DECsystem there are two commands, RUN and RUNNH, that can be used to execute (run) a program. If RUN is used, as in Figure II–1, the computer will print a header giving the name of your program (that is, the name under which it is stored in your directory, CH2FIG1.CBP in this example), the date, and the time as well as the output of the program. The RUNNH (Run No Header) command will eliminate the header and print only the output of the program. Throughout the remainder of this book we will use the RUNNH format.

```
00010   REM *** THIS PROGRAM COMPUTES AN ***
00020   REM *** EMPLOYEE'S GROSS PAY.     ***
00030   LET HOURS = 40
00040   LET RTE = 4.5
00050   LET GROSS = HOURS * RTE
00060   LET MESSAGE$ = "GROSS PAY IS"
00070   PRINT MESSAGE$;GROSS
00099   END
```

```
RUN

S2F1.CDP
Friday, October 24, 1986 17:40:00

GROSS PAY IS 180


Compile time: 0.085 secs
Run time: 0.084 secs                    Elapsed time: 0:00:00
```

● FIGURE II–1
Gross Pay Program

● Line Numbers

As we mentioned earlier, BASIC commands are executed in immediate or direct mode. BASIC statements, or instructions, may be executed in either direct mode or **indirect mode.** In indirect mode, the statements are not executed until the RUN (or RUNNH) command is given. **Line numbers** tell the computer that the statements following them are to be executed in indirect mode. Therefore, the computer does not execute these statements until it is instructed to do so.

Line numbers also determine the sequence of execution of BASIC statements. (Later on, we will learn ways to alter the order in which statements are executed.) Execution starts at the lowest line number and continues in ascending numerical order to the highest number. Line numbers must be integers between 1 and 99999, although the upper limit may be lower, depending upon the system being used (Table II–1). No commas or embedded spaces can be included in a line number. Table II–2 contains examples of valid and invalid line numbers. Line numbers in BASIC are often considered labels, because they refer to specific statements in the program. In Figure II–1, the number 70 is the label for the statement PRINT MESSAGE$; GROSS.

Line numbers do not have to be in increments of 1. In fact, it is best to use increments of 10 or 20, in order to allow for insertion of lines at a later time if necessary. Instructions need not be entered in ascending numerical order: the computer will rearrange them in this order for execution. This feature of BASIC makes it easy to insert new lines between existing lines. For example, if you type:

```
00010 LET NAM$ = "SAM"
00020 PRINT MESS$,NAM$
00099 END
```

● COMPUTERS AND INFORMATION PROCESSING

Minimum and Maximum Line Numbers

COMPUTER	LOWEST NUMBER	HIGHEST NUMBER
DECsystem	1	99999
Apple	0	63999
IBM/Microsoft	0	65529
Macintosh/Microsoft*	0	65529
TRS-80	0	65529

*Line numbers are not required

and then realize you forgot a statement that should go between lines 10 and 20, you can simply add the needed statement like this:

```
00015 LET MESS$ = "MY NAME IS "
```

Now when the program is listed, it will appear like this:

```
00010 LET NAM$ = "SAM"
00015 LET MESS$ = "MY NAME IS "
00020 PRINT MESS$,NAM$
00099 END
```

Because we incremented the line numbers by 10 in this example, it was a simple matter to insert a line. If the statements had been numbered in increments of 1 instead, we would have had to retype the entire program in order to insert a line. For this reason, programmers generally use increments of at least 10.

If you find that you have made an error on a line, simply retype the line number and the correct BASIC statement. This procedure corrects the error because, if two lines are entered with the same line number, the computer saves and executes the most recently typed one. To demonstrate this fact, assume that line 160 should print SUM, but the following was typed instead:

```
00160 PRINT SUN
```

To correct this, simply retype line 160:

```
000160 PRINT SUM
```

The computer will discard the current line 160 and replace it with the newest version of line 160.

● Table II–2
Valid and Invalid Line Number Examples

VALID	INVALID
00010 PRINT "MY NAME IS SAM"	00010.5 PRINT "MY NAME IS SAM"
00020 LET NME$ = "SAM"	02,000 LET NME$ = "SAM"
00099 END	000 99 END

● BASIC Statement Components

In the remaining portion of this chapter, we will take a closer look at numeric and character string constants and numeric and string variables.

CONSTANTS

Constants are values that do not change during the execution of a program. There are two kinds of constants: numeric and character string.

Numeric Constants

A **numeric constant** is a number that is included in a BASIC statement (other than the line number). Numbers can be represented in two ways in the BASIC language: as real numbers, which include a decimal point (also called floating-point numbers), or as integers (numbers with no decimal portion). When using numbers in BASIC, remember these rules:

1. No commas can be included in numbers. The computer interprets the digits before and after a comma as two separate numbers. For example, the computer would interpret 3,751 as the number 3 *and* the number 751. The valid form of the number is 3751.

2. If a number has no sign, the computer assumes it is positive. For example, 386 is the same as +386.

3. If a number is negative, the negative sign must precede the digits, as in the example −21.

4. Fractions must be written in decimal form. For example, 2.75 is the correct representation for 2¾.

A **real constant** is a number with a decimal part. The following are all valid real constants.

```
   6.0      6.782
    .95     0.58
 −7.234    −0.09
```

Very small or very large numbers can be represented in scientific notation (also called exponential notation). The following format is used ±x.xxxxE±n. The E represents base 10, and the signed number following the E is the power to which 10 is raised. The number preceding the E is called the mantissa and in most systems lies between 1.000 and 9.999. A plus sign (+) by the power indicates that the decimal point is to be shifted to the right that number of places, whereas a minus sign (−) indicates that the decimal point should be shifted left that number of places.

The following are examples of exponential notation:

DECIMAL FORM	POWER EQUIVALENT	EXPONENTIAL NOTATION
5278	5.278×10^3	5.278E+03
0.0000021	2.1×10^{-6}	2.1E−06
−923180	-9.2318×10^5	−9.2318E+05
−0.00069	-6.9×10^{-4}	−6.9E−04

On many BASIC systems, real numbers can be stored as either single-precision or double-precision numbers.

Single-precision numbers take less storage space than double-precision numbers, and the computer can perform single-precision number calculations more rapidly. Single-precision numbers have fewer digits and therefore are usually less accurate than double-precision numbers. This difference can be important in programs that perform a number of calculations and require a high degree of accuracy. However, caution must be used, because in some cases the BASIC internal functions might not be any more accurate with double-precision than with single-precision. You should consult the manual for your system.

An integer is a number with no decimal portion. The following numbers are examples of integer constants:

29   123434
3432   −8
205   −101

Character String Constants

A **character string** constant is simply a collection of symbols called **alphanumeric data.** These can include any combination of letters, numbers, and special characters including dashes, commas, blanks, and others. The character string is enclosed in double or single quotation marks, depending on the system. All of the systems covered in this textbook require double quotation marks to delimit character strings.

You can include single quotation marks within a string constant delimited by double quotation marks. The following are examples of valid character string constants delimited by double quotation marks:

"He said, 'Good morning.' "
"This is a string constant."
"Gary's Tennis Racket"

The following character string constant is invalid:

"The letter "A" is a vowel."

In the last example, the system would recognize the double quotation mark before the letter A as indicating the end of the string. Actually, the quotation mark at the end of the line is supposed to indicate the end of the string. This character string constant could be correctly written as:

"The letter 'A' is a vowel."

The length of a string constant is determined by counting all of its characters. For example, the two character strings below will not be stored in the computer in the same way:

"SATURDAY   "
"SATURDAY"

The first string will be stored as SATURDAY plus three blanks (the computer can store a blank, just as it can store any other character). The second string will be stored simply as SATURDAY. Therefore, the computer will store eleven characters for the first string and only eight for the second one.

The maximum number of characters allowed in a character string depends upon the system being used. On all the BASIC systems used in this textbook, the maximum character string length is 255 characters.

The program in Figure II–1 contains a character string in line 60:

```
00060 LET MESSAGE$ = "GROSS PAY IS"
```

VARIABLES

Before we explain BASIC programming any further, it is important that you understand how data is stored in the primary storage unit of a computer.

To visualize a computer's primary storage unit, imagine a block of post office boxes. Each box has an assigned number that acts as an address for that particular box (see Figure II–2). The addresses of these boxes always remain the same, but their contents will almost certainly change over a period of time. Similarly, the primary storage unit in a computer is divided into many separate storage locations, each with a specific address. A storage location containing a value that can change during program execution is referred to as a **variable.** A variable can contain only one value at a time; when a new value is assigned to a variable, the old value is lost.

In BASIC the programmer is allowed to assign names to storage locations and then refer to each location by its name. In the example in Figure II–2, HOURS and RTE are **variable names** used to identify specific storage locations. The value (or contents) of the locations named HOURS and RTE are 40 and 4.50 respectively.

The number of characters allowed in a variable name differs from computer to computer, but most computers permit variable names of various lengths. Therefore, the programmer can use descriptive variable names, that is, names that describe the value they identify. Good programming habits include the use of descriptive variable names, because

● **FIGURE II–2**
Post Office Boxes Are Similar to Variables

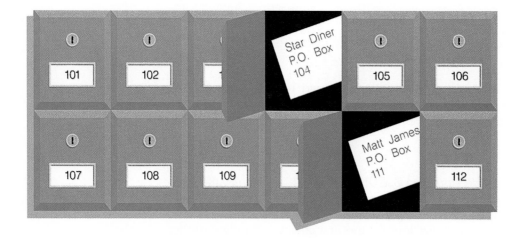

such names make programs easy to read. For example, the name STU-DENT is more descriptive than ST.

There are some BASIC systems, however, that recognize only the first two characters of a variable name (see Table II–3). These systems would recognize the variables QUANTITY and QUEUE as being identical, for example. When using these computers, the programmer must make sure that the first two characters of each variable name are unique.

Variables are classified as *numeric* or *string*. Each of these types will be discussed here.

Numeric Variables

A **numeric variable** is used to store a number that is either supplied to the computer by the programmer or internally calculated during program execution. A numeric variable name must begin with a letter, followed by letters and/or digits with no embedded blanks.

As with numeric constants, there are both integer and real numeric variables. Integer variable names must have a percent sign (%) as the last character. Table II–4 shows some valid and invalid variable names for real and integer numbers.

It is possible to assign an integer to a real variable because the computer can convert the integer to a real number without changing its value.

● **Table II–3**
Maximum Number of Characters Recognized in Variable Names

COMPUTER	MAXIMUM ALLOWED	MAXIMUM RECOGNIZED
DECsystem	30	30
Apple	238	First 2
IBM/Microsoft	Any length	First 40
Macintosh/Microsoft	40	First 40
TRS-80	40	First 40

● **Table II–4**
Valid and Invalid Numeric Variable Names

VALID	INVALID	AND REASON
SUM (real)	225	(Variable name must start with a letter)
M1% (integer)	M2&	(No special characters allowed except those used to designate type of variable)
D6E7 (real)	RT%DAY	(The percent sign must be the last symbol)
BIG47(real)	B2$	($ symbol used to designate a string variable)
AMT% (integer)	D M6	(Variable name cannot include a blank)

For example, the integer 17 can be changed to the real number 17.0. The reverse is not true, however; if a real number is assigned to an integer variable, part of the number is lost. For example, it would be impossible to store 17.65 accurately as an integer. On the DECsystem, if a real value is assigned to an integer variable, the value is cut off at the decimal point. Therefore, if the value 17.65 were assigned to the variable X%, it would be stored as 17.

String Variables

A **string variable** is used to store a character string, such as a name, an address, or a social security number. As with numeric variables, string variables can store only one value at a time.

A string variable name begins with a letter followed by letters or digits and must be terminated with a dollar sign ($). All computers require the first character to be alphabetic and the last character to be a dollar sign, which is what enables the computer to distinguish it as a string variable name. Table II-5 gives examples of string variable names.

In the sample program in Figure II-1, lines 60 and 70 contain the string variable name MESSAGE$:

```
00060 LET MESSAGE$ = "GROSS PAY IS"
00070 PRINT MESSAGE$;GROSS
```

In line 60, the character string GROSS PAY is stored in the location named MESSAGE$; in line 70, the value stored in location MESSAGE$ is printed.

RESERVED WORDS

Certain words have specific meanings to the BASIC compiler or interpreter. These are **reserved words,** which cannot be used as variable names. Table II-6 lists a few of the most common reserved words.

Some systems, such as the Apple, scan all BASIC statements for reserved words. Any reserved words embedded in a variable name are seen by the computer as reserved words and cannot be used in a variable name. For example, RATE cannot be used as a variable name on such a system because it contains the reserved word AT.

● **Table II-5**
Valid and Invalid String Variable Names

VALID	INVALID AND REASON	
C$	$	(First character must be a letter)
HEADING$	4$	(First character must be a letter)
DAY$	E2%	(A string variable name must have a $ as the last character)
EMP$	EM$P	(The $ symbol must be the last character)
M1$	M 1$	(No blanks allowed)
SSNO$	SS-NO$	(Hyphen not allowed)

ABS	END	GOSUB	LOG	REM	STEP
BASE	EXP	GOTO	NEXT	RESTORE	STOP
CALL	FN	IF	ON	RETURN	TAB
COS	FOR	INPUT	OPEN	RND	TAN
DATA	ELSE	INT	PRINT	SIN	THEN
DEF	GET	LET	PUT	SGN	TO
DIM	GO	LIST	READ	SQR	UNTIL
VAL	WHILE				

● Summary Points

● A BASIC program is a series of instructions. Each one is composed of a line number and a BASIC statement.

● The line numbers serve (1) as labels by which statements can be referenced and (2) as instructions to specify the order of execution of the statements in a program.

● Using line numbers in increments of 5 or 10 permits easy insertion of new statements.

● BASIC statements contain special reserved words (programming commands), numeric or character string constants, numeric or string variables, and formulas.

● Constants are values that do not change. A valid numeric constant is any real number expressed as an integer, a decimal fraction, or in exponential notation. Character strings are alphanumeric data enclosed in quotation marks.

● Variable names are programmer-supplied names that identify locations in storage where data values may be stored. Numeric variable names represent numbers. String variables contain alphanumeric values and their names are distinguished from numeric names by the symbol $.

● Review Questions

1. What is a BASIC program?

2. Indicate whether each of the following line numbers is valid or invalid.

  a. 000 99
  b. 136
  c. 2,893
  d. 9999

3. Convert these numbers from exponential notation to regular decimal form.

    a. 7.24396E+03

    b. 1.99E−02

    c. 4.972E+05

    d. 8.05E−04

4. Give the exponential power equivalent to these numbers using standard notation:

    a. 90206

    b. 23.785

    c. −275210

    d. .00321

5. What is a constant? Name two types.

6. Which of these are invalid numeric constants?

    a. 0.73

    b. 1072−

    c. 2.9171E−02

    d. 5.346+05

    e. 7,942

    f. +6029

7. Which of these are invalid character string constants in an expression?

    a. BOWLING GREEN, OHIO

    b. "APPLE"

    c. "7747"

    d. "PICKLE, DILL"

8. What is a variable? Name two types, and explain how they differ.

9. How many values can a memory location hold at one time?

10. Which of the following are illegal variable names, and why?

    a. 7$ f. R

    b. D   g. Z9

    c. 5B   h. W*

    d. H$ i. 25

    e. M$ j. $F

● Section III
Getting Started with BASIC Programming

● Introduction

This section describes four elementary BASIC statements—REM, the assignment statement, PRINT, and END. The assignment statement is used to assign data to variables and to perform arithmetic calculations. The PRINT statement allows the programmer to see the results of processing. Processing is stopped with the END statement. The REM statement is presented here to underscore the importance of program documentation. The section also will discuss how to place multiple statements on the same physical line.

● Documenting a Program

The REM, or remark, statement provides information for the programmer or anyone else reading the program. It is ignored by the computer; in other words, it is a nonexecutable statement. This information is referred to as documentation and its function is to explain to humans the purpose of the program, what the variable names represent, or any special instructions to the user. Because REM statements do not affect program execution, they can be placed anywhere in the program. The only restriction is that the program line must begin with the reserved word REM.

The general format of the REM statement is

line# REM comment

The comment can be any statement that the programmer regards as appropriate documentation. The word REM must be included exactly as shown; "line#" indicates that a valid line number must be inserted here.

Figure III-1 is a sample program that uses the REM statement. Lines 10 and 20 describe the purpose of the program. Lines 30 through 70 explain the major variables that are used throughout the program. These seven lines are helpful to someone who may be reading the program but who is not the original programmer. Notice that line 80 contains no comment after the REM statement. This line improves readability by separating the opening remarks from the executable statements listed later in the program.

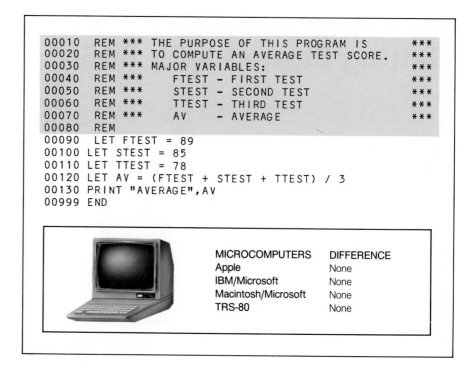

```
00010   REM *** THE PURPOSE OF THIS PROGRAM IS      ***
00020   REM *** TO COMPUTE AN AVERAGE TEST SCORE.   ***
00030   REM *** MAJOR VARIABLES:                    ***
00040   REM ***    FTEST - FIRST TEST               ***
00050   REM ***    STEST - SECOND TEST              ***
00060   REM ***    TTEST - THIRD TEST               ***
00070   REM ***    AV    - AVERAGE                  ***
00080   REM
00090   LET FTEST = 89
00100   LET STEST = 85
00110   LET TTEST = 78
00120   LET AV = (FTEST + STEST + TTEST) / 3
00130   PRINT "AVERAGE",AV
00999   END
```

MICROCOMPUTERS	DIFFERENCE
Apple	None
IBM/Microsoft	None
Macintosh/Microsoft	None
TRS-80	None

Notice also the asterisks that surround the descriptive comment. Although this device is simply a matter of personal taste, many programmers use asterisks to separate comments from the rest of the program. This technique allows the REM statement to be easily identified when the programmer is looking through long program listings.

Remarks may also be placed in the body of the program in order to explain a BASIC instruction or a series of instructions. For example, if an arithmetic calculation is performed, it is sometimes helpful to explain the purpose of that particular calculation immediately before the lines that perform it. We could add the following remark to the sample program in Figure III–1.

```
00115 REM *** COMPUTE AVERAGE OF THREE TEST SCORES ***
```

A more descriptive remark can be used for more complicated calculations.

Many systems allow comments to be placed on the same line as an executable statement. In these cases, a special symbol must be used to mark the beginning of the comment. On the DEC system this symbol is an exclamation point (!) used as follows:

```
00120 LET AV = (FTEST + STEST + TTEST) / 3      ! CALCULATE THE AVERAGE
```

The BASIC system will recognize CALCULATE THE AVERAGE as a comment because it is preceded by an exclamation point. This same type of comment can be indicated on the IBM and the Macintosh by the use of a single quotation mark (') like this:

```
120 LET AV = (FTEST + STEST + TTEST) / 3      'CALCULATE THE AVERAGE
```

Adding a comment at the end of a BASIC statement can be a very useful way to document a program.

● The Assignment Statement

The LET statement is an **assignment statement;** that is, a statement that stores a value in main memory in the location allotted to the stated variable. In a flowchart, an assignment statement is illustrated by a processing symbol ([___]). The general format of the LET statement is:

line# LET variable = expression

The variable can be a numeric or string variable. If it is a numeric variable, the expression can be a numeric constant, an arithmetic formula, or another numeric variable. If the variable is a string variable, the expression can be either a string constant or another string variable.

The LET statement can be used to assign values to numeric or string variables directly or to assign the result of a calculation to a numeric variable. In either case, the expression on the right side of the equal sign is assigned to the variable on the left side. This operation causes the value of the expression to be placed in the memory location identified by the variable name on the left side of the LET statement.

Here are some of the assignment statements from the sample program in Figure III–1:

```
00090 LET FTEST = 89
00100 LET STEST = 85
00110 LET TTEST = 78
00120 LET AV = (FTEST + STEST + TTEST) / 3
```

Lines 90 through 110 assign three numeric constants (in this case, test scores) to three numeric variables. Line 120 assigns the result of an arithmetic calculation to the numeric variable AV, which represents the average of the three scores.

The following table lists examples of assignment statements along with short descriptions of how they would be executed.

ASSIGNMENT STATEMENT	COMPUTER EXECUTION
00100 LET HOURS = 30.5	The numeric value 30.5 is assigned to the storage location called HOURS.
00110 LET SUM = A + B	The values in locations A and B are added together and the result is stored in location SUM. A and B remain unchanged.
00120 LET NUMBER = 1	The value in location 1 is also stored in location NUMBER. 1 remains unchanged.
00130 LET EMPL$ = "JON"	The character string enclosed in quotes (but not the quotation marks themselves) is placed in the location called EMPL$.
00140 LET CNT = CNT + 1	The value 1 is added to the current value in CNT. This new value replaces the previous value of CNT.

Only a variable name is permitted on the left side of the LET statement. For example,

```
00130 LET A + 1 = B
```

is *not* a valid statement.

The LET Statement is often used to assign a beginning value to a variable; this is called initialization. For example:

```
LET X = 0
LET Y = 1
LET NME$ = " "
```

BASIC, however, automatically initializes variables to a default value if the programmer does not initialize the variables to a specific value. Numeric variables default to the value zero and string variables to the null string (a blank space). Although this feature is available, it is not considered good programming practice, therefore we do not recommend the use of automatic initializations.

On most BASIC systems, including all those covered in this textbook, the use of the reserved word LET is optional. These systems see the following two statements as identical:

```
00010 LET TEST1 = 36
00020 TEST1 = 36
```

For simplicity's sake, we will discontinue using LET in programs after this section.

ARITHMETIC EXPRESSIONS

In BASIC, arithmetic expressions are composed of numeric constants, numeric variables, and arithmetic operators. The arithmetic operators that can be used are defined in the following table.

OPERATOR	OPERATION	ARITHMETIC EXPRESSION	EXPRESSION IN BASIC
+	Addition	$A + B$	A + B
−	Subtraction	$A - B$	A − B
*	Multiplication	$A \times B$	A * B
/	Division	$A \div B$	A / B
^	Exponentiation	A^B	A ^ B

Some examples of valid expressions in assignment statements follow:

```
00010 LET M = 5 + 4
00020 LET T = N1 + N2 + N3 + N4
00030 LET J = A - B
00040 LET X = 3 * C
00050 LET Y = (P * D) * C
00060 LET Q = N ^ 5
00070 LET C = 6.4 + P / X
```

● COMPUTERS AND INFORMATION PROCESSING

Again, some compilers and interpreters do not require the LET statement. If such is the case, all these statements could be written without using LET.

In an addition operation such as

```
00010 LET X = A + B
```

the value in the memory location identified by the variable A is added to the value in the memory location identified by the variable B. The result then is placed in the memory location identified by the variable X. For example, if A equals 5 and B equals 3, the computer would add 5 + 3 and place the result, 8, into the storage location identified by X.

For the example $X = A - B$, the same steps occur except that the value stored in B is subtracted from the value stored in A.

The multiplication operator (*) is used in multiplying two values. For example,

$$X = A * B$$

multiplies the value in the memory location identified by A by the value in the memory location identified by B and places the product in the memory location identified by X.

The division operator (/) is used in dividing two values. For example,

$$X = A / B$$

divides the value in the storage location A by the value in the storage location B and places the result in the storage location identified by X.

The result or product of an arithmetic operation can be used in subsequent calculations; for example,

```
00050 LET X = M + N
00060 LET Y = X * 6
00070 PRINT X,Y
```

The last arithmetic operation we will talk about here is **exponentiation,** or raising a number to a power. For example, A^3 is the same as A * A * A. The ^ operator is used in exponentiation. In the statement

```
00050 LET Y = X ^ 3
```

X would be cubed (X * X * X), and the result would be stored in the storage location identified by Y.

In the example using arithmetic operators, note that we have left a space on each side of the operators. This spacing is not necessary, but it greatly improves the readability of the program.

HIERARCHY OF OPERATIONS

When more than one operation is to be performed in a single arithmetic expression, the computer follows a **hierarchy of operations** that states the order in which arithmetic expressions are to be evaluated. When parentheses are used in an expression, the operations inside the parentheses are performed before the operations outside the parentheses. If parentheses are nested, the operations inside the innermost set are done first. Thus, in the expression

(6 + (5 * 2) / 3.12) + 10

the first operation to be performed is to multiply 5 by 2.

Parentheses aside, operations are performed according to the following rules:

Priority	Operation	Symbol
First	Exponentiation	^
Second	Multiplication/division	*, /
Third	Addition/subtraction	+, −

Operations of high priority are performed before operations of lower priority. If several operations are on the same level, they are performed from left to right. Table III–1 gives some examples of how BASIC evaluates expressions.

● The PRINT Statement

The PRINT statement is used to display or print the result of computer processing. It is flowcharted using an input/output symbol (/]). The general form of the PRINT statement is as follows:

line# PRINT $\begin{cases} \text{variable} \\ \text{literal} \\ \text{arithmetic expression} \\ \text{any combination of the above} \end{cases}$

● **Table III–1**
Examples of Evaluating Arithmetic Expressions

EXPRESSION	EVALUATION PROCESS
1. Y = 2 * 5 + 1	
First: 2 * 5 = 10	Process highest priority
Second: 10 + 1 = 11	Process next priority
Result: Y = 11	
2. Y = 2 * (5 + 1)	
First: 5 + 1 = 6	Perform process within parentheses
Second: 2 * 6 = 12	Perform next priority
Result: Y = 12	
3. Y = (3 + (6 + 2) / 4) + 10 ^ 2	
First: 6 + 2 = 8	Process innermost parentheses
Second: 8 / 4 = 2	Perform next priority
Third: 3 + 2 = 5	Process rest of outer parentheses
Fourth: 10 ^ 2 = 100	Perform next priority
Fifth: 5 + 100 = 105	Perform lowest priority

If more than one item is included in the PRINT statement, the items are separated by commas. These commas are also used to format or arrange the output; this topic will be discussed in detail in Section 4. For now, it is sufficient to know that the commas automatically space the items across the output line.

PRINTING THE VALUES OF VARIABLES

We can tell the computer to print values assigned to storage locations simply by using the reserved word PRINT with the variable name after it. If there is more than one variable to be printed, the names must be separated by commas:

```
00160 PRINT HRS,PERHR,TPAY
```

Printing has no effect on the contents of the storage location being printed. The PRINT statement only gets the value of a variable and prints it to the terminal screen.

PRINTING LITERALS

A **literal** is a group of characters containing any combination of alphabetic, numeric, and/or special characters. It is essentially the same as a constant. The term *literal*, however, is applied to constants used in PRINT statements. There are two types, character string literals and numeric literals.

Character Strings

A character string literal is a group of letters, numbers, and/or special characters enclosed in quotation marks. Whatever is inside the quotation marks is printed exactly as it is. For example,

```
00190 PRINT "SAMPLE @%OUTPUT 12"
```

would appear on the screen as

```
SAMPLE @%OUTPUT 12
```

Note that the quotation marks are not printed.

Literals can be used to print headings in output. To print column headings, for example, put each heading in quotation marks and separate them with commas. Here is an example:

```
00040 PRINT "NAME","RANK","SERIAL NO."
```

When this statement is executed, the following output will appear on the screen:

```
NAME          RANK         SERIAL NO.
```

Headings can be set off from the rest of the output in two ways: by underlining or by using a blank line. One way to underline headings is by including a separate PRINT statement that contains the necessary underscore lines, as shown below:

```
00040 PRINT "NAME","RANK","SERIAL NO."
00050 PRINT "____","____","_____"
```

The output would be:

```
NAME            RANK           SERIAL NO.
____            ____           _____
```

Note that the underline is slightly separated from the heading. This is caused by the separate PRINT statement.

A blank line in output makes the output more readable, and can be achieved by using a PRINT statement alone:

```
00140 PRINT
```

To skip more than one line, simply include more than one such statement:

```
00140 PRINT
00150 PRINT
```

Numeric Literals

Numeric literals are numbers placed within the PRINT statement which are to be printed in the output. They do not have to be enclosed in quotation marks. For example, the statement

```
00100 PRINT 103
```

will print

```
103
```

PRINTING THE VALUES OF EXPRESSIONS

The computer can print not only literals and the values of variables, but also the values of arithmetic expressions. Look at the following program:

```
00010 LET A = 15.00
00020 LET B = 26.00
00030 PRINT (A + B) / 2, A / B
00099 END
```

The computer will evaluate each expression in line 30, according to the hierarchy of operations, and then print the results:

```
20.5            .5769231
```

The computer can print only a certain number of digits for each value. Look at the second value printed. In this case, the computer cannot print more than nine digits. If the computer did not have this limit, an infinite number of digits would have been printed, because the full answer is:

.576923076923076923076 . . .

The last six digits repeat infinitely. An extremely large or small value may be printed in exponential notation instead.

● The END Statement

The END statement instructs the computer to stop program execution. In a flowchart, it is indicated by the termination symbol (⬭). The general format of the END statement is

line# END

The END statement is always the last line of a program that is executed. On the DECsystem, it must also be the last physical line of the program. To make the END statement readily identifiable, many programmers give it a line number of all 9s. All programs in this book will follow this practice.

● Multiple Statements on a Single Physical Line

Most BASIC systems allow multiple statements to be placed on a single physical line. On the DECsystem, this can be accomplished by separating the statements with backslashes (\). For example, if we wanted to skip two lines, instead of using two physical lines as illustrated previously, we could accomplish the same result more efficiently with the following line:

```
00110 PRINT \ PRINT
```

Many microcomputer systems use the colon (:) instead of the backslash (\) to place multiple logical lines on the same physical lines. For example,

```
00110 PRINT : PRINT
```

The sample program in Figure III–2 demonstrates the use of the REM and assignment statements and implements all four options of the PRINT statement.

● A Programming Problem

PROBLEM DEFINITION

A local stereo shop was advertising the following discounts:

● 5 percent off the purchase of a receiver and a pair of speakers
● 20 percent off the purchase of a receiver, a pair of speakers, and a turntable
● 40 percent off the purchase of a receiver, a pair of speakers, a turntable, and a cassette deck

Being a small shop, it only carries one model of each item. The price for each is as follows:

Item	Price
Receiver	$423.00
Pair of speakers	$300.00
Turntable	$185.00
Cassette	$210.00

Before going to the stereo shop, you decide to write a program to tell you the discounted price of each of the advertised options.

```
00010   REM ***                           PURCHASE COST                          ***
00020   REM ***                                                                  ***
00030   REM *** THIS PROGRAM PRINTS THE ITEMS AND THEIR PRICES IN A CHART.       ***
00040   REM *** IT THEN DETERMINES THE TOTAL PURCHASE COST AND PRINTS THE        ***
00050   REM *** RESULTS.                                                         ***
00060   REM *** MAJOR VARIABLES:                                                 ***
00070   REM ***      P#  - PURCHASED ITEMS                                       ***
00080   REM ***      C#  - COST OF EACH ITEM                                     ***
00090   REM
00100   REM *** ASSIGN ITEMS AND PRICES ***
00110   LET P1$ = "RECORD"
00120   LET P2$ = "SNEAKERS"
00130   LET P3$ = "BOOK"
00140   LET C1 = 8.98
00150   LET C2 = 24.82
00160   LET C3 = 6.50
00170   REM
00180   REM *** PRINT HEADINGS, CHART AND RESULTS ***
00190   PRINT "ITEM #","PURCHASE","PRICE"
00200   PRINT
00210   PRINT 1,P1$,C1
00220   PRINT 2,P2$,C2
00230   PRINT 3,P3$,C3
00240   PRINT
00250   PRINT "TOTAL PURCHASE COST",C1 + C2 + C3
00999   END
```

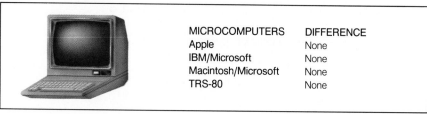

● FIGURE III–2
Purchase Cost Program

SOLUTION DESIGN

The general problem of finding the discount price can be divided into three steps: assigning the price of each component, determining the discount price by option, and printing the prices.

The first step in the program is to enter the price of each component. Next, determine the discount price for each option by adding the total

● **FIGURE III-3**
Structure Chart for Stereo Discount Price Program

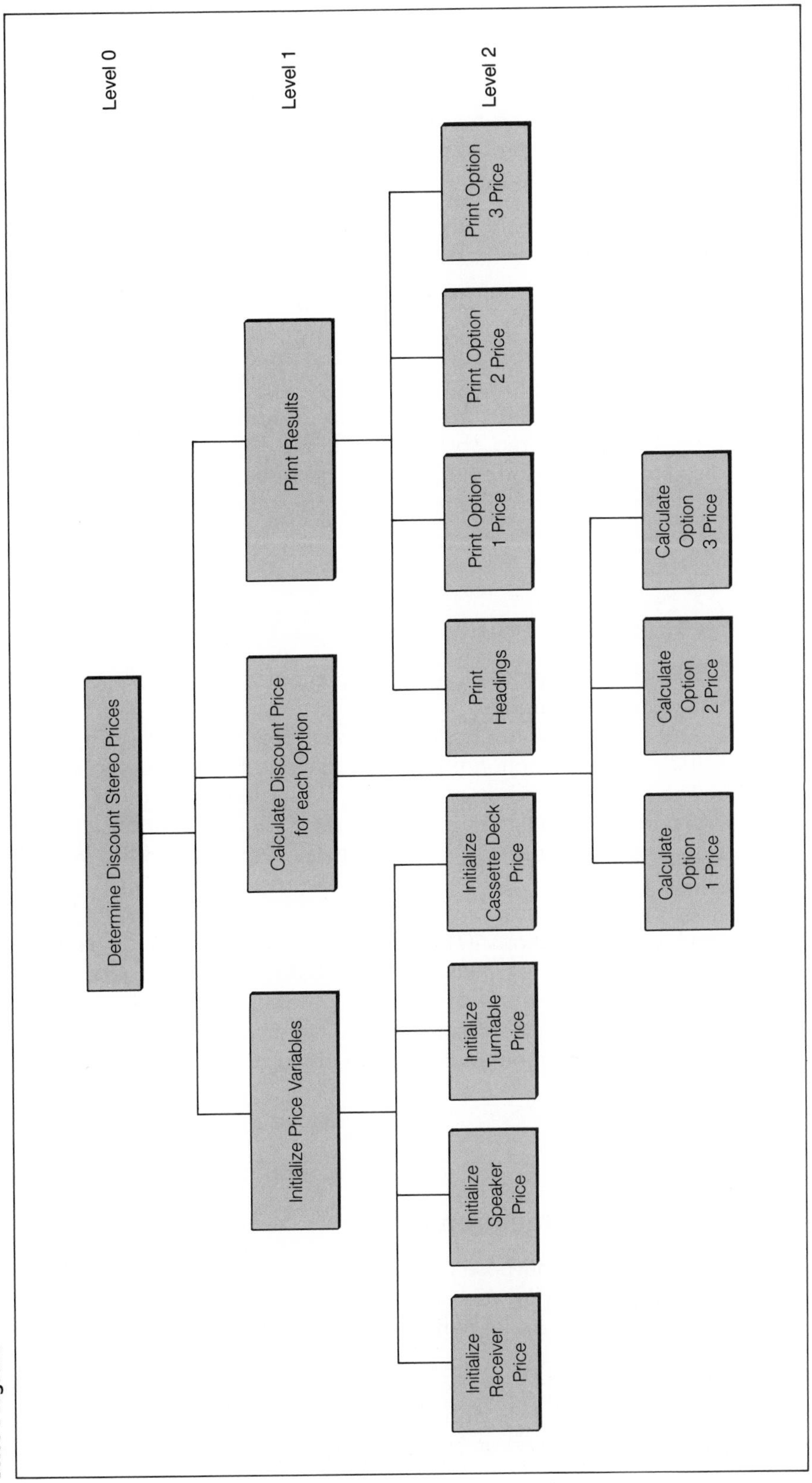

price of the items in an option and multiplying by the appropriate discount factor. You will notice we multiplied by 0.95, 0.8, and 0.6 for the respective options instead of 0.05, 0.2, and 0.4. This is because we are interested in what we have to pay rather than the discount amount itself. Finally, we want to print the results. A structure chart in Figure III–3 diagrams the outline of the problem.

THE PROGRAM

Figure III–4 shows the flowchart, the program listing and output of the program. The REM statements in lines 10 through 130 document the purpose of the program and the meaning of the variables. The REM statement in line 130 is used to set off the remarks from the executable statements. Lines 140 through 170 use assignment statements to enter the price of each stereo component. Lines 180 through 200 calculate the discounted price for each option. The headings are printed out in lines 210 through 230 and the results are printed out in lines 240 through 260.

○ Summary Points

- REM statements are used to document a program; they are not executed by the computer.
- The purpose of the assignment statement is to assign values to variables; LET is an optional keyword in some BASIC implementations.
- The assignment statement is not evaluated as an algebraic equation. The computer first evaluates the expression on the right side of the equal sign and then assigns that result to the variable on the left side of the equal sign.
- Arithmetic expressions are evaluated according to the following hierarchy of operations: (1) operations in parentheses, (2) exponentiation, (3) multiplication or division, and (4) addition or subtraction. Multiple operations at the same level are evaluated left to right.
- The PRINT statement is used to print or display the results of processing.
- The END statement indicates the physical end of a program and stops execution.

○ Review Questions

1. What is the purpose of the REM statement?
2. What is the purpose of the assignment statement?
3. In a LET statement, why can only a variable name be on the left side of the equal sign?
4. Evaluate the expression 10 LET A = 2.5 + (X * (Y ∧ 2) / C) * (8 + X) where X = 2, Y = 4, and C = 8.
5. What hierarchy, or priority, of arithmetic operations does BASIC follow?
6. What is the purpose of the PRINT statement?

● COMPUTERS AND INFORMATION PROCESSING

● **FIGURE III–4**
Stereo Discount Program and Flow-chart

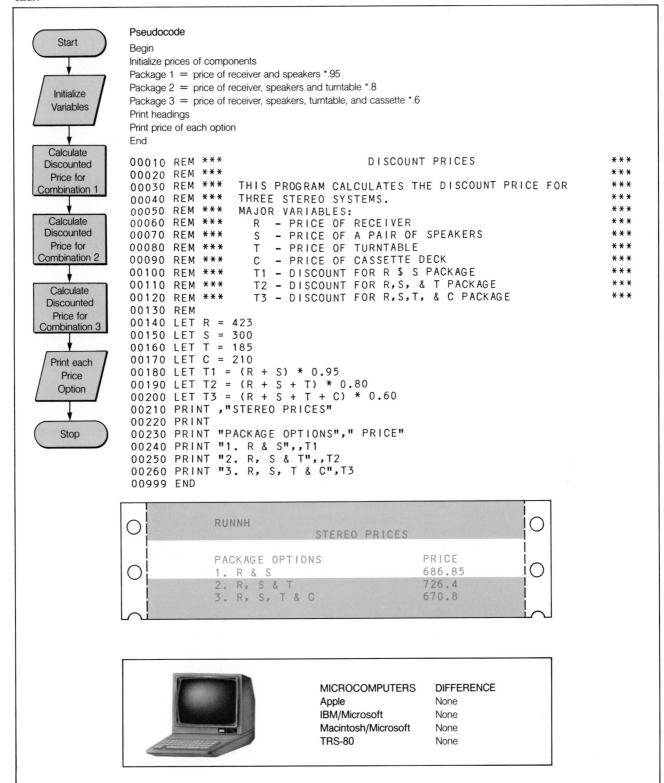

Pseudocode

Begin
Initialize prices of components
Package 1 = price of receiver and speakers *.95
Package 2 = price of receiver, speakers and turntable *.8
Package 3 = price of receiver, speakers, turntable, and cassette *.6
Print headings
Print price of each option
End

```
00010 REM ***                        D I S C O U N T   P R I C E S        ***
00020 REM ***                                                             ***
00030 REM ***    THIS PROGRAM CALCULATES THE DISCOUNT PRICE FOR           ***
00040 REM ***    THREE STEREO SYSTEMS.                                    ***
00050 REM ***    MAJOR VARIABLES:                                         ***
00060 REM ***      R  - PRICE OF RECEIVER                                 ***
00070 REM ***      S  - PRICE OF A PAIR OF SPEAKERS                       ***
00080 REM ***      T  - PRICE OF TURNTABLE                                ***
00090 REM ***      C  - PRICE OF CASSETTE DECK                            ***
00100 REM ***      T1 - DISCOUNT FOR R $ S PACKAGE                        ***
00110 REM ***      T2 - DISCOUNT FOR R,S, & T PACKAGE                     ***
00120 REM ***      T3 - DISCOUNT FOR R,S,T, & C PACKAGE                   ***
00130 REM
00140 LET R = 423
00150 LET S = 300
00160 LET T = 185
00170 LET C = 210
00180 LET T1 = (R + S) * 0.95
00190 LET T2 = (R + S + T) * 0.80
00200 LET T3 = (R + S + T + C) * 0.60
00210 PRINT ,"STEREO PRICES"
00220 PRINT
00230 PRINT "PACKAGE OPTIONS"," PRICE"
00240 PRINT "1. R & S",,T1
00250 PRINT "2. R, S & T",,T2
00260 PRINT "3. R, S, T & C",T3
00999 END
```

```
RUNNH
                    STEREO PRICES


PACKAGE OPTIONS                      PRICE
1. R & S                             686.85
2. R, S & T                          726.4
3. R, S, T & C                       670.8
```

MICROCOMPUTERS	DIFFERENCE
Apple	None
IBM/Microsoft	None
Macintosh/Microsoft	None
TRS-80	None

7. What is the output of the following program segment?
```
10 LET X = 952
20 LET Y = 56
30 PRINT 5.3 + X / (Y * 10)
```
8. Define a character string, and give three examples.
9. What is the purpose of the END statement?
10. Identify which of the following statements are invalid, and tell why:
  a. 10 LET P = 5 * (A + B)
  b. 10 PRINT TOTAL PRICE =
  c. 10 LET N = "NAN"
  d. 10 LET N = N + M
  e. 10 LET X = 5 + P$

● Debugging Exercises

Identify the following programs or program segments that contain errors, and debug them.

1.
```
00010 REM *** THIS PROGRAM CALCULATES   ***
00020 REM *** AN AVERAGE OF TWO NUMBERS. ***
00030 LET 10 = A
00040 LET 20 = B
00050 LET X = A + B / 2
00060 PRINT X
00099 END
```

2.
```
00100 REM *** THIS PROGRAM FINDS    ***
00110 REM *** THE CUBE OF A NUMBER. ***
00120 REM
00130 LET X = 5
00140 LET C$ = X ^ 3
00150 PRINT C$
00999 END
```

● Programming Problems

1. You want to know how much it would cost you to fly your plane to Hollywood for the Oscars. Hollywood is 2,040 nautical miles from your home. Your plane gets 14 miles per gallon, and you can get gas for $10.50 per gallon. Your output should have the following format:

DISTANCE	TOTAL COST
XXX	$XXX.XX

2. A cassette tape with a list price of $8.98 is on sale for 15 percent off. Write a program that will calculate and output the sale price of the tape.
3. You own an apartment building with eight identical apartments, each having two rooms that need carpeting. One room has a length of twelve feet and a width of nine feet, and the other has a length of ten feet and a width of eight feet. The carpeting costs $9.50 a square yard. Write a program that will calculate the amount of carpeting needed to carpet the entire building, as well as the total cost of the carpeting. The output should include both figures. The area of a room is equal to the length multiplied by the width. Be sure to document your program.

4. Write a program that will print the date, time, and telephone number of the following telephone log entries:

8/9/90	8:09 am	(419)353-7789
9/1/90	3:51 pm	(614)366-6443
1/7/91	6:42 am	(313)577-5864

The output should have the following format:

DATE	TIME	TELEPHONE #
X/X/X	X:XXxx	(XXX)XXX-XXXX
.	.	.
.	.	.

5. Write a program that converts 72 degrees Fahrenheit to its centigrade equivalent and prints the result, appropriately labeled. Use the formula $C = 5/9(F - 32)$, where C equals the degrees centigrade and F equals the degrees Fahrenheit.

●Section IV
Input and Output

● Introduction

The first part of this section explains ways of entering data to a program. The two methods introduced here are the INPUT statement and the READ and DATA statements. The INPUT statement allows the user to enter data while the program is running. When the READ and DATA statements are used, the data is entered as part of the program itself.

The remainder of the section discusses ways of printing program results. It explains how output can be printed so that it is attractive and easy to read. Printing output in table form is also explained.

● The INPUT Statement

In many programs, the data changes each time the program is executed. For example, think of a program that calculates the gas mileage for your car. Each time you run this program, you will want to be able to enter new values for the number of miles traveled and the amount of gas used. If such a program used assignment statements to assign these values to variables, these statements would have to be rewritten every time you wanted to calculate your gas mileage. A more practical approach to this programming problem is to use the INPUT statement.

The INPUT statement allows the user to enter data from the keyboard while the program is executing. The format of the INPUT statement is:

line# INPUT variable list

For example,

```
00140 INPUT L
00150 INPUT W
00160 INPUT H
```

These also could be combined into one line as follows:

```
00140 INPUT L,W,H
```

Note that one or more variables may be listed in a single INPUT statement. If there is more than one, the variables must be separated by commas.

The variables listed in the INPUT statements may be string or numeric. Just be sure to enter the correct value to be assigned to each variable. In other words, the type of data must be the same as that designated by the variable.

INPUT statements are placed where data values are needed in a program. This is determined by the logic of the program.

When a program is running and an INPUT statement is encountered, the program temporarily stops executing and a question mark appears on the terminal screen. The user must then enter the required data and press the RETURN key. After each value entered is stored in its corresponding variable, program execution continues to the next statement. More than one variable can be listed in the INPUT statement; the user must know how many values to enter.

On some systems when there is not enough data entered, another question mark is displayed, or a message to ?REDO FROM THE START is printed and the user must enter all data requested by the INPUT statement. On the DECsystem an error message is printed, telling the user that there is insufficient data. For example, when line 140 is executed with only one value entered, the result would look like this:

```
00140 INPUT L,W,H
RUNNH
 ? 28.5
? 59 Insufficient data at line 00140 of MAIN PROGRAM
 ?
```

The computer will continue telling the user that more data is needed until enough data has been entered. Then the program will continue executing.

If the user attempts to enter a character string to a numeric variable, another error message will appear:

```
? 52   Invalid floating point number at line 00010 of MAIN PROGRAM
```

The user can, however, assign a numeric value to a character string variable. The computer treats the numeric value as a string of characters and stores it in the corresponding string variable, but it cannot perform calculations with this value.

If the user knew what entries to make and how many, the output would look like this:

```
RUNNH
 ? 28.5,25,10
```

The variable L would have the value 28.5, W would be assigned the value 25, and H would contain 10. As you can see, the INPUT statement offers a great deal of flexibility. Each time the program is executed, new values can be entered without changing any program statements.

● Prompts

In the previous example, when the INPUT statement was executed, only a question mark (?) appeared on the terminal screen when it was time for the user to enter data. The user was not told what type of data or how many data items to enter. Therefore, the programmer should also include a **prompt** to tell the user what is to be entered. A prompt can consist of a PRINT statement, placed before the INPUT statement in the program, which tells the user the type and quantity of data to be entered.

Figure IV–1 shows a short program that calculates the volume of a box. The length, width, and height of the box are entered and the volume is output. Note the spelling of the variable names LNGTH and WDTH. It might seem more appropriate to name these variables LENGTH and

● **FIGURE IV–1**
Program Demonstrating the INPUT Statement

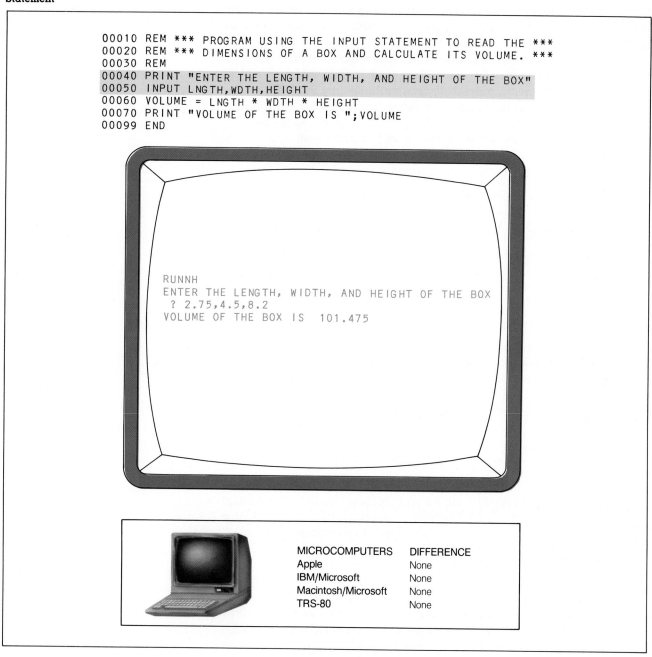

```
00010 REM *** PROGRAM USING THE INPUT STATEMENT TO READ THE ***
00020 REM *** DIMENSIONS OF A BOX AND CALCULATE ITS VOLUME. ***
00030 REM
00040 PRINT "ENTER THE LENGTH, WIDTH, AND HEIGHT OF THE BOX"
00050 INPUT LNGTH,WDTH,HEIGHT
00060 VOLUME = LNGTH * WDTH * HEIGHT
00070 PRINT "VOLUME OF THE BOX IS ";VOLUME
00099 END
```

```
RUNNH
ENTER THE LENGTH, WIDTH, AND HEIGHT OF THE BOX
? 2.75,4.5,8.2
VOLUME OF THE BOX IS  101.475
```

MICROCOMPUTERS	DIFFERENCE
Apple	None
IBM/Microsoft	None
Macintosh/Microsoft	None
TRS-80	None

WIDTH, but all or part of these words are reserved words in at least one of the BASIC implementations covered in this textbook. Therefore, it was necessary to alter these variable names to make them different from the reserved words.

Line 40 of the program in Figure IV–1 contains the prompt:

```
00040 PRINT "ENTER THE LENGTH, WIDTH, AND HEIGHT OF THE BOX"
```

Line 50 is the INPUT statement:

```
00050 INPUT LNGTH,WDTH,HEIGHT
```

After line 50 is executed, the computer will stop and wait for the user to enter the desired length, width, and height. Then execution will continue, and the volume of the box will be calculated and printed on the screen.

Most computers allow the prompt to be contained within the INPUT statement itself. If this were done for the program in Figure IV–1, lines 40 and 50 could be replaced with a single statement:

```
00040 INPUT "ENTER THE LENGTH, WIDTH, AND HEIGHT OF THE BOX";LNGTH,WDTH,HEIGHT
```

When this program is run, the question mark and the prompt appear on the same line:

```
RUNNH
ENTER THE LENGTH, WIDTH, AND HEIGHT OF THE BOX ? 2.75,4.5,8.2
VOLUME OF THE BOX IS  101.475
```

Using this format simplifies the writing of the program and makes the logic easy to follow.

This method of data entry, in which the user enters a response to a prompt printed on the screen is called **inquiry-and-response,** or **conversational mode.**

● The READ and DATA Statements

The READ and DATA statements provide another way to enter data into a BASIC program. These two statements always work together. Values contained in the DATA statements are assigned to variables listed in the READ statements.

The general format of the READ and DATA statements is this:

line# READ variable list
line# DATA value list

The READ and DATA statements differ from the INPUT statement in that data values are not entered by the user during program execution, but instead are assigned by the programmer within the program itself.

The following is a list of rules explaining the use of the READ and DATA statements.

● A program may contain any number of READ and DATA statements.
● The placement of READ statements is determined by the logic of a given program. The programmer places them in the program at the point at which data needs to be read.

• DATA statements are nonexecutable and can therefore be placed anywhere in the program before the END statement. This book follows the common practice of placing all data statements immediately before the END statement, so that they are easy to locate.

• The computer collects the values from all the DATA statements in a program and places them in a single list, referred to as the **data list.** This list is formed by taking the values from the DATA statements in order, from the lowest to the highest line number and from left to right within a single statement.

• When more than one data value is placed in a single DATA statement, the values are separated by commas. Character string values may or may not be placed in quotes. However, if the character string contains leading or trailing blanks, commas, or semicolons, it must be enclosed in quotation marks.

• When the program encounters a READ statement, it goes to the data list and assigns the next value from that list to the corresponding variable in the READ statement. If the variable is numeric, the data value must also be numeric. If it is a character string variable, however, the computer will allow a numeric value to be assigned to it, as previously explained for the INPUT statement. Again, computations cannot be performed with numbers that have been assigned to character string variables.

• If there is inadequate data for a READ statement (that is, if there are no more data values in the data list), an OUT OF DATA error message occurs and the program stops executing at that point.

• If there are more data values than variables, these extra data values simply remain unread.

Figure IV–2 shows a program segment containing READ and DATA statements. When the computer executes this program, it first encounters the READ statement in line 100. The statement instructs it to read four data values from the data list and assign these values to the corresponding variables. Therefore, the values JACOBS, 48, 60, and 53 are assigned to the variables NME$, S1, S2, and S3 respectively. After this task is completed, program execution continues to line 110, where the next value in the data list, GUINARD, is assigned to the variable NME$. This new value of NME$ replaces JACOBS, which was the previous value.

Note that the computer "remembers" where it is in the data list. Whenever it encounters another READ statement, it assigns the next value in

• **FIGURE IV–2**
Examples of READ and DATA Statements

		CURRENT VALUES OF VARIABLES			
	AT LINE#:	NME$	S1	S2	S3
00100 READ NME$,S1,S2,S3	100	JACOBS	48	60	53
00110 READ NME$	110	GUINARD	48	60	53
00120 READ S1,S2	120	GUINARD	62	58	53
00130 READ S3	130	GUINARD	62	58	54
00140 DATA JACOBS,48					
00150 DATA 60,53,GUINARD					
00160 DATA 62,58					
00170 DATA 54					

• **COMPUTERS AND INFORMATION PROCESSING**

the list to that variable. Study Figure IV–2 to make certain you understand how the READ and DATA statements are used in reading data values. Notice that the columns on the right side of the figure state the current values of each of the variables for lines 100 through 130.

The program in Figure IV–3 shows how READ and DATA statements can be used to read the dimensions of a box and to calculate and print the volume. Note that line 40 contains a single READ statement that reads all three dimensions of the box. The DATA statement in line 70 contains the three values to be assigned to the three variables in the READ statement.

● Comparison of the INPUT and the READ/DATA Statements

There are certain situations where the INPUT statement is particularly useful, and other situations in which READ/DATA statements are more suitable. As you become adept at programming in BASIC, you will easily be able to choose the most appropriate data entry method for a given situation. Here are some guidelines to help you decide which method to use:

● The INPUT statement is ideal when data values change frequently, because it allows the data to be entered at the keyboard during program execution.

● **FIGURE IV–3**
Program Demonstrating the READ and DATA Statements

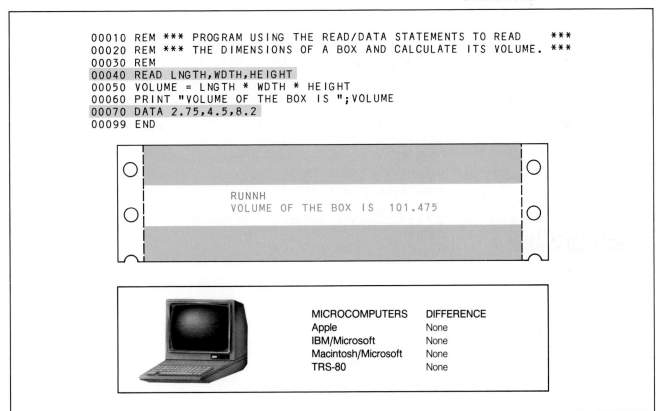

```
00010 REM *** PROGRAM USING THE READ/DATA STATEMENTS TO READ   ***
00020 REM *** THE DIMENSIONS OF A BOX AND CALCULATE ITS VOLUME. ***
00030 REM
00040 READ LNGTH,WDTH,HEIGHT
00050 VOLUME = LNGTH * WDTH * HEIGHT
00060 PRINT "VOLUME OF THE BOX IS ";VOLUME
00070 DATA 2.75,4.5,8.2
00099 END
```

```
RUNNH
VOLUME OF THE BOX IS  101.475
```

MICROCOMPUTERS	DIFFERENCE
Apple	None
IBM/Microsoft	None
Macintosh/Microsoft	None
TRS-80	None

• The READ and DATA statements are well suited for programs using large quantities of data, because the user does not have to enter a long list of data values during program execution, as would be necessary with the INPUT statement.

• The READ and DATA statements are most useful when data values will not be different for each program execution. The main disadvantage of using the READ and DATA statements is that the program itself must be altered when the data values change.

● Using Print Zones

Section 3 explained that the PRINT statement let us have the results of processing printed. When more than one item is to be printed on a line, commas can be used to control the spacing output.

The number of characters that can be printed on a line varies with the system used. On some terminals each output line consists of eighty print positions. Each line is divided into sections called print zones. The zone size and the number of zones per line depend on the system. The print zones on the DECsystem are 14 characters wide, with five zones per line. The beginning columns of the five print zones are shown below:

ZONE 1 COL 1	ZONE 2 COL 15	ZONE 3 COL 29	ZONE 4 COL 43	ZONE 5 COL 57

Commas can be used within a PRINT statement to control the format of printed output. A comma indicates that the next item to be printed will start at the beginning of the next print zone. The following example shows how this works:

```
00010 READ W1$,W2$,W3$
00020 PRINT W1$,W2$,W3$
00030 DATA "BE","SEEING","YOU"
```

The first item in the PRINT statement is printed at the beginning of the line, which is the start of the first print zone. The comma between W1$ and W2$ causes the computer to space over to the next print zone; then the value in W2$ is printed. The second comma directs the computer to space over to the next zone (Zone 3) and print the value in W3$. The output is as follows:

ZONE 1   **ZONE 3**

```
RUNNH
BE              SEEING          YOU
```

If there are more items listed in a PRINT statement than there are print zones in a line, the print zones of the next line are also used, starting with the first zone. Notice the output of the following example.

```
00010 READ SEX$,AGE,CLASS$,MAJ$,HRS,GPA
00020 PRINT SEX$,AGE,CLASS$,MAJ$,HRS,GPA
00030 DATA "M",19,"JR","CS",18,2.5
```

```
RUNNH
M               19              JR              CS              18
2.5
```

If the value to be printed exceeds the width of the print zone, the entire value is printed, regardless of how many zones it occupies. A following comma causes printing to continue in the next print zone, as shown in the following example:

```
00010 SPOT$ = "BAGHDAD"
00020 PRINT "YOUR NEXT DESTINATION WILL BE",SPOT$
```

```
RUNNH
YOUR NEXT DESTINATION WILL BE                    BAGHDAD
```

Table IV–1 presents the formatting differences among the five computer systems discussed in this book. Columns 2 and 3 give the number of columns and rows available on each system and columns 4 and 5 give the number of print zones per line and zone widths. Note that some systems enable the user to determine the screen and zone dimensions. Columns 6 and 7 indicate whether leading and trailing spaces are provided for numeric values. Column 8 gives the maximum number of digits that will be printed for a single-precision number.

A print zone can be skipped by the use of a technique that involves enclosing a space (the character blank) in quotation marks. This causes the entire zone to appear empty:

```
00010 PRINT "ARTIST"," ","ALBUM"
```

Most computers (including all those covered in this text) also enable the user to skip a zone by typing consecutive commas:

```
00010 PRINT "ARTIST",,"ALBUM"
```

Both of these techniques cause the literal ARTIST to be printed in Zone 1, the second zone to be blank, and the literal ALBUM to be printed in Zone 3:

```
RUNNH
ARTIST                         ALBUM
```

● **Table IV–1**
Computer Display Characteristics

COMPUTER	SCREEN WIDTH (CHARACTERS)	SCREEN HEIGHT (LINES)	NUMBER OF PRINT ZONES	ZONE WIDTH	SPACE FOR SIGN?	SPACE AFTER NUMBER?	NUMBER OF DIGITS PRINTED, SINGLE PRECISION
DECsystem	80/132*	24/16*	5/9*	14	Yes	Yes	7
Apple	40**	24	3	16	No	No	9
IBM/Microsoft	80	24	5	14	Yes	Yes	7
Mac/Microsoft	***	***	***	***	Yes	Yes	7
TRS-80	64/32*	15	4/2*	16	Yes	Yes	6

*The slash indicates that both options are available to the user.
**Screen width may be 80 columns if the computer is equipped with an 80-column card.
***These can be determined by the user. See your manual.

If a comma appears after the last item in a PRINT statement, the output of the next PRINT statement encountered will begin at the next available print zone. Thus, the statements

```
00010  READ NME$,AGE,SEX$,VOICE$
00020  PRINT NME$,AGE,
00030  PRINT SEX$,VOICE$
00040  DATA "SHICOFF",32,"M","TENOR"
00099  END
```

produce the following output:

```
RUNNH
SHICOFF        32             M              TENOR
```

● Using the Semicolon

Using a semicolon instead of a comma causes output to be packed more closely on a line. This alternative gives the programmer greater flexibility in formatting output. In the following examples, notice the difference in spacing when semicolons are used instead of commas:

```
00060  PRINT "JASON","JACKSON"
```

```
RUNNH
JASON           JACKSON
```

```
00060  PRINT "JASON";"JACKSON"
```

```
RUNNH
JASONJACKSON
```

The semicolon between the items tells the computer to skip to the next **column** to print the next item—not to the next print zone, as with the comma.

The above example shows what happens when semicolons are used with character strings. Since letters do not have signs, they are run together. The best way to avoid this problem is to enclose a space within the quotes:

```
00060  PRINT "JASON";" JACKSON"
```

```
RUNNH
JASON JACKSON
```

When numbers are printed, most computers (the Apple is an exception) print the number with a preceding space if the number has no sign, such as 104 or 48. If the number has a sign, such as -176 or $+32$, no preceding space is printed, because the sign is printed in that position. In either case, a space is left after the number for greater readability. Therefore, on most computers, when numeric values are separated by a semicolon, the printed digits are not adjacent as in the case of the character strings. The following example demonstrates this point:

```
00010  PRINT 100;-200;300
```

```
RUNNH
 100 -200  300
```

Notice that the output shows only one space before −200. This is because the computer left a space after printing the number 100. But there are two spaces before 300: Not only was a space left after −200 was printed, but a space was left for the sign (an assumed positive) of the number 300.

If the semicolon is the last character of the PRINT statement, carriage control is not advanced when the printing of the statement is completed; therefore, the output generated by the next PRINT statement continues on the same line. For example,

```
00060 PRINT 495207;
00070 PRINT "JASON";" JACKSON"
```

```
RUNNH
 495207 JASON JACKSON
```

Line 60 causes 495207 to be printed out. The semicolon after this number keeps the printer on the same line; then, when line 70 is encountered, JASON JACKSON is printed on the same line.

● The TAB Function

The comma causes the results of processing to be printed according to predefined print zones. The semicolon causes them to start printing in the next position on the output line. Both are easy to use, and many reports can be formatted in this fashion. However, there are times when a report should be structured differently.

The TAB function allows output to be printed in any column in an output line, providing the programmer greater flexibility to format printed output.

The general format of the TAB function is this:

TAB(expression)

The expression in parentheses may be a numeric constant, variable, or arithmetic expression; it tells the computer the column in which printing is to occur.

When a TAB function is encountered in a PRINT statement, the computer spaces over to the column number indicated in the expression. The next variable value or literal found in the PRINT statement is printed starting in that column. The TAB function is separated from the items to be printed by semicolons. For example, the statement

```
00050 PRINT TAB(10);"HI THERE!";TAB(25);"BYE!"
```

causes the literal HI THERE! to be printed starting in column 10. Then, starting in column 25, the literal BYE! is printed.

On some computers, however, such as the DECsystem and the TRS-80, the string HI THERE! would begin in column 11 and BYE! in column 26. In other words, the computer tabs to the tenth column and the semicolon instructs it to begin printing in the *next* column (column 11). Check your manual to determine how this works for your system.

It is best to have the expression in the TAB function evaluate as an integer, because this makes it clear in which column the output will start printing. However, it is possible to use a real value for an expression, as in the following statement:

```
00050 PRINT TAB(15.7);"HI THERE!"
```

On the DECsystem, the number 15.7 will be rounded to 16, the computer will tab to the sixteenth column, and the character string will be printed starting in column 17.

The program in Figure IV–4 illustrates the use of the TAB function. This program prints a simple table by using the TAB function to place the printed values in columns.

Note that we have used the semicolon as the punctuation mark with the TAB function. The semicolon separates the expression from the values to be printed. If commas were used instead, the printer would default and use the predefined print zones, ignoring the columns specified in parentheses. For example, if line 50 of the program in Figure IV–4 had been

```
00050 PRINT TAB(5),"ITEM",TAB(25),"QUANTITY"
```

the output would have been

```
RUNNH
                INVENTORY REPORT

            ITEM                        QUANTITY

        PENCILS           1000
        ERASERS           200
        PAPER             500
```

The computer spaced over the five columns indicated by the first TAB function, but when it saw the comma following the parentheses, it skipped over to the next predefined print zone to print ITEM. The same thing happens again with QUANTITY.

When using the TAB function, it is important to be aware of spacing. On the DECsystem, there can be a space between the word TAB and the left parenthesis, because the DEC recognizes the reserved word TAB. On some systems, however—for example, the IBM—there cannot be a space between TAB and the left parenthesis. This is because the reserved word that these systems recognize is TAB(. Without the opening parenthesis following it, TAB is taken as a variable name TAB and the value in parentheses is taken as an array subscript. (Arrays will be discussed in Section 9). The following statement would be invalid on systems that recognize TAB(as a reserved word:

```
00010 PRINT TAB (5);"ITEM";TAB (25);"QUANTITY"
```

The statement would be correctly written like this:

```
00010 PRINT TAB(5);"ITEM";TAB(25);"QUANTITY"
```

As another caution, remember that when the TAB function is used, the printer cannot be backspaced. Once a column has been passed, the printer cannot go back to it. This means that if more than one TAB function is used in a PRINT statement, the column numbers in parentheses must increase from left to right. For example,

Valid:

```
00020 PRINT TAB(5);3;TAB(15);4;TAB(25);5
RUNNH
      3        4        5
```

The following statement does not use the TAB function properly:

```
00020 PRINT TAB(25);5;TAB(15);4;TAB(5);3
RUNNH
                         5   4   3
```

The invalid statement above demonstrates the action taken by most systems when the column numbers do not increase from left to right. The statement instructs the computer to print the number 5 in column 25, which it does. However, because there can be no backspacing to columns 15 and 5 as the next two TAB functions instruct, the TAB function is ignored and the numbers 4 and 3 are printed where indicated by the semicolons.

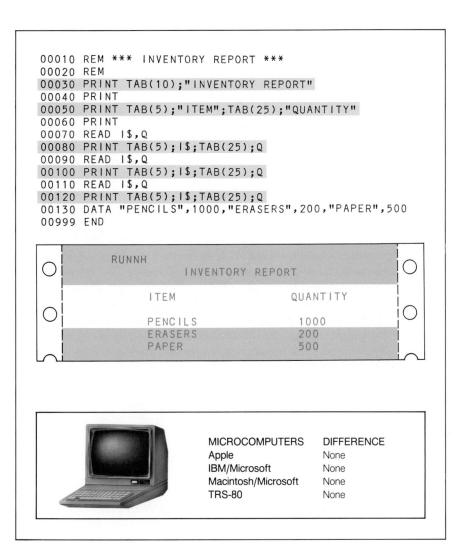

● **FIGURE IV–4**
Program Demonstrating the TAB Function

The IBM and Macintosh systems respond to this situation in a different way. When a TAB function specifies a column to the left of the current print position, the computer spaces to that column on the next line. The following BASIC statement was run on the IBM:

```
20 PRINT TAB(25);5;TAB(15);4;TAB(5);3
RUN
                              5
                    4
          3
```

● The PRINT USING Statement

Yet another convenient feature for controlling output is the PRINT USING statement. This feature is especially useful when printing table headings or aligning columns of numbers. All of the computers covered in this text, except the Apple, have a PRINT USING capability. The syntax for the PRINT USING statement varies considerably among different computers. This section briefly describes its use on the DECsystem; the principles are similar for other computers with this feature.

The general format of the PRINT USING statement on the DECsystem is as follows:

line# PRINT USING image statement line#, expression-list

The expression list in the format description consists of a sequence of variables or expressions separated by commas, similar to the expression list in any PRINT statement. The PRINT USING statement instructs the computer to print the items in this expression list using the format described by the *image statement*, the line number of which is given.

An image statement is identified in the program by a colon following the line number. Its format is as shown here:

line#: format control characters

The image statement, like the DATA statement, is nonexecutable and can appear anywhere in the program. The PRINT USING statement, however, is placed where the program logic demands. A single image statement can be referred to by several PRINT USING statements.

Special format control characters are used in the image statement to describe the output image and to control spacing. The most commonly used DECsystem format control characters are listed in Table IV–2.

The PRINT USING statement can easily be used to center character strings within a field. For example, the statements:

```
00100 PRINT USING 140,"HALSTON & LING, INC."
00110 PRINT USING 140,"ATTORNEYS AT LAW"
00120 PRINT USING 140,"749 S. MAIN"
00130 PRINT USING 140,"ALTOONA,MI"
00140 :'CCCCCCCCCCCCCCCCCCCCCCCCCCCCCC
```

will cause the following output:

```
RUNNH
          HALSTON & LING, INC.
           ATTORNEYS AT LAW
             749 S. MAIN
             ALTOONA,MI
```

● COMPUTERS AND INFORMATION PROCESSING

Format Control Characters for the DECsystem

CHARACTER	CONTROL IMAGE FOR	EXAMPLE
#	Numeric data; used in a mask*; one symbol for each digit to be printed; zeros are added to the left of the number to fill the field.	###.###
$	Dollar sign; printed exactly as is.	$###.##
$$	Causes dollar sign to be printed immediately before first digit.	$$##.##
**	Leading asterisks; printed in place of blanks.	***##.##
.	Decimal point; printed exactly as is.	####.##
E	Alphanumeric data; preceded by apostrophe ('); permits overflow to be printed to the right; if necessary, blanks are added to the left of the data to fill the field.	'E
L	Alphanumeric data; preceded by apostrophe ('); used as a mask; aligns output at the left side of the field.	'LLLLLLL
R	Alphanumeric data; preceded by apostrophe ('); used as a mask; aligns output at the right side of the field.	'RRRRRR
C	Alphanumeric data; preceded by apostrophe ('); used as a mask; centers output in the field.	'CCCC

*A *mask* specifies the maximum number of characters to be printed in a field.

The same image statement (at line 140) has been used for all four PRINT USING statements. When these headings were printed, all four were centered in a field of length 30, because the image statement in line 140 contains 30 C's. (As explained in Table IV-2, the character C causes the output to be centered within the field specified.)

Suppose the same program segment is run again, but with the image statement altered:

```
00100 PRINT USING 140,"HALSTON & LING, INC."
00110 PRINT USING 140,"ATTORNEYS AT LAW"
00120 PRINT USING 140,"749 S. MAIN"
00130 PRINT USING 140,"ALTOONA,MI"
00140 :'LLLLLLLLLLLLLLLLLLLLLLLLLLLLLL
```

The output now looks like this:

```
RUNNH
HALSTON & LING, INC.
ATTORNEYS AT LAW
749 S. MAIN
ALTOONA,MI
```

The use of the letter L in the image statement causes the output to be lined up at the left margin of the field.

PRINT USING statements are very useful in aligning columns of numbers. Consider the following program segment.

```
00010 READ V1,V2,V3,V4
00020 PRINT USING 90,V1,V2,V3,V4
00030 READ V1,V2,V3,V4
00040 PRINT USING 90,V1,V2,V3,V4
00050 READ V1,V2,V3,V4
00060 PRINT USING 90,V1,V2,V3,V4
00070 READ V1,V2,V3,V4
00080 PRINT USING 90,V1,V2,V3,V4
00090 : ######.##
00100 DATA 14.56,78.905,10234.1,0.03,6.73,12322.4,943.05,17.65
00110 DATA 65.56,945.7,125447.80,0.17,175.35,78.92,319.00,4.56
```

The output of this program segment is as follows:

```
RUNNH
     14.56       78.90    10234.10        0.03
      6.73    12322.40      943.05       17.65
     65.56      945.70   125447.80        0.17
    175.35       78.92      319.00        4.56
```

Note that all of the numbers have been aligned at the decimal point.

The program in Figure IV–5 illustrates how PRINT USING statements can be used to print a table. Notice the use of the two dollar signs in the image statement in line 290:

```
00290 : 'LLLLLLLLLLLLLLL          $$##.##            $$##.##
```

This causes the dollar sign to "float," so that it is always printed immediately before the first digit of the number following it.

The PRINT USING statements of the IBM, Macintosh, and TRS-80 are somewhat different. The general format for all of these systems looks like this:

line# PRINT USING format expression; expression-list

The format expression can be a string constant or a string variable consisting of formatting characters.

The following example illustrates this format:

```
100 A$ = "**$###,###.## DOLLARS"
110 PRINT USING A$;P
```

Figure IV–6 demonstrates how the program shown in Figure IV–5 would be implemented on these computer systems. Table IV–3 contains a list of the format control characters for the various BASIC implementations.

● A Programming Problem

PROBLEM DEFINITION

Baymont High School would like a program to generate absentee percentages per class. Design the program so that they can run it every day

```
00010 REM *** PRINT PROGRAM TO ILLUSTRATE PRINT USING ***
00020 REM
00030 PRINT
00040 PRINT USING 280,"ITEM","TOTAL","SALES"
00050 PRINT USING 280,"PURCHASED","PRICE","TAX"
00060 PRINT
00070 READ A$,X
00080 Y = X * .06
00090 PRINT USING 290,A$,X,Y
00100 READ A$,X
00110 Y = X * .06
00120 PRINT USING 290,A$,X,Y
00130 READ A$,X
00140 Y = X * .06
00150 PRINT USING 290,A$,X,Y
00160 READ A$,X
00170 Y = X * .06
00180 PRINT USING 290,A$,X,Y
00190 READ A$,X
00200 Y = X * .06
00210 PRINT USING 290,A$,X,Y
00220 REM
00230 REM *** DATA STATEMENTS ***
00240 DATA TOASTER,27.50,BLENDER,18.45
00250 DATA BLANKET,9.90,KNIVES,34.99,FAN,29.99
00260 REM
00270 REM *** IMAGE STATEMENTS ***
00280 : 'LLLLLLLLLLLL          'CCCCCCCCC           'CCCCCCCCC
00290 : 'LLLLLLLLLLLLLLL        $$##.##              $$##.##
00999 END
```

```
RUNNH

ITEM                        TOTAL                   SALES
PURCHASED                   PRICE                     TAX

TOASTER                    $27.50                   $1.65
BLENDER                    $18.45                   $1.11
BLANKET                     $9.90                   $0.59
KNIVES                     $34.99                   $2.10
FAN                        $29.99                   $1.80
```

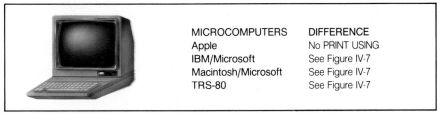

MICROCOMPUTERS	DIFFERENCE
Apple	No PRINT USING
IBM/Microsoft	See Figure IV-7
Macintosh/Microsoft	See Figure IV-7
TRS-80	See Figure IV-7

```
10   REM *** PROGRAM TO ILLUSTRATE PRINT USING ***
20   REM
30   PRINT
40   PRINT USING "\        \         \        \            \";"ITEM","TOTAL","SALES"
50   PRINT USING "\        \         \        \            \ \";"PURCHASED";"PRICE";"TAX"
60   PRINT
70   READ A$,X
80   Y = X * .06
90   PRINT USING "\        \      $$##.##        $$##.##";A$,X,Y
100  READ A$,X
110  Y = X * .06
120  PRINT USING "\        \      $$##.##        $$##.##";A$,X,Y
130  READ A$,X
140  Y = X * .06
150  PRINT USING "\        \      $$##.##        $$##.##";A$,X,Y
160  READ A$,X
170  Y = X * .06
180  PRINT USING "\        \      $$##.##        $$##.##";A$,X,Y
190  READ A$,X
200  Y = X * .06
210  PRINT USING "\        \      $$##.##        $$##.##";A$,X,Y
220  REM
230  REM *** DATA STATEMENTS ***
240  DATA TOASTER,27.50,BLENDER,18.45
250  DATA BLANKET,9.90,KNIVES,34.99,FAN,29.99
999  END
```

```
RUN

ITEM            TOTAL          SALES
PURCHASE        PRICE          TAX

TOASTER         $27.50         $1.65
BLENDER         $18.45         $1.11
BLANKET          $9.90         $0.59
KNIVES          $34.99         $2.10
FAN             $29.99         $1.80
```

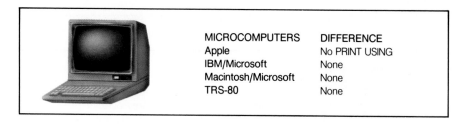

MICROCOMPUTERS	DIFFERENCE
Apple	No PRINT USING
IBM/Microsoft	None
Macintosh/Microsoft	None
TRS-80	None

IBM and MACINTOSH

CHARACTER	EXPLANATION
#	Same as DECsystem.
.	Same as DECsystem.
$$	Two dollar signs cause the dollar sign to be floating, meaning that it will be in the first position before the number.
**$	Vacant positions will be filled with asterisks, and the dollar sign will be in the first position to the left of the number.
+	When a + sign is placed at the beginning or end of a number, it causes a + sign to be printed if the number is positive and a − sign if the number is negative.
−	When a − sign is placed at the end of a number, negative numbers will be followed by a negative sign and a space will appear after the number for positive numbers.
^^^^	This causes the number to be printed in exponential format.
\spaces\	This specifies a string field to be 2 plus the number of spaces between the slashes.
!	This causes only the first string character to be printed.
&	This specifies a variable-length field. The string is output exactly as it is entered.
——	The underscore causes the next character in the format string to be printed. The character itself may be underscored by preceding it with two underscores (_____).
%	If the number to be printed is larger than the specified field, a percent sign will appear before the number. If rounding causes the number to exceed the field, the percent sign will be printed in front of the rounded number.

TRS-80

CHARACTER	EXPLANATION
#	Same as DECsystem.
.	Same as DECsystem.
$	Same as DECsystem.
$$	Two dollar signs cause the dollar sign to be floating, meaning that it will be in the first position before the number.
**$	Vacant positions will be filled with asterisks, and the dollar sign will be in the first position to the left of the number.
+	When a + sign is placed at the beginning or end of a number, it causes a + sign to be printed if the number is positive and a − sign if the number is negative.
−	When a − sign is placed at the end of a number, negative numbers will have a negative sign, and a space will appear after the number for positive numbers.
^^^^	This causes the number to be printed in exponential format.
%spaces%	This specifies a string field to be 2 plus the number of spaces between the percent signs.
!	This causes only the first string character to be printed.

in order to compare the daily figures and determine if there is any pattern. Format the output as follows:

DAILY ABSENCE REPORT FOR (current date)

CLASS	TOTAL NUMBER OF STUDENTS	NUMBER ABSENT	PERCENTAGE ABSENT
xx	xxx	xx	xx
xx	xxx	xx	xx
xx	xxx	xx	xx
xx	xxx	xx	xx

Use INPUT statements to allow the user to enter the current date and the following data:

Class	#Students	#Absent
9	345	4
10	321	28
11	367	10
12	298	32

SOLUTION DESIGN

The general problem of generating an absentee percentage per class report can be divided into two subproblems—the task of processing each class, and the task of printing the information in table format.

1. Process each class
2. Report the information in a table format

Step 1 can be further broken down into several smaller tasks that must be performed for each class:

1a. Enter the total enrollment per class
1b. Enter the number absent per class
1c. Calculate the percentages per class

Step 2 can also be divided into smaller problems:

2a. Print the headings
2b. Print the per class information
2c. Print the footer

The structure chart in Figure IV–7 diagrams this outline of the problem.

THE PROGRAM

Figure IV–8 shows the flowchart, the program listing and the output of the program. Lines 10 through 100 explain the purpose of major variables used in the program. Input statements with prompts are used in lines 120 through 200 to allow the user to enter the total enrollment and number absent per class. Lines 230 through 260 calculate the absentee percentage by dividing the number absent by the total enrolled and multiplying by

● FIGURE IV-7
Structure Chart for Absentee Report
Program

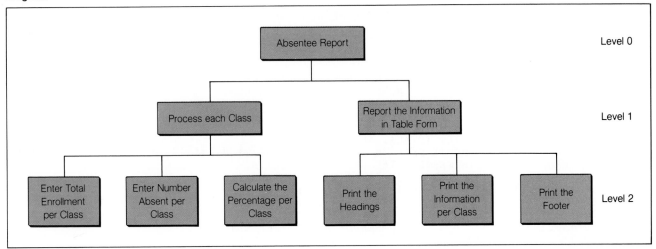

● FIGURE IV-8
Absentee Report Program and Flow-chart

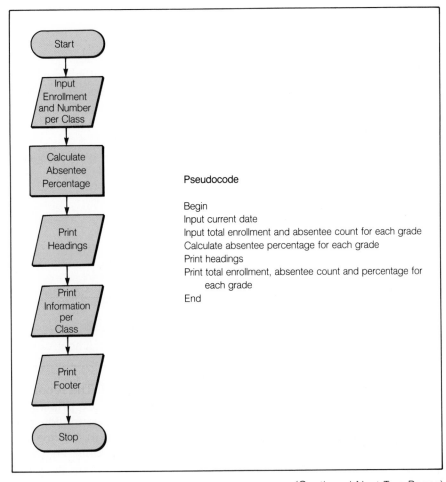

Pseudocode

Begin
Input current date
Input total enrollment and absentee count for each grade
Calculate absentee percentage for each grade
Print headings
Print total enrollment, absentee count and percentage for
    each grade
End

(Continued Next Two Pages)

```
00010 REM ***                    ABSENCE PERCENTAGES                    ***
00020 REM
00030 REM *** THIS PROGRAM GENERATES ABSENTEE PERCENTAGES PER CLASS ***
00040 REM *** FOR ANY GiVEN DAY                                     ***
00050 REM *** MAJOR VARIABLES:                                      ***
00060 REM *** DT$             DATE FOR PERCENTAGE DETERMINATION     ***
00070 REM *** TTAL            NUMBER OF STUDENTS / CLASS            ***
00080 REM *** ASENT           NUMBER OF STUDENTS ABSENT / CLASS     ***
00090 REM *** PER             PERCENTAGE OF ABSENT / CLASS          ***
00100 REM
00110 REM *** INPUT DATE, TOTALS, AND ABSENTS ***
00120 INPUT "ENTER TODAY'S DATE IN THIS FORM MM/DD/YY ";DT$
00130 INPUT "ENTER 9TH GRADE TOTAL ENROLLMENT";NTTAL
00140 INPUT "                 NUMBER OF ABSENT";NASENT
00150 INPUT "ENTER 10TH GRADE TOTAL ENROLLMENT";TTTAL
00160 INPUT "                 NUMBER OF ABSENT";TASENT
00170 INPUT "ENTER 11TH GRADE TOTAL ENROLLMENT";ETTAL
00180 INPUT "                 NUMBER OF ABSENT";EASENT
00190 INPUT "ENTER 12TH GRADE TOTAL ENROLLMENT";WTTAL
00200 INPUT "                 NUMBER OF ABSENT";WASENT
00210 REM
00220 REM *** CALCULATE PERCENTAGES ***
00230 NPER = NASENT / NTTAL * 100
00240 TPER = NASENT / TTTAL * 100
00250 EPER = EASENT / ETTAL * 100
00260 WPER = WASENT / WTTAL * 100
00270 REM
00280 REM *** PRINT HEADINGS AND RESULTS **
00290 PRINT
00300 PRINT USING 440,DT$
00310 PRINT USING 450,
00320 PRINT
00330 PRINT USING 460,
00340 PRINT USING 470,
00350 PRINT USING 450,
00360 PRINT
00370 PRINT USING 480,9,NTTAL,NASENT,NPER
00380 PRINT USING 480,10,TTTAL,TASENT,TPER
00390 PRINT USING 480,11,ETTAL,EASENT,EPER
00400 PRINT USING 480,12,WTTAL,WASENT,WPER
00410 PRINT USING 450,
00420 REM
00430 REM *** IMAGE STATEMENTS ***
00440 :               DAILY ABSENCE REPORT FOR 'LLLLLLLLL
00450 :_____
00460 :           TOTAL NUMBER         NUMBER          PERCENTAGE
00470 : GRADE     OF STUDENTS          ABSENT          ABSENT
00480 :   ##          ###               ###             ##.##
00999 END
```

100 in order to get a percentage as opposed to a decimal. The report in table format is obtained via print usings. The headings are printed in lines 290 through 360. Lines 370 through 400 print the information per class and line 410 prints the table footer. Lines 440 through 480 are the image statements to accompany the PRINT USING statements. They are nonexecutable; therefore the program goes to line 999, which stops execution.

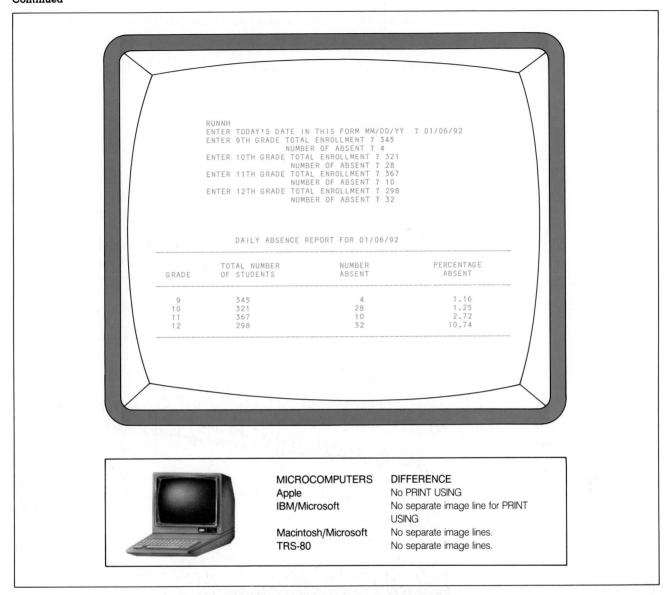

```
RUNNH
ENTER TODAY'S DATE IN THIS FORM MM/DD/YY   ? 01/06/92
ENTER 9TH GRADE TOTAL ENROLLMENT ? 345
              NUMBER OF ABSENT ? 4
ENTER 10TH GRADE TOTAL ENROLLMENT ? 321
              NUMBER OF ABSENT ? 28
ENTER 11TH GRADE TOTAL ENROLLMENT ? 367
              NUMBER OF ABSENT ? 10
ENTER 12TH GRADE TOTAL ENROLLMENT ? 298
              NUMBER OF ABSENT ? 32


              DAILY ABSENCE REPORT FOR 01/06/92
```

GRADE	TOTAL NUMBER OF STUDENTS	NUMBER ABSENT	PERCENTAGE ABSENT
9	345	4	1.16
10	321	28	1.25
11	367	10	2.72
12	298	32	10.74

MICROCOMPUTERS	DIFFERENCE
Apple	No PRINT USING
IBM/Microsoft	No separate image line for PRINT USING
Macintosh/Microsoft	No separate image lines.
TRS-80	No separate image lines.

● Summary Points

● The INPUT statement allows the user to enter data while the program is running. Therefore, the values used can change each time the program is run.

● When an INPUT statement is encountered during program execution, the program stops running until the user enters the needed data and presses the RETURN key. Each data value entered is then assigned to the corresponding variable in the INPUT statement.

- When data must be entered by the user, the program should display a prompt telling exactly what data are to be entered.
- Another way of entering data into a program is to use READ and DATA statements. The READ statement causes values contained in the DATA statements to be assigned to variables.
- READ and INPUT statements are located where the logic of the program indicates. DATA statements are nonexecutable and may be located anywhere in the program.
- The RESTORE statement causes the next READ statement to begin taking values from the top of the data list.
- Numeric values can be assigned to character variables, but character strings cannot be assigned to numeric variables.
- The INPUT statement is ideally suited for programs in which the data changes often, whereas the READ and DATA statements are particularly useful when it is necessary to read large quantities of data.
- When more than one item is to be printed on a line of output, the spacing can be indicated by the use of commas and semicolons.
- Each line of output can be divided into a predetermined number of print zones. The comma is used to cause results to be printed in the print zones.
- Using a semicolon instead of a comma to separate printed items causes output to be packed more closely on a line.
- Using the TAB function in a PRINT statement permits results to be printed anywhere on an output line.
- The PRINT USING feature provides a flexible method of producing output. The format control characteristics in the image statement define how the output will look.

● Review Questions

1. What are the advantages of the INPUT statement?

2. What is a prompt used for? What two things should a prompt tell the user?

3. Is the following a valid INPUT statement?

    10 INPUT "THE NAME OF YOUR DOG";N

4. Is the following a valid READ statement?

    20 READ N$ B6 A

5. After the following READ/DATA statements were executed, what would be the value of each variable?

    10 DATA 256,49
    20 DATA "TAMPA BAY"
    30 DATA "FLORIDA",40421
    40 READ A,B,C$
    50 READ S$,X

6. What happens when a PRINT statement ends with a comma?

7. What happens when a PRINT statement ends with a semicolon?

8. What will be the output of the following program segment?

    00230 X$ = "MOUNTAIN"
    00240 Y$ = "MOLEHILL"
    00250 PRINT X$;Y$

9. Using the TAB function, what would the PRINT statement look like that prints out NAME starting in column 1, CITY in column 20, and STATE in column 35?

10. How does the PRINT USING statement work?

● Debugging Exercises

Identify the following programs or program segments that contain errors and debug them.

1.
```
00010 INPUT "ENTER CITY AND STATE:";CITY$,ST
00020 INPUT "AND ZIP CODE:";ZIP$
00030 PRINT TAB(5);CITY$;TAB(25),ST;TAB(35);ZIP
```

2. How should these PRINT statements be corrected to match their output if X = 2, Y = 365, Z = 900, R = 52, A$ = YEARS, and B$ = WEEKS"?

Output

Z1	Z2	Z3	Z4	Z5
		TIM TUCKER		
2	365	900	52	
2	365	YEAR		

```
00060 PRINT "TIM";"TUCKER"
00070 PRINT X,Y,Z;R
00080 PRINT X,Y
00090 PRINT A$
```

● Programming Problems

1. Mrs. Mathey wants to know how much it would cost her to fertilize her garden, which measures 15 by 20 feet. The economy fertilizer costs $1.75 per pound, and one pound covers 20 square feet. She also wants to know how much it would cost if she used the deluxe fertilizer, which is $2.00 per pound, and one pound covers 20 square feet. The program should output the cost of using each and the cost difference between the two.

2. Write a program that asks for a person's name and weight in pounds and computes the weight in kilograms (1 pound = 0.453592 kilograms). The program should print the name of the person, his/her weight in pounds, and weight in kilograms, each in a different print zone.

3. Write a program that will provide the user with an arithmetic quiz. The program should ask the user to enter two numbers. Then it should print a message telling the user to press any key when ready to see the sum, difference, product, and quotient of the two numbers. The program should then print the four results mentioned. Your output should be as follows:

```
ENTER ANY TWO NUMBERS
(SEPARATE THE NUMBERS WITH A COMMA) XXX, XXX
PRESS ANY KEY WHEN READY TO SEE THE ANSWERS: X
XXX + XXX = XXXX
XXX − XXX = XXX
XXX*XXX = XXXXXX
XXXX/XXX = XX
```

4. Tod Stiles has friends across the country, and would like to have a computerized address book. Write a program to read the following sample data and print it with the headings NAME, STREET, CITY, and STATE, using the TAB function:

Irene Bulas, 124 Columbia Hts, Brooklyn, NY
Monica Murdock, 778 Riverview Dr., New Orleans, LA
Link Case, 86 Eldorado Dr., Dallas, TX
Karen Milhoan, 799 Royal St. George, Naperville, IL

5. Write a program using READ/DATA statements to tally the cost of grocery list items. The program should calculate the total of the prices, a 6 percent tax on this amount, and the final total. Make use of the PRINT USING statement to print the prices and totals. Use the following data: 12.79, 9.99, 4.57, 3.99. The output should look like this:

	12.79
	9.99
	4.57
	3.99
Subtotal	XX.XX
Tax	X.XX
	——————
Total	$XX.XX

● Section V
Control Statements

● Introduction

This section introduces the control statement, a powerful programming tool that will be used in all programs from this point on. **Control statements** allow the programmer to control the order in which program statements are executed. The GOTO, IF/THEN/ELSE, and ON/GOTO statements are the control statements introduced here. The section also introduces the technique of looping and two methods of controlling loop execution.

● The GOTO Statement: Unconditional Transfer

All of the programs we have written so far have been executed in a simple sequential manner. That is, the lowest-numbered line is executed first, then control passes to the next-lowest numbered line, and so on from the beginning to the end of the program. To solve many programming problems, however, it is necessary to alter the order in which statements are executed. Changing the normal path or flow of program execution is known as **branching,** and a statement that can make such a change is called a branch.

An example of a branch is the GOTO statement. Its general format looks like this:

line# GOTO transfer line#

The transfer line number tells the computer the line number of the next statement to be executed, and control transfers to that program line regardless of its location in the program.

When a GOTO statement is executed, there are three possible actions that may be taken:

● If the statement indicated by the transfer line number is executable, it is executed, and execution continues from that point.

● If the statement indicated by the transfer line number is not executable (such as a REM or DATA statement), control passes to the next line after it.

● If the transfer line number is not a line number of the program, an error message is displayed and execution is terminated.

The following is an example of a GOTO statement:

```
00100 GOTO 60
```

This statement causes program execution to branch or "go to" line 60, execute it if possible, and continue execution with the line following line 60.

Because control of the execution path *always* changes when the GOTO statement is encountered, such a statement is known as an **unconditional transfer.** Figures V–1 and V–2 show how execution paths are controlled with GOTO statements.

In Figure V–1, the GOTO statement in line 50 causes control to pass to line 70. Therefore, only the value of Y is printed; line 60 is skipped and left unexecuted.

In Figure V–2, control is transferred to line 50 by the GOTO statement. Line 50 contains a nonexecutable statement, so control passes to line 60. Notice that lines 30 and 40 are skipped and left unexecuted.

At this point a word of caution is in order. Although the GOTO statement gives the programmer increased control over the logical flow of a program, unconditional transfers can produce an execution path so complex and unreadable that the logic is virtually impossible to follow, and debugging becomes a nightmare. Later in this chapter and in other chapters, you will be introduced to control statements that are preferable to the GOTO statement. The GOTO should be used only when it is not feasible to use a different control statement.

● The IF/THEN Statement: Conditional Transfer

The GOTO statement always transfers control. Often, however, it is necessary to transfer control only when a specified condition exists. The IF/THEN statement is used to test for such a condition. If the condition does not exist, the next statement in the program is executed. Such a control transfer is called a **conditional transfer.** The general format of the IF/THEN statement is this:

line# IF condition THEN line#

A condition has the following general format:

expression   relational symbol   expression

● **FIGURE V–1**
GOTO Statement: Example 1

```
  ⌐  00030 X = 10
  ⌐→ 00040 Y = 20
  ⌐→ 00050 GOTO 70
  │   00060 PRINT X
  └→ 00070 PRINT Y
  └→ 00080 ------
```

● **FIGURE V–2**
GOTO Statement: Example 2

```
  ⌐  00010 X = 20
  ⌐  00020 GOTO 50
  ⌐  00030 -------
  │   00040 -------
  └→ 00050 REM *** THIS ISN'T EXECUTED ***
  └→ 00060 PRINT Y
```

For example, in the statement "110 if X < Y + 1 THEN 230," X < Y + 1 is the condition.

Conditions tested can involve either numeric or character string data. **Relational symbols** that can be used include the following:

Symbol	Meaning	Examples
<	Less than	A < B
< = or ≤	Less than or equal to	X < = Y
>	Greater than	J > 1
> = or ≥	Greater than or equal to	A > = B
=	Equal to	X = T
		N$ = "NONE"
<> or ><	Not equal to	R <> Q
		"APPLE" <> R$

The condition test of the IF/THEN statement is represented in a flowchart by a diamond-shaped decision symbol. The outcome of the test determines which flow line (path of program logic) will be followed. Figure V–3 shows the flowchart of an IF/THEN statement.

Some examples of valid IF/THEN statements follow:

Statement	Computer Execution
00010 IF X >= 6 THEN 30 00020 A = A + X 00030 PRINT X	If the value contained in X is greater than or equal to 6, the computer branches to line 30. If not, the computer executes the next sequential instruction, line 20.
00010 IF K <> N * 40 THEN 50 00020 K = N * 40	If K is not equal to N * 40, the computer transfers to statement 50. Otherwise, it executes the next statement, line 20.
00040 IF A$ = "NO" THEN 60 00050 X = X + 1 00060 PRINT X	If the value contained in A$ is NO, control is passed to line 60. If A$ contains anything else, control goes to line 50.

The program in Figure V–4 checks a student's record and prints the name of that student if he or she made the freshman honor roll. The first condition to be checked is whether the student is a freshman:

```
00120 IF CLASS$ <> "FR" THEN 999
```

If the student is not a freshman, the rest of the student record doesn't need to be checked, and the program ends by branching to line 999. Otherwise, execution continues to line 130, which is skipped because it is nonexecutable.

The second condition to be checked is whether the student's GPA is less than 3.5:

```
00150 IF GPA < 3.5 THEN 999
```

If the student's GPA is too low, control passes to line 999 as with the first condition. If the program execution reaches line 180, the student has survived both tests and his or her name is printed.

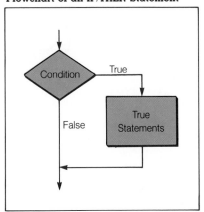

● **FIGURE V–3**
Flowchart of an IF/THEN Statement

```
00010 REM ***            FRESHMAN HONOR ROLL            ***
00020 REM
00030 REM *** PRINT STUDENT NAME IF A FRESHMAN WITH     ***
00040 REM *** A GPA OF 3.5 OR HIGHER.                   ***
00050 REM
00060 REM *** ENTER STUDENT DATA ***
00070 INPUT "ENTER NAME";NME$
00080 INPUT "ENTER CLASS (FR,SO,JR,SR)";CLASS$
00090 INPUT "ENTER GPA";GPA
00100 REM
00110 REM *** REJECT IF NOT FRESHMAN ***
00120 IF CLASS$ <> "FR" THEN 999
00130 REM
00140 REM *** REJECT IF GPA < 3.5 ***
00150 IF GPA < 3.5 THEN 999
00160 REM
00170 REM *** PRINT NAME ***
00180 PRINT
00190 PRINT NME$;" IS ON THE FRESHMAN HONOR ROLL."
00999 END
```

```
RUNNH
ENTER NAME ? LEVI TULLY
ENTER CLASS (FR,SO,JR,SR) ? FR
ENTER GPA ? 3.7

LEVI TULLY IS ON THE FRESHMAN HONOR ROLL.
```

Many BASIC implementations allow other, more general forms of the IF statement. One of these is the following:

line# IF condition THEN statement

The statement following THEN can be a BASIC statement or statements. Some examples follow:

```
00010 IF X < Y THEN A = A + 1 \ PRINT A
00050 IF M = N * P THEN PRINT M
```

IF/THEN/ELSE STATEMENTS

Another useful form of the IF statement is the IF/THEN/ELSE statement. The general format of the IF/THEN/ELSE statement is this:

line# IF condition THEN clause ELSE clause

The clause can be a BASIC statement or statements or a line number to branch to.

If the condition being tested is true, the clause following the THEN statement is executed. If the condition is false, the THEN clause is bypassed, and the clause following ELSE is executed.

The flowchart in Figure V–5 represents the logic of the IF/THEN/ELSE statement.

Some examples of valid IF/THEN/ELSE statements are given here:

```
00010 IF X = Y THEN PRINT "EQUAL" ELSE PRINT "NOT EQUAL"
00020 IF C = A * B THEN X = 1 ELSE X = 0
00030 IF M < R THEN 110 ELSE 150
```

Figure V–6 illustrates the use of an IF/THEN/ELSE statement.

● The ON/GOTO Statement: Conditional Transfer

The ON/GOTO, or computed GOTO, statement transfers control to other statements in the program based on the evaluation of a mathematical expression. The computed GOTO often operates as would multiple IF/THEN statements; any one of several transfers can occur, depending on the result computed for the expression. Since transfers depend on the expression, the computed GOTO is another conditional transfer statement. Its general format is this:

line# ON expression GOTO line#1,line#2,line#3,...,line#n

The arithmetic expression is always evaluated to an integer, and the line numbers following GOTO must identify statements in the program.

The general execution of the ON/GOTO statement proceeds as follows:

1. The expression is evaluated as an integer.
2. Depending on the value of the expression, control passes to the corresponding line number.

a. if the value of the expression is 1, control passes to the first line number listed.

● **FIGURE V–5**
Flowchart of an IF/THEN/ELSE Statement

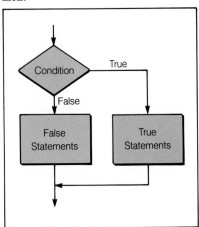

```
00010 REM ***    TEMPERATURE CONVERSION   ***
00020 REM
00030 INPUT "ENTER THE NUMBER OF DEGREES";T1TEMP
00040 PRINT "ENTER '1' FOR FAHRENHEIT TO CELSIUS"
00050 PRINT "      '2' FOR CELSIUS TO FAHRENHEIT"
00060 INPUT CODE
00070 REM
00080 REM *** CALCULATE TEMPERATURE ACCORDING TO CODE ***
00090 IF CODE = 1 THEN T2TEMP = (T1TEMP - 32) * (5 / 9) \ DEG$ = "CELSIUS"
                 ELSE T2TEMP = T1TEMP * (9 / 5) + 32 \ DEG$ = "FAHRENHEIT"
00100 REM
00110 PRINT "THE RESULT = ";T2TEMP;" DEGREES ";DEG$
00999 END
```

```
RUNNH
ENTER THE NUMBER OF DEGREES ? 50
ENTER '1' FOR FAHRENHEIT TO CELSIUS
       '2' FOR CELSIUS TO FAHRENHEIT
 ? 1
THE RESULT =  10  DEGREES CELSIUS
```

MICROCOMPUTERS	DIFFERENCE
Apple	No IF/THEN/ELSE statements
IBM/Microsoft	Multiple statements separated by "\"
Macintosh/Microsoft	None
TRS-80	None

b. If the value of the expression is 2, control passes to the second line number listed.

c. If the value of the expression is n, control passes to the nth line number listed.

Several examples are presented here to illustrate the operation of this statement:

Statement	Computer Execution
00010 ON X GOTO 50,80,100	IF X = 1, control goes to line 50. IF X = 2, control goes to line 80. IF X = 3, control goes to line 100.
00030 ON N / 50 GOTO 90,100	IF N/50 = 1, control goes to line 90. IF N/50 = 2, control goes to line 100.

If the computed expression in an ON/GOTO statement does not evaluate to an integer, the value is either rounded or truncated (digits to the right of the decimal are ignored), depending on the BASIC implementation. For example,

Statement	Value of Variable	Action
00040 ON N / 3 GOTO 60,80	N = 7	$7 \div 3 = 2.33$. The expression is evaluated as 2.33. The remainder is truncated, and the result becomes the integer 2. Control passes to statement 80.

Three additional rules apply to the ON/GOTO statement:

● If the value of the expression is zero, the DECsystem displays an error message. The other systems described in this book ignore the rest of the ON/GOTO statement, and control passes to the next statement.
● If the value of the expression is greater than the number of transfer lines listed (but still within the system's permitted range), the DECsystem displays an error message and execution stops. Other systems merely bypass the ON/GOTO.
● If the value of the expression is negative, or if it exceeds the system's permitted maximum, an error message is displayed and execution stops.

The following table illustrates what happens if the value of the expression is greater than the number of transfer lines listed.

Statement	Value of Variable	Execution
00030 ON COUNT GOTO 70,85,100 00040 COUNT = COUNT - 1	COUNT = 5	**DECsystem:** Execution stops. Error message displayed. **Microcomputers:** Control passes to line 40.

Table V–1 illustrates how various BASIC implementations respond to these conditions.

● Menus

A **menu** is a listing that displays the functions that can be performed by a program. The desired function is chosen by entering a code (typically a simple numeric or alphabetic character) from the terminal keyboard. A computer menu is like a menu in a restaurant. The user (diner) reads a group of possible selections on the screen (menu) and then enters a selection into the computer (describes the desired meal to the waiter or waitress).

TABLE V–1
ON/GOTO Actions

COMPUTER	EXPRESSION IS	ACTION IF EXPRESSION IS ZERO	ACTION IF EXPRESSION IS NEGATIVE OR GREATER THAN MAXIMUM ALLOWED	ACTION IF EXPRESSION IS GREATER THAN NUMBER OF LINES
DECsystem	truncated	"ON STMT OUT OF RANGE" error	"ON STMT OUT OF RANGE" error	Error message
Apple	truncated	ON/GOTO bypassed	"ILLEGAL QUANTITY" error	ON/GOTO bypassed
IBM/Microsoft	rounded	ON/GOTO bypassed	"ILLEGAL FUNCTION CALL" error	ON/GOTO bypassed
Macintosh/Microsoft	rounded	ON/GOTO bypassed	"ILLEGAL FUNCTION CALL" error	ON/GOTO bypassed
			"?FC" error	ON/GOTO bypassed
TRS-80	rounded	ON/GOTO bypassed	"ILLEGAL FUNCTION CALL" error	ON/GOTO bypassed

The calculator menu program (Figure V–7) illustrates a common use of the ON/GOTO statement in making a menu selection. The user tells the computer whether to add, subtract, multiply, or divide two numbers by entering either 1, 2, 3, or 4. Line 160 transfers the program execution to the appropriate operation.

In the example, after entering the value for A and B, the user indicates that multiplication is the desired operation by typing in the number 3 which is assigned to the variable code. Line 160, an ON/GOTO statement, causes program execution to branch to the third line number, 270. The operation is then performed, and the result is printed.

● Looping Procedures

Often a situation arises in which a single task must be performed several times. For example, a teacher may need a program to find the average test score of all the students in a given class. The job of processing a single student's data is simple enough:

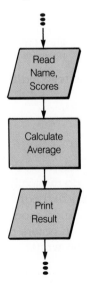

● **FIGURE V-7**
ON/GOTO Example Using a Menu

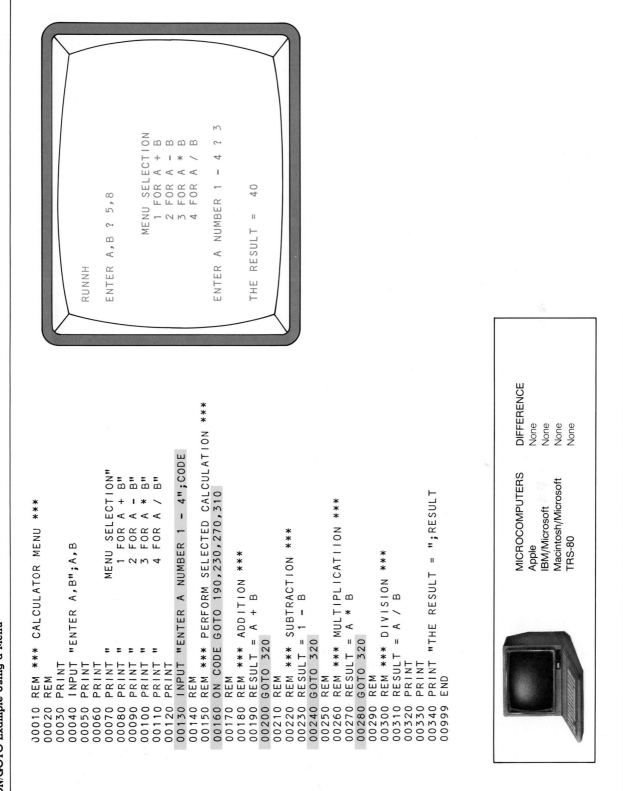

```
00010 REM *** CALCULATOR MENU ***
00020 REM
00030 PRINT
00040 INPUT "ENTER A,B";A,B
00050 PRINT
00060 PRINT
00070 PRINT "       MENU SELECTION"
00080 PRINT "        1 FOR A + B"
00090 PRINT "        2 FOR A - B"
00100 PRINT "        3 FOR A * B"
00110 PRINT "        4 FOR A / B"
00120 PRINT
00130 INPUT "ENTER A NUMBER 1 - 4";CODE
00140 REM
00150 REM *** PERFORM SELECTED CALCULATION ***
00160 ON CODE GOTO 190,230,270,310
00170 REM
00180 REM *** ADDITION ***
00190 RESULT = A + B
00200 GOTO 320
00210 REM
00220 REM *** SUBTRACTION ***
00230 RESULT = 1 - B
00240 GOTO 320
00250 REM
00260 REM *** MULTIPLICATION ***
00270 RESULT = A * B
00280 GOTO 320
00290 REM
00300 REM *** DIVISION ***
00310 RESULT = A / B
00320 PRINT
00330 PRINT
00340 PRINT "THE RESULT = ";RESULT
00999 END
```

Screen:
```
RUNNH
ENTER A,B ? 5,8

      MENU SELECTION
       1 FOR A + B
       2 FOR A - B
       3 FOR A * B
       4 FOR A / B

ENTER A NUMBER 1 - 4 ? 3

THE RESULT = 40
```

MICROCOMPUTERS	DIFFERENCE
Apple	None
IBM/Microsoft	None
Macintosh/Microsoft	None
TRS-80	None

However, consider the problem of repeating these steps for a class of thirty students:

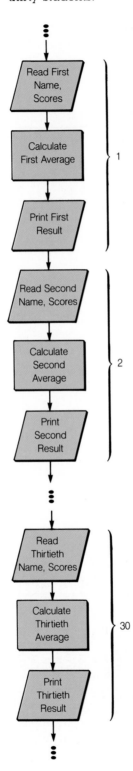

● COMPUTERS AND INFORMATION PROCESSING

The same three statements to process a single student's data would have to be written thirty times. Although such a solution would be possible, it clearly would be a tedious and taxing job for the programmer. The problem could be greatly simplified by writing the statements to process the data of just one student, then executing those statements as many times as needed. This procedure, called looping, is flowcharted below:

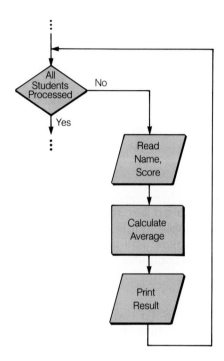

A sequence of steps executed repeatedly in this way constitutes a **loop.** One of the most important uses of control statements is the creation of loops. Control statements can determine which actions are to be repeated and the number of repetitions to be made. Some techniques for loop control include the use of trailer values, counters, and such looping statements as the FOR and NEXT statements. This section presents trailer values and counters; the FOR and NEXT statements are discussed in Section 6.

TRAILER VALUE

A loop controlled by a **trailer value** contains an IF/THEN statement that checks for the end of the data. The last data item is a dummy value that is not part of the data to be processed. Either numeric or alphanumeric data can be used as a trailer value. However, the programmer must always select a trailer value that will not be confused with real data. For example, a customer account number is never 0, which implies that zero may be safely used as a dummy value.

Here is how it works. An IF/THEN statement is placed within the set of instructions to be repeated, usually at the beginning of the loop. One of the variables to which data is entered is tested. If it contains the dummy value, control is transferred out of the loop. If the variable contains valid data (does not equal the trailer value), looping continues.

Figure V–8 contains a loop pattern controlled by a trailer value. The program calculates the commission on sales made by several employees of the Rich Rugs Company. Statement 170 tests the value NME$ for the dummy value:

```
00170 IF NME$ = "LAST" THEN 999
```

If the condition is true, the flow of processing drops out of the loop to line 999. If the condition is false, processing continues to the next line in sequence, line 180. Note that since we used the INPUT statement to enter the data, it is necessary to tell the user how to end the looping process. This is done in lines 140 and 260. The user has to enter two dummy values, LAST and 0, because the INPUT statement expects two values to be entered.

COUNTER

A second method of controlling a loop requires the programmer to create a **counter**—a numeric variable that is incremented each time the loop is executed. Normally, the increment is 1. A counter is effective only if the programmer notifies the computer how many times a loop should be repeated. The following steps are involved in setting up a counter for loop control:

1. Initialize the counter to give it a beginning value.
2. Increment the counter each time the loop is executed.
3. Test the counter to determine if the loop has been executed the desired number of times.

The sales commission program used in Figure V–8 can be modified to use a counter, as shown in Figure V–9. Since there are three salespeople, the loop must be executed three times. The counter in this example is CNTR. It is initialized to 0 in line 150. The IF/THEN statement in line 210 tests the number of times the loop has been executed, as represented by the counter CNTR. Line 280 causes CNTR to be incremented each time the loop is executed. The loop instructions will be executed until CNTR equals 3.

● A Programming Problem

PROBLEM DEFINITION

Ed Hoge, an instructor for Art 101, needs a program that will assign letter grades to students based on their test scores. In addition, he wants to know how many students are in each grade category and how many took the test.

```
00010 REM ***                    RICH RUGS CO.                  ***
00020 REM
00030 REM *** THIS PROGRAM CALCULATES THE COMMISSION FOR EACH  ***
00040 REM *** SALESPERSON ENTERED.                             ***
00050 REM *** MAJOR VARIABLES:                                 ***
00060 REM ***    NME$ - LAST NAME                              ***
00070 REM ***    RTE - RATE OF COMMISSION                      ***
00080 REM ***    SALES - VALUE OF SALES                        ***
00090 REM ***    COMMSN - COMMISSION                           ***
00100 REM
00110 RTE = .15
00120 REM *** ENTER FIRST SALESPERON'S DATA ***
00130 PRINT "ENTER NAME, SALES"
00140 INPUT "TYPE 'LAST,0' TO END";NME$,SALES
00150 REM
00160 REM *** TEST FOR TRAILER VALUE ***
00170 IF NME$ = "LAST" THEN 999
00180 COMMSN = SALES * RTE
00190 PRINT
00200 PRINT "NAME","SALES","COMMISSION"
00210 PRINT NME$,SALES,COMMSN
00220 PRINT
00230 REM
00240 REM *** ENTER NEXT SALESPERSON'S DATA ***
00250 PRINT "ENTER NAME, SALES"
00260 INPUT "TYPE 'LAST,0' TO END";NME$,SALES
00270 GOTO 170
00999 END
```

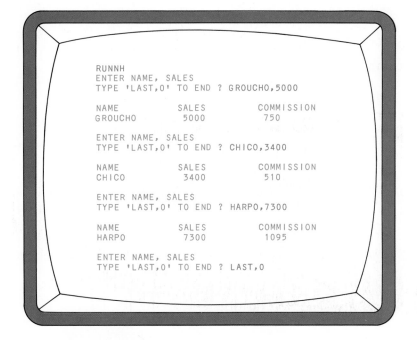

```
RUNNH
ENTER NAME, SALES
TYPE 'LAST,0' TO END ? GROUCHO,5000

NAME          SALES          COMMISSION
GROUCHO       5000           750

ENTER NAME, SALES
TYPE 'LAST,0' TO END ? CHICO,3400

NAME          SALES          COMMISSION
CHICO         3400           510

ENTER NAME, SALES
TYPE 'LAST,0' TO END ? HARPO,7300

NAME          SALES          COMMISSION
HARPO         7300           1095

ENTER NAME, SALES
TYPE 'LAST,0' TO END ? LAST,0
```

MICROCOMPUTERS	DIFFERENCE
Apple	None
IBM/Microsoft	None
Macintosh/Microsoft	None
TRS-80	None

```
00010 REM ***                    RICH RUGS CO.               ***
00020 REM
00030 REM ***   THIS PROGRAM CALCULATES THE COMMISSION FOR   ***
00040 REM ***   EACH SALESPERSON ENTERED.                    ***
00050 REM ***   MAJOR VARIABLES:                             ***
00060 REM ***      NME$ - LAST NAME                          ***
00070 REM ***      RTE - RATE OF COMMISSION                  ***
00080 REM ***      SALES - VALUE OF SALES                    ***
00090 REM ***      COMMSN - COMMISSION                       ***
00100 REM ***      CNTR - LOOP COUNTER                       ***
00110 REM
00120 RTE = .15
00130 REM
00140 REM *** INITIALIZE COUNTER ***
00150 CNTR = 0
00160 REM
00170 REM *** PRINT HEADINGS ***
00180 PRINT "NAME","SALES","COMMISSION"
00190 REM
00200 REM *** TEST COUNTER VALUES ***
00210 IF CNTR = 3 THEN 999
00220 READ NME$,SALES
00230 COMMSN = SALES * RTE
00240 PRINT
00250 PRINT NME$, SALES, COMMSN
00260 REM
00270 REM *** UPDATE COUNTER VALUE ***
00280 CNTR = CNTR + 1
00290 GOTO 210
00300 REM
00310 REM *** DATA STATEMENTS ***
00320 DATA "GROUCHO",5000,"CHICO",3400,"HARPO",7300
00999 END
```

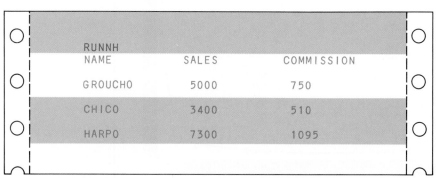

```
RUNNH
NAME          SALES          COMMISSION

GROUCHO       5000           750

CHICO         3400           510

HARPO         7300           1095
```

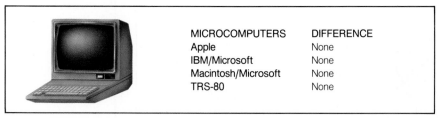

MICROCOMPUTERS	DIFFERENCE
Apple	None
IBM/Microsoft	None
Macintosh/Microsoft	None
TRS-80	None

The grading scale is as follows:

Score	Letter Grade
90 or more	A
78 to 89	B
66 to 77	C
54 to 65	D
Less than 54	F

Ed wants the program to print the name, score, and letter grade for each student entered, followed by the total number of grades in each category, and finally the total number of students. The students and their scores follow:

Student	Score
Nan Barnett	96
Bob Szymanski	93
Jim Strong	89
Bob Tynecki	78
Lynn Probst	90
Bill Brandon	51
Denise Siviy	88
Vic Flynn	66
Karen McKee	98
Anne Tate	77

SOLUTION DESIGN

The general problem of producing a grade report can be divided into two subproblems—the repeated task of processing each student, and the task of printing the summary information, which is performed only once.

1. Process each student's data.
2. Report the summary information.

A repeated task suggests a loop. Step A can be further divided into several smaller tasks that must be performed for each student:

1. a. Enter the student's data.
1. b. Determine the grade.
1. c. Update the appropriate counters.
1. d. Print the student's information.

Step B can also be divided into smaller problems:

2. a. Print a heading.
2. b. Print the grade counts.
2. c. Print the total student count.

The structure chart in Figure V–10 diagrams this outline of the problem. Since the number of students is not known, the tasks of Step 1 can be placed in a loop controlled by a trailer value. When each student has been processed, the report of the summary information can be printed. The flowchart in Figure V–11 shows the order of steps necessary to solve the problem.

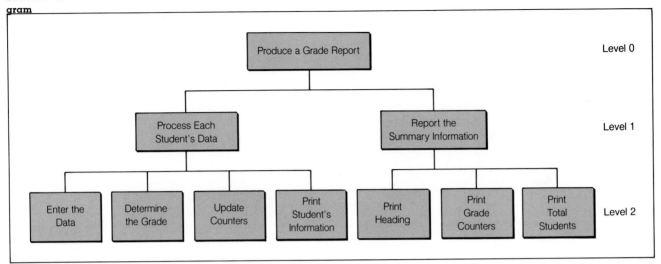

THE PROGRAM

The counter variables are initialized to 0 by the assignment statements in lines 180 through 230 of Figure V–11. The name and score for the first student are entered in line 270. Line 300 tests for the trailer value XXX. As long as the student's name does not equal XXX, the loop is reexecuted. The total number of students is accumulated in line 330. The first test to determine the grade is made in line 340. If the score is less than 90, it is not an A. Control is transferred to line 400, where the score is tested again to see if it is less than 78 (less than that required for a B.) In this fashion, scores less than the lowest number required for a particular grade are passed down to the next lowest level until the correct one is found. Line 600 requires no test; any grade less than 54 is an F. When the trailer value, XXX, is detected, control drops down to line 770, where printing of the totals occurs.

● Summary Points

● The GOTO statement is an unconditional transfer of control that allows the computer to bypass or alter the sequence in which instructions are executed.

● The IF/THEN statement permits control to be transferred only when a specified condition is met. If the condition following IF is true, the clause following the word THEN is given control; if it is false, control passes to the next line.

● The IF/THEN/ELSE statement is an extension of the IF/THEN statement. If the condition following IF is true, the clause following THEN is given control. If the condition is false, control is transferred to the clause following ELSE. IF/THEN/ELSE statements may be nested.

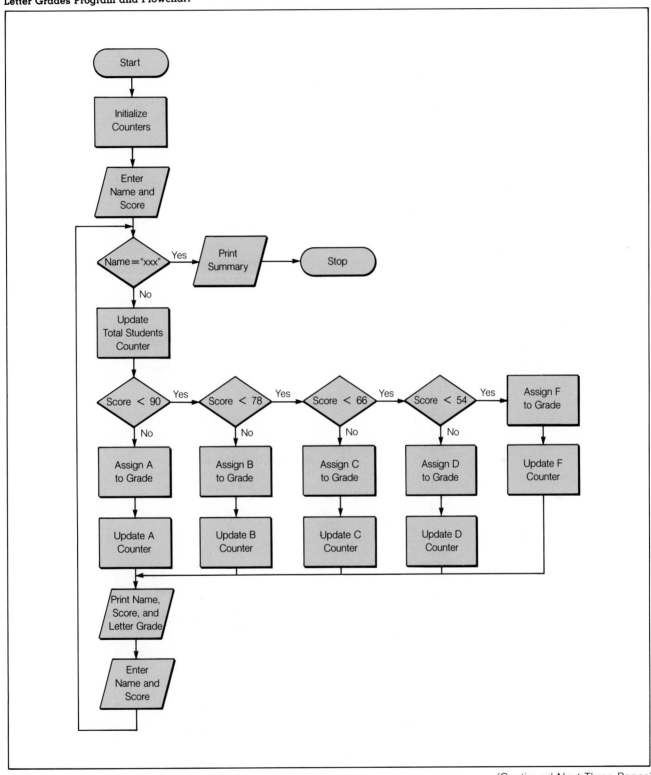

(Continued Next Three Pages)

Pseudocode

Begin

Initialize letter grade counters
Input first student's name and score
Begin loop, do until end of items
    Increment total student counter by 1
    If score is greater than or equal to 90
        Then
            Assign letter grade of "A"
            Increment "A" counter by 1
        Else
            If score is greater than or equal to 78
                Then
                    Assign letter grade of "B"
                    Increment "B" counter by 1
            End if
        Else
            If score is greater than or equal to 66
                Then
                    Assign letter grade of "C"
                    Increment "C" counter by 1
            End if
        Else
            If score is greater than or equal to 54
                Then
                    Assign letter grade of "D"
                    Increment "D" counter by 1
            End if
        Else
            Assign letter grade of "F"
            Increment "F" counter by 1
    End if
    Print student report headings
    Print student's name, score and letter grade
    Input next student's name and score
End loop
Print grade totals and total number of students
End

```
00010 REM ***                    ART 101 GRADES               ***
00020 REM
00030 REM *** THIS PROGRAM ASSIGNS LETTER GRADES BASED ON ***
00040 REM *** TEST SCORES, THEN TALLIES THE RESULTS. THE  ***
00050 REM *** SCALE USED IS AS FOLLOWS:                   ***
00060 REM ***         >= 90        = A                    ***
00070 REM ***         78 - 89      = B                    ***
00080 REM ***         66 - 77      = C                    ***
00090 REM ***         54 - 65      = D                    ***
00100 REM ***         < 54         = F                    ***
00110 REM *** MAJOR VARIABLES:                            ***
00120 REM ***    NME$ - STUDENT NAME                      ***
00130 REM ***    TESTSCR - STUDENT TEST SCORE             ***
00140 REM ***    TTAL - TOTAL NUMBER OF STUDENTS          ***
00150 REM ***    LETTR$ - LETTER GRADE                    ***
00160 REM
```

```
00170 REM *** INITIALIZE LETTER GRADE COUNTERS ***
00180 A = 0
00190 B = 0
00200 C = 0
00210 D = 0
00220 F = 0
00230 TTAL = 0
00240 REM
00250 REM *** ENTER FIRST STUDENT'S DATA ***
00260 PRINT "ENTER NAME, SCORE"
00270 INPUT "TYPE 'XXX,0' TO END";NME$,TESTSCR
00280 REM
00290 REM *** TEST FOR TRAILER VALUE ***
00300 IF NME$ = "XXX" THEN 770
00310 REM
00320 REM *** UPDATE TOTAL STUDENTS COUNTER ***
00330 TTAL = TTAL + 1
00340 IF TESTSCR < 90 THEN 400
00350 REM
00360 REM *** GRADE = A ***
00370 LETTR$ = "A"
00380 A = A + 1
00390 GOTO 650
00400 IF TESTSCR < 78 THEN 460
00410 REM
00420 REM *** GRADE = B ***
00430 LETTR$ = "B"
00440 B = B + 1
00450 GOTO 650
00460 IF TESTSCR < 66 THEN 520
00470 REM
00480 REM *** GRADE = C ***
00490 LETTR$ = "C"
00500 C = C + 1
00510 GOTO 650
00520 IF TESTSCR < 54 THEN 600
00530 REM
00540 REM *** GRADE = D ***
00550 LETTR$ = "D"
00560 D = D + 1
00570 GOTO 650
00580 REM
00590 REM *** GRADE = F ***
00600 LETTR$ = "F"
00610 F = F + 1
00620 REM
00630 REM *** PRINT STUDENT REPORT ***
00640 PRINT
00650 PRINT "NAME";TAB(25);"SCORE";TAB(35);"GRADE"
00660 PRINT NME$;TAB(27);TESTSCR;TAB(37);LETTR$
00670 PRINT
00680 REM
00690 REM *** ENTER NEXT STUDENT'S DATA ***
00700 PRINT
00710 PRINT "ENTER NAME, SCORE"
00720 INPUT "TYPE 'XXX,0' TO END";NME$,TESTSCR
00730 PRINT
00740 GOTO 300
00750 REM
00760 REM *** PRINT TOTALS ***
00770 PRINT
00780 PRINT "TOTAL # OF A'S = ";A
00790 PRINT "TOTAL # OF B'S = ";B
00800 PRINT "TOTAL # OF C'S = ";C
00810 PRINT "TOTAL # OF D'S = ";D
00820 PRINT "TOTAL # OF F'S = ";F
00830 PRINT
00840 PRINT "TOTAL # OF STUDENTS = ";TTAL
00999 END
```

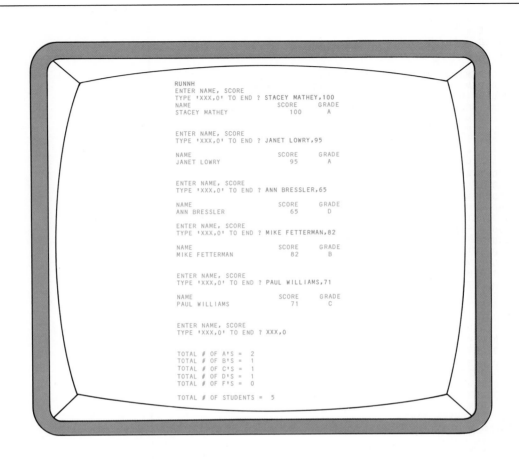

```
RUNNH
ENTER NAME, SCORE
TYPE 'XXX,0' TO END ? STACEY MATHEY,100
NAME                    SCORE     GRADE
STACEY MATHEY            100        A


ENTER NAME, SCORE
TYPE 'XXX,0' TO END ? JANET LOWRY,95

NAME                    SCORE     GRADE
JANET LOWRY              95         A


ENTER NAME, SCORE
TYPE 'XXX,0' TO END ? ANN BRESSLER,65

NAME                    SCORE     GRADE
ANN BRESSLER            65         D

ENTER NAME, SCORE
TYPE 'XXX,0' TO END ? MIKE FETTERMAN,82

NAME                    SCORE     GRADE
MIKE FETTERMAN          82         B


ENTER NAME, SCORE
TYPE 'XXX,0' TO END ? PAUL WILLIAMS,71

NAME                    SCORE     GRADE
PAUL WILLIAMS           71         C


ENTER NAME, SCORE
TYPE 'XXX,0' TO END ? XXX,0


TOTAL # OF A'S =  2
TOTAL # OF B'S =  1
TOTAL # OF C'S =  1
TOTAL # OF D'S =  1
TOTAL # OF F'S =  0

TOTAL # OF STUDENTS =  5
```

MICROCOMPUTERS	DIFFERENCE
Apple	None
IBM/Microsoft	None
Macintosh/Microsoft	None
TRS-80	None

- The ON/GOTO statement instructs the computer to evaluate an expression and, based on its value, to branch to one of several points in a program.
- A menu is a listing that displays the functions a program can perform. The user selects the desired function by entering a code from the keyboard.
- The number of times a loop is executed can be controlled by the use of a trailer value or a counter.
- The trailer value is a dummy value entered at the end of all the data.
- A counter can be set up if the programmer knows ahead of time how many times a loop is to be executed.

● Review Questions

1. Why is the GOTO statement an unconditional transfer?

2. Rewrite the following program, using a loop controlled by a trailer value:

```
00010 READ N$,X,Y
00020 Z = X + Y
00030 PRINT N$,Z
00040 READ N$,X,Y
00050 Z = X + Y
00060 PRINT N$,Z
00070 READ N$,X,Y
00080 Z = X + Y
00090 PRINT N$,Z
00100 DATA LARRY,10,5,MOE,25,7,CURLY,17,41
00999 END
```

3. Why is the IF/THEN statement a conditional transfer?

4. In an IF/THEN statement, the THEN clause may be _____.
   a. a line number
   b. a single BASIC statement
   c. multiple BASIC statements
   d. all of the above
   e. a and b only

5. Which of these are valid IF/THEN statements?
   a. 10 IF X <> "NO" THEN 30
   b. 60 IF Y = 2 THEN 100
   c. 100 IF A$ = "APPLE" THEN 150
   d. 200 IF X$ = "YES" THEN 250

6. The statement after ELSE in an IF/THEN/ELSE statement is executed when the condition is _____.
   a. true
   b. false

7. To what line number will control be transferred when this statement is encountered $(N = 51)$?

   100 ON N / 17 GOTO 150, 200, 275

8. What is a menu?

9. What is a trailer value?

10. Rewrite the program in Question 2 using a counter-controlled loop.

● Debugging Exercises

Indentify the following programs or program segments that contain errors, and debug them.

1.
```
00010 PRINT TAB(7);"WORLD CUP STANDINGS"
00020 PRINT TAB(5);"NAME";TAB(26);"POINTS"
00030 READ NME$,PTS
00040 IF NME$ = "DONE" THEN 99
00050 PRINT TAB(5);NME$;TAB(26);PTS
00060 READ NME$,PTS
00070 GOTO 40
00080 DATA BILL JOHNSON,192,PHIL MAHRE,131
00090 DATA INGMAR STENMARK,47,DONE
00999 END
```

2.
```
00010 REM *** CALCULATE SUM OF 20 NUMBERS ***
00020 Y = 1
00030 IF Y > 20 THEN 80
00040 INPUT "ENTER NUMBER";NMBR
00050 SUM = SUM + NMBR
00060 GOTO 20
00070 PRINT "SUM = ";SUM
00099 END
```

● Programming Problems

1. The Admissions Board of Blighter College conducts three interviews of every prospective student. These interviews are rated and averaged. Based on this average, a report is to be printed recommending the action to be taken by the Board. Each of the three interviews carry a maximum score of fifty points. Your job is to compute the average score for each prospective student and write a report giving the recommended action to be taken. The report also should list the total number of candidates evaluated and the total number of candidates in each category. The test data is as follows:

Name	Interview		
	1	2	3
Buz Murdock	50	45	49
Sam Hunt	35	21	42
Marie Walker	43	32	35
Stacy O'Donnell	19	35	20
Susie McKinniss	41	47	39

2. The Marvel-Vac Company is processing the monthly checks for its door-to-door sales agents. Each agent receives a 35 percent commission on his or her monthly sales. An agent whose sales exceed $1000 receives a $50 bonus, and an agent whose sales are less than $250 must pay a $25 processing charge, which is subtracted from that month's check. Each vacuum sells for $250. Write a program that will calculate each agent's total sales, straight commission, bonus or deduction if necessary, and check total. A report should print each agent's name, straight commission, bonus or deduction adjustment, and total amount to be paid. Use the following data:

Agent	Number of Vacuums Sold
Drake, J.	6
Tully, M.	3
Hendricks, R.	5
Corelli, I.	1
Cross, J.	0

3. Write a program that calculates the value of inventory on hand of each item in stock, and displays the stock number and value on hand. Use a loop controlled by a trailer value, and use the following data:

Stock Number	Price	In Stock
X3308	$13.75	31
X5500	9.50	25
X9611	20.95	14

4. Write a program that will print current weather forecasts. A menu should be used to display the choices. Use the ON/GOTO statement and the following sample data:

Date	Forecast
9/01	Cloudy; 60% chance of afternoon showers; high 70–75°
9/02	Sunny and breezy; high 80–85°
9/03	Partly cloudy; 40% chance of rain; high 65–70°

5. A styling salon manager gives each employee a year-end bonus based on the average value of retail products he or she has sold in the last three months of the year. You are to write a program to find the average of the three values and determine a bonus for each employee. Your output should include the name and bonus of each employee. Use the following data:

Susan Jones	$88	$90	$85
Stacy Matthey	65	73	81
Wendy White	50	46	65
Les Southwyk	44	75	90
Bob Green	35	43	49
Stephanie Miller	68	60	55

Use a loop controlled with a counter. The bonus scale is set up like this:

$90 or more	$50
$80 to 90	$40
$70 to 80	$30
$60 to 70	$20
$59 or less	$10

● Section VI
More About Looping

● Introduction

Section V discussed two methods of controlling loops—counters and trailer values. This section presents another method for loop control—FOR and NEXT statements. In addition, it discusses nested loops (loops within loops).

Let us review what happens when a counter is used to control a loop since the logic of FOR/NEXT loops is very similar. First, the counter variable is set to some initial value. The counter value is compared to the terminal value, and if it does not exceed the terminal value the statements inside the loop are executed once and the counter is incremented. The counter variable then is tested again to see if the loop has been executed the required number of times. When the variable exceeds the designated terminal value, the looping process ends, and the computer proceeds to the rest of the program. For example, assume we want to write a program that will multiply each of the numbers from 1 to 5 by 5 and then add 2. The program in Figure VI–1 does this using a loop controlled by the counter method. We will see later how the FOR/NEXT loop allows us to accomplish the same steps in a more efficient manner.

● The FOR and NEXT Statements

The FOR and NEXT statements allow concise loop definition. The general format of the FOR and NEXT loop is as follows:

line# FOR loop control variable = initial expression TO terminal expression STEP step value

.

.

.

line# NEXT loop control variable

The FOR statement tells the computer how many times to execute the loop. The **loop control variable** is a variable the value of which is used to control loop repetition. When the FOR statement is executed, the loop control variable (also called the **index**) is set to an initial value. This value is tested against the terminal value to determine whether or not the loop

● COMPUTERS AND INFORMATION PROCESSING

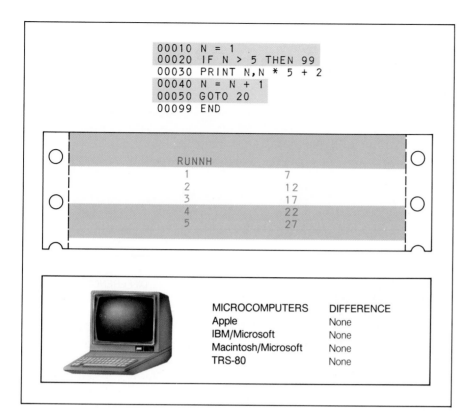

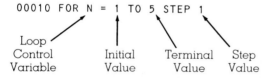

should be executed. The initial and terminal values may be constants, variables, or expressions, all of which must be numeric.

To set the initial value and test the counter took two lines (lines 10 and 20) in Figure VI–1. The FOR statement combines these two steps into one statement:

```
00010 FOR N = 1 TO 5 STEP 1
```

Loop
Control   Initial   Terminal   Step
Variable   Value   Value   Value

Lines 40 and 50 in Figure VI–1 increment the loop control variable (the counter) and send control back to line 20. The functions of these two statements are combined in the NEXT statement. In Figure VI–1, after control is transferred back to line 20, the value of the loop control variable is again tested against the terminal value. Once the value is exceeded, control passes to line 99. When FOR and NEXT are used, control goes to the statement immediately following the NEXT statement.

Thus, the loop used in Figure VI–1 can be set up to use FOR and NEXT statements, as shown in Figure VI–2. The FOR statement in line 10 tells the computer to initialize the loop variable, N, to one. Between the FOR and NEXT statements is line 20, the instruction that is to be repeated; it prints N and the result of N * 5 + 2. Line 30, the NEXT statement, increments the loop control variable by the step indicated in the FOR state-

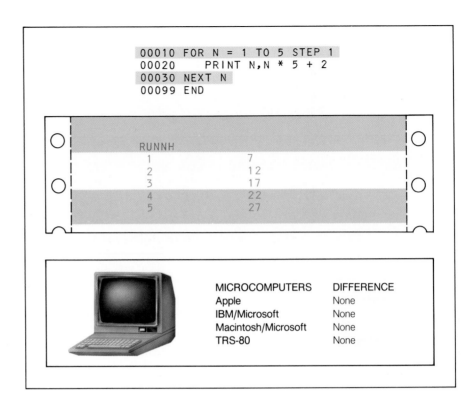

```
00010 FOR N = 1 TO 5 STEP 1
00020    PRINT N,N * 5 + 2
00030 NEXT N
00099 END
```

```
RUNNH
  1            7
  2          1 2
  3          1 7
  4          2 2
  5          2 7
```

MICROCOMPUTERS	DIFFERENCE
Apple	None
IBM/Microsoft	None
Macintosh/Microsoft	None
TRS-80	None

ment. The step value may be a constant, variable, or expression, and it must have a numeric value.

FLOWCHARTING FOR AND NEXT LOOPS

Figure VI–3a illustrates a common method of flowcharting the FOR/NEXT loop. We have developed our own shorthand symbol for FOR/NEXT loops, which is shown in Figure VI–3b. This is very convenient for representing a loop, since it shows the initial, terminal, and step values for the loop control variable in one symbol.

PROCESSING STEPS OF FOR AND NEXT LOOPS

Let us review the steps followed by the computer when it encounters a FOR statement:

1. The initial, terminal, and (if given) step value expressions are evaluated.
2. The loop control variable is assigned the initial value.
3. The value of the loop control variable is tested against the terminal value.
4. If the loop control variable is less than or equal to the terminal value, then the loop body is executed.
5. If the loop control variable is greater than the terminal value, then the loop body is skipped and control passes to the first statement following the NEXT statement. This means that the loop will not be executed at all.

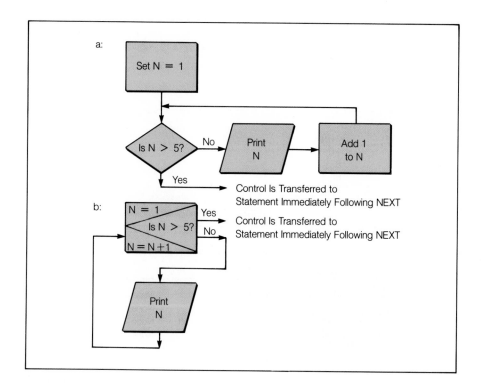

(The Apple is an exception here—it always executes a FOR/NEXT loop at least once.)

Here is what happens when the NEXT statement is found:

1. The step value indicated in the FOR statement is added to the loop control variable. If the step value is omitted, a + 1 is added.
2. A check is performed to determine if the value of the loop control variable exceeds the terminal value.
3. If the loop control variable is less than or equal to the terminal value, then control is transferred back to the statement after the FOR statement and the loop is repeated. Otherwise, the loop is exited and execution continues with the statement following the NEXT statement.

RULES FOR USING FOR AND NEXT STATEMENTS

Some rules to be aware of when you use FOR and NEXT statements follow:

1. The initial value must be less than or equal to the terminal value when using a positive step. Otherwise, the loop will never be executed. For example, a loop containing either of the following statements would not be executed at all:

```
00030 FOR X = 1 TO -10 STEP 2
00020 FOR X = 100 TO 50 STEP 5
```

2. There are times when it is desirable to use a negative step value, for example, to count backward from 10 by 2s (see Figure VI–4). The loop

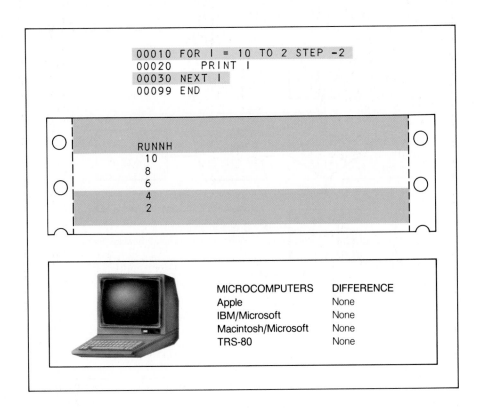

```
00010 FOR I = 10 TO 2 STEP -2
00020     PRINT I
00030 NEXT I
00099 END
```

```
RUNNH
  10
   8
   6
   4
   2
```

MICROCOMPUTERS	DIFFERENCE
Apple	None
IBM/Microsoft	None
Macintosh/Microsoft	None
TRS-80	None

is terminated when the value of the loop control variable, I, is less than the specified terminal value, 2. The initial value of the loop variable should be greater than the terminal value when using a negative step; for example,

```
00050 FOR J = 10 TO 1 STEP -2
00100 FOR K -1 TO -10 STEP -2
```

3. The step size in a FOR statement should never be 0. This value would cause the computer to loop endlessly. Such an error condition is known as an **infinite loop:**

```
00070 FOR X = 20 TO 30 STEP 0
```

4. Transfer can be made from one statement to another within a loop. For example, the program in Figure VI–5 reads in four names and the number of hours they worked. It will print out only those people who worked more than 40 hours. Note, however, that a transfer from a statement within the loop to the FOR statement of the loop is poor programming practice. Such a transfer would cause the loop variable to be reset rather than simply continuing the loop process. In the following segment, line 20 is not a proper branch:

```
00010 FOR I = 900 TO 1000
00020    IF I = 950 THEN 10
00030    PRINT I - 50
00040 NEXT I
```

If you want to continue the looping process but want to bypass some inner instruction, branch (transfer control) to the NEXT statement, as was done in Figure VI–5 (line 110).

5. It is possible to modify the loop control variable in the loop body, but this should *never* be done. Note how unpredictable the execution of the following program loop would be. The value of I is dependent on the integer entered by the user.

```
00030 FOR I = 1 TO 10
00040    INPUT "ENTER AN INTEGER";X
00050    I = X
00060 NEXT I
```

6. The initial, terminal, and step expressions can be composed of any valid numeric variable, constant, or expression. The following examples are valid where $X = 2$, $Y = 10$, and $Z = -2$:

```
00010 FOR I = X TO (Y + 20) STEP 1
00020    PRINT I + X
00030 NEXT I
```

```
00010 FOR J = Y TO X STEP Z
00020    S = S + J * 3
00030 NEXT J
```

```
00010 FOR K = (X + 1) TO (Y * 2) STEP -Z
00020    PRINT K
00030 NEXT K
```

● **FIGURE VI–5**
Transferring Control Within a FOR/NEXT Loop

```
00010 REM ***                    WORKER LIST                    ***
00020 REM ***                                                   ***
00030 REM *** THIS PROGRAM PRINTS A LIST OF FULL-TIME WORKERS.  ***
00040 REM ***    MAJOR VARIABLES:                               ***
00050 REM ***      NME$ - NAME OF WORKER                        ***
00060 REM ***      HRS - NUMBER OF HOURS WORKED IN ONE WEEK     ***
00070 REM
00080 REM *** LOOP TO CHECK FOUR WORKERS ***
00090 FOR I = 1 TO 4
00100     READ NME$,HRS
00110     IF HRS < 40 THEN 130
00120     PRINT NME$
00130 NEXT I
00140 DATA "SHELLI BECHSTEIN",42,"TONYA KNAUSS",43
00150 DATA "CHARLIE KOLDING",32,"FRANK FURTER",45
00999 END
```

```
RUNNH
SHELLI BECHSTEIN
TONYA KNAUSS
FRANK FURTER
```

MICROCOMPUTERS	DIFFERENCE
Apple	None
IBM/Microsoft	None
Macintosh/Microsoft	None
TRS-80	None

7. Each FOR statement must be accompanied by an associated NEXT statement. In addition, the loop control variable in the FOR statement must be specified in the NEXT statement.

There are some exceptions to Rule 7. Some systems allow nested loops to share a NEXT statement (check your systems manual); for example,

```
00050 NEXT I,J
```

In this case, I is the inner loop control variable, and J is the outer loop control variable and is equivalent to

```
00050 NEXT I
00060 NEXT J
```

Also, on some systems it is not necessary to follow the NEXT statement with a loop control variable. This would be a valid NEXT statement:

```
00050 NEXT
```

When a NEXT statement without a loop control variable is used, it returns control to the closest FOR statement (previous to the NEXT statement) that has not already been paired with a NEXT. The following is an example:

```
00010 FOR I = 1 TO 10
00020    FOR J = 1 TO 5
00030       PRINT I,J
00040    NEXT
00050 NEXT
```

When the computer comes to the NEXT statement on line 50, it pairs it with line 10, FOR I = 1 TO 10, because it is the closest FOR statement without a NEXT statement. Line 20, FOR J = 1 TO 5, has already been paired with the first NEXT statement on line 40.

Figure VI–6 demonstrates the application of a FOR/NEXT loop. The purpose of this program is to find the total number of passengers who ride a roller coaster in a half-hour. There are eight runs each half-hour. The FOR/NEXT loop is set to be executed eight times—once for each run of the roller coaster. Each time through the loop, the user enters the number of passengers on the roller coaster, PASSENGERS, and the computer adds that number to the total, TTAL.

● Nested FOR and NEXT Statements

Section V showed how IF/THEN and IF/THEN/ELSE statements can be nested, so that one statement makes up part of another statement. Similar nesting can be done with loops. A pair of nested FOR/NEXT loops looks like this:

```
FOR I = 1 TO 4
   FOR J = 1 TO 2
      .
      .
      .
   NEXT J
NEXT I
```

Nested loops such as this should be indented as shown to make the structure more readable. In this case, each time the outer loop (loop I) is executed once, the inner loop (loop J) is executed twice since J varies from 1 to 2. When the inner loop has terminated, control passes to the first statement after the NEXT J, which in this case is the statement NEXT I. This statement causes I to be incremented by 1 and tested against the terminal value of 4. If I is still less than or equal to 4, the body of loop I is executed again. The J loop is again encountered, the value of J is reset to 1, and the inner loop is executed until J is greater than 2. Altogether,

● **FIGURE VI–6**
Using the FOR/NEXT Loop to Calculate a Total

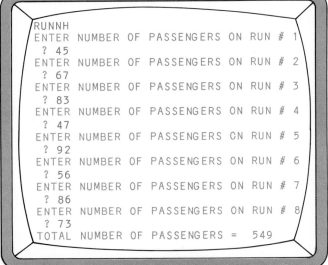

```
00010 REM ***                    ROLLER COASTER TALLY                ***
00020 REM
00030 REM *** THIS PROGRAM COMPUTES THE TOTAL NUMBER OF PASSENGERS ***
00040 REM *** FOR 8 RUNS OF A ROLLER COASTER.                       ***
00050 REM *** MAJOR VARIABLES:                                      ***
00060 REM ***    PASSENGERS - NUMBER OF PASSENGERS ON 1 RUN         ***
00070 REM ***    TTAL - TOTAL NUMBER OF PASSENGERS                  ***
00080 REM
00090 TTAL = 0
00100 FOR I = 1 TO 8
00110    PRINT "ENTER NUMBER OF PASSENGERS ON RUN #";I
00120    INPUT PASSENGERS
00130    TTAL = TTAL + PASSENGERS
00140 NEXT I
00150 PRINT "TOTAL NUMBER OF PASSENGERS = ";TTAL
00999 END
```

```
RUNNH
ENTER NUMBER OF PASSENGERS ON RUN # 1
 ? 45
ENTER NUMBER OF PASSENGERS ON RUN # 2
 ? 67
ENTER NUMBER OF PASSENGERS ON RUN # 3
 ? 83
ENTER NUMBER OF PASSENGERS ON RUN # 4
 ? 47
ENTER NUMBER OF PASSENGERS ON RUN # 5
 ? 92
ENTER NUMBER OF PASSENGERS ON RUN # 6
 ? 56
ENTER NUMBER OF PASSENGERS ON RUN # 7
 ? 86
ENTER NUMBER OF PASSENGERS ON RUN # 8
 ? 73
TOTAL NUMBER OF PASSENGERS =  549
```

MICROCOMPUTERS	DIFFERENCE
Apple	None
IBM/Microsoft	None
Macintosh/Microsoft	None
TRS-80	None

the outer loop is executed I times (4 times in this case) and the inner loop is executed I × J times (4 × 2 = 8 times).

The following rules should be remembered when using nested FOR/NEXT loops.

● Each loop must have a unique loop control variable. The following example is invalid, because execution of the inner loop modifies the value of the outer loop control variable:

```
FOR I = X TO Y STEP 2
   FOR I = Q TO R
      •
      •
      •
   NEXT I
NEXT I
```

These nested loops should be rewritten so that each uses a unique loop control variable:

```
FOR I = X TO Y STEP 2
   FOR J = Q TO R
      •
      •
      •
   NEXT J
NEXT I
```

● The NEXT statement for an inner loop must appear within the body of the outer loop, so that one loop is entirely contained within another.

Invalid

```
FOR I = 1 TO 5
   FOR J = 1 TO 10
      •
      •
      •
NEXT I
   NEXT J
```

Valid

```
FOR I = 1 TO 5
   FOR J = 1 TO 10
      •
      •
      •
   NEXT J
NEXT I
```

In the invalid example, notice that the J loop is not entirely inside the I loop, but extends beyond the NEXT I statement.

● It is possible to nest many loops within one another. (Beware of improper nesting, however, as in the preceding invalid example.) Here is a correct example of multiple nested loops:

```
FOR I = 1 TO 2
   PRINT I


      FOR J = 1 TO 3
         PRINT J;


            FOR K = 1 TO 3
               PRINT K
            NEXT K


      NEXT J


NEXT I
```

● COMPUTERS AND INFORMATION PROCESSING

In this example, each nested loop is completely within its outer loop (the brackets never cross each other). Loop 1 is executed two times, loop 2 is executed six times (2 × 3), and loop 3 is executed eighteen times (2 × 3 × 3).

The following segment illustrates the mechanics of the nested loop. The outer loop will be executed three times, because I varies from 1 to 3. The inner loop will be executed twice each time the outer loop is executed once, so the inner loop will be executed a total of six times (2 × 3):

```
        ┌─ FOR I = 1 TO 3
        │     FOR J = 1 TO 2 ┐
Outer Loop ┤       PRINT I,J   ├──    Inner Loop
        │     NEXT J          ┘
        └─ NEXT I
```

	I	J	
a. First time through	1	1	First time through inner loop; J = 1
outer loop; I = 1	1	2	Second time through inner loop; J = 2
b. Second time through	2	1	Inner loop; J = 1
outer loop; I = 2	2	2	Inner loop; J = 2
c. Third time through	3	1	Inner loop; J = 1
outer loop; I = 3	3	2	Inner loop; J = 2

Figure VI–7 illustrates an application of nested loops. The program generates three multiplication tables. The inner loop controls the printing of the columns in each row, and the outer loop controls how many rows will be printed.

First, A is initialized to 1; then execution of the inner loop begins. When B = 1, line 100 tells the computer to print "1 × 1 = 1." The comma at the end of that line tells the computer not to start the output of the next PRINT statement on a new line, but rather to continue in the next print zone of the same line. Line 110 increments B to 2 and returns control to line 90. The variable A has not changed and the terminal value of B has not been exceeded, so "2 × 1 = 2" is printed in the second print zone. The inner loop executes one more time and prints "3 × 1 = 3." After the inner loop has executed the third time, one complete row has been printed:

1 × 1 = 1   2 × 1 = 2   3 × 1 = 3

The PRINT statement in line 120 causes the remainder of the first row to remain blank, and the next output starts on the left margin of the next line. Finally, A is incremented when line 130 is encountered. The process continues until A exceeds its terminal value, 10.

```
00010 REM ***                    MULTIPLICATION TABLES                ***
00020 REM
00030 REM *** THIS PROGRAM PRINTS A MULTIPLICATION TABLE OF 1 TO 10 ***
00040 REM *** FOR EACH OF THE NUMBERS 1 TO 3.                       ***
00050 REM
00060 REM *** LOOP TO PRINT ROWS ***
00070 FOR A = 1 TO 10
00080    REM *** LOOP TO PRINT COLUMNS ***
00090    FOR B = 1 TO 3
00100       PRINT B;"X";A;"=";B * A,
00110    NEXT B
00120    PRINT
00130 NEXT A
00999 END
```

```
RUNNH
   1 X  1 =  1        2 X  1 =  2        3 X  1 =  3
   1 X  2 =  2        2 X  2 =  4        3 X  2 =  6
   1 X  3 =  3        2 X  3 =  6        3 X  3 =  9
   1 X  4 =  4        2 X  4 =  8        3 X  4 = 12
   1 X  5 =  5        2 X  5 = 10        3 X  5 = 15
   1 X  6 =  6        2 X  6 = 12        3 X  6 = 18
   1 X  7 =  7        2 X  7 = 14        3 X  7 = 21
   1 X  8 =  8        2 X  8 = 16        3 X  8 = 24
   1 X  9 =  9        2 X  9 = 18        3 X  9 = 27
   1 X 10 = 10        2 X 10 = 20        3 X 10 = 30
```

MICROCOMPUTERS	DIFFERENCE
Apple	None
IBM/Microsoft	None
Macintosh/Microsoft	None
TRS-80	None

● FIGURE VI–7
Program Using Nested Loops

● The WHILE Loop

An additional set of instructions is used to implement loops: the WHILE/ NEXT. Here is the general format for this loop.

line# WHILE expression

- •
- •
- •
- •
- •
- •

line# NEXT

● **COMPUTERS AND INFORMATION PROCESSING**

Notice that the NEXT statement in this loop is not followed by a variable. Any statements between the WHILE and NEXT statements will be executed each time the loop is repeated. The WHILE loop will be executed as long as the expression in the WHILE statement is true. When the expression is no longer true, control is transferred to the first instruction after the NEXT statement.

In contrast to the FOR/NEXT loop, the WHILE/NEXT loop involves no automatic initialization or incrementing of the loop control variable. A statement before the WHILE statement must initialize the control variable, and another statement within the loop body must at some point change the value of the control variable so that the expression of the WHILE statement can change and end the loop. Otherwise an infinite loop results, as shown here:

```
00010 WHILE CNT < 50
00020    PRINT CNT
00030 NEXT
```

This loop could be correctly written:

```
00010 CNT = 1
00020 WHILE CNT < 50
00030    PRINT CNT
00040    CNT = CNT + 1
00050 NEXT
```

The program in Figure VI–8 uses a WHILE/NEXT loop controlled by a trailer value. The program checks each student score entered to determine the name and score of the highest- and lowest-scoring student. A trailer value of XXX is used for the student name. Lines 220 through 300 set up a WHILE/NEXT loop to process the data. The WHILE statement in line 220 causes the loop to be executed as long as the condition NME$ <> "XXX" evaluates as true. When NME$ equals XXX, the condition becomes false and control passes out of the loop.

Some implementations of BASIC (such as the IBM and Macintosh) create WHILE loops with the WHILE/WEND rather than the WHILE/NEXT statements. The format of the WHILE/WEND follows:

line# WHILE expression
.
.
.
line# WEND

The execution of the WHILE/WEND is identical to that of the WHILE/NEXT.

The WHILE loop can always be used in place of the FOR/NEXT loop, but the reverse is not true. The FOR/NEXT loop executes a prespecified number of times, as given by the initial and terminal values of the loop control variable. The WHILE loop can also execute a given number of times, if the programmer initializes the loop control variable before the loop begins and tests for the given value in the WHILE statement. However, the WHILE loop can also be used when the final number of desired loop executions is not known, such as when a trailer value is used. In such a situation, a properly structured FOR/NEXT loop would not be appropriate.

● Logical Operators

So far in this text, the arithmetic operators (^,*,/, +, −) and the relational operators (=, <>, <, >, <=, >=) have been covered. Now a third group of operators will be discussed: the **logical** or **Boolean operators.** A logical operator acts on one or more expressions that evaluate as true or false to produce a statement with a true or false value. The three most commonly used logical operators are AND, OR, and NOT.

The operator AND combines two expressions and produces a value of true only when both of these conditions are true. For example, the combined logical expression in the statement.

```
00020 IF (HEIGHT > 72) AND (WEIGHT > 150) THEN PRINT NME$
```

evaluates as true only if the expressions HEIGHT > 72 and WEIGHT > 150 are both true. If one or the other is false, the entire statement is false, and the THEN clause of the statement is ignored. The parentheses in the preceding statement are not necessary, but they improve the readability of the statement.

● **FIGURE VI–8**
Program Using a WHILE/NEXT Loop

```
00010 REM ***                          GRADE RANGE                    ***
00020 REM
00030 REM *** THIS PROGRAM FINDS THE HIGHEST AND THE LOWEST STUDENT ***
00040 REM *** SCORES ENTERED.                                        ***
00050 REM *** MAJOR VARIABLES:                                       ***
00060 REM ***    NME$ - STUDENT'S LAST NAME                          ***
00070 REM ***    SCR - TEST SCORE                                    ***
00080 REM ***    HISCR - HIGHEST SCORE                               ***
00090 REM ***    LOSCR - LOWEST SCORE                                ***
00100 REM ***    HNME$ - NAME OF STUDENT WITH HIGHEST SCORE          ***
00110 REM ***    LNME$ -   "    "    "      "   LOWEST    "           ***
00120 REM
00130 REM *** ENTER FIRST STUDENT SCORE ***
00140 PRINT "ENTER LAST NAME AND SCORE"
00150 INPUT "(TYPE 'XXX,0' TO QUIT)";NME$,SCR
00160 REM
00170 REM *** INITIALIZE HIGH AND LOW SCORES TO FIRST SCORE ***
00180 HISCR = SCR \ HNME$ = NME$
00190 LOSCR = SCR \ LNME$ = NME$
00200 REM
00210 REM *** LOOP TO FIND HIGH AND LOW SCORES ***
00220 WHILE NME$ <> "XXX"
00230     IF SCR > HISCR THEN HISCR = SCR \ HNME$ = NME$
00240     IF SCR < LOSCR THEN LOSCR = SCR \ LNME$ = NME$
00250     REM
00260     REM *** ENTER NEXT SCORE ***
00270     PRINT
00280     PRINT "ENTER LAST NAME, SCORE"
00290     INPUT "(TYPE 'XXX,0' TO QUIT)";NME$,SCR
00300 NEXT
00310 REM
00320 REM *** PRINT RANGE OF SCORES ***
00330 PRINT
00340 PRINT
00350 PRINT HNME$;" RECEIVED THE HIGH SCORE OF";HISCR
00360 PRINT LNME$;" RECEIVED THE LOW SCORE OF";LOSCR
00999 END
```

The logical operator OR also combines two expressions, but only one of these expressions needs to evaluate as true for the entire statement to be true. Thus the statement

```
00020 IF (HEIGHT > 72) OR (WEIGHT > 150) THEN PRINT NME$
```

evaluates as true if either HEIGHT > 72 or WEIGHT > 150 is true, or if both are true. The entire condition is false only if the expressions HEIGHT > 72 and WEIGHT > 150 are both false. Table VI–1 shows the results for all possible values of two expressions combined by AND and OR.

The third logical operator, NOT, is a **unary operator** (an operator used with one operand) and therefore is used with a single expression. The effect of NOT is to reverse the logical value of the expression it precedes. For example, if the variable PET$ has the value DOG, the condition of the following statement is false:

```
00020 IF NOT (PET$ = "DOG") THEN 90
```

● **FIGURE VI–8**
Continued

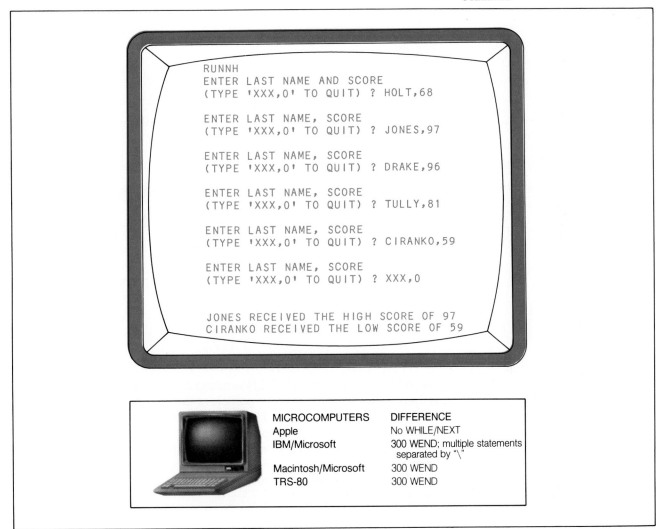

```
RUNNH
ENTER LAST NAME AND SCORE
(TYPE 'XXX,0' TO QUIT) ? HOLT,68

ENTER LAST NAME, SCORE
(TYPE 'XXX,0' TO QUIT) ? JONES,97

ENTER LAST NAME, SCORE
(TYPE 'XXX,0' TO QUIT) ? DRAKE,96

ENTER LAST NAME, SCORE
(TYPE 'XXX,0' TO QUIT) ? TULLY,81

ENTER LAST NAME, SCORE
(TYPE 'XXX,0' TO QUIT) ? CIRANKO,59

ENTER LAST NAME, SCORE
(TYPE 'XXX,0' TO QUIT) ? XXX,0


JONES RECEIVED THE HIGH SCORE OF 97
CIRANKO RECEIVED THE LOW SCORE OF 59
```

MICROCOMPUTERS	DIFFERENCE
Apple	No WHILE/NEXT
IBM/Microsoft	300 WEND; multiple statements separated by "\"
Macintosh/Microsoft	300 WEND
TRS-80	300 WEND

The AND and OR Logical Operators

CONDITION 1	CONDITION 2	CONDITION 1 AND CONDITION 2	CONDITION 1 OR CONDITION 2
true	true	true	true
true	false	false	true
false	true	false	true
false	false	false	false

Because the condition PET$ = "DOG" evaluates as true, the NOT operator reverses this value to false, making the final result of the entire condition false. If PET$ contained any other value, the condition PET$ = "DOG" would evaluate as false, and the NOT would make the value of the entire condition true.

Logical operators can be combined in a single statement, and they are evaluated in the following sequence:

1. NOT
2. AND
3. OR

For example, the following statement combines AND and OR:

```
00050 IF (PET$ = "DOG") OR (AGE = 3) AND (WT = 10) THEN 90
```

Given the predefined order of evaluation, the following diagram shows how the preceding statement would be evaluated if PET$ = "DOG", AGE = 3, and WT = 9:

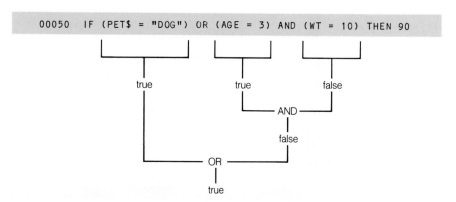

The AND portion of the IF/THEN statement is evaluated first. That result is then combined with the OR portion of the statement to determine the final value of the entire condition. In this case, the statement condition is true, so control is passed to line 90.

The precedence of logical operators (like that of arithmetic operators) can be altered using parentheses. The previous example, using the same variable values as before, could be rewritten as

```
00050 IF ((PET$ = "DOG") OR (AGE = 3)) AND (WT = 10) THEN 90
```

In this example, the OR portion of the expression is evaluated before the AND portion. Thus the parentheses can change the final result of the evaluation, as shown in the following diagram. Compare the evaluation of this statement with the previous diagram.

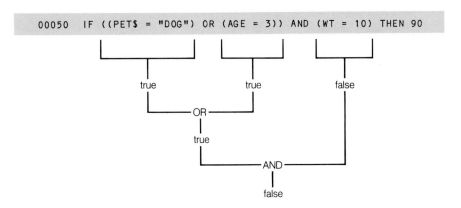

Even if the order of evaluation desired in a condition is the same as the predefined order, it is good programming practice to use parentheses in order to make the logic easier to follow.

NOT can also be combined with AND and OR in a single statement, as shown in the following diagram. Study the evaluation of the condition, making sure that you understand how the use of parentheses and the predefined order of operators has determined the final result of the evaluation. Assume that PET$ = "PIG", AGE = 6, and WT = 1500.

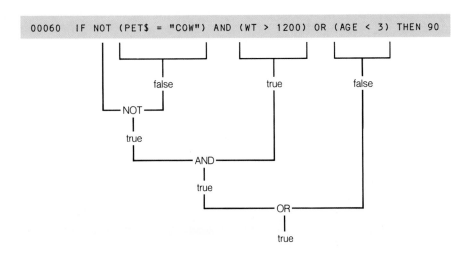

Table VI–2 shows the order in which all types of BASIC operators are evaluated. Further examples involving these operators are shown in Table VI–3.

The program shown in Figure VI–9 demonstrates how logical operators can be used to determine if a triangle is scalene, isosceles, or equilateral.

1. Anything in parentheses	6. Relational operators $(=, <>, <, >, <=, >=)$
2. Exponentiation (*)	7. NOT
3. Unary plus and minus $(+, -)$	8. AND
4. Multiplication and division $(*, /)$	9. OR
5. Addition and subtraction $(+, -)$	

Note: Operators on the same level are evaluated left to right.

Notice that the condition of the first test uses the AND operator to determine if all three sides are equal:

```
00080 IF (S1SIDE = S2SIDE) AND (S1SIDE = S3SIDE) THEN
```

The test for an isosceles triangle is more complex and involves checking for three different conditions. Only one of these conditions needs to be true for the triangle to be isosceles; therefore, this test involves the OR operator. If none of these conditions is true, the triangle must be scalene. As shown by this program, logical operators allow for a variety of conditions to be checked efficiently and simultaneously.

● A Programming Problem

PROBLEM DEFINITION

The computer science department needs a program to display a bar graph that shows the number of students enrolled in each of the computer science classes, sections 100 through 109:

100	37
101	28
102	31
103	34
104	26
105	22
106	30
107	21
108	10
109	18

The output should have appropriate headings, and the horizontal bar should be marked off by 10s.

● **TABLE VI-3**
Examples of Conditions Using Logical Operators

CONDITION	EVALUATES AS
NOT (1 * 4 = 5)	TRUE
(18 < 16) OR (7 + 2 = 9)	TRUE
(18 < 16) AND (7 + 2 = 9)	FALSE
((2 + 8) <= 11) AND (17 * 2 = 34)	TRUE
NOT (12 > 8 - 2)	FALSE

SOLUTION DESIGN

The task of displaying a student enrollment graph can be divided into two basic parts:

1. Display the graph headings.
2. Display a bar for each section.

● **FIGURE VI–9**
Triangle Test Program

```
00010 REM *** DETERMINE THE TYPE OF A TRIANGLE:    ***
00020 REM *** SCALENE, ISOSCELES, OR EQUILATERAL. ***
00030 REM
00040 INPUT "ENTER THE THREE SIDES: "S1SIDE,S2SIDE,S3SIDE
00050 PRINT "TRIANGLE IS ";
00060 REM
00070 REM *** CHECK FOR EQUILATERAL ***
00080 IF (S1SIDE = S2SIDE) AND (S2SIDE = S3SIDE) THEN PRINT "EQUILATERAL"
          \ GOTO 999
00090 REM
00100 REM *** CHECK FOR ISOSCELES; IF NOT, THEN IT'S SCALENE ***
00110 IF (S1SIDE = S2SIDE) OR (S1SIDE = S3SIDE) OR (S2SIDE = S3SIDE) THEN PRINT
          "ISOSCELES" ELSE PRINT "SCALENE"
00999 END
```

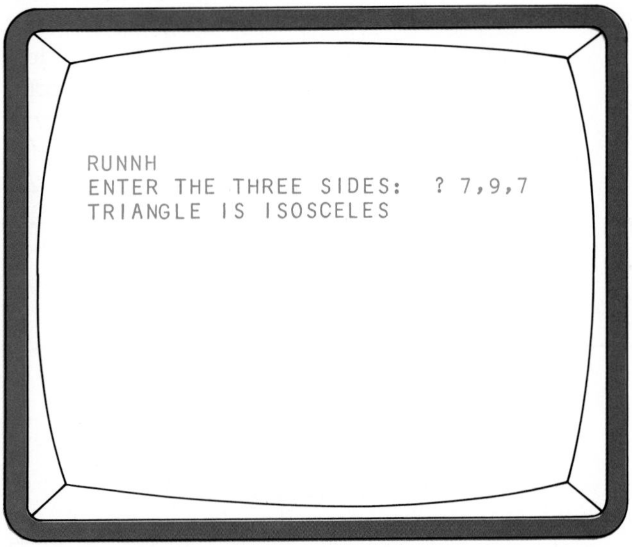

```
RUNNH
ENTER THE THREE SIDES:    ? 7,9,7
TRIANGLE IS ISOSCELES
```

MICROCOMPUTERS	DIFFERENCE
Apple	None
IBM/Microsoft	None
Macintosh/Microsoft	None
TRS-80	None

The graph headings consist of the graph title, the labels for the section numbers and student numbers, and the horizontal scale of multiples of ten.

The bar to be displayed for each class section is made up of two parts: the section number and the row of asterisks showing the number of students. Step 2 described above can therefore be further divided:

2. a. Display the section number.
2. b. Display the row of asterisks.

Figure VI–10 shows this analysis of the problem solution.

The steps, 2.a and 2.b, must be repeated for each class section, and thus should be placed in a loop. Since the second of these steps, displaying the asterisks, itself calls for a loop, this program will use a nested loop. Figure VI–11 shows the steps needed for this solution.

THE PROGRAM

Figure VI–11 is a good illustration of nested FOR/NEXT loops. Lines 90 through 150 print the headings with appropriate spacing. The outer loop (lines 180 through 250) is set to run from 100 to 109, so the variable I represents the section number. Line 190 prints the section number and tabs the printer to column 9. Line 200 reads the number of students; then the inner loop (lines 210 through 230) is set to repeat the PRINT statement (line 220) as many times as there are students. Because lines 190 and 220 end with a semicolon, the printer will print the section number and all of the asterisks on one line. After the row of asterisks has been printed and the inner loop is finished, the printer must be advanced to the next line; this is done in line 240. Because line 240 does not end with a comma or semicolon, the printer moves to the next line.

Many variations can be made to this bar graph display. The asterisk can be replaced by any other character. Also, the limitations placed by

● **FIGURE VI–10**
Structure Chart for Enrollment Program

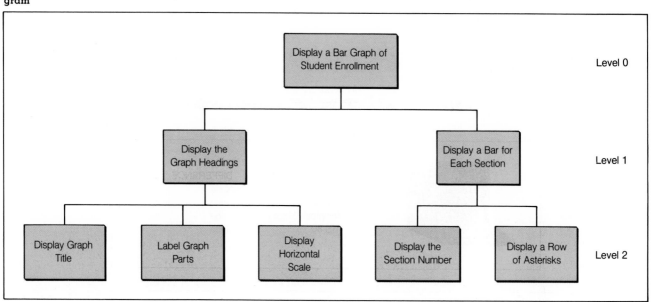

● **COMPUTERS AND INFORMATION PROCESSING**

the width of the terminal can be overcome by using appropriate scales. For example, each asterisk could represent two students.

⬤ Summary Points

⬤ The FOR/NEXT loop executes the number of times specified in the FOR statement. The NEXT statement increments the loop control variable, tests it against the terminal value, and returns control to the statement immediately following the FOR statement if another loop execution is required.

⬤ **FIGURE VI–11**
Enrollment Program and Flowchart

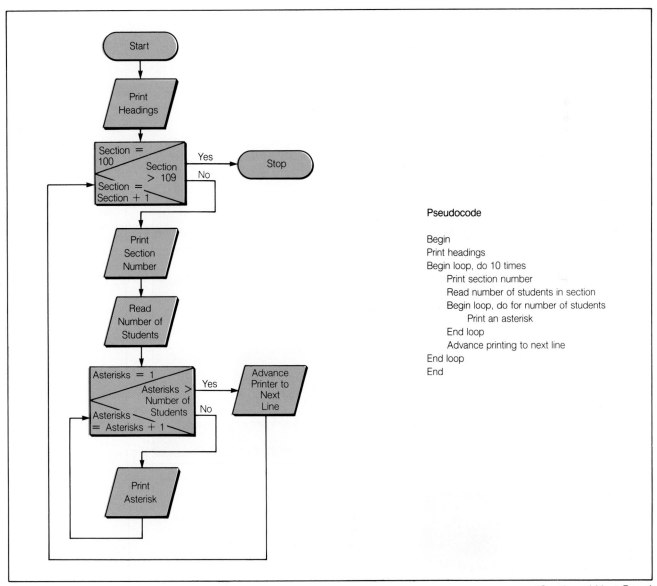

Pseudocode

Begin
Print headings
Begin loop, do 10 times
    Print section number
    Read number of students in section
    Begin loop, do for number of students
        Print an asterisk
    End loop
    Advance printing to next line
End loop
End

(Continued Next Page)

```
00010 REM ***                              ENROLLMENT GRAPH                      ***
00020 REM
00030 REM *** THIS PROGRAM DISPLAYS A BAR GRAPH THAT SHOWS THE NUMBER ***
00040 REM *** OF STUDENTS ENROLLED IN EACH COMPUTER SCIENCE SECTION. ***
00050 REM *** MAJOR VARIABLES:                                        ***
00060 REM ***    STUDENTS - NUMBER OF STUDENTS IN ONE SECTION         ***
00070 REM
00080 REM *** PRINT HEADINGS ***
00090 PRINT
00100 PRINT
00110 PRINT TAB(16);"CLASS ENROLLMENT"
00120 PRINT
00130 PRINT "SEC. #";TAB(16);"STUDENTS"
00140 PRINT TAB(8);1;TAB(17);10;TAB(27);20;TAB(37);30
00150 PRINT
00160 REM
00170 REM *** PRINT GRAPH ***
00180 FOR I = 100 TO 109
00190    PRINT I;TAB(9);
00200    READ STUDENTS
00210    FOR J = 1 TO STUDENTS
00220       PRINT "*";
00230    NEXT J
00240    PRINT
00250 NEXT I
00260 REM
00270 REM *** DATA STATEMENTS ***
00280 DATA 37,28,31,34,26,22,30,21,10,18
00999 END
```

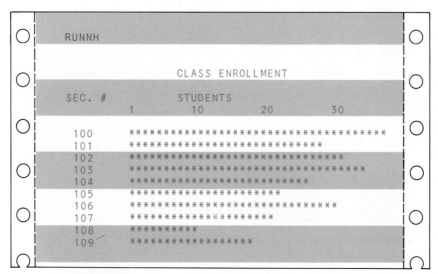

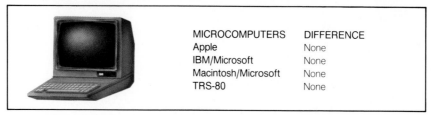

MICROCOMPUTERS	DIFFERENCE
Apple	None
IBM/Microsoft	None
Macintosh/Microsoft	None
TRS-80	None

- Some rules to remember when using FOR and NEXT loops follow:
  —The initial value must be less than or equal to the terminal value when using a positive step value. Otherwise, the loop will never be executed.
  —The step value can be negative. If it is, the initial value must be greater than or equal to the terminal value in order for the loop to execute at least once.
  —The step value should never be 0; this creates an infinite loop.
  —The loop control variable in the NEXT statement must be the same loop control variable that was used in the corresponding FOR statement.
  —Transfer can be made from one statement to another within a loop. However, transfer from a statement in the loop body to the FOR statement is poor programming practice.
  —The value of the loop control variable should not be modified by program statements within the loop.
  —The initial, terminal, and step expressions can be composed of any valid numeric variable, constant, or mathematical formula.
  —Each FOR statement must be accompanied by a NEXT statement.
  —FOR/NEXT loops can be nested.
  —The NEXT statement of the nested inner loop must come before the NEXT statement of the outer loop.
- The WHILE statement repeats execution of its loop body as long as the given condition is true.
- The logical operators NOT, AND, and OR are used with conditions. NOT is a unary operator that negates a condition. An expression containing AND evaluates as true when both conditions joined by the AND are true. A condition containing OR is true if at least one of the joined conditions is true.

● Review Questions

1. Is this a valid FOR statement?

```
00020 FOR C$ = 1 TO 10 STEP 2
```

2. When is a WHILE loop a more appropriate choice than a FOR/NEXT loop?

3. What is the output from the following statements?

```
00030 L = 10
00040 FOR L = 1 TO 6
00050     PRINT L
00060 NEXT L
```

4. Can arithmetic expressions be used as initial and terminal values?

5. If the step value is negative, will the loop be terminated when the initial value is less than or greater than the terminal value?

6. Can control be transferred from one statement to another within a loop? From a statement within a loop to the FOR statement?

7. Is this a valid FOR/NEXT loop?

```
00010 FOR I = 1 TO 10
00020    READ X
00030    IF X > 20 THEN 50
00040    S = S + W
00050 NEXT I
```

8. Which of the following is a valid WHILE loop?

```
00050 WHILE X < 10          00100 WHILE Q + 6 < R
00060    PRINT X            00110    S = S + 1
00070    X = X + 1          00120    PRINT S
00080 NEXT                  00130 NEXT
```

9. Is this a valid nested loop?

```
00090 FOR I = 10 TO 1 STEP -1
00100    PRINT I
00110    FOR J = 2 TO 6 STEP 2
00120       S = I + J
00130       FOR K = 1 TO 3
00140          S = S + K
00150          PRINT S
00160       NEXT J
00170       PRINT J
00180    NEXT J
00190 NEXT I
```

10. How many times is the following inner loop executed? How many times is the outer loop executed?

```
00060 FOR I = 1 TO (3 * 4) STEP 2
00070    FOR J = 1 TO 2 STEP .5
00080       PRINT I,J
00090    NEXT J
00100 NEXT I
```

● Debugging Exercises

Identify the following programs or program segments that contain errors, and debug them.

```
1. 00010 FOR I = 1 TO 10
   00020    READ C
   00030    IF C = 1 THEN 10
   00040    READ N
   00050 NEXT I
2. 00010 K = 1
   00020 WHILE K < 5
   00030    PRINT K
   00040    INPUT N$,AMT
   00050    IF AMT < 20.0 THEN 70
   00060    PRINT N$,AMT
   00070 NEXT
```

● Programming Problems

1. Your landlord is considering a raise in rent of 5 percent, 7 percent, or 10 percent. To determine how much additional money you and your fellow tenants cannot afford to pay, write a program to show sample rents of $200 to $600 (by increments of $50) and the three proposed increased rents for each. Create a table like the following:

RENT	+5%	+7%	+10%
200	XXX	XXX	XXX
250	XXX	XXX	XXX
.	.	.	.
.	.	.	.
.			

2. Write a program to display a multiplication table. Allow the user to enter the upper and lower limits of the table, then print the appropriate values. Use the following format for the table:

X	3	4	5	6
3	9	12	15	18
4	12	16	20	24
5	15	20	25	30
6	18	24	30	36

3. The high school tennis team is holding its annual tryouts. The coach selects the team members on the basis of the results of a series of matches. Each player is placed on a first, second, or third string team depending on his or her number of wins:

Number of Wins	Team
10 or more	First string
4 to 9	Second string
3 or less	Third string

You are to write a program using a WHILE loop that indicates on which team a player belongs. Use the following data:

Name	Wins
Sanders, S.	7
Crosby, D.	5
Casey, E.	9
Case, L.	12
Sandoval, V.	10
Coles, S.	3
Schnur, R.	2

4. Write a program to calculate X^N. This value should be found by multiplying X times itself N number of times (e.g. $X^4 = X * X * X * X$). Use the following values for X and N to test your program:

X	N
1	2
6	3
5	4
2	6

The output should have the following format:

X raised to the N = R.

A trailer value should be used to determine the end of the data.

5. The Happy Hedonist Health Spa has asked you to write a payroll program that will calculate the weekly net pay for each of its employees. The employees have the option of participating in a medical insurance plan that deducts $10 per week. The income tax rate is 25 percent. Use a FOR/NEXT loop in your program.

The following is the company pay code key:

Code	Wage Rate
1	$5.00
2	6.75
3	9.50

Use the following data:

Name	Medical Plan	Hours	Wage Code
Cochran, K.	Yes	40	2
Batdorf, D.	Yes	45	1
Jones, S.	No	38	3
Goolsby, L.	Yes	30	2
Halas, G.	No	35	1

The output should appear as follows:

NAME	NET PAY
XXXXXXXXX	$XXX.XX

● Section VII
Modularizing Programs

● Introduction

We have previously discussed the two main characteristics of structured programs: (1) they incorporate easy-to-follow logic (which is achieved mainly by using decision and looping structures whenever possible, instead of using GOTO statements), and (2) they are divided into subprograms, each of which is designed to perform a specific task.

Decision and looping structures were introduced in the two previous sections. This section will explain how programs are divided into subprograms or modules, which in BASIC are called **subroutines.** The GO-SUB and ON/GOSUB statements are the two methods of executing a subroutine in BASIC, and both will be covered here.

● The Importance of Modularizing Programs

Dividing a program into modules is useful for two reasons: (1) the logic of a program that is divided into modules, each performing a distinct task, is easier to follow, and (2) the same module can be executed any number of times. For example, if the program needs to do the same task at two different points, the subroutine that performs this task may simply be executed twice. Without the subroutine, the programmer would have to write the same program segment twice.

● Writing Subroutines

A subroutine is a sequence of statements, typically located after the main body of the program. Two statements in BASIC can be used to **call** a subroutine, that is, to cause it to be executed. These two statements are the GOSUB and the ON/GOSUB statements.

THE GOSUB STATEMENT

The GOSUB statement transfers the flow of program control from the calling program to a subroutine. A subroutine can be called either from the main program or from another subroutine. The format of the GOSUB statement is:

line# GOSUB transfer line#

The transfer line number must be the first line number of the subroutine to be executed. This is very important, because the computer will not detect an error if it is instructed to branch to an incorrect line. It will detect an error only if the transfer line number does not exist in the program. The GOSUB statement causes an unconditional branch to this specified line number. For example, the following statement will always cause a branch to the subroutine starting at line 1000:

```
00100 GOSUB 1000
```

THE RETURN STATEMENT

After a subroutine is executed, the RETURN statement causes program control to return to the line following the one that contained the GOSUB statement. The format of the RETURN statement is as follows:

line# RETURN

Note that no transfer line number is needed in the RETURN statement. The computer automatically returns control to the statement immediately following the GOSUB statement that called the subroutine. If the line returned to is a nonexecutable statement, such as a REM statement, the computer simply skips it. Each subroutine must contain a RETURN statement; otherwise, the program cannot branch back to the point from which the subroutine was called.

A PROGRAM CONTAINING MULTIPLE CALLS TO THE SAME SUBROUTINE

Look at the program in Figure VII–1. This program prints a simple multiplication table. It contains a subroutine that prints a row of asterisks to divide the multiplication table into sections to make it more readable. The subroutine is called from three places in the main program: line 70, line 90, and line 190. Each time this subroutine is called, program control transfers to line 1000. Because lines 1000 through 1050 are nonexecutable statements, execution skips down to line 1060. Lines 1060 through 1080 contain a FOR/NEXT loop that is used to print a line of 80 asterisks. Then program control returns to the line following the statement that called the subroutine. In Figure VII–1, both the main program and the subroutine are labeled. Arrows are drawn to show the flow of execution of the program.

In this example, the subroutine is very short, so it would be easy to repeat the necessary series of statements each time they are needed. If the subroutine were 10, 20, or more lines long, however, it would be tedious and wasteful to type it three times. Using the subroutine simplifies the program logic by organizing specific tasks into neat, orderly subsections.

Notice that the subroutine in Figure VII–1 begins at line 1000. To make programs more readable, programmers often start subroutines at readily

FIGURE VII–1
Program Demonstrating Multiple Calls to a Subroutine

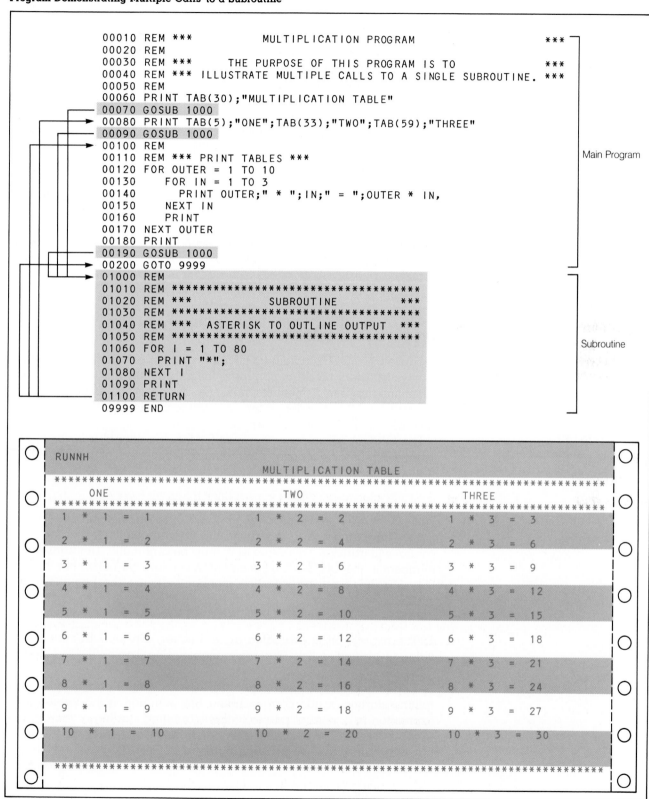

identifiable line numbers, such as multiples of 1000. For example, the first subroutine might start at line 1000, the second at line 2000, and so on. This practice of starting at readily identifiable line numbers will be followed in this textbook.

In Figure VII–1, when program execution reaches the last line of the main program (line 200) it is ready to stop. We do not want to execute the subroutine again at this point, because it has already been called where it was needed in the program. Therefore, it is necessary to branch to the END statement, which has a line number of 09999. This branch statement will skip over any subroutines that have been placed between the end of the main program and the END statement.

On the DECsystem, the END statement must be at the end of the entire program and must also have the highest line number. Not all BASIC implementations have these requirements. On many systems, the END statement may be placed immediately after the last statement of the main program and before the subroutines. If this is possible on your system, it is recommended that you use this method because it avoids the use of a GOTO statement.

THE ON/GOSUB STATEMENT

Because the GOSUB statement is an unconditional transfer statement, it always transfers program control to the subroutine starting at the indicated line number. Sometimes, however, it is necessary to branch to one of several subroutines depending on existing conditions. The ON/GOSUB statement is useful for this purpose.

The ON/GOSUB statement allows for the conditional transfer of program control to one of several subroutines. The format of the ON/GOSUB statement is:

line# ON expression GOSUB transfer line#1[,transfer line#2,...]

The ON/GOSUB is similar to the ON/GOTO statement (Section 5) in that it uses an expression to determine the line number to which program control will transfer. This expression must be arithmetic. The transfer line numbers in the ON/GOSUB statement, however, are not within the calling program. Each transfer line number indicates the beginning of a subroutine.

The general execution of the ON/GOSUB proceeds as follows:

1. The expression is evaluated as an integer. On the DECsystem, this value is truncated if it is a real number. See Table VII–1 for system differences in this respect.

2. Depending on the value of the expression, control passes to the subroutine starting at the corresponding line number. If the value of the expression is n, control passes to the subroutine starting at the nth line number listed. (For example, if the expression evaluates as 1, control transfers to the first line number in the list.)

3. After the specified subroutine is executed, control is transferred back

● **TABLE VII–1**
ON/GOSUB Differences

COMPUTER	ACTION TAKEN IF EXPRESSION IS GREATER THAN NUMBER OF LINE NUMBERS	EXPRESSION TRUNCATED OR ROUNDED?
DECsystem	"ON statement out of range at line 00120"	Truncated
Apple	Control is passed to next executable statement	Truncated
IBM/Microsoft	Control is passed to next executable statement	Rounded
Macintosh/Microsoft	Control is passed to next executable statement	Rounded
TRS-80	Control is passed to next executable statement	Rounded

to the line following the ON/GOSUB statement by a RETURN statement at the end of the subroutine.

The ON/GOSUB statement provides a more structured approach to programming than the ON/GOTO statement because the location of the return of control is determined by the BASIC system and not by the programmer. This eliminates the chance of the programmer stating the incorrect line number in the GOTO statement.

On the DECsystem, if the expression in an ON/GOSUB statement evaluates as a number larger than the number of transfer line numbers indicated, an error message is printed and program execution terminates. Table VII–1 explains how different systems handle this situation.

Figure VII–2 demonstrates a simple use of the ON/GOSUB statement. The user enters an integer value representing his or her year in college (1, 2, 3, or 4). This integer value is assigned to the variable YR, which is then used to determine which subroutine will be executed. If YR = 1, the subroutine starting at line 1000 will be executed; if YR = 2, the subroutine starting at line 2000 will be executed; if YR = 3, the subroutine starting at line 3000 will be executed; and if YR = 4, the subroutine starting at line 4000 will be executed. After the appropriate subroutine is executed, control is returned to the main program, which then stops executing.

USING THE STRUCTURE CHART TO MODULARIZE A PROGRAM

So far in this textbook, we have been using structure charts to help analyze the steps necessary to solve programming problems. Structure charts enable us to visualize the specific tasks a program must perform to achieve the desired overall result. Because structure charts represent the subtasks involved in solving a problem, they are very helpful in developing modularized programs. Once the tasks of a program are identified, each of these can be implemented in the program as a separate subroutine.

We will illustrate the use of structure charts with a simple problem. We are going to write a program that will calculate the cost of a long distance phone call based on the following table (note that the user should enter the number of miles as an integer value):

Distance of Call	Cost Per Minute
Within 99 miles	12¢ per minute for first 5 minutes, 10¢ per minute thereafter
Between 100 and 199 miles	15¢ per minute for first 5 minutes, 13¢ per minute thereafter
Between 200 and 299 miles	18¢ per minute, regardless of length of the call

● FIGURE VII-2
Program Using the ON/GOSUB Statement

```
00010 REM ***              GRADUATION PROGRAM               ***
00020 REM
00030 REM ***    THIS PROGRAM PRINTS THE CLASS A STUDENT ***
00040 REM *** BELONGS TO (FRESHMAN, SOPHOMORE, JUNIOR,   ***
00050 REM *** SENIOR) AND THE YEAR OF GRADUATION WHEN     ***
00060 REM *** THE CORRESPONDING INTEGER (1, 2, 3, OR 4)  ***
00070 REM *** IS ENTERED.                                 ***
00080 REM *** MAJOR VARIABLES:                            ***
00090 REM *** STUDENT$          STUDENT'S NAME            ***
00100 REM *** YR                YEAR                      ***
00110 REM
00120 REM *** ENTER THE NECESSARY DATA ***
00130 INPUT "ENTER THE STUDENT'S NAME ";STUDENT$
00140 INPUT "ENTER THE STUDENT'S YEAR (1,2,3, OR 4) ";YR
00150 REM
00160 REM *** BRANCH TO SUBROUTINE THAT WILL PRINT MESSAGE ***
00170 ON YR GOSUB 1000,2000,3000,4000
00180 GOTO 9999
01000 REM
01010 REM ***********************************************
01020 REM ***           SUBROUTINE FRESHMAN        ***
01030 REM ***********************************************
01040 REM
01050 PRINT STUDENT$;" IS A FRESHMAN"
01060 PRINT "AND WILL GRADUATE IN 1991"
01070 RETURN
02000 REM
02010 REM ***********************************************
02020 REM ***           SUBROUTINE SOPHOMORE       ***
02030 REM ***********************************************
02040 REM
02050 PRINT STUDENT$;" IS A SOPHOMORE"
02060 PRINT "AND WILL GRADUATE IN 1990"
02070 RETURN
03000 REM
03010 REM ***********************************************
03020 REM ***           SUBROUTINE JUNIOR          ***
03030 REM ***********************************************
03040 REM
03050 PRINT STUDENT$;" IS A JUNIOR"
03060 PRINT "AND WILL GRADUATE IN 1989"
03070 RETURN
04000 REM
04010 REM ***********************************************
04020 REM ***           SUBROUTINE SENIOR          ***
04030 REM ***********************************************
04040 REM
04050 PRINT STUDENT$;" IS A SENIOR"
04060 PRINT "AND WILL GRADUATE IN 1988"
04070 RETURN
09999 END
```

● COMPUTERS AND INFORMATION PROCESSING

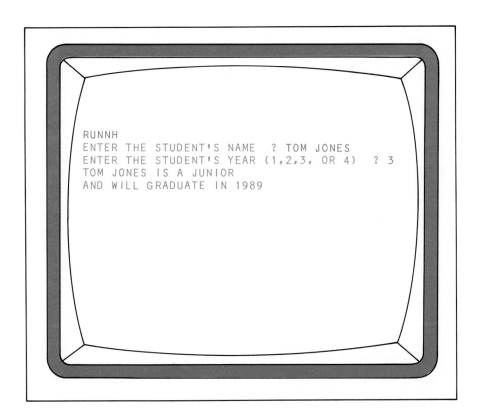

```
RUNNH
ENTER THE STUDENT'S NAME   ? TOM JONES
ENTER THE STUDENT'S YEAR (1,2,3, OR 4)   ? 3
TOM JONES IS A JUNIOR
AND WILL GRADUATE IN 1989
```

No phone calls can be placed outside the 299-mile radius.

First we need to develop an algorithm for this problem. The steps needed to solve this problem could be listed like this:

1. Enter the distance and length of time of the call.
2. Calculate the cost of the call based on the distance.
3. Print the cost of the call.

A structure chart for this problem is shown at the top of Figure VII–3. Steps 1 and 3 are simple enough to implement: Step 1 can be written as a subroutine that allows the user to enter the distance and length of time of the call, and Step 3 can be written as a subroutine that prints the final cost with an appropriate label. Because these are such simple steps, they could be included within the main program itself. In this example, however, we are including them as subroutines to demonstrate how every task in the program can be modularized.

Step 2 is more complex. We want the program to use one of three rates in determining the cost, depending on the distance. This is a situation that is well suited to the ON/GOSUB statement; three subroutines can be used to perform these calculations, as shown in Figure VII–3. The following ON/GOSUB statement will cause program control to be transferred to the needed subroutine, if the computer system being used is one that truncates the value of the ON/GOSUB expression, as the DEC-system does:

```
00120 ON (DIST + 100) / 100 GOSUB 2000,3000,4000
```

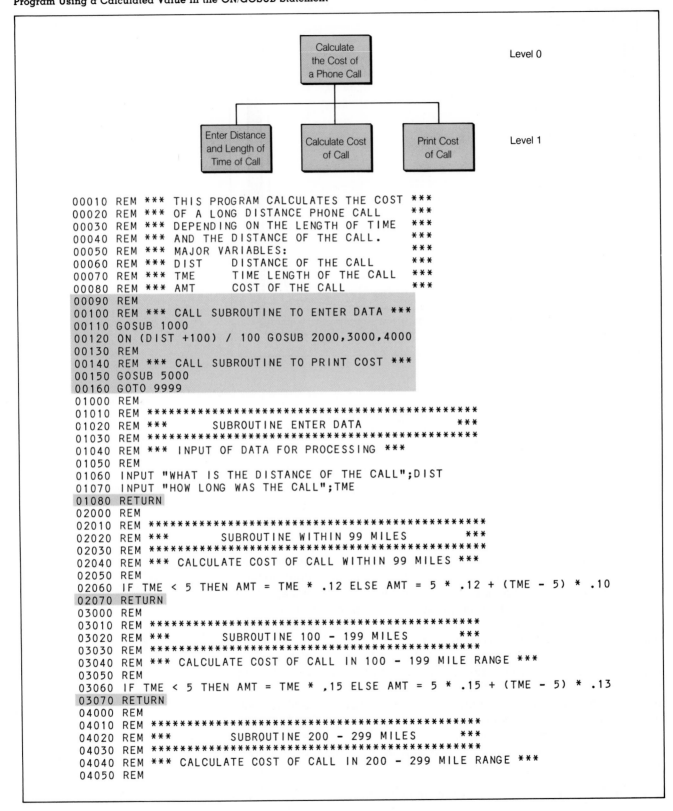

```
00010 REM *** THIS PROGRAM CALCULATES THE COST ***
00020 REM *** OF A LONG DISTANCE PHONE CALL    ***
00030 REM *** DEPENDING ON THE LENGTH OF TIME  ***
00040 REM *** AND THE DISTANCE OF THE CALL.    ***
00050 REM *** MAJOR VARIABLES:                 ***
00060 REM *** DIST    DISTANCE OF THE CALL     ***
00070 REM *** TME     TIME LENGTH OF THE CALL  ***
00080 REM *** AMT     COST OF THE CALL         ***
00090 REM
00100 REM *** CALL SUBROUTINE TO ENTER DATA ***
00110 GOSUB 1000
00120 ON (DIST +100) / 100 GOSUB 2000,3000,4000
00130 REM
00140 REM *** CALL SUBROUTINE TO PRINT COST ***
00150 GOSUB 5000
00160 GOTO 9999
01000 REM
01010 REM *******************************************
01020 REM ***          SUBROUTINE ENTER DATA       ***
01030 REM *******************************************
01040 REM *** INPUT OF DATA FOR PROCESSING ***
01050 REM
01060 INPUT "WHAT IS THE DISTANCE OF THE CALL";DIST
01070 INPUT "HOW LONG WAS THE CALL";TME
01080 RETURN
02000 REM
02010 REM *******************************************
02020 REM ***          SUBROUTINE WITHIN 99 MILES  ***
02030 REM *******************************************
02040 REM *** CALCULATE COST OF CALL WITHIN 99 MILES ***
02050 REM
02060 IF TME < 5 THEN AMT = TME * .12 ELSE AMT = 5 * .12 + (TME - 5) * .10
02070 RETURN
03000 REM
03010 REM *******************************************
03020 REM ***          SUBROUTINE 100 - 199 MILES  ***
03030 REM *******************************************
03040 REM *** CALCULATE COST OF CALL IN 100 - 199 MILE RANGE ***
03050 REM
03060 IF TME < 5 THEN AMT = TME * ,15 ELSE AMT = 5 * .15 + (TME - 5) * .13
03070 RETURN
04000 REM
04010 REM *******************************************
04020 REM ***          SUBROUTINE 200 - 299 MILES  ***
04030 REM *******************************************
04040 REM *** CALCULATE COST OF CALL IN 200 - 299 MILE RANGE ***
04050 REM
```

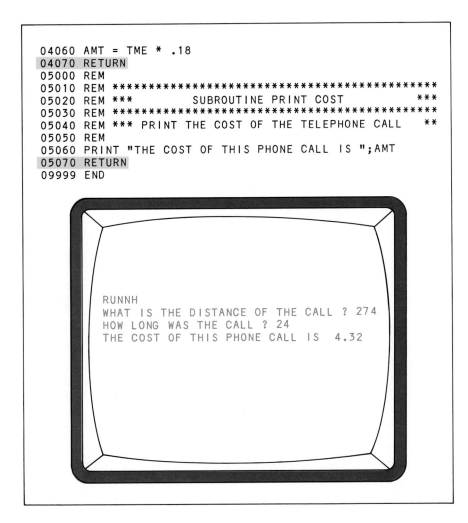

```
04060 AMT = TME * .18
04070 RETURN
05000 REM
05010 REM ************************************************
05020 REM ***             SUBROUTINE PRINT COST        ***
05030 REM ************************************************
05040 REM *** PRINT THE COST OF THE TELEPHONE CALL    **
05050 REM
05060 PRINT "THE COST OF THIS PHONE CALL IS ";AMT
05070 RETURN
09999 END
```

```
RUNNH
WHAT IS THE DISTANCE OF THE CALL ? 274
HOW LONG WAS THE CALL ? 24
THE COST OF THIS PHONE CALL IS  4.32
```

Let's test this expression by assuming that the number of miles entered is 199. With this value substituted, the statement would look like this:

```
00120 ON (199 + 100) / 100 GOSUB 2000,3000,4000
```

The expression (199 + 100) / 100 is equal to 2.99. This number is truncated to 2, so the program will branch to the second subroutine, which starts at line 3000. This is the subroutine used to calculate phone bills in the 100- to 199-mile radius.

Test this program yourself, using different values for the distance. If your BASIC system rounds the expression rather than truncating it, however, the expression must be written differently:

```
00120 ON (DIST + 50) / 100 GOSUB 2000,3000,4000
```

To check this statement, let's again assume that 199 has been entered as the value for DIST:

```
00120 ON (199 + 50) / 100 GOSUB 2000,3000,4000
```

The expression evaluates as 2.49, which rounds to 2. This value will cause the program to branch to the subroutine starting at line 3000, which is exactly what we want it to do.

It is often possible to use expressions similar to the preceding one in ON/GOSUB statements. They can often simplify the programming process, but they must be thoroughly tested to make certain that they will always evaluate as expected.

The complete program is shown in Figure VII–3. Note that this main program contains only four executable statements, three of which are used to call subroutines; the fourth statement branches to the end of the program. This is an example of a **driver program,** that is, a program the main purpose of which is to call the subprograms. These subprograms then perform the actual processing.

SINGLE-ENTRY, SINGLE-EXIT SUBROUTINES

Chapter 6 discussed the fact that program structures such as loops, decisions, and subroutines should have only one entry point and one exit point. This is an important principle of structured programming.

A subroutine may be called any number of times in a given program, but it should always be entered at the first line of the subroutine. Branching to the middle of a subroutine makes program logic virtually impossible to follow and often leads to errors.

Figure VII–4 illustrates two program segments, both of which perform the same task. The top segment is incorrectly written, because the IF/THEN/ELSE statement in line 110 can allow control to be passed either to the first line of the subroutine (line 1000) or to the middle of the sub-

● **FIGURE VII–4**
Demonstration of Single-Entry Subroutine Principle

```
00100  INPUT "ENTER YOUR SCORE";PTS
00110  IF PTS > 80 THEN GOSUB 1000 ELSE GOSUB 1060
00120  GOTO 9999
01000  REM
01010  REM ************************************
01020  REM ***              SUBROUTINE          ***
01030  REM ************************************
01040  REM
01050  PRINT "YOU DID VERY WELL!"
01060  PRINT "YOU PASSED THE COURSE."
01080  RETURN
09999  END
```
Incorrectly Written Program Segment With Branch to the Middle of Subroutine

```
00100  INPUT "ENTER YOUR SCORE";PTS
00110  GOSUB 1000
00120  GOTO 9999
01000  REM
01010  REM **************************************
01020  REM ***              SUBROUTINE            ***
01030  REM **************************************
01040  REM
01050  IF PTS > 0 THEN PRINT "YOU DID VERY WELL!"
01060  PRINT "YOU PASSED THE COURSE."
01070  RETURN
09999  END
```
Correctly Written Program Segment With a Single-Entry Point to Subroutine

● **COMPUTERS AND INFORMATION PROCESSING**

routine (line 1060). The bottom example shows how this segment can be correctly written. Note that an IF/THEN statement within the subroutine is used to control execution.

Likewise, a subroutine should contain only one RETURN statement, which should be the last statement of the subroutine. This rule is referred to as the single-exit point principle. At the top of Figure VII–5 is a program segment that is incorrectly written because it contains two RETURN statements, one in line 1050 and one in line 1080. The bottom program segment accomplishes the same task by using an IF/THEN statement (line 1050) to branch to the RETURN statement at the end of the subroutine.

MENUS

Many programming applications require that the user be presented with a list of tasks that the program is able to perform. The use of menus for this purpose has already been discussed in connection with the ON/GOTO statement. The ON/GOSUB statement is also well suited for use with menus. The user can enter a value based on the choices offered in the menu, and the correct subroutine can be executed to perform the desired task.

Figure VII–6 contains a program that uses the ON/GOSUB statement with a menu. When this program is executed, the user is asked to enter

● **FIGURE VII–5**
Demonstration of Single-Exit Subroutine Principle

```
00100 INPUT "ENTER YOUR SCORE";PTS
00110 GOSUB 1010
00120 GOTO 9999
01000 REM
01010 REM ********************************************
01020 REM ***              SUBROUTINE            ***
01030 REM ********************************************
01040 REM
01050 IF PTS < 80 THEN PRINT "YOU FAILED" \ RETURN ELSE PRINT "YOU PASSED"
01060 CREDITHR = CREDITHR + 4
01070 ST$ = "OK"
01080 RETURN
09999 END
```

Incorrectly Written Program Segment With Multiple RETURNs

```
00100 INPUT "ENTER YOUR SCORE";PTS
00110 GOSUB 1000
00120 GOTO 9999
01000 REM
01010 REM ********************************************
01020 REM ***              SUBROUTINE            ***
01030 REM ********************************************
01040 REM
01050 IF PTS < 80 THEN PRINT "YOU FAILED" \ GOTO 1080 ELSE PRINT "YOU PASSED"
01060 CREDITHR = CREDITHR + 4
01070 ST$ = "OK"
01080 RETURN
09999 END
```

Correctly Written Program Segment With a Single RETURN

```
00010 REM ***                    PROGRAM MEAL COST                      ***
00020 REM
00030 REM *** THIS PROGRAM CALCULATES THE COST OF A PURCHASE AT A        ***
00040 REM *** FAST FOOD RESTAURANT.  THE USER ENTERS AN INTEGER AT       ***
00050 REM *** THE KEYBOARD WHICH REPRESENTS THE COST OF A SPECIFIC       ***
00060 REM *** ITEM.  THE USER THEN ENTERS HOW MANY OF THAT ITEM ARE      ***
00070 REM *** DESIRED.  THE COST OF THE ITEM IS THEN CALCULATED.         ***
00080 REM *** THE USER IS THEN ALLOWED TO ENTER ANOTHER ITEM. AFTER      ***
00090 REM *** THE USER HAS ENTERED AN ORDER, THE TOTAL COST OF THE       ***
00100 REM *** ORDER IS PRINTED.                                          ***
00110 REM *** MAJOR VARIABLES:                                           ***
00120 REM *** FOOD           CODE NUMBER TO INDICATE ITEM                ***
00130 REM *** CST            COST OF AN ITEM                             ***
00140 REM *** NUMBER         HOW MANY OF THE CHOSEN ITEM                 ***
00150 REM *** TTCST          TOTAL COST OF THE ORDER                     ***
00160 REM
00170 REM *** INITIALIZE TOTAL COST TO ZERO  ***
00180 TTCST = 0
00190 REM
00200 REM *** PRINT THE MENU  ***
00210 PRINT
00220 PRINT "CODE NUMBER";TAB(25);"ITEM";TAB(52);"COST OF  ITEM"
00230 PRINT
00240 FOR I = 1 TO 80
00250     PRINT "-";
00260 NEXT I
00270 PRINT
00280 PRINT USING 6020,1,"HAMBURGER",0.75
00290 PRINT USING 6020,2,"CHEESEBURGER",0.90
00300 PRINT USING 6020,3,"DRINK",0.50
00310 PRINT USING 6020,4,"FRENCH FRIES",0.55
00320 PRINT
00330 PRINT TAB(6);"5      USED TO INDICATE END OF THE ORDER"
00340 PRINT
00350 FOR I = 1 TO 80
00360     PRINT "-";
00370 NEXT I
00380 PRINT
00390 PRINT
00400 INPUT "ENTER CODE FOR FOOD ITEM (5 TO FINISH) ";FOOD
00410 ON FOOD GOSUB 1000,2000,3000,4000,5000
00420 IF FOOD <> 5 GOTO 200 ELSE GOTO 9999
01000 REM
01010 REM ********************************************************
01020 REM ***              SUBROUTINE HAMBURGERS             ***
01030 REM ********************************************************
01040 REM ***               HAMBURGERS ORDERED               ***
01050 REM
01060 CST = 0.75
01070 INPUT "HOW MANY HAMBURGERS DO YOU DESIRE ";NUMBER
01080 TTCST = TTCST + (CST * NUMBER)
01090 RETURN
02000 REM
02010 REM ********************************************************
02020 REM ***             SUBROUTINE CHEESEBURGERS           ***
02030 REM ********************************************************
02040 REM ***              CHEESEBURGERS ORDERED             ***
02050 REM
02060 CST = 0.90
02070 INPUT "HOW MANY CHEESEBURGERS DO YOU DESIRE ";NUMBER
```

a code number depending on the food item desired. Then the statement in line 410 causes the correct subroutine to be executed depending on the item chosen. Each subroutine prompts the user for the desired quantity of that particular item, calculates the cost, and then adds it to the total cost of the food purchased. If the user enters code number 5, the total bill is printed and the program stops executing. Otherwise, the menu is displayed again so that the user can enter another choice.

USING STUBS TO ENTER PROGRAMS

So far, considerable attention has been given to top-down development of programming problem solutions. It is also possible to use a top-down method when entering a program to the computer. When writing a large program that contains many subroutines, it is poor programming practice to enter the entire program at one time. A far wiser approach is to start by entering the main program (the driver) and one or two subroutines.

● FIGURE VII-6
Continued

```
02080 TTCST = TTCST + (CST * NUMBER)
02090 RETURN
03000 REM
03010 REM ***************************************************
03020 REM ***            SUBROUTINE DRINKS              ***
03030 REM ***************************************************
03040 REM ***             DRINKS ORDERED                ***
03050 REM
03060 CST = 0.50
03070 INPUT "HOW MANY DRINKS DO YOU DESIRE ";NUMBER
03080 TTCST = TTCST + (CST * NUMBER)
03090 RETURN
04000 REM
04010 REM ***************************************************
04020 REM ***          SUBROUTINE FRENCH FRIES          ***
04030 REM ***************************************************
04040 REM ***           FRENCH FRIES ORDERED            ***
04050 REM
04060 CST = 0.55
04070 INPUT "HOW MANY FRENCH FRIES DO YOU DESIRE ";NUMBER
04080 TTCST = TTCST + (CST * NUMBER)
04090 RETURN
05000 REM
05010 REM ***************************************************
05020 REM ***           SUBROUTINE PRINT COST           ***
05030 REM ***************************************************
05040 REM ***          PRINT TOTAL COST OF ORDER        ***
05050 REM
05070 PRINT
05080 PRINT USING 6030,"THE TOTAL COST OF THIS ORDER IS",TTCST
05090 RETURN
06000 REM
06010 REM *** IMAGE STATEMENTS ***
06020 :     #                'LLLLLLLLLLLL          $#.##
06030 :'LLLLLLLLLLLLLLLLLLLLLLLLLLLLLLLL  $$##.##
09999 END
```

(Continued Next Two Pages)

```
RUNNH

CODE NUMBER                ITEM                    COST OF ITEM

--------------------------------------------------------------

        1               HAMBURGER                   $0.75
        2               CHEESEBURGER                $0.90
        3               DRINK                       $0.50
        4               FRENCH FRIES                $0.55

        5       USED TO INDICATE END OF THE ORDER


        ------------------------------------------------------

ENTER CODE FOR FOOD ITEM (5 TO FINISH)  ? 2
HOW MANY CHEESEBURGERS DO YOU DESIRE  ? 4

CODE NUMBER                ITEM                    COST OF ITEM

--------------------------------------------------------------

        1               HAMBURGER                   $0.75
        2               CHEESEBURGER                $0.90
        3               DRINK                       $0.50
        4               FRENCH FRIES                $0.55

        5       USED TO INDICATE END OF THE ORDER


        ------------------------------------------------------

ENTER CODE FOR FOOD ITEM (5 TO FINISH)  ? 3
HOW MANY DRINKS DO YOU DESIRE  ? 2

CODE NUMBER                ITEM                    COST OF ITEM

--------------------------------------------------------------

        1               HAMBURGER                   $0.75
        2               CHEESEBURGER                $0.90
        3               DRINK                       $0.50
        4               FRENCH FRIES                $0.55

        5       USED TO INDICATE END OF THE ORDER


        ------------------------------------------------------

ENTER CODE FOR FOOD ITEM (5 TO FINISH)  ? 4
HOW MANY FRENCH FRIES DO YOU DESIRE  ? 2

CODE NUMBER                ITEM                    COST OF ITEM

--------------------------------------------------------------

        1               HAMBURGER                   $0.75
        2               CHEESEBURGER                $0.90
        3               DRINK                       $0.50
        4               FRENCH FRIES                $0.55

        5       USED TO INDICATE END OF THE ORDER


        ------------------------------------------------------

ENTER CODE FOR FOOD ITEM (5 TO FINISH)  ? 5

THE TOTAL COST OF THIS ORDER IS     $5.70
```

● **FIGURE VII–6**
Continued

MICROCOMPUTERS	DIFFERENCE
Apple	No IF/THEN/ELSE; no PRINT USING; output needs reformatting.
IBM/Microsoft	No separate image statement with PRINT USING.
Macintosh/Microsoft	No separate image statement with PRINT USING.
TRS-80	No separate image statement with PRINT USING.

Subroutines that are not yet implemented are called, but each of these nonimplemented subroutines consists merely of a **stub.** A stub contains a PRINT statement that indicates a given subroutine has been called but is not yet implemented. The stub must also contain a RETURN statement to return control to the main program. The idea is to enter the program in manageable segments, which can then be executed and tested for errors in an orderly way. As segments of the program work properly, more can gradually be added and tested.

Let's see how the program in Figure VII–6 might have been developed in this manner. First, the main program would be typed into the computer. At this point the programmer might also want to enter subroutines 1 and 5. The number of subroutines entered at one time is entirely dependent upon the judgment of the programmer. We have chosen to enter a subroutine that calculates the cost of one of the food items (in this case, hamburgers), and also the subroutine that prints the total bill so that we can check to see if the results obtained by the program are accurate.

Let's assume that lines 10 through 1090 and lines 5000 through 09999 are entered exactly as they appear in Figure VII–6. The rest of the program could be entered like this:

```
02000 PRINT "SUBROUTINE 2 NOT YET IMPLEMENTED"
02010 RETURN
03000 PRINT "SUBROUTINE 3 NOT YET IMPLEMENTED"
03010 RETURN
04000 PRINT "SUBROUTINE 4 NOT YET IMPLEMENTED"
04010 RETURN
```

Therefore, it is possible for the user to order hamburgers and have the total cost of the hamburgers printed. If the user attempts to order cheeseburgers, the following message will appear on the screen.

SUBROUTINE 2 NOT YET IMPLEMENTED

Control will then return to line 420 of the main program. The user will not be prompted to enter the number of cheeseburgers desired, nor will any value be added to the variable containing the total cost of the order. This same thing will happen if the user attempts to order drinks or french fries.

The programmer is now able to determine if the main program, the hamburger subroutine, and the final printing subroutine are working properly. If the total cost printed is incorrect, or if there is some other error, it is much easier to pinpoint the problem than if the entire program had been entered at once. When the programmer is certain that the program is working properly, more subroutines can be gradually added and tested. This method of entering and testing programs greatly simplifies the debugging process, particularly for large programs.

● Checking for Invalid Data

Interactive programs should check to make certain that data entered by the user is valid. If the data is invalid, the program should ask the user to reenter it. For example, in the program in Figure VII–6, the user is asked to enter an integer between 1 and 5. If the user entered a number that was less than 1 or more than 5, the program would not be able to execute properly. In order to protect the program from such an occurrence, the program should check the data entered and make certain that it falls within the allowable range.

The following subroutine shows how this checking can be accomplished. A WHILE/NEXT loop (lines 7050–7090) is used to determine if the value of FOOD is within the valid range. This condition is checked using the logical operator OR:

```
00430 WHILE FOOD < 1 OR FOOD > 5
```

This loop will be executed only if the value of FOOD is less than 1 or greater than 5. Otherwise, the loop will be skipped. If the loop is executed, the user is instructed to reenter a code number, making certain that the number is between 1 and 5.

```
07000 REM *****************************************
07010 REM ***          SUBROUTINE CODE CHECK      ***
07020 REM *****************************************
07030 REM ***          CHECK FOR CODE OF 1 - 5    ***
07040 REM
07050 WHILE FOOD < 1 OR FOOD > 5
07060     PRINT "CODE MUST BE AN INTEGER"
07070     PRINT "BETWEEN 1 AND 5."
07080     INPUT "PLEASE REENTER CODE";FOOD
07090 NEXT
07100 RETURN
```

In programs that are not interactive, invalid data must be handled in a different manner. Suppose that the program in Figure VII–6 had been written using READ/DATA statements instead of INPUT statements. How could the programmer handle data outside the allowable range?

One method is to ignore the invalid data item and go on to the next item. An error message could be printed, stating that an invalid data item was encountered and ignored. Another method is to print an error message and stop program execution prematurely. For example, if the value 7 was entered in this example, a message such as INVALID VALUE ENTERED TO VARIABLE FOOD could be printed. Program execution could then be terminated by the STOP statement, which has the following format:

line# STOP

The STOP statement differs from the END statement in that STOP can appear as often as necessary in a program, whereas the END statement can appear only once. Also, on the DECsystem, the END statement must have the highest line number, whereas the STOP statement can have any line number. When the STOP statement is executed, the computer prints a message similar to the following:

```
STOP at line 00310 of MAIN PROGRAM
```

This type of error checking is a feature of any well-written program. From this point on, you should attempt to write programs that are protected as much as possible from invalid input.

● A Programming Problem

PROBLEM DEFINITION

The public library needs a program to calculate the total cost of the books it adds to its collection. This cost includes not only the purchase price of the book but also the cost of processing the book. The program should be interactive, allowing the librarians to enter the data at the keyboard. The total book cost should then be printed on the terminal screen.

Processing costs are dependent upon two factors: (1) the type of book (reference, circulating, or paperback), and (2) whether or not the book is a duplicate of one already in the library. It is cheaper to process books that are duplicates of those already in the library's collection, because cards for these books are already in the card catalog and the cost of card production is saved. Processing costs are as follows:

Reference book
not a duplicate	$8.50
duplicate	$7.40

Circulating book
not a duplicate	$7.82
duplicate	$6.60
bestseller	$1.75 additional

Paperback
not a duplicate	$4.60
duplicate	$3.10

The type of book should be entered using an integer code:

1—Reference
2—Circulating
3—Paperback

Note the additional $1.75 cost for processing circulating books that are also bestsellers. This cost is for a plastic cover to give the book extra protection. The necessary input and output for this program are shown in the following example:

Input:

Price	Type of Book	Duplicate	Bestseller (applies to code 2 only)
25.39	2	N	N

Needed Output:

TOTAL COST: $33.21

SOLUTION DESIGN

Each time this program is executed, it will calculate the total cost (purchase price plus processing cost) of one book. The program needs four input variables. These input variables are one numeric variable for the price of the book, another numeric variable to represent the book code, a character string variable to store a Y if the book is a duplicate and an N if it is not, and, if the book code entered is a 2, a character string variable to indicate whether the book is a bestseller. The output variable will be a numeric variable containing the total cost. The needed variables are summarized in the following table:

Input Variables

price of book	(PRICE)
code for type of book	(CODE)
duplicate indicator	(DUP$)
best seller indicator	(SELLER$)

Program Variables

processing cost	(PRCST)

Output Variables

total cost	(TTCST)

Three basic steps are necessary to determine the total book costs:

1. Enter the data for the book.
2. Calculate the correct processing cost.
3. Determine the total cost.

Step 1 can be divided into three substeps that ask the user to enter the price of the book, the code for the type of book, and the duplicate indicator. This step should also include checking to make certain that the values entered for the book code and the duplicate indicator are valid. If an invalid value has been entered, the user should be prompted to reenter that value. Since each of these substeps is relatively simple, when we write the program we will include them all in a single subroutine.

Step 2 is the most difficult part of this problem. It involves performing one of three options, depending on whether a reference, circulating, or paper book is being processed. Because only one of these options will be executed, this is an ideal situation for a conditional branch to one of three subroutines, each of which will calculate the cost for a particular type of book. The book type code can be used as the controlling expression in an ON/GOSUB statement to transfer program control from the main program to the appropriate subroutine.

Step 3 involves adding the processing cost to the purchase price of the book and printing this total.

The basic steps to solve the problem can be further divided as follows:

1. a. Enter the price of the book.
1. b. Enter the code for the type of book.
1. c. Enter the duplicate indicator.
3. a. Add processing cost to book price.
3. b. Print the total cost.

The structure chart for this solution is shown in Figure VII–7.

THE PROGRAM

Study the complete program as shown in Figure VII–8. Note that the main body of the program is a driver program and is therefore quite short.

The first subroutine enables the user to enter the necessary data. This subroutine contains two WHILE/NEXT loops that check for invalid data. The first loop (lines 1150–1180) allows the user to reenter the value of the type code if an invalid code has been entered. The second loop (lines 1220–1250) makes certain that the user has entered either a Y or an N as the duplicate book indicator. If a different value has been entered, the user is asked to reenter the data.

The value entered for the book type code must be a 1, 2, or 3. This value is then used in the ON/GOSUB statement in line 310 to determine which one of the three subroutines will be executed. Each of the subroutines calculates the processing cost for one type of book. The circulating book subroutine is a little more complicated than the other two, because it must ask the user if the book is a bestseller and include an additional charge if it is. After the processing cost of the book has been determined, control returns to the main program, where the final subroutine is called to add the processing cost to the purchase price and print the total cost.

● **FIGURE VII–7**
Structure Chart for Book Processing Cost Problem

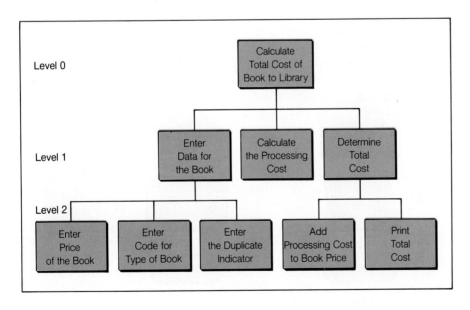

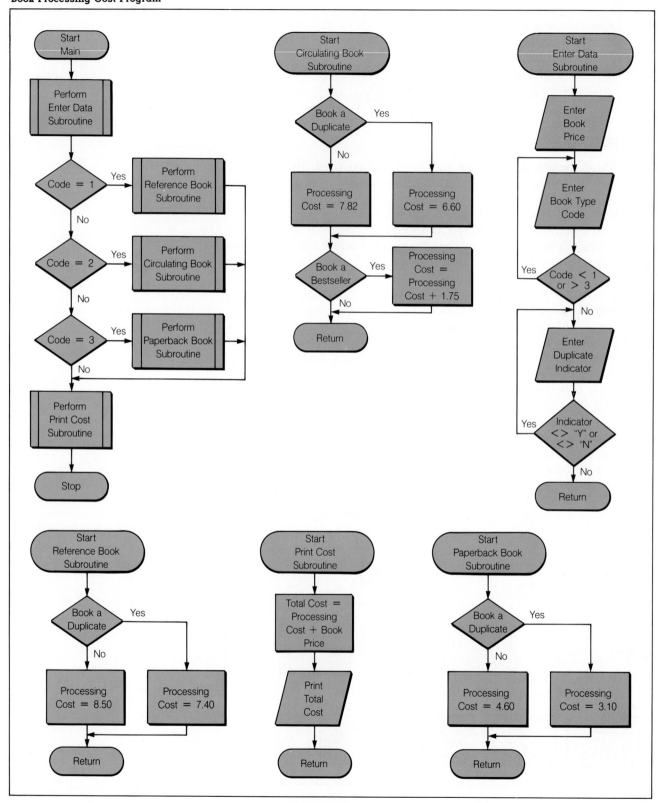

Pseudocode

Begin main program
Perform enter data subroutine
If type code = 1 perform reference book subroutine
If type code = 2 perform circulating book subroutine
If type code = 3 perform paperback book subroutine
Perform print cost subroutine
End main program

Begin enter data subroutine
Prompt user to enter price
Prompt user to enter type code
Begin loop, do until code >= 1 and <= 3
    Prompt user to reenter type code
End loop
Prompt user to enter duplicate indicator
Begin loop, do until indicator is equal to "Y" or "N"
    Prompt user to reenter duplicate code
End loop
End enter data subroutine

Begin reference book subroutine
If book is duplicate
    Then processing cost = 7.40
    Else processing cost = 8.50
End if
End reference book subroutine

Begin circulating book subroutine
If book is duplicate
    Then processing cost = 6.60
    Else processing cost = 7.82
End if
Prompt user to enter bestseller indicator
If book is a bestseller
    Then add 1.75 to processing cost
End if
End circulating book subroutine

Begin paperback book subroutine
If book is duplicate
    The processing cost = 3.10
    Else processing cost = 4.60
End if
End paperback book subroutine

Begin print cost subroutine
Total cost = processing cost + book price
Print total cost
End print cost subroutine

```
00010 REM ***                  PROGRAM BOOKCOST           ***
00020 REM
00030 REM ***   THIS PROGRAM CALCULATES THE TOTAL COST    ***
00040 REM *** OF A BOOK. THE TOTAL COST IS OBTAINED BY    ***
00050 REM *** ADDING THE PRICE OF THE BOOK TO THE PRO-    ***
00060 REM *** CESSING COST, WHICH IS BASED ON THE TYPE.   ***
00070 REM ***       1.   REFERENCE BOOK                   ***
00080 REM ***              NOT A DUPLICATE    $8.50       ***
00090 REM ***              DUPLICATE          $7.40       ***
00100 REM ***       2.   CIRCULATING BOOK                 ***
00110 REM ***              NOT A DUPLICATE    $7.82       ***
00120 REM ***              DUPLICATE          $6.60       ***
00130 REM ***              BESTSELLER         $1.75       ***
00140 REM ***       3.   PAPERBACK                        ***
00150 REM ***              NOT A DUPLICATE    $4.60       ***
00160 REM ***              DUPLICATE          $3.10       ***
00170 REM
00180 REM *** MAJOR VARIABLES:                            ***
00190 REM *** PRICE          PRICE OF THE BOOK            ***
00200 REM *** CODE           TYPE OF BOOK AS ABOVE        ***
00210 REM *** DUP$           IS BOOK A DUPLICATE(Y/N)?    ***
00220 REM *** PRCST          PROCESSING COST              ***
00230 REM *** SELLER$        IS BOOK A BESTSELLER(Y/N)?   ***
00240 REM *** TTCST          TOTAL COST OF BOOK           ***
00250 REM
00260 REM *** CALL SUBROUTINE TO ENTER DATA               ***
00270 GOSUB 1000
00280 REM
```

```
00290 REM *** CALL APPROPRIATE SUBROUTINE TO CALCULATE ***
00300 REM *** THE PROCESSING COST                       ***
00310 ON CODE GOSUB 2000,3000,4000
00320 REM
00330 REM *** CALL SUBROUTINE TO ADD PROCESSING COST    ***
00340 REM *** TO BOOK PRICE AND PRINT TOTAL COST        ***
00350 GOSUB 5000
00360 GOTO 9999
01000 REM
01010 REM *********************************************
01020 REM ***           SUBROUTINE ENTER DATA        ***
01030 REM *********************************************
01040 REM *** SUBROUTINE TO ALLOW USER TO ENTER DATA ***
01050 REM
01060 INPUT "ENTER PRICE OF THE BOOK";PRICE
01070 PRINT
01080 PRINT
01090 PRINT
01100 PRINT "1 - REFERENCE BOOK"
01110 PRINT "2 - CIRCULATING BOOK"
01120 PRINT "3 - PAPERBACK"
01130 INPUT "ENTER TYPE CODE FOR THE BOOK, USING THE CODES LISTED ABOVE";CODE
01140 REM
01150 REM ** LOOP TO ALLOW CODE TO BE REENTERED IF CURRENT ENTRY IS INVALID ***
01160 WHILE CODE < 1 OR CODE > 3
01170    INPUT "TYPE CODE MUST BE A 1, 2, OR 3.  PLEASE REENTER CODE";CODE
01180 NEXT
01190 PRINT
01200 INPUT "IS BOOK A DUPLICATE (Y/N)";DUP$
01210 REM
01220 REM *** LOOP TO ALLOW DUPLICATE INDICATOR TO BE REENTERED, IF INVALID ***
01230 WHILE DUP$ <> "Y" AND DUP$ <> "N"
01240    INPUT "IS BOOK A DUPLICATE?  PLEASE ENTER A 'Y' OR AN 'N'";DUP$
01250 NEXT
01260 RETURN
02000 REM
02010 REM *********************************************
02020 REM ***         SUBROUTINE REFERENCE BOOK      ***
02030 REM *********************************************
02040 REM *** SUBROUTINE TO CALCULATE PROCESSING COST ***
02050 REM *** OF REFERENCE BOOK                       ***
02060 REM
02070 IF DUP$ = "Y" THEN PRCST = 7.40 ELSE PRCST = 8.50
02080 RETURN
03000 REM
03010 REM *********************************************
03020 REM ***        SUBROUTINE CIRCULATING BOOK     ***
03030 REM *********************************************
03040 REM *** SUBROUTINE TO CALCULATE PROCESSING COST ***
03050 REM *** OF CIRCULATING BOOK                     ***
03060 REM
03070 IF DUP$ = "Y" THEN PRCST = 6.60 ELSE PRCST = 7.82
03080 INPUT "IS THE BOOK A BESTSELLER (Y/N)?";SELLER$
03090 IF SELLER$ = "Y" THEN PRCST = PRCST + 1.75
03100 RETURN
04000 REM
04010 REM *********************************************
04020 REM ***         SUBROUTINE PAPERBACK BOOK      ***
04030 REM *********************************************
04040 REM *** SUBROUTINE TO CALCULATE PROCESSING COST ***
```

```
04050 REM *** OF PAPERBACK BOOK                          ***
04060 REM
04070 IF DUP$ = "Y" THEN PRCST = 3.10 ELSE PRCST = 4.60
04080 RETURN
05000 REM
05010 REM *****************************************************
05020 REM ***              SUBROUTINE PRINT COST          ***
05030 REM *****************************************************
05040 REM *** SUBROUTINE TO CALCULATE AND PRINT TOTAL  ***
05050 REM *** COST                                     ***
05060 REM
05070 TTCST = PRCST + PRICE
05080 PRINT
05090 PRINT USING 5120,"***    TOTAL COST:",TTCST
05100 RETURN
05110 REM *** IMAGE STATEMENT ***
05120 : 'LLLLLLLLLLLLLLLLLLL   $$##.##
09999 END
```

```
RUNNH
ENTER PRICE OF THE BOOK ? 25.39


1 - REFERENCE BOOK
2 - CIRCULATING BOOK
3 - PAPERBACK
ENTER TYPE CODE FOR THE BOOK, USING THE CODES LISTED ABOVE ? 2

IS BOOK A DUPLICATE (Y/N) ? J
IS BOOK A DUPLICATE?  PLEASE ENTER A 'Y' OR AN 'N' ? N
IS THE BOOK A BESTSELLER (Y/N)? ? N

 ***    TOTAL COST:       $33.21
```

MICROCOMPUTERS	DIFFERENCE
Apple	No IF/THEN/ELSE, no PRINT USING
IBM/Microsoft	No separate image statement with PRINT USING
Macintosh/Microsoft	No separate image statement with PRINT USING
TRS-80	No separate image statement with PRINT USING

◉ Summary Points

● Modularizing programs involves dividing them into subprograms, each of which performs a specific task. In BASIC, these subprograms or modules are referred to as subroutines.

● The use of subroutines makes program logic easier to follow. Also, a given subroutine can be called any number of times.

● Two BASIC statements can be used to call subroutines: GOSUB and ON/GOSUB.

● The GOSUB statement is an unconditional branch that causes the flow of execution to be passed to the line number contained in the GOSUB statement.

● The RETURN statement causes control to be transferred back to the statement after the one that called the subroutine.

● The ON/GOSUB statement allows for a conditional branch to one of several stated subroutines, depending on the evaluation of the expression in the ON/GOSUB statement. If the value of the expression is n, control passes to the subroutine starting at the nth line number listed.

● An important rule in structured programming is that all subroutines should have a single entry point and a single exit point. Otherwise, the possibility of an error in the program is greatly increased. Also, entering or exiting from the middle of a subroutine makes the logic of the program convoluted and difficult to follow.

● Menus often use the ON/GOSUB statement, which provides a simple way for the program to branch to the correct subroutine depending on the code number entered by the user.

● Stubs allow a program to be developed in a methodical fashion. Rather than entering a program to the computer all at once, the programmer can add and test subroutines gradually. Once the parts already entered work properly, more of the program can be entered. This procedure makes it easier to locate program errors.

● All programs should check for invalid data and print an error message if any is found. In interactive programs, the user can be prompted to reenter the data.

Review Questions

1. Name two advantages of modularizing programs.

2. How can a structure chart help in modularizing a program?

3. Why doesn't the RETURN statement contain a transfer line number? That is, how is it possible that program control can be transferred back to the correct statement even though no transfer line number is specified in the RETURN statement?

4. Where are RETURN statements placed in programs?

5. Why is the GOSUB statement referred to as an unconditional branching statement?

6. What happens if the transfer line number in a GOSUB statement is a nonexecutable statement?

7. Why is it important that a subroutine have only one entry point and one exit point?

8. Explain how the ON/GOSUB statement works. How is it different from the GOSUB statement?

9. What is a driver program?

10. How can stubs be used when entering programs to the computer?

Debugging Exercises

Identify the following programs and program segments that contain errors and debug them.

1.
```
00100 INPUT "ENTER THE STUDENT'S GRADE";PTS$
00110 ON PTS$ GOSUB 2000,3000,4000,5000
```

2.
```
00010 INPUT "ENTER THE INTEGER VALUE OF THE MONTH";MNTH
00020 WHILE (MNTH > 1) OR (MNTH > 12)
00030    PRINT "PLEASE ENTER THE INTEGER"
00040    PRINT "BETWEEN 1 AND 12 THAT"
00050    INPUT "REPRESENTS THE MONTH";MNTH
00060 NEXT
00070 PRINT MNTH
```

Programming Problems

1. World Travel wants a program that displays a menu with a list of countries to which the agency can send a customer with special discount rates. After the user enters the name of a particular country, the program should print all cities in that country in which the special rates are available. Use the following data:

Country	Cities
France	Nice
	Cannes
	Nantes
	Chamonix
Italy	Milan
	Verona
	Venice
	Naples
U.S.A.	Chicago
	San Francisco
	New York
	Miami

2. Budget Balloons provides hot-air balloon rides for fairs, parties, and other special occasions. The basic fee is $65.00 for the first hour and $45.00 for every additional hour. The company needs a program to help calculate its clients' bills. The program should call a subroutine to do the actual calculating, and use a loop to allow as many bills to be calculated as desired. The output of the program should include the name of the client and his or her total bill.

3. The R & R Railways wants a program to determine the cost for passengers to various cities. The cost per person for the following cities is as follows:

Columbus	$ 39.00
Denver	142.00
New York	108.00
New Orleans	158.00

A menu should display the names of the cities and ask how many people would like to purchase tickets. If a customer wants first-class tickets, there is an additional $30.00 flat fee. The cost of the needed tickets should be calculated in subroutines. Develop your own data to test the program.

4. As the manager of an apartment building, you need a program to help you keep track of the various apartments for rent. Write a program using subroutines which will give the user a choice of a studio, one-bedroom, or two-bedroom apartment. The monthly rent depends on the size of the apartment and whether it is to be furnished or unfurnished (this data should also be entered by the user). Use the following data:

Type	Rent Deposit	Furnished	Unfurnished
Studio	$ 75	$150	$135
One-bedroom	150	275	250
Two-bedroom	200	325	315

The program should print the apartment description, required deposit, and monthly rent according to the choices entered, using the following format:

Description: One-bedroom furnished
Deposit $150
Rent: $275

5. Dan's yard care business needs a program to help with the billing of its customers. The user should be able to enter the due date for all bills to be processed. For each customer, enter a name, address, and the applicable charges selected from the following list:

Lawn mow	$15.00
Tree trim	12.00
Hedge/bush trim	10.00
Edging	7.00

All customers receive the standard service of a lawn mow. The program should print an itemized bill showing the total amount due and the amount owed for late payment, which is the total plus 5 percent. Use your own test data. Your output should resemble the following:

Name: Cummings, E.   Due Date: 09/17/87
Address: 445 Cherry St.

Services:

Lawn mow	$15.00
Hedge/bush trim	10.00
Edging	7.00
Total amount due:	$32.00
After due date:	$33.60

●Section VIII
Functions

● Introduction

A useful feature of BASIC is the **function,** a subprogram designed to perform a specific task and return a single value. BASIC has numerous **library functions,** or built-in functions, which perform common mathematical operations, such as finding the square root of a number or its absolute value. Other library functions operate on character strings, performing tasks such as finding the length of a string. These functions are also called **intrinsic** or **predefined functions.** They are useful to the programmer, who is spared the necessity of writing the sequence of statements otherwise needed to perform these operations. In some cases, however, it is useful for the programmer to write a function to meet a particular need. Functions that are written by the programmer are called **user-defined functions.** This section discusses both library functions and user-defined functions.

● Library Functions

Library functions are those that have been built into the BASIC language and included in the BASIC language library, where the programmer can easily reference them. In order to use a library function in a program, the programmer must call or reference the function, just as a subroutine must be called by the main program. The general format of a function call is as follows:

function name (argument)

The **argument** required within the parentheses is the value needed by the function to obtain a result, and can consist of the following:

- A constant
- A variable
- Another function
- Expressions involving any of the preceding

The type of argument depends on the function used. The function performs its specific task, using the argument value, and returns a single value to the calling program.

A function call can be used in a BASIC statement in the place of a constant, a variable, or an expression. A function call evaluates as a single value and cannot be used to the left of an equal sign. For example, the function that finds the square root of a number, SQR, could be used in the following statement that assigns the value 5 to the variable SUM:

```
00060 SUM = SQR(4) + 3
```

The following statement would be invalid, however, because it attempts to assign the value of SUM plus 3 to the value 2 (the square root of 4):

```
00060 SQR(4) = SUM + 3
```

When a function call occurs in a statement, it is evaluated before any other operations in the statement are evaluated. Therefore, a function call has a higher priority than arithmetic, relational, and logical operators.

There are two categories of BASIC library functions: numeric functions and string functions. Some of the numeric functions available on most systems will be discussed first.

NUMERIC FUNCTIONS

Table VIII–1 shows eleven common numeric functions that are available on most systems and used by all of the systems discussed in this text.

The Trigonometric Functions

Four of these functions—SIN, COS, TAN, and ATN—are trigonometric functions used in mathematical, engineering, and scientific applications. The argument for these functions is an angle measure given in radians; however, often a trigonometric problem is more easily understood using degrees. You may convert from one unit to the other as follows.

Radians to degrees:
1 radian = 57.29578 degrees
N radians = N * 57.29578 degrees

● **TABLE VIII–1**
Numeric Functions

FUNCTION	OPERATION
ABS (X)	Absolute value of X
ATN (X)	Trigonometric arc tangent of X radians
COS (X)	Trigonometric cosine of X radians
EXP (X)	e^x
INT (X)	Greatest integer less than or equal to X
LOG (X)	Natural logarithm (if $x = e^y$, LOG (X) = Y)
RND	Random number between 0 and 1
SGN (X)	Sign of X: $+1$ if $X > 0$, 0 if $X = 0$, -1 if $X < 0$
SIN (X)	Trigonometric sine of X radians
SQR (X)	Square root of X
TAN (X)	Trigonometric tangent of X radians

To convert 2.5 radians to degrees, for example, multiply 2.5 by 57.29578. The product is approximately 143 degrees.

Degrees to radians:
1 degree = 0.01745 radians
N degrees = N * 0.01745 radians

To convert 180 degrees to radians, multiply 180 by 0.01745. The result is equal to π (approximately 3.14 radians).

The Exponential Function

The exponential or EXP function performs the calculation EXP $(X) = e^x$. The constant e is equal to approximately 2.718. For example, the following statement assigns the value e^x to Y:

```
00050 Y = EXP(X)
```

The Natural Logarithm Function

The natural logarithm or LOG function is the reverse of the EXP function. For example, if $X = e^y$, then LOG $(X) = Y$. In other words, Y (the natural logarithm of X) is the power that e is raised to in order to find X. If we know X but need to know the value of Y, we can use the following statement to assign the natural logarithm of X to Y:

```
00030 Y = LOG(X)
```

The argument of the LOG function must be a positive real number.

The Square Root Function

The square root or SQR function determines the positive square root of its argument. In most BASIC implementations, the argument must be a nonnegative number (the Apple, which requires that the argument be greater than zero, is the only exception among the systems discussed in this book). The following examples illustrate the SQR function:

Statement	Result
`00020 Y = SQR(X)`	$Y = \sqrt{X}$
`00050 Z = SQR(SQR(16))`	$Z = 2$
`00030 T = SQR((A * B) / (A - C))`	$T = \sqrt{\dfrac{AB}{A - C}}$

The Integer Function

The integer, or INT, function computes the largest integer less than or equal to the argument value. For example:

X	INT (X)
8	8
5.34	5
16.9	16
-2.75	-3
-0.5	-1

If the argument is a positive value with a fractional part, the digits to the right of the decimal point are truncated (cut off). Notice from the preceding examples that truncation does not occur when the argument is negative. For instance, when the argument equals −2.75, the INT function returns −3, the largest integer *less than or equal to* that value. This fact can be seen on the number line, where the farther to the left a number lies, the less value it has:

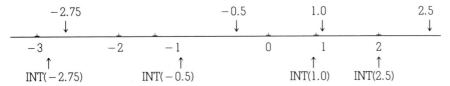

Although the INT function alone does not round its argument, it can be used in an expression that rounds to the nearest integer, nearest tenth, or nearest hundredth, or to any other degree of accuracy desired. The program in Figure VIII–1 rounds a number to the nearest integer, as shown in line 50. Line 60 rounds the same number to the nearest tenth, by adding 0.05 to the number and multiplying the result by 10. Then the INT function is applied and the result is divided by 10. The steps to round the number to the nearest hundredth follow the same pattern in line 70, but instead add 0.005 and multiply and divide by 100.

The Sign Function

The sign or SGN function determines the sign of a number. If $X > 0$, then SGN $(X) = 1$; if $X = 0$, then SGN $(X) = 0$; and if $X < 0$, then SGN $(X) = -1$. For example:

X	SGN (X)
8.5	1
0	0
−5.02	−1
−1005	−1

The Absolute Value Function

The absolute value or ABS function returns the absolute value of its argument. Remember that the absolute value is always positive or zero; if the argument has a negative value, the ABS function serves to remove the negative sign. For example:

X	ABS (X)
−2	2
0	0
3.54	3.54
−2.75	2.75

This function is often used to identify significant differences between given values. For example, the Internal Revenue Service may want to know which individuals owe the government a substantial sum or are owed a substantial sum by the government. The program in Figure

VIII–2 demonstrates how the absolute value function might be used to identify such individuals. Line 50 tests for persons who either owe or are being refunded at least $1,000.00.

The Random Number Function

The random number or RND function produces a random number between 0 and 1. The term **random** means that any value in a given set of values is equally likely to occur. The function is useful for any situation requiring an input quantity of which the exact value is unpredictable.

● **FIGURE VIII–1**
Rounding with the INT Function

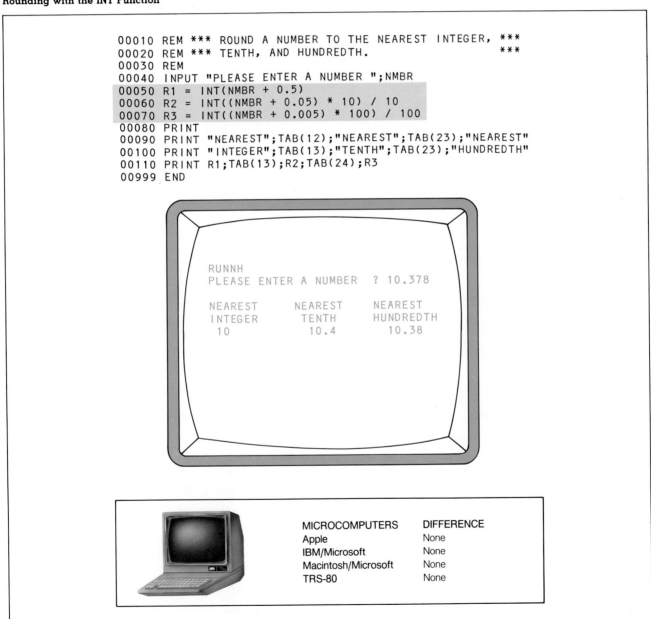

```
00010 REM *** ROUND A NUMBER TO THE NEAREST INTEGER, ***
00020 REM *** TENTH, AND HUNDREDTH.                   ***
00030 REM
00040 INPUT "PLEASE ENTER A NUMBER ";NMBR
00050 R1 = INT(NMBR + 0.5)
00060 R2 = INT((NMBR + 0.05) * 10) / 10
00070 R3 = INT((NMBR + 0.005) * 100) / 100
00080 PRINT
00090 PRINT "NEAREST";TAB(12);"NEAREST";TAB(23);"NEAREST"
00100 PRINT "INTEGER";TAB(13);"TENTH";TAB(23);"HUNDREDTH"
00110 PRINT R1;TAB(13);R2;TAB(24);R3
00999 END
```

```
RUNNH
PLEASE ENTER A NUMBER  ? 10.378

NEAREST       NEAREST       NEAREST
INTEGER       TENTH         HUNDREDTH
 10            10.4          10.38
```

MICROCOMPUTERS	DIFFERENCE
Apple	None
IBM/Microsoft	None
Macintosh/Microsoft	None
TRS-80	None

● **COMPUTERS AND INFORMATION PROCESSING**

The RND function is particularly important in applications involving statistics, computer simulations, and games.

At first it might not seem hard to produce random values. This task is difficult, however, for machines of very precise structure and logic (such as computers). The numbers produced by a computer are not truly random, such as those resulting from a throw of dice, but are more accurately described as pseudorandom. In order to produce a sequence of seemingly unrelated numbers, the RND function uses a special algorithm that differs among the various computer manufacturers. The particular sequence of numbers generated by this algorithm depends on a value

● **FIGURE VIII–2**
Program Demonstrating the ABS Function

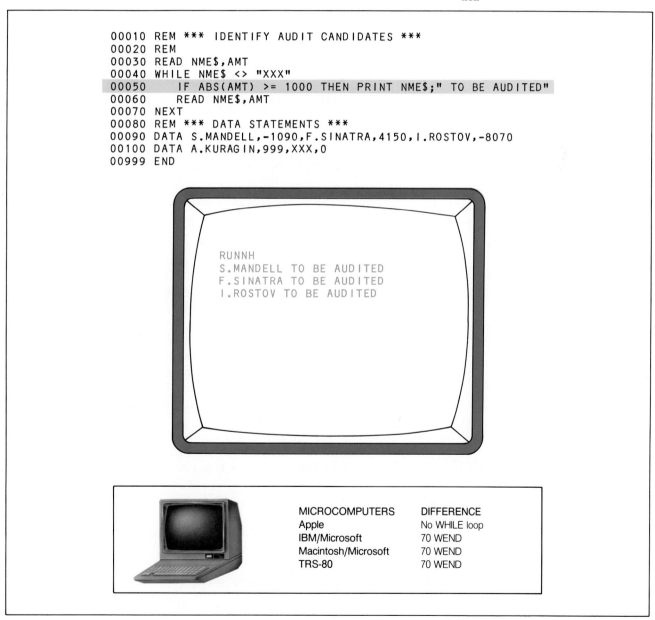

```
00010 REM *** IDENTIFY AUDIT CANDIDATES ***
00020 REM
00030 READ NME$,AMT
00040 WHILE NME$ <> "XXX"
00050    IF ABS(AMT) >= 1000 THEN PRINT NME$;" TO BE AUDITED"
00060    READ NME$,AMT
00070 NEXT
00080 REM *** DATA STATEMENTS ***
00090 DATA S.MANDELL,-1090,F.SINATRA,4150,I.ROSTOV,-8070
00100 DATA A.KURAGIN,999,XXX,0
00999 END
```

```
RUNNH
S.MANDELL TO BE AUDITED
F.SINATRA TO BE AUDITED
I.ROSTOV TO BE AUDITED
```

MICROCOMPUTERS	DIFFERENCE
Apple	No WHILE loop
IBM/Microsoft	70 WEND
Macintosh/Microsoft	70 WEND
TRS-80	70 WEND

● BASIC Extensions
CINT Function

The Apple Macintosh and the IBM/Microsoft allow the use of the CINT function which is useful when rounding. The format of the CINT function is shown below:

line# Y = CINT(X)

The CINT function converts X to an integer by rounding the fraction portion of the number. X must be within the range of −32768 to 32767 or else an overflow error will occur.

An example of the CINT function is shown below.

```
10 PRINT "NUMBER","INTEGER"
20 FOR I = 1 TO 3
30    READ N
40    C = CINT(N)
50    PRINT N,C
60 NEXT I
70 DATA 5.2980734,778.98,64.5
99 END


RUN
NUMBER          INTEGER
 5.298074       5
 778.98         779
 64.5           65
```

known as a seed. When a new seed value is supplied to the algorithm, a new sequence of numbers is produced. If the seed is never changed, however, a program containing the RND function produces the same series of "random" numbers each time it is run.

The method used to reseed the random number generator varies among different computers. Often the seed is obtained from the computer's internal clock (e.g., the number of seconds after midnight) or is supplied by the program user. Some systems require that the RND function be used with an argument; other systems do not. The box "Random Numbers" shows how you can obtain random numbers between 0 and 1 on the systems considered in this text.

Random numbers greater than 1 can be produced by combining the RND function with other mathematical operations. The following formula generates a real random number R between L (low limit) and H (high limit):

R = RND * (H − L) + L

A formula to generate a random integer 1 between L and H is:

1 = INT (RND * (H − L) + L)

If the range of the random integer should include L and H, the value 1 is added to H − L as follows:

1 = INT (RND * (H − L + 1) + L)

● COMPUTERS AND INFORMATION PROCESSING

● Random Numbers

Random numbers between 0 and 1 can be obtained as follows.

DECSYSTEM

The RND function needs no argument with the DECsystem. The function gives the same numbers each time the program is run unless it is reseeded: therefore, these numbers are not truly random. Once a program is working correctly, the RANDOMIZE statement can be inserted before the statement containing RND. The RANDOMIZE statement automatically reseeds the random number generator, thus causing the RND function to produce different numbers each time the program is run. An example follows:

```
00030 RANDOMIZE
      .
      .
      .
00060 X = RND
```

APPLE

Only one statement is needed with the Apple computer to produce different numbers each time the program runs. The RND function requires one argument; the sign and value of the argument affect the result. A positive argument, as in the following example, returns a random real number greater than or equal to 0 and less than 1:

```
10 X = RND(3)
```

If the argument is 0, as in the following example, the most recently generated random number is returned.

```
10 X = RND(0)
```

If the argument is negative, a particular random number sequence is started that is the same every time RND is used with that negative argument:

```
10 X = RND(-4)
```

If a RND call with a positive argument follows a RND call with a negative argument, it will generate the particular, repeatable sequence of numbers peculiar to the negative argument. Each different negative argument starts a different repeatable sequence.

IBM

As with the DECsystem, the RND function used alone on the IBM produces the same sequence of numbers each time the program runs. Used without an argument or with an optional positive argument, the RND function generates a random number between 0 and 1.

As with the Apple, an argument of 0 gives the last random number generated, and a negative argument begins a particular sequence that is the same every time that negative argument is used.

The RANDOMIZE statement is needed to provide a new random number seed and therefore give a truly random result. The format of this statement with the IBM is as follows:

RANDOMIZE [integer]
    or
RANDOMIZE TIMER

The integer, if used, must be changed each time the program runs to produce new numbers. If the integer is omitted, the prompt message

Random Number Seed (−32768 to 32767)?

asks the user to enter a number within this range.

If the function name TIMER is specified, a new number seed determined by the computer's clock is generated for each program run and no prompt appears. For example:

```
10 RANDOMIZE TIMER
20 PRINT RND
```

MACINTOSH

The RND function on the Macintosh works in the same manner as described for the IBM.

TRS-80

The RND function requires an argument of 0 to obtain a number between 0 and 1. The RANDOM statement serves to reseed the random number generator, and must precede the RND to give a truly random result. An example follows:

```
20 RANDOM
     .
     .
     .
60 X = RND(0)
```

The program in Figure VIII–3 shows how these formulas can be used to generate random numbers in any given range.

STRING FUNCTIONS

Up to this point, we have manipulated numbers but have done little with strings except print them out or compare them in IF and THEN tests. Many business applications require more sophisticated manipulations of strings.

A string is simply a series of alphanumeric characters such as #OJQ$P or HORNBLOWER, H. Usually, BASIC requires that quotation marks be placed around strings.

BASIC string functions allow programmers to modify, **concatenate** (join together), compare, and analyze the composition of strings. These functions are useful for sorting lists of names, finding out subject matter in text, printing mailing lists, and so forth. For example, we can help the computer understand that John J. Simmons is the same as Simmons, John J. The most common string functions are listed in Table VIII–2.

Concatenation

It is possible to join strings together using the concatenation function. In business this is often desirable when working with names or addresses. The plus sign (+) serves as the concatenation operator. For example, the statement

```
00020 A$ = "NIGHT" + "MARE"
```

● **FIGURE VIII–3**
Random Number Program

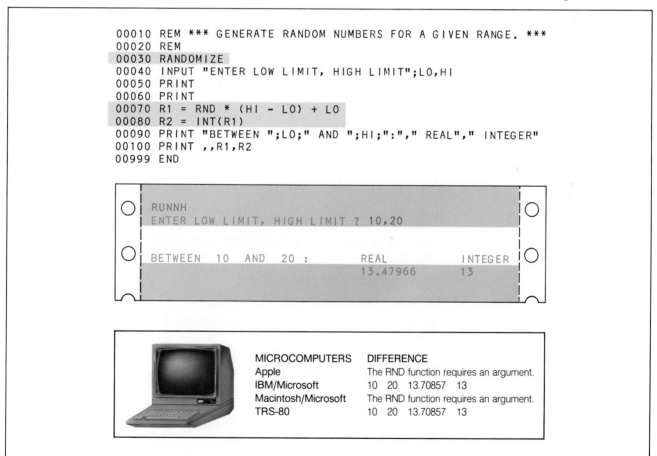

```
00010 REM *** GENERATE RANDOM NUMBERS FOR A GIVEN RANGE. ***
00020 REM
00030 RANDOMIZE
00040 INPUT "ENTER LOW LIMIT, HIGH LIMIT";LO,HI
00050 PRINT
00060 PRINT
00070 R1 = RND * (HI - LO) + LO
00080 R2 = INT(R1)
00090 PRINT "BETWEEN ";LO;" AND ";HI;":"," REAL"," INTEGER"
00100 PRINT ,,R1,R2
00999 END
```

```
RUNNH
ENTER LOW LIMIT, HIGH LIMIT ? 10,20


BETWEEN   10   AND   20 :        REAL            INTEGER
                                 13.47966        13
```

MICROCOMPUTERS	DIFFERENCE
Apple	The RND function requires an argument.
IBM/Microsoft	10 20 13.70857 13
Macintosh/Microsoft	The RND function requires an argument.
TRS-80	10 20 13.70857 13

FUNCTION	OPERATION	EXAMPLE
string1 + string2	Concatenation; joins two strings	"KUNG" + "FU" is "KUNG FU"
ASCII (string) or ASC (string)	Returns the ASCII code for the first character in the string	IF A$ = "DOG", THEN ASCII (A$) is 68
CHR$ (integer expression)	Returns the string representation of the ASCII code of the expression	CHR$(68) is "D"
LEFT$ (string, integer expression)	Returns the number of leftmost characters of a string specified by the expression	LEFT$("ABCD",2) is "AB"
LEN (string)	Returns the length of a string	IF N$ = "HI THERE", THEN LEN(N$) is 8
MID$ (string, expression1, expression2)	Starting with the character at expression1, returns the number of characters specified by expression2	MID$("MARIE",2,3) is "ARI"
RIGHT$(string, expression)	*DEC:* Returns the rightmost characters of a string, starting with character specified by the expression *Micros:* Returns the number of rightmost characters specified by the expression	RIGHT$("ABCDE",2) is "BCDE" RIGHT$("ABCDE",2) is "DE"
STR$(expression)	Converts a number to its string equivalent	STR$(123) is "123"
VAL(string)	Returns the numeric value of a number string	IF N$ = "352 63" THEN VAL(N$) is 35263

assigns the string NIGHTMARE to the variable A$. Similarly, the following segment results in X$ containing the value SAN FRANCISCO:

```
00020 A$ = "SAN"
00030 B$ = " FRAN"
00030 C$ = "CISCO"
00040 X$ = A$ + B$ + C$
```

The LEN Function

The length or LEN function returns the number of characters in the single string that is its argument. (Remember that blanks in quoted strings are counted as characters.) The following statement assigns the value 9 to NMBR:

```
00080 NMBR = LEN("YOUR NAME")
```

An example of how the LEN function might be used is given in the statements that follow, which print a centered heading for an 80-column screen:

```
00090 INPUT "ENTER HEADING";HEAD$
00100 X = LEN(HEAD$)
00110 CNTR = (80 - X) / 2
00120 PRINT TAB(CNTR);HEAD$
```

The LEFT$ and RIGHT$ Functions

The LEFT$ function returns a string that consists of the leftmost portion of the string argument, from the first character to the character position specified by the expression. For instance, the following statement assigns to X$ the value BE SEEING:

```
00030 X$ = LEFT$("BE SEEING YOU!",9)
```

The program in Figure VIII–4 demonstrates the LEFT$ function. Notice that the length of the string, which controls the number of times the FOR loop is executed, is determined in line 50 by the LEN function.

The microcomputer discussed in this book handle the RIGHT$ function differently than the DECsystem does. On the DECsystem, the RIGHT$ function returns the rightmost part of the string, from the *character po-*

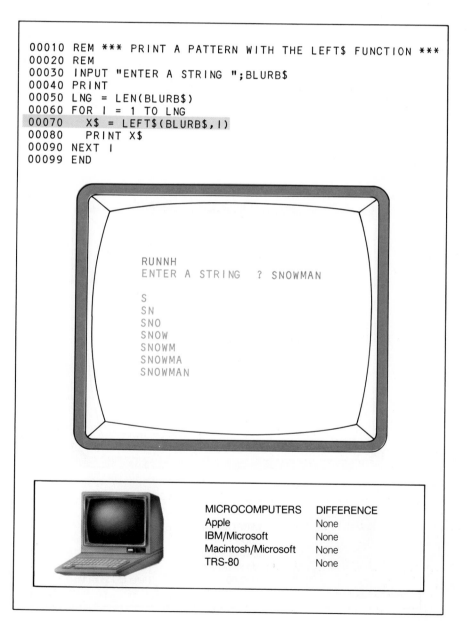

● **FIGURE VIII–4**
The LEFT$ Function

```
00010 REM *** PRINT A PATTERN WITH THE LEFT$ FUNCTION ***
00020 REM
00030 INPUT "ENTER A STRING ";BLURB$
00040 PRINT
00050 LNG = LEN(BLURB$)
00060 FOR I = 1 TO LNG
00070   X$ = LEFT$(BLURB$,I)
00080   PRINT X$
00090 NEXT I
00099 END
```

```
RUNNH
ENTER A STRING   ? SNOWMAN

S
SN
SNO
SNOW
SNOWM
SNOWMA
SNOWMAN
```

MICROCOMPUTERS	DIFFERENCE
Apple	None
IBM/Microsoft	None
Macintosh/Microsoft	None
TRS-80	None

sition given by the expression to the end of the string. Thus the following statement assigns the value SEEING YOU! to X$:

```
00030 X$ = RIGHT$("BE SEEING YOU!",4)
```

With the microcomputers, however, this function returns the *number of characters* specified by the expression from the right end of the string. On these systems, the following instruction would assign to X$ the last nine characters of the string. In this case the value EING YOU!:

```
30 X$ = RIGHT$("BE SEEING YOU!",9)
```

The programs in Figures VIII–5 and VIII–6 demonstrate the RIGHT$ func-

● **FIGURE VIII–5**
The RIGHT$ Function on the DECsystem

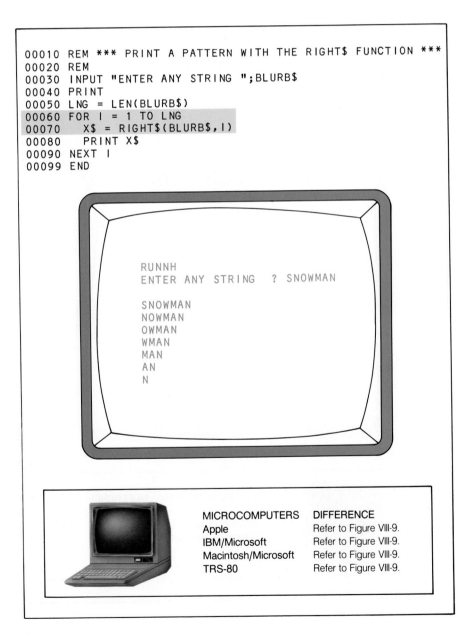

```
00010 REM *** PRINT A PATTERN WITH THE RIGHT$ FUNCTION ***
00020 REM
00030 INPUT "ENTER ANY STRING ";BLURB$
00040 PRINT
00050 LNG = LEN(BLURB$)
00060 FOR I = 1 TO LNG
00070    X$ = RIGHT$(BLURB$,I)
00080    PRINT X$
00090 NEXT I
00099 END
```

```
RUNNH
ENTER ANY STRING   ? SNOWMAN

SNOWMAN
NOWMAN
OWMAN
WMAN
MAN
AN
N
```

MICROCOMPUTERS	DIFFERENCE
Apple	Refer to Figure VIII-9.
IBM/Microsoft	Refer to Figure VIII-9.
Macintosh/Microsoft	Refer to Figure VIII-9.
TRS-80	Refer to Figure VIII-9.

● **COMPUTERS AND INFORMATION PROCESSING**

tion as used on the DECsystem and the IBM respectively. Notice how line 60 differs between the two programs to produce the same output.

The LEFT$ function is often useful when comparing character strings. Suppose a program asks the user to answer a yes or no question but does not specify whether the question should be answered by typing the entire word YES or NO or just the first letter Y or N. We can use the LEFT$ function to compare just the first character of the user's response, allowing the user to type either YES/NO or Y/N. The example that follows illustrates this:

```
00010 INPUT "ARE YOU MARRIED ";A$
00020 A$ = LEFT$(A$,1)
00030 IF A$ = "Y" THEN PRINT "YES" ELSE PRINT "NO"
```

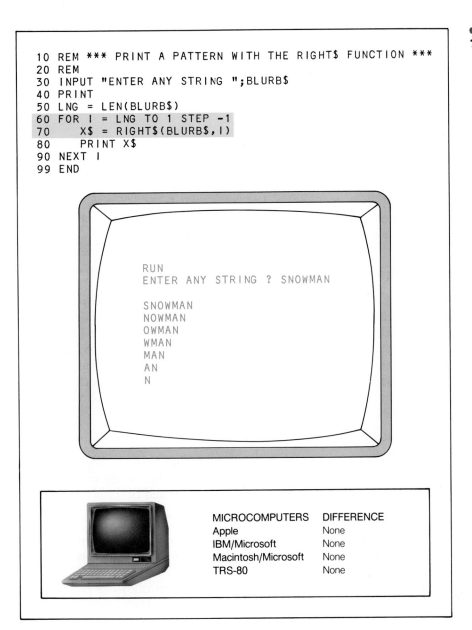

● **FIGURE VIII–6**
The RIGHT$ Function on the IBM

```
10 REM *** PRINT A PATTERN WITH THE RIGHT$ FUNCTION ***
20 REM
30 INPUT "ENTER ANY STRING ";BLURB$
40 PRINT
50 LNG = LEN(BLURB$)
60 FOR I = LNG TO 1 STEP -1
70    X$ = RIGHT$(BLURB$,I)
80    PRINT X$
90 NEXT I
99 END
```

```
RUN
ENTER ANY STRING ? SNOWMAN

SNOWMAN
NOWMAN
OWMAN
WMAN
MAN
AN
N
```

MICROCOMPUTERS	DIFFERENCE
Apple	None
IBM/Microsoft	None
Macintosh/Microsoft	None
TRS-80	None

The MID$ Function

The MID$ function is more complicated. Here is the general format:

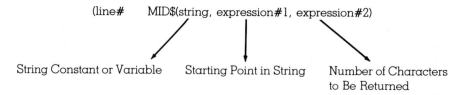

(line#   MID$(string, expression#1, expression#2)

String Constant or Variable   Starting Point in String   Number of Characters
to Be Returned

Sometimes expression 2 is omitted; in that case, the characters—from the starting point to the end of the string—are returned. The following statement assigns to X$ a string four characters long, starting at the fifth character: NDIP.

```
00020 X$ = MID$("SERENDIPITY",5,4)
```

The MID$ function is useful when you want to look at some middle characters of a string. For instance, assume you have a file of telephone numbers, and you want to print out only those with an exchange of 352. Here are the telephone numbers:

491-354-1070
491-353-0011
491-352-3520
491-352-1910
491-352-7350
491-353-9822

The program in Figure VIII–7 will compare the exchange of "352" and print the telephone numbers that qualify.

The ASCII and CHR$ Functions

The ASCII function returns the ASCII value of the first character of its string argument, which can be a string constant, variable, or expression.

On the DECsystem, the function name is ASCII; the same function on the microcomputers discussed in this book is called ASC, and its format is the same as for the DEC. Table VIII–3 lists characters and their corresponding ASCII values. For example, the following statement examines the first character of the argument, R, and assigns its ASCII value of 82 to the variable RVALUE:

```
00030 RVALUE = ASCII("RETURN A VALUE")
```

The CHR$ function performs the reverse operation of the ASCII function: It returns the single character that corresponds to a given ASCII value. The following statement assigns to MES$ the value HI!

```
00070 MES$ = CHR$(72) + CHR$(73) + CHR$(33)
```

The ASCII and CHR$ functions are demonstrated in the program in Figure VIII–8, which prints a listing of the alphabet with its corresponding ASCII codes.

The ASCII and CHR$ functions are helpful in allowing programs to respond to both lowercase and uppercase input. Using these functions,

● COMPUTERS AND INFORMATION PROCESSING

a program can allow the user to answer a yes or no question with y, Y, n, or N. Table VIII–3 shows that the codes for the lower case letters range from 97 through 122, and those for uppercase letters range from 65 through 90. An IF/THEN statement can be used to compare the ASCII value of the user response to 96. If the value is greater than 96, a lowercase letter has been typed; if the value is less than 96, the letter is uppercase.

Once the program has determined the type of letter, it can convert the letter to either uppercase or lowercase for comparison. An uppercase letter can be changed to lowercase by adding 32 to the ASCII value, and a lowercase letter can be made uppercase by subtracting 32. The fol-

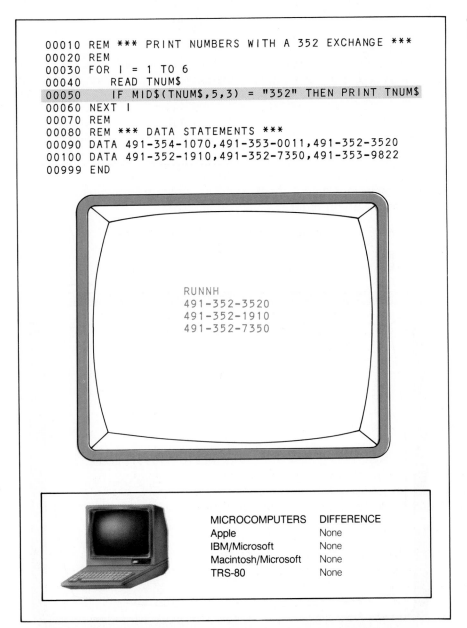

● **FIGURE VIII–7**
The MID$ Function

```
00010 REM *** PRINT NUMBERS WITH A 352 EXCHANGE ***
00020 REM
00030 FOR I = 1 TO 6
00040    READ TNUM$
00050    IF MID$(TNUM$,5,3) = "352" THEN PRINT TNUM$
00060 NEXT I
00070 REM
00080 REM *** DATA STATEMENTS ***
00090 DATA 491-354-1070,491-353-0011,491-352-3520
00100 DATA 491-352-1910,491-352-7350,491-353-9822
00999 END
```

```
RUNNH
491-352-3520
491-352-1910
491-352-7350
```

MICROCOMPUTERS	DIFFERENCE
Apple	None
IBM/Microsoft	None
Macintosh/Microsoft	None
TRS-80	None

	32	!	33	"	34	#	35
$	36	%	37	&	38	'	39
(	40	)	41	*	42	+	43
,	44	-	45	.	46	/	47
0	48	1	49	2	50	3	51
4	52	5	53	6	54	7	55
8	56	9	57	:	58	;	59
<	60	=	61	>	62	?	63
@	64	A	65	B	66	C	67
D	68	E	69	F	70	G	71
H	72	I	73	J	74	K	75
L	76	M	77	N	78	O	79
P	80	Q	81	R	82	S	83
T	84	U	85	V	86	W	87
X	88	Y	89	Z	90	[	91
\	92	]	93	^	94	_	95
`	96	a	97	b	98	c	99
d	100	e	101	f	102	g	103
h	104	i	105	j	106	k	107
l	108	m	109	n	110	o	111
p	112	q	113	r	114	s	115
t	116	u	117	v	118	w	119
x	120	y	121	z	122	{	123
	124						

lowing program segment checks a user's reply and converts it to upper-case if necessary in order to compare it.

```
00030 INPUT "ARE YOU ALLERGIC TO ANY MEDICATIONS? (Y/N) ";AN$
00040 X = ASCII(AN$)
00050 IF X > 96 THEN AN$ = CHR$(X - 32)
00060 IF AN$ <> "Y" THEN PRINT "NO ALLERGIES"
```

```
RUNNH
ARE YOU ALLERGIC TO ANY MEDICATIONS? (Y/N) ?
```

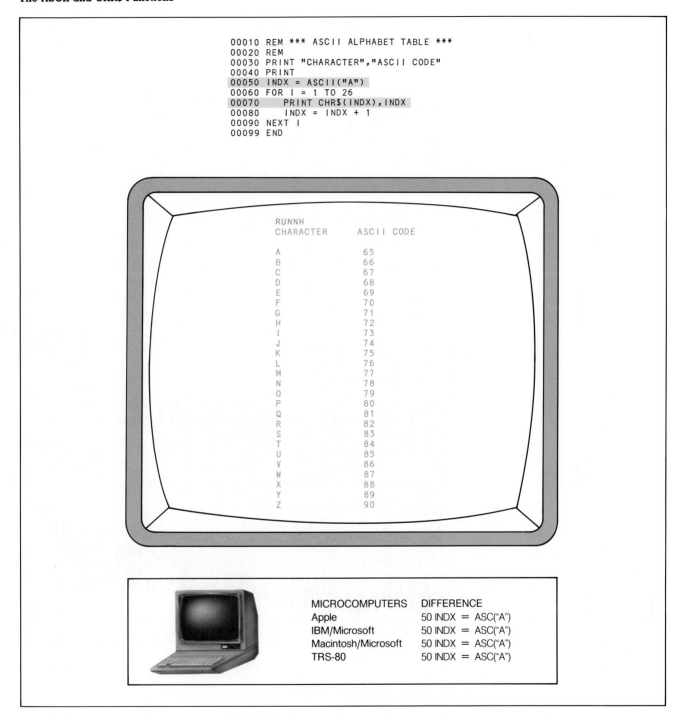

```
00010 REM *** ASCII ALPHABET TABLE ***
00020 REM
00030 PRINT "CHARACTER","ASCII CODE"
00040 PRINT
00050 INDX = ASCII("A")
00060 FOR I = 1 TO 26
00070    PRINT CHR$(INDX),INDX
00080    INDX = INDX + 1
00090 NEXT I
00099 END
```

```
RUNNH
CHARACTER      ASCII CODE

A              65
B              66
C              67
D              68
E              69
F              70
G              71
H              72
I              73
J              74
K              75
L              76
M              77
N              78
O              79
P              80
Q              81
R              82
S              83
T              84
U              85
V              86
W              87
X              88
Y              89
Z              90
```

MICROCOMPUTERS	DIFFERENCE
Apple	50 INDX = ASC("A")
IBM/Microsoft	50 INDX = ASC("A")
Macintosh/Microsoft	50 INDX = ASC("A")
TRS-80	50 INDX = ASC("A")

The VAL and STR$ Functions

The VAL function converts a numeric string expression (such as "12.34") into its equivalent numeric value.

The characters of the argument string can include the digits 0 through 9, the plus and minus signs, and the decimal point. Any leading blanks in the string are ignored. The microcomputers discussed in this book also allow the string argument to contain nonnumeric characters; see the box "VAL Function Differences."

By using the VAL function, it is possible to change a number in a character string to a number that can be used in mathematical computations. The program in Figure VIII–9 reads an integer value to a string variable and uses the VAL function to compute the sum of its digits.

The STR$ function performs the reverse of the VAL function operation: it converts a real number to a string. Its general format is as follows, where the expression evaluates as a numeric value:

STR$ (expression)

The program in Figure VIII–10 demonstrates the STR$ function. Remember that once a number has been converted to a string, it can no longer be used in mathematical computations unless it is converted back to a numeric value.

● VAL Function Differences

If the string argument of the VAL function contains nonnumeric characters (other than leading blanks), the DECsystem gives an error message. Such a string is handled differently on the Apple, IBM, Macintosh, and TRS-80: If the first nonblank character of the string is nonnumeric, the function returns a value of zero. For example, the following statement would output 0:

```
00070 PRINT VAL(" BG, OH  43402")
```

Otherwise, the function examines the string one character at a time until an unacceptable character is encountered. On all of the systems mentioned above, a blank is acceptable within a numeric string; it is simply ignored. The following statement would be valid and would assign to N1 the value 1084:

```
00070 N1 = VAL(" 1084 WELSH VIEW DR.")
```

● User-Defined Functions

The DEF, or definition, statement can be used by the programmer to define a function not already included in the BASIC language. Once a function has been defined, the programmer can use it as many times as necessary in the program. The DEF statement can be placed anywhere in the program before the function is first called, but in the interests of clarity and organization, all DEF statements should appear near the beginning of the program. The general format of the DEF statement is as follows:

line# DEF function name (argument list) = expression

The function name consists of the letters FN followed by a valid variable name (e.g., FNROUND, FNAREA, or FNX). The arguments are one or

● **FIGURE VIII–9**
The VAL Function

```
00010 REM *** FIND THE SUM OF THE DIGITS OF AN INTEGER ***
00020 REM *** MAJOR VARIABLES:                          ***
00030 REM ***     NSTR$      -      NUMBER STRING        ***
00040 REM ***     DIG$       -      SINGLE DIGIT CHARACTER ***
00050 REM ***     NDIG       -      NUMERIC VALUE OF DIGIT ***
00060 REM
00070 SUM = 0
00080 INPUT "ENTER A NON-NEGATIVE INTEGER ";NSTR$
00090 LONG = LEN(NSTR$)
00100 FOR I = 1 TO LONG
00110    DIG$ = MID$(NSTR$,I,1)
00120    NDIG = VAL(DIG$)
00130    SUM = SUM + NDIG
00140 NEXT I
00150 PRINT "SUM = ";SUM
00999 END
```

```
RUNNH
ENTER A NON-NEGATIVE INTEGER  ? 145
SUM =  10
```

MICROCOMPUTERS	DIFFERENCE
Apple	None
IBM/Microsoft	None
Macintosh/Microsoft	None
TRS-80	None

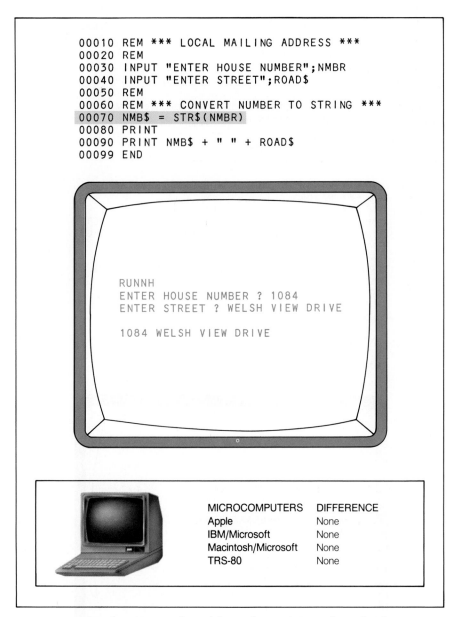

```
00010 REM *** LOCAL MAILING ADDRESS ***
00020 REM
00030 INPUT "ENTER HOUSE NUMBER";NMBR
00040 INPUT "ENTER STREET";ROAD$
00050 REM
00060 REM *** CONVERT NUMBER TO STRING ***
00070 NMB$ = STR$(NMBR)
00080 PRINT
00090 PRINT NMB$ + " " + ROAD$
00099 END
```

```
RUNNH
ENTER HOUSE NUMBER ? 1084
ENTER STREET ? WELSH VIEW DRIVE

1084 WELSH VIEW DRIVE
```

MICROCOMPUTERS	DIFFERENCE
Apple	None
IBM/Microsoft	None
Macintosh/Microsoft	None
TRS-80	None

more variables that are replaced by values given when the function is called (the Apple allows only one argument). The expression contains the operations performed by the function; it evaluates as a single value, which is returned by the function. The entire DEF statement cannot exceed one logical line. (The DECsystem also limits it to 33 characters.)

A call to a user-defined function has the following format:

function name (expression list)

The function name matches a function name appearing in a previous DEF statement. The one or more expressions are evaluated, and the results are used to replace the arguments of the DEF statement on a one-to-one basis.

The following segment demonstrates the use of a simple user-defined function. When the computer encounters line 10, it stores in memory the definition for the function FNR. Line 20 initializes PRICE to 5.50. When the computer encounters line 30, it evaluates the expression in parentheses at 5.50; then, using the definition for FNR, it substitutes this value for X. Therefore the expression (X + 20)/2 evaluates as 12.75. This value becomes the function value, which is printed by line 30.

```
00010 DEF FNR(X) = (X + 20) / 2
00020 PRICE = 5.50
00030 PRINT FNR(PRICE)
```

```
RUNNH
12.75
```

The arguments in the DEF statement are sometimes called dummy arguments because they have no real values; they only show how the input values of the function will be used. A dummy argument can have the same name as a regular program variable without affecting the value of the regular variable, as shown in the following example.

```
00010 N = 3
00020 DEF FNCUBE(N) = N * N * N
00030 PRINT N
00040 Y = 4
00050 PRINT FNCUBE(Y)
00060 PRINT N
```

```
RUNNH
 3
 64
 3
```

The expression of the function definition can contain variables that do not appear in the argument list. When the function is called, the most current values of these variables are used, as demonstrated in Figure VIII–11.

The expression of the function definition can also contain calls to previously defined functions or library functions. For example, the definition of line 60 is valid:

```
00050 DEF FNMULT(X,Y) = X * Y
00060 DEF FNCALC(X,Y) = SGN(X) + FNMULT(X,Y)
```

However, a function definition cannot call itself. The following statement is invalid:

```
00060 DEF FNMULT(X,Y) = FNMULT(X,Y) + X + Y
```

Many systems (including those discussed in this book, with the exception of the Apple) also allow the programmer to define string functions. The type of a function, like that of a variable, is indicated by its name. For example, the function FNA$ specifies a string function, while FNA is a real value function. Figure VIII–12 demonstrates a user-defined string function that prints a name in the format of last name, first initial.

● A Programming Problem

PROBLEM DEFINITION

Create an interactive program that generates a mathematical sequence and allows a player to guess the next number in the sequence. The program should show the player the first three numbers of the sequence and offer him or her the option of seeing the next number. If so desired, it should print the next number in the sequence; the player may see as many numbers as he or she requests. The player should then be asked for a guess as to the next number, and the program should print appropriate messages in response to the guess. If the guess is correct, the game is over; otherwise, the player is again given the option of seeing more numbers.

The program should allow for upper- or lowercase responses of either

● FIGURE VIII–11
User-Defined Numeric Function

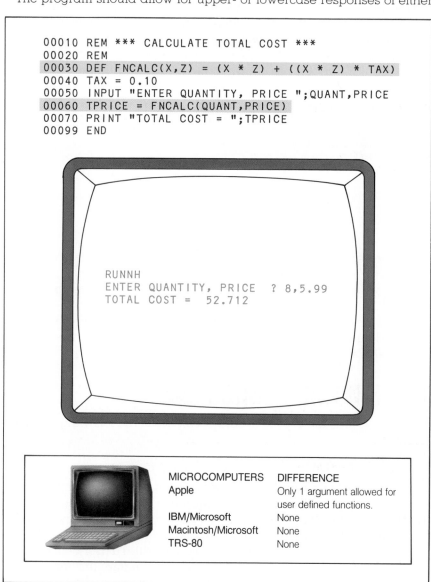

```
00010 REM *** CALCULATE TOTAL COST ***
00020 REM
00030 DEF FNCALC(X,Z) = (X * Z) + ((X * Z) * TAX)
00040 TAX = 0.10
00050 INPUT "ENTER QUANTITY, PRICE ";QUANT,PRICE
00060 TPRICE = FNCALC(QUANT,PRICE)
00070 PRINT "TOTAL COST = ";TPRICE
00099 END
```

```
RUNNH
ENTER QUANTITY, PRICE  ? 8,5.99
TOTAL COST =  52.712
```

MICROCOMPUTERS	DIFFERENCE
Apple	Only 1 argument allowed for user defined functions.
IBM/Microsoft	None
Macintosh/Microsoft	None
TRS-80	None

● COMPUTERS AND INFORMATION PROCESSING

a full word or a first letter, and guesses should be input as character strings to guard against an error in case the player enters a nonnumeric guess. The values of the sequence should be such that the nth member is generated by multiplying n times itself and adding to it the value $n - 1$. A sample game is shown below:

```
RUNNH
CURRENT SEQUENCE
  1    5   11
DO YOU WANT TO SEE THE NEXT NUMBER  ? Y
CURRENT SEQUENCE
  1    5   11   19
DO YOU WANT TO SEE THE NEXT NUMBER  ? N
ENTER YOUR GUESS:  ? 29
THAT'S CORRECT
```

● **FIGURE VIII–12**
User-Defined String Function

```
00010 REM *** REVERSE A NAME ***
00020 REM
00030 DEF FNREV$(A$,B$) = B$ + "," + LEFT$(A$,1) + "."
00040 INPUT "ENTER FIRST NAME ";FIRST$
00050 INPUT "ENTER LAST NAME ";LAST$
00060 RNAM$ = FNREV$(FIRST$,LAST$)
00070 PRINT
00080 PRINT RNAM$
00099 END
```

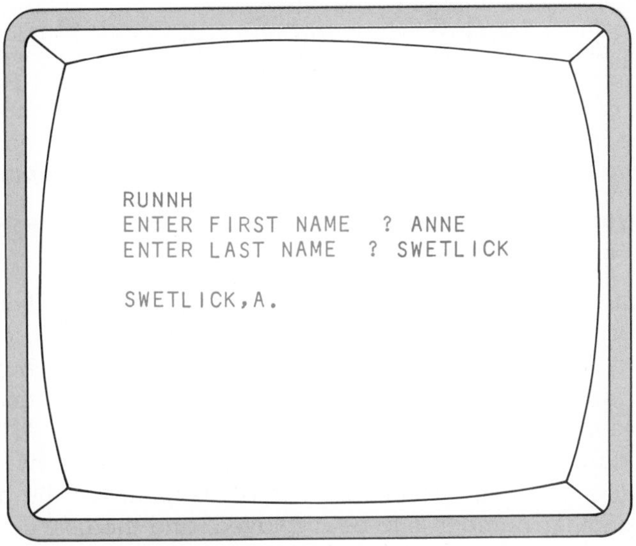

```
RUNNH
ENTER FIRST NAME  ? ANNE
ENTER LAST NAME   ? SWETLICK

SWETLICK,A.
```

MICROCOMPUTERS	DIFFERENCE
Apple	Only 1 argument allowed for user defined functions.
IBM/Microsoft	None
Macintosh/Microsoft	None
TRS-80	None

SOLUTION DESIGN

Because this is an interactive program, it is helpful to consider what steps must be taken to enable the player to enter a correct guess—the action that ends the program. In order to begin, the player must be able to see a part of the sequence. Each element is calculated according to the same formula, so a user-defined function could be used in generating the sequence.

The second major step, and therefore a second subroutine of the program, must give the player the option of seeing another number. In order to do this, the program must prompt the player with a yes or no question. The player's response at this point could be converted to a Y or N and checked by another subroutine. If the answer is yes, then the first step of the program (printing the current number sequence) must be performed again. This process of prompting the player and displaying the sequence can continue until the player answers no; the repetition should suggest a loop.

The third major step of the program is to allow a guess to be entered. This step involves prompting the user, checking to see if the guess is correct (and therefore generating the next number of the sequence), and then printing an appropriate message. The needed steps thus far are as follows:

1. Print first three numbers of sequence
2. Offer to show the player the next number
3. Offer the player the chance to guess

A correct guess ends the game; otherwise, the program must continue to offer the player more numbers and accept guesses until a correct guess is entered. These two processes could therefore be initiated within a loop.

2.a. Convert player response
2.b. Print next number in sequence

The structure chart for this solution is shown in Figure VIII–13. Each of the steps on the second level of the diagram represents a subroutine. Notice that the subroutine which offers the player another number calls two other subroutines, and that one of these is a subroutine that has already been called by the main program.

The variables needed by the program are relatively few. The input variables consist of the user's input, a Y/N response to the question of whether another number is to be displayed, and the user's guess. Program variables needed are a counter to keep track of the numbers in the currently displayed sequence, and a flag to indicate a correct guess. The only output is a message to the user, so no variable is required. The needed variables are summarized below:

Input variables

player response	(AN$)
player guess	(GUES$)

Program variables

count of numbers generated	(CNT)
flag for correct guess	(OK$)

THE PROGRAM

The program in Figure VIII–14 uses four subroutines and one user-defined function (defined in line 90) to solve the problem. The variable CNT is used to keep track of the quantity of numbers which have been displayed; this is initially set to 3 in line 120 to begin the game. The variable OK$, initialized to "N," is used as a flag that indicates whether a correct guess has been given and the game is to end.

The WHILE loop of lines 190 through 220 allows the player to see numbers and make guesses until the answer flag equals "Y." The subroutine of lines 1000 through 1100 displays the current sequence by calling the user-defined function FNNXT. The second subroutine asks the player if another number is needed; the answer is converted to a Y or N by calling the fourth subroutine in lines 4000 through 4090. Each time the player responds to a yes/no question, his or her answer is checked in this way.

When the player does not want to see more numbers, the subroutine beginning at line 3000 is called to accept a guess, which is entered as a string in line 3060. The next number of the sequence is computed in line 3100 and converted to a string to be compared to the guess. In line 3110, the flag OK$ is set to reflect a correct or incorrect guess, and control is passed back to the main program at line 220. The WHILE statement then checks the flag and either repeats the entire process or terminates the game.

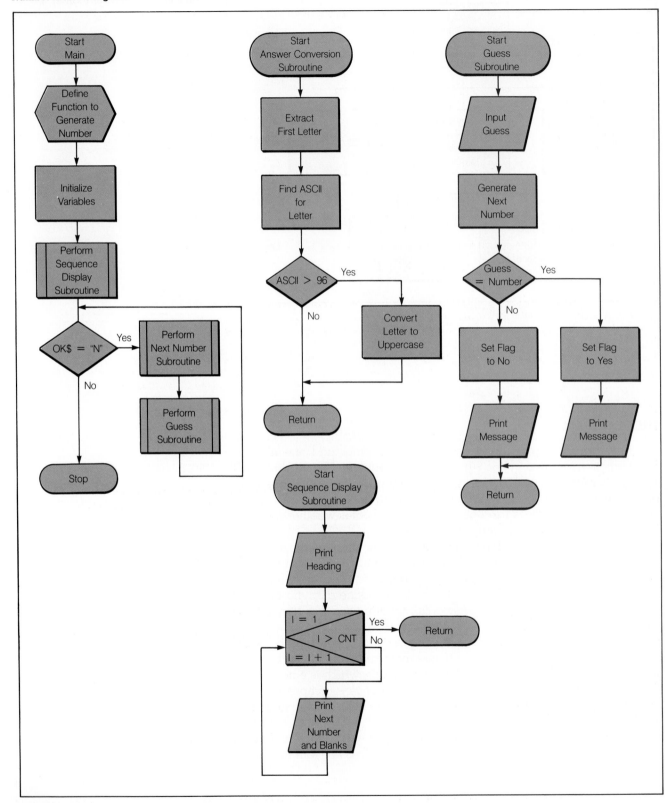

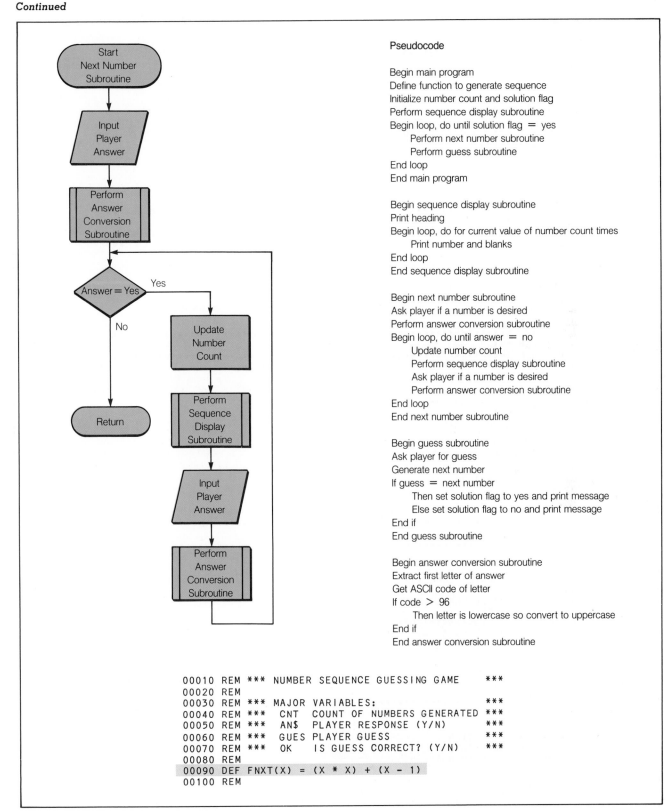

Pseudocode

Begin main program
Define function to generate sequence
Initialize number count and solution flag
Perform sequence display subroutine
Begin loop, do until solution flag = yes
    Perform next number subroutine
    Perform guess subroutine
End loop
End main program

Begin sequence display subroutine
Print heading
Begin loop, do for current value of number count times
    Print number and blanks
End loop
End sequence display subroutine

Begin next number subroutine
Ask player if a number is desired
Perform answer conversion subroutine
Begin loop, do until answer = no
    Update number count
    Perform sequence display subroutine
    Ask player if a number is desired
    Perform answer conversion subroutine
End loop
End next number subroutine

Begin guess subroutine
Ask player for guess
Generate next number
If guess = next number
    Then set solution flag to yes and print message
    Else set solution flag to no and print message
End if
End guess subroutine

Begin answer conversion subroutine
Extract first letter of answer
Get ASCII code of letter
If code > 96
    Then letter is lowercase so convert to uppercase
End if
End answer conversion subroutine

```
00010 REM *** NUMBER SEQUENCE GUESSING GAME    ***
00020 REM
00030 REM *** MAJOR VARIABLES:                 ***
00040 REM ***   CNT   COUNT OF NUMBERS GENERATED ***
00050 REM ***   AN$   PLAYER RESPONSE (Y/N)     ***
00060 REM ***   GUES  PLAYER GUESS              ***
00070 REM ***   OK    IS GUESS CORRECT? (Y/N)   ***
00080 REM
00090 DEF FNXT(X) = (X * X) + (X - 1)
00100 REM
```

```
00110 REM *** INITIALIZE VARIABLES ***
00120 CNT = 3
00130 OK$ = "N"
00140 REM
00150 REM *** DISPLAY INITIAL SEQUENCE ***
00160 GOSUB 1000
00170 REM
00180 REM *** LOOP TO DISPLAY NUMBERS AND ACCEPT GUESSES UNTIL CORRECT ***
00190 WHILE OK$ = "N"
00200  GOSUB 2000
00210  GOSUB 3000
00220 NEXT
00230 GOTO 9999
01000 REM
01010 REM ************************************************************
01020 REM ***                    SUBROUTINE 1                    ***
01030 REM ************************************************************
01040 REM ***               DISPLAY CURRENT SEQUENCE            ***
01050 REM
01060 PRINT "CURRENT SEQUENCE "
01070 FOR I = 1 TO CNT
01080    PRINT FNXT(I);"  ";
01090 NEXT I
01100 RETURN
02000 REM
02010 REM ************************************************************
02020 REM ***                    SUBROUTINE 2                    ***
02030 REM ************************************************************
02040 REM ***              PROVIDE ADDITIONAL NUMBERS           ***
02050 REM
02060 PRINT
02070 INPUT "DO YOU WANT TO SEE THE NEXT NUMBER ";AN$
02080 GOSUB 4000
02090 WHILE AN$ = "Y"
02100    CNT = CNT + 1
02110    GOSUB 1000
02120    PRINT
02130    INPUT "DO YOU WANT TO SEE THE NEXT NUMBER ";AN$
02140    GOSUB 4000
02150 NEXT
02160 RETURN
03000 REM
03010 REM ************************************************************
03020 REM ***                    SUBROUTINE 3                    ***
03030 REM ************************************************************
03040 REM ***              ACCEPT AND TEST PLAYER'S GUESS       ***
03050 REM
03060 INPUT "ENTER YOUR GUESS: ";GUES$
03070 REM
03080 REM *** GENERATE NEXT NUMBER AND TEST GUESS ***
03090 TEMP = CNT + 1
03100 NXT$ = STR$(FNXT(TEMP)
03110 IF NXT$ = GUES$ THEN OK$ = "Y" \ PRINT "THAT'S CORRECT"
       ELSE OK$ = "N" \ PRINT "SORRY, INCORRECT "
03120 RETURN
04000 REM
04010 REM ************************************************************
04020 REM ***                    SUBROUTINE 4                    ***
04030 REM ************************************************************
04040 REM ***              CONVERT PLAYER RESPONSE TO Y/N       ***
04050 REM
04060 AN$ = LEFT$(AN$,1)
04070 B = ASCII(AN$)
04080 IF B > 96 THEN AN$ = CHR$(B - 32)
04090 RETURN
09999 END
```

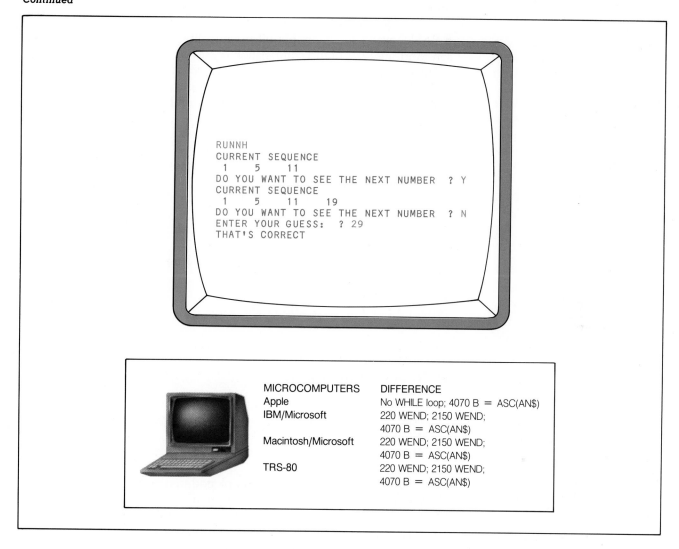

```
RUNNH
CURRENT SEQUENCE
  1    5    11
DO YOU WANT TO SEE THE NEXT NUMBER  ? Y
CURRENT SEQUENCE
  1    5    11    19
DO YOU WANT TO SEE THE NEXT NUMBER  ? N
ENTER YOUR GUESS:   ? 29
THAT'S CORRECT
```

MICROCOMPUTERS	DIFFERENCE
Apple	No WHILE loop; 4070 B = ASC(AN$)
IBM/Microsoft	220 WEND; 2150 WEND;
	4070 B = ASC(AN$)
Macintosh/Microsoft	220 WEND; 2150 WEND;
	4070 B = ASC(AN$)
TRS-80	220 WEND; 2150 WEND;
	4070 B = ASC(AN$)

● Summary Points

● The BASIC language includes several library functions that can make complicated mathematical operations easier to program.

● The trigonometric functions are SIN (X), COS (X), TAN (X), and ATN (X), where X is in radians.

● The exponential or EXP function calculates EXP (X) = e^x, and the natural logarithm or LOG (X) function is the reverse of that function.

● The SQR (X) function returns the square root of its argument.

● The INT (X) function computes the greatest integer less than or equal to the value specified as the argument.

● The SGN (X) function produces a 1, 0, or −1, depending on whether the argument is positive, zero, or negative respectively.

● The ABS (X) function returns the absolute value of its argument.

- The programmer can define functions by using the DEF statement. A user-defined function definition cannot exceed one line and must precede any reference to it in a program.
- BASIC string functions permit modification, concatenation, comparison, and analysis of the composition of strings.
- The concatenation operation (+) joins two strings together.
- The LEN function is used to find the number of characters in a string.
- The LEFT$ function returns a specified number of leftmost characters of a string.
- The RIGHT$ function returns the specified rightmost characters of a string.
- The MID$ function enables the programmer to gain access to characters in the middle of a string.
- The ASCII function returns the ASCII code for the first character in a string.
- The CHR$ function returns the string representation of the ASCII code of the expression.
- The VAL (X) function is used to find the numeric equivalent of a string expression.
- The STR$ function acts as a reverse of the VAL (X) function by converting a number to its string equivalent.

● Review Questions

1. What are the allowable arguments of a function?
2. How many values can be returned by a function?
3. What is the result of INT (−3.4)?
4. Write a BASIC statement using the INT (X) function to round a number to the nearest hundredth.
5. Where is the function definition placed in a program?
6. What is meant by string concatenation?
7. The _____ function returns the number of characters in a string.
8. Explain the use of the LEFT$, RIGHT$, and MID$ functions.
9. What will the output from this instruction be?

00030 PRINT STR$(342) + STR$(58)

10. Give the output from the following statement:

00020 PRINT MID$("MICHAEL JACKSON",9,4)

● Debugging Exercises

Identify the following program segments that contain errors and debug them.

```
1. 00010 READ X
   00020 PRINT FNA(X)
   00030 DEF FNA(Y) = EXP(Y) + 5
   00040 DATA 22
```

● COMPUTERS AND INFORMATION PROCESSING

2.
```
00010 FOR I = 1 TO 5
00020    READ N$
00030    N = STR$(N$)
00040    N = N * .5
00050    PRINT N
00060 NEXT I
```

● Programming Problems

1. Write an interactive program that accepts a Fahrenheit temperature and prints the centigrade equivalent. Define one function to use the following formula:

$$C = 5 / 9 (F - 32)$$

A second function should round the results to the nearest tenth of a degree. Let the user enter temperatures as long as desired. Test the program with the following data: 32, 77, 120.

2. Write a program to print the trigonometric functions sine, cosine, and tangent for 1° to 15°. Define a function to convert degrees to radians and another function to round the results to four decimal places. The output should be printed in a format similar to this:

DEGREES	SIN X	COS X	TAN X
XX	X.XXXX	X.XXXX	X.XXXX
•	•	•	•
•	•	•	•

3. Write a program to simulate the throwing of a dice twenty times. After the twenty throws, print the total occurrence of each number (1 to 6). Generate random numbers to represent the tosses. Define a function to generate the needed random numbers.

4. Write a program that reads a list of words and prints only those words that begin with whatever prefix is entered by the user. Use the following data: EXCESS, EXCOMMUNICATE, EXCELLENT, REWARD, RENUMERATE, REWORD, RECEIVE, PREPARE, PREFIX, PREVIEW, SUBTOTAL, SUBMARINE, SUBTRACT.

5. An auto parts store has a system to help detect errors in recording inventory. The last two digits of every stock number must be the sum of the preceding three digits. For example, the stock number QB412.07 is valid because 07 is the sum of 4 + 1 + 2. Write a program that inputs stock numbers and prints a message for any invalid numbers. Use the following data:

QB371.11
UT491.14
UT307.11

● Section IX
Arrays

● Introduction

All of our programs thus far have used simple variables such as LBS, TITLE$, or HRS to represent single values. If a program was required to handle many single values of the same type (such as 100 student scores), a loop was used to allow one variable to represent these values one at a time. Now consider the problem of a TV network poll. A program is needed to read and retain the daily viewing times of ten random viewers, calculate the average viewing time, and print the difference between each person's viewing time and the average in the following format:

NAME	HRS	DIFFERENCE FROM AVG
P. BUSCH	1	−3
C. CARSTENS	5	1
J. DRAKE	0	−4
H. POIROT	2	−2
M. BULAS	7	3
D. ZONGAS	3	−1
C. HASTINGS	4	0
T. ZEKLEY	11	7
S. MCKINNIS	3	−1
G. BALDUCCI	4	0

AVERAGE VIEWING TIME = 4

Our past procedure for calculating averages has been to set up a loop to read and accumulate each value in a single variable. Each time a new value is read by this method, however, the previous value stored in the variable is destroyed. Thus, in the problem involving the TV poll, we would not be able to compare each person's viewing time with the calculated average viewing time. To make the comparison, we must store each person's viewing time in a separate memory location. It is possible to use ten different variables to hold these values, but this clearly is a cumbersome solution that would be even more impractical when dealing with a larger number of values.

There is an easier way: BASIC permits us to deal with many related data items as a group by means of a structure known as an **array.** This chapter shows how arrays can be used in a situation such as the television poll program, in which groups of data items must be stored and

● **COMPUTERS AND INFORMATION PROCESSING**

manipulated efficiently. Both one-dimensional and two-dimensional arrays are presented in Section 9. Various methods of sorting and searching arrays are also discussed.

● Subscripts

The individual data items within an array are called **elements.** An array consists of a group of consecutive storage locations in memory, each location containing a single value. The entire array is given one name; the programmer indicates an individual element in the array by referring to its position in the array. To illustrate, suppose that there are five test scores to be stored: 97, 85, 89, 95, 100. The scores could be put in an array called TESTS, which we might visualize like this:

Array TESTS

97	85	89	95	100

The array name TESTS now refers to all five storage locations containing the test scores. To gain access to a single test score within the array, an array **subscript** or **index** is used. A subscript is a value enclosed in parentheses that identifies the position of a given element in the array. For example, the first element of array TESTS (containing the value 97) is referred to as TESTS(1). The second test score is in TESTS(2), the third test score is in TESTS(3), and so on. Therefore, the following statements are true:

TESTS(1) = 97
TESTS(2) = 85
TESTS(3) = 89
TESTS(4) = 95
TESTS(5) = 100

The subscript enclosed in parentheses does not have to be an integer constant; it can consist of any legal numeric expression. When an array element subscript is indicated by an expression, the computer carries out the following steps:

● It evaluates the expression within the parentheses.
● It converts the result to an integer value. (This is done either by truncation, as on the DECsystem and the Apple, or by rounding, as on the IBM, Macintosh, and TRS-80).
● It accesses the indicated element in the array. Keep in mind that the subscript value of an array element is entirely different from the contents of that element. In the previous example, the value of TESTS(4) is 95; the subscript 4 tells where the value 95 is located in the array.

Variables that refer to specific elements of arrays (such as TESTS(4)) are called **subscripted variables.** In contrast, simple variables such as we have used in previous chapters are called **unsubscripted variables.** Both kinds of variables store a single value, numeric or string, and both can be used in BASIC statements in the same manner. The important difference between the two is that a subscripted variable refers to one value in a group; it is possible to access a different value in the group simply by changing the subscript. An unsubscripted variable, on the other hand, does not necessarily have any special relationship to the values stored before or after it in memory.

The same rules that apply to naming simple variables also apply to naming arrays. Remember that only numeric values can be stored in arrays with numeric variable names, and that character string arrays can contain only string values. It is possible to use the same name for both a simple variable and an array in a program, but this is not a good programming practice because it makes the logic of the program difficult to follow.

Assume that the array X and the variables A and B have the following values:

$X(1) = 2$ $A = 3$
$X(2) = 15$ $B = 5$
$X(3) = 16$
$X(4) = 17$
$X(5) = 32$

The following examples show how the various forms of subscripts are used.

Example	Reference
$X(3)$	Third element of X, or 16.
$X(B)$	$B = 5$; thus the fifth element of X, or 32.
$X(X(1))$	$X(1) = 2$; thus the second element of X, or 15.
$X(B - SQR(X(3)))$	$X(3) = 16$, $SQR(16) = 4$, $B - 4 = 1$; thus the first element of X, or 2.

● Dimensioning an Array

When a subscripted variable is found in a program, the BASIC system recognizes it as part of an array and automatically reserves a standard number of storage locations for the array. On most systems (including all those discussed here), space is set aside for eleven array elements, the subscripts of which run from 0 through 10. (Some systems reserve space for ten elements, 1 through 10.) The programmer does not have to fill all of the reserved array storage spaces with values; it is illegal, however, to refer to an array element for which space has not been reserved.

The DIM, or dimension, statement enables the programmer to override this standard array space reservation and reserve space for an array of any desired size. A DIM statement is not required for arrays of eleven or fewer elements, but it is good programming practice to specify DIM statements for all arrays to help document the array usage.

The general format of the DIM statement follows:

line# DIM variable1(limit1)[, variable 2(limit2),...]

The variables are the names of arrays. Each limit is an integer constant that specifies the maximum subscript value possible for that particular array. For example, if space is needed to store 25 elements in an array ITEM$, the following statement reserves the necessary storage locations:

```
00010 DIM ITEM$(24)
```

Although it may seem that this statement sets aside only 24 positions, remember that array positions 0 through 24 are actually equal to 25 locations. For the sake of clarity and program logic, programmers often ignore the zero element. If we choose not to use the zero position, we would dimension the array ITEM$ as shown below in order to have 25 positions:

```
00010 DIM ITEM$(25)
```

There is no problem if fewer than 25 values are read into array ITEM$. Array subscripts can vary in the program from 0 to the limit declared in the DIM statement, but no subscript can exceed that limit.

As indicated in the statement format, more than one array can be declared in a DIM statement. For example, the following statement declares ACCNT, NAM$, and OVERDRWN as arrays:

```
00010 DIM ACCNT(100),NAM$(150),OVERDRWN(50)
```

Array ACCNT may contain up to 101 elements, NAM$ up to 151 elements, and OVERDRWN up to 51 elements. (If the index begins at 1, then 100, 150, and 50 elements can be stored respectively.)

DIM statements must appear in a program before the first references to the arrays they describe; a good practice is to place them at the beginning of the program. The following standard preparation symbol is often used to flowchart the DIM statement:

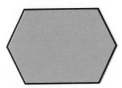

● One-Dimensional Arrays

READING DATA TO AN ARRAY

A major advantage of using arrays is the ability to use a variable rather than a constant as a subscript. Because a single name such as TESTS(I) can refer to any element in the array TESTS, depending on the value of I, this subscripted variable name can be used in a loop that varies the value of the subscript I. A FOR/NEXT loop can be an efficient method of reading data to an array if the exact number of items to be read is known in advance. The following program segment reads a list of five numbers into the array TESTS:

```
00010 FOR I = 1 TO 5
00020    READ TESTS(I)
00030 NEXT I
00040 DATA 85,71,63,51,99
```

The first time this loop is executed, the loop variable I equals 1. Therefore, when line 20 is executed, the computer reads the first number from the data list (which is 85) and stores it in TESTS(I), which evaluates as TESTS(1) during this loop execution. The second time through the loop, I equals 2. The second number is read to TESTS(I), which now refers to TESTS(2)—the second location in the array. The loop processing continues until all five numbers have been read and stored. This process is outlined as follows:

FOR I =	Action	Array TESTS:				
		85				
1	READ TESTS(1)	85	71			
2	READ TESTS(2)	85	71	63		
3	READ TESTS(3)					
4	READ TESTS(4)	85	71	63	51	
5	READ TESTS(5)	85	71	63	51	99

An array can also be filled with values using an INPUT statement or an assignment statement within a loop. To initialize an array of ten elements to zero, the following statements could be used:

```
00050 FOR I = 1 TO 10
00060     SCORES(I) = 0
00070 NEXT I
```

It is often possible to read data to several arrays within a single loop. In the following segment, each data line contains data for one element of each of three arrays:

```
00010 DIM NAM$(5),AGE(5),SSN$(5)
00020 FOR I = 1 TO 5
00030    READ NAM$(I),AGE(I),SSN$(I)
00040 NEXT I
00050 DATA "TOM BAKER",41,"268-66-1071"
00060 DATA "LALLA WARD",28,"353-65-2861"
00070 DATA "MASADA WILMOT",33,"269-59-9064"
00080 DATA "PATRICK JONES",52,"255-65-9375"
00090 DATA "BERYL JONES",56,"249-50-8736"
```

When the exact number of items to be read to an array is unknown, a WHILE/NEXT loop and a trailer value can be used. This method is demonstrated in the following segment, where the data contains a trailer value of −1. Care must be taken, however, that the number of items read does not exceed the size of the array.

```
00010 DIM X(50)
00020 I = 1
00030 INPUT X(I)
00040 WHILE (I < 50) AND (X(I) <> −1)
00050     I = I + 1
00060     INPUT X(I)
00070 NEXT
```

PRINTING THE CONTENTS OF AN ARRAY

The FOR/NEXT loop can be used to print the contents of the array TESTS, as shown in the following segment.

● COMPUTERS AND INFORMATION PROCESSING

```
00070 FOR T = 1 TO 5
00080     PRINT TESTS(T)
00090 NEXT T
```

RUNNH
  85
  71
  63
  51
  99

Because there is no punctuation at the end of the PRINT statement in line 80, each value will be printed on a separate line. The values could be printed on the same line instead by placing a semicolon at the end of the line:

```
00070 FOR T = 1 TO 5
00080     PRINT TESTS(T);
00090 NEXT T
```

RUNNH
  85 71 63 51 99

As the loop control variable T varies from 1 to 5, so does the value of the array subscript, and the computer prints elements 1 through 5 of array TESTS.

PERFORMING CALCULATIONS ON ARRAY ELEMENTS

Now consider again the problem of the TV network viewing poll presented earlier in this chapter. The output format required that each line contain the viewer's name, his or her number of viewing hours, and the difference between those hours and the average hours of all the viewers. This problem is solved in the program in Figure IX–1. The solution can be broken into the following steps:

1. Read the data to two arrays: a character string array for the names and a numeric array for the hours.
2. Calculate the average viewing hours.
3. Calculate for each viewer the difference between his or her hours and the average; these differences can be stored in a third array.
4. Print the required information from the three arrays.

The viewers' names and hours are read to their appropriate arrays in line 200 as part of a FOR/NEXT loop. Line 210 performs an accumulation of all the elements of the array HRS. As I varies from 1 to 10, the elements 1 through 10 of HRS are added to the total hours (THRS). Therefore, when this loop is exited, the arrays NME$ and HRS are filled with values, and the unsubscripted variable THRS contains the sum of all the values contained in HRS. The average number of viewing hours is then calculated in line 230.

The FOR/NEXT loop starting in line 260 calculates the difference from the average viewing time for each viewer and stores the results in the array DAVG. Thus the first element of each array contains some information about the first viewer, the second element of each array concerns the second viewer, and so on. All of the information can then be printed in the required format by the FOR/NEXT loop of lines 320 through 340.

```
00010 REM ***           NETWORK VIEWING TIME SURVEY          ***
00020 REM
00030 REM *** THIS PROGRAM DETERMINES THE AVERAGE VIEWING  ***
00040 REM *** TIME BY A GROUP OF VIEWERS. IT THEN DETER-   ***
00050 REM *** MINES THE DIFFERENCE FOR EACH VIEWER FROM    ***
00060 REM *** THE AVERAGE AND THEIR ACTUAL VIEWING TIME.   ***
00070 REM *** MAJOR VARIABLES:                             ***
00080 REM ***     NME$      ARRAY OF VIEWERS               ***
00090 REM ***     HRS       ARRAY OF HOURS                 ***
00100 REM ***     DAVG      ARRAY OF DIFFERENCES FROM AVG  ***
00110 REM ***     AVG       AVERAGE VIEWING HRS            ***
00120 REM ***     THRS      TOTAL VIEWING HRS              ***
00130 REM
00140 REM *** DIMENSIONING THE ARRAY SIZES ***
00150 DIM NME$(10), HRS(10), DAVG(10)
00160 THRS = 0
00170 REM
00180 REM *** READ DATA AND CALCULATE TOTAL HOURS ***
00190 FOR I = 1 TO 10
00200    READ NME$(I),HRS(I)
00210    THRS = THRS + HRS(I)
00220 NEXT I
00230 AVG = THRS / 10
00240 REM
00250 REM *** CALCULATE DIFFERENCES ***
00260 FOR I = 1 TO 10
00270    DAVG(I) = HRS(I) - AVG
00280 NEXT I
00290 REM
00300 REM *** PRINT RESULTS ***
00310 PRINT "NAME","HRS";TAB(22);"DIFFERENCE FROM AVG"
00320 FOR I = 1 TO 10
00330    PRINT NME$(I),HRS(I),DAVG(I)
00340 NEXT I
00350 PRINT
00360 PRINT "AVERAGE VIEWING TIME = ";AVG
00370 REM
00380 REM *** DATA STATEMENTS ***
00390 DATA P. BUSCH, 1, C. CARSTENS, 5, J. DRAKE, 0, H. POIROT, 2
00400 DATA M. BULAS, 7, D. CSONGAS, 3, C. HASTINGS, 4, T. ZEKLY, 11
00410 DATA S. MCKINNIS, 3, G. BALDUCCI, 4
00999 END
```

```
RUNNH
NAME            HRS     DIFFERENCE FROM AVG
P. BUSCH        1             -3
C. CARSTENS     5              1
J. DRAKE        0             -4
H. POIROT       2             -2
M. BULAS        7              3
D. CSONGAS      3             -1
C. HASTINGS     4              0
T. ZEKLY        11             7
S. MCKINNIS     3             -1
G. BALDUCCI     4              0

AVERAGE VIEWING TIME =  4
```

Sometimes not every element of an array needs to be manipulated in the same way. If we wanted to find the product of only the odd-numbered entries in an array K containing 25 numbers, we could use the following statements:

```
00090 PROD = 1
00100 FOR I = 1 TO 25 STEP 2
00110    PROD = PROD * K(I)
00120 NEXT I
```

● Two-Dimensional Arrays

The arrays shown so far in this chapter have all been one-dimensional arrays; that is, arrays that store values in the form of a single list. Two-dimensional arrays enable a programmer to represent more complex groupings of data. For example, suppose that a fast-food restaurant chain is running a four-day promotional T-shirt sale at its three store locations. It might keep the following table of data concerning the number of shirts sold by each of the three restaurants.

		Store		
		1	2	3
	1	12	14	15
	2	10	16	12
Day	3	11	18	13
	4	9	9	10

Each row of the data refers to a specific day of the sale, and each column contains the sales data for one store. Thus, the number of shirts sold by the second store on the third day of the sale (18) can be found in the third row, second column.

Data items that can be grouped into rows and columns such as this can be stored easily in a two-dimensional array. A two-dimensional array named SHIRTS containing the preceding data can be pictured like this:

Array SHIRTS

12	14	15
10	16	12
11	18	13
9	9	10

The array SHIRTS consists of twelve elements arranged as four rows and three columns. In order to reference a single element of a two-dimensional array such as this, two subscripts are needed: one to indicate the row and a second to indicate the column. For instance, the subscripted variable SHIRTS(4,1) contains the number of shirts sold on the fourth day by the first store (9). In BASIC, the first subscript gives the row number and the second subscript gives the column number.

The rules regarding one-dimensional arrays also apply to two-dimensional arrays. Two-dimensional arrays are named in the same way as other variables, and cannot use the same name as another array (of one or two dimensions) in the same program. A two-dimensional array can contain only one type of data; numeric and character string values cannot be mixed.

As with one-dimensional arrays, subscripts of two-dimensional arrays can be indicated by any legal numeric expression:

```
SHIRTS(3,3)
SHIRTS(1,2)
SHIRTS(I,J)
SHIRTS(1,I + J)
```

Assume that $I = 4$ and $J = 2$, and that the array X contains the following 16 elements:

Array X:

10	15	20	25
50	55	60	65
90	95	100	105
130	135	140	145

The following examples show how the various forms of subscripts are used:

Example	Refers to
X(4,I)	X(4,4)—The element in the fourth row, fourth column of X, which is 145.
X(J,I)	X(2,4)—The element in the second row, fourth column of X, which is 65.
X(3,J+1)	X(3,3)—The element in the third row, third column, which is 100.
X(I−1,J−1)	X(3,1)—The element in the third row, first column, which is 90.

As with one-dimensional arrays, most computers automatically reserve space for a two-dimensional array. Usually this default reservation allows for 11 elements (0 through 10) for each dimension, making 11 rows and 11 columns. (Some computers reserve 10 elements (1 through 10) per dimension.) Thus the default space for a two-dimensional array is usually $11 \times 11 = 121$ elements. As mentioned earlier, often the 0 elements (those in the 0 row and 0 column) are ignored.

The DIM statement can also be used to set the dimensions of a two-dimensional array. The general format of such a DIM statement is as follows:

line# DIM variable (limit1,limit2)

where the variable is the array name, and the limits are the highest possible values of the subscripts for each dimension. For example, the following statement reserves space for the two-dimensional character array STDNT$, with up to 16 rows and 6 columns, for a total of $16 \times 6 = 96$ elements (or $15 \times 5 = 75$ elements if the subscripts begin at 1):

```
00030 DIM STDNT$(15,5)
```

● **COMPUTERS AND INFORMATION PROCESSING**

READING AND PRINTING WITH TWO-DIMENSIONAL ARRAYS

Recall from the previous sections of this chapter that a FOR/NEXT loop is a convenient means of accessing all the elements of a one-dimensional array. The loop control variable of the FOR statement is used as the array subscript, and as the loop control variable changes value, so does the array subscript:

```
00030 DIM X(5)
00040 FOR I = 1 TO 5
00050    READ X(I)
00060 NEXT I
```

FOR/NEXT loops can also be used to read data to and print information from a two-dimensional array. It may be helpful to think of a two-dimensional array as a group of one-dimensional arrays, with each row making up a single one-dimensional array. A single FOR/NEXT loop can read values to one row. This process is repeated for as many rows as the array contains; therefore, the FOR/NEXT loop that reads a single row is nested within a second FOR/NEXT loop controlling the number of columns being accessed.

The array SHIRTS of the previous example can be filled from the sales data table one row at a time, moving from left to right across the columns. The following segment shows the nested FOR/NEXT loops that do this:

```
00030 FOR I = 1 TO 4
00040    FOR J = 1 TO 3
00050       READ SHIRTS(I,J)
00060    NEXT J
00070 NEXT I
00080 DATA 12,14,15
00090 DATA 10,16,12
00100 DATA 11,18,13
00110 DATA 9,9,10
```

Notice that each time line 50 is executed, one value is read to a single element of the array; the element is determined by the current values of I and J. This statement is executed $4 \times 3 = 12$ times, which is the number of elements in the array.

The outer loop (loop I) controls the rows, and loop J controls the columns. Each time the outer loop is executed once, the inner loop is executed three times. While I = 1, J becomes 1, 2, and finally 3 as the inner loop is executed. Therefore, line 50 reads values to SHIRTS(1,1), SHIRTS(1,2), and SHIRTS(1,3), and the first row is filled:

| | J = | |
1	2	3
12	14	15

I = 1

While I equals 2, J again varies from 1 to 3, and line 50 reads values to SHIRTS(2,1), SHIRTS(2,2) and SHIRTS(2,3) to fill the second row:

	J =		
	1	2	3
	12	14	15
I = 2	10	16	12

I is incremented to 3 and then to 4, and the third and fourth rows are filled in the same manner.

To print the contents of the entire array, the programmer can substitute a PRINT statement for the READ statement in the nested FOR/NEXT loops. The following segment prints the contents of the array SHIRTS, one row at a time:

```
00040 BLANK = 10
00050 FOR I = 1 TO 4
00060    FOR J = 1 TO 3
00070       PRINT TAB(BLANK * J);SHIRTS(I,J);
00080    NEXT J
00090    PRINT
00100 NEXT I
```

The semicolon at the end of line 70 tells the computer to print the three values on the same line. After the inner loop is executed, the blank PRINT statement in line 90 sets the carriage return so that the next row is printed on the next line. The program in Figure IX–2 shows how the data table for the T-shirt sales results can be read to a two-dimensional array and printed in table form with appropriate headings.

ADDING ROWS

Once data has been stored in an array, it is often necessary to manipulate certain array elements. For instance, the sales manager in charge of the T-shirt promotional sale might want to know how many shirts were sold on the last day of the sale.

Because the data for each day is contained in a row of the array, it is necessary to total the elements in one row of the array (the fourth row) to find the number of shirts sold on the fourth day. The fourth row can be thought of by itself as a one-dimensional array. One loop is therefore required to access all the elements of this row:

```
00030 D4SALES = 0
00040 FOR J = 1 TO 3
00050    D4SALES = D4SALES + SHIRTS(4,J)
00060 NEXT J
```

Notice that the first subscript of SHIRTS(4,J) restricts the computations to the elements in row 4, while the column,J, varies from 1 to 3. The process performed in line 50 is pictured in the following diagram:

● COMPUTERS AND INFORMATION PROCESSING

Array SHIRTS:

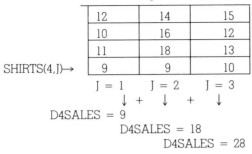

12	14	15
10	16	12
11	18	13
9	9	10

SHIRTS(4,J)→

J = 1   J = 2   J = 3
↓   +   ↓   +   ↓

D4SALES = 9

D4SALES = 18

D4SALES = 28

● **FIGURE IX-2**
Two Dimensional Array

```
00010 REM ***                    T-SHIRT SALES REPORT                 ***
00020 REM
00030 REM *** THIS PROGRAM PRINTS A REPORT ON THE NUMBER OF           ***
00040 REM *** T-SHIRTS SOLD PER STORE FOR 4 DIFFERENT DAYS.           ***
00050 REM *** MAJOR VARIABLES:                                        ***
00060 REM ***    TSHIRT          ARRAY OF T-SHIRTS SOLD               ***
00070 REM ***    I,J             LOOP CONTROLS                        ***
00080 REM
00090 REM *** DIMENSION ARRAY ***
00100 DIM TSHIRT(4,3)
00110 REM
00120 REM *** READ THE DATA ***
00130 FOR I = 1 TO 4
00140     FOR J = 1 TO 3
00150         READ TSHIRT(I,J)
00160     NEXT J
00170 NEXT I
00180 REM
00190 REM *** PRINT TABLE OF QUANTITIES SOLD ***
00200 PRINT "DAY #";TAB(10);"STORE 1";TAB(20);"STORE 2";TAB(30);"STORE 3"
00210 FOR I = 1 TO 4
00220     PRINT I;
00230     FOR J = 1 TO 3
00240         PRINT TAB(J*10);TSHIRT(I,J);
00250     NEXT J
00260     PRINT
00270 NEXT I
00280 REM
00290 REM *** DATA STATEMENTS ***
00300 DATA 12,4,15,10,6,12,11,8,13,9,9,10
00999 END
```

```
RUNNH
DAY #      STORE 1    STORE 2    STORE 3
  1          12          4         15
  2          10          6         12
  3          11          8         13
  4           9          9         10
```

ADDING COLUMNS

To find the total number of T-shirts sold by the third store, it is necessary to total the elements in the third column of the array. This time we can think of the column by itself as a one-dimensional array of four elements. This operation calls for a FOR/NEXT loop, as shown here:

```
00040 S3SHOP = 0
00050 FOR I = 1 TO 4
00060     S3SHOP = S3SHOP + SHIRTS(I,3)
00070 NEXT I
```

In line 60, the second subscript (3) restricts the computations to the elements in the third column, while the row, I, varies from 1 to 4. This process is pictured in the following diagram:

Array SHIRTS

SHIRT(I,3)
↓

12	14	15
10	16	12
11	18	13
9	9	10

I = 1 → S3SHOP = 15
I = 2 → S3SHOP = 27
I = 3 → S3SHOP = 40
I = 4 → S3SHOP = 50

TOTALING A TWO-DIMENSIONAL ARRAY

Consider now the problem of finding the grand total of all T-shirts sold during the entire four-day special offer. The program must access all the elements of the array one at a time and add them to the grand total. Remember that nested FOR/NEXT loops were used to print or read values to a two-dimensional array. This same method can be used to total the elements of an array by substituting an addition operation for the READ or PRINT statement:

```
00050 TSHIRT = 0
00060 FOR I = 1 TO 4
00070     FOR J = 1 TO 3
00080         TSHIRT = TSHIRT + SHIRTS(I,J)
00090     NEXT J
00100 NEXT I
```

This segment adds the elements in a row-by-row sequence. While I equals 1, the inner loop causes J to vary from 1 to 3, thus adding the contents of the first row elements to the total accumulated in TSHIRT. When the outer loop terminates, the contents of all four rows will have been added to the total.

This totaling of all the elements of the array can also be performed in a column-by-column sequence:

```
00050 TSHIRT = 0
00060 FOR J = 1 TO 3
00070     FOR I = 1 TO 4
00080         TSHIRT = TSHIRT + SHIRTS(I,J)
00090     NEXT I
00100 NEXT J
```

Note that the two loops have been interchanged from the first example. Now the outer loop, loop J, controls the columns, and the inner loop, loop I, controls the rows. While J equals 1, I varies from 1 to 4 and the elements of the first column are added to the total: SHIRTS(1,1), SHIRTS(2,1), SHIRTS(3,1) and SHIRTS(4,1). J is then incremented to 2, the second column is added, and so on.

● The Bubble Sort

Many applications require that data items be sorted, or ordered, in some way. For example, names must be alphabetized, Social Security numbers arranged from lowest to highest, basketball players ranked from high scorer to low scorer, and the like.

Suppose that an array, X, contains five numbers that we would like ordered from lowest to highest:

It is a simple matter for us to mentally reorder this list as follows:

Array X (Unsorted)	Array X (Sorted)
10	2
30	10
15	15
100	30
2	100

What if there were seven hundred numbers instead of five? Then it would not be easy for us to order the number list. However, the computer is perfectly suited for such tasks. One method of sorting with the computer is illustrated in Figure IX–3. The **bubble sort** works by comparing two adjacent values in an array and then interchanging them according to the desired order—either ascending or descending order.

The program in Figure IX–3 sorts ten U.S. cities into alphabetical order. To the computer, the letter A is less than the letter B, B is less than C, and so on. Lines 110 through 140 simply read the city names into an array called C$ and print them. Lines 200 through 280 perform the bubble sort. Let us examine them carefully to see what happens.

Line 200 refers to the variable F, short for flag. It is initialized to 0. Its value is checked later by the computer to determine if the entire array has been sorted.

Notice the terminal value of the FOR/NEXT loop that sorts the array. The terminal value is one less than the number of items to be sorted. This is because two items at a time are compared. I varies from 1 to 9, which means that the computer eventually will compare item 9 and item 9 + 1. If the terminal value were 10 (the number of cities), the computer would try to compare item 10 with item 11, which does not exist in our array.

The IF/THEN statement in line 220 tells the computer whether to interchange two compared values. For example, when I = 1, the computer compares LOS ANGELES with CHICAGO. Since C comes before L in the alphabet, the positions of these two items must be switched:

LOS ANGELES	I = 1	CHICAGO	
	Switch		
CHICAGO	I = 2	LOS ANGELES	DETROIT
	Switch		
DETROIT	I = 3	LOS ANGELES	
	No Switch		
NEW YORK CITY	I = 4		

•

•

•

DENVER

Then I is incremented to 2, and LOS ANGELES is compared with DE-TROIT. These two names must be interchanged. This is performed by lines 230 through 250. Note that we have created a holding area, H$, so that the switch can be made. We move LOS ANGELES to the holding area, H$, and then move DETROIT to LOS ANGELES'S previous position.

● FIGURE IX–3
Bubble Sort Program

```
00010 REM ************************************************************
00020 REM ***   THIS PROGRAM SORTS THE CITIES INTO ALPHABETIC ORDER ***
00030 REM ************************************************************
00040 REM
00050 DIM C$(10)
00060 PRINT "UNSORTED LIST OF CITIES"
00070 PRINT
00080 REM ***********************************************
00090 REM ***     READ THE NAMES INTO AN ARRAY     ***
00100 REM ***********************************************
00110 FOR I = 1 TO 10
00120    READ C$(I)
00130    PRINT C$(I)
00140 NEXT I
00150 PRINT
00160 PRINT
00170 REM ***********************************************
00180 REM ***              THE BUBBLE SORT          ***
00190 REM ***********************************************
00200 F = 0
00210 FOR I = 1 TO 9
00220    IF C$(I) <= C$(I + 1) THEN 270
00230    H$ = C$(I)
00240    C$(I) = C$(I + 1)
00250    C$(I + 1) = H$
00260    F = 1
00270 NEXT I
00280 IF F = 1 THEN 200
00290 PRINT "SORTED LIST OF CITIES"
00300 PRINT
00310 FOR I = 1 TO 10
00320    PRINT C$(I)
00330 NEXT I
00340 DATA LOS ANGELES,CHICAGO,DETROIT,NEW YORK CITY,DALLAS
00350 DATA CLEVELAND,BOSTON,WASHINGTON,MIAMI,DENVER
00999 END
```

● COMPUTERS AND INFORMATION PROCESSING

Now LOS ANGELES is placed in the position previously occupied by DETROIT. Whenever the computer interchanges two values, F is set to 1 in line 260. This loop continues until every item in the array has been examined. After once through this entire loop, the array C$ looks like this:

CHICAGO
DETROIT
LOS ANGELES
DALLAS
CLEVELAND
BOSTON
NEW YORK CITY
MIAMI
DENVER
WASHINGTON

● **FIGURE IX–3**
Continued

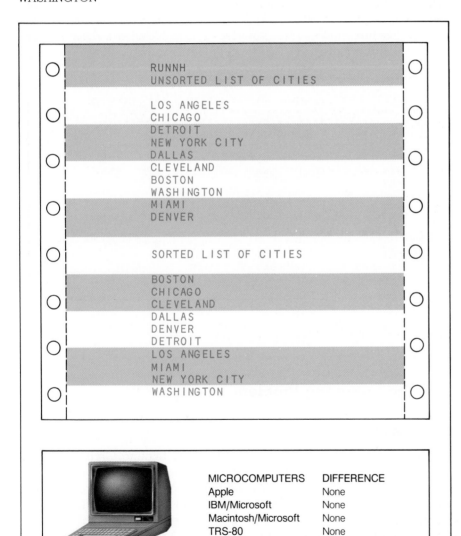

```
RUNNH
UNSORTED LIST OF CITIES

LOS ANGELES
CHICAGO
DETROIT
NEW YORK CITY
DALLAS
CLEVELAND
BOSTON
WASHINGTON
MIAMI
DENVER


SORTED LIST OF CITIES

BOSTON
CHICAGO
CLEVELAND
DALLAS
DENVER
DETROIT
LOS ANGELES
MIAMI
NEW YORK CITY
WASHINGTON
```

MICROCOMPUTERS	DIFFERENCE
Apple	None
IBM/Microsoft	None
Macintosh/Microsoft	None
TRS-80	None

Although several switches have been made, the list is not sorted completely. That is why we need line 280. As long as F equals 1, the computer knows that switches have been made, and the sorting process must continue. When the computer loops through the entire array without setting F equal to 1—that is, when no switches are made—the computer finds F equal to 0 and knows that the list is ordered.

Numbers, of course, can be sorted by this same method. Two-dimensional arrays can be sorted with nested loops.

● SWAP

The Macintosh and the IBM/Microsoft have additional capabilities which allow the use of the SWAP statement. The SWAP statement exchanges the values of two variables and is useful when sorting. The general format of the SWAP statement is shown below.

line# SWAP variable 1, variable 2

Following is a sorting subroutine using the SWAP statement.

```
01000 REM **************************************
01010 REM ***        SUBROUTINE BUBBLE SORT     ***
01020 REM **************************************
01030 REM *** SORT ARRAY D$ IN ASCENDING        ***
01040 REM *** USING THE SWAP STATEMENT.         ***
01050 REM
01060 FLAG = 0
01070 FOR K = 1 TO 9
01080     IF D$(K) <= D$(K + 1) THEN 1110
01090     SWAP D$(K),D$(K + 1)
01100     FLAG = 1
01110 NEXT K
01120 IF FLAG = 1 THEN 1060
01130 RETURN
```

● A Programming Problem

PROBLEM DEFINITION

The scorekeepers of the Centrovian Open Ice Skating Championships need a program to determine the winner of the final round. Each competitor is given six scores, of which the highest and lowest are discarded. The remaining four scores are then averaged to obtain the final score. The maximum score for each event is 6.0. Write a program that will read the names and scores of the ten finalists and produce a listing of the skaters' names and final scores in order of finish. Sample input and needed output are shown in the following table.

● COMPUTERS AND INFORMATION PROCESSING

Input:

BALDUCCI, G.	5.7	5.3	5.1	5.0	4.7	4.8
CREED, A.	3.1	4.9	4.1	3.7	4.6	3.9
WILLIAMS, E.	4.1	5.3	4.9	4.4	3.9	5.4
HAMILTON, S.	5.1	5.7	5.6	5.5	4.4	5.3
LORD, P.	5.9	4.8	5.5	5.0	5.7	5.7
STRAVINSKY, I.	5.1	4.7	4.1	3.1	4.6	5.0
MONTALBAN, R.	5.1	5.1	4.9	3.4	5.5	5.3
SCHELL, M.	4.9	4.3	5.2	4.5	4.6	4.9
CRANSTON, T.	6.0	6.0	5.7	5.8	5.9	5.9
CROWLEY, S.	4.3	5.2	6.9	5.3	4.3	6.0

Needed Output:

PLACE	NAME	SCORE
1	BALDUCCI, G.	5.7
.	.	.
.	.	.
.	.	.

SOLUTION DESIGN

The problem provides us with seven items of data for each skater—a name and six scores—and asks for a list of names and averages, sorted by average. Once the data items have been read (the first step), two basic operations must be performed in order to produce the listing: the averages must be calculated, and these averages with their associated names must be sorted. Thus, the problem can be broken into four major tasks: (1) read the data, (2) calculate the averages, (3) sort the names and averages, and (4) print the sorted information. The stepwise refinement is shown below.

1. Read names and scores
2. Calculate averages
3. Sort by averages
4. Print results

The structure chart for this problem is shown in Figure IX–4.

The input for this problem consists of two types of data, alphabetic and numeric, so two arrays must be used to store them. The output calls for

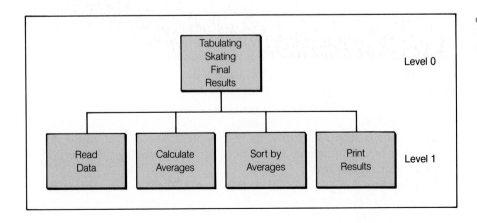

● **FIGURE IX–4**
Structure Chart for Skating Scores Program

the names already stored plus a new set of values, the averages, so another array can be used to store these averages. In calculating the averages, variables will also be needed to keep track of the high and low scores. The main variables needed can be summarized as follows.

Input variables

array of names   (SKNM$)
array of scores   (PTS)

Program variables

high score for a competitor   (HI)
low score for a competitor   (LO)
total of four scores   (TPTS)

Output variables

array of averages   (AVG)

In order to calculate the averages, each of the six scores of each skater must be examined to find the high and low scores. For any given skater, each score must be compared with the highest and lowest score found so far for that skater.

A sort is required in the third step of our algorithm. A descending-order bubble sort could be effective here, because the number of items to be sorted is relatively small. A crucial point is that, as the averages are rearranged, the corresponding skater's name must be carried with each average. This means, for example, that the average for the fourth skater (SKNM$(4)) must be stored in AVG(4).

THE PROGRAM

The program of Figure IX–5 shows the solution to the problem. Line 140 of the main program reserves space for a two-dimensional array for the scores. Each row of array PTS contains the scores for one skater, so ten rows with six columns each are needed.

The first subroutine called by the main program reads the names and scores to their respective arrays. The second subroutine finds the average score of each skater. It does this by performing a sequential search on each row of the scores array (array PTS) in lines 2050 through 2110. When the low and high scores for the row have been found, lines 2150 through 2170 add all the scores for that row, except the low and high, to the total; then the average for that row is calculated.

The sorting of the final averages is performed in the bubble sort of the third subroutine. Notice that the flag indicating that a switch has been made can be a string variable, as in line 3050. The actual value stored in the flag is unimportant; the critical factor is whether that value is changed during the sort.

The condition AVG(I) > AVG(I + 1) in line 3070 causes the averages to be sorted from highest to lowest. Every time an average is moved, its corresponding name from the array SKNM$ is also moved. The sorted results are printed by the fourth subroutine in lines 4000 through 4090.

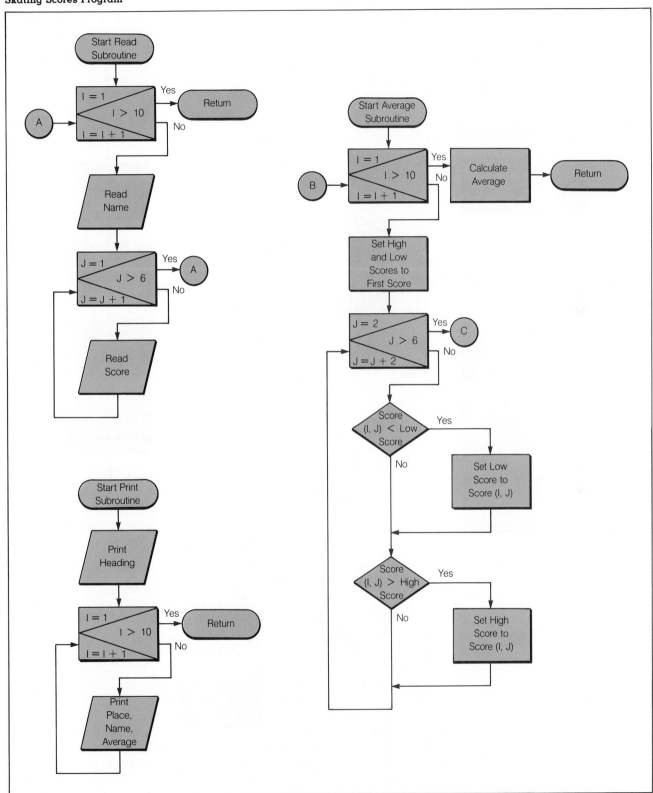

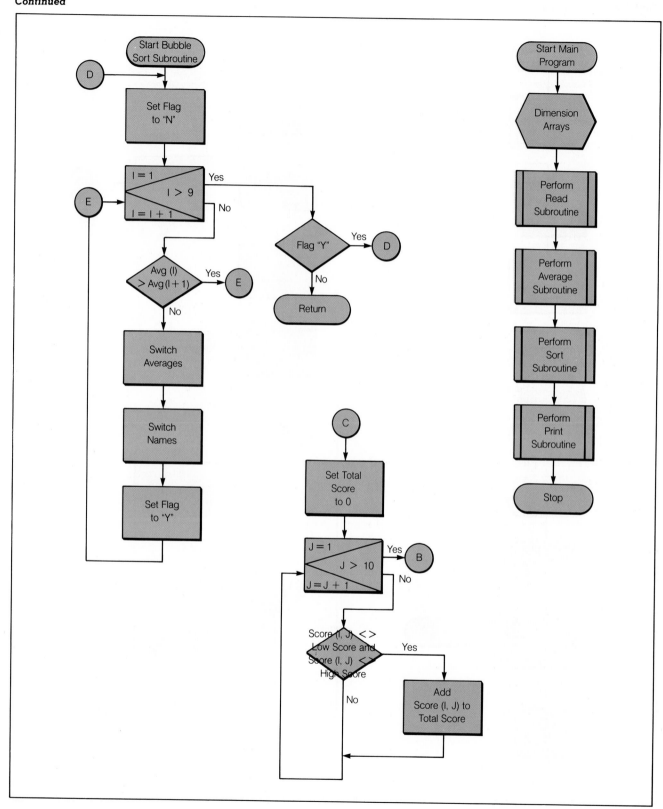

● **COMPUTERS AND INFORMATION PROCESSING**

Pseudocode

Begin main program
Dimension arrays
Perform subroutine to read data
Perform subroutine to calculate averages
Perform subroutine to sort information
Perform subroutine to print information
End main program

Begin read subroutine
Begin loop, do 10 times
    Read name
    Begin loop, do 6 times
        Read score
    End loop
End loop
End read subroutine

Begin average subroutine
Begin loop, do 10 times
    Set low and high scores to first score
    Begin loop, do 5 times
        If current score < low score
            Then set low score to current score
        End if
        If current score > high score
            Then set high score to current score
        End if
    End loop

Set total of scores to 0
    Begin loop, do 6 times
        If current score is not low or high score,
            Then add current score to total score
        End if
    End loop
    Calculate average
End loop
End average subroutine

Begin sort subroutine
Initialize flag
Begin loop, do 9 times
    If adjacent scores are already in ascending order
        Then proceed to next pair
    End if
    Switch scores and corresponding names
    Set flag to indicate switch
End loop
If flag indicates switch
    Then repeat entire process
End if
End sort subroutine

Begin print subroutine
Print headings
Begin loop, do 10 times
    Print place, name, average
End loop
End print subroutine

```
00010 REM ***              SKATING FINAL RESULTS           ***
00020 REM
00030 REM *** THIS PROGRAM COMPUTES THE AVERAGES OF SKATING ***
00040 REM *** SCORES, USING SIX SCORES AND DROPPING THE LOW ***
00050 REM *** AND HIGH SCORES. IT THEN SORTS ALL THE AVERAGE***
00060 REM *** SCORES IN ASCENDING ORDER.                    ***
00070 REM *** MAJOR VARIABLES:                              ***
00080 REM ***      SKNM$          ARRAY OF SKATERS NAMES    ***
00090 REM ***      PTS            ARRAY OF SCORES           ***
00100 REM ***      AVG            ARRAY OF AVERAGES         ***
00110 REM ***      HI,LO          HIGHEST/LOWEST SCORES     ***
00120 REM
00130 REM *** DIMENSION THE ARRAYS ***
00140 DIM SKNM$(10),PTS(10,6),AVG(10)
00150 REM
00160 REM *** READ NAMES AND SCORES ***
00170 GOSUB 1000
00180 REM
00190 REM *** CALCULATE FINAL AVERAGE ***
00200 GOSUB 2000
00210 REM
00220 REM *** SORT BY AVERAGE ***
00230 GOSUB 3000
00240 REM
00250 REM *** PRINT RESULTS ***
00260 GOSUB 4000
```

```
00270 GOTO 9999
01000 REM *********************************************************
01010 REM ***                  SUBROUTINE READ                  ***
01020 REM *********************************************************
01030 REM ***        READS THE NAMES AND SIX SCORES             ***
01040 REM
01050 FOR I = 1 TO 10
01060     READ SKNM$(I)
01070     FOR J = 1 TO 6
01080         READ PTS(I,J)
01090     NEXT J
01100 NEXT I
01110 RETURN
02000 REM *********************************************************
02010 REM ***                SUBROUTINE AVERAGE                 ***
02020 REM *********************************************************
02030 REM ***   DROP HIGH/LOW SCORES, THEN AVERAGE SCORE        ***
02040 REM
02050 FOR I = 1 TO 10
02060       HI = PTS(I,1)
02070       LO = PTS(I,1)
02080       FOR J = 2 TO 6
02090          IF PTS(I,J) < LO THEN LO = PTS(I,J)
02100          IF PTS(I,J) > HI THEN HI = PTS(I,J)
02110       NEXT J
02120       REM
02130       REM *** AVERAGE REMAINING SCORES ***
02140       TPTS = 0
02150       FOR J = 1 TO 6
02160          IF PTS(I,J) <> LO OR PTS(I,J) <> HI THEN
                   TPTS = TPTS + PTS(I,J)
02170       NEXT J
02180       AVG(I) = TPTS / 4
02190 NEXT I
02200 RETURN
03000 REM *********************************************************
03010 REM ***              SUBROUTINE BUBBLE SORT               ***
03020 REM *********************************************************
03030 REM ***        SORT AVERAGES IN ASCENDING ORDER           ***
03040 REM
03050 SWITCH$ = "N"
03060 FOR I = 1 TO 9
03070     IF AVG(I) > AVG(I + 1) THEN 3150
03080     TEMP = AVG(I)
03090     STEMP$ = SKNM$(I)
03100     AVG(I) = AVG(I + 1)
03110     SKNM$(I) = SKNM$(I + 1)
03120     AVG(I + 1) = TEMP
03130     SKNM$(I + 1) = STEMP$
03140     SWITCH$ = "Y"
03150 NEXT I
03160 IF SWITCH$ = "Y" THEN 3050
03170 RETURN
04000 REM *********************************************************
04010 REM ***                 SUBROUTINE PRINT                  ***
04020 REM *********************************************************
04030 REM ***     PRINT THE HEADINGS AND THE RESULTS            ***
04040 REM
04050 PRINT "PLACE";TAB(10);"NAME";TAB(30);"SCORE"
04060 PRINT
```

```
04070 FOR I = 1 TO 10
04080    PRINT I;TAB(10);SKNM$(I);TAB(30);AVG(I)
04090 NEXT I
04100 RETURN
04200 REM
04210 REM ***  DATA STATEMENTS  ***
04220 DATA "BALDUCCI,G",5.7,5.3,5.1,5.0,4.7,4.8
04230 DATA "CREED,A",3.1,4.9,4.1,3.7,4.6,3.9,
04240 DATA "WILLIAMS,E.",4.1,5.3,4.9,4.4,3.9,5.4,
04250 DATA "HAMILTON,S",5.1,5.7,5.6,5.5,4.4,5.3
04260 DATA "LORD,P",5.9,4.8,5.5,5.0,5.7,5.7
04270 DATA "STRAVINSKY,I",5.1,4.7,4.1,3.1,4.6,5.0
04280 DATA "MONTALBAN,R",5.1,5.1,4.9,3.4,5.5,5.3
04290 DATA "SCHELL,M",4.9,4.3,5.2,4.5,4.6,4.9
04300 DATA "CRANSTON,T",6.0,6.0,5.7,5.8,5.9,5.9
04310 DATA "CROWLEY,S",4.3,5.2,6.9,5.3,4.3,6.0
09999 END
```

```
RUNNH
PLACE     NAME                SCORE

  1       CRANSTON,T          8.825
  2       LORD,P              8.15
  3       CROWLEY,S           8
  4       HAMILTON,S          7.9
  5       BALDUCCI,G          7.65
  6       MONTALBAN,R         7.325
  7       SCHELL,M            7.1
  8       WILLIAMS,E.         7
  9       STRAVINSKY,I        6.65
 10       CREED,A             6.075
```

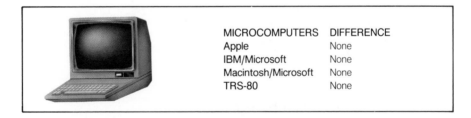

MICROCOMPUTERS	DIFFERENCE
Apple	None
IBM/Microsoft	None
Macintosh/Microsoft	None
TRS-80	None

● Summary Points

● Arrays are lists or tables of related values stored under a single variable name.

● Access to individual elements in an array can be gained through the use of subscripts.

● A subscript of an array element can be any legal numeric expression.

● The DIM statement sets up storage for arrays and must appear before the first reference to the array it describes.

- Array manipulation is carried out through the use of loops.
- A two-dimensional array stores values as a table or matrix, grouped into rows and columns.
- The first subscript of a two-dimensional array refers to the element's row, and the second subscript refers to the column.
- The bubble sort places elements of an array in ascending or descending order by comparing adjacent elements.

● Review Questions

1. What is an array?

2. We can make reference to individual elements in an array by referring to their position. This is done through the use of _____.

3. What is the purpose of the DIM statement?

4. DIM statements must appear where in a program?

5. Only one array can be dimensioned in a DIM statement. True or false?

6. Assume X = 1, Y = 2, and Z = 3. What are the values of the variables A(X), A(Y − X), and A(X*Z) if array A contains the following values?

Array A

11
42
37
90
17

7. Write a set of instructions that will find the sum of the four elements in array A.

8. Reading data into and printing data from two-dimensional arrays can be accomplished using _____statements.

9. Give two advantages of arrays.

10. Describe how a bubble sort works.

● Debugging Exercises

Identify the following programs or program segments that contain errors, and debug them.

```
1. 00010 DIM L(15)
   00020 FOR I = 1 TO 16
   00030     PRINT L(I)
   00040 NEXT I
2. 00100 DIM X(3,2)
   00110 FOR I = 1 TO 2
   00120     FOR J = 1 TO 3
   00130         READ X(I,J)
   00140     NEXT J
   00150 NEXT I
```

● Programming Problems

1. A stereo equipment store is holding a sale. The manager needs a program that will place the prices of all sale items in one array and the corresponding rate of discount in a second array. A third array should be used to hold the sale price of each item (sale price = price − (rate * price)). Use the following data:

Price	Rate of Discount
$178.89	0.25
59.95	0.20
402.25	0.30
295.00	0.25
589.98	0.30
42.99	0.20

Print the original prices and their corresponding sale prices.

2. Read 12 numbers to array A and 12 numbers to array B. Compute the product of the corresponding elements of the two arrays, and place the results in array C. Print a table similar to the following:

A	B	C
2	3	6
7	2	14

3. Your teacher has a table of data concerning the semester test scores for your class:

Name	Test 1	Test 2	Test 3
Mathey, S.	88	83	80
Sandoval, V.	98	89	100
Haggerty, B.	75	65	79
Drake, J.	60	85	99
Jenkins, J.	75	89	89

Your teacher would like to know the test average for each student, and the class average for each test. The output should include the preceding table.

4. The following list of employee names and identification numbers is in alphabetical order. Use a bubble sort to print the list in ascending order by I.D. number. (Remember that when you change the position of a number in the array, the position of the name also must be changed so that they correspond.)

Name	I.D. #
Altt, D.	467217
Calas, M.	624719
Corelli, F.	784609
Kanawa, K.	290013
Lamas, F.	502977
Lehman, B.	207827
Shicoff, N.	389662
Talvela, M.	443279
Tousteau, J.	302621
Wymer, E.	196325

5. The manager of the Epitome Books store would like a program that will generate a report regarding the sales of the various types of books the store carries. The program should use the following data:

Year	Pop. Fiction	Classics	Biography	Instruction
1982	4,561	549	973	3,702
1983	5,140	632	1,375	4,300
1984	5,487	581	1,798	4,345
1985	5,952	605	2,204	5,156

The report should indicate what percentage of each year's total sales consisted of each book type. The format for the report is as follows:

SALES PERCENTAGES FOR EACH YEAR:

YEAR	POP. FICTION	CLASSICS	BIOGRAPHY	INSTRUCT.
1982	XX.XX%	XX.XX%	XX.XX%	XX.XX%
1983				
1984				
1985				

● Section X
File Processing

● Introduction

Up to this point, we have been storing data in variables using either
DATA statements or INPUT statements. The storage locations where these
variables are kept are in the primary storage unit of the computer. This
method of storing data is adequate for some applications, but not for
others.

Suppose that a large amount of data needs to be stored. Two problems
arise: the data is difficult to organize, and the computer's primary storage
unit may be too small to hold all of it. These problems occur often in
business and scientific applications. For instance, a large insurance corporation needs many pieces of data for each of its policy holders. This
data might include the policyholder's name, address, age, social security
number, the type of policy, the amount of the policy, what the policy
covers, and so on. The amount of memory in the corporation's computer
would almost certainly be too small to store all of this data, and the data
would not be organized in a useful fashion.

Another problem also arises. What if the same data needs to be accessed by more than one program? For example, the data used by the
accounting department in one program might need to be used by the
sales department in a different program. It would not be efficient to have
duplicate DATA statements in both programs, and updating all the DATA
statements would likely result in some errors.

Using files can help us solve these problems. A **file** is a collection of
related data items organized in a meaningful way and kept in secondary
storage. In this section, you will learn to use files in BASIC programs.
Unfortunately, however, there is no standardized method for performing
operations on files. Many BASIC implementations include unique file
manipulation commands, although the principles on which these commands are based are similar. We will discuss the general concepts of
file handling before explaining how the necessary commands are implemented on each of the BASIC systems discussed here.

● What Is a File?

Files provide an alternative means of organizing and storing related
data. A major advantage of using files is that they make use of secondary

storage, which is virtually unlimited; thus the problem of inadequate space in the primary storage unit is solved. Another advantage is that the data contained in a file can be organized and stored using a variety of methods, depending on the needs of the user. Also, many users can access the same file. Thus, data can be used more efficiently, and updating data is simpler and less error-prone.

Although files help to solve these problems, they have one major disadvantage. It takes longer to retrieve data stored in a file than data stored in the computer's primary storage unit. When using files, the computer must locate the data in secondary storage, move it into the primary storage unit, and then retrieve it. Even though program execution is slower using files, the advantages of greater storage space and data organization outweigh this disadvantage.

There are two major divisions within a file. The smallest of these divisions, the *field*, contains a single unit of information. A student's name is an example of a **field** value. Fields are grouped together to form the second major division, the **record.** A record consists of one or more fields that describe a single entity. Therefore, an example of a record might contain a name field, a course field, and a grade field; together, these fields would constitute a student's record for a single course. The finished product, a file, consists of a group of records. An example of a file is a group of student records, each containing a name field, a course field, and a grade field.

A computer file can be compared to a drawer in a filing cabinet. A particular file drawer usually contains related information about one general topic. For example, it might contain information about a company's employees. A computer file also contains information about a single subject. Within each file cabinet drawer there are probably folders, each containing information regarding a single employee. Records for computer files also contain information about individual entities. Each record in file drawer folder consists of a collection of individual pieces of information, such as an employee's name, address, and so on. Each field in a computer file also contains a single piece of information. Figure X–1 illustrates this concept.

Now that the divisions of a computer file have been explained, the organization within a file can be described. In many companies or or-

● **FIGURE X–1**
Parts of a File

Name:	George C. Schott	Field 1		
			Record 1	
Address:	1632 Arrowhead Dr.	Field 2		
Name:	Ellen B. McGold	Field 1		
			Record 2	File
Address:	112 E. Reed #16	Field 2		
Name:	Karen L. Milhoan	Field 1		
			Record 3	
Address:	215 Colorado Blvd.	Field 2		

ganizations, special filing systems are used. For example, the records within a file cabinet might be arranged alphabetically or from the oldest to the newest. Computer records can also be organized in several different ways. This organization of records within a file is referred to as **file organization.**

● File Organization

The method used to organize records within a file determines how these records will be stored and retrieved by the BASIC system. The method of organization is specified when a file is created. Three possible methods of file organization are implemented on BASIC systems, although some systems allow only two of them to be used.

The first method of organization, **sequential organization,** stores records in a sequence. The order in which records are written to a file determines the order in which the records are stored. In order to access a record with sequential organization, all preceding records must be accessed before the record needed can be accessed. Therefore, if the fifth record of a file needs to be accessed, the first four records must be sequentially accessed first.

To help in understanding this concept, imagine four rooms, each with one door that connects it to the room next to it:

1	2	3	4

In order for a person to enter the third room, he or she must open the door at the left and walk through the first room, open the next door and walk through the second room, and then open the third door and walk through the third room. This concept is analogous to sequential organization of files.

A second method of organization, **relative organization,** stores each record in a numbered location in secondary storage. A record can be accessed either in order from the first record to the needed record, or randomly by using the record's numbered location. Now imagine that there is a hallway adjacent to the four connected rooms. Each room still has a door that connects it to the next room, but now each room also has another door that enters in the hallway:

1	2	3	4

In order for a person to enter the third room, he or she can walk through the first two rooms and enter the third room, or enter the hallway and open the door to the third room. This concept is similar to that of relative organization of computer files.

The third method of file organization, **indexed organization,** stores records according to a primary key. A **primary key** is a field that uniquely identifies a particular record and by which that record is accessed. Records cannot be accessed by their physical order when using indexed organization. The primary key field of each record must be different from that of every other record in the file. An example of a primary key is a person's social security number. Because no two people have the same social security number, an individual's record can be uniquely identified by this value.

Records in a file using indexed organization may contain more than one key. The additional keys, called **secondary keys,** are unique or nonunique fields that can also be used to access and retrieve records. However, a record must be accessed through its primary key before the secondary key can be used.

Let's now compare indexed organization with our analogy of the four rooms. The rooms now have no doors between them; there is only the hallway with a door entering into each room. In order for a person to find a specific room, he or she must know the room number (that is, the primary key value). By knowing the room number, a person can find the needed room and enter it. This concept is illustrated as follows:

| 1 | 2 | 3 | 4 |

Because records are organized within files using different methods, it might seem that the retrieval of records for each type of file organization would be different. This is not the case, however; only two access methods exist. One access method can be used with all three types of file organization, and the other can be used with two types of file organization. We will discuss these methods next.

● Methods of Accessing Files

An **access method** is a way in which the computer transmits data between secondary storage and the primary storage unit when reading data to or writing data from a file. Two types of access methods are used in BASIC: random access and sequential access.

Random access allows the BASIC program, not the manner in which the file is organized, to control which record is to be accessed. The record is accessed directly because the program specifies which record is to be retrieved. A record location number is used if the record is in a relative file, and a key value is used if the record is in an indexed file. Random access cannot be used with a record in a sequential file, because there is no primary key field or record location number by which to access it.

The other access method, **sequential access,** retrieves a record based on its sequential position within the file. Sequential access uses the physical ordering of the sequential file or the position number of the relative file to access a record sequentially. Note that a sequential file is not the same as sequential access. The term "sequential file" refers to the organization of a file, whereas "sequential access" refers to the manner in which individual records within the file are retrieved.

The next section discusses the type of secondary storage medium that is used by the computer to store the file. The type of medium is an important factor in file organization and access.

● Secondary Storage

Secondary storage refers to storage media outside the primary storage unit on which files are permanently kept. Some forms of secondary storage media are magnetic tapes, magnetic disks, and floppy diskettes. Home computers such as the Macintosh, Apple, IBM PC, and TRS-80 most frequently use floppy diskettes. Larger computers, such as the DEC-system, use magnetic tapes or disks.

A reel of magnetic tape looks similar to a reel of movie film. Magnetic tape is usually 2400 feet long and is spun by a tape drive, as shown in Figure X–2. Because of the design of a tape drive, records must be read sequentially. The read/write head, which performs the actual reading and writing of the data, cannot skip to a particular record on the tape; the tape must spin until the read/write head locates the needed record. Figure X–3 shows how records are stored on magnetic tape.

A magnetic disk looks like a record album. Data is stored on the disk in tracks, which are series of concentric circles on the surface of the magnetic disk (see Figure X–4). A collection of concentric disk tracks with

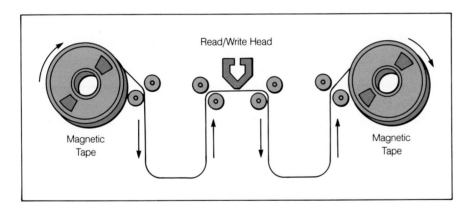

● **FIGURE X–2**
Read/Write Head

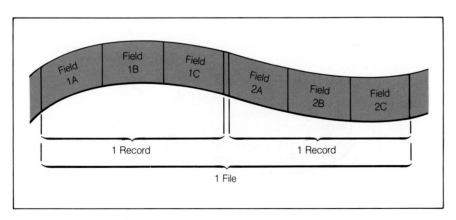

● **FIGURE X–3**
Data Storage on Magnetic Tape

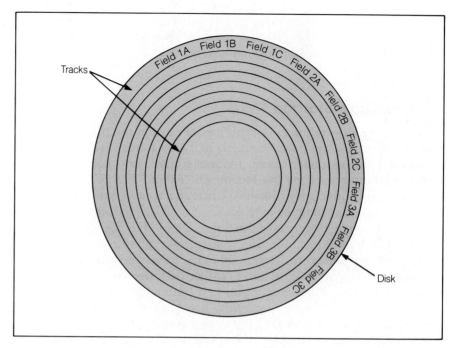

the same radius is called a cylinder. Both cylinders and tracks are numbered. A group of disks is a disk pack, which looks like a stack of record albums with a spindle passing through the middle, as shown in Figure X–5. Notice that there are two read/write heads for each disk: one for the upper surface and one for the lower surface. (The top and bottom disk in the disk pack each have only one read/write head for control purposes.) The read/write arm, which holds the read/write heads, can move backward and forward, and the disk pack can rotate on the spindle as well. By using the numbered tracks and cylinders and the movement of the disk pack, the computer can find a record randomly or sequentially.

A floppy diskette (Figure X–6) looks like a small record album in its cover. To locate a record, the computer uses tracks that are located on the diskette. Each track is divided into sectors. The diskette contains an index hole, which the computer uses to calculate the location of a particular sector by timing the diskette's rotation. Figure X–7 shows the parts of a floppy diskette.

Data file programs never have to specify the physical address when accessing a record. However, the file organization and the access method

● FIGURE X–5
A Disk Pack

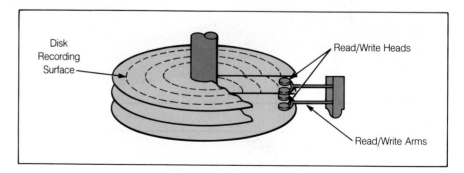

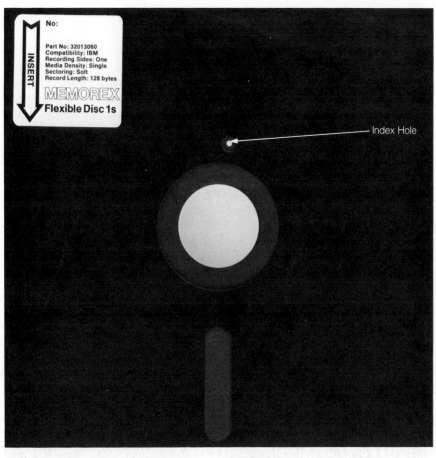

Index Hole

must be determined before the program is written. Not all file organizations can be used with all access methods on all types of secondary storage, as shown in Figure X–8.

● Using Sequential Files With Sequential Access and Relative Files With Random Access

Now that we have explained the general concepts of what a file is, how it is organized, and how it is stored, we can describe specific applications. This section will not explain how to use all the possible file organizations with all the types of BASIC systems presented in this textbook. An entire book could be written on this subject. We will explain only the most

● FIGURE X–7
Parts of a Floppy Diskette

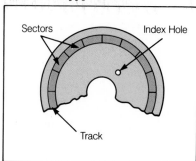

Sectors

Index Hole

Track

● FIGURE X–8
Possible Combinations of Storage Media, File Organizations, and Access Methods

FILE ORGANIZATION	ACCESS METHOD	STORAGE MEDIA
Sequential	Sequential	Tape, Disk, Diskette
Relative	Random or Sequential	Disk, Diskette

frequently used combinations: sequential files with sequential access and relative files with random access.

In sequential files, records are stored in the order in which they were written to the file. Therefore, when a programmer needs to write to or read from a sequential file, all records that precede the needed one must be accessed first. This is referred to as a predecessor-successor record relationship. For each successfully accessed record (except the last) there is a succeeding record somewhere in the file.

Sequentially organized files allow only sequential access. In these files, the predecessor-successor relationship is physical (that is, each record except the last is physically adjacent to the next record). Sequential access to a sequential file means that records are accessed in the order in which they were inserted into the file. A record can be processed only after each preceding record has been successfully accessed. Similarly, once a record is processed, you must start at the beginning of the file before preceding records can be accessed. For example, imagine four houses on a one-way street where house number one is the first house as you enter the street. For a driver to get to the third house he or she would have to turn on to the one-way street and drive past the first and the second house. If the driver should then wish to go to the first house it would be necessary for him or her to go around the block and return to the beginning of the one-way street.

Programs that use random access to relative files must specify a particular record number, which represents the record location. Remember that a relative file consists of records in numbered locations: location 1 contains the first record relative to the start of the file, location 2 contains the second record, and so forth. Because the record locations are numbered, records do not have to be read or written in sequential order. The records are still in sequential order from the beginning of the file, however, so they can be sequentially accessed. Relative files that use random access are referred to as random files by all of the BASIC systems. Specific instructions for sequential files will be explained for the DECsystem 20/ 60, Apple, IBM, Macintosh, and TRS-80.

● File Position Pointers

Associated with each file is a file position pointer that indicates the current position in the file; i.e., the next record to be processed. The computer itself manipulates this pointer when a file command is executed in a program. For instance, when a file is accessed the pointer is moved to the beginning of the specified file so that the first record in the file is available for processing. If a program then retrieves a record, the file pointer is automatically advanced, after the operation is performed, to the next record. For example, in the diagram below of file NAMES the file pointer points to the name MIKE after the file is accessed.

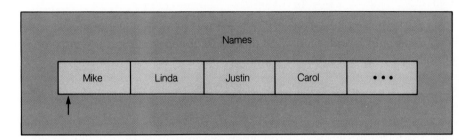

If a record retrieval is then executed, the name MIKE would be read and the file pointer would advance to the next record; the pointer would then be at LINDA.

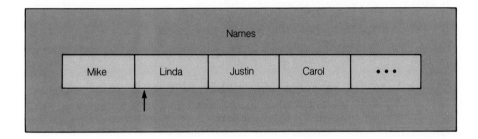

The file position pointer has no effect on the data contained in the file; it simply indicates the current position in the file. This information will be useful when processing sequential and relative files.

● DECsystem 20/60

MAPPING

Before a file is opened, a buffer must be created in memory. A buffer is a space set aside in main memory that contains a record that has been read from secondary storage or a record that will be written to secondary storage. The MAP statement establishes and names this buffer, and also describes the fields contained in each of the records in the file. It lists the variables into which each of these fields will be placed. The general format of the MAP statement is as follows:

line# MAP (buffer-name) fieldname,fieldname

Buffer-name is the name given to the buffer (the parentheses around it are optional). **Fieldname** assigns a name to each field of the record. The length of each string field must be specified by the syntax:

string variable fieldname = n

where string variable **fieldname** is any string variable, and *n* is the maximum number of characters that will ever need to be placed in that field. An example of the MAP statement is as follows:

```
00010 MAP BUFF1 P$ = 16,H$ = 2
```

This MAP statement indicates that each record in this file has two fields. The maximum length of the first field is 16 characters, and the maximum length of the second field is 2 characters.

CREATING AND ACCESSING A FILE

The OPEN statement enables you to create a new file or access an existing file. The following syntax is used when opening an existing file or creating a new sequential file:

line# OPEN filename FOR $\begin{Bmatrix} \text{INPUT} \\ \text{OUTPUT} \end{Bmatrix}$

AS FILE #integer,SEQUENTIAL,MAP mapname

MAP mapname

(The braces ({}) indicate a choice. Choose one from the enclosed options.) where:

filename	is a string expression representing the name of the file.
FOR INPUT	requires that the specified file exists. If the file does not exist, an error results.
FOR OUTPUT	creates a new file with the specified name.

(If you leave the FOR INPUT/OUTPUT clause out entirely, BASIC searches for an existing file of the specified name. If the search fails, BASIC creates a new file. It is good programming practice always to specify this clause in the OPEN statement.)

AS FILE #integer	Associates the file with a file number; zero is invalid.
SEQUENTIAL	Arranges the records in the file by order of input.
MAP mapname	References a MAP statement that defines the record layout buffer used to store the file's data temporarily.

The following example opens a sequential file:

```
00020 OPEN "COMMITTEE" FOR OUTPUT AS FILE #2,
            SEQUENTIAL MAP BUFF1
```

Because the file is opened FOR OUTPUT, a new file named COMMITTEE is created. BUFF 1 is the mapname for the buffer that contains the record layout.

CLOSING A FILE

Files should be closed when no longer needed. The CLOSE statement closes all types of files. It has the following format:

● **COMPUTERS AND INFORMATION PROCESSING**

line# CLOSE #filenumber 1[,filenumber 2...]

For example:

```
00070 CLOSE #1
00080 CLOSE #2,#4
```

These statements close the three files represented by the filenumbers 1, 2, and 4. If you do not specify a file number, BASIC closes all files, as shown below:

```
00070 CLOSE
```

FILE OPERATIONS

There are several operations that you can perform on individual records in a file. These operations allow you to add, modify and examine the records within a file. The following section describes the available options for sequential file organization.

Writing to a File

When a file is opened for output, a new file is created; however, no records are in the file. To place records in a newly created file, the PUT statement is used. The PUT statement writes a new record from the buffer to the file. The general format of the PUT statement for sequential files is as follows:

line# PUT #filenumber

Figure X–9 is an example of a program creating a new file and adding records to it. Notice that the input variables are the same as the MAP (buffer) variables. This causes the buffer to be filled with the record's data, so that when line 110 is encountered the buffer data is written to the file represented by the file number 2.

When sequential files are used, the order in which the records occur in the file is determined by the order in which they were written to the file. This is because each time a PUT statement is executed, the record in the buffer is written to the file and the file position pointer points to the end of the newly inserted record (also referred to as the next available record position). In Figure X–9 the record SARA 21 is the first record in the file COMMITTEE because it was entered first, TONY 43 is second, and so forth.

If it is necessary to append (add to the end) records to an existing file, a few alterations to the OPEN statement are necessary. Because the file is already created, the file must be opened for INPUT. The reason for this is that if an existing file is opened for OUTPUT the file is deleted and a new file is created. When a file is opened for INPUT, the file position pointer points to the first record in the file; however, records can only be added to the end of a sequential file. Thus it becomes necessary to have the file position pointer point to the end of the file. This can be done by adding an ACCESS APPEND clause to the statement:

line# OPEN filename FOR INPUT ,AS FILE #integer,SEQUENTIAL, MAP map-name, ACCESS APPEND

```
00060 MAP BUFF1 NME$ = 15, HRWK
00070 OPEN "COMMITTEE" FOR OUTPUT AS FILE #2, SEQUENTIAL, MAP BUFF1
00080 INPUT "ENTER THE NAME (FINISH TO QUIT) ";NME$
00090 WHILE NME$ <> "FINISH"
00100   INPUT "ENTER THE HOURS WORKED ";HRWK
00110   PUT #2
00120   INPUT "ENTER THE NAME (FINISH TO QUIT) ";NME$
00130 NEXT
00140 CLOSE #2
00999 END
```

```
RUNNH
ENTER THE NAME (FINISH TO QUIT)   ? SARA
ENTER THE HOURS WORKED   ? 21
ENTER THE NAME (FINISH TO QUIT)   ? TONY
ENTER THE HOURS WORKED   ? 43
ENTER THE NAME (FINISH TO QUIT)   ? JAY
ENTER THE HOURS WORKED   ? 31
ENTER THE NAME (FINISH TO QUIT)   ? DANNY
ENTER THE HOURS WORKED   ? 23
ENTER THE NAME (FINISH TO QUIT)   ? LORRAINE
ENTER THE HOURS WORKED   ? 16
ENTER THE NAME (FINISH TO QUIT)   ? FINISH
```

● **FIGURE X–9**
Writing to a Sequential File

This clause sets the file pointer initially to the end of the file. Now records can be appended in the same manner as they are added to a new file.

Figure X–10 shows a program adding records to the file COMMITTEE, which was created in Figure X–9. The only change made was in the OPEN statement; the file is opened for INPUT and the ACCESS APPEND clause has been added.

Reading from a File

To read a record from a file you need to open the file for input and then use the GET statement. The general format of the GET statement for sequential files is as follows:

```
00060 MAP BUFF1 NME$ = 15, HRWK
00070 OPEN "COMMITTEE" FOR INPUT AS FILE #2, SEQUENTIAL, MAP BUFF1,
         ACCESS APPEND
00080 INPUT "ENTER THE NAME (FINISH TO QUIT) ";NME$
00090 WHILE NME$ <> "FINISH"
00100   INPUT "ENTER THE HOURS WORKED ";HRWK
00110   PUT #2
00120   INPUT "ENTER THE NAME (FINISH TO QUIT) ";NME$
00130 NEXT
00140 CLOSE #2
00999 END
```

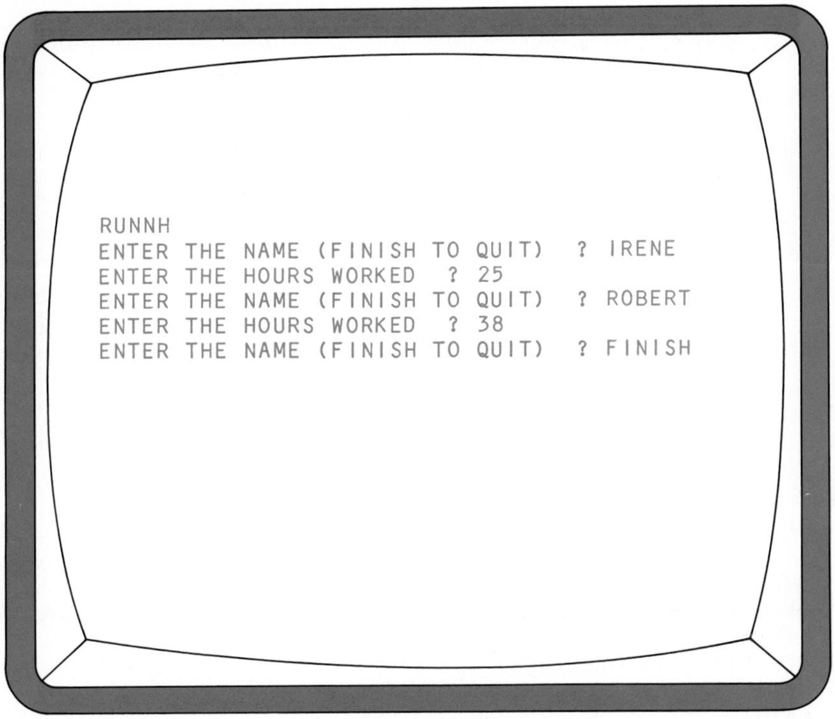

```
RUNNH
ENTER THE NAME (FINISH TO QUIT)  ? IRENE
ENTER THE HOURS WORKED  ? 25
ENTER THE NAME (FINISH TO QUIT)  ? ROBERT
ENTER THE HOURS WORKED  ? 38
ENTER THE NAME (FINISH TO QUIT)  ? FINISH
```

● FIGURE X–10
Appending Records to a Sequential File

line# GET #filenumber

This statement reads the record pointed to by the file position pointer, from the file specified, and places it in the buffer. After the GET statement is executed, the file position pointer is automatically advanced to the next record.

In a sequential file a GET operation is performed on succeeding records starting at the beginning of the file (because the OPEN statement sets the pointer at the first record). Each successive GET statement retrieves the next record in the file and places it in the buffer. Unless the user knows the exact number of records in a file, it is impossible to know how many GET statements should be executed in order to read the entire file. If the program attempts to read more than the number of records in a file an error will occur and the program will stop executing prematurely.

This situation can be avoided by an ONERROR statement. This statement allows the user to read the file until the end of the file is found, and then continue with the rest of the program. This syntax is as follows:

line# ONERROR GOTO line number

Figure X–11 reads the data records stored in the file COMMITTEE, which was created and added to Figures X–9 and X–10.

Line 130 causes the program flow to branch around the printing of the records when the end of the file is found. Line 140 retrieves a record from the file and places it in the buffer; notice that the variables printed are the same as those in the buffer.

Within a subroutine, a RESUME statement must be used in conjunction with the ONERROR statement. The RESUME statement has the following format:

line # RESUME transfer line number

The transfer line number, which is optional, specifies the line to which control is transferred. If the transfer line is omitted, control passes to the line where the error occurred. If the program code appearing in Figure X-11 were used in a subroutine, a RESUME statement would be included to cause execution to continue beyond the end of the loop:

```
00130 ONERROR GOTO 170
00140    GET #2
00150     PRINT NME$;TAB(15);HRWK
00160 GOTO 130
00170 RESUME 180
00180 CLOSE #2
00190 RETURN
```

● **FIGURE X11**
Reading a Sequential File

```
00060 MAP BUFF1 NME$ = 15, HRWK
00070 OPEN "COMMITTEE" FOR INPUT AS FILE #2, SEQUENTIAL, MAP BUFF1
00090 REM
00100 REM *** PRINT THE HEADINGS ***
00110 PRINT "NAME";TAB(15);"HOURS WORKED"
00120 PRINT
00130 ONERROR GOTO 170
00140    GET #2
00150     PRINT NME$;TAB(15);HRWK
00160 GOTO 130
00170 CLOSE #2
00999 END
```

```
RUNNH
NAME          HOURS WORKED

SARA          21
TONY          43
JAY           31
DANNY         23
LORRAINE      16
IRENE         25
ROBERT        38
```

● IBM/Microsoft and Macintosh/Microsoft

For our purposes here the IBM/Microsoft and Macintosh/Microsoft implementations of files are very similar. Therefore, we will discuss these two implementations together, noting any differences. (Remember that line numbers are optional on the Macintosh.)

CREATING AND ACCESSING A FILE

The OPEN statement enables the programmer to create a new file or access an existing file. The following syntax is used when creating a new, or accessing an existing, sequential file:

$$\text{line\# OPEN ''filename'' FOR} \left\{ \begin{array}{l} \text{INPUT} \\ \text{OUTPUT} \\ \text{APPEND} \end{array} \right\} \text{AS \#filenumber}$$

where:

filename	is a string expression representing the name of the file.
FOR INPUT	requires that the specified file exist; if not, an error results. Used for sequential files.
FOR OUTPUT	creates a new file with the specified name. Used for sequential files.
FOR APPEND	used for sequential files. Sets the file pointer to the end of the file.

If the FOR INPUT/OUTPUT/APPEND is omitted, the computer defaults to random files and searches for an existing random file of the specified name. If found, the file is opened for input; if the search fails, BASIC creates a new random file.

AS #filenumber   associates a file with a number; zero is invalid.

For example, the following statement opens a sequential file named COMMITTEE and gives it filenumber 3:

```
470 OPEN "COMMITTEE" FOR INPUT AS #3
```

CLOSING A FILE

Files need to be closed when no longer needed. The CLOSE statement closes all types of files. It has the following format:

920 CLOSE #filenumber[,#filenumber...]
where:
#filenumber   represents the file to be closed.
For example:
```
70 CLOSE #1
80 CLOSE #2,#3,#5
```

These statements close the four files represented by the filenumbers 1,2,3, and 5. If no filenumber is supplied, as shown below, BASIC closes all files.

```
70 CLOSE
```

FILE OPERATIONS

Several operations can be performed on individual records in a file, depending on the file's organization. These operations allow you to add, modify, and examine the records within a file. The following section describes the available options in relation to sequential file organization.

Writing to a File

When a file is opened for output, a new file is created; however no records are in the file. To place records in a newly created file the WRITE# statement is used. The WRITE# statement writes a new record to the file. The general format is as follows:

WRITE #filenumber,expression-list

The filenumber is the number under which the file was opened with the OPEN statement. The expressions in the list can be either string or numeric expressions. They must be separated by commas.

Figure X–12 is an example of a program creating a new file and adding records to it. With sequential files the order in which the records occur in the file is the order in which they are written to the file. This is because each time a WRITE# statement is executed, the record is written to the file and the file position pointer is advanced to the next record position. Therefore, in Figure X–12 the record SARA 21 is the first record in the file COMMITTEE because it was entered first, TONY 43 is second, and so on.

If it is necessary to add records to an existing file the OPEN statement must contain the FOR APPEND clause. When a file is opened for input or output the file position pointer is placed at the first record in the file; however, you can only write records at the end of a sequential file. The FOR APPEND clause sets the file position pointer to the end of the specified file and permits the user to insert new records.

Figure X–13 shows a program adding records to the file COMMITTEE, which was created in the program in Figure X–12. The only change made was in the OPEN statement; the file is opened for APPEND.

Reading from a File

To read a record from a file, the file must be opened for input; then the INPUT# statement is used. The general format of this statement is as follows:

line# INPUT #filenumber,variable-list

The filenumber is the number used when the file was opened for input. The variable-list contains the names used that will be assigned to the items in the file (the data types must match).

This statement reads the record pointed to by the file position pointer from the file specified and places its contents in the variables in the variable list. After the INPUT# statement is executed, the file position pointer is automatically advanced to the next record.

```
70 OPEN "COMMITTEE" FOR OUTPUT AS #3
80 INPUT "ENTER THE NAME (FINISH TO QUIT) ";NME$
90 WHILE NME$ <> "FINISH"
100     INPUT "ENTER THE HOURS WORKED ";HRWK
110     WRITE #3,NME$,HRWK
120     INPUT "ENTER THE NAME (FINISH TO QUIT) ";NME$
130 WEND
140 CLOSE #3
999 END
```

```
RUN
ENTER THE NAME (FINISH TO QUIT) ? SARA
ENTER THE HOURS WORKED ? 21
ENTER THE NAME (FINISH TO QUIT) ? TONY
ENTER THE HOURS WORKED ? 43
ENTER THE NAME (FINISH TO QUIT) ? JAY
ENTER THE HOURS WORKED ? 31
ENTER THE NAME (FINISH TO QUIT) ? DANNY
ENTER THE HOURS WORKED ? 23
ENTER THE NAME (FINISH TO QUIT) ? LORRAINE
ENTER THE HOURS WORKED ? 16
ENTER THE NAME (FINISH TO QUIT) ? FINISH
```

In a sequential file, an INPUT# operation is performed on succeeding records starting at the beginning of the file (because the OPEN statement sets the pointer to the first record). Each successive INPUT# statement retrieves the next record in the file and places it in the variable list. Unless the user knows the exact number of records in a file it is impossible to know how many INPUT# statements should be executed in order to read the entire file. If the program attempts to read more records than are in the file, an error will occur and program execution will stop prematurely. This can be avoided by the EOF function. This function tests for the end-of-the-file, thus allowing the user to read the file until the end is found. The syntax is as follows:

EOF (filenumber)

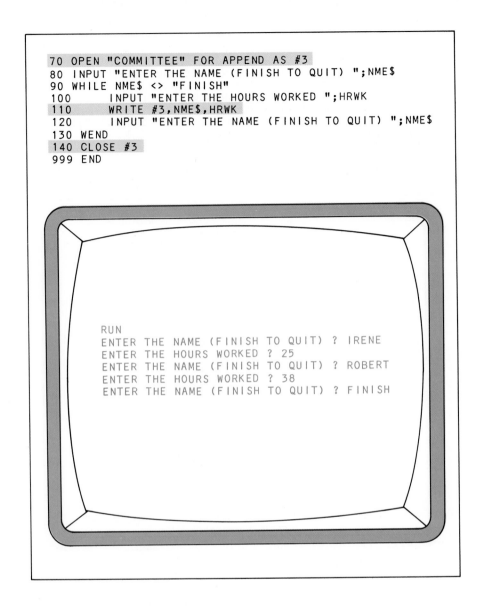

```
70 OPEN "COMMITTEE" FOR APPEND AS #3
80 INPUT "ENTER THE NAME (FINISH TO QUIT) ";NME$
90 WHILE NME$ <> "FINISH"
100     INPUT "ENTER THE HOURS WORKED ";HRWK
110     WRITE #3,NME$,HRWK
120     INPUT "ENTER THE NAME (FINISH TO QUIT) ";NME$
130 WEND
140 CLOSE #3
999 END
```

```
RUN
ENTER THE NAME (FINISH TO QUIT) ? IRENE
ENTER THE HOURS WORKED ? 25
ENTER THE NAME (FINISH TO QUIT) ? ROBERT
ENTER THE HOURS WORKED ? 38
ENTER THE NAME (FINISH TO QUIT) ? FINISH
```

Figure X–14 reads the data records stored in the file COMMITTEE, which was created and added to in Figures X–12 and X–13.

The WHILE statement in line 120 uses the EOF function to find the end of the file. Once the WHILE condition is false (that is, the end of the file has been reached), the file is closed and execution stops. Line 130 retrieves a record from the file and places its contents in the variables listed.

● TRS-80 Model 4

CREATING AND ACCESSING A FILE

The OPEN statement enables the programmer to create a new file or access an existing file. The following is used when creating a new or accessing an existing sequential file:

```
 70 OPEN "COMMITTEE" FOR INPUT AS #3
 80 REM
 90 REM *** PRINT THE HEADINGS ***
100 PRINT "NAME";TAB(15);"HOURS WORKED"
110 PRINT
120 WHILE NOT EOF(3)
130     INPUT #3,NME$,HRWK
140     PRINT NME$;TAB(15);HRWK
150 WEND
160 CLOSE #3
999 END
```

● **FIGURE X–14**
Reading a Sequential File

● FIGURE X–14
Reading a Sequential File

```
RUN
NAME            HOURS WORKED

SARA            21
TONY            43
JAY             31
DANNY           23
LORRAINE        16
IRENE           25
ROBERT          38
```

$$\text{line\# OPEN} \begin{Bmatrix} ``I" \\ ``O" \\ ``E" \end{Bmatrix} \text{,filenumber,filename}$$

where:

I   instructs the computer to open for input an existing sequential
                    file. If the file specified does not exist, an error results.

O   instructs the computer to create a new sequential file with the
                    filename specified.

E   is used with sequential files; it opens an existing file and sets
                    the file pointer to the end of the file.

filenumber   associates a file with a number; zero is invalid.

filename   is a string expression representing the name of the file.

For example, the following statement opens a sequential file named
COMMITTEE and gives it filenumber 3:

```
130 OPEN "I",3,"COMMITTEE"
```

CLOSING A FILE

Files need to be closed when no longer needed. The CLOSE statement
closes all types of files. It has the following format:

line# CLOSE filenumber[,filenumber...]

where filenumber represents the file to close. For example:

```
70 CLOSE 1
80 CLOSE 2,3,5
```

BASIC SUPPLEMENT ●   **B-221**

These statements close the four files represented by the filenumbers 1, 2, 3, and 5. If you do not specify any filenumber, all files are closed:

```
70 CLOSE
```

FILE OPERATIONS

Several operations can be performed on individual records in a file. These operations allow you to add, modify, and examine the records within a file.

The following section describes the options in relation to sequential file organization.

Writing to a File

When a file is opened for output, a new file is created; however, no records are in the file. To place records in a newly created file you use the WRITE# statement. The WRITE# statement writes a new record to the file. The general format of this statement for sequential files is as follows:

WRITE# filenumber, expression-list

The filenumber is the number under which the file was opened with the OPEN statement. The expressions in the list are string or numeric expressions. They must be separated by commas.

Figure X–15 is an example of a program creating a new file and adding records to it. With sequential files the order in which they are written to the file is the order in which they occur in the file. This is because each time a WRITE# statement is executed the record is written to the file and the file pointer is advanced to the next record position. Therefore, in Figure X–15 the record SARA 21 is the first record in the file COMMITTEE because it was entered first; TONY 43 is second, and so on.

If it is necessary to add records to an existing file, the OPEN statement must be formatted as follows:

line# OPEN "E",filenumber,filename

When a file is opened for input/output, the file position pointer is placed at the first record in the file; however, records can only be appended to the end of a sequential file. Thus it becomes necessary to have the file position pointer point to the end of the file. Opening the file with "E" sets the file position pointer to the end of the specified file and permits the user to append new records.

Figure X–16 shows a program adding records to the file COMMITTEE, which was created in the program in Figure X–15. The only change made was in the OPEN statement.

Reading from a File

To read a record from a file, the file must be opened for input:

line# OPEN "I",filenumber,filename

● COMPUTERS AND INFORMATION PROCESSING

```
70    OPEN "O",2,"COMMITTEE"
80    INPUT "ENTER THE NAME (FINISH TO QUIT) ";NME$
90    WHILE NME$ <> "FINISH"
100     INPUT "ENTER THE HOURS WORKED ";HRWK
110     WRITE #2,NME$,HRWK
120     INPUT "ENTER THE NAME (FINISH TO QUIT) ";NME$
130   WEND
140   CLOSE 2
999   END
```

```
RUN
ENTER THE NAME (FINISH TO QUIT) ? SARA
ENTER THE HOURS WORKED ? 21
ENTER THE NAME (FINISH TO QUIT) ? TONY
ENTER THE HOURS WORKED ? 43
ENTER THE NAME (FINISH TO QUIT) ? JAY
ENTER THE HOURS WORKED ? 31
ENTER THE NAME (FINISH TO QUIT) ? DANNY
ENTER THE HOURS WORKED ? 23
ENTER THE NAME (FINISH TO QUIT) ? LORRAINE
ENTER THE HOURS WORKED ? 16
ENTER THE NAME (FINISH TO QUIT) ? FINISH
```

Then the INPUT# statement is used to read the needed data:

line# INPUT #filenumber,variable-list

The filenumber is the number used when the file was opened for input. The variable list contains the names used that will be assigned to the items in the file (the data types must match).

This statement reads the record pointed to by the file position pointer, from the file specified, and places its contents in the variables of the variable list. After the INPUT# statement is executed, the file position pointer is automatically advanced to the next record.

In a sequential file, an INPUT# operation is performed on succeeding records starting at the beginning of the file (because the OPEN statement sets the pointer at the first record). Each successive INPUT# statement retrieves the next record in the file and places it in the variable list.

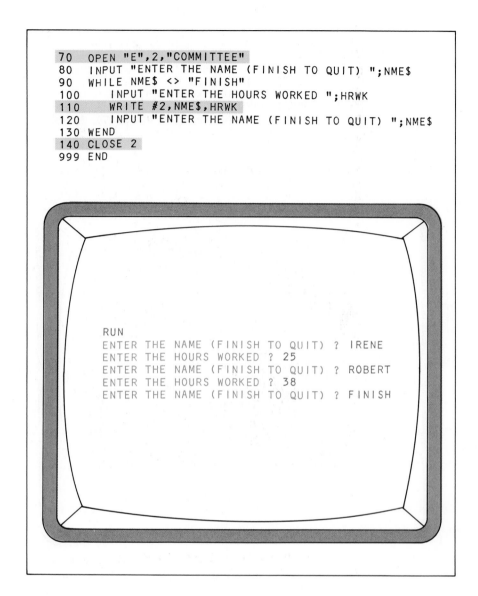

```
70   OPEN "E",2,"COMMITTEE"
80   INPUT "ENTER THE NAME (FINISH TO QUIT) ";NME$
90   WHILE NME$ <> "FINISH"
100     INPUT "ENTER THE HOURS WORKED ";HRWK
110     WRITE #2,NME$,HRWK
120     INPUT "ENTER THE NAME (FINISH TO QUIT) ";NME$
130  WEND
140  CLOSE 2
999  END


RUN
ENTER THE NAME (FINISH TO QUIT) ? IRENE
ENTER THE HOURS WORKED ? 25
ENTER THE NAME (FINISH TO QUIT) ? ROBERT
ENTER THE HOURS WORKED ? 38
ENTER THE NAME (FINISH TO QUIT) ? FINISH
```

Unless the user knows the exact number of records in a file it is impossible
to know how many INPUT# statements should be executed in order to
read the entire file. If the program attempts to read more records than
are in the file, an error will occur and the program will stop executing
prematurely. This can be avoided by using the EOF (*End Of File*) function. This function tests for the end of a data file, thus allowing the program to read the file until the end is encountered. The syntax is as follows:

EOF (filenumber)

Figure X–17 reads the data records stored in the file COMMITTEE,
which was created and added to in Figures X–15 and X–16.

The WHILE statement in line 120 uses the EOF function to find the end
of the file. Once the WHILE condition is false (that is, the end of the file
is reached), the file is closed and execution stops. Line 130 retrieves a
record from the file and places its contents in the variables listed.

```
70  OPEN "I",2,"COMMITTEE"
80  REM
90  REM *** PRINT THE HEADING ***
100 PRINT "NAME";TAB(15);"HOURS WORKED"
110 PRINT
120 WHILE NOT EOF(2)
130    INPUT #2,NME$,HRWK
140    PRINT NME$;TAB(15);HRWK
150 WEND
160 CLOSE 2
999 END
```

```
RUN
NAME              HOURS WORKED

SARA              21
TONY              43
JAY               31
DANNY             23
LORRAINE          16
IRENE             25
ROBERT            38
```

● Apple

CREATING AND ACCESSING A FILE

Data files, referred to as text files by Apple, are stored on floppy diskettes. In order to access a disk for text files from within a BASIC program, the user must press the CTRL key and the D key simultaneously. An alternative method of accessing files is to have the program reference a string variable that has been set equal to CHR$(4), the ASCII code character for <CTRL><D>. It is common practice to call this variable D$. The following statement should come at the beginning of a text file program:

```
10 D$ = CHR$(4)
```

(We will use D$ from here on, and assume it has been initialized to CHR$(4).) Next, the file must be opened. The general format for the OPEN statement on the Apple when creating a new, or accessing an existing, sequential file is as follows:

line# PRINT $\left\{ \begin{array}{c} \text{D\$} \\ \text{<CTRL><D>} \end{array} \right\}$; "OPEN filename"

where:

PRINT $\left\{ \begin{array}{c} \text{D\$} \\ \text{<CTRL><D>} \end{array} \right\}$ tells the computer that a file on disk is going to be accessed. D$ must have been initialized to CHR$(4).

OPEN   opens the specified file.

filename   identifies the file.

For example, the following statement opens a sequential file named COMMITTEE.

```
290 PRINT D$;"OPEN COMMITTEE"
```

CLOSING A FILE

Files need to be closed when no longer needed. The CLOSE statement closes all types of files. It has the following format:

line# PRINT D$;"CLOSE filename"

where filename represents the file to be closed. For example:

```
80 PRINT D$;"CLOSE COMMITTEE"
```

This statement closes the file COMMITTEE. If no filename is specified, then all opened files will be closed.

FILE OPERATIONS

Several operations can be performed on individual records in a file. These operations allow the programmer to add, modify, and examine the records within a file. The following section describes the available options in relation to sequential file organizations.

Writing to a File

Before data can be written to a file, the operating system must be instructed that all subsequent PRINT statements are to write to the file instead of the display screen. The syntax for the statement to do this is as follows:

line# PRINT D$;"WRITE filename"

This statement does not write anything to the file; it just indicates to the operating system that any data is now to be written to the stated file. Now PRINT statements can be used to write data to the file. However, there is one difference between the standard PRINT statement and the PRINT statement used for files. An example is shown below:

```
70 PRINT "MONDAY",31,"MARCH"
```

The above PRINT statement appears to write three values. However, when the program tries to read the first data item back (MONDAY), all the values will come back combined into one value:

```
MONDAY31MARCH
```

In Applesoft, fields must be separated in the file by a comma or a carriage return. To solve the above problem, the programmer must assign a comma to a string variable and write that variable between every value in the PRINT statement, separated by a semicolon as follows:

```
60 C$ = ","
70 PRINT "MONDAY";C$;31;C$;"MARCH"
```

● COMPUTERS AND INFORMATION PROCESSING

A PRINT statement always generates a carriage return, thus indicating the end of a record.

Remember that the WRITE command causes all output to be written to the file, including any output that would normally appear on the display screen. Therefore, if you use an INPUT statement such as a prompt after the WRITE command has been executed, the prompt which would normally be output to the display screen would be written to the file instead. If an INPUT statement needs to be used with a prompt after the WRITE command has been executed, the WRITE command must first be cancelled by issuing the PRINT D$ statement:

```
50 PRINT D$
```

In order to continue writing data to the file you must reissue the WRITE command. Figure X–18 is an example of a program creating a new file and adding records to it.

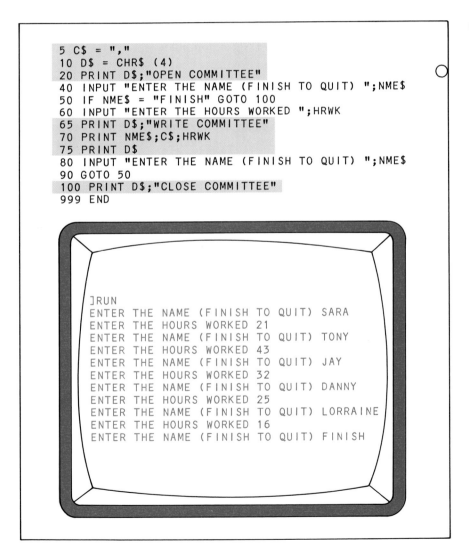

● **FIGURE X–18**
Writing to a Sequential File

```
5 C$ = ","
10 D$ = CHR$ (4)
20 PRINT D$;"OPEN COMMITTEE"
40 INPUT "ENTER THE NAME (FINISH TO QUIT) ";NME$
50 IF NME$ = "FINISH" GOTO 100
60 INPUT "ENTER THE HOURS WORKED ";HRWK
65 PRINT D$;"WRITE COMMITTEE"
70 PRINT NME$;C$;HRWK
75 PRINT D$
80 INPUT "ENTER THE NAME (FINISH TO QUIT) ";NME$
90 GOTO 50
100 PRINT D$;"CLOSE COMMITTEE"
999 END
```

```
]RUN
ENTER THE NAME (FINISH TO QUIT) SARA
ENTER THE HOURS WORKED 21
ENTER THE NAME (FINISH TO QUIT) TONY
ENTER THE HOURS WORKED 43
ENTER THE NAME (FINISH TO QUIT) JAY
ENTER THE HOURS WORKED 32
ENTER THE NAME (FINISH TO QUIT) DANNY
ENTER THE HOURS WORKED 25
ENTER THE NAME (FINISH TO QUIT) LORRAINE
ENTER THE HOURS WORKED 16
ENTER THE NAME (FINISH TO QUIT) FINISH
```

Line 5 assigns a comma to the variable string C$ and the PRINT statement in line 70 uses the variable string to separate the fields in the record written to the file. The WRITE command is issued in line 65 directly prior to the PRINT statement in line 70, which indicates the data to be written to the file. Line 75, however, cancels the WRITE command. This is so that the INPUT prompts will not be written to the file, but rather to the display screen.

Each time this program is executed, whatever is in the PRINT statement will overwrite the old file, thus deleting the data already stored in the file. If fewer characters are written than are already in the file, the tail end of the previous data will remain following the new data. To avoid this problem, the old file should be erased before new data is stored in it. To delete the file, type DELETE filename at the system prompt (]). This process is only necessary when a given file is created more than once.

With sequential files the order in which the records occur in the file is the order in which they are written to the file. If you wish to add records to an existing file you must add the records to the end of the file. Because the OPEN statement sets the file pointer to the first record in the file, it cannot be used when adding records. The APPEND statement is used instead. The format of the APPEND statement is:

line# PRINT D$;"APPEND filename"

The APPEND statement places the pointer at the end of the file; therefore records can be added to an existing file. The APPEND statement requires that the specified file already exists; if it does not, the error message FILE NOT FOUND is printed. Figure X–19 shows a program adding records to the file COMMITTEE, which was created in the program in Figure X–18. The only change made was that the OPEN statement was replaced by the APPEND statement.

Reading from a File

Just as output can be directed to a file, so input can be accepted from a file. Again, it is necessary to tell the operating system that all subsequent INPUT statements are to receive data from the specified file until the READ command is cancelled. The format is as follows:

line# PRINT D$;"READ filename"

This command does not read anything from the file; it just indicates to the operating system that data is now to be read from the file. After the READ command is executed, all subsequent input will be read from the file. Once the computer has been directed to read input from the specified file, the INPUT statement is used to read the data from the file.

All data values in a record must be read by a single INPUT statement. Each INPUT statement always reads all the data up to the next carriage return (which marks the next record's starting point), no matter how many values that may involve. The values are assigned one by one to the variables listed in the INPUT statement. If the INPUT statement does not list enough variables for all the values, the extra values are lost and the message EXTRA IGNORED appears.

● COMPUTERS AND INFORMATION PROCESSING

```
  5 C$ = ","
 10 D$ = CHR$ (4)
 20 PRINT D$;"APPEND COMMITTEE"
 40 INPUT "ENTER THE NAME (FINISH TO QUIT) ";NME$
 50 IF NME$ = "FINISH" GOTO 100
 60 INPUT "ENTER THE HOURS WORKED ";HRWK
 65 PRINT D$;"WRITE COMMITTEE"
 70 PRINT NME$,C$,HRWK
 75 PRINT D$
 80 INPUT "ENTER THE NAME (FINISH TO QUIT) ";NME$
 90 GOTO 50
100 PRINT D$;"CLOSE COMMITTEE"
999 END
```

```
]RUN
ENTER THE NAME (FINISH TO QUIT) IRENE
ENTER THE HOURS WORKED 25
ENTER THE NAME (FINISH TO QUIT) ROBERT
ENTER THE HOURS WORKED 13
ENTER THE NAME (FINISH TO QUIT) FINISH
```

For example, assuming the WRITE command is in effect, the following PRINT statement would write one record to the file, but three data values (record fields).

```
390 C$ = ","
400 PRINT "MONDAY";C$;31;C$;"MARCH"
```

The INPUT statement necessary to read this record from the file is as follows:

```
420 INPUT DY$,DTE,MNTH$
```

In Applesoft, the INPUT statement interprets every comma it encounters in a file's record as the end of a value; therefore, the commas separate data in the records. This is the reason why commas must be used in the PRINT statement when writing to the file.

In a sequential file, an INPUT operation is performed on succeeding records starting at the beginning of the file (because the OPEN command sets the pointer to the first record). Each successive INPUT statement retrieves the next record in the file and places it in the variable list. Unless the user knows the exact number of records in a file it is impossible to know how many INPUT statements should be executed in order to read the entire file. If the program attempts to read more than the number of records in the file an error will occur and your program will stop executing prematurely. This situation can be avoided by an ONERR statement. This statement allows the user to read the file until the end of the file is found and then continue with the rest of the program. The syntax is:

line# ONERR GOTO line#

Figure X–20 reads the data records stored in the file COMMITTEE, using the ONERR statement to find the end of the file. Without this statement, when the end of the file is encountered, the program would stop executing and an error message would be printed. With the statement, the file will be closed and then program execution stopped because the error causes the program to branch to line 85.
Line 40 activates the READ command so the INPUT statement in line 50 will read from the file.

● A Programming Problem

PROBLEM DEFINITION

Safeway National Bank keeps a file of all its customers and their savings account balances. They have asked you to write a program that will update their master file by using a transaction file they have processed for you. Up to twenty customers and their account balances are described on a file called MASTER. Twenty or fewer customers and the amounts

● **FIGURE X–20**
Reading a Sequential File

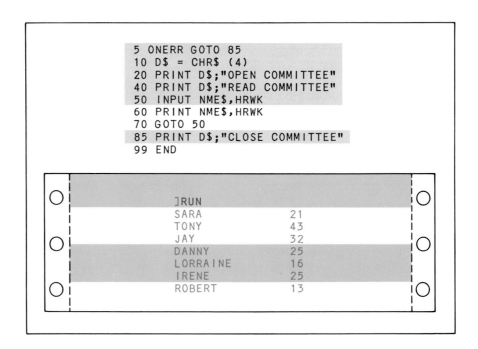

```
5 ONERR GOTO 85
10 D$ = CHR$ (4)
20 PRINT D$;"OPEN COMMITTEE"
40 PRINT D$;"READ COMMITTEE"
50 INPUT NME$,HRWK
60 PRINT NME$,HRWK
70 GOTO 50
85 PRINT D$;"CLOSE COMMITTEE"
99 END
```

```
]RUN
SARA          21
TONY          43
JAY           32
DANNY         25
LORRAINE      16
IRENE         25
ROBERT        13
```

● **COMPUTERS AND INFORMATION PROCESSING**

of their transactions are on a file called TRANSACTN. A negative amount on the TRANSACTN indicates a withdrawal, while a positive amount shows a deposit. Your program will be run on the DECsystem 20/60.

SOLUTION DESIGN

In order to produce an updated account file, the data in the master file and transaction file must be compared. This can be done by copying data from these files into arrays. Next, the transaction amounts must be added to the appropriate accounts. To find the needed account in the master arrays, each name in the transaction array can be compared to a master name array until a match is found. Then the transaction amount can be added to the old balance and placed in another array. Finally, the old customer names and the new balances can be written to the new updated file and printed. Thus, the steps needed are as follows:

1. Place the contents of the master file into arrays and print them.
2. Place the contents of the transaction file into arrays and print them.
3. Add the transaction amounts for the appropriate accounts.
4. Write the customer names and new balances from the arrays to a file and print them.

These steps are shown in the diagram in Figure X–21.

THE PROGRAM

Figure X–22 gives the program listing. Line 300 sets the dimensions for the arrays that will hold the data from the files. Lines 350 and 360 open the master and transaction files, respectively, to be read. Line 370 opens for output the new master file that will be an updated version of the master file. The appropriate buffers for each of these files are set in lines 320 through 340.

The first subroutine puts data from the master file into the arrays CUSTARAY$ and BALARAY, prints the contents of those arrays, and counts the customers in that file. Line 1170 closes the master file. The second subroutine does the same for the transaction file, putting the data in the arrays TRANSARAY$ and AMTARAY.

● **FIGURE X–21**
Structure Chart for Savings Account Update Problem

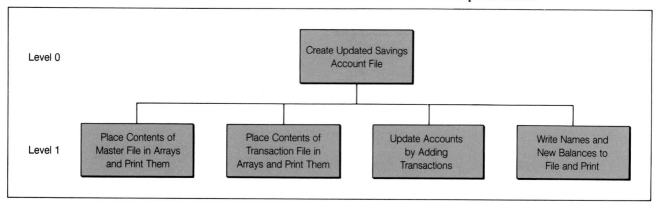

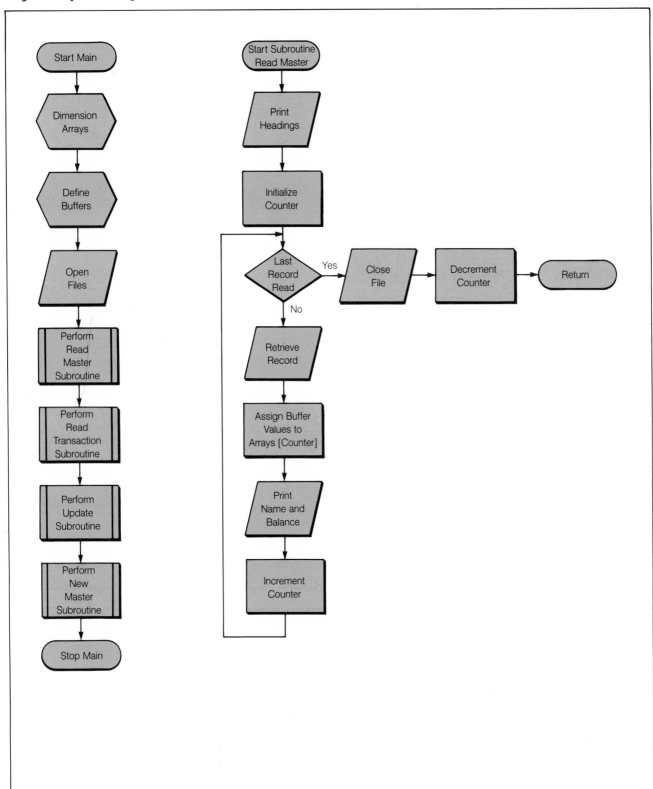

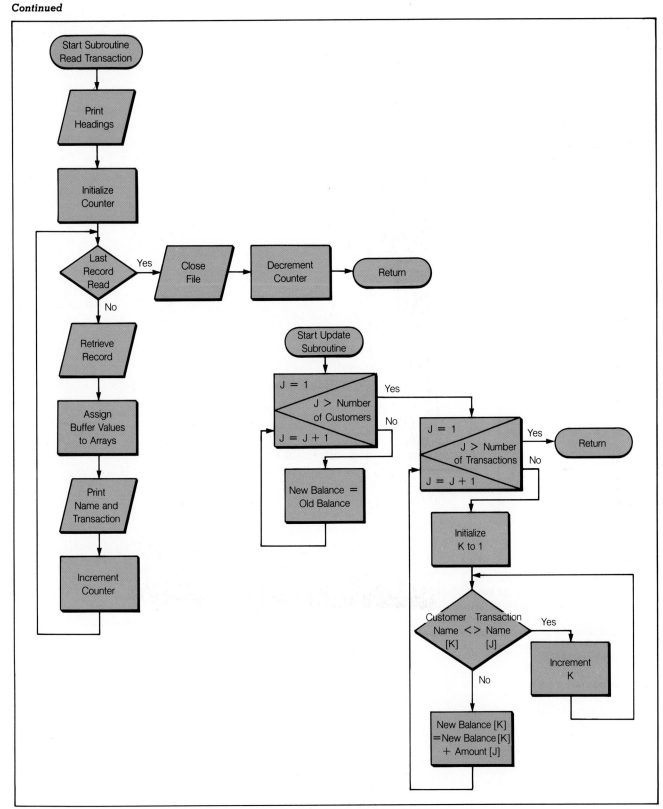

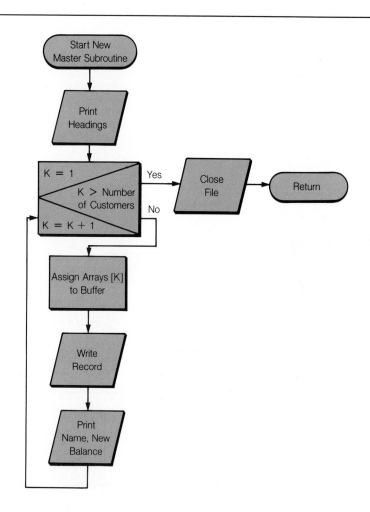

Pseudocode

Begin main program
Dimension arrays
Define buffers
Open master file, transaction file, and new master file
Perform subroutine to read master file to arrays and print them
Perform subroutine to read transaction file to arrays and print them
Perform subroutine to update account balance data
Perform subroutine to write updated data to new master file and print
End main program

Begin read master subroutine
Print headings
Begin loop, repeat until no more records
    Retrieve record
    Assign buffer values to arrays
    Print name and balance
    Update count of records
End loop

Close master file
End read master subroutine

Begin read transaction subroutine
Print headings
Begin loop, repeat until no more records
    Retrieve record
    Assign buffer values to arrays
    Print name and transaction amount
    Update count of records
End loop
Close transaction file
End read transaction subroutine

Begin update subroutine
Begin loop, repeat for number of master records
    Copy old balance to new balance
End loop

Begin loop, repeat for number of transaction records
    Initialize master array index
        Begin loop, repeat until master array name equals transaction array name
            Increment master array index
        End loop
        New balance equals old balance plus transaction amount
    End loop
    End update subroutine

    Begin new master subroutine
    Print headings
    Begin loop, repeat for number of master records
        Assign name from master array to new master buffer
        Assign new balance from array to new master buffer
        Write record
        Print name and new balance
    End loop
    Close new master file
    End new master subroutine

```
00010 REM ***                    SAVINGS ACCOUNT UPDATE                    ***
00020 REM
00030 REM *** THIS PROGRAM ACCESSES A SEQUENTIAL FILE CALLED MASTER         ***
00040 REM *** AND UPDATES ITS DATA USING THE SEQUENTIAL FILE TRANS-         ***
00050 REM *** ACTN.  THE CONTENTS OF THE FILES ARE READ INTO ARRAYS,        ***
00060 REM *** THE TRANSACTION AMOUNTS ARE ADDED TO THE APPROPRIATE          ***
00070 REM *** CUSTOMER ACCOUNTS, AND THE RESULTS ARE PLACED IN A            ***
00080 REM *** THIRD SEQUENTIAL FILE CALLED NMASTER.                         ***
00090 REM
00100 REM
00110 REM *** FIELDS OF THE FILE MASTER:                                    ***
00120 REM ***     CUST$ - CUSTOMER NAME                                     ***
00130 REM ***     BAL   - CURRENT ACCOUNT BALANCE                           ***
00140 REM *** FIELDS OF THE FILE TRANSACTN:                                 ***
00150 REM ***     NME$ - CUSTOMER NAME                                      ***
00160 REM ***     AMOUNT - AMOUNT OF TRANSACTION                            ***
00170 REM *** FIELDS OF THE FILE NMASTER:                                   ***
00180 REM ***     NCUST$ - CUSTOMER NAME                                    ***
00190 REM ***     NBAL - NEW BALANCE OF ACCOUNT                             ***
00200 REM
00210 REM *** MAJOR VARIABLES:                                              ***
00220 REM ***     MCOUNT - COUNT OF CUSTOMERS IN MASTER                     ***
00230 REM ***     TCOUNT - COUNT OF CUSTOMERS IN TRANSACTN                  ***
00240 REM ***     CUSTARAY$ - ARRAY OF CUSTOMER NAMES                       ***
00250 REM ***     BALARAY$ - ARRAY OF CURRENT BALANCES                      ***
00260 REM ***     TRANSARAY$ - ARRAY OF TRANSACTION CUSTOMERS               ***
00270 REM ***     AMTARAY - ARRAY OF TRANSACTION AMOUNTS                    ***
00280 REM ***     NBALARAY - ARRAY OF UPDATED BALANCES                      ***
00290 REM
00300 DIM CUSTARAY$(20),BALARAY(20),TRANSARAY$(20),AMTARAY(20),NBALARAY(20)
00310 REM
00320 MAP BUFF1 CUST$ = 10,BAL
00330 MAP BUFF2 NME$ = 10,AMOUNT
00340 MAP BUFF3 NCUST$ = 10,NBAL
00350 OPEN "MASTER" FOR INPUT AS FILE #1,SEQUENTIAL, MAP BUFF1
00360 OPEN "TRANSACTN" FOR INPUT AS FILE #2,SEQUENTIAL, MAP BUFF2
00370 OPEN "NMASTER" FOR OUTPUT AS FILE #3,SEQUENTIAL, MAP BUFF3
00380 REM
```

```
00390 REM *** READ FILES INTO ARRAYS ***
00400 GOSUB 1000
00410 GOSUB 2000
00420 REM
00430 REM *** DETERMINE UPDATED ACCOUNTS ***
00440 GOSUB 3000
00450 REM
00460 REM *** WRITE UPDATED ARRAY TO FILE AND PRINT ***
00470 GOSUB 4000
00480 GOTO 9999
00490 REM
01000 REM ************************************************************
01010 REM ***                    SUBROUTINE READ MASTER          ***
01020 REM ************************************************************
01030 REM *** READ FILE MASTER TO ARRAYS AND PRINT ARRAYS.       ***
01040 REM
01050 PRINT TAB(5);"MASTER FILE"
01060 PRINT "ACCOUNT","BALANCE"
01070 PRINT
01080 K = 1
01090 ONERROR GOTO 1160
01100    GET #1
01110    CUSTARAY$(K) = CUST$
01120    BALARAY(K) = BAL
01130    PRINT CUSTARAY$(K),BALARAY(K)
01140    K = K + 1
01150 GOTO 1090
01160 RESUME 1170
01170 CLOSE #1
01180 MCOUNT = K - 1
01190 RETURN
01200 REM
02000 REM ************************************************************
02010 REM ***                  SUBROUTINE READ TRANSACTION       ***
02020 REM ************************************************************
02030 REM ***   READ FILE TRANSACTN TO ARRAYS AND PRINT THEM.    ***
02040 REM
02050 PRINT
02060 PRINT TAB(2);"TRANSACTION ACCOUNT"
02070 PRINT "ACCOUNT","AMOUNT"
02080 PRINT
02090 K = 1
02100 ONERROR GOTO 2170
02110    GET #2
02120    TRANSARAY$(K) = NME$
02130    AMTARAY(K) = AMOUNT
02140    PRINT TRANSARAY$(K),AMTARAY(K)
02150    K = K + 1
02160 GOTO 2100
02170 RESUME 2180
02180 TCOUNT = K - 1
02190 CLOSE #2
02200 RETURN
02210 REM
03000 REM ************************************************************
03010 REM ***                    SUBROUTINE UPDATE               ***
03020 REM ************************************************************
03030 REM ***   COPY ALL BALANCES INTO ARRAY NBALARAY AND ADD TRANS- ***
03040 REM ***   ACTION AMOUNTS TO UPDATED ACCOUNTS.              ***
03050 REM
```

```
03060 FOR J = 1 TO MCOUNT
03070    NBALARAY(J) = BALARAY(J)
03080 NEXT J
03090 REM
03100 REM *** SEARCH MASTER ARRAY FOR ACCOUNTS TO BE UPDATED ***
03110 FOR J = 1 TO TCOUNT
03120    K = 1
03130    WHILE CUSTARAY$(K) <> TRANSARAY$(J)
03140       K = K + 1
03150    NEXT
03160    NBALARAY(K) = NBALARAY(K) + AMTARAY(J)
03170 NEXT J
03180 RETURN
03190 REM
04000 REM *****************************************************************
04010 REM ***                    SUBROUTINE NEW MASTER               ***
04020 REM *****************************************************************
04030 REM *** WRITE THE NEW BALANCE ARRAY TO THE FILE NMASTER WITH   ***
04040 REM *** THE OLD MASTER NAMES AND PRINT THEM.                   ***
04050 REM
04060 PRINT
04070 PRINT TAB(3);"NEW MASTER FILE"
04080 PRINT "ACCOUNT","BALANCE"
04090 PRINT
04100 FOR K = 1 TO MCOUNT
04110    NCUST$ = CUSTARAY$(K)
04120    NBAL = NBALARAY(K)
04130    PUT #3
04140    PRINT CUSTARAY$(K),NBALARAY(K)
04150 NEXT K
04160 CLOSE #3
04170 RETURN
09999 END
```

Now we must update the master file. Lines 3060 through 3080 set each new customer balance (NBALARAY) equal to each old account balance (BALARAY). If the name from the master file (CUSTARAY$) does not equal the name from the transaction file (TRANSARAY$) in line 3130, then the next master file name is checked until the two names are equal. When the names are equal, then line 3160 replaces the number in NBALARAY with the result of the transaction amount (AMTARAY) added to the old balance.

The fourth subroutine writes each customer's name and new balance to the file NMASTER and prints the contents of the new file. Line 4160 closes NMASTER.

● Summary Points

● Files are used to organize large amounts of data. Because they are kept in secondary storage, they solve the problem of limited space in the computer's primary storage unit.

● A given file can be accessed by many different programs.

● Files are divided into records, which in turn are divided into fields.

● Files can be organized in one of three ways: sequential organization, relative organization, or indexed organization.

● In sequential organization, records are stored in a sequence, one after another.

● In relative organization, each record is stored in a numbered location.

● When indexed organization is used, records are stored according to a primary key that uniquely identifies each record.

● Two access methods exist: random access and sequential access.

● Random access allows a program to access a particular record within a file directly, regardless of its position.

● Sequential access retrieves a record based on the record's sequential order within the file. If it is necessary to access the fifth record, for example, records 1 through 4 must be accessed first.

● Secondary storage media are a factor in determining the type of file organization and access method that will be used.

● Before a file can be accessed, it must be opened.

● When processing is completed on a file, it must be closed so that its contents are not lost.

● No standardized method exists among the various BASIC systems for performing operations on files. Therefore, it is necessary to become familiar with the specific statements used on your system.

● Review Questions

1. What is a data file?
2. What are the advantages and disadvantages of using a data file?
3. Name the divisions of a file, explain how they are related to each other, and give an example of each.
4. Explain sequential file organization.

5. Explain relative file organization.
6. Explain indexed file organization.
7. What is meant by an access method?
8. Differentiate between random access and sequential access.
9. Why can a magnetic tape only contain sequential files?
10. Why must a file be closed?

● Debugging Exercises

Identify the following programs and program segments that contain errors and debug them. These exercises are written for the DECsystem 20/60 implementation of files.

```
1. 00010  MAPP BUFF J$ = 20,PS = 5
   00020  OPEN "PAYSCALE" FOR OUTPUT AS FILE #4,SEQUENTIAL,MAP BUFF
   00030  FOR I = 1 TO 4
   00040      PRINT "JOB TITLE?"
   00050      INPUT J$
   00060      PRINT "HOURLY WAGE?"
   00070      INPUT HW
   00080      PUT #2
   00090  NEXT I
   00100  CLOSE
   00999  END
```

```
2. 00010  MAP BUFF S$ = 20,A$ = 20
   00020  OPEN "SUBSCRIBERS" FOR OUTPUT AS FILE #4,SEQUENTIAL,
                 MAP BUFFER
   00030  FOR X = 1 TO 20
   00040      GET #4
   00050      PRINT S$
   00060      PRINT A$
   00070      PRINT
   00080  NEXT X
   00099  END
```

● Programming Problems

1. The Hoytville Hardware store has just taken inventory. Create a sequential file using the following data:

Stock #	Unit Price	Quantity
A1123	$4.82	50
B2132	9.73	70
C2134	5.00	20
D1955	4.35	60
D3356	0.55	90

Write the contents of the file to the screen, with appropriate headings.

2. Using the file created in Problem 1, determine the value of inventory on hand for each item and the total inventory value. Print these values using appropriate headings.

3. Create a sequential file with the following information:

SSN	Name	Sex	Height	Birthday
269670053	Cochran, K.	M	75	04/04/62
268441124	Veryser, A.	F	64	07/08/63
267768456	Simpson, L.	F	66	02/19/57
268770786	Bulas, M.	M	68	06/24/60
269556874	Rivera, P.	M	71	11/23/63

4. Print the average age and height of all females, and the average age and height of all males, from the file created in Problem 3.

5. Write a program to determine if a student is eligible for graduation from Washington High School. Read 10 students' names, ages, credits, and grade point averages. To qualify for graduation, a student must be at least 16 years old, have 20 credits, and a grade point average of at least 2.5. Print all eligible students' records to a sequential file. Create your own data for this program. Then access the file and print it to the display screen.

BASIC GLOSSARY

Access method A way in which the computer transmits data between secondary storage and the primary storage unit.

Algorithm The sequence of steps needed to solve a problem. Each step must be listed in the order in which it is to be performed.

Alphanumeric data Any combination of letters, digits, and/or special characters.

Argument A value used by a function to obtain its final result.

Array A group of related data items, stored in consecutive storage locations, with a single variable name.

Assignment statement A statement that causes a value to be stored in a variable.

Boolean operator See **Logical operator.**

Branching Altering the normal flow of execution.

Bubble sort A sort that progressively arranges the elements of an array in ascending or descending order by making a series of comparisons of the adjacent array values and exchanging values that are out of order.

Character string A group of alphanumeric characters enclosed in quotation marks.

Concatenation The joining of data items, such as character strings, to form a single item.

Conditional transfer Program control is transferred to another point only if a stated condition is satisfied.

Constant A value that does not change during program execution.

Control statement A statement that allows the programmer to alter the order in which program instructions are executed.

Conversational mode See **inquiry-and-response mode.**

Counter A method of loop control in which a numeric variable is assigned a specific value that is tested each time the loop is executed until the desired number of repetitions is reached.

Data Facts that have not been organized in a meaningful way.

Data list A single list containing the values in all of the data statements in a program. The values appear in the list in the order in which they occur in the program.

Debug To locate and correct program errors.

Documentation Comments that explain a program to people; documentation is ignored by the computer. In BASIC, the REM statement is used to denote a comment.

Driver program A program whose main purpose is to call subroutines, which do the actual work of the program.

Element A single data item within an array; elements are referred to by using a subscript along with the variable name.

Exponentiation The process of raising a number to a stated power.

Field The smallest division within a file, consisting of a single unit of data. Fields group together to form records.

File A collection of related data items, organized in a meaningful way and kept in secondary storage.

File organization The method used to arrange records within a file. There are three types of file organization: sequential organization, relative organization, and indexed organization.

Flowchart A graphic representation of the solution to a programming problem.

Function A subprogram that performs a specific task and results in a single value.

Hierarchy of operations The order in which arithmetic operations are performed in BASIC; the order is (1) anything in parentheses; (2) exponentiation; (3) multiplication and division; (4) addition and subtraction.

Immediate-mode commands A command executed as soon as the RETURN or ENTER key is pressed; it is used without line numbers.

Index See **Loop control variable.**

Indexed organization Records are stored according to a primary key.

Indirect mode The mode in which statements are not executed until the RUN command is given. The statements must have line numbers (except in those implementations, such as Macintosh/Microsoft, in which line numbers are optional).

Infinite loop A loop with no exit point; it therefore will never stop executing.

Information Data that has been processed so that it is meaningful to the user.

Input Data that is entered into the computer for processing.

Inquiry-and-response mode A mode of operation in which the program asks a question and the user enters a response.

Library function A function that is prewritten as part of the language.

Line number A number preceding a BASIC statement which is used to reference that statement and which can determine its order of execution.

Literal Any expression containing any combination of letters, numbers, and/or special characters.

Logical operator An operator that acts on one or more conditions to produce a value of true or false.

Loop A structure that allows a given section of a program to be repeated as many times as necessary.

Loop control variable A variable the value of which is used to determine the number of loop repetitions.

Menu A screen display of a program's functions. The user enters a code at the keyboard to make a selection.

Module See **Subprogram.**

Numeric constant A number (excluding line numbers) that is included in a statement.

Numeric variable A variable used to store a number.

Predefined function See **Library function.**

Primary key A field that uniquely identifies a particular record; the record can then be accessed by this field.

Programming The process of writing instructions for a computer to use to solve a problem.

Programming process The steps used to develop a solution to a programming problem.

Prompt A message telling the user what data should be entered at this point.

Pseudocode An English-like description of a program's logic.

Random A term describing a set (such as a set of numbers) in which every member has an equal chance of occurring.

Random access Accessing a record directly by means of a record location number or a primary key.

Record One or more fields that together describe a single entity. Records group together to form files.

Relational symbol A symbol used to specify a relationship between two values.

Relative organization Each record is stored in a numbered location.

Reserved word A word that has a specific meaning to the BASIC system and therefore cannot be used as a variable name.

Secondary key A field that can be used to access a record after it has been accessed through its primary key.

Secondary storage Storage that is used to supplement the primary storage unit. Because it is external to the computer, it takes longer to access than primary storage, but it is less costly.

Sequential access Accessing a record by accessing all records sequentially until the needed record is reached.

Sequential organization A method of organizing records within a file, whereby the records are stored in the same order in which they are written to the file.

Software A program or a series of programs.

Stepwise refinement The process used in top-down design to divide a problem into smaller and smaller sub-problems.

String variable A variable used to store a character string. In BASIC, the last character in a string variable name must always be a $.

Structure chart A diagram that visually illustrates how a problem solution has been developed using stepwise refinement. The structure chart not only displays the modules of the problem solution but also the relationships between modules.

Structured programming A method of programming in which programs have easy-to-follow logic and are divided into subprograms, each designed to perform a specific task.

Stub A subroutine containing only a PRINT statement, which indicates that the subroutine has not yet been implemented, and a RETURN statement. Stubs are used when implementing a program in a top-down fashion.

Subprogram A distinct part of a larger program, designed to perform a specific task. In structured programming, subprograms are used to make a program's logic easier to follow.

Subroutine A module in a BASIC program containing a sequence of statements designed to perform a specific task; it follows the main program.

Subscript A value enclosed in parentheses that identifies the position in an array of a particular element.

Subscripted variable A variable that refers to a specific element of an array.

Syntax The grammatical rules of a language.

Syntax error A violation of the grammatical rules of a language.

System command A command that instructs the computer's operating system to manipulate a program.

Top-down design   A method of solving a problem that proceeds from the general to the specific.

Trailer value   A method of controlling loop repetition in which a unique data value signals the termination of the loop.

Unary operator   An operator used with one operand.

Unconditional transfer   Program control is always passed elsewhere, regardless of any program conditions.

Unsubscripted variable   A simple variable; one that does not refer to an array element.

User-defined function   A function that is written by the programmer.

Variable   A storage location containing a value that can change during program execution.

Variable name   The name used to represent the memory location in which a variable is stored.

BASIC INDEX

GLOSSARY

Abacus An early device used for mathematical calculations; it consists of a rectangular frame with beads strung on wires.

Access To get or retrieve data from a computer system.

Access mechanism The device that positions the read/write head of a direct-access storage device over a particular track.

Accounting machine A mechanically operated forerunner of the computer; could read data from punched cards, perform calculations, rearrange data, and print results in varied formats.

Acoustic-coupler modem A device used in telecommunications that is attached to a computer by a cable and that connects to a standard telephone handset.

Action entries One of four sections of a decision logic table; specifies what actions should be taken.

Action stub One of four sections of a decision logic table; describes possible actions applicable to the decision being made.

Activity The proportion of records processed during an update run.

Ada A high-level programming language developed for use by the Department of Defense. Named for Augusta Ada Byron, Countess of Lovelace and daughter of the poet Lord Byron, Ada is a sophisticated structured language that supports concurrent processing.

Add A data-manager feature that allows the user to add a record to an existing file.

Address A unique identifier assigned to each memory location within primary storage.

American Standard Code for Information Interchange

(ASCII) A seven-bit standard code used for information interchange among data-processing systems, communication systems, and associated equipment.

Amount field The field where a clerk manually inserts the amount of the check; used in the processing of bank checks.

Analog computer A computer that measures the change in continuous electrical or physical conditions rather than counting data; contrast with digital computer.

Analog transmission Transmission of data over communication channels in a continuous wave form.

Analytical engine A machine (designed by Charles Babbage) capable of addition, subtraction, multiplication, division, and storage of intermediate results in a memory unit. Too advanced for its time, the analytical engine was forgotten for nearly a hundred years.

APL (A Programming Language) A terminal-oriented high-level programming language that is especially suitable for interactive problem solving.

Application program A sequence of instructions written to solve a specific user problem.

Arithmetic Logic Unit (ALU) The section of the processor or CPU that handles arithmetic computations and logical operations.

Artificial intelligence (AI) Field of research currently developing techniques whereby computers can be used to solve problems that appear to require imagination, intuition, or intelligence.

ASCII-8 An eight-bit version of ASCII developed for computers that require eight bit rather than seven-bit codes.

Assembler program The translator program for an

assembly language program; produces a machine-language program (object program) which can then be executed.

Assembly language A low-level programming language that uses convenient abbreviations called mnemonics rather than the groupings of 0s and 1s used in machine language. Because instructions in assembly language generally have a one-to-one correspondence with machine-language instructions, assembly language is easier to translate into machine language than are high-level language statements.

Attribute A characteristic field within a record in a computer file.

Audio conferencing A conference call that links three or more people.

Audit trail A means of verifying the accuracy of information; a description of the path that leads to the original data upon which the information is based.

Augmented audio conferencing A form of teleconferencing that combines graphics and audio conferencing.

Automatic page numbering A print formatting feature in word processors that automatically produces pages with printed page numbers.

Automatic spillover A feature of electronic spreadsheets that allows labels that are too long for one cell to spill over into the next cell.

Automatic teller machine (ATM) Remote terminal that allows bank customers to make transactions with the bank's central computer; user can check account balances, transfer funds, make deposits, and so forth.

Auxiliary storage See Secondary storage.

Back-end processor A small CPU serving as an interface between a large CPU and a large data base stored on a direct-access storage device.

Background partition In a multiprogramming system, a partition handling a lower-priority program that is executed only when high-priority programs are not using the system.

Background program In a multiprogramming system, a program that can be executed whenever the facilities of the system are not needed by a high-priority program.

Bandwidth Also known as grade; the range of width of the frequencies available for transmission of a given channel.

Bar-code reader A device used to read a bar code by means of reflected light, such as a scanner that reads the Universal Product Code on supermarket products.

BASIC (Beginners' All-purpose Symbolic Instruction Code) A high-level programming language commonly used for interactive problem solving by users; it is widely implemented on microcomputers and is often taught to beginning programmers.

Batch file access An access method in which all transactions are accumulated for a given period of time and then processed all at once.

Batch processing A method of processing data in which data items are collected into a group (or "batch") to be executed in a continuous stream without user intervention. Batch processing makes efficient use of computer time but can be slow.

Binary number system Number system used in computer operations that uses the digits 0 and 1 and has a base of 2; corresponds to the two possible states in machine circuitry, "on" and "off."

Binary representation Use of a two-state, or binary, system to represent data, as in setting and resetting the electrical state of semiconductor memory to either 0 or 1.

Binary system See Binary number system.

Biochip In theory, a chip whose circuits will be built from the proteins and enzymes of living matter such as *E. coli* bacteria.

Bit Short for BInary digiT; the smallest unit of data that the computer can handle and that can be represented in the digits (0 and 1) of binary notation.

Bit cells The name for storage locations in semiconductors.

Block See Blocked record.

Block copy A word-processing feature that allows the user to mark a section (block) of text and duplicate it at a new location.

Block delete A word-processing feature that allows the user to mark a section (block) of text and then issue a single command to remove the entire section of text from the screen.

Block merge A word-processing feature that reads a file from disk and merges the file with the document currently in memory.

Block move A word-processing feature that allows the user to define a section (block) of text and then move it from one location to another.

Block operations Word-processing features which allow the user to define a section of text and then perform a specific operation on the entire section. Common block operations include block move, block copy, block save, and block delete.

Block save A word-processing feature that allows the user to mark a section (block) of text and save it as a new file on a disk.

Blocked record Records grouped together on magnetic tape or magnetic disk to reduce the number of interrecord gaps and more fully utilize the storage medium.

Boldface A character enhancement feature of word processors that makes individual characters or words appear darker than regular text.

Boot To load instructions into the computer's memory.

Branch A statement used to alter the normal flow of program execution.

Breach of contract The instance when goods fail to meet the terms of either an express warranty or implied warranty.

Broad-band channel A communication channel that can transmit data at rates of up to 120,000 bits per second; for example, microwaves.

Bubble memory A memory medium in which data is represented by magnetized spots (magnetic domains) resting on a thin film of semiconductor material.

Buffer Storage used to compensate for a difference in the rate of flow of data, or time of occurrence of events; used when transmitting data from one device to another.

Bug A program error.

Bus configuration A configuration often used with local-area networks in which multiple stations connected to a communication cable can communicate directly with any other station on the line.

Byte A fixed number of adjacent bits operated on as a unit.

C A high-level structured programming language that includes low-level language instructions, C is popular because it is portable and is implemented on a wide variety of computer systems.

Cache memory Also known as a high-speed buffer; a working buffer or temporary area used to help speed the execution of a program.

Cell The unique location in an electronic spreadsheet where a row and a column intersect.

Center A print formatting feature in word processors that places text in the exact middle of a line.

Central processing unit (CPU) Acts as the "brain" of the computer; composed of three sections—arithmetic/logic unit (ALU), control unit, and primary storage unit.

Centralized design An information structure in which a separate data-processing department is used to provide data-processing facilities for the entire organization.

Chain printer An output device that has the character set engraved in type and assembled in a chain that revolves horizontally past all print position; prints when a print hammer (one for each column of the paper) presses the paper against an inked ribbon that presses against the characters on the print chain.

Channel A limited-capacity computer that takes over the tasks of input and output in order to free the CPU to handle internal processing operations.

Character A single letter, digit, or special sign (like $, #, or *). Characters are represented by bytes in computer storage.

Charge-coupled device (CCD) A storage device made of silicon that is nearly 100 times faster than magnetic bubble storage.

Check bit See Parity bit.

Chief Programmer Team (CPT) A method of organization used in developing software systems in industry in which a chief programmer supervises the development and testing of software; programmer productivity and software reliability are increased.

Clock speed The number of electronic pulses a microprocessor can produce each second.

Clustered key-to-tape device The tying together of several keyboards to one or two magnetic-tape units.

COBOL (COmmon Business-Oriented Language) A high-level programming language generally used for business applications; it is well suited to manipulating large data files.

Coding The processing of writing a programming problem solution in a programming language.

Common law Law that is based on customs and past judicial decisions in similar cases.

Communication channel A medium for carrying data from one location to another.

Compatibility The ability to use equipment or software produced by one manufacturer on a computer produced by another manufacturer.

Compiler program The translator program for a high-level language such as FORTRAN or COBOL; translates the entire source program into machine language, creating an object program that is then executed.

Composite color monitor A computer monitor offering composite color and resolution slightly better than a TV.

Computer General-purpose electronic machine with applications limited only by the creativity of the humans who use it; its power is derived from its speed, accuracy, and memory.

Computer-aided design (CAD) Process of designing, drafting, and analyzing a prospective product using computer graphics on a video terminal.

Computer-aided manufacturing (CAM) Use of a computer to simulate or monitor the steps of a manufacturing process.

Computer-assisted instruction (CAI) Use of a computer to instruct or drill a student on an individual or small-group basis.

Computer anxiety A fear individuals have of the effects computers have on their lives and society in general.

Computer conferencing A form of teleconferencing that uses computer terminals for the transmission of messages; participants need not be using the terminal in order to receive the message—it will be waiting the next time they use the terminal.

Computer crime A criminal act that poses a greater threat to a computer user than to a non-computer user, or a criminal act that is accomplished through the use of a computer.

Computer ethics A term used to refer to the standard of moral conduct in computer use; a way in which the "spirit" of some laws are applied to computer-related activities.

Computer-integrated manufacturing (CIM) An arrangement that links various departments within an organization to a central data base for the purpose of improving the efficiency of the manufacturing process.

Computer literacy General knowledge about computers; includes some technical knowledge about hardware and software, the ability to use computers to solve problems, and awareness of how computers affect society.

Computer phobia Fear of computers and their effects on society.

Computer security Instituting the technical and administrative safeguards necessary to protect a computer-based system against the hazards to which computer systems are exposed and to control access to information.

Computerized axial tomography (CT or CAT) scanning Form of noninvasive physical testing that combines x-ray techniques and computers to aid diagnosis.

Concentrator A device that systematically allocates the use of communication channels among several terminals.

Concurrent Taking place within the same time interval. In multiprogramming, concurrency occurs when processing alternates between different programs.

Condition entries One of four sections of a decision logic table; answers question in the condition stub.

Condition stub One of four sections of a decision logic table; describes all options to be considered in making a decision.

Continuous form A data-entry form, such as cash register tape, utilized by OCR devices.

Control program A routine, usually part of an operating system, that aids in controlling the operations and management of a computer system.

Control unit The section of the CPU that directs the sequence of operations by electrical signals and governs the actions of the various units that make up the computer.

Coprocessor A microprocessor that can be plugged into a microcomputer to replace or work with the microcomputer's original microprocessor.

Copy A feature of electronic spreadsheets that allows the user to duplicate a cell or group of cells on another part of the spreadsheet.

Corporate planning model See Simulation decision support system.

Crash conversion A method of system implementation in which the old system is abandoned and the new one implemented at once.

Cursor Usually a flashing character such as an underline or a block that shows where the next typed character will appear on the computer display screen.

Cut form Data-entry form such as a phone or utility bill; used by OCR devices.

Daisy-wheel printer An output device resembling an office typewriter; it employs a flat disk with petal-like projections, each having a character at its tip; printing occurs one character at a time.

Data Facts; the raw material of information.

Data base Collection of data that is commonly defined and consistently organized to fit the information needs of a wide variety of users in an organization.

Data-base analyst The person responsible for the analysis, design, and implementation of the data base.

Data-base management system (DBMS) A set of programs that serves as the interface between the data base and the programmer, operating system, and users; also programs used to design and maintain data bases.

Data buffering Reading data into a separate storage unit normally contained in the control unit of the input/output system.

Data communication The electronic transmission of data from one site to another, usually over communication channels such as telephone or microwave.

Data definition language (DDL) The language in which the schema, which states how records within a data base are related, is written. This language differs depending on the type of data-base management system being used.

Data manipulation language (DML) The language used to access a hierarchical or a relational data base to provide a way for users to access the data base. The data manipulation language is different for each type of data-base management system.

Data processing A systematic set of procedures for collecting, manipulating, and disseminating data to achieve specified objectives.

Data redundancy The repetition of the same data in different files.

Data set See Modem.

Data structure A particular relationship between the data elements in a computer file.

Datacom handler Another name for multiplexer and concentrator.

Debugging The process of locating, isolating, and correcting errors in a program.

Decentralized design An information structure in which the authority and responsibility for computer support are placed in relatively autonomous organization operating units.

Decimal number system A number system based on the powers of ten.

Decision logic table (DLT) A table that organizes relevant facts in a clear and concise manner to aid a decision-making process.

Decision support system (DSS) An integrated system that draws on data from a wide variety of sources such as data bases to provide a supportive tool for managerial decision-making. Generally, managers use fourth-generation programming languages to access decision support systems.

Decrypted Data that is translated back into regular text after being encrypted for security reasons.

Default setting Programmed parameters a software package automatically uses when no other parameter is specified; for example, margin settings for printing.

Demodulation The process of retrieving data from a modulated carrier wave.

Desk checking A method used in both system and application program debugging in which the sequence of operations is mentally traced to verify the correctness of program logic.

Detail diagram Used in HIPO packages to describe the specific functions performed and data items used in a given module.

Digit rows The lower ten rows, numbers 0 through 9, that are found on an eighty-column punched card.

Digital computer Type of computer commonly used in business applications; operates on distinct data (for example, digits) by performing arithmetic and logic processes on specific data units.

Digital transmission The transmission of data as distinct on and off pulses.

Direct-access file design Records are organized in a file in any order, with record keys providing the only way to access data.

Direct-access storage device (DASD) Auxiliary storage device that allows data to be stored and accessed either randomly or sequentially.

Direct-connect modem A device used in telecommunications that is attached to a computer by a cable and that connects directly to a telephone line by plugging into a standard phone jack.

Direct conversion See Crash conversion.

Directory Contains record keys and their corresponding addresses; used to obtain the address of a record with a direct-access file design.

Disk address The method used to identify a data record on a magnetic disk; consists of the disk surface number, track number, and record number.

Disk-based word processor A word processor that places the entire document in RAM.

Disk drive The mechanical device used to rotate a disk pack during data transmission.

Disk pack A stack of magnetic disks.

Diskette See Floppy disk.

Distributed computing A system in which processing is done at a site other than that of the central computer.

Distributed data processing (DDP) See distributed computing.

Distributed design An information structure in which independent operating units have some data-processing facilities but there is still central control and coordination of computer resources.

Dot-matrix printer A type of impact printer that creates characters through the use of dot-matrix patterns.

Download To transmit or copy information from a mainframe computer, such as a network's computer, and store it on a disk.

Drum printer An impact printer that consists of a metal cylinder with rows of characters engraved on its surface; one line of print is produced with each drum rotation.

Dump A hard-copy printout of the contents of computer memory; valuable in debugging programs.

Edit checks Processing statements designed to identify potential errors in the input data.

Editing window The area on a computer screen that contains the typed words in a document; also the area inside of which changes can be made in a document.

EDVAC (Electronic Discrete Variable Automatic Computer) A stored-program computer developed at the University of Pennsylvania.

Eighty-column punched card See Hollerith card.

Electronic bulletin board A communication network used to send messages to members of a group which share a common interest; uses existing communication networks.

Electronic data processing (EDP) Data processing performed largely by electronic equipment, such as computers, rather than by manual means.

Electronic funds transfer (EFT) A cashless method of managing money; accounts involved in a transaction are adjusted by electronic communications between computers.

Electronic mail Transmission of messages at high speeds over telecommunication facilities.

Electronic spreadsheet An electronic ledger sheet used to store and manipulate any type of numeric data.

Electrostatic printer A nonimpact printer in which electromagnetic impulses and heat are used to affix characters to paper.

Electrothermal printer A nonimpact printer that uses a special heat-sensitive paper; characters are formed when heated rods in a matrix touch the paper.

Encrypted A term describing data that is translated into a secret code for security reasons.

End-user development tools Tools that allow the end-user to develop an application package, usually through the use of a fourth-generation programming language. Examples of end-user development tools are simulation software, statistical packages, and data-base management systems.

ENIAC (Electronic Numerical Integrator and Calculator) The first general-purpose electronic digital computer; it was developed by John W. Mauchly and J. Presper Eckert at the University of Pennsylvania.

Erasable programmable read-only memory (EPROM) A form of read-only memory that can be erased and reprogrammed, but only by being submitted to a special process such as exposure to ultraviolet light.

Ergonomics The method of researching and designing computer hardware and software to enhance employee productivity and comfort.

Even parity A method of coding in which an even number of 1 bits represent each character; used to enhance the detection of errors.

Executive See Supervisor program.

Expert system Form of artificial intelligence software designed to imitate the same decision-making and evaluation processes of experts in a specific field.

Express warranty Created when the seller makes any promise or statement of fact concerning the goods being sold, which the purchaser uses as a basis for purchasing the goods.

Extended Binary Coded Decimal Interchange Code (EBCDIC) An eight-bit code for character representation.

External storage See Secondary storage.

Facsimile system Produces a picture of a page by scanning it.

Feedback A check within a system to see whether predetermined goals are being met; the return of information about the effectiveness of the system.

Fiber optics A data transmission concept using laser pulses and cables made of tiny threads of glass that can transmit huge amounts of data at the speed of light.

Field A meaningful collection of characters, such as a social security number or a person's name.

File A grouping of related records, such as student records; sometimes referred to as a data set.

File manager An application package designed to duplicate the traditional manual methods of filing records.

First-generation computer Computer that used vacuum tubes; developed in the 1950s; much faster than earlier mechanical devices, but very slow in comparison to today's computers.

Flexible disk See Floppy disk.

Floppy disk A low-cost direct-access form of data storage made of plastic and coated with a magnetizable substance upon which data are stored; disks come in varying sizes.

Floppy diskette See Flexible diskette.

Flowchart Of two kinds: the program flowchart, which is a graphic representation of the types and sequences of operations in a program; and the system flowchart, which shows the flow of data through an entire system.

Foreground partition Also called foreground area; in a multiprogramming system, a partition containing high-priority application programs.

Foreground program In a multiprogramming system, a program that has high priority.

Formal design review Also called a structured walkthrough; an evaluation of the design of a software system by a group of managers, analysts, and programmers to determine completeness, accuracy, and quality of the design.

Formula A mathematical expression that can contain numbers from other cells in an electronic spreadsheet as well as constant numbers.

FORTH A high-level programming language that includes low-level language instructions, FORTH is the standard language used in astronomical observatories around the world.

FORTRAN (FORmula TRANslator) The oldest high-level programming language, it is used primarily in performing mathematical or scientific operations.

Four-bit binary coded decimal (BCD) A four-bit computer code that uses four-bit groupings to represent digits in decimal numbers.

Fourth-generation computer Computer that uses chips made by large-scale integration and offers significant price and performance improvements over earlier computers.

Fourth-generation software development tools See End-user development tools.

Front-end processor A small CPU serving as an interface between a large CPU and peripheral devices.

Full-duplex A type of communication channel through which data can be transmitted in both directions simultaneously.

Fully distributed configuration A network design in which every set of nodes in the network can communicate directly with every other set of nodes through a single communication link.

Functional tools A category of application software packages that perform specific tasks or functions, such as inventory control.

Game paddle An input device that is normally used with microcomputers for game applications; it is used to position a figure that is required to move across or up and down the display screen.

Garbage in-garbage out (GIGO) A phrase illustrating the fact that the meaningfulness of computer output relies on the accuracy or relevancy of the data fed into the processor.

Global search and replace A word-processing feature that allows the user to enter a command that will cause the computer to locate a specified word or phrase and replace it with another word or phrase throughout the document. Once the initial command is entered, no additional intervention is required for the computer to carry out the action.

Grade See Bandwidth.

Graphic display device A visual-display device that projects output in the form of graphs and line drawings and accepts input from a keyboard or light pen.

Graphics package An application software package designed to allow the user to display images on the display screen or a printer.

Graphics tablet A flat board-like object that, when drawn on, transfers the image to a computer screen.

Grid chart (tabular chart) A chart used in system analysis and design to summarize the relationships between functions of an organization.

Hacking A term used to describe the activity of computer enthusiasts who are challenged by the practice of breaking computer security measures designed to prevent unauthorized access to a particular computer system.

Half-duplex A type of communication channel through which data can be transmitted in both directions, but in only one direction at a time.

Hard copy Printed output.

Hardware Physical components that make up a computer system.

Hard-wired Memory instructions that cannot be changed or deleted by other stored-program instructions.

Hashing See Randomizing.

Hexadecimal number system A base 16 number system commonly used when printing the contents of primary storage to aid programmers in detecting errors.

Hidden cells A security feature of electronic spreadsheets that conceals the contents of a cell so that they are not shown on the screen.

Hierarchical configuration A network design for multiple CPUs in which an organization's needs are divided into multiple levels that receive different levels of computer support.

Hierarchical design An information structure in which each level within an organization has necessary computer power; responsibility for control and coordination goes to the top level.

Hierarchical structure Also called tree structure; the data structure in which one primary element may have numerous secondary elements linked to it at lower levels.

High-level language Languages that are oriented more toward the user than the computer system (contrast with low-level languages). High-level languages generally contain English words such as READ and PRINT. These statements must be translated into machine language before execution. A single high-level language statement may translate into several machine-language statements.

HIPO (Hierarchy plus Input-Process-Output) package A collection of diagrams, typically consisting of a visual table of contents, an overview diagram, and a detail diagram, that describes the inputs, processing, and outputs of program modules.

Hollerith card An eighty-column punched card; a commonly used, sequential-storage medium in which data is represented by the presence or absence of strategically placed holes.

Hollerith code A method of data representation named for the man who invented it; delineates numbers, letters, and special characters by the placement of holes in eighty-column punched cards.

Icon A picture or graphic image representing a command or menu choice; appears on the screen of many brands of microcomputers; used in conjunction with a mouse.

Impact printer A printer that forms characters by physically striking a ribbon against a paper.

Implied warranty A warranty that provides for the automatic inclusion of certain warranties in a contract for the sale of goods.

Implied warranty of fitness A situation in which the purchaser relies on a seller's expertise to recommend a good that will meet his or her needs; if the good later fails to meet the purchaser's needs the seller has breached the warranty.

Implied warranty of merchantability Guarantees the purchaser that the good purchased will function properly for a reasonable period of time.

Indent A word-processing feature that places the cursor at a predetermined number of spaces in from the left margin; used at the beginning of a paragraph.

Indexed-sequential file design Records are organized sequentially in a file and also in an index; allows for both sequential and direct-access processing.

Informal design review An evaluation of a software system by selected management, analysts, and programmers prior to the actual coding of program modules to determine necessary additions, deletions, and modifications to the system design.

Information Data that has been organized and processed so that it is meaningful.

Information processing The conversion of data to information that is used for decision making.

Information service A collection of information accessible over communication lines to paying subscribers.

In-house An organization's use of its own personnel or resources to develop programs or other problem-solving systems.

Ink-jet printer A nonimpact printer that uses a stream of charged ink to form dot-matrix characters.

Input Data submitted to the computer for processing.

Input/output bound A situation in which the CPU is slowed down because of I/O operations, which are extremely slow in comparison to CPU internal processing speeds.

Input/output control unit   A device located between one or more I/O devices that performs code conversion.

Input/output management system   A subsystem of the operating system that controls and coordinates the CPU while receiving input from channels, executing instructions of programs in storage, and regulating output.

Insert   A word-processing feature that allows the user to enter new characters into a document.

Instruction set   The fundamental logical and arithmetic procedures that the computer can perform, such as addition, subtraction, and comparison.

Integrated circuit   An electronic circuit etched on a small silicon chip less than ⅛-inch square, permitting much faster processing than with transistors and at a greatly reduced price.

Interactive processing   A processing method in which the user is able to interact directly with the computer during program execution. Input is usually entered at the keyboard during execution and output is then displayed on the terminal screen.

Interactive video   A multimedia learning concept that merges computer text, sound, and graphics by using a videodisk, videodisk player, microcomputer with monitor and disk drive, and computer software.

Interblock gap (IBG)   A space on magnetic tape that facilitates processing; separates records grouped together on the tape.

Internal memory   See Primary storage.

Internal modem   A modem that plugs into the internal circuitry of a computer; no external cables or connections are needed.

Internal storage   See Primary storage.

Interpreter   A high-level language translator that evaluates and translates a program one statement at a time; used extensively on microcomputer systems because it takes up less primary storage than a compiler.

Interrecord gap (IRG)   A space that separates records stored on magnetic tape; allows the tape drive to regain speed during processing.

Interrupt   A condition or event that temporarily suspends normal processing operations.

Inverted structure   A structure that indexes a simple file by specific record attributes.

Job-control language (JCL)   A language that serves as the communication link between the programmer and the operating system.

Job-control program   A control program that translates the job-control statements written by a programmer into machine-language instructions that can be executed by the computer.

Josephson junction   A primary storage unit that will be housed in liquid helium to reduce the resistance to the flow of electricity that currently exists in semiconductor memory.

Joystick   An input device that is normally used with microcomputers for game applications; it is used to position some object, such as a cursor, on the display screen.

K (kilobyte)   A symbol used to denote 1,024 (2^{10}) storage units (1,024 bytes) when referring to a computer's primary storage capacity; often rounded to 1,000 bytes.

Key   The unique identifier or field of a record; used to sort records for processing or to locate specific records within a file.

Keypunch   A keyboard device that punches holes in a card to represent data.

Key-to-disk   Hardware designed to transfer data entered via a keyboard to magnetic (hard) disk.

Key-to-diskette   Hardware designed to transfer data entered via a keyboard to a floppy disk instead of the conventional hard disk.

Key-to-tape   Hardware designed to transfer data entered via a keyboard to magnetic tape.

Label   A name written beside a programming instruction that acts as an identifier for that instruction; also, in spreadsheets, information used to describe some aspect of the spreadsheet.

Language-translator program   Software that translates the English-like programs written by programmers into machine-executable code.

Large-Scale Integration (LSI)   Method by which circuits containing thousands of electronic components are densely packed on a single silicon chip.

Laser printer   A type of nonimpact printer that combines laser beams and electrophotographic technology to form images on paper.

Laser storage system   A secondary storage device using laser technology to encode data onto a metallic surface; usually used for mass storage.

Librarian program   Software that manages the storage and use of library programs by maintaining a directory of programs in the system library and appropriate procedures for additions and deletions.

Library programs   User-written or manufacturer-supplied programs and subroutines that are frequently used in other programs; they are written and stored in secondary storage and called into primary storage when needed.

Light pen   A pen-shaped object with a photoelectric cell at its end; used to draw lines on a visual display screen.

Line spacing   A word-processing feature that allows the user to choose the amount of space between lines.

Linear structure A data structure in which the records in a computer file are arranged sequentially in a specified order.

Link A transmission channel that connects nodes.

Linkage editor A subprogram of the operating system that links the object program from the system residence device to primary storage.

LISP (LISt Processing) A high-level programming language commonly used in artificial intelligence research and in the processing of lists of elements.

Local-area network (LAN) A specialized network of computers that operates within a limited geographic area, such as a building or complex of buildings, with the stations being linked by cable.

Local system Peripherals connected directly to the CPU.

Locked A security feature of electronic spreadsheets that prevents unauthorized users from altering or destroying a template or cells containing formulas; a password is needed to make any changes to locked cells.

Logo An education-oriented, procedure-oriented, interactive programming language designed to allow anyone to begin programming and communicating with computers quickly.

Loop A structure that allows a specified sequence of instructions to be executed repeatedly as long as stated conditions remain constant.

Machine language The only set of instructions that a computer can execute directly; a code that designates the proper electrical states in the computer as combinations of zeros and ones.

Magnetic core Iron-alloy, doughnut-shaped ring about the size of a pinhead of which memory can be composed; individual cores can store one binary digit (its state is determined by the direction of an electrical current); the cores are strung on a grid of fine wires that carry the current.

Magnetic disk A direct-access storage medium consisting of a metal platter coated on both sides with a magnetic recording material upon which data are stored in the form of magnetized spots.

Magnetic domain A magnetized spot representing data in bubble memory.

Magnetic drum Cylinder with a magnetic outer surface on which data can be stored by magnetizing specific positions on the surface.

Magnetic-ink character reader A device used to perform magnetic-ink character recognition (MICR).

Magnetic-ink character recognition (MICR) A process that involves reading characters composed of magnetized particles; often used to sort checks for subsequent processing.

Magnetic tape A sequential storage medium consisting of a narrow strip of plastic upon which spots of iron-oxide are magnetized to represent data.

Mainframe A type of large, full-scale computer capable of supporting many peripheral devices.

Main memory See Primary storage.

Main storage See Primary storage.

Management information system (MIS) A formal network that uses computers to provide information used to support structured managerial decision making; its goal is to get the correct information to the appropriate manager at the right time.

Mark I First automatic calculator.

Mark sensing See Optical-mark recognition.

Master file A file that contains all existing records organized according to the key field; updated by records in a transaction file.

Materials requirement planning (MRP) A manufacturing system that ties together different manufacturing needs such as raw materials planning and inventory control into interacting systems. The interacting systems allow a manufacturer to plan and control operations efficiently.

Megahertz (MHz) One million times per second; the unit of measurement for clock speed.

Memory-based word processor A word processor that loads only the part of the document that is being edited into memory. The remaining part of the document is stored in temporary files.

Memory management In a multiprogramming environment, the process of keeping the programs in primary storage separate.

Memory protection See Memory management.

Menu driven An application program is said to be menu-driven when it provides the user with "menus" displaying available choices or selections to help guide the user through the process of using the software package.

Message switching The task of a communications processor of receiving messages and routing them to appropriate destinations.

Microcomputer A small, low-priced computer used in homes, schools, and businesses; also called a personal computer.

Microprocessor A programmable processing unit (placed on a silicon chip) containing arithmetic, logic, and control circuitry; used in microcomputers, calculators, and microwave ovens and in many other applications.

Microprogram A sequence of instructions wired into read-only memory; used to tailor a system to meet the user's specific processing requirements.

Minicomputer A type of computer with the components of a full-sized system but with smaller primary storage capacity.

Mnemonics   A symbolic name (memory aid); used in symbolic languages (for example, assembly language) and high-level programming languages.

Model   A mathematical representation of an actual system, containing independent variables that influence the value of a dependent variable.

Modem   Also called a data set; a device that modulates and demodulates signals transmitted over communication facilities.

Modula-2   A high-level structured programming language that is a descendant of Pascal; it is based on the concept of modules that are nested within one another. Modula-2 supports concurrent processing and also incorporates low-level language commands.

Modular approach   A method of simplifying a programming project by breaking it into segments or subunits referred to as modules.

Modulation   A technology used in modems to make data processing signals compatible with communication facilities.

Module   Part of a whole; a program segment or subsystem; a set of logically related program statements that perform one specified task in a program.

Monitor   See Supervisor program.

Monochrome monitor   A computer monitor that displays amber, green, or white characters on a black background.

Mouse   A desk-top input device that controls cursor movement, allowing the user to bypass the keyboard.

Multiphasic health testing (MPHT)   Computer-assisted testing plan that compiles data on patients and their test results, which are compared with norms or means to aid the physician in making a diagnosis.

Multiplexer   A device that permits more than one I/O device to transmit data over the same communication channel.

Multiplexor channel   A limited-capacity computer that can handle more than one I/O device at a time; normally used to control slow-speed devices such as card readers, printers, or terminals.

Multiprocessing   A multiple CPU configuration in which jobs are processed simultaneously.

Multiprogramming   A technique whereby several programs are placed in primary storage at the same time, giving the illusion that they are being executed simultaneously; this results in increased CPU active time.

Napier's Bones   A portable multiplication tool (described by John Napier) consisting of ivory rods that slide up and down against each other; forerunner of the slide rule.

Narrow bandwidth channel   A communication channel that can transmit data only at a rate between 45 and 90 bits per second; for example, telegraph lines.

Natural language   Designed primarily for novice computer users; uses English-like statements usually for the purpose of accessing data in a data base.

Network   The linking together of several CPUs.

Network structure   The data structure in which a primary data element may have many secondary elements linked to it and any given secondary element may be linked to numerous primary elements.

Next-sequential-instruction feature   The ability of a computer to execute program steps in the order in which they are stored in memory unless branching takes place.

Node   The endpoint of a network; consists of CPUs, printers, CRTs, or any other physical devices.

Nondestructive read/destructive write   The feature of computer memory that permits data to be read and retained in its original state, allowing it to be referenced repeatedly during processing.

Nondestructive testing (NDT)   Testing done electronically to avoid breaking, cutting, or tearing apart a product to find a problem.

Nonimpact printer   The use of heat, laser technology, or photographic techniques to print output.

Nonmonotonic logic   A type of logic that adapts to exceptions to ordinary monotonic logical statements and allows conclusions to be drawn from assumptions.

Nuclear magnetic resonance (NMR)   A computerized, noninvasive diagnostic tool that involves sending magnetic pulses through the body to identify medical problems.

Numeric bits   The four rightmost bit positions of six-bit BCD used to encode numeric data.

Numerically controlled machinery   Manufacturing machinery that is driven by a magnetic punched tape created by a tape punch that is driven by computer software.

Object program   A sequence of machine-executable instructions derived from source-program statements by a language-translator program.

Octal number system   Number system in which each position represents a power of eight.

Odd parity   A method of coding in which an odd number of 1 bits is used to represent each character; facilitates error checking.

Office automation   Integration of computer and communication technology with traditional office procedures to increase productivity and efficiency.

Online file access   An access method in which records are updated when transactions are made; current information can be retrieved at any time.

Online storage   In direct communication with the computer.

On-us field   The section of a check that contains the customer's checking-account number.

Op code The part of a machine or assembly language instruction that tells the computer what function to perform.

Operand The part of an instruction that tells where to find the data or equipment on which to operate.

Operating system A collection of programs designed to permit a computer system to manage itself and to avoid idle CPU time while increasing utilization of computer resources.

Operation code (op code) The part of an instruction that indicates what operation is to be performed.

Optical character A special type of character that can be read by an optical-character reader.

Optical-character recognition (OCR) A method of electronic scanning that reads numbers, letters, and other characters and then converts the optical images into appropriate electrical signals.

Optical disk A secondary storage device that stores data as the presence or absence of a pit burned into the surface of the disk by a laser beam.

Optical-mark page reader A device that senses marks on an OMR document as the document passes under a light source.

Optical-mark recognition (OMR) Mark sensing; a method of electronic scanning that reads marks on a page and converts the optical images into appropriate electrical signals.

Output Information that comes from the computer, as a result of processing, into a form that can be used by people.

Output devices Hardware that receives information from a computer in hard or soft copy.

Overview diagram Used in an HIPO package to describe in greater detail a module shown in the visual table of contents.

Packaged software A set of standardized computer programs, procedures, and related documentation necessary for solving specific problems.

Page Material that fits in one page frame of primary storage.

Page frame In a virtual storage environment, one of the fixed-sized physical areas into which primary storage is divided.

Paging A method of implementing virtual storage: data and programs are broken into fixed-sized blocks, or pages, and loaded into real storage when needed during processing.

Parallel conversion A system implementation approach in which the new system is operated side by side with the old one until all differences are reconciled.

Parallel processing A type of processing in which instructions and data are handled simultaneously.

Parity bit A bit added to detect incorrect transmission of data; it conducts internal checks to determine whether the correct number of bits is present.

Partition In multiprogramming, the primary storage area reserved for one program; it may be fixed or variable in size; see also Region.

Pascal A high-level structured programming language that was originally developed for instructional purposes and that is now commonly used in a wide variety of applications.

Pascaline A device invented by Blaise Pascal used to add and subtract; a series of rotating gears performed the calculations.

Peripheral device Device that attaches to the central processing unit, such as a secondary storage device or an input or output device.

Phased conversion A method of system implementation in which the old system is gradually replaced by the new one.

Pilot conversion The implementation of a new system into an organization on a piecemeal basis.

Piracy The unauthorized copying of a computer program written by someone else.

Point-of-sale (POS) system A computerized system that records information required for such things as inventory control and accounting at the point where a good is sold; see also source-data automation.

Point-of-sale (POS) terminal An input device that records information at the point where a good is sold.

Poll The process used by a concentrator to determine if an input/output device is ready to send a message to the CPU.

Portable The characteristic of a program that can be run on many different computers with minimal changes.

Portable computer A computer light enough to be carried; does not require an external power source.

Primary key A unique field for a record; used to sort records for processing or to locate a particular record within a file.

Primary storage/memory Also known as internal storage/memory and main storage/memory; the section of the CPU that holds instructions, data, and intermediate and final results during processing.

Primary storage The section of the CPU that holds instructions, data, and intermediate results during processing.

Print-wheel printer An impact printer with 120 wheels each containing 48 characters. To produce characters on paper, the wheels rotate into position, forming an entire line of characters, then a hammer presses paper against the wheels.

Printer A device used to produce permanent (hard copy) computer output; impact printers are designed to work mechanically; nonimpact printers use heat, laser, or chemical technology.

Printer-keyboard An output device similar to an office

typewriter; prints one character at a time and is controlled by a program stored in the CPU of the computer.

Privacy   An individual's right regarding the collection, processing, storage, dissemination, and use of data about his or her personal attributes and activities.

Process   To transform data into useful information by classifying, sorting, calculating, summarizing, or storing.

Process-bound   A condition that occurs when a program monopolizes the processing facilities of the computer, making it impossible for other programs to be executed.

Processing program   A routine, usually part of the operating system, that is used to simplify program preparation and execution.

Processor   The term used collectively to refer to the ALU and control unit.

Productivity tools   Application software packages that can increase the productivity of the user. Examples are text processors and graphics packages.

Program   A series of step-by-step instructions that tells the computer exactly what to do; of two types, application and system.

Program specifications   The documentation for a programming problem definition; it includes the desired output, needed input, and the processing requirements.

Programmable communications processor   A device that relieves the CPU of the task of monitoring data transmission.

Programmable read-only memory (PROM)   Read-only memory that can be programmed by the manufacturer or by the user for special functions to meet the unique needs of the user.

Proper program   A structured program in which each individual segment or module has only one entrance and one exit.

Pseudocode   An informal design language used to represent the logic of a programming problem solution.

Public domain software   Programs unprotected by copyright law for free, unrestricted public use.

Punched card   A heavy paper storage medium on which data is represented by holes punched according to a coding scheme much like that used on Hollerith's cards.

Query language   See Natural language.

Random-access memory (RAM)   A form of primary storage into which instructions and data can be read, written, and erased; directly accessed by the computer; temporary memory that is erased when the computer is turned off.

Random-access memory (RAM) disk   A portion of RAM memory that is temporarily treated as a secondary storage device.

Randomizing   A mathematical process applied to the record key that produces the storage address of the record.

Read-only memory (ROM)   The part of computer hardware containing items (circuitry patterns) that cannot be deleted or changed by stored-program instructions because they are wired into the computer.

Read/write head   An electromagnet used as a component of a tape or disk drive; in reading data, it detects magnetized areas and translates them into electrical pulses; in writing data, it magnetizes appropriate areas and erases data stored there previously.

Real storage   See Primary storage: contrast with virtual storage.

Recalculation   A feature of electronic spreadsheets that automatically adjusts the result of a formula when a cell used in the formula changes.

Record   A collection of data items, or fields, that relates to a single unit, such as a student.

Region   In multiprogramming, with a variable number of tasks, a term often used to mean the internal space allocated for a particular program; a variable-sized partition.

Register   An internal computer component used for temporary storage of an instruction or data; capable of accepting, holding, and transferring that instruction or data very rapidly.

Relational structure   The data structure that places the data elements in a table with rows representing records and columns containing fields.

Reliability   The ability of a program to consistently obtain correct results.

Remote terminal   A terminal that is placed at a location distant from the central computer.

Remote system   A system in which terminals are connected to the central computer by a communication channel.

Replace   A word-processing feature that allows the user to correct spelling or typing mistakes by moving the cursor to the incorrect characters and typing over them.

Resident routine   A frequently used component of the supervisor that is initially loaded into primary storage.

Retrieve   To access previously stored data.

RGB (red-green-blue) monitors   A computer monitor that displays in three colors with high resolution.

Ring configuration   A network design in which a number of computers are connected by a single transmission line in a ring formation.

Robotics   The science that deals with robots, their construction, capabilities, and applications.

RPG (Report Program Generator) A problem-oriented high-level language that requires little skill on the part of the programmer to use. RPG was originally designed to produce business reports and requires the programmer to fill out specification forms; the generator program then builds the needed program.

Schema Determines how records within a data base will be organized and how they will be related to one another.

Screen-oriented word processor A type of word processor that exactly matches what is printed on paper with what appears on the computer screen; also referred to as the what-you-see-is-what-you-get feature.

Script theory An approach to artificial intelligence that links memories of past situations with behavior or action in a new situation.

Search and replace A word-processing feature that allows the user to enter a command that will cause the computer to locate a specified word or phrase and substitute it with another word or phrase.

Secondary key Fields that are used to gain access to records on a file; may not be unique identifiers.

Secondary storage Also known as external or auxiliary storage; supplements primary storage and is external to the computer; data is accessed at slower speeds.

Second-generation computer A computer that used transistors; it was smaller, faster, and had larger storage capacity than the first-generation computers.

Segment A variable-sized block or portion of a program used in a virtual storage system.

Segmentation A method of implementing virtual storage; involves dividing a program into variable-sized blocks, called segments, depending on the program logic.

Selection A logic pattern that requires the computer to make a comparison; the result of the comparison determines which execution path will be taken next.

Selector channel A channel that can accept input from only one device at a time; generally used with high-speed I/O devices such as a magnetic tape or magnetic-disk unit.

Semiconductor memory Memory composed of circuitry on silicon chips; smaller than magnetic cores and allows for faster processing; more expensive than core memory and requires a constant power source.

Sequential file design Records are organized in a file in a specific order based on the value of the key field.

Sequential processing The process of creating a new master file each time transactions are processed; requires batch file access.

Serial processing A method of processing in which programs are executed one at a time; usually found in simple operating systems such as those used on the earliest computer systems.

Shareware Programs that are distributed to the public; the author retains the copyright to the programs with the expectation that users will make donations to the author based upon the value of the program to the users.

Silicon chip Solid-logic circuitry on a small piece of silicon used to form the primary storage of third- and fourth-generation computers.

Simple sequence A logic pattern in which one statement is executed after another, in the order in which they occur in the program.

Simple structure A data structure in which the records in a computer file are arranged sequentially.

Simplex A type of communication channel that provides for unidirectional, or one-way, transmission of data.

Simulation software Application software that uses a model to project the outcome of a particular real-world situation.

Simultaneous decision support system A decision support system that attempts to incorporate into one system the decision making of various functional areas of an organization so that consistent, overall decisions can be made by management.

Six-bit Binary Coded Decimal (BCD) A data representation scheme that is used to represent the decimal digits 0 through 9, the letters A through Z, and twenty-eight special characters.

Soft copy A temporary, or nonpermanent, record of machine output; for example, a CRT display.

Software Program or programs used to direct the computer in solving problems and overseeing operations.

Software copying See Piracy.

Software development process A sequence of four steps used to develop the solution to a programming problem in a structured manner. The steps are: (1) Define and document the problem. (2) Design and document a solution. (3) Write and document the program. (4) Debug and test the program and revise the documentation if necessary.

Software package A set of standardized computer programs, procedures, and related documentation designed to solve problems of a specific application; often acquired from an external supplier.

Sort/merge program A type of operating system utility program; used to sort records to facilitate updating and subsequent combining of files to form a single, updated file.

Source-data automation The use of special equipment to collect data at its source.

Source program A sequence of instructions written in either assembly language or high-level language that is translated into an object program.

Spelling checker Application software that checks words in a document against a dictionary file. Any words in the document that are not in the file are flagged. Spelling checkers are often included in text processing packages.

Stand-alone key-to-tape device A self-contained unit that takes the place of a keypunch device.

Star configuration A network design in which all transactions must go through a central computer before being routed to the appropriate network computer.

Statistical package A software package that performs statistical analysis of data. Examples are SAS, SPSS, and Minitab.

Status line A message line above or below the text area on a display screen that gives format and system information.

Stepped reckoner Machine designed by von Liebniz that could add, subtract, multiply, divide, and calculate square roots.

Stored program Instructions stored in the computer's memory in electronic form; can be executed repeatedly during processing.

Stored-program concept The idea that program instructions can be stored in primary storage (computer memory) in electrical form so that no human intervention is required during processing; allows the computer to process the instructions at its own speed.

Structure chart A graphic representation of the results of the top-down design process, displaying the modules of the solution and their relationships to one another; of two types, system and process.

Structured programming A collection of techniques that encourages the development of well-designed, less error-prone programs with easy-to-follow logic. Structured programming techniques can be divided into two categories: (1) structured design techniques, such as top-down design, that are used in designing a problem solution, and (2) structure coding techniques, which state the rules that are followed when a program is actually coded.

Structured walkthrough See Formal design review.

Subroutine A sequence of statements not within the main line of the program; saves the programmer time by not having to write the same instructions over again in different parts of the program.

Supercomputer The largest, fastest, most expensive type of computer in existence, capable of performing millions of calculations per second and processing enormous amounts of data; also called maxicomputer or monster computer.

Supermicrocomputer A microcomputer built around a 32-bit microprocessor that is powerful enough to compete with low-end minicomputers.

Supervisor program Also known as a monitor or executive; the major component of the operating system; coordinates the activities of all other parts of the operating system.

Swapping In a virtual-storage environment, the process of transferring a program section from virtual storage to real storage, and vice versa.

Symbolic language The use of mnemonic symbols to represent instructions; must be translated into machine language before being executed by the computer.

Synergism The interaction that the combined efforts of all parts of an information system have to achieve a greater effect than the sum of the individual efforts.

Syntax The grammatical rules of a language.

System analysis A detailed, step-by-step investigation of an organization and one or more of its information systems for the purpose of solving an information-related problem.

System analysis report A report given to top management after the system analysis phase has been completed to report the findings of the system study; includes a statement of objectives, constraints, and possible alternatives.

System analyst The person who is responsible for system analysis, design, and implementation of computer-based information systems and who is the communication link or interface between users and technical persons.

System design report The phase of the system life cycle in which information system design alternatives are developed and presented to management. These alternatives should contain information on system inputs, processing, and outputs.

System flowchart The group of symbols that represents the general information flow; focuses on inputs and outputs rather than on internal computer operations.

System implementation The phase of the system life cycle in which the new or revised information system is put into service. This process involves training and system conversion.

System library A collection of files in which various parts of an operating system are stored.

System program Programs that coordinate the operation of computer circuitry and assist in the development of application programs. System programs are designed to facilitate the efficient use of the computer's resources.

System residence device An auxiliary storage device (disk, tape, or drum) on which operating-system programs are stored and from which they are loaded into primary storage.

Tab A word-processing feature that locates the cursor at predetermined column settings when the user enters a command that usually consists of pressing a key.

Tabular chart See Grid chart.

Tape cassette A sequential-access storage medium used in small computer systems for high-density digital recording.

Tape drive A device that moves magnetic tape past a read/write head.

Telecommunication The combined use of communication facilities, such as telephone systems and data-processing equipment.

Telecommuting Method of working at home by communicating via electronic-machine telecommunication facilities.

Telecomputing A term referring to the use of online information services that offer access to one or more data bases; for example, CompuServe, The Source, and Dow Jones News/Retrieval.

Teleconferencing The method of two or more remote locations communicating via electronic and image-producing facilities.

Telecopier system See Facsimile system.

Teletypewriter system Transmits messages as strings of characters.

Terminals An input/output device through which data can be input or output from a system.

Test When applied to software development, to run a given program using a wide variety of data to determine if it will always obtain correct results.

Text processor An application software package that is used to create documents. Tasks such as correcting, editing, and manipulating text can be performed efficiently.

Third-generation computer A computer characterized by the use of integrated circuits, reduced size, lower costs, and increased speed and reliability.

Thrashing Programs in which little actual processing occurs in comparison to the amount of swapping.

Time-sharing system An arrangement in which two or more users can access the same central computer resources and receive what seem to be simultaneous results.

Time slicing A technique used in a time-sharing system that allocates a small portion of processing time to each user.

Title A feature of electronic spreadsheets that shows the labels used in a spreadsheet on the screen at all times.

Top-down design A method of defining a solution in terms of major functions to be performed, and further breaking down the major functions into subfunctions; the further the breakdown, the greater the detail.

Touch-tone device A terminal used with ordinary telephone lines to transmit data.

Track A horizontal row following the length of a magnetic tape on which data can be recorded; one of a series of concentric circles on the surface of a magnetic disk.

Transaction file A file containing changes to be made to the master file.

Transient routine A supervisor routine that remains in primary storage with the remainder of the operating system.

Transistor A type of circuitry characteristic of second-generation computers; smaller, faster, and more reliable than vacuum tubes but inferior to third-generation, large-scale integration.

Transit field The section of a check, preprinted with magnetic ink, that includes the bank number.

Transportable computer A computer that is larger than a portable, but is still small enough to be carried; requires an external power source.

Tree structure See Hierarchical structure.

Turnkey system An integrated system including hardware, software, training, and support developed for particular businesses.

Uniform Commercial Code (UCC) A set of provisions proposed by legal experts to promote consistency among state courts in the legal treatment of commercial transactions between sellers and purchasers.

Unit record One set of information; the amount of data on one punched card.

UNIVAC I (UNIVersal Automatic Computer) One of the first commercial electronic computers; became available in 1951.

Universal Product Code (UPC) A machine-readable code consisting of thirty dark bars and twenty-nine spaces that identifies a product and its manufacturer; commonly used on most grocery items.

Update A data-manager feature that allows the user to change data contained in a record.

Upload To transmit information to a mainframe computer from a microcomputer.

User friendly An easy-to-use, understandable software design that makes it easy for noncomputer personnel to use an application software package.

User's group An informal group of owners of a particular brand of microcomputer who meet to exchange information about hardware, software, service, and support.

Utility program A program within an operating system that performs a specialized function.

Vacuum tube A device (resembling the light bulb) from which almost all air has been removed and through which electricity can pass; often found in old radios and televisions; used in first-generation computers to control internal operations.

Value A single piece of information used in the calculations of a spreadsheet.

Variable   A meaningful name assigned by the programmer to storage locations of which the values can change.

Variable column width   A feature of electronic spreadsheets that allows the user to set the width of columns; useful when entering long descriptive labels.

Verification   Mathematically proving that a program or a program module is correctly designed.

Very-Large-Scale Integration (VLSI)   A type of circuitry replacing large-scale integration in fourth-generation computers; smaller, faster, and less costly than large-scale integration.

Videoconferencing   A technology that employs a two-way, full-motion video plus a two-way audio system for the purpose of conducting conferences between two remote locations through communication facilities.

Video seminar   A form of teleconferencing that employs a one-way, full-motion video with two-way radio.

Virtual memory   See Virtual storage.

Virtual storage   An extension of multiprogramming in which portions of programs not being used are kept in secondary storage until needed, giving the impression that primary storage is unlimited; contrast with real storage.

Visual display terminal   A terminal capable of receiving output on a cathode-ray tube (CRT) and, with special provisions, capable of transmitting data through a keyboard.

Visual table of contents   Used in HIPO packages; includes blocks with identification numbers that are used as a reference in other HIPO diagrams.

Voice mail   See Voice message system.

Voice message system (VMS)   The sender activates a special "message" key on the telephone, dials the receiver's number, and records the message. A button lights on the receiver's phone, and when it is convenient, the receiver can activate the phone and listen to the message.

Voice-grade channel   A communication channel that has a wider frequency range and can transmit data at rates between 300 and 9,600 bits per second; for example, a telephone line.

Volatility   The frequency of changes made to a file during a certain period of time.

Wand reader   A device used in reading source-data represented in optical bar-code form.

Wire-matrix printer   See Dot-matrix printer.

Word   A memory location in primary storage; varies in size (number of bits) from computer to computer.

Word processing   The use of computer equipment in preparing text; involves writing, editing, and printing.

Word processor   See Text processor.

Word size   The number of bits that can be manipulated at one time.

Xerographic printer   A type of nonimpact printer that uses printing methods similar to those used in common xerographic copying machines.

Zone bit   A bit used in different combinations with numeric bits to represent numbers, letters, and special characters.

Zone rows   The upper three rows, numbered 12, 11, and 0, that are found on an eighty-column punched card.

INDEX

CAT scan, 480, 481
Cells, 564
Cellular phones, 228
Central processing unit (CPU), 14, 77–78
Chain printer, 120
Channels, 220–221
   multiplexor, 221
   selector, 221
Character, 11
Charge-coupled devices (CCDs), 144–145
Check bit, 94
Chief Programmer Team (CPT), 288
Clock speed, 192
Clustered key-to-tape devices, 105–106
Code checking, 94
Coding, 289
Comments, 290–291
Commercial application software, 341–356
   advantages and disadvantages, 341–342
   categories of, 342
   end-user development tools, 349–352
   expert systems, 352–355
   functional tools, 346–349
   productivity tools, 342–346
   selection of, 355–356
Common law, 461–462
Communication channel, 221–227
   grades of, 223–224
   modes of, 224
   types of, 221–223
Communication hardware, 228–229
   multiplexers and concentrators, 228
   programmable communications processors, 228
Comparisons, 292
Compatible, 200–201
Compiler program, 330
Composite color monitors, 204
Computations, 291
Computer-aided design (CAD), 432–433
Computer-aided manufacturing (CAM), 433
Computer anxiety, 417–418
Computer-assisted diagnosis, 478–482
   computerized axial tomography (CAT scan), 480–481

multiphasic health testing, 480
   nuclear magnetic resonance (NMR), 481–482
Computer-assisted instruction (CAI), 493–494
Computer-assisted treatment, 482–483
Computer chips, *see* Silicon chips
Computer codes, 91–94
   four-bit binary coded decimal (BCD), 91–92
   six-bit BCD, 92
Computer conferencing, 427–428
Computer crimes, 246–247, 442–456
   definition of, 443–444
   financial crimes, 446–447
   prevention and detection, 447–450
   sabotage, 444–445
   security, 450–454
   theft of property, 446
   theft of services, 445–446
Computer ethics, 455–456
Computer-integrated manufacturing (CIM), 434
Computerized axial tomography (CAT scan), 480–481
Computer literacy, 420
Computer phobia, 417–418
Computer-related careers, 499–505
   computer operator, 504
   data-base specialists, 503–504
   data-entry operator, 505
   librarian, 504
   MIS manager, 499–500
   programmers, 500–502
   remote terminal operator, 505
   system analysts, 502–503
Computers, 3
   advantages of, 17–18
   analog, 16–17
   in banking, 4, 230–231
   in business, 4–7, 231–232
   careers in, 499–505
   digital, 17
   for disabled people, 206
   in education, 10, 216, 493–494
   evolution of, 29–49
   first-generation, 36–38
   fourth-generation, 41–42
   in government, 7, 429–432
   hardware, 76–96
   impact on society, 2–10
   as an industry, 42–46
   in industry, 432–436
   in law, 230

mainframes, 21–22
   in medicine, 10, 478–483
   micro-, 23–24, 180–211
   mini-, 22–23
   operation of, 16–17
   professional associations, 46–49
   second-generation, 38–39
   supercomputers, 19–21
   third-generation, 40–41
   types of, 19–24
Computer security, 450–454
Concentrator, 228
Concurrently, 257
Condition entries, 372
Condition stub, 372
Continuous form, 112
Control programs, 251–253
Control unit, 77
Conversion, 386
   crash, 386
   direct, 386
   parallel, 386
   phased, 386
   pilot, 386
Coordinate, 566
Coprocessor, 200–201
Copyright law, 463
Corporate planning models, 409
Crash conversion, 386
Cursor, 201
Cut forms, 112

Daisy-wheel printer, 119
Data, 10
Data base, 13, 168–175, 551–552
   analyst, 169
   management systems, 174–175
   packages, 551–552
   structuring data, 169
Data-base analyst, 169
Data-base management system (DBMS), 174–175, 354–355
Data-base packages, 551–552
Data buffering, 219
Datacom handler, 228
Data communication, 217–221
   analog transmission, 217–218
   applications, 230–232
   communication channels, 221–227
   digital transmission, 218
   hardware for, 228–229
   input/output operations, 219–221
Data definition language (DDL), 355
Data managers, 548–562
   business uses of, 553

PHOTO CREDITS

pany; **179 (bottom)** Courtesy of Apple Computer Inc.; **182** Courtesy of Blyth Software; **183** Reproduced with permission of AT & T Corporate Archive; **184** Courtesy of Apple Computer, Inc.; **185** Courtesy of International Business Machines Corporation; **186** The Dow Chemical Company; **187 (top)** Photo courtesy of Hewlett-Packard Company; **187 (bottom)** Courtesy of Blyth Software; **188** Courtesy of Blyth Software; **189 (top)** Photo courtesy of Hewlett-Packard Company; **189 (bottom)** Courtesy of Radio Shack, a Division of Tandy Corporation; **190** Courtesy of Apple Computer, Inc.; **191** The Tower 1632 from NCR Corporation; **197** Courtesy of Blythe Software; **198** Courtesy of Nissan Motor Company; **199 (top)** Courtesy of Comp-U-Card; **199 (middle)** Courtesy of Perkin-Elmer Corporation; **199 (bottom)** Courtesy of Blythe Software; **202 (top)** Courtesy of Corona Data Systems, Inc.; **202 (lower left)** Courtesy of Commodore Business Machines, Inc.; **202 (lower right)** Courtesy of Apple Computer, Inc.; **203 (top)** Courtesy of Blythe Software; **203 (bottom)** Courtesy of GTCO Corporation, Rockville, Maryland; **204** Courtesy of N.A.P. Consumer Electronics Corporation; **205** Courtesy of Maxtor Corporation; **207** Reprint permission granted by computer Associates Micro Products division, October, 1985; **213** Courtesy of Apple Computer, Inc.; **215 (top)** Courtesy of RCA Corporation; **215 (middle)** Courtesy of COMSAT; **215 (bottom)** Courtesy of Gould, Inc.; **219 (left)** Photo courtesy of Hewlett-Packard Company; **219 (middle)** Photo courtesy of Anderson Jacobson, Inc.; **219 (right)** Photo courtesy of Hayes Microcomputer Products; **222 (top)** Courtesy of BRIntec Corporation; **222 (bottom)** Courtesy of Gould, Inc.; **226** Photo courtesy of RCA Corporation; **227 (top left)** Courtesy of COMSAT; **227 (top right)** Western Union Corporation; **227 (bottom)** Courtesy of International Business Machines Corporation; **231** Courtesy of Anacomp, Inc.; **232** Courtesy of Apple Computer, Inc.; **240** Courtesy Bank America Corporation; **245 (top)** Courtesy of Information Systems of America; **245 (middle)** Courtesy of International Business Machines Corporation; **245 (bottom)** Photo courtesy of Hewlett-Packard Company; **267** Courtesy of NCR Corporation; **269 (top)** Courtesy of Lear Siegler; **269 (middle)** Courtesy of International Business Machines Corporation; **269 (bottom)** Courtesy of Crown Zellerbach; **296** Courtesy of Eli Lilly and Company; **299 (top)** Courtesy of NASA; **299 (middle)** Courtesy of Dow Chemical Company; **328** Courtesy of NASA; **329 (top)** National Optical Astronomy Observations; **329 (bottom)** Courtesy of NASA; **337** Reprinted courtesy of Sperry Corporation; **339 (top)** Courtesy of Borland International; **339 (middle)** Courtesy of SAS Institute Inc., Cary, N.C.; **339 (bottom)** Courtesy of Execucom Systems Corporation; **344 (top)** Courtesy of SAS Institute Inc., Cary, N.C.; **344 (lower left)** Courtesy of SAS Institute Inc., Cary, N.C.; **344 (lower right)** Courtesy Execucom Systems Corporation; **345** Photo courtesy of Software International Corp.; **352** Courtesy of SAS Institute Inc., Cary, N.C.; **353** Courtesy of Execucom Systems Corporation; **355** Courtesy of SAS Institute Inc., Cary, N.C.; **360** Courtesy of Microsoft Corporation; **361 (bottom)** Courtesy of Honeywell, Inc.; **391** Courtesy of Marathon Oil Company; **395 (top)** Courtesy of Bank of America; **395 (middle)** Courtesy of Mead; **395 (bottom)** Courtesy of AT & T Bell Laboratories; **412** Courtesy of Execucom Systems Corporation; **415 (top)** Courtesy of Cincinatti Milacron; **415 (middle)** Courtesy of International Business Machines Corporation; **415 (bottom)** Courtesy of Combustion Engineering; **418** NYSE/Jeff Aranita; **419 (top)** Chicago Tribune Company; **419 (middle)** Courtesy of Honeywell; **419 (bottom)** Courtesy of Honeywell; **422** The Dow Chemical Company; **423 (top)** Photo courtesy of TRW, Inc.; **423 (bottom)** This photo supplied courtesy of Lear Siegler, Inc./Data Products Division; **425** Photo courtesy of CPT Corporation; **426** Photo courtesy of Northern Telecom Inc.; **428** Courtesy of AT & T Bell Laboratories; **429** CompuServe Incorporated; **430** Courtesy of News Net, Inc.; **432 (top)** Courtesy Houston Instrument; **432 (bottom)** Courtesy of International Business Machines Corporation; **433** Courtesy of Combustion Engineering; **434** Photo courtesy of Automation Technology Products-"CIMPLEX"; **436** Courtesy of Cincinatti Milacron; **439** Courtesy of Decision